"These chapters show that the Companion is not just a status quaestionis of the established theory and practice of interreligious dialogue: it actually tries to contribute to its theoretical and practical development."

—*Journal of Empirical Theology*, 2014

"In summation, Cornille has served up what must surely establish itself as one of the core reference texts in any serious library on interreligious dialogue, encounters, and relations."

—*Journal of Religious History*, 3 September 2014

"Instructively, the volume's impressive breadth and scholarship serve to orient readers to the future and its possibilities rather than to an alleged final word on a given dialogue. Every library and student in this and related disciplines should hold a copy."

—*Religious Studies Review*, 16 June 2014

"Summing Up: Highly recommended. Upper-division undergraduates through professionals/practitioners."

—*Choice*, 1 February 2014

"*The Wiley Blackwell Companion to Inter-Religious Dialogue* is a landmark accomplishment that offers a definitive map of the terrain of a robust field and its growing literature. But the internationally recognized experts gathered herein do far more than report on the already known. This treasure trove of essays opens onto new vistas and poses vital questions that must be answered as scholars venture into terra incognita. Comprehensive, authoritative, creative and cutting-edge – this is a must read collection for beginners and experts alike."

—John J. Thatamanil, Union Theological Seminary

The Wiley Blackwell Companions to Religion

The Wiley Blackwell Companions to Religion series presents a collection of the most recent scholarship and knowledge about world religions. Each volume draws together newly commissioned essays by distinguished authors in the field, and is presented in a style which is accessible to undergraduate students, as well as scholars and the interested general reader. These volumes approach the subject in a creative and forward-thinking style, providing a forum in which leading scholars in the field can make their views and research available to a wider audience.

Published

Forthcoming

The Wiley Blackwell Companion to Inter-Religious Dialogue

Edited by

Catherine Cornille

WILEY Blackwell

This paperback edition first published 2020
© 2013 John Wiley & Sons Ltd

Edition history: John Wiley & Sons, Ltd. (hardback, 2013)

Registered Offices
John Wiley & Sons, Inc., 111 River Street, Hoboken, NJ 07030, USA
John Wiley & Sons Ltd, The Atrium, Southern Gate, Chichester, West Sussex, PO19 8SQ, UK

Editorial Office
The Atrium, Southern Gate, Chichester, West Sussex, PO19 8SQ, UK

For details of our global editorial offices, customer services, and more information about Wiley products visit us at www.wiley.com.

Wiley also publishes its books in a variety of electronic formats and by print-on-demand. Some content that appears in standard print versions of this book may not be available in other formats.

Library of Congress Cataloging-in-Publication Data

The Wiley Blackwell companion to inter-religious dialogue / edited by Catherine Cornille.
    pages   cm
  Includes index.
  ISBN 978-0-470-65520-7 (hardback) 978-1-119-57259-6 (paperback)
1. Religions–Relations.   2. Dialogue–Religious aspects.   I. Cornille, C. (Catherine), editor of compilation.
  BL410.W545 2013
  201′.5–dc23

                                                        2012048006

Cover image: © Diana Ong/SuperStock
Cover design by Wiley

Set in 10/12.5 pt Photina by SPi Global, Pondicherry, India

10 9 8 7 6 5 4 3 2 1

Contents

List of Contributors

Michael Amaladoss, SJ is Director of the Institute for Dialogue with Cultures and Religions, Chennai, India.

Mary Anderson is an interdisciplinary artist, writer, and scholar, currently an Associate at the Mahindra Humanities Center at Harvard University and Visiting Faculty in the Visual and Critical Studies Department at the School of the Museum of Fine Arts, Boston.

Yaakov Ariel is Professor of Religious Studies at the University of North Carolina at Chapel Hill.

John Azumah is Associate Professor of World Christianity at Columbia Theological Seminary.

John Berthrong is Associate Professor of Comparative Theology at Boston University.

Pierre-François de Béthune, OSB is a monk of the monastery of Saint-André de Clerlande in Belgium and former Secretary General of the Commissions for Inter-monastic Dialogue.

Anna Bigelow is Associate Professor of South Asian Religions at North Carolina State University.

William Chittick is Professor of Religious Studies at the State University of New York, Stony Brook.

Francis X. Clooney, SJ is the Parkman Professor of Divinity and Professor of Comparative Theology at Harvard Divinity School.

Catherine Cornille is Professor of Comparative Theology at Boston College.

Reuven Firestone is Professor of Medieval Judaism and Islam at Hebrew Union College in Los Angeles.

Jeannine Hill Fletcher is Associate Professor of Theology at Fordham University.

Barbara A. Holdrege is Professor of Religious Studies, South Asian Traditions and Jewish Traditions at the University of California, Santa Clara.

Paul Ingram is Professor of Religion Emeritus at Pacific Lutheran University.

S. Ayse Kadayifci-Orellana is Visiting Assistant Professor in the MA program in Conflict Resolution at Georgetown University.

Nathan Katz is the Bhagwan Mahavir Professor of Jain Studies in the School of International Affairs and Research Professor at Florida International University.

Paul Knitter is the Paul Tillich Professor of Theology, World Religions and Culture at Union Theological Seminary.

Aasulv Lande is Professor Emeritus of Missiology and Ecumenics at the University of Lund and Senior Researcher at the Senior Center, Agder University.

David Peter Lawrence is Associate Professor of Religion and Philosophy at the University of North Dakota.

Daniel Madigan, SJ is the Ruesch Family Associate Professor of Theology at Georgetown University.

Robert Millet is Professor of Ancient Scripture and Emeritus Dean of Religious Education at Brigham Young University.

Marianne Moyaert is Professor of Comparative Theology and the Hermeneutics of Interreligious Dialogue at the Free University of Amsterdam, and post-doctoral researcher at the Catholic University of Louvain.

Sachiko Murata is Professor of Religion and Asian Studies at the State University of New York, Stony Brook.

Galia Patt-Shamir is Professor of Comparative Philosophy and Religion at Tel-Aviv University.

Achiel Peelman, OMI is Professor of Theology at Saint Paul University, Ottawa.

Anantanand Rambachan is Professor of Religion, Philosophy and Asian Studies at Saint Olaf College.

Tinu Ruparell is Associate Professor of Religious Studies at the University of Calgary.

Leonard Swidler is Professor of Catholic Thought and Interreligious Dialogue at Temple University.

Imtiyaz Yusuf is Professor of Islamics and Religion at the College of Religious Studies, Mahidol University, Salaya, Thailand.

Ping Zhang is Professor of Chinese and East Asian studies at Tel-Aviv University.

Introduction

Catherine Cornille

Since the middle of the twentieth century the notion of dialogue has become increasingly common in describing or prescribing the proper relationship between religions. Rather than competing with one another over territories, converts or claims, religions have generally come to adopt a more conciliatory and constructive attitude toward one another, collaborating in social projects and exchanging views on common religious questions. Centers for interreligious dialogue have emerged in different parts of the world, and high-profile international meetings have been organized, bringing together leaders and/or scholars from any number of religious traditions to engage in mutually respectful conversation about various religious topics. This has led in turn to increased reflection on the nature of inter-religious dialogue and on its many forms and manifestations.

The term *dialogue* tends to be used to cover a wide range of engagements between religious traditions, from daily interaction between believers living in the same neighborhoods to organized discussions and debates between expert scholars, and from formal or casual exchanges between spiritual or institutional leaders to inter-religious activism around social issues. The goals of particular dialogues may differ, from peaceful coexistence to social change, and from mutual understanding to actual religious growth. But the common denominator in all these forms of inter-religious engagement is mutual respect and openness to the possibility of learning from the other. The category of *inter-religious dialogue* may then be used to refer to any form or degree of constructive engagement between religious traditions.

In this, dialogue between religions may be distinguished from other types of inter-religious engagement that lack an actively constructive element, such as the neutral study of religion, or more traditional apologetics. It differs from religious studies approaches in that participants engage one another from a faith position, and in that the goal of dialogue lies not only in mutual understanding, but also in the pursuit of truth and of personal and religious growth. Such growth may take the form of deeper self-understanding or of appropriating new insights and practices from the other religion. It may also lead to confession and repair of past misdeeds committed against the other, or to the actual prevention of violent conflict.

While dialogue is often thought of as the peaceful and amicable exchange of views, it also often entails argument and fierce debate. If true to their convictions, believers will naturally wish to witness not only to the contents, but also to the truth of their faith. And since no two religions are ever perfectly compatible, the exchange and discussion of religious views cannot but involve some level of disagreement and some measure of defense of the plausibility of one's own beliefs and practices. Apologetics may thus form part of advanced forms of dialogue. However, while classical apologetics is mainly oriented toward defeating the other, dialogue also involves openness and receptivity to the witness of the other. As such, dialogue between religions involves a delicate and often difficult balance between commitment to one's own tradition and openness to the other.

The very possibility of dialogue between religious traditions signals, or perhaps requires significant shifts in the self-understanding of religious traditions. While religions tend to be naturally convinced of the superior, if not exclusive truth of their own teachings, dialogue presupposes some degree of humility about one's own conception of truth and a certain receptivity, even hospitality to the truth of the other. The attitudes of humility and hospitality reinforce one another and have come to affect most religious traditions as these have come to terms with the reality of religious diversity. Direct encounter with and deeper knowledge of the teachings and practices of other religions tends to preclude an easy dismissal of their validity and truth. And the very conception of religious truth has undergone a significant paradigm shift, as Leonard Swidler points out in his contribution to this volume. While most religions have come to a basic recognition and acceptance of the reality of religious plurality, degrees of religious tolerance and openness toward the religious other continue to vary, not only between religious traditions but also within them. As such, inter-religious dialogue remains a challenge for religious traditions, often requiring considerable hermeneutical effort and the retrieval of internal textual or traditional resources to facilitate such constructive exchange.

While the systematic effort to bring people from different religions into dialogue with one another may be a relatively recent phenomenon, the history of religions is replete with examples of more or less constructive engagement between religions. The articles in this volume give ample testimony to this fact. Some form of dialogue already takes place whenever a new religion attempts to define its own identity through a process of acceptance, rejection and reinterpretation of the parent religion or religions. While this may be seen to lack the reciprocity of genuine dialogue, the emergence of a new offshoot religion often challenges the parent religion to redefine its own teachings or sharpen its own beliefs. The same process occurs when religions move from one cultural context to another and tend to naturally borrow teachings and practices from the traditional religion of the culture. The processes of appropriation and reinterpretation of teachings and practices of other religions which takes place in the process of acculturation may be regarded as a form of implicit dialogue. In addition to these forms of unintentional dialogue and unavoidable engagement of other religions, one may also find isolated historical examples of more conscious attempts at dialogue and debate between religions. While often serving political or social interests, such dialogues do involve peaceful exchanges of views and attempts at adjudicating the truth of these views in fairly transparent ways. Some of the historical dialogues discussed in this volume (e.g. the Buddhist–Hindu dialogue) in fact display a level of reflectivity about dialogue itself rarely encountered even in modern instances. Indeed, though dialogue is often thought of as a modern phenomenon and the relationship between religions as evolving toward greater openness, some contributions also suggest the opposite movement, from original intimacy and mutuality to growing animosity. Not only does religious self-understanding change in often unpredictable ways, but religions are also commonly used to bolster nationalistic and ethnocentric ideologies. As such, history provides not only examples of past dialogue, but also food for further dialogue.

This Companion focuses on the phenomenon of inter-religious dialogue in general and in concrete cases. The first part of the volume deals with focal topics in inter-religious dialogue. These topics bring to the fore some of the areas which have been particularly relevant in the pursuit and performance of inter-religious dialogue, as well as some critical issues arising from that dialogue. Some contributions deal with topics internal to the dialogue (comparative theology, scriptural reasoning, interstitial theology, etc.) while others deal with the relationship between of dialogue and broader social issues.

We start with a discussion of the history of inter-religious dialogue by Leonard Swidler, himself one of the pioneers of such dialogue in the West. This is followed by a closer exploration of the fundamental conditions for a constructive dialogue between religions. Monastics from different religions have played a crucial role in the development of inter-religious dialogue, not only in exemplifying openness and hospitality toward the religious other, but also in pointing to a deeper level of spiritual connection from which all actual dialogue may spring. One of the main architects and advocates of intermonastic dialogue, Pierre de Béthune, offers a thorough discussion of the background, the principles and the fruits of this dialogue.

Among scriptural traditions, inter-religious dialogue has often taken the form of the reading of sacred texts of another tradition. This may happen in solitary form, as a scholar of one tradition reads and engages in theological reflection on a text of another. But it may also happen in more communal fashion, as scholars from different religious traditions enter into dialogue on the meaning of a particular text. The first type of dialogue has been called comparative theology, and the latter scriptural reasoning. Francis Clooney, who is a pioneer and strong proponent of comparative theology, discusses the nature of this discipline and its relation to inter-religious dialogue. Marianne Moyaert offers an overview of the background, principles and practices of scriptural reasoning together with some critical reflections.

While dialogue is generally understood as verbal exchange, the act of participating in the rituals of another religion or of worshipping together also constitutes a form of dialogue. In his article, Michael Amaladoss deals with various types of inter-religious worship as practiced mainly in India, while also pointing to some of the contested issues in this dialogue. Art represents another powerful non-verbal vehicle for inter-religious exchange. Mary Anderson draws some beautifully evocative connections between the artistic relationship to the world and the openness, empathy and receptivity required for genuine dialogue between religions.

Among the different religious or theological innovations spawned by inter-religious dialogue, one of the most radical or extreme is that of interstitial theology. Tinu Ruparell, himself one of its vocal proponents, discusses the philosophical foundations and religious justifications of this type of theology which he defines as "the construction of hybrid perspectives for continuing the conversation between religions in an open and constructive way."

The constructive dimension of inter-religious dialogue may involve direct learning from the insights and practices of another religion. But it may also entail collaboration between religions to bring about social change, either through the prevention of conflict (religious or other) or through the building of a more just society, drawing from the resources and the visions of different religions. Paul Knitter, one of the foremost advocates of inter-religious dialogue, offers an impassioned argument for the necessary interconnection between inter-religious dialogue and social action. Focusing specifically on the role of inter-religious dialogue in peace building, Ayse Kadayifci-Orellana discusses the various ways in which collaboration between religions may help prevent war and build a more sustainable peace.

One of the critical questions in inter-religious dialogue is that of women's participation. While women have played and continue to play a crucial role in many forms of informal dialogue, they are rarely at the center of the more formal and institutional dialogues between religions. Jeannine Hill-Fletcher sheds a critical light on this situation, pointing to the reasons why women's voices may have been overlooked or ignored, and why they matter.

The second part of the book deals with case studies in inter-religious dialogue. These cases are, of course, far from exhaustive, or representative of all of the dialogues which have taken place in the course of history or which are taking place today. They do, however, offer a sample of the dialogues which are taking place in different parts of the world and between different types of religions: old and new, large and small, scriptural and oral, ethnic and universalistic, theistic and nontheistic. Each of the case studies deals variously with the history of a particular dialogue, important thinkers and ideas, contemporary developments and/or future challenges. Some of the dialogues discussed in this volume have a very long history, while others are fairly new. Some are enmeshed in deep-seated social and political tensions, while others take place on a purely speculative and theological level. This diversity is reflected in the different approaches and contents of the particular case studies. Some offer an overview of the history of a particular dialogue, while other focus primarily on the contemporary engagement between two religions. One contribution even engages in actual live dialogue on a topic central to Judaism and Confucianism.

Most of the authors of the case studies approach the dialogue mainly from the perspective of one or the other religion, and even from the perspective of a particular school or tradition within a certain religion. This is inevitably the case, as most of the authors are themselves active participants in the dialogue, engaging the other religion constructively from their own religious perspective. Robert Millet, for example, is one of the first Mormons to engage with Evangelical Christians, and Anant Rambachan has become one of the favorite Hindu dialogue partners for Christians, just as Daniel Madigan and John Berthrong are often called upon to represent Christianity in the dialogue with, respectively, Islam and Confucianism. Each of these authors has a profound knowledge of and sympathy for the other religion, and for the other's perspective on the dialogue. But one must keep in mind that the essay on the Christian–Buddhist dialogue that appears here would have been quite different if it had been written by a Buddhist, or for that matter by a Roman Catholic Christian, while a Muslim author might have shed a different light or taken a different approach to the Jewish–Muslim dialogue. A notable exception to the one-sidedness of the approaches to dialogue is the article on the Confucian–Jewish dialogue, which was co-authored by a Jewish scholar of Confucianism and a Confucian scholar of Judaism. Some authors do display a remarkable capacity to approach the dialogue "from the middle" between the two traditions, either because they are somewhat removed from either tradition, or, on the contrary, because they have come to identify with both.

The case studies are arranged roughly in order of antiquity, or according to the length of history of their engagement. As might be expected, the oldest dialogues are mostly between religions with some family relationship: Hinduism and Buddhism, Judaism and Christianity, Christianity and Islam. But there are also unrelated religions with a long tradition of mutual engagement: Shinto and Buddhism, or Hinduism and Islam. Until the twentieth century, engagement between religions was largely determined by physical proximity and the vicissitudes of territorial expansion. In the contemporary globalized context, however, dialogues may take place between any two or more religions, across territorial and ideological boundaries. The antiquity of a dialogue is of course no guarantee for its continuity or success. Relationships between religions change, often due to political and social factors, and religions which were once quite intimate (such as Shintoism and Buddhism) may grow apart, while religions with scant historical connection (such as Buddhism and Christianity) may come to engage in very active and productive dialogue. Dialogue is in fact often easier between religions with little or no family relationship, since there is less need to come to terms with directly opposing views or interpretations, and with a history of mutual rejection. As such, the dialogue between Christianity and Buddhism is considerably less contentious and encumbered than the dialogue between Christianity and Islam. However, as the fascination with novelty and difference wanes and as the burden of history is somewhat lifted, one may expect similar challenges and advances in both types of dialogue.

Relative to the long history of religions, the experience of genuine dialogue or constructive engagement between religions is still in fact in its infancy. While much may be learned from the history of encounter between two religions and from the evidence of conscious or unconscious borrowing, dialogue still constitutes for most religions a future promise, rather than a past accomplishment. The possibilities for inter-religious dialogue are virtually infinite, not only in terms of possible dialogue partners, but also in terms of unending and unpredictable possibility for growth and change. There are undoubtedly limits to the constructive potential of any dialogue between particular religions. But few, if any of the dialogues discussed in this volume have reached those limits. As such, it cannot represent a summary or an afterword to the history of inter-religious dialogue, so much as a preamble.

In closing, I wish to thank each and every scholar who has contributed to this volume. The task of writing a history of a particular dialogue was in many cases daunting and the authors have accepted the challenge with generosity and grace. Though every dialogue is ongoing and constantly changing, each article represents an invaluable record of certain important facts, an account of their emergence and their meaning, and an important contribution to scholarship on inter-religious dialogue. I also want to thank Glenn Willis for his expert help in editing this collection. This volume may be regarded as a companion to a series of books I have recently edited on various critical topics in inter-religious dialogue, each approached by scholars from different religious traditions.[1] Together they point to the real challenges, the wide range of possibilities, the important achievements, and the enduring promise of genuine dialogue between religions.

Note

1   The volumes in the series are Catherine Cornille, ed. *Criteria of Discernment in Interreligious Dialogue*. Eugene, OR: Wipf and Stock, 2009; Catherine Cornille and Chris Conway, eds. *Interreligious Hermeneutics*. Eugene, OR: Wipf and Stock, 2010; Catherine Cornille and Glenn Willis, eds. *The World Market and Interreligious Dialogue*. Eugene, OR: Wipf and Stock, 2011; Catherine Cornille and Stephanie Corigliano, eds. *Interreligious Dialogue and Cultural Change*. Eugene, OR: Wipf and Stock. 2012); and Catherine Cornille and Jillian Maxey, eds. *Women and Interreligious Dialogue* (Eugene: Wipf and Stock, 2013).

PART I
Focal Topics

CHAPTER 1

The History of Inter-Religious Dialogue

Leonard Swidler

The world has always needed dialogue, but after the 1989 "Fall of the Wall," and even more after 9/11, the world increasingly *realizes* that it needs dialogue. At the heart of dialogue is inter-religious dialogue, because religion is the most comprehensive of all the human "disciplines": "an explanation of the *ultimate* meaning of life, and how to live accordingly" (Swidler and Mojzes 2000). Until the slow emergence of inter-religious dialogue out of Modernity, out of the eighteenth-century Enlightenment of the West, religion was also the most absolutist, exclusivist of all the disciplines. Thus, dialogue – fundamentally meaning "I can learn from you" – is a dagger pointed at the heart of absolutist religion/ideology. But, let's start briefly at the beginning.

As long as there has been *Homo sapiens sapiens* (perhaps since 70,000 BCE.) there have been attempts – however meager – to explain "the ultimate meaning of life and how to live accordingly": religions. When small groups of humans gathered into large enough collectivities to form cities, each of these civilizations had at its heart a religion which both shaped and expressed that civilization. All of these ancient religions were "primary religions," that is, were coterminous with the civilization or "state"; for instance, all members of the Israelite "nation," and only they, were devotees of the Israelite religion.

That began to change drastically in the four ancient civilizations of Greece, Israel, India, China during the Axial Age (800–200 BCE). A shift occurred whereby some individuals began to identify no longer primarily with the collective, but with the personal conscience, to focus no longer primarily on the exterior, but on the interior. These religions increasingly tended to claim not just particularist but universal validity, that is, not just for, for instance, Athenians, but for all humans – which gave rise to religious absolutism. Still, the link between the state and religion remained strong, for as the state expanded the religion also tended to expand; and conquered peoples tended eventually to adopt the religion of the victors. For example, as the Christian, or later Muslim, armies were victorious, so too Christianity and Islam spread. Hence, the

The Wiley Blackwell Companion to Inter-Religious Dialogue, First Edition. Edited by Catherine Cornille.
© 2013 John Wiley & Sons Ltd. Published 2020 by John Wiley & Sons Ltd.

universalist claims of Axial and post-Axial religions led to at times peaceful, but also bellicose encounters among the various religions, with the latter by far dominating. There were occasional leading devotees of such religions who stand out as models of irenicism, like Ashoka the Great (304–232 BCE), the quasi-Buddhist Emperor of India, St. Francis of Assisi (1181–1226 CE), Akbar the Great, Muslim Emperor of India (1542–1605 CE). Their peaceful impacts on inter-religious relations were, however, limited, geographically and in other ways, and inter-religious encounters during the subsequent age of European exploration and colonization were marked primarily by proselytization.

This slowly began to change, though at first not noticeably, with the rise of Modernity and the Enlightenment, which was characterized by freedom, reason, history, and later dialogue (Swidler 2011). The Enlightenment put forth a breakthrough thesis: at the heart of being human is freedom and rationality, and to that was added by the Late Enlightenment (German scholars write of *die Spät Aufklärung*) a sense of history and dynamism. Embedded in the clarion call written in 1776 in Philadelphia (Greek: Brotherly/Sisterly Love), "All men are created equal" was the soft whisper, "therefore dialogue." It became a public voice at the inter-religious encounter of the 1893 Parliament of the World's Religions in Chicago.

The Christian Ecumenical Movement

Before directing our attention to the turning point of the Parliament of the World's Religions, I would like to draw attention to a slightly later development that provided a solid underpinning for the expansion of inter-religious dialogue subsequent to the parliament. I am referring to the launching of the Christian Ecumenical Movement in 1910 in Edinburgh.

As a delegate to the 1910 World Missionary Conference in Edinburgh, Bishop Charles H. Brent, a Missionary Episcopal Bishop in the Philippines, felt there was a need to discuss the questions of faith and ecclesiastical order deliberately excluded from the conference. Speaking from the floor, he announced his intention to found an organization for that purpose (eventually the Movement for Faith and Order) (Michael 1958: 21).

In the following fall, Bishop Brent addressed the Protestant Episcopal Church of the United States, telling the members about the Edinburgh Conference and urging them to take the lead in founding a Conference on Faith and Order. As a consequence, a committee was appointed. The response was extraordinarily favorable throughout the United States and other parts of the world. Even the response of the Vatican was very sympathetic, though indefinite. However, the plans were almost completely disrupted by the outbreak of the First World War (Sasse 1929: 5). Immediately after the war, in the spring of 1919, a deputation from the American Episcopal Church Commission left on a European trip in an attempt to contact the leaders of the Orthodox Churches and the Roman Catholic Church, and a date for the first World Conference of the Movement for Faith and Order was set for August 3, 1927, when 394 representatives from 108 Protestant and Orthodox Churches met in Lausanne, Switzerland (Tatlow 1954: 409–419).

Almost simultaneously a parallel effort was playing out. The genesis of the second large ecumenical organization, the Movement for Life and Work, was intimately bound up with the First World War, and the World Alliance of Churches for Promoting International Friendship, which was launched by the Protestant Churches early in 1914 as war was looming. The leader of both the Alliance and the Movement for Life and Work was the Lutheran Archbishop of Uppsala, Nathan Søderblom. He maintained that a common organ of expression was necessary for the churches, and that its formation could not wait until they had achieved unity on matters of faith and order. This was shown by the helplessness of the churches during the crisis of the war. "We cannot afford to remain separated and in a state of unnecessary impotence caused by our separation, up to the time when we shall be truly united in faith and Church organization" (Søderblom 1923: 1). This Ecumenical Council would not encroach on the independence of the churches and would deal, not with matters of faith and order, but with social and international problems. As the planning committee of Life and Work expressed it in 1922, "Doctrine divides, but service unites" (Kalstroem: 540). The first international conference of Life and Work was held in Stockholm on August 19, 1925.

In the wake of these two huge ecumenical gatherings, the sentiment arose that they themselves needed an "ecumenical movement" to unify them. Plans were then eventually made to allow the second meetings of the two organizations to take place very near each other in time and place so that many delegates could attend both. This happened in the summer of 1937 in Oxford and Edinburgh. The two organizations each voted to merge, and joint committees were set up. The newly formed joint organization, named the World Council of Churches, was to have its first world conference in 1941, but, as in 1914, when the outbreak of war prevented the launch of the Movement for Faith and Order, so the formal coming into existence of the World Council of Churches was postponed by war; it had to wait until 1948, in Amsterdam.

Protestant leaders tried mightily to include the Catholic Church in their efforts toward Christian unity. However, the Pope's own words in the early 1920s made it extremely clear that he had no intention of participating in ecumenical organizations. "Therefore, worthy brethren, it is clear why this Apostolic See never allows its own members to take part in the conferences of non-Catholic Christians. One may foster the reunion of Christians only insofar as one fosters the return of those standing outside to the one true Church from which they once unfortunately separated themselves" (Pius XI 1928: 58). Similar attitudes persisted in the Vatican for the next 40 years, repeatedly forbidding Catholic participation in dialogue (e.g., 1928 *Mortalium animos*; 1948 *Monitum*; 1949 *Instructio*; 1954 barring of Catholics at the Evanston World Council of Churches World Assembly). Clearly, the repeated Vatican condemnations were actually in reaction to the rising Catholic interest and participation in ecumenical dialogue – most notably through the *Una Sancta Movement*, starting in Germany after World War I (1914–18), expanding under Nazi oppression, and becoming a popular movement after World War II (1935–45) (see Swidler, 1966).

Why spend so much time reviewing the intra-Christian ecumenical movement when laying out the development of inter-religious dialogue? Inter-religious dialogue as it is now understood in each of its three primary modes – that is, reaching out to learn from other religions/ideologies more fully the meaning of life (Dialogue of the Head); joining with the Other to make the world a better place in which to live (Dialogue of the Hands); and an awe-filled embrace of the inner spirit and aesthetic expressions of the Other (Dialogue of the Heart) – grew out of the Enlightenment West, former Christendom. It is this magnetic lodestone that has been drawing the rest of the globe into its paradigm shift. It first drew splintered Christianity into its orbit, moving it to a search for greater unity in response to the ever-expanding intellectual challenge of the Enlightenment and its spun-off new scholarly disciplines: scientific history, sociology, anthropology, psychology. The growing Enlightenment moved on to begin to pull all the religions/ideologies of the world into its growing "Field of Force," eventually ushering in by the latter part of the twentieth century the Age of Global Dialogue. Hence, it is vital to see some of the historical context whence this incredible world-changing global force derived.

The Move to Dialogue with Other Religions

As noted above, we can date the "public" launching of modern inter-religious dialogue to the 1893 Parliament of the World's Religions in Chicago (Barrows 1893). It was by far the most prominent gathering at the Columbian World Exhibition celebrating the 400th anniversary of Columbus's discovery of America. What is stated about the parliament's importance is accurate: "Today it is recognized as the occasion of the birth of formal inter-religious dialogue worldwide."[1] The "trigger" of the positive explosion of inter-religious dialogue at the parliament was provided by the Indian Hindu Swami Vivekananda. He began his address: " 'Sisters and brothers of America!' To these words he got a standing ovation from a crowd of seven thousand, which lasted for two minutes" (Bhuyan 2005: 5). Though Vivekananda was a devotee of a particular branch of Hinduism (Advaita Vedanta), he was not on a conversion trip to America. His aim clearly was dialogic in the modern sense: " 'I do not come,' said Swamiji on one occasion in America, 'to convert you to a new belief. I want you to keep your own belief; I want to make the Methodist a better Methodist; the Presbyterian a better Presbyterian; the Unitarian a better Unitarian. I want to teach you to live the truth, to reveal the light within your own soul' " (Vivekananda). A number of other well-known religious leaders also participated in the parliament, including Virchand Gandhi, a Jain scholar from India, Anagarika Dharmapala from Sri Lanka representing Theravada Buddhism, and D.T. Suzuki from Japan representing Zen Buddhism. They and many other religious teachers and leaders toured or taught in the West for years, spreading their teachings, gaining new followers in some instances, and promoting a new openness to other religions.

The *fin de siècle* parliament, massively reinforced by the subsequent inflow of the intra-Christian Ecumenical Movement at the beginning of the new century described earlier, opened the dam for the dialogue among the religions of the world. From this point forward only the outstanding events that most recognize as major markers in the development of inter-religious dialogue can be, albeit all too briefly, discussed. Since, as it happened, I personally "stumbled" into the "dialogue" in the middle of the twentieth century and was carried along with the expanding dialogic flood tide, I will now largely use my own direct experience as the "thread" with which to follow developments in inter-religious dialogue from the middle of the last century onward.

The first half of the twentieth century had seen a huge global Armageddon conflict in two stages referred to as the First and Second World Wars. Following the Second World War, with the beginning of the "Long Peace," (Pinker 2011) most Protestant and Orthodox Churches were finally able to gather together in the World Council of Churches in 1948. However, as noted above, the great majority of Christians – Catholics – remained mired in isolation through the next decade and a half. Individual Catholic thinkers, and larger efforts like the German Una Sancta movement, nevertheless persisted against Vatican condemnations and silencings. Then suddenly, seemingly miraculously, the elderly Cardinal Angelo Roncalli was elected as a "safe interim" pope, (Saint) John XXIII. Shortly after his installation he called together the Cardinals in Rome and announced "I had a dream" (before Martin Luther King) in which he went around the Vatican throwing open the windows. He announced that he was calling a new Ecumenical Council (Vatican II) to follow the "signs of the times," as he put it, to "bring the Catholic Church up to date (*aggiornamento*)" so it could engage in dialogue with the world.

Vatican Council II (1962–65) ushered in a revolution in the literal sense; it turned things around in many areas, including Catholic relations with non-Catholics. At the Council a "Declaration on Religious Liberty" (*Dignitatis humanae*) was passed, solemnly affirming that religious liberty was a central part of Catholic teaching (after it had been formally condemned by Pope Gregory XVI in 1832, and Pope Pius IX in 1864, as *deliramentum*, "madness"). Secondly, a "Decree on Ecumenism" (*Unitatis reintegratio*) was passed committing all Catholics to engage in dialogue: "Exhorting *all* the Catholic faithful to recognize the signs of the times and to take an active and intelligent part in the work of ecumenism." Not being content with this exhortation, the Catholic bishops went on to say that, "in ecumenical work, [all] Catholics must . . . make the *first approaches* toward them [non-Catholics]." In case there were some opaque minds or recalcitrant wills out there, the bishops once more made it ringingly clear that ecumenical dialogue "involves the whole Church, faithful and clergy alike. It extends to everyone, according to the talent of each" (Article 5). Thirdly, all the Catholic bishops of the world, including the Bishop of Rome, the Pope, passed a "Declaration on the Relation of the Church to Non-Christian Religions" (*Nostra Aetate*) in which the Catholic Church "reflects at the outset what humans have in common and what tends to promote fellowship among them. All humans form but one community."

The third paragraph of *Nostra aetate* expressed with such clarity the human search for meaning that it merits citation in full here:

Humans look to their different religions for an answer to the unsolved riddles of human existence. The problems that weigh heavily on the hearts of humans are the same today as in the ages past. What is the human? What is the meaning and purpose of life? What is upright behavior, and what is sinful? Where does suffering originate, and what end does it serve? How can genuine happiness be found? What happens at death? What is judgment? What follows death? And finally, what is the ultimate mystery, beyond human explanation, which embraces our entire existence, from which we take our origin and toward which we tend?

The Declaration then drew positive practical conclusions from these questions:

> The Catholic Church rejects nothing of what is true and holy in these religions. It has a high regard for their manner of life and conduct, their precepts and doctrines . . . The Church therefore urges its members to enter with prudence and charity into dialogue and collaboration with members of other religions. . . . preserving and encouraging the moral truths found among non-Christians, as well as their social life and culture.

Further, the Catholic Church immediately acted on these words by setting up in the Vatican – and requiring every national conference of bishops around the world, and indeed, every diocese to set up – secretariats for dialogue with 1) other Christian Churches and the Jews, 2) non-Christian religions, and 3) non-believers. In 1964, even before the close of the Vatican II Council, I myself was invited to be a participant in the US Catholic-Reformed & Presbyterian Dialogue, and a little later to be a member of the US Catholic Bishops' Committee on Dialogue with the Jews.

During the Council in 1964 Pope Paul VI in his first encyclical made it clear that:

> dialogue is *demanded* nowadays. . . . It is *demanded* by the dynamic course of action which is changing the face of modern society. It is *demanded* by the pluralism of society, and by the maturity man has reached in this day and age. Be he religious or not, his secular education has enabled him to think and speak, and to conduct a dialogue with dignity (*Ecclesiam suam*, no. 78).

Following up on these extraordinary initiatives, shortly after the Council ended, the Vatican's Secretariat for Dialogue with Non-believers wrote that even "doctrinal dialogue should be initiated with courage and sincerity, with the greatest freedom and with reverence." It then went further to make a statement that is mind-jarring in its liberality:

> Doctrinal discussion requires perceptiveness, both in honestly setting out one's own opinion and in recognizing the truth everywhere, *even if the truth demolishes one so that one is forced to reconsider one's own position, in theory and in practice, at least in part.* . . . [I]n discussion the truth will prevail by no other means than by the truth itself. Therefore, the liberty of the participants must be ensured by law and reverenced in practice. All Christians should do their best to promote dialogue between men of every class as a duty of fraternal charity suited to our progressive and adult age. . . . The willingness to engage in dialogue is the measure and the strength of that general renewal which must be carried out in the Church. (*Humanae personae dignitatem* II.2)

This full-bore entrance of the Catholic Church into dialogue exponentially increased the involvement of all the other Christian Churches as well as the Jews. Every Church either expanded or created new agencies to foster dialogue.

The pages of the *Journal of Ecumenical Studies* (JES) serve as an excellent bellwether marking the progress of the Interreligious Dialogue Movement. It was in the middle of Vatican II (1964) that my wife Arlene Anderson Swidler and I launched her idea, JES, a scholarly periodical devoted to religious dialogue. The original subtitle of the journal was "Protestant, Catholic, Orthodox," but as soon as its second year we dropped it and took on our first non-Christian Associate Editor, Rabbi Arthur Gilbert. In the next three years JES continued to expand the dialogue (adding Muslim, Hindu, Buddhist . . . Associate Editors) so that the initial dialogue among Christians quickly spread to dialogue among all religions and beyond to all ideologies, cultures, and societal institutions.

Thus, what I had started to study as a graduate student in the 1950s – the dialogue between Catholics and Protestants – naturally moved on to Jewish–Christian dialogue, then Jewish–Christian–Muslim dialogue, and further to dialogue with Hinduism, Buddhism . . . and even Marxism. One of the new endeavors was the launching in the 1980s of the "Third Search for the Historical Jesus" among Christian and Jewish scholars (Swidler 1988; Swidler et al. 1990) followed by my involvement in the dialogue with Buddhism, (Swidler and Fernando, 1984) and then the launching of the Christian-Confucian Dialogue, June 8–15, 1988 (Swidler et al. 2005). Then, as part of this wave, some who were involved in individual dialogues began to reflect on "dialogue" itself. As this was happening the Berlin Wall came down in November, 1989, and the Soviet Union – which everybody (including the CIA and the KGB) thought would last well into the third millennium – teetered into oblivion.

Shortly afterward, Samuel Huntington argued that the world had settled back in to a "Clash of Civilizations" (Huntington 1993, 1996). He was right. There was/is a "clash of civilizations," but that did not, and does not, describe the entire contemporary global scene. The world also dramatically began to move into the "Age of Global Dialogue," which my work, as just one scholar, reflected. In that same time period, between 1990 and 1992, I published twelve books dealing with inter-religious dialogue (see the reference list).

In 2007, six years after Al Qaeda's attack on America, Islam began to join global inter-religious dialogue in a massive way. This *volte-face* is analogous to the full-force entry of the Catholic Church into inter-religious dialogue beginning with Vatican II. Positive events suddenly began to erupt exponentially. This embrace of "*global* inter-religious dialogue" by Islam came first from 138 Muslim scholars and religious leaders from around the world on October 13, 2007, when they issued the amazing public letter "A Common Word Between Us," inviting Christians leaders and scholars to join with them in Dialogue (see: www.acommonword.com).[2]

Then, onto the stage of world inter-religious dialogue strode King Abdullah of Saudi Arabia, the heart-land of Islam! Having met Pope Benedict XVI in 2007, King Abdullah launched a World Conference on Dialogue with all the religions of the world in Spain, the land of the medieval "Golden Age" of inter-religious dialogue – Convivencia – on July 16–18, 2008 (www.saudi-us-relations.org/articles/2008/ioi/080719-madrid-declaration.html). Further, King Abdullah supported, and even lent his name, to the establishment of the King Abdullah Center for the Study of Contemporary Islam and the Dialogue of Civilizations within Imam University, Riyadh, Saudi Arabia. The very name sends a loud and clear message, that if you wish to be a serious Muslim in the contemporary world, you need to be involved in dialogue with the other civilizations of the world. As an initial down-payment on that pledge, in 2009 the King Abullah Center sent fourteen professors of Islamics from Imam University to study dialogue and democracy with the Dialogue Institute: inter-religious, intercultural, international (DI is the outreach arm of JES). In March, 2011, I lectured at Baku, Azerbaijan, Sulaimani, Iraqi Kurdistan, and Beirut, Lebanon, establishing new "Dialogue Institutes" in each place, as well as one in Kinshasa, Congo, as part of the expanding Dialogue Institutes Network – DIN – linked to DI/JES (http://institute.jesdialogue.org/programs/network).

There are, of course, now vastly many more instances of Muslim involvement in dialogue around the world. Contrast this with the fact that the ten Muslim scholars whom I and Gene Fisher were able to gather for the International Scholars Annual Trialogue (ISAT), starting in 1978 and still running, could not find any kindred-spirit Muslims worldwide, until 2007. This burgeoning of inter-religious, interideological dialogue around the world is engaging all the religions and ideologies. For example, the most famous of contemporary Confucian scholars, Weiming Tu, was professor at Harvard University for decades, until 2011, when he was brought to China's equivalent, Beijing University, to start the Institute for Advanced Humanistic Studies, dedicated in a major way to the "Dialogue of Civilizations." Even many agnostics and atheists are recognizing the importance of the exploding inter-religious dialogue and want to be part of it. Without a doubt, inter-religious, interideological dialogue has gained cultural, academic and religious relevance in a variety of ways. The plethora of bilateral dialogues among the religions of the world that has sprung up in the latter half of the twentieth century is reflected in manifold essays on these multiple dialogues in the rest of this volume, and doubtless will only increase expontially.

Reasons for the Rise of Dialogue

How after thousands of millennia of absolutistic exclusivism – I alone possess all the truth, and anyone who disagrees with me obviously is mistaken – did large portions of humanity start to reverse its attitude and begin to think that they could learn from each other, particularly in that hypersensitive area of religion? Why did humanity begin in the last hundred years or so to reach out in dialogue?

Of course there are circumstantial reasons why dialogue is becoming more and more important today as world travel has been expanding massively. But there are also numerous internal reasons for this most radical shift. Thomas Kuhn revolutionized our understanding of the development of scientific thinking with his notion of the paradigm shift. He painstakingly showed that fundamental "paradigms" or "exemplary models" are the large thought-frames within which we place and interpret all observed data, and that scientific advancement inevitably brings about paradigm shifts – from geocentricism to heliocentrism, for example, or from Newtonian to Einsteinian physics, which are always vigorously resisted at first but finally prevail (Kuhn 1970).

Since the eighteenth-century European Enlightenment, Christendom has been undergoing a major epistemological paradigm shift in how we humans understand our process of understanding and what meaning and status we attribute to "truth," that is, our epistemology. This new epistemological paradigm is increasingly determining how we perceive, conceive, think about, and subsequently decide and act in the world. Whereas the Western notion of truth was largely absolute, static, and monologic or exclusive up to the eighteenth/nineteenth-centuries Enlightenment, it has since become deabsolutized, dynamic, and dialogic – in a word, it has become "relational." Already two millennia and more ago some Hindu and Buddhist thinkers held a nonabsolutistic epistemology, but that fact had no significant impact on the West owing to the relative cultural eclipse of those civilizations in the early modern period and the dominance of the Western scientific worldview. Since the middle of the nineteenth century, Eastern thought has become increasingly well-known in the West, and proportionately influential. This knowledge and influence appears to be increasing geometrically in recent decades. This "new" view of truth came about in at least six different, but closely related, ways. In brief they are historicism, intentionality, sociology of knowledge, limits of language, hermeneutics and dialogue.

Historicism

Before the nineteenth century in Europe truth, that is, *a statement about reality*, was conceived in quite an absolute, static, exclusivistic either-or manner. If something was true at one time, it was always true; not only empirical facts but also the meaning of things or the ought-ness that was said to flow from them were thought of in this way. At bottom, the notion of truth was based exclusively on the Aristotelian principle of non-contradiction: a thing could not be true and not true in the same way at the same time. Truth was defined by way of exclusion; A was A because it could be shown not to be not-A. Truth was thus understood to be absolute, static, exclusivistically either-or. This is a *classicist* or *absolutist* view of truth.

In the nineteenth century many scholars came to perceive all statements about the truth of the meaning of something as partially the products of their historical circumstances. Those concrete circumstances helped determine the fact that the statement under study was even called forth, that it was couched in particular intellectual categories (for example, abstract Platonic, or concrete legal, language), in particular literary forms (for example, mythic or metaphysical language), and in particular psychological settings (for example, a polemic response to a specific attack). These scholars argued that only if the truth statements were placed in their historical situation, their historical *Sitz im Leben*, could they be properly understood. The understanding of the text could be found only in *context*. To express that same original meaning in a later *Sitz im Leben* one would require a proportionately different statement. Thus, all statements about the meaning of things were now seen to be deabsolutized in terms of time. This is a *historical* view of truth. Clearly at its heart is a notion of *relationality*: any statement about the truth of the meaning of something has to be understood in *relation*ship to its historical context.

Intentionality

Later thinkers like Max Scheler (1874–1928) added a corollary to this historicizing of knowledge; it concerned not the past but the future. Such scholars also saw truth as having an element of intentionality at its base, as being oriented ultimately toward action, praxis. They argued that we perceive certain things as questions to be answered, and that we set goals to pursue specific knowledge because we wish to do something about those matters; we intend to live according to the truth and meaning that we hope to discern in the answers to the questions we pose, in the knowledge we decide to seek. The truth of the meaning of things was thus seen as de-absolutized by the action-oriented intentionality of the thinker-speaker. This is an *intentional* or *praxis* view of truth, and it too is basically *relational*: a statement has to be understood in *relation*ship to the action-oriented intention of the speaker.

The sociology of knowledge

Just as statements of truth about the meaning of things were seen by some thinkers to be historically deabsolutized in time, so too, starting in the twentieth century with scholars like Karl Mannheim (1893–1947), such statements began to be seen as deabsolutized by such things as the culture, class, and gender of the thinker-speaker, regardless of time. All reality was said to be perceived from the perspective of the perceiver's own world view. Any statement of the truth of the meaning of something was seen to be perspectival, "standpoint-bound," *standort-gebunden*, as Karl Mannheim put it, and thus deabsolutized. This is a *perspectival* view of truth and is likewise *relational*: all statements are fundamentally *related* to the standpoint of the speaker.

The limitations of language

Following Ludwig Wittgenstein (1889–1951) and others, many thinkers have come to see that any statement about the truth of things can be at most only a partial description of the reality it is trying to describe. Although reality can be seen from an almost limitless number of perspectives, human language can express things from only one perspective at once. If we ask a question in legal thought-categories, for example, we will naturally receive answers in legal categories, which will not necessarily answer questions of ethics, or of empirical reality. Further, when we are dealing with religious questions, the very fact of dealing with the truth of the "meaning" of something indicates that the knower is essentially involved, and hence reflects the perspectival character of all such statements. A statement may be true, of course – it may accurately describe the extramental reality it refers to – but it will always be cast in particular thought-categories, language, concerns, etc., of a particular "standpoint," and in that sense will be limited, deabsolutized. This is a *perspectival* view of truth, and therefore also *relational*. This limited and limiting, as well as liberating, quality of language is especially clear in talk of the transcendent. the transcendent is by definition that which goes beyond our experience.

Any statements about the transcendent must thus be de-absolutized and limited far beyond the perspectival character seen in ordinary statements.

Hermeneutics

Hans-Georg Gadamer (1900–2002), Bernard Lonergan (1904–1984), and Paul Riceour (1913–2005) recently led the way in developing the science of hermeneutics, which, by arguing that all knowledge of a text is at the same time an *interpretation* of the text, further de-absolutizes claims about the "true" meaning of the text. But this basic insight goes beyond knowledge of texts and applies to all knowledge. When I come to know something the object comes into me in a certain way, i.e. through the lens that I use to perceive it. This is an *interpretive* view of truth. It is clear that *relationality* pervades this hermeneutical, interpretative, view of truth.

Dialogue

A further development of this basic insight is that I learn not by being merely passively open or receptive to, but in dialogue with extramental reality. I not only "hear" or receive reality, but I also – and, I think, first of all – "speak" to reality. I ask it questions, I stimulate it to speak back to me, to answer my questions. In the process I give reality the specific categories and language in which to respond. The "answers" that I receive back from reality will always be in the language, the thought-categories, of the questions I put to it. It can "speak" to me, can really communicate with my mind, only in a language and categories that I understand. When the speaking, the responding, grows less and less understandable to me, if the answers I receive are sometimes confused and unsatisfying, then I probably need to learn to speak a more appropriate language when I put questions to reality. If, for example, I ask the question, "How far is yellow?" I will receive a non-sense answer. Or if I ask questions about living things in mechanical categories, I will receive confusing and unsatisfying answers. This is a *dialogic* view of truth, whose very name reflects its *relationality*.

In sum, our understanding of truth and reality has been undergoing a radical shift. This new paradigm which is being born understands all statements about reality, especially about the meaning of things, to be historical, intentional, perspectival, partial, interpretive and dialogic. What is common to all these qualities is the notion of *relationality*, that is, that all expressions or understandings of reality are in some fundamental way *related* to the speaker or knower. It is while bearing this paradigm shift in mind that we proceed with our analysis.

The contribution of the "scientific" study of religion to inter-religious dialogue

For thousands of years almost the only religion "taught" was by the adherents themselves. When for one reason or another a religion other than the "true" one was taught, it was almost always taught by the outsider. Example: for centuries Judaism was taught to Jews by Jews, but when Judaism was taught at the University of Paris, Oxford, or Cambridge, it was taught by Christians. The same was true concerning Islam in Paris as well as concerning the teaching of Christianity at Al-Khasar in Cairo. The study of "religion" was done from the perspective of the religion of the teacher/student. Thus, there was Christian "theology," Muslim *kalam*, etc. After the eighteenth-century Enlightenment in the West and the subsequent development of the "critical" science of history, and then the various social sciences (sociology, anthropology, psychology, etc.) in the course of the nineteenth century, the "scientific" study of religion (*Religionswissenschaft*) was born – Max Müller (1823–1900) being recognized as its "grandfather" – in its last quarter.

The study of religion largely continued in departments of theology for the rest of the nineteenth century and more than half of the twentieth century. When religions other than the "home" religion (in the West, almost always Christianity) were studied and taught, it was almost inevitably by a Christian theologian. This began to change when Temple University became a state-related university, divested itself of its Divinity School, and established its Department of Religion in 1964 (other state universities, for example, the University of Iowa, had developed various symbioses with religious bodies in the teaching about religion). Temple University's Department of Religion pioneered a new way to study and teach religion, namely, by gathering professors who were critical scholars of the religions they were teaching, in addition to professors whose approach was more *Religionswissenschaft*. Thus, the world's religions were studied/taught by critical scholars who knew the religion from "the inside" and "the outside."

One can begin here to discern the differences between the study of and teaching about religion via one of the various forms of *Religionswissenschaft* on the one hand, and, as noted above, what occurs when "religious insiders," that is, members of two or more religions, come together primarily to learn from each other what the other thinks/does and why.

The epistemological assumption underlying dialogue is that "Nobody knows everything about anything" – which clearly includes that most complicated of all disciplines, religion. Hence, the primary aim of inter-religious dialogue is for the dialogue partners to learn something about the ultimate meaning of life that they did not know solely from their own religious perspective. Whether or not one agrees with one's dialogue partner's view of something, learning more about how and why she or he understands, and hence acts in, the world necessarily influences how the first partner perceives, and therefore acts in, the world. Thus, ultimately, the philosophy guiding the early stages of inter-religious dialogue can be said to be pragmatism: The participants of inter-religious dialogue were interested in what William James and other pragmatists designated the "cash value" of the ideas discussed – what difference they make in how they see life and, hence, live it.

In the higher education study of religion, inter-religious dialogue *itself* occured, as did also the study *of* it. There are a number of philosophical, social-scientific, and religious issues that underlie inter-religious dialogue that needed to be studied in order to understand the other. The results of this study, in turn, came to significantly influence the actual dialogues that occurred, whether in a university setting or elsewhere.

Comparative religion, on the other hand, engages in a historical cross-cultural study of religious phenomena with the emphasis being on comparison. Scholars "observe similar phenomena from religions laid side by side and draw conclusions from such comparison." (Swidler and Mojzes 2000: 135) Concepts and categories are examined for similarities and differences, at times hypothesizing about their origins – whether there was a historical connection or an independent origin of recurrent themes. Some scholars seek universal structures, while others reject this as an unwarranted imposition upon diverse religious phenomena. Comparative religion did not *per se* promote inter-religious dialogue, but insights from it came to be useful in dialogue.

Thus, comparative religion, or more broadly, *Religionswissenschaft*, made valuable contributions to the understanding of religion and the influences it has in human life. It provided extremely helpful resources for inter-religious dialogue, helping religious and nonreligious persons and groups to understand themselves and others better, and consequently to act with greater respect for one's own religious self and that of the Other. Inter-religious dialogue came to utilize these resources from *Religionswissenschaft* and elsewhere to engage in that respectful, learning encounter with the religious Other which is the very definition of inter-religious dialogue.

The Deepening and Expanding of Inter-Religious Dialogue

Inter-religious dialogue has not remained bilateral, or even multilateral, but has also become global. Let me mention just four examples: http://jes/dialogue

First, was the founding in 1970 in Kyoto, Japan, of the World Conference on Religion and Peace (WCRP, en.wikipedia.org/wiki/World_Conference_of_Religions_for_Peace – also known as Religions for Peace) by Nikkyo Niwano. It has affiliates in 75 countries around the world, and, among other activities, holds an international conference every five years. Nikkyo Niwano was also the co-founder in 1938 of a Japanese Buddhist sect, Rissho Kosei Kai, which today has 6.5 million members (en.wikipedia.org/wiki/Rissh%C5%8D_K%C5%8Dsei_Kai). In the early 1960s Niwano met Joseph Spae, a Belgian Catholic priest scholar of Buddhism and inter-religious dialogue – he had established the Oriens Institute for Religious Research in Tokyo – who introduced him to Pope Paul VI during Vatican Council II (1962–1965). This led Niwano to focus much of his personal energy and that of Rissho Kosei Kai on inter-religious dialogue, one result of which was the launching of the WCRP (current Secretary General, William Vendley – wvendley@wcrp.org), and in 1976 the related Asian Conference on Religion and Peace (ACRP (rk-world.org/acrp.aspx), current Secretary General, Sunggon Kim (drkim123@yahoo.co.kr).

Second, the United Religions Initiative (URI) was launched. The charter of the organization mentions that "The idea for *URI* came to California Episcopal Bishop William Swing in 1993, after an invitation by the United Nations to host a large interfaith service in San Francisco, marking the 50th anniversary of the signing of the UN Charter. He asked himself, 'If the nations of the world are working together for peace through the UN, then where are the world's religions?'" (uri.org/about_uri/charter). It also has affiliates in 75 countries around the world.

Third, in 1971, a year after the founding of the WCRP, Taesan (1916–1998), the second Head Dharma Master of a new sect of Buddhism founded in Korea in 1916, Won Buddhism, proposed a United Religions Organization (URO) parallel to the United Nations. Taesan's vision was for United Religions "to develop spiritual power through the cooperation of the world religions and to promote human happiness and world peace through the balance and harmony of political power and spiritual strength." Thus reported Rev. Dr. Bokin Kim, daughter of Master Sotaesan and President of the Won Institute of Graduate Studies (soninstitute.edu) in Philadelphia, as well as a former doctoral student of mine at Temple University Department of Religion (Bokin Kim 2000). For a number of years in the latter part of the twentieth century URO had a representative at the UN in New York, but eventually folded its work into that of the URI.

Fourth, the launching of the Movement for a Global Ethic. In the fall of 1990, while my wife Arlene and I were teaching at Temple University Japan, my longtime friend and colleague Hans Küng sent me a copy of his new book *Projekt Weltethos* (Küng 1990). The message of the book was that the world needs a common ethical foundation. I immediately drafted an editorial for the *Journal of Ecumenical Studies* and faxed it to Hans, as one of the founding Associate Editors, asking whether he wished to co-sign the editorial. The editorial argued that the next step toward realizing a global ethic was to attempt to articulate a "Universal Declaration of a Global Ethic," analogous to the Universal Declaration of Human Rights of the UN, which every religious and nonreligious group and individual could, and eventually would, publicly commit to. Hans did co-sign and we published the editorial – along with simultaneous publication in various international publications, as well as Hans's announcing it at a September, 1991 lecture at UNESCO in Paris – with the additional signatures of twenty-four more scholars from various religions.[3] I then brought the idea to *ISAT*, who asked me to consult as widely as possible and bring back to the next annual meeting a proposed draft of a Universal Declaration of a Global Ethic, which I did. About the same time Hans was asked by the committee in Chicago preparing for the second Chicago Parliament of the World's Religions to develop a similar draft of a declaration for them, which he did. It was signed by the two-hundred-plus religious leaders at the September, 1993 Chicago World Parliament, and subsequently circulated (weltethos.org), as was also the one created for/at ISAT. They and other versions, as well as an extensive list of two dozen organizations and web sites fostering a global ethic, can be found at: globalethic.org. The latest Institute for World Ethics was launched as part of the Institute for Advanced Humanistic Studies (Director, Weiming Tu at Beijing University in relationship with the University of Tübingen, Germany, in November, 2012.

Conclusion: The Current State of Inter-Religious Dialogue

For millennia religion was at the very heart of all human societies, but with the Enlightenment it both was driven out of, and abandoned, civil society; now it is coming back in (Micklethwait and Wooldrige 2009) – both in very destructive ways – "9/11," Palestine–Israel, Sri Lanka, Northern Ireland, Kashmer, Sudan . . ., – but also in constructive ways – the peace movement, reconciliation movements, as in South Africa, Ghandi,

Martin Luther King, and especially inter-religious dialogue. This, then, is the twenty-first-century state of inter-religious dialogue. It is no longer confined to the reservation of theological/religious reflection and cultic activity; it is moving ever more broadly and deeply and bringing religion back into all the opinion-shaping institutions of society: business, education, politics, the arts. Thus, flowing out of its dim beginning in the Enlightenment, inter-religious dialogue is now spreading in all the societal structures of the globe, moving humanity in the direction of a Global Dialogical Civilization.

Notes

1   http://en.wikipedia.org/wiki/Parliament_of_the_World%E2%80%99s_Religions accessed December 1, 2012.
2   This was quickly followed up by a major scholarly conference at Yale University, which also deliberately included Jewish scholars: "The 'Common Word' letter was drafted by Muslim leaders and addressed specifically to leaders of 'Christian churches everywhere' in order to address concrete issues and problems between Christians and Muslims. Given the extent, however, to which Jewish concerns are intertwined with those of Christians and Muslims, and given the historic Christian and Muslim tendency inappropriately to exclude the Jewish community, we are deeply committed to seeking out Jewish leaders and scholars to play a central role in the ongoing Common Word dialogue." (Saperstein et al. in Wolf et al. 2010).
3   Swidler and Küng (1991). The additional signatories were Mohammed Arkoun (Muslim), Julia Ching (Confucian/Catholic, John Cobb (Methodist), Kkalid Duran ((Muslim), Claude Geffré (Catholic), Irving Greenberg (Jewish), Norbert Greinacher (Catholic), Riffat Hassan (Muslim), Rivka Horwitz (Jewish), John Hick (Presbyterian), Adel Khoury (Catholic), Paul Knitter (Catholic), Karl-Josef Kuschel (Catholic), Pinchas Lapide (Jewish), Johannes Lähnenmann (Lutheran), Dietmar Mieth (Catholic), Paul Mojzes (Methodist), Jürgen Moltmann (Reformed), Fathi Osman (Muslim), Raimundo Panikkar (Hindu/Buddhist/Catholic), Daniel Polish (Jewish), Rodolfo Stavenhagen (sociologist), Theo Sundermeier (Lutheran), Knut Walf (Catholic/Taoist).

Bibliography

Barrows, John Henry (ed.). *The World's Parliament of Religions.* 2 vols. Chicago: Parliament Publishing Company, 1893.

Beversluis, Joel D. (ed.). *Sourcebook of the World's Religions: An Interfaith Guide to Religion and Spirituality.* Navato, CA: New World Library, 2000.

Bhuyan, P. R. *Swami Vivekananda.* Atlantic Publishers & Distributors, 2003.

Bokin Kim. "The Il-Won Symbol and Its Ecumenical Significance," in *Concerns and Issues in Won Buddhism,* ed. Bokin Kim. Philadelphia: Won Publications, 2000, p. 133, note 41; originally published as an article in *Buddhist–Christian Studies,* 14 (1994).

Eck, Diana. *A New Religious America: How a "Christian Country" Has Become the World's Most Religiously Diverse Nation.* San Francisco: HarperCollins, 2001.

Heckman, Bud, with Rori Picker Neiss (eds.). *Interactive Faith: The Essential Interreligious Community-Building Handbook.* Woodstock, VT: Skylight Paths Publishing, 2008.

Hick, John. *An Interpretation of Religion: Human Responses to the Transcendent.* New Haven, CT: Yale University Press, 2nd edn., 2004.

Huntington, Samuel. "Clash of Civilizations," *Foreign Affairs*, July, 1993, pp. 22–49.

Huntington, Samuel. *The Clash of Civilizations and the Remaking of World Order*. New York: Simon & Schuster, 1996.

Karlstroem, Nils. "Movements for international Friendship," in *A History of the Ecumenical Movement*, ed. Ruth Rouse. London, 1954.

Knitter, Paul. *No Other Name? A Critical Survey of Christian Attitudes Toward the World Religions*. Maryknoll, NY: Orbis Books, 1985.

Kuhn, Thomas S. *The Structure of Scientific Revolutions*. Chicago: University of Chicago Press, 2nd edn, 1970.

Küng, Hans. *Christianity and the World Religions: Paths of Dialogue with Islam, Hinduism, and Buddhism*. Garden City, NY: Doubleday, 1986.

Küng, Hans. *Projekt Weltethos*. Munich: Pieper Verlag, 1990. The slightly later English version was titled, *Global Responsibility: In Search of a New World Ethic*. New York: Crossroad, 1991.

Küng, Hans and Karl-Josef Kuschel (eds.). *A Global Ethic*. New York: Continuum, 1993.

Magonet, Jonathan. *Talking to the Other: Jewish Interfaith Dialogue with Christians and Muslims*. London: I.B. Tauris, 2003.

Michael, J. P. *Christen suchen eine Kirche*. Freiburg, 1958.

Micklethwait, John and Adrian Wooldridge. *God Is Back. How the Global Revival of Faith Is Changing the World*. New York: The Penguin Press, 2009.

Pinker, Steven. *The Angel of Our Better Nature. Why Violence Has Declined*. New York: Viking Press, 2011.

Pius XI. "Über die Förderung der wahren Religionseinheit," *Die Friedenstadt*, II, 1928.

Saperstein, Andrew, Rick Love and Joseph Cumming. "Answers to Frequently Asked Questions Regarding the Yale Response to 'A Common Word Between Us and You'," in *A Common Word*, eds. Miroslav Wolf, Ghazi bin Muhammad, and Melissa Yarrington. Grand Rapids, MI: Eerdmans, 2010, pp. 179f.

Sasse, H. *Die Weltkonferenz für Glaube und Kirchenverfassung*. Berlin, 1929.

Søderblom, Nathan. *Christian Fellowship, or the United Life and Work of Christendom*. New York, 1923.

Swami Vivekananda. *The Sayings & Utterances of Swami Vivekananda, The Complete Works*, vol. 5, no. 82., found at http://www.ramakrishnavivekananda.info/vivekananda/volume_5/vol_5_frame.htm (accessed December 1, 2012).

Swidler, Leonard. *The Ecumenical Vanguard*. Pittsburgh: Duquesne University Press, 1966.

Swidler, Leonard. *Yeshua: A Model for Moderns*. Kansas City: Sheed & Ward, 1988.

Swidler, Leonard (ed.). *Human Rights: Christians, Marxists, and Others in Dialogue*. Paragon House, 1991.

Swidler, Leonard. *Die Zukunft der Theologie im Dialog der Religionen und Weltanschauungen*. Pustet/Kaiser Verlag, 1992.

Swidler, Leonard. *The Meaning of Life at the Edge of the Third Millennium*. Paulist Press, 1992.

Swidler, Leonard. *Introduzione al buddismo. Paralleli con l'etica ebraico-cristiana*. Co-authored with Antony Fernando). Edizioni Dehoniane, 1992.

Swidler, Leonard (ed.). *Muslims in Dialogue: The Evolution of a Dialogue over a Generation*. Lewiston, NY: Edwin Mellen Press, 1992.

Swidler, Leonard. *Der umstrittene Jesus*. Quell Verlag, 1991; Chr. Kaiser/Gütersloher Verlagshaus, 1993.

Swidler, Leonard. *After the Absolute: The Dialogical Future of Religious Reflection*. Fortress Press, 2000.

Swidler, Leonard. *Club Modernity. For Reluctant Christians*. Philadelphia, PA. The Ecumenical Press, 2011).

Swidler, Leonard and Antony Fernando. *Buddhism Made Plain for Christians and Jews*. Maryknoll, NY: Orbis Books, 1984.

Swidler, Leonard, John Cobb, Monika Hellwig and Paul Knitter, *Death or Dialogue: From the Age of Monologue to the Age of Dialogue*. Trinity Press International, 1990.

Swidler, Leonard and Paul Mojzes. *Attitudes of Religions and Ideologies towards the Outsider: The Other*. Lewiston, NY: Edwin Mellen Press, 1990.

Swidler, Leonard and Paul Mojzes. *Christian Mission and Interreligious Dialogue*. Lewiston, NY: Edwin Mellen Press, 1990.

Swidler, Leonard, Gerard Sloyan, Lewis Eron and Lester Dean. *Bursting the Bonds. A Jewish–Christian Dialogue on Jesus and Paul*. Maryknoll, NY: Orbis Books, 1990.

Swidler, Leonard and Hans Küng. "Toward a 'Universal Declaration of Global Ethos,'" *Journal of Ecumenical Studies*, 28(1) (Winter, 1991): 123–125.

Swidler, Leonard and Paul Mojzes. *The Study of Religion in an Age of Global Dialogue*. Philadelphia: Temple University Press, 2000.

Swidler, Leonard, co-ed. and author with Shu-hsien Liu and John Berthrong. *Confucianism in Dialogue Today. West, Christianity, and Judaism*. Philadelphia: Ecumenical Press, 2005.

Tatlow, Tissington. "The World Conference on Faith and Order," in Ruth Rouse, ed., *A History of the Ecumenical Movement*. London, 1954.

Organizations Promoting Inter-Religious Dialogue

The book by Heckman and Neiss, *Interactive Faith*, has a helpful listing as of 2008 of over 60 organizations dealing with inter-religious dialogue, with a brief description and website of each.

Arts & Spirituality Center: www.artsandspirituality.org

Beliefnet: www.beliefnet.com

Council for a Parliament of the World's Religions: www.cpwr.org

Dialogue Institute: www.jesdialogue.org

Fellowship of Reconciliation: www.forusa.org

Hartford Institute for Religion Research: www.hirr.hartsem.edu

The Interfaith Alliance: www.interfaithalliance.org

Interfaith Youth Core: www.ifyc.org

International Association for Religious Freedom: www.iarf.net

North American Interfaith Network: www.nain.org

Pluralism Project: www.pluralism.org

Religions for Peace: www.religionsforpeace.org

Temple of Understanding: www.templeofunderstanding.org

United Religions Initiave: www.uri.org

CHAPTER 2

Conditions for Inter-Religious Dialogue

Catherine Cornille

In the encounter between members from different religious traditions, the term "dialogue" tends to be used in many ways, ranging from peaceful coexistence and friendly exchanges, to active engagement with the teachings and practices of the other, and from cooperation toward social change to common prayer and participation in the ritual life of the other. Each of these different types of dialogue will naturally involve differing sets of conditions or requirements (for other lists of conditions for dialogue see Dupuis 1997; Panikkar 1999; Swidler et al. 1990; and Timmerman and Segaert 2005). Whereas a peaceful social and political context will play an important role in promoting peaceful coexistence and friendly exchanges, a basic sense of human solidarity and a commitment to the common good may be sufficient to engage in joint social projects. Common worship, on the other hand, requires a particular conception of the nature and the goal of prayer or worship, and some recognition of the authenticity and effectiveness of the ritual practices of the other. This latter understanding of dialogue illustrates that the more dialogue touches upon distinctively religious elements, such as ritual, the more difficult or challenging it becomes.

In this article, I will discuss the conditions for dialogue focused specifically on the teachings and practices of religious traditions. Dialogue, in its ideal form, involves a conversation or exchange in which participants are willing to listen to and learn from one another. It is the possibility of mutual learning which makes dialogue more than a luxury or benevolent pastime for the curious, and renders it a matter of internal religious necessity or opportunity. Dialogue is here thus understood as comparative theology in the broad sense of the term, as a constructive engagement between religious texts, teachings, and practices oriented toward the possibility of change and growth. To be sure, far from every dialogue between religions will actually yield religious fruit. But it is the very possibility that one may learn from the other which moves religious traditions from self-sufficiency to openness to the other.

The possibility of learning from the religious other, however, involves a demanding set of conditions. It first of all requires recognition that there is still room for growth in one's understanding of the truth, and it also presupposes a regard of the other religion as a potential source or occasion for such growth. In the language of virtues, the first may be called epistemological humility and the latter generosity or hospitality toward the truth of the other. In addition to these two fundamental conditions, dialogue between religions also presupposes identification with a particular religion from which one engages in dialogue, trust that the other religion addresses the same ultimate truth or fundamental questions in a mutually relevant way, and belief that one may actually understand the teachings and practices of another religion in a way that might open up one's own religion to new insights and actions. The latter conditions I have designated as commitment, interconnection, and empathy respectively.

If phenomenologically sound, these conditions apply equally to any religious tradition engaged in dialogue, even though their concrete form and expression may vary. In *The Im-Possibility of Interreligious Dialogue*, I developed these conditions in greater detail and discussed them in light of the possible resources available within the Christian tradition (Cornille 2008). But it is up to each tradition to discover in their teachings and traditions a religious motivation to engage in dialogue with other religions.

Humility

The first condition for inter-religious dialogue is recognition of the very possibility of change or growth within one's own tradition. This presupposes a humble recognition of the limited or finite way in which the ultimate truth is grasped or expressed within one's religion. Such humility may be applied to doctrines, rituals, and/or ethical systems. It may express itself in terms of the relativity of all historical and cultural expression and/or in terms of a progression toward final clarity and understanding at some future point in time. But the possibility of learning from another religion presupposes at least a recognition that one may still grow in understanding or expressing the fullness of truth.

Such epistemological humility goes against the grain of most religious self-understanding. Religions tend to claim the fullness of truth and the definitive and unquestionable way to the highest goal. Most religions refer to a transcendent source for their fundamental teachings and practices, which forms the basis for religious confidence and certainty. This generates commitment and surrender, which most religions regard as the basis for religious and spiritual growth. For some religions, the locus of absoluteness is situated in particular teachings which must be accepted on faith. For others, it involves particular ritual actions or rules for daily life which must be executed precisely and followed unfailingly. Most religions exhibit a combination of unquestionable teachings, prescriptions, and rules. To be sure, every religion is subject to historical and cultural changes and developments, and to internal disagreement and schism. But each new interpretation pretends to preserve the original and unchanging truth revealed to its founder. As such, the reality of change and growth tends to be minimalized, ignored, or effaced, as every new tradition or school of interpretation claims to offer a more authentic or faithful interpretation of the original revelation.

Epistemological humility thus requires a shift in most religious self-understanding. Some religions do have ready resources for recognizing the limits of their claims to absolute and final truth. Mahayana Buddhism, for example, is based on the explicit recognition of the fallibility of language in expressing ultimate truth (Garfield 2002), and Christianity's notion of the *eschatological proviso* should, at least theoretically, guard against identifying any historical forms with ultimate reality (*Dei Verbum* 8). But most religions may need to engage in a creative retrieval of resources which would permit some degree of doctrinal humility.

One area which offers a ready basis for epistemological humility in many religions is that of mysticism, in so far as it acknowledges the impossibility of fully expressing the experience of the ultimate reality. Mystical texts and teachings admit the radical transcendence of ultimate reality and the impossibility of fully expressing that reality in finite human terms. This recognition of the distinction between the ultimate reality itself and the finite categories in which it is expressed may come to reinforce epistemological humility and open up space for the possibility of growth. Pluralist thinkers have mined those traditions to argue for the unity of all mystical experiences and/or to call for an abandonment of all religious claims to absolute truth (Hick 1989). They tend to hold fast to the distinction between Eckhart's God and Godhead, or between Nirguna and Saguna Brahman, or between the known and the unknown names of God in Islam as the basis for abandoning all religious claims to absolute and final truth. While one need not go so far as to abandon all religious claims to superiority or exclusivity, this affirmation of the transcendence of ultimate reality may at least serve as the basis for doctrinal humility and openness to the possibility of growth and change in one's understanding of ultimate truth. This is probably one of the reasons why monastics in different religious traditions, whose life is oriented toward the cultivation and reflection of such spiritual or mystical experiences, have been at the forefront of the dialogue between religions.

A second basis for doctrinal humility may be found in the emergence of historical-critical and social-scientific study of religion. While believers often regard their religious teachings and practices as transmitted in pure and unaltered form since the beginning, the subjection of religious traditions to historical approaches tends to reveal human and finite hand in the emergence and development of particular teachings and practices. This awareness of the historical and cultural particularity of certain teachings and practices may come to loosen attachment to particular formula or forms of expression and open the way for accepting the possibility of change and growth. This also accords with the cultural-linguistic understanding of doctrine which, in the words of George Lindbeck, opposes "the boasting and sense of superiority that destroys the possibility of open and mutually enriching dialogue" (Lindbeck 1984: 64).

However, this approach to religious teachings and practices is often regarded as suspect or dangerous by those who seek to safeguard firm adherence to the teachings of a particular tradition. Pressed to their extreme, historical critical methods, like the emphasis on the radical transcendence of ultimate truth, may lead to relativism, and to the erasure of the cognitive or propositional nature of all religious claims or of faith in the efficacy of all ritual gestures and practices. However, recognition of the finite and relative nature of religious language does not necessarily lead to relativism, or to the reduction of religious truths to their historical and cultural contexts. One may recognize the limitation of religious expressions while still holding on to their truth, and even superiority. As such, religious conviction does not preclude doctrinal humility, nor does doctrinal humility erode religious conviction.

Commitment

The second condition for inter-religious dialogue is commitment to a particular religious tradition. It is such commitment which distinguishes dialogue between religions from a purely personal exploration of the teachings of different religious traditions for spiritual enrichment. Whereas the latter form of engagement is guided purely by personal taste and judgment, the former involves a sense of representing a particular tradition, being accountable to that tradition and submitting one's judgment to that of a larger whole. Speaking from and for a particular religion plays an important role, both for the partner in dialogue and for the religion itself. For the partner, it offers a sense of confidence that one is not only engaging personal opinion, but rather a whole tradition of reflection on important religious questions. And for religious traditions, it offers the opportunity to reap some of the fruits of dialogue. It is true that serious inter-religious dialogue takes place between individuals. But it is only in so far as those individuals are willing to engage their own traditions with the insights and experiences gained through dialogue that traditions are also likely to grow and change.

Though the idea of representing a whole religious tradition in dialogue may seem daunting, it involves various qualifications. First, dialogue occurs between individuals located within particular sub-traditions of religions. As such dialogue takes place not between a Muslim and a Buddhist, but rather between a Shi'ite Muslim and a Tibetan Buddhist, or between a Mennonite Christian and a Conservative Jew. Second, dialogue does not presuppose a comprehensive knowledge of the tradition. While a basic knowledge and understanding of traditional teachings would be expected, dialogue itself can become an occasion to gain a deeper knowledge of one's own tradition as one attempts to answer probing questions raised by the religious other.

The act of representing a particular tradition in dialogue involves attesting not only to the contents, but also to the truth of particular teachings. This touches upon the much disputed question of the relationship between dialogue and mission (see from a Roman Catholic perspective the document "Dialogue and Proclamation" (Vatican Council for Interreligious Dialogue 1991)). While dialogue is often regarded as a friendly exchange of information about beliefs and practices, mission or evangelization is seen to involve an attempt to convince the other of the truth of those teachings and practices. As I have argued elsewhere, this tends to create a false dichotomy or a divided consciousness in those engaging religious others and a sense of suspicion in the partner in dialogue (Cornille 2011a). It also tends to deprive dialogue of its energy and zeal. In so far as its ultimate goal is the advancement of truth, dialogue may be regarded as a form of mutual or reciprocal witnessing.

In its ideal form, dialogue involves a back and forth between engaging in dialogue with the other and with one's own tradition. The latter movement takes place not only through internal confrontation and integration of different teachings in an intra-religious dialogue (Panikkar 1999), but also through second order dialogue with fellow believers, theologians, and representatives of the religious establishment. Traditions play an important role as a place of return for those involved in dialogue. Ideally, they provide a broader basis for discernment of insights gained in dialogue, and they allow for the fruits of the dialogue to be enjoyed by a larger community. However, the return to one's own tradition often forms a challenging moment in the process of dialogue. First, it is not always evident how to communicate the fruits of dialogue to the larger tradition. While some religions have a teaching authority (who may or may not support inter-religious dialogue), others do not have a clear structure of doctrinal oversight or evident channels through which the insights gained through dialogue might be disseminated. Scholars engaged in dialogue may publish their insights, but it often remains a challenge to translate those insights for the benefit of people in the pews.

A second challenge lies in the fact that religious traditions tend to be resistant to change and less than receptive to the new insights and experiences gained through dialogue. The admission of learning from another religion through dialogue may be perceived as an expression of weakness or insufficiency. This often leaves individuals engaged in dialogue in the margins of their respective traditions, either by necessity or choice. Inter-religious dialogue thus requires, on the part of participants, willingness to openly and humbly engage the larger tradition with the fruits of the dialogue, and on the part of official representatives of the traditions encouragement and openness toward the fruits of the dialogue.

Interconnection

In addition to the basic requirements of openness and commitment, inter-religious dialogue also presupposes belief that religions actually do have something to do with one another, that they deal with some of the same fundamental religious and existential questions or that they somehow connect in common concerns or on some higher plane. If the term religion is actually vacuous (as some argue) or if the religions are so different as to be entirely unrelated, then dialogue between religions could be regarded as futile or irrelevant.

Though the term religion has become a contested category, it would be disingenuous to deny that, at least from a historical or phenomenological perspective, the forms of belief and practice that have come to be called religions have nothing in common. While there are indeed many different definitions of religion, they all point to the ways in which humans have given expression (in myth, ritual, ethical systems, and institutional structures) to their relationship with some transcendent reality. Religions provide varying answers to many of the same fundamental questions and they attend in different ways to some of the same moments of existential crisis. This recognition of the other as engaged with the same or similar religious questions and desires offers a basic foundation as well as a starting point for inter-religious dialogue.

Participants in dialogue may find their common ground or goal in various places, either inside or outside of the religion proper. Often, religions have come together around common social or political causes: poverty, hunger, homelessness, war, or natural disasters (see this volume Chapter 9 on inter-religious dialogue and social action, and Chapter 10 on inter-faith dialogue and peace building). These common causes not only require a communal response, but they also allow religions to engage one another in practical terms and to connect on a basic human level. Such collaboration may in some cases lead to further dialogue on the reasons for engaging in social action, on the conceptions of the ideal society informing the pursuit of social change, or on any other topic of interest to both parties. Cooperation in common causes tends to establish a level of trust and friendship necessary for further fruitful and constructive exchange. However, the focus on a common cause *outside* of any tradition does not necessarily lead to enduring dialogue focused on the contents of religious faith and practice. First, the level of exchange between members of different religions may never go beyond attending to the practical matters at hand. And second, the actual occurrence of dialogue would remain dependent on the existence of common external challenges or crises.

Sustained dialogue between religions thus requires a sense of interconnection which is *intrinsic* to the religions themselves. Some search for this religious basis for interconnection in an experience or goal common to all religions involved. As such, mystical experiences have often been regarded as a meeting point between religions. Perennialist philosophers such as Aldous Huxley and essentialist scholars of mysticism such as Robert Forman argue that all religious traditions derive from or are oriented toward the same mystical experience (Huxley 1945; Forman 1999). This common experience then provides the reason for engaging in dialogue as well as the goal of dialogue.

Rather than a common mystical experience, pluralist thinkers such as John Hick have postulated the existence of a common ultimate reality as the basis and reason for dialogue between religions. Since all religions are partial expressions of this same ultimate reality (called the Real), dialogue between religions may be regarded as the only way to advance toward this ultimate reality and to approach the truth (Hick 1989).

While these notions of an interconnection between religious traditions in a spiritual experience or transcendent reality *common* to all religions may represent an important impulse and ground for dialogue, they also contain some limitations. First, the very idea that all religions meet in a common experience is difficult, if not impossible, to argue definitively, as is evident in the ongoing debate between essentialists and constructivists in the area of comparative mysticism. While the former assume a unified mystical experience, the latter argue that all mystical experiences are shaped by the categories and practices which lead up to the experience. The idea of a transcendent reality beyond all religious traditions has also been subject to critique in the area of theology of religion (D'Costa 2000, Heim 1999). Not only do most religions affirm a continuity between their conception of the ultimate reality and that reality itself, but they also tend to affirm the truth of their own claims, even when conflicting with those of others, and take such claims as the ultimate basis for judging the truth of others.

In addition to the question of the plausibility of a common experience and goal, the problem with such a conception of interconnection lies in the fact that it is not conducive to genuine interest in the particulars of other religions (Heim 1999: 28 ff.). If all religious teachings and practices are ultimately regarded as pointing to an experience or goal which is radically beyond any religious conception, then the expressions which make up the particularity and the identity of religious traditions do not matter very much. As such, the idea of a common spiritual ground or goal does not constitute a sufficiently compelling basis for engaging in dialogue about such particularities.

Rather than attempting to establish interconnection in a ground or goal common to religions, I would argue that what is required for dialogue is a sense of interconnection grounded in the concrete beliefs of any particular religion. It is not the belief in a common experience, but the conviction that all sentient beings possess Buddha-nature which will form the basis for engaging other religions from a Buddhist perspective, just as Christians will need to believe that the Biblical God is also revealed (in some form or to some degree) in the texts and teachings of other religions. The possibility of constructive inter-religious dialogue thus requires that every religious tradition involved develop a religious self-understanding in which (at least some of) the teachings of other religions are somehow related to or relevant for one's own religious conception of truth. As such, different religions will have different conceptions of how they are connected to other religious traditions. But it is through such various conceptions of interconnection that dialogue takes place.

Empathy

In addition to the more reflexive or self-referential conditions, dialogue between religions also requires the possibility of understanding one another across religious traditions. This epistemological condition for dialogue has been the subject of considerable debate in the study of religion (McCutcheon 1999). The importance of this condition may seem self-evident. If one is locked conceptually and experientially within one's own religion, then dialogue would never be able to yield any new insights or experiences. While constructive dialogue may not require perfect understanding of the religious other, it does presuppose some capacity to stretch one's religious imagination beyond the categories of one's own religion and gain some understanding of, and resonance with, religious teachings and practices other than one's own.

In so far as historical data are available, it has become more commonly accepted in the history of religions that an outsider to a particular religion may attain a level of knowledge and understanding of a tradition equal or at times even superior to that of an insider. A good number of classical scholarly studies in the history of religions were written by individuals who did not belong to the religion involved. Given proper linguistic and historical competency, there is thus no *a priori* reason to doubt the possibility of intellectually understanding the texts, teachings, practices, and philosophical traditions of another tradition. However, constructive dialogue also requires some level of empathic understanding of, or affective resonance with the other. Not only does this yield a deeper understanding of the meaning of particular teachings and practices, but it also provides a measure for what may eventually become the object of constructive dialogue. It is only insofar as one is able to resonate positively with particular beliefs and experiences in another religion that one will be disposed to entertain the possibility of integrating such teachings in one's own religion. Religious teachings or practices which leave one cold, or which elicit a negative response will probably not invoke much creative energy and initiative, save perhaps to demonstrate the superior value and power of one's own teachings. Empathy thus plays an important role in inter-religious dialogue.

The notion of empathy has become all but taboo in the study of religion. It is usually associated with the bygone days of romantic hermeneutics (Dilthey) and of early phenomenology of religion (Van der Leeuw). Empathy is indeed a highly elusive category and skill. However, insofar as it does play an important role in dialogue, one cannot but focus attention on some of its constituent dimensions. The term empathy has been generally understood as transposition into the mental lives of others or as "the experience of foreign consciousness" (Stein 1964: 11). Max Scheler defined empathy in cognitive terms as "all such attitudes as merely contribute to our apprehending, understanding, and in general, reproducing (emotionally) the experiences of others, including their states of feeling" (Scheler 1954: 8). The human capacity for empathy has been variously grounded in universal mental structures (Van der Leeuw 1930: 675), in the fundamental inter-connectedness of self and other (Ricoeur 1992: 372), and more recently in the existence of "mirror neurons" (Stueber 2006). In her work on empathy, Edith Stein refers to one's mental and emotional disposition or "structure" as the basis for empathy, arguing that "all foreign experience permitting itself to be derived from my own structure can be fulfilled, even if this structure has not actually unfolded" (Stein 1964: 104). This may suggest that one's actual religious beliefs and practices also play a role in the process of comprehending the religious life of the other. Most empathy involves some degree of analogical apprehension, or relation of the meaning of a particular teaching or ritual to one's given reservoir of religious experiences. As such, one's religious tradition plays a constitutive role in inter-religious empathy.

However, the possibility of empathic understanding of the other is not necessarily limited to the array of religious experience and insight already given in one's religious tradition and in one's personal experiential repertoire. Referring to the despair of Jesus on Gethsemane, Max Scheler argued that this experience "can be understood and shared regardless of our historical, racial and even human limitations. And for every candid heart which steeps itself in that desolation it operates, not as a reminder or revival of personal sufferings, great or small, but as the revelation of a new and greater suffering hitherto undreamed of" (Scheler 1954: 47). The study of and immersion in another tradition at times offers access to experiences and insights hitherto unknown. These may become the occasion for genuine religious learning and for further consideration of the possibility of engaging such beliefs and practices in a constructive dialogue with one's own tradition.

To be sure, not every religious belief or practice with which one resonates will become food for constructive engagement and dialogue. One may, for example, empathize with religious teachings and practices which offer little new or distinctive content for dialogue, and one may also develop a negative empathic response to certain teachings or practices. Constructive dialogue may also require more than a strictly personal positive resonance. It would probably take a more widespread appeal for a religion to consciously appropriate elements from another religious tradition.

Empathic understanding of another religion may be enhanced through direct participation in the religious life of the other. Ritual participation and direct access to the sources of religious and spiritual authority of a tradition raises one's sense of awareness and undoubtedly adds to one's ability to resonate, either positively or negatively, with the other. But it also points to the limits of full understanding of the other (Cornille 2011b; Moyaert 2013). Not only are there often limits to participation in the ritual life of the other, such participation also draws attention to the importance of actual faith in the process of understanding the other. While I may understand devotion to the Hindu Gods Krishna or Ganesha by way of analogy with my own devotion to Jesus Christ, I will never gain full access to the contents of the other's faith, insofar as it is essentially shaped by the object of faith. However, participation in Hindu devotion may still reveal levels of intensity of love of God and ritual expressions hitherto unknown, and positively inspiring.

Though empathy may not provide full access to the experience of an insider, it does allow for an expansion of one's religious imagination and experience. Whether or not the insights and experiences gained through the understanding of another tradition actually lead to constructive dialogue will depend on their compatibility with one's given religious framework, and a broader religious resonance.

Hospitality

The final, and sole sufficient condition for dialogue involves recognition of actual truth in another religion and hospitality toward integrating that truth in one's own tradition. This condition may be seen to include or presuppose most of the other conditions for dialogue: the recognition of truth in another religion presupposes some humility about the truth of one's tradition, commitment to a tradition which exercises hospitality, a general sense of the interconnectedness between religions, and genuine understanding of the other. The very discovery of truth in another religion may in and of itself be seen as a sufficient reason to engage that religion in a constructive dialogue.

Generosity or hospitality toward recognizing and integrating truth found in another religion does not necessarily require recognition of truth in all religions, or in every dimension of a particular religion. This would hardly be possible insofar as religions often espouse mutually exclusive or conflicting teachings. However, the discovery of any single inspiring thought or practice may or should lead to a constructive engagement.

In the process of discerning truth in other religions, it is evident that one's own religious tradition will serve as a starting point or basic norm. Teachings or practices which are in direct contradiction with one's own will unlikely be regarded as true. In functioning as criteria of truth, one's basic teachings may operate as minimal or maximal norms, or as negative or positive norms (Haight 1999: 409). This will determine the degree and the kind of truth present in other religions.

When the teachings of one's tradition operate as maximal or positive norm, only those teachings or practices in the other tradition which are identical to one's own will be regarded as valid or true. This approach to the question of alien truth is fairly common in religious traditions. It is unthreatening in so far as the presence of elements of truth in the other tradition does not challenge or call into question one's claim to possessing the fullness of truth. It also avoids the problem of logical incoherence in that it does not deny the truth of alien teachings which are identical to one's own. The recognition of truth in teachings which are no different than those already proclaimed in one's own tradition, however, leaves little room for constructive dialogue. It merely confirms or reinforces what one already knows, allowing for little or no possibility for change and growth. To be sure, teachings which seem similar are never identical insofar as they are embedded in different religious contexts and larger interpretative frameworks. As such, selflessness, though an ideal in many religious traditions, may have very different connotations, depending on particular anthropological presuppositions. Attention to the reality of differences-in-similarity may thus still allow for the possibility of learning from the other tradition, provided those differences in context and interpretation are not *a priori* rejected.

In functioning as a minimal or negative norm, one's tradition serves as a basis to exclude only those teachings and practices which are irreconcilable with one's own, or – stated positively – to affirm teachings and practices with are compatible with one's own. This leaves considerable room for recognizing truth in teachings which are different from those already present in one's tradition, and for genuine growth through learning from the other. Of course, not every teaching or practice which is in principle reconcilable with one's tradition will necessarily become the object of constructive reflection. Some differences between religions are more interesting or meaningful than others. Whereas dietary restrictions in one tradition may not contradict another, neither are they likely to be engaged in a constructive manner. Constructive engagement will thus depend on whether certain teachings or practices are seen to respond to certain practical or theoretical questions or needs, or whether they provide access to genuine religious knowledge or experience.

Some pluralist thinkers involved in the dialogue between religions reject altogether the use of religion-specific norms in the process of dialogue as patronizing (Hick 1981: 463). Instead, they attempt to propose generic or neutral norms agreed upon by all participants in dialogue. While this may work for a dialogue in which all participants agree upon certain criteria (such as the degree to which religions promote gender equality), religious traditions are unlikely to substitute their own revealed criteria for those attained by human reason and agreement.

It is clear that every religion judges others on the basis of their own particular criteria or norms. It is in this process of mutual judgment that a certain equality between religions is established. Though the implicit or explicit use of religion-specific criteria is thus natural and omnipresent, it is not always clear which set of criteria represent the essence of a particular religious tradition, and which are to be called upon to assess particular religious teachings and practices. Most often, the criteria operative are discovered in the process of dialogue, in negative reactions to or in the appeal of certain teachings and practices. Religions often tend to focus on ethical consequences as the measure of the truth of certain teachings (Cornille 2009). But many different teachings may have the same ethical results, and constructive dialogue requires a somewhat more explicit set of norms according to which one may productively engage the teachings and practices of another tradition.

The existence of such norms does not necessarily imply a static and defined understanding of religious identity and criteria. Criteria may themselves change or evolve in the process of dialogue, as one may come to a deeper understanding of one's very norm or norms in the process of dialogue.

Conclusion

Though framed in terms of personal virtues, the conditions for dialogue discussed above represent epistemological requirements which are to be applied to religious traditions, as much as to individuals involved in the dialogue. The conditions of humility, interconnection, and hospitality in particular involve attitudes toward the religious other which must be generated from within a particular religious self-understanding. It is only insofar as religions find within themselves the resources for dialogue that constructive engagement with religious others will bear fruit in those traditions.

It is clear that most religions are not by nature disposed to constructive dialogue with other religious traditions. The conditions discussed above represent varying challenges for religious traditions. While doctrinal humility may form a difficult challenge for religions based on strong propositional claims to truth or on firmly defined religious practice, doctrinal hospitality may represent a particular problem for religions which attach less importance to doctrinal development and ritual precision. Hence, the possibility of inter-religious dialogue always involves some degree of hermeneutical effort and a commitment to mining the resources of one's own tradition in order to open the tradition up for constructive engagement with others.

Rather than a set of requirements which must be perfectly achieved in order for dialogue to be possible, these conditions for dialogue represent a heuristic device which may help to understand the limits and the possibility of interreligious dialogue. They may offer a basis for understanding why certain dialogues fail, and for recovering the religious resources necessary for constructive dialogue. Moreover, it is often only in the process of engaging other religions that the conditions for dialogue come to be cultivated. The dialogue with Buddhism, for example, has inspired some Christian theologians to a deeper understanding of doctrinal humility, just as the Christian notion of interconnection in the Trinity has inspired some Buddhists to develop their own alternative conceptions of the interconnection between religions.

The focus on mutual learning as the goal of inter-religious dialogue still raises the question as to the kind of learning taking place through dialogue. In general, learning may take the form of remembering or of appropriating. One of the most common and innocuous fruits of dialogue is that of remembering or rediscovering neglected or forgotten dimensions of one's own tradition. The other religion then serves as a catalyst to remind one of certain analogous beliefs, teachings, or practices in one's own tradition. An immediate fruit of the Christian dialogue with Asian religious traditions has been the recovery of contemplative Christian traditions and practices. While such renewed attention to particular aspects of the tradition may be regarded as a simple recovery, it may also at times include some degree of innovation, or reinterpretation of the tradition in light of the other. This type of mutual learning may also take the form of renewed commitment to particular teachings and practices. This may arise from an experience of contrast of from inspiration in which engagement with another religion serves to reinforce particular religious beliefs and practices. Here, the other thus serves as a mirror offering a new lens through which to understand one's own religion.

Mutual learning may also involve the appropriation of new teachings and practices. This may take various forms, from integrating new practices to adopting a new worldview or philosophical framework, and from adding new meanings to traditional symbols or teachings to appropriating new symbols and religious models. There is no *a priori* limit to the possibility of new learning from other religions, except that imposed by the need for coherence and continuity with the established tradition. This type of religious borrowing is not new: throughout history, religions have appropriated elements from one another, often without acknowledging their source. Inter-religious dialogue, however, offers the opportunity to consciously learn from other religions and to recognize the origin of such learning. To be sure, this process of learning from other religions does not necessarily imply wholesale appropriation of the original meaning of a particular teaching or practice. All borrowing involves a certain semantic shift in which the meaning of particular teachings or practices is adapted to the new context. However, this may still lead to genuinely new insight and to real religious development and growth.

Bibliography

Bernhardt, Reinhold. *Ende des Dialogs? Die Begegnung der Religionen und ihre theologische Reflexion.* Zurich: Theologischer Verlag, 2005.

Clooney, Francis. *Comparative Theology. Deep Learning Across Religious Borders.* Oxford: Wiley-Blackwell, 2010.

Cornille, Catherine. *The Im-Possibility of Interreligious Dialogue.* New York: Crossroad/ Herder & Herder, 2008.

Cornille, Catherine (ed.). *Criteria of Discernment in Interreligious Dialogue.* Eugene, OR: Wipf and Stock, 2009.

Cornille, Catherine (ed.). *Interreligious Hermeneutics.* Eugene, OR: Wipf and Stock, 2010.

Cornille, Catherine. "The Role of Witness in Interreligious Dialogue." *Concilium* 1 (2011a): 61–70.

Cornille, Catherine. "Interreligious Hospitality and its Limits," in *Hosting the Stranger*

Between Religions, ed. R. Kearney and J. Taylor. New York: Continuum, 2011b, 35–45.

Cobb, John. *Beyond Dialogue: Toward a Mutual Transformation of Christianity and Buddhism.* Philadelphia: Fortress Press, 1982.

Cobb, John (ed.). *The Dialogue Comes of Age. Christian Encounters with Other Religions.* Minneapolis: Fortress Press, 2010.

D' Costa, Gavin. *The Meeting of Religions and the Trinity.* Maryknoll, NY: Orbis, 2000.

de Béthune, Pierre-Francois. *Par la foi et l'hospitalité.* Clerlande: Publications de Saint-André, 1997.

Dupuis, Jacques. *Toward a Christian Theology of Religious Pluralism.* Maryknoll, NY: Orbis, 1997.

Forman, Robert. *Mysticism, Mind, Consciousness.* Albany: State University of New York Press, 1999.

Garfield, Jay. *Empty Words: Buddhist Philosophy and Cross-Cultural Interpretation.* Oxford: Oxford University Press, 2002.

Griffiths, Paul. *Problems of Religious Diversity.* Oxford: Blackwell, 2001.

Haight, Roger. *Jesus, Symbol of God.* Maryknoll, NY: Orbis, 1999.

Heim, Mark. *Salvations. Truth and Difference in Religion.* Maryknoll, NY: Orbis, 1999.

Heim, Mark. *The Depth of the Riches. A Trinitarian Theology of Religious Ends.* Grand Rapids, MI: Eerdmans, 2001.

Hick, John. "On Grading Religions." *Religious Studies* 17 (1981): 451–467.

Hick, John. *An Interpretation of Religion.* New Haven, CT: Yale University Press, 1989.

Huxley, Aldous. *The Perennial Philosophy.* New York: Harper and Brothers, 1945.

Jeanrond, Werner and Aasulv Lande (eds.) *The Concept of God in Global Dialogue.* Maryknoll, NY: Orbis, 2005.

Keenan, John. *The Meaning of Christ. A Mahayana Theology.* New York: Orbis, 1989.

Keenan, John. *The Gospel of Mark: A Mahayana Reading.* Maryknoll:, NY: Orbis, 1995.

Lefebure, Leo and Peter Feldmeier. *The Path of Wisdom. A Christian Commentary on the Dhammapada.* Leuven: Peeters, 2011.

Lindbeck, George. *The Nature of Doctrine. Religion and Theology in a Postliberal Age.* Philadelphia: Westminster, 1984.

McCutcheon, Russell. *The Insider–Outsider Debate in the Study of Religion.* London: Cassell, 1999.

Moyaert, Marianne. *Fragile Identities, Toward a Theology of Interreligious Hospitality.* Amsterdam: Rodopi, 2011.

Moyaert, Marianne. "Inappropriate Behavior: On the Ritual Core of Religions and the Limits to Interreligious Hospitality," in *Interreligious Theology*, ed. Reinhold Bernhardt and Perry Schmidt-Leukel. Zurich: Theologischer Verlag, 2013.

O'Leary, Joseph. *Religious Pluralism and Christian Truth.* Edinburgh: Edinburgh University Press, 1996.

Panikkar, Raimon. *The Intra-Religious Dialogue.* New York: Paulist, 1999.

Pratt, Douglas, David Cheetham, and David Thomas. *Understanding Interreligious Relations.* Oxford: Oxford University Press, 2013.

Ricoeur, Paul. *Oneself as Another.* Chicago: University of Chicago Press, 1992.

Scheler, Max. *The Nature of Sympathy.* London: Routledge and Kegan Paul, 1954.

Schmidt-Leukel, Perry. *Transformation by Integration. How Inter-faith Encounter Changes Christianity.* London: SCM Press, 2011.

Sheridan, Daniel. *Krishna and Christ. A Christian Commmentary on the Narada Sutras.* Leuven: Peeters, 2007.

Stein, Edith. *On the Problem of Empathy.* The Hague: Martinus Nijhoff, 1964.

Steinkerchner, Scott. *Beyond Agreement. Interreligious Dialogue Amid Persistent Differences.* Lanham, MD: Rowman & Littlefield, 2011.

Stueber, Karsten. *Rediscovering Empathy: Agency, Folk Psychology and the Human Sciences.* Cambridge, MA: MIT Press, 2006.

Sugirtharajah, Sharada. *Religious Pluralism and the Modern World. An Ongoing Engagement with John Hick.* Basingstoke: Palgrave, 2012.

Swidler, Leonard, John Cobb, Paul Knitter, and Monika Hellwig. *Death or Dialogue? From* the Age of Monologue to the Age of Dialogue. London: SCM Press, 1990.

Timmerman, Christian and Barbara Segaert. How to Conquer the Barriers to Intercultural Dialogue: Christianity, Islam and Judaism. Brussels: Peter Lang, 2005.

Tracy, David. Dialogue with the Other. The Inter-Religious Dialogue. Leuven: Peeters, 1990.

Van der Leeuw, Gerardus. Religion in Essence and Manifestation. Princeton, NJ: Princeton University Press, 1986 (original 1930).

Vroom, Hendrick. Religions and the Truth. Philosophical Reflections and Perspectives. Grand Rapids, MI: Eerdmans, 1989.

Yong, Amos. Hospitality and the Other. Maryknoll, NY: Orbis, 2005.

CHAPTER 3

Monastic Inter-Religious Dialogue

Pierre-François de Béthune, OSB

The formation in 1978 of commissions for monastic inter-religious dialogue (MID) or, in French, dialogue interreligieux monastique (DIM) has been one of the most important developments in the area of inter-religious dialogue, giving concrete expression to a constitutive element of all true dialogue, namely, encounter at the level of spiritual experience. Obviously, monks are not the only ones to engage in this form of dialogue. Later on I shall mention the many lay-people, Christians as well as those of other traditions, who practice such dialogue. However, monks have engaged in it more intentionally, and have written extensively about their experience. A closer look at the initiative undertaken by Benedictines will make it possible to come to a better understanding of dialogue at this level.

I shall begin by first describing the history of the formation of the DIM/MID commissions, a history that shows how thinking about dialogue has evolved over the past decades. Second, this evolution would not have been possible without the commitment of the pioneers of dialogue. Third, the history of DIM/MID from 1978 to 2011 will demonstrate the growing acceptance of dialogue that was possible and necessary over the course of these years. Fourth, and finally, I will conclude by looking at the challenges and promise of this form of dialogue.

The Creation of Commissions for Monastic Inter-Religious Dialogue

The establishment of commissions for monastic inter-religious dialogue was made possible by an evolution – or better, a revolution – of the Catholic attitude to other religions. What was involved was nothing less than a new conversion to the Gospel. The change took place over the past century, and is evident when we consider the monastic foundations in that period of time. The few Christian monasteries that were founded in Africa or in the Far East at the end of the nineteenth century were outposts of Western civi-

The Wiley Blackwell Companion to Inter-Religious Dialogue, First Edition. Edited by Catherine Cornille.
© 2013 John Wiley & Sons Ltd. Published 2020 by John Wiley & Sons Ltd.

lization. There was no contact with the local religions. By way of illustration, consider this episode that took place in 1931 at the Chinese monastery of Si-shan, founded by the Belgian abbey of Saint André: "One day during a walk, a Chinese novice and ex-bonze by the name of Wang said he thought there were similarities between Buddhism and Christianity. The prior, Dom Joliet, felt that he needed to retract this statement and insisted that the novice explicitly affirm the pre-eminence of Christianity, doing so on his knees in front of those who were with him on the walk. The guilty novice did as he was told, but a few days later he left the monastery" (Delcourt 1988: 209). Daring to express any perception of similarities between Christian and Buddhist monasticism was regarded as an expression of apostasy; blindness to such issues, instead, was considered a monastic virtue.

But a major evolution was taking place, mainly because there were those who dared to look kindly and objectively on other spiritual traditions. A change of mentality came about quickly. After the Second World War the Christian missionary movement started up again, but this time with much greater respect for the actual situation in which the so-called "young churches" existed.

It was at this time that some Benedictine and Cistercian monks began to pay more attention to the culture and spiritual life of other continents. Thus, when Abbots Cornelius Tholens and Theodore Ghesquière recommended at a meeting of Benedictine abbots in 1959 that they needed to find better ways to coordinate the establishment of monasticism in the young churches, their proposal was well received and an opening to dialogue was assured. With the establishment of the "Secretariat to Aid the Implantation of Monasticism" (AIM) two years later, Christian monks became much more conscious of the life – more precisely, the spiritual life – of monasteries in Africa and Asia. But this awareness was still driven by a missionary purpose, a concern to spread the faith through monasticism.

In 1965, inspired by the Second Vatican Council and its declaration on non-Christian inter-religious relations, *Nostra Aetate*, the Secretariat of AIM drew attention to the presence of Hindu or Buddhist monasticism in the countries where it was preparing to establish Christian monasteries. The founders of AIM went so far as to suggest that coming to know these other monastic traditions could contribute to the renewal of the spiritual life of Christians.

The first pan-Asiatic Congress that took place in Bangkok in 1968 had an especially significant impact on this consciousness. Ardent proponents of monastic renewal such as Abbot Primate Rembert Weakland, Abbot Cornelius Tholens, and Father Jean Leclercq were deeply impressed by the massive presence of Buddhist monks in Thailand. Indeed, the recognition of Christian minority status in certain cultural contexts made Christian monastics all the more aware of the necessity of dialogue. Moreover, the accidental death of Father Thomas Merton during the course of this congress made people take even more notice of his own evolution during the last years of his life, and his profound interest in other religions.

"The experience of God in the different religions" was the theme chosen for the second pan-Asiatic Congress, this one held in Bangalore in 1973 (Secretariat AIM 1974). Many speakers were asked to collaborate in developing this theme, especially religious such as Hugo Enomiya Lassalle, S.J., Vincent Shigeto Oshida, O.P., Edmond

Verdière, M.E.P., and also Raimon Panikkar. At the conclusion of this monastic gathering, however, Abbot Primate Weakland noted, with some chagrin, that relatively few monks played an active role in the congress.

His concern produced results, and a year later there was an official letter, signed by Cardinal Sergio Pignedoli, President of the Secretariat for Non-Christians, asking the Abbot Primate to arrange for inter-monastic dialogue. Pignedoli noted that "the monk represents a point of contact and of mutual comprehension between Christians and Non-Christians. The presence of monastics in the Catholic Church is therefore, in itself, a bridge that joins us to all other religions" (Pignedoli 1974).

The two people who played a leading role in this undertaking were Monsignor Piero Rossano, secretary of the Secretariat, and Abbot Tholens, who had just spent a year at Shantivanam in India. Abbot Primate Weakland asked the latter to lay the groundwork in Europe and North America for the establishment of monastic inter-religious dialogue commissions within AIM. Many of those he contacted expressed interest in this project and he was able to secure the collaboration of monks like Mayeul de Dreuille and Armand Veilleux.

His efforts came to fruition in two important meetings that took place in 1977, one at Petersham, Massachusetts, and the other at Loppem in Belgium. These meetings brought together scores of monks and nuns to discuss their contacts with the East. At the beginning of the following year two commissions were set up, the North American Board for East–West Dialogue (NABEWD) and the commission for Dialogue Interreligieux Monastique (DIM) for Europe.

The Pioneers of Dialogue at the Level of Spiritual Experience

This evolution would not have been possible without the witness of a large number of pioneers of dialogue. They did not have any canonical authority or mandate, but they had a decisive impact on the mentality of those who were in a position to make decisions.

With the perspective made possible by the passing of time, we can now see that these pioneers had much in common, even if they had almost no contact with one another. Almost all of them were Westerners and monks, or at least members of religious congregations. During the 30 or so key years that followed the Second World War, they contributed mightily to the creation of a positive attitude toward the spiritualities of the East. Along with other Westerners – explorers, archaeologists, artists, philosophers – who were captivated by the East, they felt an attraction to Hinduism and Buddhism and did what they could to gather the treasures of these religious traditions and place them at the service of Christianity. Indeed, what motivated most of them was the missionary impulse that was dominant in the churches at that time. They went to Asia with the intention of working towards a deeper "inculturation" of Christianity. At the beginning, they made contact with other spiritualities in order to enrich the Christian life, as well as to convert pagans. Little by little, however, their way of thinking evolved. Their fascination with the religions of Asia led them to examine them without ulterior motives and finally to give themselves, body and soul, to a respectful encounter with those religions.

Even though they were rather marginal members of the orders to which they belonged, the sincerity of their spiritual quest obliged their superiors to respect their peculiar ways, and at the same time their religious vocation prevented them from breaking away from the Church. For these reasons, their writings and especially their personal witness were able to affect a large number of Christians.

One of the first to set out on this new way of living the Gospel was Charles de Foucauld (1859–1916), whom we can therefore consider the precursor of the pioneers. He was converted to the Christian faith of his parents because of the example of Moroccan Muslims and later became a Cistercian monk. In 1901 he left the monastery to live with the Touaregs of the Saharan desert. He did not attempt to enter into explicit dialogue with Muslims. Rather, his intention was to witness to the Gospel by the simple expression of hospitality, given and received. In this way he inaugurated a different model of Christianity and became an inspiration for many Christians.

By the middle of the twentieth century, there were already a large number of Christians who opted for this approach. Their undertaking was audacious, especially in the years prior to Vatican II, for they were setting out on ways that were new and even forbidden. But an inner conviction urged them forward. During their journey they suffered deeply from the conflicts that arose between their inner experiences and the traditional doctrines of the Church. In the end, however, they were able to give witness to a Christian faith that had been profoundly reaffirmed and renewed by this very encounter.

Some names: Jules Monchanin (Swami Paramarubyananda), Henri Le Saux, OSB (Swami Abhishiktananda), Francis Mahieu, OCSO (Acharya), Bede Griffiths, OSB, Thomas Merton, OCSO, Aelred Graham, OSB, John Main, OSB, Edmond Verdière, MEP, Serge de Beaurecueil, OP, Hugo Lassalle, SJ (Enomiya Makibi), Yves Raguin, SJ, Christian de Chergé, OCSO; also the Islamic scholar Louis Massignon, and Dr Raimon Panikkar. We should also mention some priests and religious who were born in Asia, such as Vincent Shigeto Oshida, OP, Augustine Okumura, OCD, John Kakishi Kadowaki, SJ, and Aloysius Pieris, SJ. They represent a further stage, about which we shall speak in more detail below.

I should also mention the many "pioneers" who came from other religions, spiritual leaders who made their traditions known to Westerners and who were interested in learning more about Christianity. For example, the Swamis Vivekānanda, Aurobindo, and Chidānanda; Dr. Suzuki Daisetz Teitaro; Buddhist monks such as the Dalai Lama, Thich Nhat Hanh, Chögyam Trungpa, Kalu Rimpoche, and Buddhadāsa; or even the Tea Master Nojiri Michiko. Describing the kinds of dialogue engaged in by these practitioners would require another essay, one that, to the best of my knowledge, has not yet been written.

The History of DIM/MID, 1978 to 2012

Once they were set up, the North American and European commissions for monastic inter-religious dialogue began to function with a great deal of enthusiasm, especially the North American Board for East-West Dialogue. Right after its inaugural meeting in January 1978, NABEWD began publishing a Bulletin. Thanks to its first editor, Sister

Pascaline Coff, this publication was largely responsible for raising awareness throughout the United States of the importance of dialogue at the spiritual level. This work continues: in January 2011, DIM/MID launched *Dilatato Corde*, its online, multilingual journal (http://www.dimmid.org, accessed December 4, 2012).The content of *Dilatato Corde* includes personal testimonies and reflections on monastic inter-religious dialogue, scholarly articles, and helpful information.

At first, the mandate of the "sub-commissions of AIM for dialogue" was quite limited. According to Father Paul Gordan, a member of the Board of Directors of AIM, "Inter-religious dialogue is beyond the competence of the monks who are directly or indirectly involved in it. The DIM sub-commissions should limit themselves to concrete issues that may arise from contact with non-Christian monasticism in those areas where Christian monasteries have been established" (Gordan 1980). But these edicts, issued in 1980, were already out of date.

By 1979, Catholic missionaries in Japan who wanted to organize an "East–West Spiritual Exchange" between Buddhists and Christians had requested the collaboration of the European DIM to arrange for Japanese monks to spend some time in European Christian monasteries. This experience of hospitality was eye-opening for both guests and hosts. It became clear that this kind of meeting, much of it devoted to silence and held in a setting dedicated to the spiritual life, allowed for a deep level of communion. At the end of their sojourn the Pope addressed some important words to the participants: "I thank you for coming to Europe for an East–West exchange on the spiritual level. I congratulate those among you who have lived in small groups in the great Christian monasteries and have shared fully their life of prayer and work for three weeks. Your experience is truly an epoch-making event in the history of interreligious dialogue" (*L'Osservatore Romano*, September 27, 1979).

For its part, NABEWD organized an important monastic symposium on "The Monk as Universal Archetype," at which the main speaker was Raimon Panikkar. He later published a book based on his presentations at this meeting: *Blessed Simplicity* (Panikkar 1982).

In 1980, AIM, this time working together with DIM, held the third pan-Asiatic congress in Kandy, Sri Lanka. The meeting was marked by the well-integrated participation of Buddhists, Hindus, and Muslims. At the end of the congress some participants organized a meeting of Christian monks from Asia, specifying that participation at this meeting was limited to monks born in Asia. This was not an act of defiance with regard to those great pioneers who had come from the West – and whom the Asians themselves venerated – but rather an expression of the desire of Asian monks to take charge of monastic inter-religious dialogue in Asia and to work together towards this end. Their initiative marks the end of the age of the pioneers. Some years later the movement of monastic inter-religious dialogue would find a *modus agendi* that was proper to Asia and Oceania with the creation of commissions on these two continents.

In the meantime the "East–West Spiritual Exchanges" continued. In 1983 the Reverend Hirata Seiko, President of the Institute of Zen Studies, invited Christian monks to spend time in Zen monasteries in Japan. This second "Spiritual Exchange" proved to be a decisive event in the history of the European DIM. The 17 participants – among them three abbots – were deeply moved by the experience. They understood that exchanges like this could not be "limited to concrete questions." It was not enough simply to enter the house of the other; one had to enter their spirituality as well, making a serious attempt to understand and appreciate their reasons for following a monastic way of life. In order to do this, a high level of reciprocal trust is essential. A description of this memorable voyage is given in a book written by one of the participants, Father Benoît Billot (Billot 1987).

A significant fact: some months later, in May 1984, the Secretariat for non-Christians, with the collaboration of Father Abbot Simone Tonini, one of the participants of the Spiritual Exchange, was able to draw up a precise text about inter-religious dialogue at this level:

> At a deeper level, persons rooted in their own religious traditions can share their experiences of prayer, contemplation, faith and duty, as well as their expressions and ways of searching for the Absolute. This type of dialogue can be a mutual enrichment and fruitful cooperation for promoting and preserving the highest values and spiritual ideals of man. It leads naturally to each partner communicating to the other the reason for his own faith. (Secretariatus pro non christianis 1984: 138)

Referring to this paragraph, Pope John Paul II added in his conclusive speech, "Here I think especially of intermonastic dialogue" (*ibid.*: 24).

The day of prayer for peace held in Assisi on October 27, 1986, showed that it was possible for followers of different religions to encounter one another at the deepest level. As consulter to the Secretariat for non-Christians, I was invited to take part in this gathering, including a common prayer for peace offered by all who came together at the entrance to the basilica of Saint Francis. All of us, followers of different religions, were praying. Unless one identifies prayer with its formulation, it was obvious that we were united in one prayer. The following day I met the Zoroastrian delegate, Mr. Homi Dhalla, who told me, "I will no longer be able to pray as I used to; from now on I will always pray in communion with all who pray."

What John Paul proposed to do at Assisi II was not well received by some of his advisors. His decision to go ahead came from a personal conviction that he had expressed in 1981: the prayer of believers, whatever their religious affiliation, is inspired by the same Spirit. In response to criticism received for inviting followers of other religions to pray together, he explained his thinking in an allocation he gave to the cardinals and the Roman Curia on December 22 of that same year, 1986. This text (Secretariatus pro non christianis 1987) is one of the foundations for the encounter of monks with other religions because, without neglecting other approaches, the principal objective of DIM is to foster inter-religious exchange at the level of prayer and meditation.

The "East–West Spiritual Exchanges" between Christian and Zen Buddhist monks are still taking place (S.E. XII 2011). However, the third exchange, in 1987, needs to be singled out for its particular importance. Forty Japanese monks were hosted in European monasteries and then came together in Rome for a symposium at Sant' Anselmo, the centre of Benedictine monasticism. Following the symposium, the Pope granted them a private audience. In his discourse, which was also addressed to the Christian monks who accompanied them, he said:

Your specific contribution to these initiatives consist not only in maintaining an explicit dialogue, but also in promoting a deep spiritual encounter, for your life is above all one devoted to silence, prayer, and a witness of community life. There is much you can do through *hospitality*. In opening your houses and your hearts, as you have done these days, you follow well the tradition of your spiritual father, Saint Benedict. To your brother monks coming from across the world and from a very different religious tradition you apply the beautiful chapter of the Rule concerning the reception of guests. In doing so you offer a setting wherein a meeting of mind and heart can take place, a meeting characterized by a shared sense of brotherhood in the one human family that opens the way of ever deeper spiritual dialogue. (Secretariatus pro non christianis 1988: 5–6)

This text clearly defines the specific character of monastic dialogue and demonstrates the confidence that the Catholic hierarchy has invested in the work of the DIM/MID commissions.

Another occasion to clarify this way of encountering other contemplative traditions was given in 1989, when the Congregation for the Doctrine of the Faith published a *Letter to the Bishops of the Catholic Church on some Aspects of Christian Meditation*. Its purpose was to warn Catholics of the danger involved in the practice of Eastern forms of meditation. The document recalled some fundamental aspects of Christian prayer, but an overall tone of suspicion regarding the spiritual practices of other religions and a haughty ignorance of these practices prevented it from being very useful. At the request of the Pontifical Council for Interreligious Dialogue, which was surprised that it had not been consulted about the matter, I made a close study of the document and argued in an unpublished article that any attempt to deal with matters pertaining to another religion that is not carried out in a spirit of dialogue ends up by doing more harm than good. After presenting my critique of the document to the staff of the Pontifical Council for Interreligious Dialogue, its president, Cardinal Francis Arinze, wrote me an official letter requesting that DIM undertake a new study of this subject. What followed was an extensive consultation of the members of DIM throughout Europe as well as in the United States and India on the practice of dialogue in and through meditation. A team of monks and nuns synthesized their responses in a small document entitled *Contemplation and Interreligious Dialogue: References and Perspectives Drawn from the Experience of Monastics*, recommending prudence and boldness. This document was officially approved and published by the Pontifical Council for Interreligious Dialogue (Pontificium Consilium pro Dialogo inter Religiones 1993).

Up until this point DIM was a sub-commission of AIM. However, the differences between their methods and objectives, inter-monastic dialogue, and monastic foundations, were becoming more and more evident. In addition, two new commissions had been created, one for India and Sri Lanka, the other for Australia. Thus, in 1994 Abbot Primate Jerome Theisen set up DIM/MID as an independent secretariat, but always in liaison with AIM.

The witness of the monks of Tibhirine helped DIM to further widen its horizons. The European DIM invited the prior of Tibhirine, Father Christian de Chergé, to its annual meeting in 1995, which was held at the abbey of Montserrat (Spain). There he introduced us to his practice of communion in prayer with all who pray. Until that point we had confined ourselves to contact with monks of other religions, which meant that we essentially limited ourselves to dialogue with Buddhists and Hindus. But the testimony of de Chergé called us to open our hearts to all who pray. One year later the tragic deaths of the monks of Tibhirine and the way in which their witness has radiated throughout the world was a sign of God's blessing on this kind of dialogue.

Finally, I should mention a number of important conferences organized by the North American commission in recent years. In the mid-1990s the Dalai Lama expressed a desire to continue the dialogue he had had with Thomas Merton. Thus far, three conferences for Buddhist and Catholic monks have been held at Merton's monastery, Gethsemani in Kentucky. The first took place in 1996 and dealt with monastic spiritual practices (Mitchell and Wiseman 1997). The two that followed were on suffering (Mitchell and Wiseman 2003) and on monasticism and the environment (Mitchell and Skudlarek 2010). Nuns in North America have created an original form of encounter called "Nuns in the West" that brings together Christian, Buddhist, and Hindu nuns living in North America. Monks have followed with "Monks in the West" (Skudlarek 2008). This kind of exchange on concrete issues of monastic life has proven to be very fruitful.

In concluding this initial overview, we can recognize how much DIM/MID has been able to – or more exactly, has had to – evolve. Among other experiences of dialogue, they were able to articulate a method of inter-religious encounter based on the spirit of Benedictine hospitality. Monks, obviously, are not the only ones who engage in this kind of dialogue, but the "monastic" way of engaging in it has now been recognized throughout the Christian world and beyond.

We can notice now that a "dialogical movement" has gradually taken shape alongside the liturgical movement and the ecumenical movement. To say that inter-religious dialogue has become a "movement" implies that it is no longer the sole concern of a small group of committed individuals. For this reason the present concern of DIM/MID is to ensure that the movement for dialogue is well grounded as well as widespread, involving more and more of the faithful in a dialogical consciousness crucial for the future of religion. While inter-monastic dialogue is not essentially different from any other kind of dialogue between religions, there are a few dimensions of monastic life and experience which may have some value for all forms of inter-religious dialogue. Two aspects of dialogue which Thomas Merton developed in his Asian journal on the day of his departure were: communication and communion (Merton 1975: 5). In its beginning stages dialogue can bring about a relationship of empathy expressed by intense communication. We will see that it is, however, possible to go much further and to create a sincere bond, a true communion of mutual recognition.

Communication

With its emphasis on the virtue of silence, monastic life would not appear to be a very good training ground for dialogue. As Saint Jerome noted, "A monk is not known by his speech, but by his sitting in silence" (Letter 50,4). Nonetheless, as we have observed, the contribution of monks to inter-religious dialogue has been important. Their normal way of contributing, however, has not been by means of talks or writings, but through the witness they have given, the paradoxical witness of a "dialogue of silence" (Walker 1987). And yet, words are necessary to describe this kind of dialogue.

At the basis of this inter-monastic encounter there is what we might call a tacit connivance. Thomas Merton called attention to this in a talk he gave at a conference organized by the "Temple of Understanding" in Calcutta toward the end of his time in Asia. He noted that a marvellous communication takes place among people who are engaged in a spiritual quest (Merton 1975: 308). In fact, when a Christian monk is welcomed into a Zen or Thai monastery, he feels right at home! He likes the fact that its location is a bit withdrawn; he finds the same monastic simplicity, the same respect for nature and care for beauty. He recognizes that in monks who belong to a very different religious tradition there is the same love of silence and the same reliance on traditional sacred scriptures. He also notes the important role of the Master in the spiritual development of the community. Within all monastic traditions there exists the same tension between the love of solitude and openness to the outside world, between radical detachment and respect for culture. At the end of his stay in a Zen monastery, a Christian monk remarked, "We had discovered how profoundly we were in agreement about what constituted the ideal life. As we were saying our good-byes, it became clear that we had just taken part in a reunion of long-lost brothers. How could we have been so unaware of this for such long a time?" (Billot 1987: 176).

It has been suggested that the monastic traditions of the West and the East may have a common origin (de Dreuille 1999: 70). The existence of Hindu, Jain, or Buddhist monks was already well known in the third century BCE. Alexander the Great brought back from India the so-called "gymnosophists," that is to say, naked wise men, probably Jains. In ancient Greek and Latin literature there are hundreds of allusions to India and its inhabitants, including dozens of descriptions of the monks who lived there (Majumdar 1981). Among the thirteen authors who describe the life of these monks in more detail, two Fathers of the Church are especially significant: Clement of Alexandria (Stomata III, 194) and Jerome (Adversus Jovinianum, 14). Moreover, we know that in Alexandria there was an Indian quarter that housed merchants from the west coast of India who came to Egypt via the Red Sea. Indian culture and ideals may also have had some influence on the first Christian monks.

Christian monks may be quite reluctant to acknowledge the originary influence of other religions. But we cannot hide a troubling fact about the decision of those first monks to live in the desert. The desert is often referred to in the Judeo-Christian tradition, but it is always a place to traverse. One may live there for forty years or forty days, only to return to human society. The invitation of Christ to the young man who wanted to be his disciple (Matthew 19, 21) is very clear: "If you wish to be perfect, go, sell your possessions, give the money to the poor and then come, follow me." According to Saint Athanasius (Life of Antony, 2, 2–5), Saint Antony (d. 355), considered to be the founder of Christian monasticism, recognized his vocation when he heard this verse from the Gospel of Matthew. However, after hearing these words, rather than following the example of Christ and the apostles, he retired once and for all to the desert, continually seeking out places that were more remote. He heard the words, "Follow me," and his response was to separate himself from other human beings. How is one to explain this – to say the least – curious interpretation of the Gospel? By way of contrast, when Saint Francis of Assisi heard this same text in the thirteenth century, he too recognized his vocation, but he understood it as a call to proclaim the Good News in the surrounding towns and countryside, only withdrawing now and then to spend a few days in the mountains. It is difficult to understand Saint Antony's way of responding to the Gospel without hypothesizing the existence of foreign influences, for example the Indian ideal of perfection, which involves a progressive turning away from the world of illusion (*maya*) and a permanent withdrawal to a desert area or to the source of the Ganges. Of course, it will never be possible to prove that this ideal did in fact influence early Christian monasticism. Regardless, it seems that the sense of "being at home" that Christian monks experience today when hosted by Buddhist or Hindu monastic communities is probably not merely incidental. Whatever the case, we can be glad that Antony's way of coming to understand the Gospel made it possible for monasticism to develop in the Church. At the very time that Christianity became a state religion, this monastic movement – in all likelihood the result of outside influences – provided the Church with a way of being faithful to the Gospel without becoming overwhelmed by the cares of the world.

In the same way of reflexion we should also recall the theme of the monk as a universal archetype that Raimon Panikkar developed during a conference sponsored by NABEWD at Holyoke, Massachussetts, in 1980. With the collaboration of monks and nuns of different religions, Panikkar reflected on the call addressed to monks in every country, inviting them to continue their common search for "Blessed Simplicity" (Panikkar 1982).

However, these many similarities and connections supporting communication between monks of different religions are not the most decisive factor in inter-monastic encounter. The monastic world is certainly a favourable environment (in the strongest sense of the term) for dialogue. It is the setting where the dialogue of spiritual experience can flourish. Monastic commitment, moreover, provides the time necessary for arriving at spiritual maturity. But the most decisive agreement between monks is found at a deeper level than that of the monastic institution or spiritual anthropology.

The most fundamental characteristic of all monastic traditions is their dedication to the spiritual quest. The awareness that another monk is engaged in this zealous search is what makes real communication possible. And when we look at the different features of a life consecrated to the spiritual quest, we see how they prepare the way for a particularly fruitful encounter.

The beginning of the monastic way of life is directed to awakening the heart. The Rule of Saint Benedict opens with the words, "Listen, my son, and open the ear of your heart." The 16 ideograms of the Zen manifesto, attributed to Bodhidharma, proclaim, "Go straight to the human heart." Everything a monk does is intended to reach his heart, to strip it, to purify it by transforming his "heart of stone" into a "heart of flesh." The Christian tradition even speaks of a "pierced heart," opened by a wound that cannot be healed (See Acts 2,37 and John 19,34). When someone whose heart has become vulnerable meets an authentic witness from another religious tradition, he or she can be profoundly moved and be led to an "intra-religious" dialogue, to use the expression of Raimon Panikkar to which we will return.

If monks of all traditions recognize one another as companions on the path, it is because they are all involved in the same quest. A *mondo* of Mazu, a Chan Master of the eighth century, offers a good example of this characteristic of the monastic life (Despeux 1980):

When Dazhu made his first visit to Mazu, the latter asked him,

–Where do you come from?
–I come from the Great Clouds monastery in Yue prefecture.
–What brings you here?
–I come in search of the treasure of Buddha's teaching.
–Do you not see the treasure hidden in your own dwelling? What is the point of wandering around so far from home?
–What is the treasure of my own dwelling?
–Your very question at this moment. That is your treasure!

At these words Dahzu was awakened to his "Original Heart."

It is there, in the question, or more exactly, in the space between the question and the response, that monks meet one another. In this silent space where the question resounds profoundly, the answer is not necessarily given, but the partners in dialogue experience an intense encounter, one that goes beyond words and similarities.

It should be noted that this space is not a topography, some well-defined area. Interreligious dialogue is often described as a coming together in a place that we have in common, like a mountaintop that we come to by different paths. That image is too simplistic. If we want to use an image, a better one would be a bottomless well whose opening cannot be measured, a well that draws to itself those who are in search of the absolute. They are united in their quest, but the only thing they have in common is their movement towards this abyss of silence and emptiness. What they have in common is not some possession, a patrimony they share, but a great desire. That which unites them is what surpasses them.

Moreover, the monk has no place he can call his own. Like Christ, he has "nowhere to lay his head" (Luke 9: 58). The *sanyasi* and the gyrovagues represent an extreme form of this renunciation. In relation to the "world," monks are marginal figures. They regard themselves as "aliens and exiles" (1 Peter 2: 11). They give witness to impermanence and universal relativity. For this reason they are not too attached to dogmatic formulations and thus run the risk of being labeled as relativists. But in the presence of the absolute, nothing else can be regarded as having any absolute value.

In fact they are not loners, spiritual isolationists. At least for Christian and Buddhist monks, it is clear that their commitment is not made in isolation, but is related to the church or the *sangha*, particularly when they encounter believers of other faiths (Cornille 2008: 80).

The most ancient account about a monk can be found in the Rig Veda (X, 136, translation of Panikkar 1977). In a hymn it offers an evocative description of the wandering and naked ascetic known as a *kesin*:

Ridden by the wind, companion of its blowing,
Pushed along by the Gods,
He is at home in both seas, the East
And the West – the silent ascetic.

Thus, by the eighth century BCE the monk is recognized as someone who travels great distances to unite East and West!

To complete this catalogue of the ways the monk has traditionally been understood and how these characteristics favor an in-depth inter-religious encounter, I should mention one final distinctive feature: poverty, or – in the Buddhist world – emptiness. When Thomas Merton and Dr. Suzuki Daisetz exchanged letters, they instinctively treated the place of poverty and innocence in the spiritual life (Merton 1968: 109).

It is also true that those who are firmly committed to this kind of encounter discover that they become even poorer. We might think that the insights gained through interaction with great religious traditions would be experienced as enrichment. In fact, the encounter with other spiritualities and the wonder that they arouse involve the loss of many of our points of reference. Many of the cultural and theological riches garnered by Christianity to defend and illustrate the faith are henceforth seen to be less essential than had been thought. The practice of dialogue at the level of spiritual experience, precisely because it involves an encounter with the ineffable, produces a certain deconstruction of doctrinal formulations. The most precious fruit of this kind of dialogue is the grace of poverty, the blessed poverty of the Gospel Beatitudes.

Therefore, when monks and others become involved in this determined spiritual quest and interact with people who are filled with the same desire, communication at a spiritual level takes place quite naturally. By giving witness to the possibility of dialogue at this highest level, they point to the ultimate goal of all dialogue. Such encounter is, in fact, the keystone of the entire dialogical edifice. But this keystone does not close off the building. Like the keystone of the Pantheon in Rome, it is an opening to the sky.

At this point we can see how, beyond this intense communication, a concrete link can be established. Indeed, the experience of monks in dialogue has revealed a particularly fruitful method of encounter.

Communion

The most promising inter-monastic exchanges have taken place in the context of reciprocal hospitality. As we have seen above, the DIM/MID commissions have sponsored conferences, colloquia, and lectures by experts in the field of inter-religious dialogue. But I believe it will be more helpful to limit my description here to their method of welcoming the other, which is more specific.

Of course hospitality is not a prerogative of monks. In recent times, numerous authors have written about the need to face the "risk of hospitality" (Marty 2005: 124–148) if we want to go to the end of the road in our encounters with the followers of other religions (Cornille 2008: 177–210). Offering such hospitality does involve a risk, as the word "host" itself suggests: both "hospitality" and "hostility" share the same Indo-European root, "ghost." The guest, the stranger, may also be an enemy; he always arouses a certain anxiety. To extend hospitality, one has to overcome fear and go beyond one's comfort zone. If hospitality is always sacred, is it not because it involves a reaching out, a going beyond?

In any case, this way of proceeding is especially suited to the encounter with followers of other religions because it means receiving the stranger *as stranger*, respecting differences rather than trying to smooth them over. The guests who are thus received recognize that they are not at home and therefore have to show a certain reserve *vis-à-vis* their host. This kind of inter-religious encounter, by its very nature, is weary of any kind of syncretism.

Hospitality is known and honored by all cultures and religions. The Taittiriya Upanishad (1,11,2) says, "Let your guest be a god unto you" (Clooney 2011). One could cite innumerable parallel texts. Accordingly, to adopt this kind of encounter for inter-religious exchanges seems a beautiful opportunity. It should be noted, however, that sacred hospitality, so honored within all religious traditions, has almost never been extended to those who belong to another religion. Rather, in the inter-religious situation, hostility and rejection seem to often be regarded as a sacred duty. Religions, therefore, need to undergo a radical conversion in order to become truly hospitable (de Béthune 2010: 11–15).

This conversion is particularly needed today. The time has come to pass beyond mere talk. It was already a major point of progress to be able to speak peacefully with believers of other religious traditions. But after several decades of inter-religious dialogue we detect a certain weariness for meetings which remain at the level of words.

Philosophical insights (Levinas 1979; Derrida 2000; Ricoeur 2006) and socio-political positions (Volf 1996; Yong 2008) have provided new ways of looking at the encounter between religions when situated at the level of hospitality (Kearney 2010). Theology is also being summoned to renew itself (Monge 1997). Is it able to "rejoice in the truth" (1 Cor 13: 6), no matter where it comes from? The question is how theology can maintain "hospitable truths," expressing convictions which seriously take in account the truth of others? Raimon Panikkar's expression "intra-religious dialogue" may be of use here (Panikkar 1978). Such dialogue occurs not only between two partners, but inside the person who receives a question in his own heart and undergoes an interior struggle when coping with this challenge. It is then a shared interiority, another kind of hospitality. As Panikkar himself put it, "Intrareligious dialogue and hospitality always go together" (Panikkar 2010).

Monks may offer their expertise in giving concrete expressions of hospitality. As we have seen, from their initial establishment, American and European inter-monastic initiatives have sought ways to offer inter-religious hospitality, notably by welcoming Buddhist monks in Christian monasteries. This was their way of putting into practice the Benedictine charism of hospitality as set forth in the Rule of Saint Benedict (RB 53), which is a kind of résumé of the ancient Christian teaching on this subject. Basing his teaching on the hospitality of Abraham (Genesis 18) and the teaching of the Gospel (Matthew 25), Saint Benedict says that the monks should receive "all the guests" as messengers of God, and even "adore Christ" in those who visit. Thus, when the abbot of the monastery carries out the ancient rite of washing the feet of the guests, the Rule specifies that the following verse of Psalm 47 [48] is to be sung: "We receive your mercy, O God, in the midst of your temple." The visit of the stranger is indeed a blessing of the Lord.

By applying these proposals to Buddhist monks, Christian monks have discovered just how deep this kind of encounter can be. By simple, wordless gestures, an intense communion takes place, as is shown by the following anecdote. As he was leaving, a Zen monk remarked, "I have spent two weeks in this Trappist monastery. The monks work hard. They don't eat very well, nor do they get a lot of sleep. So where does this joy come from that I see in their faces?" Because of the difficulty of communication, it was not possible to respond adequately to this Japanese monk, but it was clear that during his silent stay in that monastery, without receiving any explanation, he experienced the essence of their life.

The discoveries of Christian monks who were received in Zen, Tibetan, or Thai monasteries were even more significant than what they learned when they welcomed Buddhist monks to their own monasteries. The number of Christian monks who have taken part in this kind of "immersion program" is already quite large. Being a helpless stranger, unable to make oneself understood, obliged to eat unfamiliar food, being confined to a setting that is completely foreign, makes one feel very vulnerable. But it is precisely this situation of vulnerability that makes the spiritual experience of encounter so powerful. The Biblical tradition is very clear on this point. In the Law of Moses it is written, "You shall love the alien as yourself, for you were aliens in the land of Egypt" (Leviticus 19: 34; see Exodus 22: 20; 23: 9; Deuteronomy 10: 19). That means that to be a good host you must have had the experience of being in need of shelter.

Here we need to remember that hospitality, in the strict sense, is intended for strangers, for people who have no rights at all. Such foreign guests are not welcomed because of family or nationality ties, nor because of their financial standing – their ability to pay for a hotel or hospital room – but only because of their need. They are human beings, brothers and sisters in need. It is, therefore, impossible to understand the essence of hospitality and to put it into practice unless one has also experienced the need to be welcomed.

To *offer* hospitality is a moral duty; it is even the basis of any morality. But to *receive* hospitality is an experience of grace, a spiritual experience. Therefore it is in such situations that the so called "inter-religious encounter at the spiritual level" is most promising.

All the pioneers of inter-religious dialogue attest to this. Actually, anyone who has been the recipient of unexpected and undeserved hospitality knows how overpowering such an experience is. Father Le Saux's inter-religious breakthrough came the day he left Shantivanam, his normal dwelling place, to live at the ashram of Ramana Maharshi at Tiruvanamalai, and then with Swami Gnānānda at Tirukkoyilur (Le Saux 1970, 1978, 1998). For each of these pioneers it would be possible to point to the decision they made one day to uproot themselves in order to dwell with the followers of another religion and learn from them. When we read their writings, it is obvious that their decision was not made out of disregard for their own Christian religion. They wanted only to show their great respect for a religious tradition that they had discovered and admired. They were possessed by a great desire to see how the Holy Spirit was at work there.

This dimension of hospitality thus also requires humility. All traditions of hospitality insist on the necessity of humility. For example, to take part in the *cha no yu*, the Japanese tea ceremony, one has to enter the room by a small door that is only 70 cm high, the *nijiri guchi*, the "door of humility."

The teaching of the Gospels is equally clear. When Jesus sent his disciples to announce the coming Kingdom, he told them to present themselves helpless and in need of hospitality (see Matthew 10 and Luke 9 and 10). The reason he asked them to "take nothing" with them, "no gold, or silver, or copper in your belts, no bag for your journey, or two tunics, or sandals, or a staff," was not, as is usually understood, because he wanted them to practice *detachment*. Rather, it was because he wanted them to be concretely *dependent* on the goodness of others, compelled to count on the generosity of their hosts. He ordered them to "enter the house" with the words "peace to this house," adding, "Remain in the same house, eating and drinking whatever they provide." This way of conducting themselves, so carefully described, is not just an expression of *captatio benevolentiae*. Nor is it a description of what they should do before they announce the Reign of God, and therefore something external to it. No! To act in this way is already a proclamation of the Reign of God. Hospitality asked for and received constitutes the prelude of the Good News; it shows a "God who is in need of people." Only after this will it be possible for those who welcomed the disciples to hear "The kingdom of God has come near to you" (Tassin 2011).

To begin asking for aid is typically Jesus's way of encountering people (cf. John 4: 7: Jesus said to her: "Give me a drink!"). But, curiously this attitude has not been much followed. The initial missionaries who were so eager to announce the Gospel did not mind following its recommendations. However, recent monastic inter-religious experiences have proven anew the spiritual fecundity of such a way.

In fact there are two sides to hospitality. Christian monks and nuns who were hosted in Japanese monasteries and could later on receive Zen monks in their own monasteries bear witness to the fecundity of this reciprocal welcome. We should always respect both sides of hospitality, because they are complementary, and both are essential. If one is lacking, hospitality is not only incomplete, but it is denatured. The first side, the offering of hospitality, has been more often studied. But if this is the only kind of hospitality we are engaged in, we are running the risk of want of balance. We ought to ask our self regularly if we have already asked hospitality from our partners before we offer it. Only when we have enough received from them, can we in our turn offer them our best.

In conclusion, we can say that the specific contributions made by monastics to inter-religious dialogue are twofold.

The monastic way of engaging in this dialogue is an invitation never to renounce to situate the encounter with religions at the spiritual level, because only in this way can we accept them as such, and not only as historical or sociological phenomena.

Furthermore, monks and nuns remind us of the necessity of reciprocity in the encounter, and more specifically, they show us that the entrance to mutual recognition is through the humble request for hospitality.

The contribution of monks is nothing extraordinary, something nobody else could succeed in offering. Rather, their way of engaging in dialogue simply accentuates the essential elements of all inter-religious encounter, and this reminder is important.

In any case, while practising inter-religious encounter as monks do, we can wholeheartedly accept what Thomas Merton said in Calcutta some days before his death: "And the deepest level of communication is not communication, but communion. It is wordless. It is beyond words, and it is beyond speech, and it is beyond concepts. Not that we discover a new unity. My dear brothers, we are already one. But we imagine that we are not. And what we have to recover is our original unity. What we have to be is what we are." (Merton 1975)

Bibliography

Åmell, Katrin. *Contemplation et dialogue.* Upsala: The Swedish Institute of Missionary Research, 1998.

Billot, Benoît. *Voyage dans les monastères zen.* Paris: Desclée de Brouwer, 1987: 176.

Blée, Fabrice. *The Third Desert: The story of Monastic Interreligious Dialogue.* Collegeville, MN: Liturgical Press, 2011.

Clooney, Frank. "Food, the Guest and the *Taitiriya Upanishad*: Hospitality in the Hindu Tradition," in *Hosting the Stranger: Between Religions*, ed. Richard Kearney. New York: Continuum, 2011: 140.

Commissions pour le Dialogue Interreligieux Monastique. *Contemplation et Dialogue Interreligieux: Repères et perdspectives puisés dans l'expérience des moines.* PCID Bulletin 84 (2003), 250–270. Vatican City. English version in: *The Attentive Voice.* New York: Lantern, 2011: 143–164.

Congregation for the Doctrine of the Faith. *A Letter on some aspects of Christian Meditation.* Vatican City, 1989.

Cornille, Catherine. *The Im-Possibility of Interreligious Dialogue.* New York: Crossroad/Herder & Herder, 2008.

de Beaurecueil, Serge de Laugier. *Mes enfants der Kaboul.* Paris: Cerf, 2004.

de Béthune, Pierre-François. Monks in dialogue. *Studies in Formative Spirituality*, Pittsburgh, Duquesne University XIV, 1, 129 (1993).

de Béthune, Pierre-François. *Interreligious Hospitality: The Fulfillment of Dialogue.* Collegeville, MN: Liturgical Press, 2010.

de Dreuille, Mayeul. *From East to West: A History of Monasticism.* New York: Gracewing, 1999: 70.

Delcourt, Henri-Philippe. "Dom Jehan Joliet: un projet de monachisme bénédictin chinois." Thèse de Doctorat en théologie à la Faculté de Lille, Paris: Cerf, 1988: 209.

Derrida, Jacques. *Of Hospitality.* Stanford, CA: Stanford University Press, 2000.

Despeux, Catherine (ed.). *Les entretiens de Mazu.* Paris: Lers Deux Océans, 1980.

du Boulay, Shirley. *The Cave of the Heart.* Maryknoll, NY: Orbis, 2005.

Dupuis, Jacques. *Toward a Christian Theology of Religious Pluralism.* Brescia: Editrice Queriniana, 1997.

Gioia, Francesco. *L'accoglienza dello Straniero nel Mondo Antico.* Roma: Editrice Borla, 1986.

Gordan, Paul. "Le dialogue interreligieux et l'A.I.M." *Bulletin AIM*, Vanves 27 (1980): 44.

John-Paul II. Address to the Roman Curia. *Bulletin of the Secretariatus pro non christianis* 64 (1986): 54–62, Vatican City.

Kearney, Richard. *Anatheism*, New York: Columbia University Press, 2010.

Kuttianimattathil, Jose. *Practice and Theology of Interreligious Dialogue: A critical study of the Indian Christian attempts since Vatican II.* Bangalore: Kristu Jyoti, 1995.

Lassalle, Hugo-Enomiya. *Zen – Weg zur Erleuchtung*. Wien: Herder, 1960.

Le Saux, Henri. *Un maître spirituel du pays tamoul*. Chambéry: Présence, 1970.

Le Saux, Henri. *Souvenirs d'Arunâchala: récit d'un ermite chrétien en terre hindoue*. Paris: Epi, 1978.

Le Saux, Henri. *Ascent to the Depth of the Heart: The Spiritual Diary of Swami Abhishiktananda*. Delhi: ISPCK, 1998.

Leclercq, Jean. *Nouvelles pages d'histoire monastique*. Vanves: Secrétariat AIM, 1986.

Levinas, Emmanuel. *Totality and Infinity*. The Hague: Martinus Nijhoff, 1979.

Majumdar, R.C. *The Classical Accounts of India*. Calcutta: Firma KLM, 1981.

Marty, Martin E. *When Faiths Collide*. Oxford: Blackwell, 2005,124.

Merton, Thomas. *Zen and the Birds of Appetite*. New York: New Directions, 1968.

Merton, Thomas. *The Asian journal of Thomas Merton*. New York: New Direction, 1975, 308.

Mitchell, Donald W. and William Skudlarek, OSB (eds.). *Green Monasticism*. New York: Lantern Books, 2010.

Mitchell, Donald W. and James Wiseman, OSB (eds.). *The Gethsemani Encounter: A Dialogue on the Spiritual Life by Buddhist and Christgian Monastics*. New York: Continuum, 1997.

Mitchell, Donald W. and James Wiseman, OSB (eds.). *Transforming Suffering: Reflections on Finding Peace in Troubled Times*. New York: Doubleday, 2003.

Moffit, John. *A New Charter For Monasticism: Proceedings of the Meeting of the Monastic Superiors in the Far East, Bangkok, 9 to 15 December*. Notre Dame: University of Notre Dame Press, 1970.

Monge, Claudio. *Dieu Hôte: Recherche historique et théologique sur les rituels de l'hospitalité*. Bucarest: Zeta Books, 1997.

Mott, Michael. *The Seven Mountains of Thomas Merton*. Boston, MA: Houghton Mifflin, 1984.

Panikkar, Raimon. *The Vedic Experience: Mantramanjari*. Berkeley: University of California Press, 1977.

Panikkar, Raimon. *The Intrareligious Dialogue*. New York: Paulist Press, 1978.

Panikkar, Raimon. *Blessed Simplicity: The Monk as Universal Archetype*. New York: Seabury Press, 1982.

Panikkar, Raimon. "Foreword" to P.-F. de Béthune, *Interreligious Hospitality*. Collegeville, MN: Liturgical Press, 2010.

Pignedoli, Sergio. "Lettre à l'Abbé Primat," *Bulletin AIM*, 17, 62 (1974), Vanves.

Pohl, C.D. *Making Room: Recovering Hospitality as a Christian Tradition*. Grand Rapids, MI: Eerdmans, 1999.

Pontificium Consilium pro Dialogo inter Religiones. *Contemplation et Dialogue Interreligieux: Repères et perspectives puisées dans l'expérience des moines*. Bulletin 84 (1993) 250–270. Vatican City.

Ricoeur, Paul. *On Translation*. London: Routledge, 2006.

Salenson, Christian. *Christian de Chergé: Une théologhie de l'espérance*. Paris: Bayard, 2009.

Secrétariat AIM. *Les Moines Chrétiens face aux Religions d'Asie, Bangalore 1973*. Vanves: Secrétariat AIM, 1974.

Secretariatus pro non christianis. *Dialogue and Mission: The attitude of the Church towards the followers of other religions*. Bulletin, 56, 35 (1984): 138. Vatican City.

Secretariatus pro non christianis. *Pope's Christmas address to the Roman curia*. Bulletin 64 (1987): 54–62. Vatican City.

Secretariatus pro non christianis. *Discourse of the Pope to Zen and Christian monks*. Bulletin, 67 (1988): 5–6. Vatican City.

Skudlarek, William. *Demythologizing Celibacy: Practical Wisdom from Christian and Buddhist Monasticism*. Collegeville, MN: Liturgical Press, 2008.

Tassin, Claude. "Au commencement était la maison." *Spiritus* 201 (2011): 415–428.

Volf, Miroslav. *Exclusion and Embrace: A theological Exploration of Identity, Otherness and Reconciliation*. Nashville, TN: Abington, 1996.

Walker, Susan (ed.). *Speaking of Silence: Christian and Buddhists on the Contemplative Way*. New York: Paulist, 1987.

Yong, Amos. *Hospitality and the Other: Pentecost, Christian Practices and the Neighbor*. Maryknoll, NY: Orbis, 2008.

CHAPTER 4

Comparative Theology and Inter-Religious Dialogue

Francis X. Clooney, SJ

To begin on a personal note: I have always been most content as a scholar when I am studying some classical text and its commentaries; I return to the deep past of our traditions, to make sense of the world in which we live now. Given my decades of the study of Hindu texts in light of my Catholic Christian education, it is not decisive whether I start with a Hindu text or a Christian. In one way, of course, I always start with the Christian, but after decades of studying Hinduism, I never read without the Hindu dimension being present too, and from the start. Reading in either tradition rather quickly prompts me to see a way to read in the other tradition as well. In accord with this dynamic of interior encounter, it is important to note from the start that my expertise is in the field of comparative theology; although I am very much in favor of open and honest communication among faith traditions and often enough find myself in conversations with Hindus, for instance I rarely seek out formal occasions to engage in dialogue.[1] While I prefer comparative theology to inter-religious dialogue, I do not contend that the former is in any absolute way more important than the latter.

My distance from formal dialogues and commitment to comparative theology is because my primary work is academic, and because long years of study complicate how one relates to the religions one studies. It would be hard for me at this point in my life to imagine leaving aside my studies, in order to be a Catholic Christian representative in the dialogue with Hindus, particularly if "representation" is taken to mean standing for a "purely Roman Catholic" position that is not deeply informed by the study of Hinduism. I have on occasion even had to suggest to organizers that most dialogues work best if those invited are open-minded but not particularly learned about the other tradition involved, and thus all the more eager to listen and learn. Since I am not an official religious leader, dialoguing with religious leaders is best left to other religious leaders and their delegates. Others speak confidently and with authority for the Church, to those outside it. As an academician, I already meet a wide range of scholars of Hinduism, including scholars who are Hindu, either born Hindu or converted to that faith. So inter-religious dialogue is neither a required nor urgent form of practice for me, in light of the

The Wiley Blackwell Companion to Inter-Religious Dialogue, First Edition. Edited by Catherine Cornille.
© 2013 John Wiley & Sons Ltd. Published 2020 by John Wiley & Sons Ltd.

work I already do; my own encounters occur within the intellectual frame of comparative theology, even if that comparative theology relies on an internal dialogue.

I have never found that study, however solitary, remains closed in upon itself, as if somehow the polar opposite to dialogue. Study is today a great topic for conversation and controversy, often across religious boundaries. Rather, as a teacher and writer who visits India on a regular basis, I have many Hindu friends and colleagues. There are also Hindu critics who take exception to my work and question the propriety of a Christian studying Hinduism so persistently and, for a non-Hindu, in such depth. In all of this, one might say that a conversation occurs in my study, in the classroom, in publications, on the web, and in personal conversations, though not because I see the wider conversation as a goal in itself. It is confirmed for me over and again that comparative theology is a robust form of inter-religious learning that is neither to be confused with nor separated from inter-religious dialogue. Now let me step back and put the preceding general reflections in a wider context.

Comparative Theology and Inter-Religious Dialogue: Some Starting Points

First, I propose some distinctions that I have found useful in my work. In my 2010 book *Comparative Theology*, I made a number of distinctions, including the following, which are relevant here:

> "Theology" indicates a mode of inquiry that engages a wide range of issues with full intellectual force, but ordinarily does so within the constraints of a commitment to a religious community, respect for its scriptures, traditions, and practices, and a willingness to affirm the truths and values of that tradition. More deeply, and to echo more simply an ancient characterization of theology, it is *faith seeking understanding*, a practice in which all three words – the faith, the search, the intellectual goal – have their full force and remain in fruitful tension with one another. (Clooney 2010a: 9)

In the context of theology, two discourses belong together but must be distinguished. On the one hand,

> "Interreligious dialogue points to actual conversations, sometimes formal and academic, sometimes simply interpersonal conversations among persons of different religious traditions willing to listen to one another and share their stories of faith and values. "Dialogical" or "interreligious" theology grows out of interreligious dialogue, as reflection aimed at clarifying dialogue's presuppositions, learning from its actual practice, and communicating what is learned in dialogue for a wider audience. (Clooney 2010a: 10)

On the other,

> "Comparative theology" – comparative and theological beginning to end – marks acts of faith seeking understanding which are rooted in a particular faith tradition but which, from that foundation, venture into learning from one or more other faith traditions. This

learning is sought for the sake of fresh theological insights that are indebted to the newly encountered tradition/s as well as the home tradition. (Clooney 2010a: 10)

In the same context I explain why there are good reasons to keep comparative theology and inter-religious dialogue closely connected but also clearly distinguished:

> As actual, living interaction among people of different faith traditions that enhances mutual understanding, personal encounters in dialogue should remind us that religions flourish in the lives, beliefs, and activities of real people living out their faith day by day. Dialogue also reminds us that we must be accountable to other communities when we speak about their religion, even as we must give an account of ourselves to our own community.

Nevertheless, "even a seriously theological dialogue among learned believers is not enough," were the implication to be that those who meet in this way do not change, as if in some simple way they continue only to represent their respective own home traditions. The comparative theologian ideally does more than listen to others explain their faith; she or he must be willing to study their traditions deeply alongside her own, taking both to heart and thus incorporating the wisdom of the other into her own. But still, it is not a problem to say that this comparative theology opens into a kind of dialogue, simply in accord with the demands of good scholarship: "As essentially interreligious, each particular comparative theology is by itself always incomplete, and theologians need to hear from others how they understand and interpret the beliefs of their traditions, and how they think we ought to correct what we say about them." All of this might be counted as inter-religious dialogue, but "in the process [of study], [the theologian] will begin to theologize as it were from both sides of the table, reflecting personally on old and new truths in an interior dialogue." (Clooney 2010a: 13)

John Sheveland aptly captured the relation of comparative theology and inter-religious dialogue by drawing our attention to the musical practice of polyphony and treating inter-religious dialogue and comparative theology as two instances of such polyphony. In both, we are called to appreciate "an individual religious speaker with greater nuance and sophistication when her speech is heard communally in a shared context with other speech." Like dialogue, "comparative theology acknowledges difference as a *sine qua non* for engaging the other with hospitality and integrity." Thus, "the dynamics of counterpoint within polyphony assist us with the moral imperative of taking our companions in dialogue seriously precisely in their difference, but not isolation, from us." Two main features of polyphony – "recognition of difference and attention to an emergent structure of intelligibility" – are prized by comparative theologians and, I would add, by those practitioners of dialogue who prefer to allow theological understanding to emerge from the dialogue rather than be superimposed on it (Clooney 2010b: 172).

Comparative theology and inter-religious dialogue are of course different in obvious ways. Comparative theology is ordinarily to be understood as a form of academic theology, scholarly work, while inter-religious dialogue can occur through technical theological conversations but also in a much wider variety of less formal exchanges.

Comparative theology is primarily and usually a form of reading; inter-religious dialogue is usually a form of conversation. That comparative theology is a mode of study should not be surprising, since in this it is like other forms of theology, which are also typically exercises in study. Such learning is not necessarily, at least in the short run, dependent on conversation. While this should *not* be interpreted as a way of devaluing inter-religious dialogue as less intellectual, it does remind us that inter-religious dialogue is never a substitute for comparative theology, as if a conversation is always better than solitary study. Yet even if comparative theology is a form of reading, it can also become an internal inter-religious dialogue, a learning from the other tradition, questioning it and being questioned by it. Given its textual base, it is a premier opportunity for a deeper learning of how to learn, and for reflection on actual learning. If one is taking the other religion seriously, the study itself is accountable to the other, and in both reading and talking, the challenge of the other is present.

Yet, differences aside, in both comparative theology and in dialogue there is a serious learning from the other. As a form of study, comparative theology can find a place in the standard list of options for inter-religious dialogue, as a form of what is usually fourth on a list that includes the dialogues of life, work, spirituality, and study. As study, comparative theology is an interior inter-religious dialogue; the other is mediated by text, study, whether or not one sits and discusses that study with another person directly. Comparative theology may also be a subsequent, interiorized version of a kind of inter-religious dialogue, arising after interests are stimulated by dialogue. It can also be put the other way: inter-religious dialogue in its fourth form is an exterior form of comparative theology, in which the study takes place either in conversation or as the "sharing of notes" of the several scholars. In this light, comparative theology and inter-religious dialogue ought not to be seen as alternatives, as if exclusive of one another.

A Note on the Historical Interconnections of Comparative Theology and Inter-Religious Dialogue

It is arguable that inter-religious learning, including comparative theology, and inter-religious dialogue have never been entirely separable, given the natural interconnection between study and conversation. To study another religion invites encounter, and encounter raises questions ordinarily addressed in careful study. Here, even in ancient times in Christian and Hindu contexts, we find practices resembling comparative theology and inter-religious dialogue in relation to one another, for example, the Patristic appropriation of Greek pagan sources, in conscious continuity with and divergence from how those texts were read outside the Christian context, and in Brahminical and Buddhist interactions Such deep learning – theologically sophisticated, taken to heart, and connected to direct communication with members of the religion that is being studied – is also evident in the studies undertaken by missionaries in the era of European expansion, signally represented by Catholics like Mateo Ricci (sixteenth century, China) and Roberto de Nobili (seventeenth century, India), and by Protestants such as Bartholomaeus Ziegenbalg (eighteenth century, India).

It is illuminating also to realize that the term "comparative theology" itself apparently arose in the context of a quest for religious harmony. In 1700 James Garden (1645–1726) published *Comparative Theology; or The True and Solid Grounds of Pure and Peaceable Theology*. In explaining his project, Garden distinguishes two kinds of theology. First, there is *absolute* theology, "that knowledge of religion [which] considers its Object only as revealed and enjoined, or instituted, by God." Second, there is *comparative* theology, wherein "the respective Knowledge of Religion ponders the weight or importance, and observes the Order, Respect and Relation of things belonging to Religion." (As quoted in Clooney 2010a: 31.) The point of a comparative theology in Garden's context was to identify more important, basic truths and values which deserved our fuller attention. By contrast, according to Garden, in accentuating differences absolute theology leads to ongoing conflict about such differences, whereas comparative theology creates a space in which common truths and values can be shared.

Garden was thinking of differences among Christians and not across wider religious boundaries, but it is interesting that even at its earliest mention "comparative theology" was named a discipline by which to identify and privilege common ground, so as to enhance the possibility of constructive exchange. This irenic usage is predictive of some of the more hopeful and vital comparative work that has appeared over the centuries, particularly in the present, and clearly opens the door to what today we would term ecumenical or inter-religious dialogue.

While the nineteenth-century comparative theologians were largely Europeans and North Americans who were *not* in direct dialogue with members of other religions, it is clear that their work was in part motivated by a growing awareness of the vastness and intellectual depth of the various religions of the world. The need to understand other traditions, to collect and systematize knowledge about them, became important to their essentially Christian practices. Their comparative theologies, though not directly inter-religious dialogue, were already on the edge of dialogue, since the "other" had clearly entered into the consciousness of such scholars writing in Europe and North America.

Comparative Theology as the Right Theological Practice to go with Inter-Religious Dialogue

In a perceptive review of standard positions in the field of the theology of religion that goes on to seek an adequate theological practice to go with dialogue, Marianne Moyaert (2012) makes a strong case that comparative theology is a practice very appropriate to the reception of real, ongoing dialogue. Comparative theology can both support and be nourished by inter-religious dialogue, since "comparative theology presents itself as a genuine and adequate way to understand and appreciate the otherness of the religious other without losing sight of one's own identity." Because it can be conceived of as "a never-ending hermeneutical circle which moves between identity and openness, conviction and critique, commitment and distanciation . . .," comparative theology offers a distinctive balance between openness and commitment. It "sees interreligious encounter, first and foremost, as an ongoing conversation process which can yield preliminary results only;" and this is the mark of "real and authentic dialogue." In Moyaert's view, comparative theology avoids the *a priori* and insists on comprehension of the other, in the particular, before judgment. It is deeply dialogical, since it "sets out to understand the meaning of Christian tradition by exploring it in light of the teachings of other religious traditions" (39). As a form of critical analysis, it thus leaves room for questions of meaning, the actualization of what is learned in the life of the believer, after she or he is exposed to the meanings of the text, in a sense surrendering excessive "mastery, sufficiency, and autonomy" (44). It is always in process and unfinished, open to further experiments"; this patience, moreover, is also an expression of *hermeneutical* openness, which is the *conditio sine qua non* of real dialogue" (46).

The New Contexts of Comparative Theology and Inter-Religious Dialogue

Against this background, we can notice the context in which we need to today review the relationship of comparative theology and inter-religious dialogue. In the past, scholars "here" were usually studying religions "there," with a fairly neat divide between the world of scholarship about non-Christian religions and the societies in which members of those religions live. In our era, crossover between the study of two traditions together in comparative theology and the conversation of believers in inter-religious dialogue is almost inescapable, given the diversity and dynamism that is now characteristic of the dissemination of knowledge, and the fact of accountability to tradition and to our neighbors today. The religions that are studied are no longer far away; the presence of an increasingly diverse cultural and religious population in the West means that some of our neighbors, colleagues, and students belong to those traditions, and are often in a position to ask us about what we have written or are teaching. Even if comparative theology is still carried out primarily in the (Christian) West and is stimulated primarily by the interests of (Christian) Westerners, this does not mean that it is merely an academic discipline practiced far from situations of real dialogue. The West itself is now a place where educative and academic inter-religious dialogues, as well as dialogue on the ground, occur amidst a real and lively pluralism.

The environment for any kind of inter-religious reflection is today all the more complicated. The internet has been changing the way we communicate with one another, and this surely affects inter-religious dialogue and comparative theology, individually and in relation to one another. Even if I write a book on Hinduism from a Christian perspective and intend it for a rather limited audience, any such book would still be announced on the publisher's website promoting the book, and by online bookstores giving at least some information about it. Even people not likely to read any given book will form opinions about it from web materials. Scholarship has always impinged on multiple audiences, of course, but now the global audience for books that cross religious boundaries is growing, and this further blurs the boundary between comparative theology and the implied inter-religious dialogue. The private is now also public, and so comparative theology is open to wide scrutiny, simply because even academic writing is more widely known, commented on, even read and studied by outsiders to the academy. If so, we are in a situation where the pressures on comparative theology and inter-religious dialogue individually will keep bringing them closer to each other.

Comparative Theology and Scriptural Reasoning at the Margins of Inter-Religious Dialogue

To clarify still more closely the comparative theology–inter-religious dialogue relationship, it is helpful to consider the relationship of comparative theology to another discipline that has both reading and dialogical features – scriptural reasoning, a practice of close textual reading shared most often by small groups of Jews, Christians, and Muslims who cooperate in reading together selected passages from the scriptures of the three traditions. They do this for the sake of deeper mutual understanding. As such, it is a sophisticated form of inter-religious dialogue and also a kind of study. As a way of reading, scriptural reasoning resonates well with comparative theology. For an elaboration of the similarities and differences, see Michael Barnes' insightful 2011 essay on comparative theology and scriptural reasoning. Most pertinent for our purposes is a shared scriptural and reading-based starting point and basis for the sharing of traditions, along with the benefits and risks incurred in venturing to learn seriously the scriptures of another tradition. Ben Quash has highlighted four characteristics of scriptural reasoning: particularity, provisionality, sociality, and surprise (Quash 2006: 404). These elements, validated in the ongoing experience of scriptural reasoning, are also relevant to the differently configured dialogue that occurs in comparative theology. Comparative theology too is highly particular, limited to a reading of several texts at a time; it is provisional, in the sense that it is an exercise that can be repeated, extended, improved, tested in other unanticipated circumstances with other texts; it is social, though in the limited sense that the voices of two traditions must be heard together, neither simplified nor generalized to fit the expectations of the other; and it is likely to be surprising, since there is no already settled framework in which its meaning can be adjudicated or the outcome predicted. The same virtues, marking the distinctiveness of both scriptural reasoning and comparative theology, often apply in inter-religious dialogue as well, where fluidity and a resistance to definitive conclusions enhance the desired exchanges.

But while scriptural reasoning and comparative theology share basic intentions, there are some differences. As I have already suggested, my own comparative theology offers primarily an interior dialogue constituted by my reading of Catholic and Hindu texts together. In a sense, the sociality of learning is minimized; for example, I have been primarily reading books, but very rarely do I read them with members of Hindu traditions. However, I have been learning from the Hindu commentarial tradition and from Hindu friends for decades, and such friends have often enough generously read my manuscripts and offered criticisms. In reading the works of our own and another tradition, we begin to enter a conversation with communities inseparable from their holy texts and theological wisdom, and we begin to become (at first unexpectedly) bonded to both communities, even as long-term guests (Barnes: 403–405).

On a substantive level, in my interior dialogue as reader and as writer, my intention is not simply to listen to or learn from Hindus who speak of their scripture and interpretive traditions. Rather, as a Christian reader and writer, I myself read conscientiously and take to heart some theologically substantive and (usually) spiritually rich classic of a Hindu tradition, and allow its ideas and arguments, affective states and movement toward transformation of life to infuse and affect my Christian faith. Even if the process begins by my choice of some Hindu text that makes sense from a Catholic Christian perspective, thereafter my reading of any Christian text is, I hope, irreversibly informed by the insights, strategies, affects, intentions, and practices of that chosen Hindu text and the literature surrounding it. Boundaries are ideally blurred, echoes and references multiplied, lineages interwoven. Reaching beyond comparison, in a respectful sense my work also moves beyond inter-religious dialogue as ordinarily understood; there are no longer settled groups of interlocutors, neatly sorted out on either side by religious identification, who then play expected roles in a dialogue.

Comparative Theology in Critical Relationship with Inter-Religious Dialogue

Comparative theology is a kind of study, and of course many instances of study are indeed merely academic and can hardly be counted as inter-religious or dialogical. So how can awareness of inter-religious dialogue deepen the work of the scholar who engages in comparative theology? Each field requires and critiques the other. Comparative theology can provide answers to questions arising in relation to inter-religious dialogue, pushing us to think about what we need to know – and can easily learn – in order to engage in inter-religious dialogue in a mature, constructive way. So too, comparative theology may in some instances be a kind of follow-up, the further study that addresses questions raised in inter-religious dialogue.

Moreover, today there is always the uncomfortable question of who has the right to study and interpret the sacred texts of a tradition, a concern about the relative lack of accountability of Western scholars in interpreting the sacred texts of other traditions as they wish. Contested too would be the often presumed higher status of modern Western scholarship and the presumption that modern scholars read texts better than do the insiders to a tradition. The idea of mutual enrichment and accountability invites conversation at a deeper level. Face to face encounters among concerned religious persons of multiple traditions may then be the necessary forum for airing concerns about comparative theology, as insiders to traditions under discussion are given the opportunity to critique the views of outsiders, and re-emphasize criteria for right learning – criteria that may well not mesh smoothly with Western scholarly expectations. Religious insiders can then hear back from scholars about the reasons for their admittedly different approach to the same texts; not every difference is a mistake or ill-intentioned, after all. And so inter-religious dialogue may help and test comparative theology, making it more directly accountable in the court of dialogue.

Above I referred to John Sheveland's essay in *The New Comparative Theology*, a volume featuring reflections on comparative theology by a younger generation of scholars.

Many of the essays there address the anxieties common in the academy today regarding orientalist and hegemonic interpretations of Asian religions by Western academics who, whether writing in a positive or a negative vein, assume the position of determining what the other religion means, what is important, and how even insiders to the religion ought to understand it. For these younger scholars, the study of the other religion "on one's own" is a dangerous activity, while the corrective of dialogue will diminish the dangers of misconstrual. Comparative theology therefore needs inter-religious dialogue, on ethical grounds. For example, Hugh Nicholson highlights this ethical component by detecting the alliance of comparative theology and inter-religious dialogue in the face of several key problems:

> The correlative practices of interreligious dialogue and comparative theology mobilize members of different religious traditions against two troubling symptoms of our present situation of late-stage, global capitalism: on the one side, a proliferating consumer culture that has eroded the bonds of community and tradition; on the other, virulent forms of religious militancy that threaten the peaceful coexistence of different religious and cultural populations in today's pluralistic societies. Clooney 2010b, 55, 58

In this way, out of shared needs, the new comparative theology becomes more closely linked to inter-religious dialogue than were the older forms of comparative theology common in the nineteenth and twentieth centuries.

Yet comparative theology does not in any certain way lead straight to inter-religious dialogue. Sometimes the more you know, the harder ordinary dialogue may be. The practitioner of comparative theology may know too much, in a way, to enter upon ordinary dialogues, which may become more difficult when the practitioner of comparative theology knows very much about the other tradition in the dialogue. The comparative theologian may know things even insiders to the other tradition may not know. Some will prefer instead to dialogue only with those who have learned their tradition only from a distance, who have not studied both religions already.

In my relationship with Srivaisnavas, for instance, the connections with dialogue have been mixed. To some, the majority, it seems a very good thing that I have studied their tradition in depth, and they welcome my respectful learning. Some recognize that I have studied, but also note that I have not been educated within the tradition, as an insider and guided by a teacher. It may also be that my education in theology and Western academic study is jarring, as I study their sacred and familiar tradition in a way that, while respectful, still surprises them. And then there are a few who seem particularly uneasy that I have studied in depth, and not stayed away, inside my own tradition.

If the members of the dialogue from the other tradition know only their own tradition, and have never done the integral work of comparative theology, they will not be in a particularly authoritative position from which to judge the contribution of the comparative theologian who has studied both his/her own and this other tradition. At some point, comparative theology may then itself become the topic of an inter-religious dialogue that asks about the meaning of inter-religious study and the way in which learning changes how the traditions involved are understood. For there to be inter-religious dialogue after comparative theology, there may have to be in place parallel comparative theological practices, reaching in each direction – in my case, for example, a balancing of my work by a parallel Hindu comparative theology.

On another level, both comparative theology and inter-religious dialogue challenge ordinary – that is, nondialogical, noncomparative – theology, particularly if that theology seeks to decide the meaning of other religious traditions without dialogue and solely by the study of one's own tradition. Reflection internal to a tradition, in meditation on its own sources, is crucial and primary, but this legitimate turn inward will fall short if insiders find no way to take into account the fruits of comparative theology and inter-religious dialogue – that is, if what is learned from elsewhere is forever treated merely as information extrinsic to theology. But once those other perspectives are taken into account, it is by no means easy for a theology to return neatly to its own predialogical condition, as if innocent of the deeper theological study of other traditions.

Is Inter-Religious Dialogue Unsettled by Comparative Theology?

What is inter-religious dialogue like *after* comparative theology? How does comparative theology change inter-religious dialogue? One benefit is the dispelling of the notion that in a dialogue designated participants will be ordinarily informed about their own traditions but not about the other traditions at the table. If comparative theology has been practiced by those engaged in dialogue, everyone will already know something about the other traditions and have assimilated this learning and brought it into dialogue with their own traditions. Comparative theology may promote the transformation of the persons who engage in inter-religious dialogue, even before the inter-religious dialogue is carried forward. It may also instigate more depth of study in one's own tradition, so that even prior to inter-religious dialogue, a deepening occurs. Comparative theology raises the bar, and may seem at least to suggest that much inter-religious dialogue is superficial because the participants are presumably learned regarding their own tradition but not regarding the other, and because the dialogues are quick and occasional, neither deeply prepared for nor seriously followed up on. But what would be the value of inter-religious dialogue, if it never leads to a richer curiosity that turns into acts of study across religious boundaries, such as leave one as it were participant in both sides of the dialogue? Comparative theology may diminish the urgency for inter-religious dialogue by making it clear that the dialogue is not to be the primary source of information about the other tradition or traditions. New learning is always appreciated, and if dialogue is a good means of gaining it, all the better. In any case, after comparative theology one must learn how to pursue the dialogue differently, depending on how much learning across religious borders is already present in the room.

In Conclusion

In the preceding pages I have argued for the necessary distinction between comparative theology and inter-religious dialogue, and likewise the inevitable and complex interconnections of the fields. In the end, all of this has also to do with the kinds of person involved, who is doing the learning and the talking. We learn by interior reflection and by exchange with one another. The scholar and the theologian, in her or his personal research or in a teaching role, inevitably moves back and forth between study and private work and social exchange, today frequently with readers and students of multiple religions. It should not be surprising then that both comparative theology and inter-religious dialogue figure in *all* our efforts at inter-religious understanding. Some of us are more the readers and writers, and others more apt for face to face exchange; the former are more likely to be called "comparative theologians," and the latter "participants in dialogue." We have also seen that a turn within for the sake of comparative theological reflection is not an abandonment of inter-religious dialogue. If I have undertaken the study of Hindu texts for the sake of learning, and in that learning have also purified and clarified my own Christian beliefs, it nonetheless remains true that the fact of comparative theology has opened for me various opportunities for inter-religious dialogue, specific instances of conversation and exchange that have also been valuable and crucial for the wholeness of my understanding of my Christian and Catholic identity in light of Hindu wisdom. Inter-religious dialogue and comparative theology, respected as distinct, inevitably open into one another.

Note

1   It is also the case that relatively speaking, official Catholic–Hindu dialogues are less frequent than other dialogues in which the Church engages. It seems that the Roman Catholic Church, my community, is unsure how to dialogue with Hindus, given the rather different way in which Hindu communities are organized, their authoritative voices put forward, and issues of truth, self and other negotiated. Others, devoted to inter-religious dialogue, will have greater insights regarding dialogue with Hindus. And since I write as a North American, I do not wish to be thought to be trying to speak for the Christian communities of India, for whom dialogue will be seen as a greater priority. Certainly too, I do not wish to prejudice what might be said about the great importance of Jewish–Christian or Muslim–Christian dialogue as dialogues with their own histories.

Bibliography

Bartel, T.W. *Comparative Theology: Essays for Keith Ward*. London: SPCK, 2003.

Barnes, Michael. "Reading Other Religious Text, Intratextuality and the Logic of Scripture." *Journal of Ecumenical Studies* 46(3) (2011, summer): 389–410.

Burrell, David. *Knowing the Unknowable God: Ibn-Sina, Maimonides, Aquinas*. Notre Dame, IN: University of Notre Dame Press, 1986.

Carman, John B. *Majesty and Meekness*. Grand Rapids, MI: Eerdmans, 1994.

Clarke, James F. *Ten Great Religions: An Essay in Comparative Theology*. Boston, MA: Houghton Mifflin, 1871.

Clarke, James F. *Ten Great Religions Part II: A Comparison of All Religions*. Boston, MA: Houghton Mifflin, 1884.

Clooney, Francis X. "Extending the Canon: Some Implications of a Hindu Argument about Scripture." *Harvard Theological Review* 85(2) (1992): 197–215.

Clooney, Francis X. *Theology after Vedanta: An Experiment in Comparative Theology*. Albany: State University of New York Press, 1993.

Clooney, Francis X. "The Emerging Field of Comparative Theology: A Bibliographical Review (1989–95)." *Theological Studies* 56(3) (1995): 521–550.

Clooney, Francis X. *Seeing through Texts: Doing Theology among the Srivaisnavas of South India*. Albany: State University of New York Press, 1996.

Clooney, Francis X. *Hindu God, Christian God: How Reason Helps Break Down the Boundaries between Religions*. Oxford: Oxford University Press, 2001.

Clooney, Francis X. *Divine Mother, Blessed Mother: Hindu Goddesses and the Blessed Virgin Mary*. Oxford: Oxford University Press, 2005.

Clooney, Francis X. "Comparative Theology," in *The Oxford Handbook to Systematic Theology*, ed. John Webster, Kathryn Tanner, and Iain Torrance. Oxford: Oxford University Press, 2007: 653–669.

Clooney, Francis X. *Beyond Compare: St. Francis de Sales and Sri Vedanta Desika on Loving Surrender to God*. Washington, DC: Georgetown University Press, 2008.

Clooney, Francis X. *The Truth, the Way, the Life: Christian Commentary on the Three Holy Mantras of the Srivaisnavas*. Leuven: Peeters, 2008.

Clooney, Francis X. *Comparative Theology: Deep Learning Across Religious Borders*. Wiley-Blackwell, 2010a.

Clooney, Francis X. (ed.). *The New Comparative Theology: Voices from the New Generation*. New York: Continuum, 2010b.

Cornille, Catherine. *Song Divine: Christian Commentaries on the* Bhagavad Gita. Leuven: Peeters, 2006.

Dadosky, John. *The Structure of Religious Knowing. Encountering the Sacred in Eliade and Lonergan*. Albany: State University of New York, 2004.

Fredericks, James. *Buddhists and Christians: Through Comparative Theology to Solidarity*. Maryknoll, NY: Orbis, 2004.

Garden, James. *Comparative Theology*. 1700.

Jordan, Louis Henry. *Comparative Religion*. London: T & T Clark, 1905.

Joslyn-Semiatkoski, Daniel. *Christian Memories of the Maccabean Martyrs*. London: Palgrave Macmillan, 2009.

Kiblinger, Kristin Beise. *Buddhist Inclusivism: Attitudes Toward Religious Others*. London: Ashgate, 2005.

Kochumuttom, Thomas. *Comparative Theology: Christian Thinking and Spirituality in Indian Perspective*. Bangalore: Dharmaram, 1985.

Laksana, A. Bagus. *Muslim and Catholic Pilgrimage Practices: Walking through Java*. London: Ashgate, 2013.

Locklin, Reid. *Liturgy of Liberation: A Christian Commentary on Shankara's Upadesasahasri*. Leuven: Peeters, 2011.

MacCulloch, John A. *Comparative Theology*. London: Methuen, 1902.

Molleur, Joseph. *Divergent Traditions, Converging Faiths: Troeltsch, Comparative Theology, and the Conversation with Hinduism*. New York: Peter Lang, 2000.

Moyaert, Marianne. "Recent Developments in the Theology of Interreligious Dialogue: From Soteriological Openness to Hermeneutical Openness." *Modern Theology* 28(1) (January 2012): 25–52.

Müller, F. Max. *Introduction to the Science of Religion*. New York: Longmans, Green, and Company, 1873.

Myers, Michael W. *Brahman: a Comparative Theology*. London: Routledge, 2000.

Neville, Robert. *Behind the Masks of God*. Albany: State University of New York Press, 1991.

Neville, Robert (ed.). *The Human Condition*. Albany: State University of New York Press, 2000.

Neville, Robert (ed.). *Ultimate Realities*. Albany: State University of New York Press, 2000.

Neville, Robert (ed.). *Religious Truth*. Albany: State University of New York Press, 2000.

Neville, Robert. *Ritual and Deference: Extending Chinese Philosophy in a Comparative Context*. Albany: State University of New York Press, 2008.

Nicholson, Hugh. "A Correlational Model of Comparative Theology." *The Journal of Religion*, 85, 2 (2005): 191–213.

Nicholson, Hugh. "The New Comparative Theology and the Problem of Hegemonism," in *The New Comparative Theology: Voices from the New Generation*, ed. Francis X. Clooney. New York: Continuum, 2010.

Nicholson, Hugh. *Comparative Theology and the Problem of Religious Rivalry*. Oxford: Oxford University Press, 2011.

Panikkar, Raimon. *The Intrareligious Dialogue*. New York: Paulist, 1999.

Quash, Ben. "Heavenly Semantics: Some Literary-Critical Approaches to Scriptural Reasoning." *Modern Theology* 22(3) (July 2006): 403–20.

Roberts, Michelle. *Dualities: A Theology of Difference*. Louisville, KY: Westminster John Knox, 2010.

Sheveland, John. "Solidarity Through Polyphony," in *The New Comparative Theology: Voices from the New Generation*, ed. Francis X. Clooney. New York: Continuum, 2010.

Steinkerchner, Scott. *Watching Clouds: Engaging in Dialogue across Disparate World-Pictures*. Saarbrucken: VDM Verlag, 2009.

Thatamanil, John. *The Immanent Divine: God, Creation and the Human Predicament. An East–West Conversation*. New York: Fortress Press, 2006.

Tracy, David. "Comparative Theology," in *Encyclopedia of Religion*, ed. Lindsay Jones. 2nd edn. Detroit: Macmillan Reference USA, 2005: Vol. 13, 9125–9134.

Tsoukalas, Steven. *Krsna and Christ: Body-Divine Relation in the Thought of Sankara, Ramanuja and Classical Christian Orthodoxy*. Eugene, OR: Wipf and Stock, 2011.

Ward, Keith. *Religion and Revelation*. Oxford: Clarendon Press, 1994.

Ward, Keith. *Religion and Creation*. Oxford: Clarendon Press, 1996.

Ward, Keith. *Religion and Human Nature*. Oxford: Clarendon Press, 1998.

Ward, Keith. *Religion and Community*. Oxford: Clarendon Press, 2000.

Ward, Keith. *Religion and Human Fulfilment*. London: SCM Press, 2008.

Warren, William. *The Quest of the Perfect Religion*. Boston, MA: Rand Avery Company, 1887.

CHAPTER 5

Scriptural Reasoning as Inter-Religious Dialogue

Marianne Moyaert

In this contribution I will examine a particular form of inter-religious dialogue called scriptural reasoning, in which Jews, Christians, and Muslims temporarily suspend their sibling rivalries to become guests in one another's rich scriptural traditions.[1] If within each of these traditions scripture is, as a rule, studied and discussed within a *monoreligious* setting, scriptural reasoners want to promote a practice of *inter-religious* reading in the hope that this can also contribute to reconciliation between "people of the book" (Kavka 2007: 133). This focus on scripture – the Tanakh, Bible, and Qur'an – is unusual in inter-religious circles, and assures scriptural reasoning a special place in the current dialogue landscape.[2]

Originating in the early 1990s, this inter-religious movement (Bailey 2006: 36) now consists of about 20 official groups, primarily in North America (Duke, Virginia, Colgate, Princeton)[3] and in Great Britain (Cambridge), although there are also groups in Europe, the Middle East, Pakistan, Russia, and Australia (Ford 2011). Within a relatively short period, scriptural reasoning has expanded into a well-organized movement, with its own digital journal, academic centers devoted to research on the relationship between the Abrahamic religions, short- and long-term educational programs (Cambridge), and a PhD curriculum (Virginia). Perhaps this rather quick rise has to do with the fact that scriptural reasoning "seeks to reproduce itself in a variety of new contexts and a variety of different forms" (Adams 2011: 62).

Scriptural reasoners are primarily Jewish, Christian, and Islamic academics – scholars in biblical studies, exegetes, theologians, and philosophers – who meet a few times a year for the intensive study of authoritative scriptural texts. There are also annual meetings – both closed and open sessions – during American Academy of Religion conferences. But interest in scriptural reasoning is not limited to the academic environment. Schools, hospitals, and prisons are also taking up this practice (Ford 2011). Chaplains and other ministers are looking into how far this dialogue practice can be used in these kinds of institutions (Ochs and Ziad 2010). Recently, in London and other

The Wiley Blackwell Companion to Inter-Religious Dialogue, First Edition. Edited by Catherine Cornille.
© 2013 John Wiley & Sons Ltd. Published 2020 by John Wiley & Sons Ltd.

places, there have been citizens' initiatives as well, intended primarily to offer a coun-terweight to the dominant liberal political assumption that political consensus can be reached only through banning inter-religious differences from public debate.[4] By for-mulating a "scripturally reasoned response" to contemporary challenges, these initia-tives intend to show that it can be politically fruitful to give religious traditions a voice in the public domain.[5]

Scriptural reasoners believe in the power of serious, deep, collegial, and inter-reli-gious study of texts, the aim of which is not so much to obtain agreement beyond differences, but to make respectful disagreement possible. They believe dialogue is meaningful only when the "core identities" of the three faiths concerned are brought into conversation with one another. Instead of downplaying inter-religious differences, scriptural reasoning even seeks "to articulate and preserve the separate identities of each of the three religions" (Kepnes 2006: 372). Perhaps this rather "conservative" inclination explains why this form of dialogue is attractive to believers who object to the liberal presuppositions that often undergird inter-religious encounters (Winter 2006: 449–463). "Rather than turning aside from [inter-religious] differences in an attempt to preserve some putative peace (not really peace at all), [Scriptural Reasoning proposes that it] is precisely through exploring these differences together that [Jews, Christians and Muslims] learn the meaning of [their] profound interdependence" (Taylor 2008: 5). For them, participating in the interpretation and questioning of the scriptures of another faith tradition does not mean a relativization of their own faith commitment, but forms an incentive to read their own scripture anew, and to under-stand them anew.

From Liberal Pluralism to Postliberal Particularism

Scriptural reasoners are convinced that this practice offers an original and necessary alternative to the dominant liberal discourse on inter-religious dialogue that all too often ends up undermining particular religious traditions (Bailey 2006: 39). If the liberal tradition focuses on the commonalities beyond inter-religious differences, scrip-tural reasoning advances a postliberal particularism that argues for a dialogue founded in faith commitment.[6]

Scriptural reasoning is opposed primarily to John Hick's pluralist hypothesis, which claims that all religions are historically and culturally determined interpretations of the ineffable Real, and which is seen to exemplify the more liberal approach to religion (Hick 1989: 235–236). On this view, the diverse religions participate in a similar soteriologi-cal process, understood as the liberating transformation from ego-centeredness to reality-centeredness. All religions are more or less equal contexts of salvation, so that they enjoy a "rough parity" (Gilkey 1987: 37). Pluralism seeks to establish commonali-ties, similarities, and overlaps between two or more religions, seeking a "common ground in a deeper sense" (Cobb 1990: 604). There is one single religious ultimate reality that can be expressed effectively by a wide variety of doctrines (Griffiths 1991: 48). Pluralism presupposes unity in diversity, and the hypothesis of a common ground, which is ineffable and mysterious, leads to a de-absolutization of truth. Here, readiness to accept the contingency and relativity of one's own perspective is a prerequisite for inter-religious dialogue. "[I]f each [tradition] represents a different human perspective on the Real, each may be able to enlarge its own vision by trying to look through the lenses that others have developed" (Hick 1993: 178).

Although Hick's faith in the possibility of an enriching inter-religious encounter is praiseworthy, his view of dialogue has been criticized for not paying enough attention to the particularity of religions. Pluralism considers religious traditions to be merely different interpretations of the *same* common ground, variations on the *same* soteriological theme. Pluralism, according to a common criticism, pushes troublesome, changeable religious realities into a procrustean bed of unrestricted homogeneity (Barnes 2002: 10). As a result, the particularity of each religious tradition is undermined (Geddes 2004: 91).

Against the liberal–pluralist perspective, scriptural reasoning embodies a form of postliberal particularism, an approach to dialogue that emphasizes the irreducible particularity of religious traditions. Scriptural reasoning "does not seek to find 'underlying conceptual unities', 'overarching principles,' or 'universal essences' into which scriptures and traditions can be dissolved."[7] In all this, scriptural reasoning shows a great deal of affinity with the cultural-linguistic theory of religions, which understands religions to be analogous to languages and cultures (Ford 2006: 347).

According to George Lindbeck, who first formulated the cultural-linguistic theory of religion, "it is just as hard to think of religions as it is to think of cultures or languages as having a single generic or universal experiential essence of which particular religions – or cultures or languages – are varied manifestations or modifications" (Lindbeck 1984: 23). Just like cultures and languages, religions are irreducibly particular. Lindbeck regards religions as self-sufficient "idioms for construing reality" (Lindbeck 1984: 47). Meaning is inseparably connected with context, and is intra-textually constituted. To determine what "God" means, for example, one should investigate how the word actually functions in the Christian religion, how it gives shape to reality and experience (Lindbeck 1984: 114). The cultural-linguistic model excludes the possibility that the same experience lies at the basis of the different religions.

> Adherents of different religions do not diversely thematize the same experience, rather they have different experiences. Buddhist compassion, Christian love and . . . French revolutionary *fraternité* are not diverse modifications of a single human awareness, emotion, attitude, or sentiment, but are radically (i.e., from the root) distinct ways of experiencing and being oriented toward self, neighbor, and cosmos. (Lindbeck 1984: 40)

And, Lindbeck continues, it is even possible that "different religious and/or philosophies may have incommensurable notions of truth. . . ." (Lindbeck 1984: 55).

If religious words, practices, and experiences derive their meaning from the religious language game in which they function, they can be understood only within their own religious context. Understanding demands an intra-textual hermeneutics, which corresponds to what Clifford Geertz has called "thick description" (Geertz 1973: 3–30). Only through a "detailed familiarity with the imaginative universe in which acts are signs can one comprehend and describe the meaning of these acts for the adherents of a religion. Drawing from this postliberal particularist perspective, scriptural reasoners are concerned to preserve religious particularities and protect religious communities, without lowering the curtain on dialogue. On the contrary, they believe this will produce a more authentic *and* challenging dialogue. As Kepnes puts it:

> Beginning with scriptural forms of reasoning [scriptural reasoning is] intended to move inter-faith discussion away from conceptual and doctrinal categories of analysis. These categories often force the complex religious traditions into artificial and abstract theological concepts and dilute the complexity and specificity of the cultural-linguistic religions systems. . . . Scriptural reasoning is not against theology or philosophy, but it endeavors to use scripture to find a new/old philosophical idiom that is better attuned to religious particularity. It offers a more supple tool to lead to a richer, more complex and sensitive inter-faith dialogue. (Kepnes 2006: 373)

How Scriptural Reasoning Works

Scriptural reasoning groups are small, not only to promote interaction between participants but also to encourage the growth of friendships between them. Usually they consist of six to nine people, and a balance is sought between the three Abrahamic traditions.[8] Plenary sessions are sometimes organized, in which different scriptural reasoning groups come together to share their findings with one another.

There is no "fixed rule" that determines the course of these meetings, just as there is no "prescribed outcome" (Adams 2006a: 240). Nevertheless, a scriptural reasoning meeting is usually organized as follows:[9] First, a topic, problem, story, or image is chosen by a small committee. Next, a set of sacred texts (and perhaps commentaries) that address the chosen topic are selected: texts from the Tanakh are chosen by Jews, Biblical (New Testament) texts by Christians, and Qur'anic texts by Muslims. The texts are distributed beforehand among the participants, who are asked to study them on their own in advance. The actual meeting, which generally takes a few days, is led by a "convener." She guides the discussion, making sure everyone is offered a chance to share, question, and interpret. There are always three "presenters" who read the text aloud and possibly give a brief introduction to it with the goal of starting a discussion in the group (Taylor 2007). The presenters direct attention to prominent themes, unexpected narrative turns, and difficult passages. In this dialogue form, asking questions is often more important than formulating answers.

An important place is reserved here for so-called *deep reasonings* within each tradition. Nicholas Adams, who introduced this term in the theory of scriptural reasoning, defined it as follows: "Deep reasonings are not merely the grammars and vocabularies of a tradition, but the relatively settled patterns of their use transmitted from generation to generation. It concerns the histories of interpretation of scripture and histories of their application to particular problems in particular times and places" (Adams 2006b: 398). These deep reasonings are not only an important aspect of the interpretative process, but also give insight into the imaginative universes of the respective traditions.

What makes this practice unique is that Jews, Christians, and Muslims can read and discuss *one another's* texts on an equal basis without having to bracket their own faith commitments. Thus, for example, Jews are not the only ones who can make statements about the (final) meaning of a text from the Tanakh. Every text is read, studied, and critiqued inter-religiously. There is no room here for possessive claims and exclusivist demands. The protection reflex is contradicted right from the start.[10] To justify the "democratic" character of this practice, scriptural reasoners refer to the superabundance of textual meaning in view of which no one can claim to know or possess the *final* meaning of the text under study (Fiorenza 2009: 146).

> The text is revered and sacred, but even though its words are authoritative, its meaning has to emerge out of the give and take of dialogue . . . This means that debate is not hierarchically ordered: readers do not debate in order to recapture the one true meaning of the text, but to recommend meanings that seem more fruitful than other meanings. In this way, participants are democratized not in relation to each other, but in relationship to the text. . . . But the rule of the game is that once members of the group agree that they been introduced to a given text, then members of that text tradition relinquish their authority over the discussion. . . . Two Muslim readers may therefore debate over the biblical text and believe that they have the better reading; a Christian reader may enter in with another interpretation, but everyone has equal voice (Geddes 2004: 95).

Not infrequently, frictions, conflicts, and interpretative differences appear whenever scriptural reasoners explore different religious texts. The experience is, however, that after thorough study, the texts from the various scriptural traditions begin to affect one another, leading to astonishing, powerful, and sometimes very surprising new insights. Disagreement is an opportunity, rather than a problem. Ben Quash remarks in this regard that this approach to scripture seems more *Jewish*. Unlike the Christian tradition(s), where there is an "internal imperative to find the right interpretation" with which everyone has to agree, the Jewish tradition "has a sophisticated account of how texts can yield *a vast range* of meanings, and a robust account of how argument is the best way to make it happen" (Quash 2006b: 9) This "Jewish" fingerprint is bound up with the roots of scriptural reasoning.

The Roots of Scriptural Reasoning

Scriptural reasoning grew out of another text-oriented but exclusively Jewish practice, namely, textual reasoning.[11] The founders of textual reasoning, Steven Kepnes, Peter Ochs, and Robert Gibbs, are all postmodern thinkers from the 'Academy of Jewish Philosophy.' The question they have been concerned with until now is how to give form to Jewish thinking after the Shoah (Ochs and Levene 2002). These thinkers are very critical of the pure and abstract thinking of modernity, revealed as bankrupt during the Nazi regime. After the Shoah, and in response to modern thought, what is most needful is a re-assessment of Jewish textual traditions and the traditional practices of reading, study, and commentary.[12] Jewish thinking is thinking with and on the basis of texts (the Tanakh, rabbinic commentaries, and philosophical texts) – and it is in these rich Jewish text traditions that textual reasoners find the dialogical and exegetical ways of thinking that help them formulate answers to all kinds of contemporary challenges.

Still, textual reasoners do not intend to re-establish a kind of premodern, precritical thinking. Rather, textual reasoning claims to be *postcritical*. Let me explain what this postcritical approach entails by quoting Peter Ochs at length. According to Ochs textual reasoners:

> employ modern methods of critical inquiry to clarify the language, the historical contexts and the didactic messages of the biblical traditions of religious and moral instruction. They do not however find these methods sufficient. They argue in various ways that the biblical traditions communicate to their practitioners some rules of action that cannot be deciphered within the terms set by the canons of critical reason that emerged in the European renaissance and Enlightenment. This does not mean, however, that the biblical traditions are in this respect irrational for among their unique rules of actions are rules for interpreting the traditions themselves, including the traditions' primary texts of scriptures and scriptural commentary. In their efforts to identify these indigenous rules of interpretation the scholars represented here have begun to articulate rules of interpretation that expand and transform the modern critical canons. In some ways, these *postcritical* rules appear *postmodern*: they emerge out of criticisms of the modern search for sources of individual self-certainty, and they emphasise the communal, dialogic and textual contexts of knowledge and the meanings of what they interpret. In other ways, however, the postcritical rules are *premodern*: they describe themselves as rules of reasoning that serve the theological and moral purposes of particular traditions of scriptural interpretation. The postcritial rules belong, in other words, neither to postmodernity nor to premodernity, but rather to the dialogue now unfolding between a contemporary family of scholars and their scriptural traditions. (Ochs 1993: 1–2)

Taking inspiration from the hermeneutical and dialogical Jewish philosophers Emmanuel Levinas, Franz Rosenzweig, and Martin Buber, textual reasoners have attempted to integrate both philosophic and religious textual practices without forgetting the irreducible particularity of the Jewish tradition. On the one hand, textual reasoning is philosophy, and thus recognizes the ideal of critical rationality, but remains simultaneously critical of the self-sufficiency asserted by modern and Western thinking. The latter unjustly claims to be a privileged and normative model for "the way reason works." On the other hand, textual reasoning also responds to certain sectarian strands within Judaism, which do not have much interest in what is happening in the broader society, and which place textual study outside the scope of modern thinking. The position of textual reasoners is somewhere in between: they want to bring the Jewish scriptural tradition(s) and critical philosophical thinking together, according to the dialogical method of the classical rabbinic academies (Ochs 2002: 4).

While active participants in both Jewish communities and Western universities, textual reasoners describe themselves as troubled by dogmatic – or what they call "totalizing" – tendencies in both environments: tendencies to promote the academic disciplines as self-sufficient methods of knowledge *or* to promote any particular tradition of Judaism as an infallible means of discerning God's will (Ochs 2002: 5).

This critical attitude with respect to sectarian movements and modern universality claims, as we will see, is also present in scriptural reasoning, which chooses a postcritical approach as well. That is why practitioners are asked to bring their "internal libraries" to the table (Nayed 2005: 48–53). "These internal libraries include the diligent work scholars have done in language, textual study, philosophy, history, theology, and so on; to lack the depth and breadth of these internal libraries is surely to impoverish the reading [of these religious texts]" (Eklund 2010).

From Textual Reasoning to Scriptural Reasoning

Textual reasoners gradually came to understand the need for a deep engagement with those of other faiths who are also wrestling with giving meaning, on the basis of their scriptural tradition, to life in times of secularization and pluralization. This understanding did not arise so much through theoretical considerations as "out of a happenstance and friendship" (Belli 2011).

At the beginning of the 1990s, a number of Christian theologians, including David Ford and Daniel Hardy, attended the sessions of the textual reasoning group that were held annually during the American Academy of Religion conferences.[13] Their presence was experienced as a chance to deepen and strengthen the relations between Jews and Christians in a post-Shoah age. In addition, according to Kepnes, who was involved in this project at its initiation, there was also the idea that "it was the combination of Judaism and Christianity together with Greek culture that produced what is sometimes called Western culture" (Kepnes 2007: 118).

In the early 2000s, Muslims (Basit Koshul, Aref Nayed) also started to attend the textual reasoning meetings. This broadening was, on the one hand, anticipated from the start: Islam shares with Judaism and Christianity a faith in the one God, creator of heaven and earth, and also lives in the hopeful expectation of an end time of peace and reconciliation. Moreover, it is also a scriptural tradition: Jews, Christians, and Muslims are the "people of the book." On the other hand, the involvement of Muslims was not a matter of course: "As a religious tradition of the 'East,' Islam has often been portrayed as 'other' to the Western, Jewish, or Christian 'self'" (Koshul and Kepnes 2007: xi). Certainly after September 11, 2001, this image of Islam as *alien* to the West has become even stronger. This difficult inter-Abrahamic relationship is a reality, but it does not have to be so. By including Islam and the Qur'an, scriptural reasoning actually seeks to offer an alternative to the long history of inter-faith conflicts. This practice is intended to move beyond the popular discourse of the clash of civilizations by focusing on the existing attitudes of reverence and awe for scripture that are cultivated in each of these religions. In other words, this practice uses "the underlying allegiance to scripture of Islam, Judaism and Christianity to underscore the deep affinities between the three monotheistic traditions and at the same time preserve the respect for differences between the traditions" (Koshul and Kepnes 2007: xi).

Scripture: Source of Conflict; Source of Reconciliation?

This choice to make scriptural traditions central to inter-religious dialogue is not an obvious one. Scriptures are usually seen as an insurmountable obstacle to the success of inter-religious dialogue. There are various reasons for this. First, holy texts function as a foundational, authoritative, and often even compulsory category within their respective religious communities. Each of these traditions claims that *its* scripture is holy and gives access to the *Word* of God (Ford 2006: 349). Moreover, traditionally, there has been little appreciation for the scripture of the other. If a certain appreciation for the scripture of the other has arisen, it is seen at best as being fulfilled and at worst as being superseded by one's own scripture.[14] Finally, intra- and inter-confessional disputes have, until the present, often been fought quite literally with scripture in hand. History confirms that each of these texts, the Tanakh, the Bible, and the Qur'an, has been used to legitimize violence and justify oppression. Scriptural reasoner David Ford admits that "[e]ven for many of those who do believe it right to engage in dialogue and collaboration the scriptures are where they find what is most distinctive, most difficult, and least negotiable. So to study together anything other than very carefully selected passages might seem a recipe for increasing tensions and meeting many impasses" (Ford 2006: 346).

Still, scriptural reasoners prefer to consider the reality and seriousness of these conflicts as an extra motivation to make scriptures central in Abrahamic dialogue. Scriptures are the center around which the whole of the life of faith is organized: they are determinative for the understanding of God; they continue to be a source of inspiration for one's prayer life and liturgical practice; they nourish the religious imagination and orient moral life. An inter-religious dialogue that wishes to address the beating heart of each of these three religions must also bring in their scriptural traditions. That, moreover, will also be a primary way to help address (and possibly transform) the deeply rooted conflicts that exist between them.

Alluding to a statement by Chief Rabbi Jonathan Sacks, Hardy confirms that scriptures are the fire of the Abrahamic traditions, a fire that can both consume and warm. In addition to being the sources of conflict that they undeniably are, these scriptural traditions also constitute "sources of reason, compassion, and divine spirit for healing [these] separate communities" (Kepnes 2006: 370). That is why believers and their religious leaders must develop practices that are able to channel the warmth of the scriptural fire. In a certain respect, that is the challenge that scriptural reasoners have set for themselves: "to see if and how their three scriptural traditions offer both the warmth of faith in God *and also* protection against faith's burning fire" (Ochs and Johnson 2009: 2).

Some "Rules of Conduct"

Scriptural reasoners do not formulate grand *theories* in response to the question of how the different respective truth and revelation claims of scriptural traditions are related.

They also reject any attempt to ground the possibility of this scripture-oriented form of dialogue. Scriptural reasoning, it is invariably emphasized, is not a theory that is turned into practice but rather a practice about which one can theorize (Kepnes 2006: 370). Up until the present there does not exist an encompassing theological, philosophical, and/or hermeneutical framework in which the principles of this practice are theorized (Moyaert 2011c).[15]

Scriptural reasoners do not stand alone in their suspicion regarding grand theories. Since the postmodern turn, reliance on foundationalism is refuted. The idea is that "we should not stress navigation as much as the journey itself" (Stiver 2003: 170). Nicholas Adams especially emphasizes that scriptural reasoning is a "non-grounded discourse" (Adams 2006b: 386). He holds that inter-religious dialogue occurs and that mutual understanding is possible, but he finds it particularly futile to reflect on the metaphysical presuppositions that "explain" this possibility. For him, it is sufficient to view the inter-religious dialogue between Jews, Christians, and Muslims as a "given" without grounding this possibility metaphysically. In this sense scriptural reasoning is anti-foundational.

> Reasoning practices an empathic "taking-as-true" metaphysics and tries to cure itself of any tendencies towards "grounding" metaphysics. It treats intuitions and demonstrations as useful and informative claims but never as guarantees. What one takes as true is indeed metaphysical in the sense that it structures and informs one's knowing: there is no getting around it. This does not make it a guarantee of the truth of one's claims (Adams 2006b: 389).

Hiding behind the striving for metaphysical grounding, according to Adams, is not seldom a desire for control, a desire that is indeed human but in the end at odds with what true encounter entails. A grand theory makes the problem of the other "manageable," "containable," and "graspable," but is it not precisely part of true encounter that there is also room for what cannot be managed, contained, and grasped, for the unexpected and unpredictable?

From this perspective, scriptural reasoners claim that what makes their encounters fruitful is not theory but a form of *practical wisdom*: it is a *knowing how*, rather than a *knowing that*. To be more precise, the success of this inter-religious dialogue presupposes that the participants hold to a number of rules of conduct that revolve primarily around the search for a precarious balance between one's own commitment and a sensitive concern for the concrete other and her scriptural tradition. David Ford is one of several to translate this practical wisdom into a number of guidelines.[16]

First, one should "acknowledge *the sacredness* of the others' scriptures to them (without having to acknowledge its authority for oneself) – each believes in different ways (which can be discussed) that their scripture is in some sense from God and that the group is interpreting it before God, in God's presence and for God's sake" (Ford 2007: 279–280). Thus, Jews, for example, can acknowledge that the New Testament can be sacred for Christians without having to accept its equal footing with the Tanakh. What scriptural reasoners appear to argue here is more a kind of recognition of non-recognition, which confirms the actual asymmetry between the religious traditions. But this asymmetry does not need to stand in the way of a deep encounter. Clearly, scriptures are not always confirmed as the sources of revelation they claim to be, but in this dialogue practice they are nevertheless recognized as a source of wisdom that can also challenge outsiders. The fact that the latter ask to be received as guests in these strange religious scriptural practices corroborates this.

Second, inter-religious hospitality offers a response to believers who act like security guards or gatekeepers for their own scriptural tradition. "'Native speakers' hosting a scripture and its tradition need to acknowledge that they do not exclusively own their scriptures – they are not the *experts* on its final meaning" (Ford 2007: 280). Scriptures have a public character; they are accessible to everyone. Possessive claims are not acceptable in the practice of scriptural reasoning. Nonetheless, an expression of practical wisdom that "the hosts are to be questioned and listened to attentively as the *court of first (but not last) appeal*" obtains (Ford 2007: 280).

Third, in this practice it is not the striving for consensus that is primary but the conviction that differences of opinion can also be enriching when discussed in a respectful way. Following the Jewish tradition of Chevruta, scriptural reasoning involves a form of dialogue that revolves around respectful disagreement, "friendly competition," (Geddes 2004: 99), "a harmony of opposing voices" (Lindbeck 2002). Ben Quash formulates this as follows: "What is taught here is that dramatic tension between a plurality of perspectives is not always a sign of failure in the human appropriation of truth; it may be the disclosure of a deeper level of truthful reality than our rational minds are accustomed to allow us to appreciate" (Quash 2006a: 412). In line with this view, scriptural reasoners are not out to produce a harmonizing reading. They seem to prefer hermeneutic diversity. It is certainly not their intention to dissolve the stubbornness of the texts they have studied – to the contrary. There is something that comes to light in the stubbornness of these texts with respect to what it means to believe: namely, wrestling with God by wrestling with the texts that claim to speak about Him. The scriptural fields of tension are like an invitation to a still stronger faith commitment. Indeed, they ask, why not regard intra- and inter-religious textual frictions as divine invitations to use human creativity and reason in the search for meaning?

Finally, whenever Jews, Christians, and Muslims are guests in one another's scriptural traditions, there is more at stake than finding a balance between openness and commitment. Theologically speaking, God is at stake. He is their ultimate orientation in whom they continue to trust. *Deus semper maior est*: precisely the plurality of texts and the conflict of interpretations testify to His greatness. That is why:

> [their] ultimate desire to hallow the name of God, to bless, praise and thank God, to acknowledge that God is great, compassionate, forgiving, holy, and has whatever other perfections are expressed in worship, to relate to God all that we are and think and hope and do, and read and live in ways that please God (Ford 2005: 10).

Scriptural Reasoning Between Identity (House) and Openness (Tent)

In her book, *The Im-possibility of Interreligious Dialogue*, Catherine Cornille remarks that "the main challenge in any dialogue between religions remains that of finding a proper balance between commitment to one's own religion and openness to the other" (Cornille 2008: 84). This also obtains for scriptural reasoners: they too wrestle with the question of how their engagement in this practice of inter-religious dialogue is related to their faith commitment within a particular community. In trying to negotiate this twofold commitment, a typology of meeting places has been formulated that precisely addresses the dialogical tension between openness and identity. This typology plays with the distinction between houses (synagogue, church, and mosque) and the tent (the scriptural reasoning group).

House

Scriptural reasoners belong first and foremost to a particular house of faith where the ordinary life of faith occurs. There believers pray, sing, and study; there the major and minor events of life are celebrated; there God is praised and worshipped. In doing so, the religious identity of the community and its individual believers are formed and molded. If scriptural reasoning is cut off from the faith community, it is cut off from its source of nutrition and its reason for existence. Getting lost in an endless dialogical wandering without returning home should be avoided at all costs. The tent of meeting cannot replace the house where "ordinary" life of faith happens.

> [W]e assume that each scriptural reasoner belongs, first, to a "House" – whether Jewish, Christian or Muslim – and to the specific tradition of scriptural text-interpretation, language, history and social behavior that informs and sustains it. Whatever might lie beyond such a "House," and how Jews, Christians and Muslims may find this together, will remain supplementary to participation in this "House."[17]

The particular faith community forms the "base camp" from which scriptural reasoners are ready to move outward with their scripture and "deep reasonings" (Adams 2006b: 398). Although this particular faith commitment can sometimes carry a lot of weight, it is precisely commitments like these that make dialogue fascinating. The house of faith is also the "home" to which scriptural reasoners return to catch their breath after these inspiring, challenging, and perhaps also confusing wanderings. Scriptural reasoners will tell their travel stories to this community, hoping not only that those who stayed "at home" will feel addressed by what they have learned but also that those who stayed "home" can help them to better understand the meaning of these new insights.

From the perspective of *ordinary faith life*, scriptural reasoning is not an obvious choice for religious practice. There is no tradition of inter-religious textual study between Christianity, Judaism, and Islam, even though scripture is so central to these traditions. "So scriptural reasoning is a complex combination of what is at the core of each tradition with what is novel for each. As with any innovation it needs to be discussed and tested, not least with reference to scripture" (Ford 2007: 282). That is why, next to inter-religious dialogue, an intra-religious dialogue on the question of the theological legitimacy of scriptural reasoning must begin. But this discussion must not be carried out *a priori*. Moreover, there should not be any consensus on what precisely its rationale is. Rather, participants are to acquaint themselves with this practice from inside out, so that each will be able to formulate his or her own "justification" of what this dialogue practice exactly means. But a kind of "authoritative overview" that would apply to everyone is rejected:

> Because scriptural reasoning by definition draws people of very different commitments and disciplines into engagement with each other it is a phenomenon which is bound to be described differently even (perhaps especially) by those who know it best: part of its own approach is to resist "authoritative overviews" of the three scriptures and traditions of interpretation that are being brought into conversation, and so its own character likewise calls for diverse descriptions (Ford 2006: 347).

But more is at stake than just theological legitimacy. "There is," according to Ford, "also a case to be made for the positive enhancement of each house" (Ford 2007: 287). To be a guest in another tradition is not without consequence – consciously or not, people glean certain insights from other traditions. They learn to read their own scriptural traditions through the eyes of the other. Shifts in meaning, new interpretations, unexpected insights flow out of this practice. What was strange becomes familiar, and what was familiar becomes strange. "Far from interfaith engagement being in competition with involvement in one's own tradition, the depths of one evoke the depths of the other" (Ford 2007: 284). Studying another textual tradition is seen as an "incentive" to bury oneself in one's own scriptural tradition. It is important that believers do not keep these new insights "for themselves" but take them with them to their particular house of faith and share them with their fellow believers. The fruits of the inter-religious encounter must also be reflected upon intra-religiously. But the fact is that the dialectic between home and tent is not obvious. As is often the case, scriptural reasoners do not find it easy to report back on the insights they acquire during their inter-religious encounters to their own house of faith. Daniel Hardy, who was involved in this effort from the start, says about this:

> But the Group has also found it very difficult to "debrief" afterward, or to discuss how to identify, "hold," "agree" or "transfer" the insights generated. It is clear enough that *for those present* the "interactive particularity" of Jews, Christians and Muslims interpreting their scriptures together *is* highly generative of probing insight into both texts and their constitutive importance for the Abrahamic traditions and their contribution to today's world, both severally and together. But *how* are the results to be communicated? (Hardy 2006: 532).

Tent

Under the canopy of sacred scripture(s), a space for encounter arises where love for postcritical textual study is central (Taylor 2008: 6). It is, as it were, a "liminal space," representing "a space for study and conversation wherever they actually happen" (Ford 2007: 356). The image that is used for this is the "tent."

The category of the "tent" is symbolically packed with meaning, resonating in the first place with the culture of the ancient Near East where nomads wander through the desert. The tent thus calls up the image of being "under way" and of "moving from place to place." To respond to the populist discourse of a clash of civilizations, we need people who are prepared to set up a tent as a place to meet others, who have the skill required to move between traditions, who are prepared to substantiate the virtue of hospitality as guest and host during their journey, who do not view themselves as treasurers riveted to one spot but as people with a temporary residence in search of wisdom they will never completely grasp. Scriptural reasoning counts on people who do not flinch from reinterpreting traditions from the past with a view to the future; people who understand their faith commitment much more as a spiritual journey than as simple agreement with clearly defined doctrines; people who resist the (understandable) temptation:

> always to speak empathically in the indicative and imperative moods, when it might be more appropriate to use the interrogative mood, or the exploratory subjunctive mood of "may be" or "might be," or the optative mood, the "if only" of desire to see face to face in the future while acknowledging that now we see through a glass darkly (Ford 2005: 4).

As noted above, the tent is also strongly connected with the virtue of hospitality, which occupies such an important place in these three Abrahamic traditions. For scriptural reasoners, Abraham, called the father of hosts (*abû l-dhifân*), sets the example for what it means to be hospitable to strangers. His tent, so the tradition goes, was always open to unexpected and uninvited visitors.[18] What is more, Abraham taught that hospitality is not simply an ethical virtue but also has theological implications. Every believer in the Abrahamic tradition knows that a stranger asking for hospitality is not necessarily an intruder nor an enemy – although both are always possible –[19] but can be a messenger from God. The other might be someone who has been put on one's path by God and who helps to guide one towards the path of God (Moyaert 2011b: 95–108). Where one welcomes the stranger, one welcomes God. When love of the divine presence leads us to love our neighbor, and when loving our neighbor brings us back to the divine presence, this circular motion of love is where God dwells. Then the tent, in which the strangers are welcomed, becomes a sacred tent, a *mishkan*. In Hebrew this word is related to two other words: *shekhinah*, meaning divine presence; and *shakhen*, meaning a neighbor (Taylor 2008: 6). Welcoming others is not merely good manners and a sign of civility, it is an expression of faith and an act of worshiping God (Valkenberg 2006). Here, conversation becomes a form of prayer. Scriptural reasoning endorses this tradition.

A tent is a temporary shelter by design. It is open to the elements, temporary, insubstantial; in short, it provides little real shelter. It thus reminds us of our reliance on the will of God in a hostile world. Ultimately, scriptural reasoners argue, it is God to whom we must look for shelter. Scriptural reasoning is a wisdom-seeking practice, guided by God's spirit. Instead of looking for safety and security in repeating past traditions of interpretation, scriptural reasoning is ultimately about relying on God and trusting that building community today is worth more in God's eyes than clashing over the one true interpretation of his revelation.

What brings Jews, Christians, and Muslims together in this tent of meeting is not simply their deep reverence for sacred texts or their trust in God: the ethical command to repair the world (*tikkun olam*) is also operative. Scriptural reasoning shows its redemptive character especially in view of the conflicted nature of inter-Abrahamic relations: to bring peace where there is conflict, to create communion where there is division, to bring understanding where there is misrecognition. Its redemptive nature exists in the fact that it temporarily brings an end to inter-religious struggle. As Kepnes bluntly puts it, "in the 'tent of meeting,' people whose communities are otherwise at war with each other, are sitting down in peaceful conversation" (Kepnes 2006: 381). In doing so, this practice offers a horizon of hope that opens up a utopian perspective of what could be.

Might a privileged look into each other's worlds give us an eye-opening experience of roads not taken? Some of these roads we will be relieved not to have traveled – and this is valuable self-knowledge. But in other roads we may see terrain we wish our traditions had guided us into but did not, and we may discover otherwise hidden potentialities in our own worlds (Cobb 2007: 4).

As a rare shared state of peace, scriptural reasoning is believed to have the power to transform future relations between the Abrahamic traditions. In this sense, it is one of the ways Jews, Christians, and Muslims can answer the call to work together for the Kingdom of God in the full awareness that this will not come about by human hands alone.

Scriptural Reasoning as a Postsecular Project

Scriptural reasoning is intended to be more than a dialogue practice; it is also presented as a "new model" for dealing with religion in the public domain. More precisely, this model is meant as an alternative to the secular liberalism that preaches privatization of faith as an answer to inter-religious conflicts. Practitioners are convinced that political problems cannot be solved if religious commitments are bracketed. This "academic" practice, therefore, also has a political dimension, and thus scriptural reasoners align themselves with other postsecular movements within political philosophy, rejecting the social marginalization of religious traditions:

> It is argued that, rather than pushing religion into the private sphere and asserting a purely secular polis, there is an urgent need to devise more authentic (and responsible) conversations in the public square where the comprehensive reasons for our actions can be expressed (Cheetham 2010: 346).

The modern privatization of religion finds its origin in the many inter-Christian conflicts that have plagued Europe since the sixteenth century (Horton and Mendus 1985: 1–15). The Reformation revealed not only the deep divisions within the church; it also revealed the inability of Christians of different persuasions to find agreement on any authoritative text, doctrine, conciliar statement, or papal decree. This lack of agreement became even worse when these differences in worldview became more polemic and finally resulted in violent confrontations (Katangole 2000: 8). The religious wars especially, which ravaged Europe in the sixteenth and seventeenth centuries, showed how destructive inter-religious opposition could be.[20] These wars have been (called) 'hermeneutical civil wars' because the exegesis of scripture and the divine command-ments led to a hopeless struggle and the cruelest acts" (De Wit 2001: 88). This was the origin of the now widespread assumption that the best way to prevent conflicts is to avoid deep discussions that touch the heart of different traditions.

Freedom of religion and tolerance form the political answer to inter-Christian abso-lutism, violence, and conflict. The government and its institutions are expected to display an attitude of neutrality. The state creates the space for worldview systems to govern themselves and establishes a few ground rules for interaction, but stays out of discussions on content and value judgments. In that sense, secular liberalism can also be called a passive pluralism: tolerance is understood as a passive respect for the indi-vidual and collective rights to religious freedom, and ends in the ideas of mutual non-interference and the (strict) neutrality of the government, public institutions, and public space. At the bottom of this is an ethical concern: people can never be permitted to kill one another in the "name of God."

Admittedly, secular liberalism has succeeded in defusing the inter-religious powder keg. Nevertheless, there are reasons, according to scriptural reasoners, to suspect that holding exclusively to this *conflict avoidance* model of inter-religious relations threatens to become counterproductive.

> The major shortcoming of this epoch was a kind of reverse discrimination against particu-larity and local identity, which were misinterpreted to be the source of failures of the former epoch, rather than elements of the human condition itself. Attempting, on the whole, to elide these elements, rather than respect-but-redeem them, [secular liberalism] was ultimately utopic – unconstrained, that is, by a realistic sense of human limits and unwarmed by affection for communal traditions and folkways (Geddes 2004: 91).

Traditions are not ballast. The world can be meaningfully illuminated only because people are anchored in a particular tradition that determines to a large degree what is important, valuable, and worthy of pursuit. Traditions, in other words, also give direc-tion and support. Who we are, and who we long to become, is inseparably connected to ideas concerning the good and the true. Hence, a tradition forms the *horizon from which* a religious person faces the world and makes concrete choices and decisions. Authentic life requires one to be connected with traditions that give meaning and direc-tion to the past, present, and future. The modern illusory ideal of neutrality has uprooted people, and one of the consequences of that disruption is that they no longer know where they come from, or where they are going, not to mention why they are going anywhere.

Moreover, scriptural reasoners argue, it is one thing to "contain" inter-religious violence; it is quite another to develop a society with a social project. Society benefits from profound reflection communication, enabling people to make their fundamental worldviews more explicit and confront them with one another instead of privatizing them, silencing them, or ridiculing them. What obtains for scriptural reasoning in the academic milieu also obtains for the public space: true plurality brings these different

SCRIPTURAL REASONING AS INTER-RELIGIOUS DIALOGUE   79

voices into dialogue, and does not impose silence beforehand. Secular liberalism is not adequate for building a multicultural and multireligious society precisely because, according to David Ford, "secularized societies have generally failed to mobilize religious resources for public wisdom and for peace" (Ford 2007: 301).

Scriptural reasoning does not reject this modern tradition but nuances, corrects, and complements this passive-pluralistic discourse. Actually, scriptural reasoners strive for a centrist position: on the one hand, they want to "protect" religious traditions from a liberal discourse that all too often leads to the undermining of religious particularities. On the other hand, they guard against a further marginalization: the price for the emphasis on particularity should not be the absence of dialogue with wider modern society. They want to make a contribution to the public debate precisely from the perspective of their particular traditions, in the hope of transforming the public sphere. In this way, scriptural reasoning is also concerned with making "deep reasonings" public.

> For Jews, Christians, and Muslims committed to this the best way forward is through simultaneously going deeper into their own scriptures and traditions, deeper into wisdom-seeking conversation with each other and with all who have a stake in the public good, and deeper into activity dedicated to the common good. So one promise of scriptural reasoning is the formation of people through collegial study, wise interpretation, and friendship who might be exemplary citizens of the twenty-first century, seeking the public good for the sake of God and God's peaceful purposes. (Ford 2007: 301)

In that sense, they argue for a postsecular society: this is a society that takes the public debate into account with both secular and religious voices and believes that a meaningful discussion is possible. The model that they have in view is precisely that of the scriptural reasoning meetings where the highest good is not the consensus but that of respectful disagreement.

To Conclude: Some Unanswered Theological Questions

It is striking that there is not much critical secondary literature on scriptural reasoning, certainly in comparison with the ever-growing body of critical literature on the theology of religions. This is all the more remarkable because this form of dialogue nevertheless raises a number of fundamental questions. That scriptural reasoning moves in the margins of the theological debate is connected perhaps with the way in which this practice is related to theorization. As stated above, scriptural reasoning is in the first place a practice and only secondarily a theory. Theorizing is essentially *a posteriori*. Although this practice arose in the 1990s, it was not until 2006 that the first detailed discussion of scriptural reasoning appeared.[21] Particularly striking about this publication is the fact that it appeals to very different philosophers to explain what this particular form of inter-religious dialogue is about. Reference is made to Levinas, Buber, Lindbeck, Peirce, and Ricoeur, among others. This plurality of voices, it is argued, testifies to the wealth of this practice (Kavka 2007: 135), as well as to the enriching diversity of its practitioners. Be that as it may, it does give a certain impression of eclecticism.

Scriptural reasoners repeat time and again that striving for consensus often leads to superficiality, but diversity can also have the same effect. After all, one can ask how it is possible that this practice can be reflected upon from so many different perspectives, and what that says about its consistency (Lambkin 2010: 51). The fact that there is no critical discussion among the various theoreticians concerning these divergent reflections can strengthen the impression of a lack of self-critical depth. On this issue, I agree with Dan Stiver that "in a time of transition in philosophy and in a time of flux in theology, being clear about one's [hermeneutical] commitments and presuppositions continues to be desirable" (Stiver 2003: 175). I believe this also holds true for scriptural reasoning, which will gain in credibility only when it is thought through properly. Hence, I would like to pose a few questions that show precisely the importance of further reflection on scriptural reasoning. If scriptural reasoning wants to gain in theological relevance, there should be fundamental reflection on its relationship especially with: (1) postliberalism; (2) the theology of religions; and (3) inter-religious dialogue in a wider sense.

Although I myself have a great deal of sympathy for this form of dialogue and also appreciation for the way in which scriptural reasoners attempt to offer a counterweight to inter-religious practices inspired more by a modern liberal search for commonalities, I have my doubts about the presentation of scriptural reasoning as a postliberal particularist project. To a great extent, I would applaud postliberalism's attention to the wealth of particular religious languages, as well as its criticism of the liberal tendency to translate those specific religious meanings into a kind of all-comprehensive philosophical and/or theological framework, the outcome of which is too often loss of meaning. Postliberalism rightly points to the particularity of religious meanings that are determined intra-textually. It is correct in pointing to the importance of the deep reasonings that make the understanding of religious texts possible. Only by becoming deeply engaged in a tradition does it become possible to understand and evaluate a religious text of another tradition. The particularist awareness of differences that places the "core identities" of different religious traditions at the heart of inter-religious dialogue is an important correction to pluralistic inter-religious dialogue that focuses too much on commonalities.

None of this detracts, however, from the fact that the alliance between scriptural reasoning and postliberalism is less obvious than seems to be generally accepted. It is, in particular, not entirely clear how the postliberal urge to protect scriptural traditions and their deep reasonings against excavation and loss of meaning (Knitter 2002: 183) can be squared with what scriptural reasoners themselves report about what actually happens in the Tent of Abraham. More to the point, there is at least a tension between, on the one hand, the postliberal concern to protect the core identities of religious traditions – a concern that scriptural reasoners claim to support – and, on the other hand, the dynamic that belongs to the practice of scriptural reasoning as described by these same scriptural reasoners. Scriptural reasoning seems to be much more dynamic than the postliberalism with which it claims affinity. Postliberalism offers, in particular, few incentives for an inter-religious dialogue that also recognizes the possibility of mutual enrichment (Moyaert 2012). Cornille remarks: "If different religions and doctrinal systems are truly incommensurable, as [Lindbeck] certainly seems to think, then dialogue could never go beyond mutual affirmation (or denial)"Cornille 2008: 187). It sometimes seems as if scriptural reasoners are content with this articulation of limitation, when, for example, they cite Lindbeck's view of dialogue's purpose as a place where Jews should become better Jews, Buddhists better Buddhists, and Muslims better Muslims (Lindbeck 1984: 54). But this description is difficult to relate to the presentation of scriptural reasoning as an "open-ended," "generative" (Adams 2006b), and "wisdom-seeking" practice (Ford 2006). This is not the place to explore this relation further, but it seems to me that it is a point that needs further reflection. Not only can it give occasion for a better understanding of scriptural reasoning, but it can also lead to a fundamental reflection on the precise contribution of postliberal particularism to inter-religious dialogue.

Questions also arise with respect to the relationship between scriptural reasoning and the theology of religions. Scriptural reasoners do not intend to formulate a kind of *theology of religions*. The decades-long debate within theology of religions regarding which of the three soteriological models – exclusivism, inclusivism, or pluralism – best succeeds in "finding a balance" between identity and openness, is seen as a sterile debate that does not advance inter-religious dialogue. The question of salvation is a Christian question that does not do justice to the otherness of the other traditions. Ochs describes this theological discussion as an "unhappy dialectic of the old millennium," in which believers are forced to choose between "either our House alone or the identity of all houses, either revealed truth or some universal humanity" (Ochs 2005: 9). While the theology of religions in the end concerns a kind of intra-Christian dialogue, scriptural reasoning wants to make a true inter-religious dialogue possible, one that focuses primarily on the wealth of the different scriptural traditions:

> Beginning with scriptural forms of reasoning is . . . intended to move inter-faith discussion away from conceptual and doctrinal categories of analysis. These categories often force the complex religious traditions into artificial and abstract theological concepts and dilute the complexity and specificity of the cultural-linguistic religions systems. Scriptural reasoning . . . offers a more supple tool to lead to a richer, more complex and sensitive inter-faith dialogue (Kepnes 2006: 373).

But the question of the precise relationship between the various scriptural traditions is invariably postponed, and the attempt to resolve the conflicting truth claims of each tradition is rejected. Not infrequently, reference is made to the end time in which these complex questions will receive their definitive answer, an answer that is now not within the reach of human possibility. But the fact is that asking these questions and searching for answers belongs precisely to the particular traditions. A practice that claims to do so much justice to the particularity of the traditions should grant a place to this search for truth. Here I agree with Magdalen Lambkin who claims:

> It is not only the feelings of the dialogue partners that are at stake, but the integrity of the practice. To seek to engage seriously with a text claimed to contain revealed truth together with its adherents without evaluating those claims to truth – and one's tradition's rejection of them – is to fall short of a coherent theological approach (Lambkin 2010: 51).

The question of the precise relationship between the religions and their scriptures will become all the more urgent when this practice is opened to other non-Abrahamic traditions. It is somewhat surprising to note that most scriptural reasoners are in principle open to this broadening and see no problems worth mentioning in the possibility. Although "there are good reasons for these three [Judaism, Christianity, and Islam] to read together . . . there is not an a priori exclusion of other religions, traditions, say Confucian or Hindu or Buddhist" (Gibbs 2006: 526). Kepnes also confirms in his "Handbook for Scriptural Reasoning" that "SR members have and will continue to move beyond the borders of monotheistic scriptures by reading Buddhist, Hindu and other scriptures with representatives of these traditions" (Kepnes 2006: 378). But what will this broadening mean for the religious character of scriptural reasoning as a "prayerful event" where God's name is hallowed and his presence experienced? Cheetham asks if such a broadening will not change the whole dynamic of scriptural reasoning: could such broadening not shift the focus more to the *event* of the encounter rather than on the sacred texts? Perhaps this encounter will then revolve around the ethical command *to repair the world*, in which other religions can also involve themselves (Rashkover 2008: 444). But, according to Cheetham, this would entail a shift from text to tent, and would thus concern the creation of a "sense of familiarity: a tent of familiarity, that facilitates a dialogical ease or revelry for particular groups . . . It is simply about finding a particular common world that is shared between religious groups" (Cheetham 2010: 352). If this turns out to be the case, my question would be: How would scriptural reasoning then differ from the more liberal approaches to dialogue it has criticized?

The originality of this practice is not a matter of debate – it is clear that scriptural reasoning is a valuable dialogue practice, a practice that "is perhaps more fruitful because they have not begun with the question of the truth of the other traditions" (Lambkin 2012). Nevertheless, I think that this practice will gain in power and value if more is invested in theological and/or philosophical reflection on it.

Notes

1   The English word scripture connotes the sacred writings of a tradition, see P. Ochs, "It Has Been Taught: Scripture in Theological and Religious Studies," in *Fields of Faith*, eds. D. Ford, R. Muers, and J. Soskice. (Cambridge: Cambridge University Press, 2005).

2   In recent years, two important inter-religious practices have come to the fore: scriptural reasoning and comparative theology (e.g., Clooney). However different these approaches may be – and despite their internal diversity as well – both place the reading of sacred texts at the center of dialogue, although in different ways. Comparative theology is a solitary enterprise, whereas scriptural reasoning is a communal inter-religious practice. Both comparative theology and scriptural reasoning seem promising theologically because they constitute a truth-seeking and open-ended dialogue that would lead to the recognition that the scriptures of the religions of the book are "sources of divine spirit." For a comparison of both scripture-oriented dialogue practices see M. Barnes, "Reading Other Religious Texts: Intratextuality, and the Logic of Scripture," *Journal of Ecumenical Studies*, 46 (2011): 389–411.

3   One of the best-known institutes is the Children of Abraham Institute (CHAI) in Virginia. See http://berkleycenter.georgetown.edu/resources/organizations/children-of-abraham-institute (accessed December 10, 2012).

4   I will return to this below.

5   See, e.g., the Faith and Citizenship programme of London Metropolitan University: http://www.londonmet.ac.uk/news/latest-news/citizenship-and-faith-initiative.cfm (accessed December 10/ 2012).

6   For an extended discussion of postliberal particularism, see M. Moyaert, *Fragile Identities: Towards a Theology of Interreligious Hospitality* (Amsterdam/New York: Rodopi, 2011a).

7   Peter Ochs holds that with scriptural reasoning a "new age" has dawned that is breaking with the liberal approach to religious plurality and *the view of dialogue with which the latter operates*. Ben Quash assents here and speaks of a "new paradigm of interfaith encounter." Steven Kepnes also emphasizes that scriptural reasoning is intended to be an alternative to the dominant liberal understanding of dialogue between the religions. Geddes, "Peacemaking among the Abrahamic Faiths," 91; Quash, "Deep Calls to Deep: The Practice of Scriptural Reasoning," 6; Kepnes, "A Handbook for Scriptural Reasoning," 373.

8   Power differences are to be avoided at all cost. In 2007 the London Central Mosque Trust and the Islamic Cultural Centre issued a *fatwa*, i.e. legal opinion, on the participation of Muslims in scriptural reasoning. The *fatwa* primarily expressed concern about possible unequal power relations at these meetings and emphasized that Muslims, Christians, and Jews need to be one another's equals. But the *fatwa* was positive about the basis for this inter-religious textual study, reminding its readers that Muhammad himself entered into discussions with Jews and Christians on the scriptures. That is why it was suitable, even recommended, for Muslims to follow that example today. http://www.scripturalreasoning.co.uk/fatwa_english.pdf (accessed December 10, 2012).

9   Kepnes rightly remarks that every meeting is special because the choice of texts that are read, the participants, and the place and time leave their mark on them. See Kepnes, "A Handbook for Scriptural Reasoning," 370.

10 At a later stage I will show that there is a certain tension between scriptural reasoning's self-understanding as a postliberal and particularist project, on the one hand, and the way this practice develops as a rather open-ended dialogue practice, revolving around scripture, on the other hand.

11 The Society of Textual Reasoning was founded in 1991.

12 "Scriptural Reasoning actually has its recent origin in a conversation between two different camps within modern Judaism: Jewish text scholars and Jewish philosophers/theologians. The text scholars thought the philosophers had become rootless – theoretically remote and overly speculative; whilst the philosophers considered that the text scholars, scrupling over arcane word meanings, had simply lost the plot – they had become 'route-less'." Taylor, *How to Pitch a Tent*: 5.

13 From the reports by various practitioners the same image constantly emerges: Scriptural reasoning as the logical outcome of textual reasoning. Perhaps this explains why there is so much affinity between both practices. "My father-in-law Dan Hardy and I were invited to sit in on the sessions of a group called Textual Reasoning at annual meetings of the American Academy of Religion. They were Jewish text scholars (Tanakh and Talmud) and philosophers, and had extraordinarily lively discussions in small groups around classic Jewish texts and works by modern Jewish philosophers. Some of them joined with us to begin scriptural reasoning, and soon afterwards we were joined by some Muslims. In

retrospect, I can see that it was fulfilling a need that I had felt during my 15 years in the very multi-faith city of Birmingham but had not been met by the forms of inter-faith relations I had known there." See Marco Belli, "Wisdom of Difference."

14   The scriptural reasoner Harvey Barry describes Jews and Christians as, for example, "two peoples separated by a common text." Harvey Barry, "Eschatology and Social Ethics: The Limits of Typology," *The Journal of Scriptural Reasoning*, 1. [online journal].

15   This reluctance with respect to "grand theories" is typically postmodern and can also be found in other text-oriented dialogue practices and in comparative theology. Cf. Marianne Moyaert, "Comparative Theology in Search for a Hermeneutical Framework."

16   There are different "guidelines." See also Kepnes, "A Handbook for Scriptural Reasoning"; Ochs, "The Society of Scriptural Reasoning: The Rules of Scriptural Reasoning"; Adams, *Habermas and Theology*.

17   D.W. Hardy, Peter Ochs, and David F. Ford, "The Tent of Meeting," cited in Quash, "Deep Calls to Deep," 8.

18   In Jewish tradition it is said that Abraham's tent had four entrances so that he could invite guests from every direction.

19   In Latin, *hospes* and *hostis* are etymologically related. As Richard Kearney puts it, "The Latin root for both hostility and hospitality is the same. And the term 'host' may in fact be used to designate one who welcomes of one who invades." Richard Kearney, *Strangers, Gods and Monsters: Interpreting Otherness*: 68.

20   One of the best-known is the Thirty Years' War (1618–1648), which was ended by the Peace of Westphalia.

21   The most important contribution to the theorizing of this practice has, until now, been *The Promise of Scriptural Reasoning*, in which different Scriptural Reasoners engage in a theoretical reflection on the practice in which they were been involved for several years already. D. Ford and C.C. Pecknold, *The Promise of Scriptural Reasoning*.

Bibliography

Adams, N. *Habermas and Theology*. Cambridge: Cambridge University Press, 2006a.

Adams, N. "Making Deep Reasonings Public." *Modern Theology* 22 (2006b): 385–401.

Adams, N. "Scriptural Reasoning and Inter-faith Hermeneutics," in *Interreligious Hermeneutics in Pluralistic Europe: Between Texts and People*, eds. D. Cheetham, O. Leirvik, U. Winkler, and Judith Gruber. New York: Rodopi, 2011: 59–78.

Barnes, M. *Theology and the Dialogue of Religions*. Cambridge: Cambridge University Press, 2002.

Barnes, M. "Reading Other Religious Texts: Intratextuality, and the Logic of Scripture." *Journal of Ecumenical Studies* 46 (2011): 389–411.

Bailey, J. "New Models for Religion in Public: Interfaith Friendship and the Politics of Scriptural Reasoning." *Christian Century* 123 (2006): 36–42.

Barry, H. "Eschatology and Social Ethics: The Limits of Typology." *The Journal of Scriptural Reasoning* 1 (2001) [online journal].

Belli, M. "Wisdom of Difference: Christians, Jews and Muslims and the practice of 'Scriptural Reasoning' in an interview with Anglican theologian David Ford." *Osservatore Romane* March 25, 2011.

Cheetham, D. "Scriptural Reasoning: Texts or/and Tents?." *Islam and Christian Relations* 21 (2010): 343–356.

Cobb, J. "Responses to Relativism: Common Ground, Deconstruction and Reconstruction." *Soundings* 73 (1990): 595–616.

Cobb, K. "Introduction: Studying the Western 'Other', Understanding the Islamic Self," in *Scripture, Reason and the Contemporary Islam–West Encounter. Studying the Other, Understanding the Self*, eds. B. Koshul and S. Kepnes. New York: Palgrave MacMillan, 2007: 1–9.

Cornille, Catherine. *The Im-Possibility of Inter-religious Dialogue*. New York: Crossroad/Herder & Herder, 2008.

De Wit, T.W.A. "De trivialisering van de tolerantie," in *De lege Tolerantie. Over vrijheid en vrijblijvendheid in Nederland*, ed. M. ten Hooven. Amsterdam: Boom, 2001: 85–110.

Eklund, R.A. "The Goods of Reading: Theological Interpretation and Scriptural Reasoning," *The Journal of Scriptural Reasoning* 9 (2010) [online journal].

Fiorenza, E.S. *Democratizing Biblical Studies: Towards an Emancipatory Educational Space*. Louisville, KY: Westminster John Knox, 2009.

Ford, D. "Faith in the Third Millennium: Reading Scriptures Together." Address at the Inauguration of Dr. Iain Torrance as President of Princeton Theological Seminary and Professor of Patristics, Thursday, March 10, 2005.

Ford, D. "An Interfaith Wisdom: Scriptural Reasoning Between Jews, Christians and Muslims." *Modern Theology* 22 (2006): 345–367.

Ford, D., *Christian Wisdom: Desiring God and Learning in Love*. Cambridge: Cambridge University Press, 2007.

Ford, D., "Jews, Christians and Muslims Meet around their Scriptures: An Inter-faith Practice for the 21st Century," The Fourth Pope John Paul II Annual Lecture on Inter-Religious Understanding. The Pontifical University of St. Thomas Aquinas "Angelicum" with The Russell Berrie Foundation, Rome, April 5, 2011.

Ford, D. and C.C. Pecknold. *The Promise of Scriptural Reasoning*. Oxford: Wiley-Blackwell, 2006. Republished as a special issue in *Modern Theology* 22 (2006).

Geddes, J.L. "Peacemaking among the Abrahamic Faiths: An Interview with Peter Ochs." *The Hedgehog Review* (2004): 90–102.

Geertz, C. *The Interpretation of Cultures: Selected Essays*. New York: Basic Books, 1973: 3–30.

Gibbs, R. "Reading with Others: Levinas' Ethics and Scriptural Reasoning." *Modern Theology* 22 (2006): 526.

Gilkey, Langdon. "Plurality and its Theological Implications," in *The Myth of Christian Uniqueness*, eds. J. Hick and P. Knitter. Maryknoll, NY: Orbis, 1988.

Griffiths, P. *An Apology for Apologetics: A Study in the Logic of Interreligious Dialogue*. New York: Orbis, 1991.

Hardy, D.W. "The Promise of Scriptural Reasoning." *Modern Theology* 22 (2006): 529–551.

Hardy, D.W., P. Ochs, and D. Ford. "The Tent of Meeting," unpublished paper, 2003.

Hick, J. *An Interpretation of Religion: Human Responses to the Transcendent*. New Haven, CT: Yale University Press, 1989.

Hick, J. *Disputed Questions in Theology and the Philosophy of Religion*. London: MacMillan, 1993.

Horton, J.P and S. Mendus. *Aspects of Toleration: Philosophical Studies*. London: Methuen, 1985.

Katongole, E. *Beyond Universal Reason: The Relation Between Religion and Ethics in the Work of Stanley Hauerwas*. Notre Dame: University of Notre Dame Press, 2000.

Kavka, M. "Is Scriptural Reasoning Senseless?," in *Scripture, Reasoning and the Contemporary Islam-West Encounter*, eds. S. Kepnes and B. Koshul. New York: Palgrave, 2007: 133–148.

Kearney, R. *Strangers, Gods and Monsters: Interpreting Otherness*. London: Routledge, 2003.

Kepnes, S. "A Handbook for Scriptural Reasoning." *Modern Theology* 22 (2006): 367–383.

Kepnes, S. "Islam as Our Other, Islam as Ourselves," in *Scripture, Reasoning and the Contemporary Islam-West Encounter*, eds. S. Kepnes and B. Koshul. New York: Palgrave, 2007: 107–122.

Knitter, P. *Introducing Theologies of Religions.* Maryknoll, NY: Orbis, 2002.

Koshul, B.B. and S. Kepnes. "Preface," in *Scripture, Reasoning and the Contemporary Islam-West Encounter*, eds. S. Kepnes and B. Koshul. New York: Palgrave, 2007: xi–xix.

Lambkin, M. "Can Scriptures Unite?" *eSharp* 15 (2010): 42–64.

Lindbeck, G. *The Nature of Doctrine: Religion and Theology in a Postliberal Age.* Philadelphia: Westminster Press, 1984.

Lindbeck, K. "A Harmony of Opposing Voices: Testing the Limits of Scriptural Reasoning." *The Journal of Scriptural Reasoning* 2 (2002) [online journal].

Moyaert, M. *Fragile Identities: Towards a Theology of Interreligious Hospitality.* New York: Rodopi, 2011a.

Moyaert, M. "Abraham's Strangers: A Hermeneutic Wager," in *Hosting the Stranger between Religions*, eds. R. Kearney and J. Taylor. London: Continuum, 2011b: 95–108.

Moyaert, M. "Comparative Theology in Search for a Hermeneutical Framework," in *Interreligious Hermeneutics in Pluralistic Europe*, eds. D. Cheetham, O. Leirvik, U. Winkler, and Judith Gruber. Amsterdam: Rodopi, 2011c: 161–186.

Moyaert, M. "Postliberalism, Religious Diversity and Interreligious Dialogue: A Critical Analysis of Lindbeck's Fiduciary Interests." *Journal of Ecumenical Studies* 47 (2012): 44–66.

Nayed, A.A. "Reading Scripture Together: Towards a Sacred Hermeneutics of Togetherness." *The Princeton Seminary Bulletin*, Vol. XXVI, No. 1, new series (2005): 48–53.

Ochs, P. *The Return to Scripture in Judaism and Christianity.* Mahwah: Paulist Press, 1993.

Ochs, P. "The Society of Scriptural Reasoning: The Rules of Scriptural Reasoning." *Journal of Scriptural Reasoning* 2 (2002) [online journal].

Ochs, P. "It Has Been Taught: Scripture in Theological and Religious Studies," in *Fields of Faith*, eds. D. Ford, R. Muers, and J. Soskice. Cambridge: Cambridge University Press, 2005: 104–118.

Ochs, P. and N. Levene (eds.). *Textual Reasoning: Jewish Philosophy and Text Study at the End of the Twentieth Century.* Cambridge: Eerdmans, 2002.

Ochs, P. and W.S. Johnson. "Introdcution," in *Crisis, Call and Leadership in the Abrahamic Traditions.* New York: Palgrave Macmillan, 2009: 1–10.

Ochs, P. and H. Ziad. "Grassroots Scriptural Reasoning on Campus." *Journal of Interreligious Dialogue* 4 (2010): 38–45.

Quash, B. "Heavenly Semantics: Some Literary-Critical Approaches to Scriptural Reasoning." *Modern Theology* 22 (2006a): 403–420.

Quash, B. "Deep Calls to Deep: The Practice of Scriptural Reasoning," 6, 2006b. http://themathesontrust.org/papers/comparative religion/Quash-DeepCallstoDeep.pdf, accessed December 23. 2012.

Rashkover, R. "Introducing the work of Peter Ochs." *Modern Theology* 24 (2008): 439–445.

Stiver, D. "Theological Method," in *The Cambridge Companion to Postmodern Theology*, ed. J. Vanhoozer. Cambridge: Cambridge University Press, 2003: 170–185.

Taylor, W. *How to Pitch a Tent: A Beginner's Guide to Scriptural Reasoning.* London: St. Ethelburga's Centre for Reconciliation and Peace, 2008.

Taylor, W. "Organising a Scriptural Reasoning Group," St. Ethelburga's Centre for Reconciliation and Peace, 2007. http://www.stethelburgas.org/sites/default/files/How%20to%20pitch%20a%20Tent%20Lo%20res.pdf, accessed 31 December 2012.

Valkenberg, W. "Sharing the Lights on the Way to God: Muslim-Christian Dialogue and Theology in the Context of Abrahamic Partnership." *Currents of Encounter* 26. Amsterdam: Rodopi, 2006.

Winter, T. "Qur'anic Reasoning as an Academic Practice." *Modern Theology* 22 (2006): 449–463.

CHAPTER 6

Inter-Religious Worship

Michael Amaladoss, SJ

I focus in this essay on the emerging phenomenon of inter-religious worship. Let me start defining my terms. By worship I mean any ritual symbolizing a relationship to a transcendent dimension of reality and life. Worship is not limited to prayer as such, and can involve rituals of life and cosmic (natural) cycles, such as healing ceremonies, marriages, and harvest festivals.

Religion, defined for the purposes of this essay, is a social institution characterized by specific creeds or affirmations of belief, codes or norms of conduct, and cult or ways of worship. Participation in a religious cult is normally restricted to those who subscribe to its creed and are governed by its code. The cult symbolically expresses, celebrates, and confirms the group identity of its celebrants in the context of its beliefs concerning the cosmos, humans, and the transcendent.

My reflection is based on India, where Hinduism, Islam, Christianity, Sikhism, and Jainism are present and active. The Buddhist community is small, though the Dalai Lama and his followers are prominent. The Muslims and the Jains are not too active in the inter-religious scene, though they would come when specially invited. Encounters between Hindus, Christians, and Sikhs are more frequent.

This article will focus on the role of worship in inter-religious dialogue, and of inter-religious dialogue in worship. There are of course other kinds of dialogue between religions. During his visit to Chennai in February 1986, Pope John Paul II spoke of the dialogue in which "As followers of different religions we should join together in promoting and defending common ideals in the spheres of religious liberty, human brotherhood, education, culture, social welfare and civic order" (Origins 1986). In addition to this dialogue of social action, dialogue may also occur when different groups come together to share information about beliefs and practices. This might involve an introduction to each other's scriptures, a more intellectual discussion bordering on comparative theology, or other investigations capable of deepening mutual knowledge and understanding.

The Wiley Blackwell Companion to Inter-Religious Dialogue, First Edition. Edited by Catherine Cornille.
© 2013 John Wiley & Sons Ltd. Published 2020 by John Wiley & Sons Ltd.

Inter-Religious Worship: The Individual Level

The practice of inter-religious worship can be seen at two different levels: individual and social. An individual may be called to be present at the religious ceremony accompanying a friend's life-cycle event, such as an initiation, a marriage, or the blessing of a house or official building. This sort of presence may involve mere physical attendance, or something more sympathetic, as when an individual feels a sense of the divine blessing at hand. In recent times we also have instances of inter-monastic dialogue in which a monk lives, for a time, in the monastery of another religion, being present at their worship.

An individual in pursuit of her own spiritual goals may participate in the prayer traditions of a religion not her own. There are many Christians practicing meditation or yoga under Buddhist and Hindu masters. Here, obviously, there is recognition of the positive value in following the prayer tradition of another religion, even though the religious institution of the concerned individual may itself discourage such practice. The Congregation of the Doctrine of the Faith of the Catholic Church has, for instance, discouraged Catholics from following oriental methods of contemplation (CDF 1989). On the other hand, Hindu or Buddhist masters may welcome and initiate such individuals, extending a certain inter-religious hospitality. The individuals themselves feel free to do what they wish, and may profit from it. Some seem to integrate the two religious ways. Bernard Sénecal, a Canadian practicing Zen in Korea, describes how he discovered Christ at the heart of his Zen experience. But others find such integration difficult. Swami Abhishiktananda (Henri Le Saux) practiced Advaitic meditation for many years and claims to have experienced, after sustained practice, a full vision of nonduality. But his efforts to integrate that experience with Christian Trinitarianism were not successful, and he came to understand Advaita Vedanta and Trinitarian Christianity as two different experiences of the divine, without trying to integrate them artificially. He was a Hindu-Christian (Abhishiktananda 1998).

At a more popular level, people visit shrines of other religions, motivated by benefits like healing and general wellbeing. Christians welcome the members of other religions in their shrines generally, only warning non-Christians not to participate in the Eucharistic sharing of the body and blood of Christ. However, some theologians, myself included, have argued that even Eucharistic hospitality is possible in some cases (Pushparajan 1988; Puthanangady 1988; Amaladoss 2008: 79–96). When a multireligious group, with Catholics constituting its core, is engaged in the struggle for justice for the poor, Eucharistic sharing could be meaningful. Many ordinary Hindus, however, are not bothered by the scruples of the Catholic clergy and participate fully in the Eucharist. In their case, an implicit faith seems to play a role in their participatory orientation, allowing them to visit Sikh and Christian shrines, the tombs of Islamic Sufi saints, reading the Bible and other sacred writings, etc. Christians, too, have been inspired by the scriptures of others. A Jesuit priest, Sebastian Painadath, for instance, has been preaching retreats based on the Bhagavad Gita to Christians. A person who has no problem in visiting a shrine of another religion and in participating in its festival may have no problem in taking part in inter-religious worship. Such participation implicitly affirms that the divine or absolute is present in, but also beyond, the symbolic manifestations in a particular religion – one's own or that of another.

Inter-Religious Worship and the Community

When we speak of inter-religious prayer or worship, we do not normally refer to such individual practices. These depend on the freedom of the concerned individuals. Inter-religious practice may not be accepted easily by either religious community, especially when one seeks to participate in the official cult of another religion. The official cult is the symbolic action of a religious community, its collective self-expression in action. A life-cycle rite such as an initiation, for instance, concerns the individual and the community that receives him or her as a member, and so participation by an outsider has no meaning. But communities also have rituals that focus more explicitly on the transcendent in prayer or worship, praising, thanking, asking forgiveness, expressing love, and seeking communion. Participation in such rituals may be open to people who are not members of the community, because in these rituals the community reaches out beyond itself to the transcendent. Such participation is inter-religious only because one has not become a full member through a process of initiation, but is functionally accepted by the community as a temporary member under particular circumstances.

The community may lay down conditions for such hospitality. The Muslim community would not allow a non-Muslim to participate in its official prayer. As a matter of fact, participating in official prayer and repeating the Muslim faith affirmation that Allah is great and Mohammed is Allah's prophet is a way of becoming a Muslim. So they would not like non-Muslims, who do not want to become Muslim, to join them in their official prayer. Some Sufi Muslims, however, have shown a readiness to participate in common prayer, with Trappist monks, for instance, at Tibhirine in Algeria (Bethune 2011). Some Hindu temples would prohibit non-Hindus as well as Hindus belonging to some subaltern castes, from entering the sanctuary. Such prohibition rests not so much on a judgment of faithful qualifications, but rather on requirements of appropriate ritual purity. Roman Catholics do not mind members of other religions being present during their celebration of the Eucharist. But they would not like them to participate by sharing in the consecrated bread and wine. They only allow members of some Churches, under strict conditions, to participate.

An interesting experiment with common prayer may be found in the ecumenical and inter-religious group at Christa Prema Seva ashram in Pune, India. Writing in 1988, Sara Grant, a leading participant, describes its membership: seven Catholics, (four of whom belonged to the Syro-Malabar Rite), one Anglican, three Evangelicals, and four Hindus, with another ten to fifteen short- or long-term visitors belonging to various religious backgrounds. Every day the community chose readings from the Upanishads, the Bhagavad Gita or the bhakta poets, the Qur'an, the Sufi tradition, and, more rarely, from other sources corresponding to the Biblical liturgical readings of the day (Grant 1988: 467). Many members also participated in various ways in the Christian liturgy of the ashram. This ongoing sharing in the life and prayer of the ashram acquired a special depth on particular occasions. Sara Grant describes in detail an

Easter celebration around a fire, enriched by a reading from the Katha Upanishad and an image of *Nataraja* or the "Lord of the Dance." Both Hindus and Christians found the celebration to be deeply meaningful from their own religious perspectives (Grant 1988: 475–478). From a Christian perspective, the quest for life beyond death described in the Katha Upanishad and the image of the *Nataraja* may be seen to throw light on the risen Jesus as the "Lord of the Dance." It is an experience and celebration of life and joy in which Hinduism and Christianity may be seen to merge. Such a celebration is meaningful only in a community that has been sharing their life and prayer together for some time. It can lead towards mutual transformation and integration.

Religion, Communion, and Transcendence

Rituals are community symbolic actions through which a community expresses and celebrates its faith. It is not a totally open structure. As we have seen above, while some rituals, such as rituals of initiation, are self-expressive and constructive of the community, others are open to the transcendent. Members of other religions may be attracted to such rituals precisely by this dimension of transcendence, without feeling called to belong to the community itself, with its specific social structures.

Here we find a complex relationship between religion and community. For a believer, a religious community is not simply an association of humans. It is called into existence by a special event experienced as a revelation. The particular religious community is only responding to this divine manifestation. The response of the community may be conditioned by its historical and sociocultural circumstances. But it is always reaching out to the revelatory experience that transcends it. This is what constitutes its dynamism. An individual, as a social and historical being, is normally attracted by and committed to, not merely the self-revealing transcendent, but also its sociohistorical and cultural manifestation. This is what constitutes his religious roots and identity.

But a person may also be attracted by another self-manifestation of the transcendent, and he or she may seek to relate to it without abandoning his or her roots. On such occasions, a certain crossing of religious borders gives rise to inter-religious phenomena. But this does not and need not mean that a person's basic or primary identity must be abandoned. People familiar with religious conversions suggest that they happen, not by abandoning one identity and taking up another, but by the loss of one, for whatever reason, and the discovery of another. What is perhaps new is that, as inter-religious encounter increases, there may be more attempts to cross religious borders without permanently relinquishing one's identity. The distinction between the social and transcendent dimensions of religion also suggests the possibility that religious groups may seek to converge at the level of transcendence without abandoning their particular religious roots. This is what makes inter-religious prayer or worship possible. However, such universalism does not always take seriously the socioreligious roots of religious identity. Therefore, a general principle like, "God is one, but is manifested through various symbols, and so God can be approached through any symbol" is not enough to justify participation in the official worship of another community (Puthanangady 1988: 784–801).

Beginnings of Inter-Religious Worship: Mahatma Gandhi

It is now time to look more closely at the phenomenon of inter-religious prayer or worship itself. To my knowledge, the first instance of communal inter-religious prayer was the practice of Gandhi's community in South Africa (Pushparajan), where Gandhi was involved in a struggle against apartheid. For Gandhi, such a struggle was not merely a political movement but also a social and religious one. In order to train his activists, he founded an ashram, or a simple form of community living, centered on a farm which sought self-sufficiency for the nascent movement. Prayer was a part of life in the ashram, and because the community was inter-religious, the prayer was inter-religious as well, consisting of readings from scriptures, devotional songs, and prayers. The aim was to spend time together in prayer before God as a source of strength and inspiration. Gandhi was persuaded that God is one, though called by many names. That is why he was against people converting from one religion to another. The practice of inter-religious prayer continued when Gandhi came to India. He lived in a series of ashrams with disciples from different religions, where common prayer was a regular practice. Toward the end of his life, when Hindu–Muslim riots ravaged the subcontinent following partition (1947–1948), Gandhi used the practice of inter-religious prayer as a means of promoting peace between religious groups, specifically Hindus and Muslims. Actually he was shot on his way to one such prayer session in Delhi on January 30, 1948. The spirit of his prayer sessions is well expressed by the well known bhajan often heard in them: *Bhagawati Raghava Raja Ram . . .*

> Chief of the house of Raghu, Lord Rama,
> Uplifter of those who have fallen.
> O beloved, praise Sita and Rama.
> God and Allah are your names,
> Bless everyone with this wisdom, Lord.

In this song, the word "God" in line four – *Ishwara* – refers to the Christian God. These inter-religious prayer sessions were largely welcome by Indians in general, though they were opposed by a Hindu fundamentalist fringe group.

The Background of the Indian Tradition

Such an inter-religious practice can be fully understood only in the inter-religious atmosphere of India itself. Hinduism, Buddhism, Jainism, and Sikhism were born here, while Christianity and Islam arrived quickly after their initial formations. Though conflict between religious groups has never been absent in India, a general spirit of tolerance was in the air for over two millennia. More than a thousand years before the Common Era, the Rig Veda noted: "Truth (Reality) is one, though the sages call it by various names" (Rig Veda 1.164.46). Ashoka was a Buddhist Emperor who ruled most of north India in the third century BCE. In a rock-cut edict he instructs the people:

King Priyadarsi honours men of all faiths . . . The faiths of others all deserve to be honoured for one reason or another. By honouring them, one exalts one's own faith and at the same time performs a service to the faith of others . . . Therefore concord alone is commendable (Nikam and McKeon 1959: 49–50).

Kabir was a medieval bhakti poet. He sang:

If God is within the mosque, then to whom does this world belong? If Ram be within the image which you worship upon your pilgrimage, then who is there to know what happens without? Hari is in the East, Allah is in the West. Look within your heart, for there you will find both Karim and Ram. All the men and women of the world are his living forms (Tagore 1915: 54).

The sixteenth-century Muslim emperor Akbar invited scholars of all religions, including Jesuit missionaries from Goa, to converse together about religious questions. He even sought to found a new religion, *Din-i-Ilahi*, taking whatever he considered good in the various religions. In the nineteenth and early twentieth centuries, Swami Ramakrishna and his disciple Swami Vivekananda espoused an inclusive religious pluralism, and suggested that all religions lead to God, just as all rivers lead to the sea. This is the tolerant and pluralist tradition that Gandhi had inherited.

Dialogue and the Second Vatican Council

Within the Christian tradition, the Second Vatican Council defended religious freedom, suggested that God is the common origin and goal of all and encouraged dialogue between religions. Following the establishment of a special secretariat for the promotion of dialogue between religions at the Vatican, the Catholic Bishops in India also had a secretariat to promote inter-religious dialogue in India in the early 1970s. It prepared a set of guidelines to promote such activity. Encouraging inter-religious prayer, it says:

The purpose of such common prayer is primarily the corporate worship of the God of all who has created us to be one large family. We are called to worship God not only individually but also in community, and since in a very real and fundamental manner we are one with the whole of humanity, it is not only our right but our duty to worship him together with others. (CBCI 1989)

This attitude was supported by the Federation of Asian Bishops' Conference (FABC) which met in Calcutta for its second general assembly on "Prayer" in 1978. The Bishops declared:

Sustained and reflective dialogue with them in prayer (as shall be found possible, helpful and wise in different situations) will reveal to us what the Holy Spirit has taught others to express in a marvellous variety of ways. These are different perhaps from our own, but through them we too may hear His voice, calling us to lift our hearts to the Father. (Rosales and Arevalo 1997: 35)

There were a number of dialogue groups which met periodically in some places in India. The Secretariat for Interreligious Dialogue of the Catholic Bishops' Conference of India (CBCI) used to organize three-day live-ins in different parts of the country (Nambiaparambil 1988). The FABC also organized a few inter-religious dialogue meetings at the Asian level. These live-ins included common prayer sessions. I have participated at some of these meetings. After a period in which the participants tried to understand each other and speak about the need to work together to promote mutual understanding and peace between religious groups, common prayer came as a natural consequence. This was undoubtedly facilitated by the fact that the participants were people who were motivated and committed to a joint project of promoting peace and harmony in the world. In 1989 the leaders of Catholic schools in India came together at various levels, regional and national, to explore the theme of religious education and came to the conclusion that formation in religion was an important part of human development. As a consequence of such reflection many schools began having a brief session of common morning prayer in which all students, whatever their religion, could participate. This continues in schools and colleges even today. A brief passage from one of the religious scriptures is read and a general prayer is said, addressed to God without any specific religious name. It is interesting to note that there are daily newspapers in Tamilnadu, India that quote brief passages from the scriptures of the various religions together every day. Others at the national level have brief religious reflections that are written by different religious leaders every day. Inter-religious prayer is a common occurrence in India even today, either at special dialogue meetings or on special occasions like social and cosmic disasters and common celebrations of festivals.

The Initiative of Pope John Paul II

At the international level, two events seem to have triggered the movement towards inter-religious prayer. In 1986, Pope John Paul II invited leaders of various religions in the world to come to Assisi, Italy, to pray for peace. The delegates were welcomed in the morning. Then each religious group retired to a different church to pray for peace, each according to its religious tradition. In the evening all came together in the square before the tomb of St. Francis. Each religious leader came forward to say a prayer for peace, while the others listened to the prayers silently and respectfully. As the Pope carefully explained, the believers of different religions *came together to pray* for peace, *not to pray together*. Though they did not pray together, their silence and respectful presence when others prayed was perhaps a form of implicit participation. Such a common gesture is meaningful only if everyone believes that others can pray or reach out to the divine or the absolute, and that others' prayers will be effective. The Pope himself clarified that every authentic prayer is from the Holy Spirit. He further affirmed, in a talk to the Roman Curia:

> If it is the order of unity that goes back to creation and redemption and is therefore, in this sense, "divine," such differences – and even religious differences – go back rather to a "human fact," and must be overcome in progress towards the realization of the mighty plan of unity which dominates the creation . . . The entire human race, in the infinite complexity of its history, with its different cultures, is "called to form the new people of God" (LG 13) in which the blessed union of God with man and the unity of the human family are healed, consolidated, and raised up. (December 22, 1986)

Though inter-religious dialogue meetings and even prayer sessions were going on in India and Asia even earlier, the fact that the Pope, the supreme authority in the Catholic Church, did this openly and officially was of great significance. It confirmed and galvanized inter-religious initiatives in Asia, and deepened interest in inter-religious dialogue and prayer in Europe. Assisi was a fillip to a number of European centers, catering to an increasing group of people interested in oriental spiritualities. However, it was the last straw that caused the group led by Archbishop Lefevre to break away from the Catholic Church.

Dimensions of Inter-Religious Prayer

The possibility of inter-religious prayer and worship is based on certain principles or beliefs. First, inter-religious worship often proceeds from the conviction that there is only one God, and that anyone who prays is praying to the same God. While each group's way of understanding God and giving expression to their understanding through their cultural and historical symbols may be different, there is an underlying assumption of unity, based on the unity of God.

Second, this strong affirmation of the oneness of the absolute does not deny the possibility of pluralism at the level of God's self-manifestation and at the level of human responses, conditioned by human limitation, history, and culture. God is infinite and can manifest Godself in different ways to different groups of people, though God transcends all these forms. This is pluralism, not relativism. Relativism normally implies that objective truth is unknowable and that each knower sets up his or her own "truth," which, of course, is relative to his or her context. This is relativism that cannot reach out to the absolute truth. Pluralism affirms that truth is knowable, but may be perceived differently by different people depending on their context. It is relative perception of the absolute truth. Each group does not make up its own truth, but perceives and expresses the one Truth in its own way. Such perception and expression may be limited and partial and mixed up with falsehoods, and so discernment may be necessary. But such conditioning does not imply fundamental misapprehension of the divine.

Third, the so-called world religions have a goal that is universal and cosmic. They may call it salvation or *moksha* or *umma* or *nirvana*. This transcendent goal has a historic expression in building up a community of justice, fellowship, peace, and harmony, a community that also reaches out to creation. The religions come together to pray for peace in the world precisely because they see it as a shared and collective responsibility.

If any of these three dimensions are missing, the coming together of religious groups can only be a political gesture, not a religious one. On October 27, 2011, different religious groups came together in Assisi in response to an invitation of Benedict XVI to commemorate the 25th anniversary of Assisi 1986. But these groups largely reflected in private and then made public commitments. It is significant that agnostics, too, were invited. This was not, then, inter-religious prayer, and was not meant to be. It was a gathering of religious and other groups interested in world peace. Though it was described as a pilgrimage, the stated orientation toward peace and harmony was not matched by a common orientation toward the transcendent or absolute.

The second event supporting the movement for inter-religious prayer, especially in the USA, was the attack on the twin towers of the World Trade Center in New York on September 11, 2001. This tragedy provoked many inter-religious groups to come together to pray for peace. A variety of religious communities also felt the need to assert that they were not party to the violence of fundamentalist groups. Inter-religious prayer may respond to similar events of inter-religious violence, but may also happen on occasions of natural disasters like tsunamis and earthquakes. When people feel helpless or hopeless, they turn to prayer, not as a kind of "opium" or to unload unbearable burdens on God, but rather to enter more deeply into a mystery of life and death in the world beyond their comprehension and power.

Ways of Praying Together

When religious groups have been meeting together for dialogue over a longer period of time, they may venture into a different form of inter-religious worship in which they come together not merely to pray, but to pray together. Such common inter-religious prayer can have different components. Normally, a theme is selected for the common prayer: praise, thanksgiving, reconciliation, peace, prosperity, fellowship, etc.

One component of such worship often includes reading from the scriptures of various religions. If we recognize a religion as a legitimate way to the divine, such a positive appreciation should also embrace its scriptures and rituals. Hebrew scripture can be encountered by Christians, for instance, in two different ways. Christians can read and interpret Hebrew scripture in the light of the New Testament, as they usually do within their own communities. They can also listen to Hebrew scriptures as they are read and expounded by Jews, in a Jewish–Christian dialogue group. The interpretive accents and emphases may be very different. Both kinds of reading can be profitable. But the second kind of reading in a mixed community of Jews and Christians is properly inter-religious. This can also happen in multireligious groups in which a Hindu, a Jew, a Buddhist, a Jain, a Christian, and a Muslim read texts from their respective scriptures relevant to a chosen theme, leading either to silent listening or to a lively exchange.

A second component of inter-religious worship may include prayers chosen from different religious traditions, whose formulations do not refer to any special symbol or name, but are accessible to all believers. One example of such a prayer is the

"Hindu" prayer: "Lead me from the unreal to the Real, from darkness to Light, from death to Immortality." The Christian "Our Father," too, is such a prayer. We could also think of hymns or poems that have an inter-religious tone, such as the poems of Rabindranath Tagore, which have been widely adopted by Christians in India. The Canticle of the Creatures or the prayer for peace of St. Francis of Assisi are other such texts.

A third approach to inter-religious worship may highlight special prayer or prayers on the chosen theme of the gathering for the particular inter-religious occasion. All can pray together using such a formula. Certain symbols may also have universal meaning. I have been present in inter-religious prayer services in India where general symbols (e.g., light, to indicate the divine presence, and flowers and incense, to indicate a praying attitude and intention) have been used to great effect.

A special form of inter-religious worship can be silent meditation. Each person's focus in meditation may vary from symbols to an empty mind. But the common effort may create and facilitate an energy flow that becomes a powerful force for integration and communion. The meditators can direct healing energies towards each other that lead to harmony. This is a kind of deep prayer beyond words and images. This form may be more advisable and convenient when Buddhists are present.

Prayer with Non-Theistic Religions

One issue that presents a problem in inter-religious worship is the difference between theistic and non-theistic religions. Buddhists, for example, do not believe in a personal creator God. So it is sometimes suggested that the Buddhists may feel uncomfortable in any prayer that is directed to God. I believe, however, that the problem should not be exaggerated. There may be inter-religious groups where there is no Buddhist present. If we only come together to pray when each group prays according to its tradition in the presence of the other, Buddhists can engage in a period of silent meditation. Whatever their theological position, at the popular level Buddhist temples, both in the Mahayana and Hinayana traditions, are full of prayer wheels and flags and altars to offer flowers and incense. Buddhists may not speak of a substantive absolute, but they do have Bodhisattvas and heavenly beings to whom they pray and make offerings. Much depends, therefore, on what sort of Buddhists are present in a particular prayer group. In any case, courtesy requires that each group defers to the majority of the believers present and participate in silence, if necessary.

Normally, inter-religious prayer takes place among people who have been dialoguing for some time, and who know each other well. However, various challenges and problems may still come to the fore. One such problem is that of leadership or representation. When organizing an official inter-religious prayer service, it is not always evident who can act as a representative of certain religions. While Christianity has a well-defined structure of leadership, prayer in other religions is not always based on a clearly defined order of presiders. This may cause some tension and may resort in a return to more rigidly formal types of celebration

Conclusion

Broadly, we can say that inter-religious worship or prayer can be of two kinds, and at two levels. On the one hand, different religious groups can come together to pray, without actually praying together. In such contexts, each participating group may offer its prayer in the sympathetic and attentive presence of others. The occasion is likely to be inspired by a common general goal, such as peace and harmony in the world, though a given focus for worship and prayer may also include local issues – a particular conflict, or natural and man-made catastrophes. On the other hand, religions may actually come to pray together when an inter-religious community has been sharing their spiritual life, interacting deeply with scriptural texts, symbols, songs, and prayers, communal prayer is possible and capable of deepening the common experience of the transcendent.

Bibliography

Abhishiktananda, Swami (Henri Le Saux). *The Further Shore*. Delhi: ISPCK, 1984.

Abhishiktananda, Swami (Henri Le Saux). *Ascent to the Depth of the Heart*. Delhi: ISPCK, 1998.

Amaladoss, Michael. "Other Scriptures and the Christian," *Indian Theological Studies* 22 (1985): 62–78.

Amaladoss, Michael. "Praying Together." *Indian Theological Studies* 29 (1992): 109–124.

Amaladoss, Michael. *Beyond Dialogue. Pilgrims to the Absolute*. Bangalore: Asian Trading Corporation, 2008.

Amaladoss, Michael. "Double Religious Identity: Is It Possible? Is It Necesssary?" *Vidyajyoti Journal of Theological Reflection* 73 (2009): 519–532.

Anonymous. Harmony. *Inter-faith Prayer Services for Various Occasions*. Bangalore: Loyola Mandir, 2011.

Bethune, Pierre-François de. *Une prière inter-religieuse?* Clerlande: Parole au fil du temps, 2011: 44.

CBCI Commission for Dialogue and Ecumenism. "Guidelines for Interreligious Dialogue," 2nd revised edition. New Delhi: CBCI Centre, 1989: 68.

CDF: Congregation for the Doctrine of the Faith (Vatican). "Letter to the Bishops of the Catholic Church on some aspects of Christian Meditation," October 15, 1989. *Acta Apostolicae Sedis* 82 (1990): 362–379.

Dupuis, Jacques. "The Use of Non-Christian Scriptures in Christian Worship in India." *Studia Missionalia* 23 (1974): 127–143.

Gira, Dennis and Jacques Scheuer (eds.). *Vivre de plusieurs religions. Promesse ou illusion?* Paris: L' Atelier, 2000.

Grant, Sara. "Shared Prayer and Sharing of Scriptures," in *Sharing Worship. Communicatio in Sacris*, P. Puthanangady. Bangalore: National Biblical, Catechetical and Liturgical Centre, 1988: 459–481.

Hirudayam, Ignatius. "Get-Together and Live-Together of Ashramites." *Word and Worship* 11 (1978): 272–273.

Multi-Faith Worship? Questions and Suggestions from the Inter-Faith Consultative Group. London: Church House Publishing, 1992.

Nambiaparambil, Albert. "Guidelines for Inter-Religious Prayer." *Word and Worship* 19 (1986): 211–226, 236.

Nambiaparambil, Albert. "Inter-Faith Worship or Inter-Religious Fellowship," in *Sharing Worship. Communicatio in Sacris*, P. Puthanangady. Bangalore: National Biblical, Catechetical and Liturgical Centre, 1988: 597–604.

Nikam, N.A. and Richard McKeon (eds.). *The Edicts of Ashoka*. Mumbai: Asia Publishing House, Rock Edict 12 (1959): 49–50.

Origins 15 (1986): 598.

Panikkar, Raimundo (ed.). *The Vedic Experience: Mantramanjari. An Anthology of the Vedas for Modern Man and Contemporary Celebration*. London: Darton, Longman and Todd, 1977.

Potter, Jean and Marcus Braybrooke (eds.). *A Resource Book for Multi-Faith Prayer*. The World Congress of Faiths: Great Britain, 1997.

Pratt, Douglas. "Parameters for Interreligious Prayer: Some Considerations," www.wcc-coe.org/wcc/what/interreligious/cd31-03.html (accessed December 10, 2012).

Pro Dialogo 98 (1998/2). (Many articles.)

Pushparajan, A. "Prayer Meetings with Gandhiji," in *Sharing Worship. Communicatio in Sacris*, P. Puthanangady. Bangalore: National Biblical, Catechetical and Liturgical Centre, 1988: 624–646.

Puthanangady, Paul. *Sharing Worship. Communicatio in Sacris*. Bangalore: National Biblical, Catechetical and Liturgical Centre, 1988.

"Respectful Presence: An Understanding of Interfaith prayer and celebration from a Reformed Christian Perspective," http://worldinterfaithharmonyweek.com/wp-content/uploads/2010/11/respectfulpresence.pdf (accessed December 10, 2012).

Rosales, Gaudencio and C.G. Arevalo (eds.). *For All the Peoples of Asia*, Vol. 1. Quezon City: Claretian, 1997.

Ryan, Thomas. *Interreligious Prayer. A Christian Guide*. New York: Paulist Press, 2008.

Senécal, Bernard. *Jésus le Christ à la rencontre de Gautama le Bouddha*. Paris: Cerf, 1998.

Tagore, Rabindranath. *Poems of Kabir*. New Delhi: Rupa, 1915 (Republished 2002).

Thomas, M.M. "Christ-Centred Syncretism." *Religion and Society* 26 (1979): 26–35.

Tosh, Araj and Wesley Ariarajah (eds.). *Spirituality in Interfaith Dialogue*. Geneva: WCC Publications, 1989.

CHAPTER 7

Art and Inter-Religious Dialogue

Mary Anderson

> Religion, like poetry, is not a mere idea, it is expression. The self-expression of God is in the endless variety of creation; and our attitude toward the Infinite Being must also in its expression have a variety of individuality – ceaseless and unending
>
> (Tagore 1921: 74).

> The task of the poet and the artist is to keep the Infinite before our eyes and to remind us that it ever dwells within our souls
>
> (Novak 1961: xi).

In his collection of aphorisms entitled *Thought Relics*, Rabindranath Tagore recounts a childhood experience in which, by chance, he put on a pair of eyeglasses. Doubly revealing – of an impairment in his vision and of a world suddenly, exponentially, much closer – his renewal of sight is described by him as gaining "the world twice as much as in the moment before" (Tagore 1921: 4).[1] Through the mediate lens of the eyeglasses Tagore experienced an immediate increase in the proximity of the world. He had, in his own words, "come nearer to everything" (*ibid.*). This early recognition of a changed and infinitely changeable relation between the world and himself, effected through a shift in perception, leads Tagore to this analogous insight:

> There is such a thing as coming to the nearer presence of the world through the soul. It is like a real home-coming into this world. It is gaining the world more than can be measured – like gaining an instrument, not merely by having it, but by producing upon it music (*ibid.*).

In words that resound with an embodied aesthetic sensibility, Tagore offers us a view to the dialogical imperative within art and religion – what I think of as a constitutive narrative at the heart of creation and representation. Unveiling the generative

The Wiley Blackwell Companion to Inter-Religious Dialogue, First Edition. Edited by Catherine Cornille.
© 2013 John Wiley & Sons Ltd. Published 2020 by John Wiley & Sons Ltd.

possibility of a truly incarnate life – a real home-coming into this world through the soul – Tagore's experience and metaphor of the eyeglasses attests to this shared truth within art, religion, and dialogue: that we come home to the world, gain its nearer presence, through the difference of "the other." Our inmost relations to the world and to ourselves are mediated and made real through our dialogue with the particular difference of the other person – her vision, his speech, their worldview. The world is given to us, opens and becomes immeasurable, through myriad differential encounters in which we see and are seen – actually, spiritually, and metaphorically – through the eyes of an other whose presence in the world authenticates our own.

John Berger's now classic, *Ways of Seeing*, identifies the ethical core of this intersubjective relation represented within art and religion, which is the core – or perhaps more precisely, *le coeur* – of real dialogue. Art, in its role as mediator and interlocutor, performs (lit. *per-* "through" + *form*) and reiterates our fundamental dependence upon the other whose "eye combines with our own eye to make it fully credible that we are part of the visible world" (Berger 1972: 9). In dialogue, and in art as a form and an expression of dialogue, we not only see differently – gaining an increase in perception, an oblique angle, an enlargement in worldview – we see that which we cannot see alone. The intervention of alterity experienced through dialogue, *dia-logos*, – her eyeglasses, his voice, their aesthetic or religious expression – gives us a vantage point – an ekstasis or "standing outside of oneself" – from which we begin to see ourselves.

Gaining this vantage point, however, on the part of an individual or a community of individuals, can be doubly disclosive. The moment of true dialogue, described by Pierre-François de Béthune as "encounter at the level of spiritual experience" (this volume, Chapter 3), is ambivalent and incarnate in its effects: at the same moment that the world is given to me beyond measure, the impairment in my own vision is exposed. ("Ambivalent" here carries the positive significance of two values or aspects coexisting [L. *ambi-* both + *valere* to be strong] and intertwining, without either aspect having dominion over the other and without the common, negative connotations of indecision or doubt). In true dialogue the other's presence aligns and decenters the self, orienting me to a reality that exposes my "imaginary position as the center" (Weil 1951: 159).

This intersubjective recognition – a real seeing and being seen through the eye of the other – is transformative, sometimes radically so. Genuine dialogue opens an interstitial space of intersubjective and intrasubjective exchange. It is a space of differential relation between self and other, aptly signified by the prefixes *inter-* and *intra-* and their Latin meanings: *between, betwixt, in the midst of, among, mutually, with one another*; and, *on the inside, within*. Whether it takes place in the studio process between the artist and her material, in the viewer's perception of a work of art, in religious ritual and veneration, or in the diurnal pieties of everyday life, true dialogue – like true art – is revelatory; it risks exposing the log in my own eye (cf. Matthew 7: 3–4, Luke 6: 41–2). At the level of spiritual experience, dialogue not only creates authentic bonds and engagement among its participants – the fruitful outcome of a genuine hospitality between the other and the self – it also becomes, in the course of this engagement, an intimate agent of creation, generating within its participants subliminal, incremental, and even sudden, changes in awareness of self, other, and world. Art and dialogue, as spiritual and thus embodied practices, incorporate this double aspect of creation. They iterate and make sensible the dialectic of revelation and concealment intrinsic to representation and religiosity (Anderson 2011: 395), which is operative intersubjectively, between and among persons, and intrasubjectively, within individuals.

It is then, clearly, not by chance that I put on Tagore's eyeglasses to treat, albeit quite partially, the expansive topic of art and inter-religious dialogue. By way of narrative and metaphor Tagore's aphorism symbolically incorporates key notes and nodes of relation between the two that will guide our reflections here, from its initial emphasis on the sense of sight to a fullness of sensibility within one's whole being. We will thus approach our topic through the narrow gate of vision and visuality, highlighting aspects of art and the artist's practice that are resources for thinking inter-religious dialogue in a spiritual, aesthetic, intellectual and, or, ethical sense. There are many modes of access and egress when pondering the role of art within inter-religious practice, how art has contributed to interreligiosity, and art's efficacy as a tool for inter-religious learning. Yet rather than a historical chronicling of inter-religious art, specific artworks that intend inter-religious dialogue, or engagements between art, artists, and the religious other (Bird 1995; Illman 2012; Kearney and Rizo-Patron 2011) – all worthy of detailed attention elsewhere – our focus here is philosophical and spiritual, addressing root meanings within the act of creation and the dialogical nature of aesthetic representation. From this inclusive perspective, art will be seen as a dialogical event that can, and does, model avenues of practice for inter-religious thought and engagement.

In the broad strokes that follow, this essay will first (and then repeatedly, like a softening echo) address the alterity of art in relation to the academic field of inter-religious dialogue. Thereafter it will consider the phenomenon of creation, and then, mine its significance for inter-religious dialogue through two thematic and interleaving aspects of art: Mediation and Empathic Relation. By illumining the difference of art – as an expression of human intention, voice, and sensibility in the world – through these two lenses and their internal foci, we hope to offer a vantage point, a foothold, from which art's relevance to inter-religious dialogue may be considered anew.

The Difference of Art

First, a word about the difference that art presents to the subject and practice of inter-religious dialogue. As a hermeneutical effort and a field of scholarship, inter-religious dialogue is primarily realized in, and engaged through, verbal language – in speech or writing. In relation to this overtly linguistic terrain, visual art both presents and represents an alterity – the visible, sensible, and often unworded other – which more closely resembles a spiritual discipline than a critical, objectifying endeavor. As a sensible and intelligible activity, art inhabits a richly hybrid space between the two, bringing to expression the liminal stasis that defines human being. Though often unrecognized as such – from the perspective of the arts and of religion – art is a spiritual discipline, a way of life, a mode of contemplation, and, yet it is equally a critical, translational endeavor, actively disseminating knowledge to, and engendering culture in, the world at large.

This capacity of art to limn between contemplative and active, intrasubjective and intersubjective, orientations makes it a particularly well suited resource for dialogue among religions, most of which have rich traditions of material culture. The difference of art – its beautiful, potent, and sometimes transgressive, otherness – has the ability to awaken uncharted pathways for understanding the increasingly multiple event called "inter-religious dialogue." As the visible yet often wordless other, art offers to inter-religious dialogue a vocabulary and practice of the interstitial, the ambivalent, the hybrid, the sensible, and the liminal, advancing a positive discussion of difference as the progenitor, and vivifying agent, of dialogue. In its material grammar alone, art presents inter-religious dialogue with visual, sensory, poetic, aural, and performed instances of meaning-relations established through and across formal, perceptual, and conceptual differences, without erasing, appropriating or rejecting the other. As a practice, art demands what the sculptor Anne Truitt described as the "strict discipline of forcing oneself to work steadfastly along the nerve of one's own most intimate sensitivity" (Dillard 1989: 68). This intentional discipline of the artist is intrinsically dialogical and intrasubjective, and is brought to visible expression in myriad ways within the work of art. Contemporary interdisciplinary art practices that center on a social aesthetics of interaction outside the white cube, relational aesthetics, performance and installation formats that configure junctures between disparate mediums and methods, provide visual examples of art as innovative dialogues that may be insightful templates for thinking across religious difference. Examples of art from modern and postmodern perspectives in the West – the poems of Emily Dickinson, the social sculpture of Joseph Beuys, the sound compositions of John Cage, the sculptures of Eva Hesse and Louise Bourgeois, the drawings of William Kentridge, and the performance art of Marina Abramović – readily come to mind.

Contrary to a Gadamerian hermeneutic that emphasizes a "fusion of horizons," art and the artist's process enfold a differential hermeneutic that draws relation to Emmanuel Levinas' ethical philosophy of alterity, and David Tracy's description of the limit or end of dialogue, what he characterizes as the "more than real," "the Real," the "positive experience of a new reality (the Impassable) at the limit to hermeneutics . . ." (Tracy 2010: 20). Rather than a fusing of horizons, the processes of art court alterity and its generative affects in the effort to bring to expression that which is present yet resists representation. In its capacity to engage "a sensed reality beyond or at the limit of discursive reason" (ibid.), art is a living of faith and the artwork may be thought of as its articulation in matter. This is as true for those works of art which self-define as religious and those that may be considered non-religious, spiritual, or secular. With respect to art, which includes the facture and manufacture of material culture from the dawn of humankind, these terminologies at best become fluid or risk the terrain of the irrelevant, the redundant, and the problematic.

In this sense art "may indeed offer a glimpse or a taste of a different way of being religious" (Cornille 2008: 175), a way of being in dialogue with the unexpected, the untranslated, the yet unrecognized, beneath and beyond and within human existence. In its capacity to think within and through a material sensibility that neither excludes nor depends upon discursive thought, art instructs modes of permeable engagement that foster dialogue across, within, and on account of, difference. The work of art, its labors to originate, translate, and make visible, opens affective and cognitive horizons that invite, as David Tracy posits for the end of dialogue, "a new postdialogical way of thinking within the new experience of the Incomprehensible" (*ibid.*). Whether religious in the institutional sense or unaffiliated with organized religion, art can be a productive form of – and forum for – inter-religious dialogue.

As a process of creating, an ontological praxis, a cultural mirror and product, an existential inquiry, an empathetic response, a consecration of sense and materiality, a manifestation of belief, an act of contemplation, a form of prayer, a vocation, a sacrament or ritual, and an affirmation of the heart-and-mind – art is kaleidoscopic in aspect and yet definitive in its evocation and depiction of a humanity that otherwise would remain unpictured, unshared, unacknowledged, or unexplored. Deeply and mutually interwoven in the fabric of human histories and in the chronicling of faith in diverse cultural forms, art and religion represent sometimes parallel, sometimes antithetical, worlds. Each is an expression of human desire for, and response to, an immanently transcendent alterity – that which provokes and nourishes the ultimate and intimate questions of human life. Each witnesses to a faith and humanity, whether it is spoken through the beauty of a creed or through the grace of the artist's eye and hand. At the level of spiritual experience, art and religion reach for, and emerge from, the human heart, its searching for integrity amidst diversity. Art and religion represent our need for imaginative and participatory forms of dialogue within a wondrous, pluralistic, and hyphenated world.

The Act of Creation

Art testifies to a beginning that is irrefutable, and, in this context, insightful for understanding art's significance for inter-religious dialogue. As is often noted, art and its processes mime a primordial beginning of the world, a world of relation that emerges through differentiation. Ferdinand de Saussure's theory of language as a system of differential signs identified this relational and ultimately dialogical truth of creation. Difference, not identity, is the origin of meaning (Johnson 1995: 41), and thus is the requisite condition for dialogue, for meaning, to take place. In this light, the myriad differences among religious traditions, beliefs, creeds, and between aesthetic and religious points of view, can be seen as the harbingers of meaning. They are not perverse obstacles to be feared, transmuted, hurdled over, converted, ignored, or dissolved, but invitations, prevenient signs, pointing to an infinitely rich and enigmatic ground from which genuine listening, seeing, and speaking emerge.

Tilling this ground of difference and its meaning-making potential is a shared intention of art and inter-religious dialogue. Difference is the generative possibility through which dialogue, art, and representation enter human life, and its innumerable forms – differences of gender and sexual orientation, ethnicity, national identity, race, age, occupation, religion, faith – teach a multifaceted understanding of identity rather than a monolithic one. Many religions, and particularly the religions of the book, testify to this fact of creation in their efforts to account for an originary separation of heaven and earth, light and darkness, day and night, sun and moon. As the Hebrew Torah narrates, "God saw that the light was good, and God separated the light from the darkness" (Genesis 1: 4; Tanakh 1995, 3). Through separation a world of relation comes into being, a world of seeming opposites that speaks through and across the interstice of its origin. It is a prismatic world of relation-through-difference that is experienced intersubjectively, in our relations with other persons and things, and intrasubjectively, within ourselves.

"I came to realize the truth that something 'spiritual' only exists to the extent it becomes incarnate" (Béthune 2010: 5). So writes Pierre-François de Béthune in his personal account of inter-religious dialogue, written in the body at the level of spiritual and aesthetic practice. In Béthune's life, speaking across religious differences meant becoming a novice in the Zen Buddhist discipline of the tea ceremony. To be hospitable to the religious other was to become a beginner, making space and time for a dialogue between spiritual traditions to be rendered incarnate within his own being. This imperative of embodiment, the incarnate necessity of the "spiritual," is wordlessly professed in the practical discipline of art. By surrendering to the ritual practice, the art, of the religious other, Béthune offered himself – his body, soul, mind-and-heart, spirit – as the tent of meeting between his Roman Catholic Benedictine way of life and his fledgling Zen Buddhist practice. His realization that the "spiritual" exists only to the extent that it becomes incarnate, represents a vital instance of speaking across perceived differences, the Cartesian chasm between body and spirit, highlighting instead their inextricable relation-through-difference. Béthune's statement also points to an often negated or unrecognized aspect of religious life – that a "spiritual" life aspires to an embodied consciousness, a real home-coming into this world through the soul. As a spiritual and aesthetic practice, Béthune's hospitality is an example of living a commitment to inter-religious dialogue that is formational, shaping the whole person.

Art teaches this same truth variously. "The art must enter the body too," Annie Dillard wisely observes, in a statement that affirms the formative dialogue within the artist's process and world (Dillard 1989: 69). Her writing that the body of literature "with its limits and edges, exists outside some people and inside others," implicates the body as a liminal site of exchange between interior and exterior, private and public, worlds. Art is, in a sense, an aesthetic process of formation that exposes the permeability and boundary of the body; the work of art is a dialogue between artist and material that encompasses and penetrates the whole person. In vibrant prose, Dillard comments:

> A painter cannot use paint like glue or screws to fasten down the world. The tubes of paint are like fingers; they work only if, inside the painter, the neural pathways are wide and clear to the brain. Cell by cell, molecule by molecule, atom by atom, part of the brain changes physical shape to accommodate and fit paint. You adapt yourself, Paul Klee said, to the contents of the paintbox. Adapting yourself to the contents of the paintbox, he said, is more important than nature and its study. The painter, in other words, does not fit the paints to the world. He most certainly does not fit the world to himself. He fits himself to the paint. The self is the servant who bears the paintbox and its inherited contents. Klee called this insight, quite rightly, "an altogether revolutionary new discovery." (ibid.: 69–70)

The poet Paul Valéry shared this insight: The artist "takes his body with him," (Merleau-Ponty 1964: 162) and where there is a body there is difference, the boundary of the skin, outside and within. In the act of creation the artist's body is the permeable matter, the instrument that mediates form and world into art. "It is by lending his body to the world," Merleau-Ponty writes of the painter, "that the world is turned into paintings" (*ibid.*). This intuition is echoed in Shri Ganapati Sthapati's discussion of the sculptor in the Vaastu tradition of Indian art and architecture:[2]

> Not only in the sculptures he creates, but in everything around him. The savouring of the inner being . . . should reach the hands. . . . In my case, this savouring stays . . . as a tangible, physical form. I was able to see this for myself. I saw the image within me take shape outside. "Feelings do take form!" When I saw this, I realized that, the figure that stood before me was really myself. In a flash, I understood the statement from my tradition: "The sculptor becomes the sculpture." (Sashikala 2004)

The artist, like the monastic or "spiritual" aspirant, is an ontological site of transformation. Her work is a dialogue with matter; it is concerned with an act, an affirmation, of her being (Buber 1958: 10). As a spiritual practice and way of seeing, art offers visibility to these intricate, implicit, and yet foundational dialogues of creation. In Martin Buber's *I and Thou* we read of the artist speaking the primary word with his whole being. The work of art arises from this dialogical event; it is a bodying forth of form that incorporates both a risk and a sacrifice.

> This is the sacrifice: the endless possibility that is offered up on the altar of form. For everything which just this moment in play ran through the perspective must be obliterated; nothing of that may penetrate the work. The exclusiveness of what is facing it demands that it be so. This is the risk: the primary word can only be spoken with the whole being. He who gives himself to it may withhold nothing of himself. The work does not suffer me, as do the tree and the man, to turn aside and relax in the world of *It*; but it commands. If I do not serve it aright it is broken, or it breaks me. (*ibid.*)

In the context of inter-religious dialogue how might we utilize these insights of the creative process, the procreative tensions of difference for which dialogue is the sign? Can the processes of inter-religious engagement be understood in these aesthetic terms? Might they incorporate a similar risk and sacrifice? To be effective and take shape in the world inter-religious dialogue must, like all forms of engagement, sacrifice endless possibility to an incarnate necessity – a hospitality that holds the creative tension of relation-through-difference. Equally so, each participant in inter-religious dialogue must risk speaking with his or her whole being, surrendering to an inspired, receptive effort that welcomes the creative process – with all of its beauty, exigency, humility, and liberty – in receiving the religious other. If we imagine the dialogue between religions as a participatory aesthetics akin to Buber's artist speaking the primary word, such that it places her "in the cradle of the Real life" (*ibid.*, 9), what kinds of dialogue, what forms of art, personhood, and prayer, and what varieties of inter-religious converse, might be given to us and the world at least twice as much as the moment before? (cf. Miles-Yepez 2006).

Mediation

As Buber's dialogical philosophy suggests, the risk of art is one of being imminently present to the other and sacrificing infinite possibility to the finite imperative of form.

This distillation of the work of art to two criteria – risk and sacrifice – emphasizes the mediatory nature of art, art's ability to hold seeming opposites in generative, asymmetrical relation to each other. In the work of art – "work" signifying the translational labor of making and the formal effects of that labor in the world – dialogue is both the creative event and the creative agent of transformation. The labor of art mediates between ambivalent contraries that require each other – spiritual–incarnate, idea–form, concept–material, inspiration–concretization, subject–object, difference–dialogue. Art negotiates a terrain of differential perceptions and relations, within which it traces the ethical trajectory of art as it "bodies forth" into form. This mediation of art from an ideal to a world is a dialogical discernment through matter. It is a listening and a speaking with one's whole being, a presencing that attends the pace toward expression and reflects the ethical exigencies of an incarnate world. Inter-religious dialogue as a "bodying forth" of creation requires these same discernments. Its interpersonal mediation of the differential relations between words and bodies and beliefs, between religious commitments and their representations in the world, must be honored and at the same time illuminated for more nuanced and informed perspectives on religiosity, and the human condition to which it witnesses, to emerge into full view.

In an ekphrasis on Bruegel the Elder's sixteenth-century painting, *Icarus*, the poet W. H. Auden acknowledges the human position of suffering, its taking place "while someone else is eating or opening a window or just walking dully along" (Auden 1970: 1100). His poem, "Musée des Beaux Arts," represents in poetic form, the imbrication of amazement – the miraculous birth, the dreadful martyrdom, a boy falling out of the sky – within the pulse and intention of somatic life, its having "somewhere to get to and sail[ing] calmly on" (*ibid.*). Auden's art, and Bruegel's beforehand, testify to the mediation of difference in the work of art. Through their eyes and artifice we see a quotidian coincidence of apparent contradictories – the miracle and the unimportant failure – as they are depicted pictorially, linguistically, and as they exist in human life. Reflecting on this ambivalence in the work of art "and its dialogic interface with the world in which it dwells," Homi Bhabha writes of art as a form of address whose peculiar power "arises through its mediation between sublime silence and the din of everyday sight and sound" (Bhabha 1996: 10).

> For art has the capacity to reveal the almost impossible, attenuated limit where aura and agora overlap, to find a language for the high horizons of humanity itself and – in its finest selves, its inspired othernesses, its visionary styles, its vocabularies of vicissitude – to reveal its own fabulation, its fragility, at the moment of its articulation. (*ibid.*)

In reaching toward representation, art, like Icarus and true dialogue, articulates its own fragility. As with Tagore's doubly disclosive experience of the other's eyeglasses, art reveals its impairment even as it opens us to reality, brings us nearer to the world. The infinite aspiration of art reveals this, its finite measure. Yet this limitation of art, its artifice, is its salvation – the lie that tells the truth. Like the end of dialogue of which David Tracy wrote, the fragility of art, its revealing of its own fabulation, "provides an opportunity for a new experience of the Real beyond ordinary reality – the Infinite, the Incomprehensible, the Impossible" (Tracy 2010: 20).

This mediation of the work of art, its formal interlocution between perceived oppo-sites – heaven and earth, darkness and light, aura and agora – lends sustenance to forms of inter-religious engagement in which trust and creativity are, if held differently, still held in common. Dialogue between religious faiths requires a commitment to mediation that counsels faith, accepting a similar risk and sacrifice that Buber observes in the artist. For each participant, inter-religious dialogue will mean an investment in a process of negotiation that affirms and enlarges one's being, while also disclosing one's own fragility and fabulation. Yet it is not only an individual fragility that concerns us here. What would it mean for a religious community, a religion or religions, to reveal their own fabulation, to unveil or confront the edge and frame of their belief?

Can we ask of religions, as we do of art, to reveal the lie that tells their truth? Art offers to inter-religious dialogue a generous template for recognizing truth – in the religious other, in the other religion – that is born in the humble kenosis of self-disclosure. Religions engaging each other in dialogue need to look within, to excavate and honor their *religious* commitment to host the other as the harbinger of true dia-logue, genuine relation. What life – a religious community or individual must ask – will be nourished in me at the breast of the other's truth? And its corollary: Might this truth be my own, known under a different aspect, name, or practice? Further still and in response to an invitation to rethink one's own faith tradition: What fabulation must I surrender, be stripped of, in order to recognize the truth of my sister's, my brother's, religion? If held in common and receptive humility, such a commitment to inter-religious mediation will involve, within the particularity of differing religious orienta-tions, a disclosure of humanity clothed "in all its mystery and its ordinariness" (*ibid.*). Art's lie enfolds such truths.

A mediate lens

Jitish Kallat's recent installation, *Public Notice 3* (2010–11), is one example of the dia-logical mediation of meaning across differences and through visual form. A contempo-rary work of installation art, it is, like Auden's poem and Bruegel's painting, a formal disclosure of the ambivalent tensions within the human position. With a precision of form and intent, *Public Notice 3* negotiates between the borders of cultures – East and West, India and the United States – between signifying registers (spatial, visual, linguis-tic, temporal, experiential, relational, contemplative), and systems of belief (religious, aesthetic, political, and historical) (Ghose: 2011). Installed in the Woman's Board Grand Staircase of the Chicago Art Institute, from September 11, 2010 through September 2011, *Public Notice 3* visually implants Swami Vivekananda's "Welcome Address to the World's Parliament of Religions," given in Chicago at the World's Columbian Exposition exactly 108 years earlier. On the 118 risers of the Grand Staircase, Vivekananda's words calling for "universal toleration" and the "death-knell of fanaticism" (*ibid.*: 95) are illuminated by LED lights in a declension of colors – red, orange, yellow, blue, and green – that comprise the threat coding system of the US Department of Homeland Security.

Integrating visual, textual, and architectural, dialogues that alternately memorial-ize, interrogate, and critique the events of September 11, 1893, 2001, and 2012,

Kallat's *Public Notice 3* creates a palimpsest of meaning in the spatio-temporal layering of its material form. Through its sculptural, linguistic, and religious interlocutions we are invited to contemplate the gulf of difference between the hope of "all lead to Thee" (*ibid.*) and the insidious violence of a truncated rainbow in which orange and red – two of the most auspicious and religiously significant colors in South Asia – denote a "high" and "severe" risk of terrorist attack. In the LED lights and their reflections on the surface of each step, Vivekananda's words doubly illuminate a dialogue between each word and its attendant reflection; each step represents a mobile, imminent threshold, oscillating between hope and fear, insight and blindness, actuality and illusion, then and now. As people climb up and down the fourfold architecture of the Grand Staircase they become a part of the speech's environment, a participant in the escalation of, and breach between, its languages that alternately greet, "Sisters and Brothers of America" (*ibid.*), and warn – in uncannily bright-hued cheer – of impending terror. Each viewer becomes – amidst this dialogue that coincides religious, aesthetic, and barbaric signifi-cations – a human measure, incarnate instruments that calibrate and align two histori-cal moments 108 years apart.

Kallat's seamless installation translates and extends this measure, poignantly inter-leaving the remembrance of a national tragedy that shattered a worldview with an inaugural inter-religious dialogue and its hopeful "first attempt to create a global con-vergence of faiths (not nations)" (*ibid.*: 86). Speaking with history through architec-tural form and human scale, *Public Notice 3* demands that we walk along these edges of meaning that lie between a "spiritual" aspiration set forth in words and the visual rhetoric of terror adopted by the United States in the wake of 9/11. In this meaningful sense, the ascending and descending steps of the Grand Staircase physically and meta-phorically signify the ascendancy of hope and its decline, or as the Chicago Art Insti-tute's website declares, "the evolution, or devolution, of religious tolerance across the 20th and 21st centuries." As a work of art that adheres to no institutional religious frame (that I know of), *Public Notice 3* claims a space of alterity outside religion and yet within its bounds, speaking directly to the global necessity for inter-religious tolerance and mediation.[3]

Mediate images

The material cultures of religious traditions richly exhibit the mediatory capacities of art. In the Hindu and Christian traditions, the iconic image is believed to establish a locus of mediation, a threshold that maintains a dynamic relation-through-difference with its source. The Christian icon literally materializes, in an incarnate and thus spir-itual sense, a space of intercession between God's self-revelation and the faithful observer. As an image believed to present a likeness of God without circumscription or diminishment, the Christian icon "invites the viewer into the prayerful intercession that it materially re-presents" (Anderson 2011: 404). Similarly the iconic image in Hindu-ism – in the Sanskrit, *murti* "an embodiment, incarnation, manifestation," or *vigraha*, "body," "that form which enables the mind to grasp the nature of God" – is understood to be "the deity itself taken 'form'" (Eck 1998: 38). In each

instance, Hindu and Christian, the mediation of the religious image inscribes a differential relation of absence and presence intrinsic to the act of creation, to representation, and in a linguistic sense, to the production of meaning itself. The icon and murti,
respectively, are works of art, human artifice, that afford a state of encounter – a seeing
and being seen by the eye of the other.

In this relational, intersubjective event of a holy seeing, the religious image represents and incorporates a space of intercession and *darśan*, respectively. The image
becomes a liminal, differential site in which apparent contradictories are held in creative tension with one another. For the Christian, the icon is the visible image of the
invisible God; and for the Hindu, it is the body and form in which the uncircumscribable
deity presents itself to be seen. Visualizing and performing a true dialogue at eye level,
the iconic image opens an interstitial space in which self and other see and are seen.
In Hindu darśan, the image is venerated and beheld with the eyes, and through these
same eyes divine blessings are received. Enfolding an asymmetrical event of reverence
and reception of divine presence through the gaze, the iconic image mediates a non-
appropriative, non-grasping event that is procreative, disclosive, and auspicious. As
Diana Eck writes, "It is this fact of presence which is at the basis of *darśan*. People come
to see because there is something very powerful there to see" (*ibid.*, 51).

This fact of presence that is given form through mediation – aesthetically in the
religious image and ontologically through the body and its perceiving – is an event of
witness that both instantiates one's presence in the world and incarnates the presence
of the divine within the believer's heart. This act of witness dialogically and thus, ethically, orients us; it enacts our essential dependence upon the eye or voice of an intermediary other to combine with our own and validate our presence in the world (Berger
1972: 9). Inter-religious dialogue aspires to give and receive such a witness, hosting
the religious other in ways that privilege and intend a listening, which offers credible
witness between self and other in an ontological sense. To give and receive darśan is an
imaginative and originary act, an intersubjective moment of recognition in which the
believer touches and is touched by the presence of the divine. The religious image, in
its ritual, liturgical, and formal mediations, makes possible an art that is *"para-rupa,*
'trans-form'," (Coomaraswamy 1934: 165), an event that takes place immediately and
imminently in the face of the other. Modeling an asymmetrical, non-appropriative act
of engagement within and across difference, darśan offers a religious and aesthetic
example for a dialogue that is both hospitable and kenotic. Through the alterity and
boundary of an image, a space is made for the other to be present, for the other's habi-
tation, thereby securing a vantage point from which to see, and be seen by, the other.
Through the mediation of art and its nourishment of the religious imagination, veneration of a formless other may cultivate an attitude of reverence for, and deference
towards, the human other with whom I speak.

Sensibility

In Philip Gröning's film *Into Great Silence* (*Die Große Stille*, 2005), there is a scene in
which the Carthusian elders are discussing a ritual cleansing of their hands, a brief

gesture, a dipping into water, before entering the chapel and prayer. When it is mentioned that another Carthusian monastery has eliminated this ritual practice, one of
the elder brothers responds, "When we abolish the signs we lose our orientation."

Spoken in the context of a Christian monastic community noted for its rigorous observance of silence, the elder monk's words point to a principal function of art by calling
attention to the human reliance on signs and symbols for orientation in the world. As
with the *murti* or *vigraha* in which the deity presents itself, art offers visible, symbolic
form for that which is formless. In doing so it sensitizes and extends our capacities for
seeing the non-visible, or that which is other than visible, within the visible world. Like
Tagore's eyeglasses, art is an other that increases our acuity and sensibility – both in the
material and intelligible sense of this word – that we might be oriented to the nearer
presence of self, other, and world. Where there is increased sensibility there can be an
attunement to the subtleties of relation in an interpersonal, material, linguistic, and
phenomenological sense. Refinements of sensibility gained through the aesthetic perception of differences in the surfaces of the phenomenal world – light and shade, sight
and sound, weight and contour, texture and color – orient us to affective, inter-relational
topographies in which we are touched by the incarnate intelligence of the other – by
their words, their eyes, their presence, their hands. In the mind of the artist, Anne Truitt,
a landscape becomes the sensible and intelligent other:

> Seen whole from the air, circumscribed by its global horizon, the earth confronted me
> bluntly as a context all its own, echoing that grand sweep. I had the startling impression
> that I was looking at something intelligent. Every delicate pulsation of color was met,
> matched, challenged, repulsed, embraced by another, none out of proportion, each at once
> unique and a proper part of the whole. (Truitt 1982, 10)

From art and the artist's eye, inter-religious dialogue might borrow this relational intelligence that grounds human perception. When I look at an object – the lamp, a table,
a person – I perceive, not the lamp or table as an isolated entity, but the relation between
that object and myself. The distance between myself and an other, our relation, is the
real object of my perception. Art, as a process and as a work to be experienced, is
an existential laboratory for somatic and visual literacy, for training the senses to recognize – cognitively, affectively, physically, intuitively – this intelligent land. When Louis
Dupré writes, "[t]o realize itself in and through the other is constitutive of the embodied
mind" (Dupré 2000: 3), he implies this proximate space of relation-through-difference
between self and other, the formless interstice of relation, which is the ground of
authentic dialogue. If truly oriented to this space *between*, human beings may become
images – like the icon and *murti* – embodying, presenting, and representing this relational reality that extends into unworded realms.

As with a Hindu image awaiting the ritual spark of divine life, human beings represent a boundless reality beyond and yet within themselves. More akin to a symbol that
"stands in a more intimate relation to the signified" (*ibid.*, 2) than the sign which merely
points to it, human beings are bearers of meaning; we constitute meaning in the vital
articulation of self *as a relation* to an other. Inter-religious dialogue may thrive where
there is a symbolic understanding not only of ritual practices, religious sacrament,

ornament, and vestiture – those signs that preserve one's orientation through aesthetic relation – but of representation itself, in its broadest sense, inclusive of human being. Inter-religious practitioners engaged in the tensions of dialogue – those incurred within the borders, the boundaries, the limitations, of religious difference – may benefit from this cinematic awareness of the interstitial image:

> The image always takes place at the border of two force fields, it is meant to bear witness to a certain *otherness*; and although it always has a hard core, it always lacks something. The image is always *more and less than itself.* (Daney 2006: 28)

Empathic Relation

Religions enact, and trace their roots to, the dialectic of revelation and concealment, a dialectic of the "always *more and less than itself*" that is intrinsic to art and symbolic representation. Religious aspirants may strive to become icons, to represent and incarnate through ascetic, aesthetic, and devotional means, what non-religious language identifies as an absent, transcendent signifier. At the heart of religions there resides a symbolic dialogue of present absence, immanent transcendence, meaning-through-difference. It traces an axis of affective encounter, the reverent observance of a formlessness that constitutes a relational reality between and beyond and within human beings. In persons this ongoing dialogue of form, formless, and forming, which is always *more and less than itself*, is a path of inner transformation cultivated through the embodied practices of art, ritual, sacrament. As Pierre-François de Béthune observes from his residency in the Zen Buddhist tradition:

> The thing to look out for in a calligraphic painting is the extent to which it bears witness to a man who is really free: a freedom mirrored in his brushstrokes. Zen art is not so much a means through which an artist finds expression but rather an opportunity given him to work on his inner self, thus refining his approach to reality. This is especially true of *chado* [the way of tea], where the material used is neither ink, nor paper, nor flowers but rather the welcome of one another. In such a case the spiritual journey resides in essence within the movements that are essential to the making and serving of the tea. No less is at stake than the embodiment (incarnation) of an unconditional openness to the other person within a hospitality ritual that is pushed to the limits of perfection [my insertion]. (Béthune 2010: 8)

Inter-religious dialogue, when understood as an art and spiritual discipline, is a relational refining of each individual's approach to reality. Such dialogue, for the individual person or religious community, is truly oriented, truly relational, when it does not seek an end or an object, but only the art, the practice itself. Dialogue among religions would then be a process of developing beginners' mind, a continual emptying of self that is generative of humility, hospitality, and genuine love of the other. Inter-religious dialogue has this potential and what stores, what extraordinary resources, it holds in the palms of its many hands – the wisdom of the world's spiritual and aesthetic traditions need only be tapped, translated into a dialogical practice of love for each other. "To me," writes Thich Nhat Hanh, "religious life is life. I do not see any reason to spend one's whole life tasting just one kind of fruit. We human beings can be nourished by the best values of many traditions" (Hahn 1995: 2). *Chado*, the way of tea, as one exquisitely rigorous example of an art that is also a spiritual practice, instructs love as its insight and source; with this love of one's art a person lives it as a spiritual journey, an incarnate commitment to love (Béthune 2010: 9). Approached in this way, as an art, interreligious dialogue becomes a commitment of heart, an aesthetic practice in which love is its source, its means, and its end.

In *The Philosophy of the Act* Mikhail Bakhtin acknowledges this aesthetic truth in a discussion of un-self-interested love and its antithesis – the indifference and hostility that impoverishes and decomposes its object.

> Lovelessness, indifference, will never be able to generate sufficient power to slow down and *linger intently* over an object, to hold and sculpt every detail and particular in it, however minute. Only love is capable of being aesthetically productive; only in correlation with the loved is fullness of the manifold possible. (Bakhtin 1999: 64)

In Bakhtin's words we find the empathic source of creation to which language, art, and religion, bear symbolic witness. When art is a practice of listening, a slowing down, a lingering intently over a beloved object, it teaches a mindfulness that extends attention from the material object – held and sculpted in every detail – to an awareness of interhuman relations, personhood, human desires and needs. Noting this ethics of care that evolves from material objects to persons, Michael Barnes writes "To see things as they really are is to become sensitive to all sentient beings, building up the qualities of the *bodhisattva*, the saint who vows to work for the well-being and enlightenment of all people" (Barnes 2012: 150). At heart, aesthetic productivity cultivates an empathic sensibility that extends between the material world and the enlightenment of persons. "Only in correlation with the loved" is a lucid description of the ethical responsibility that art and dialogue intend and enfold. For in Bakhtin's statement we also discover hospitality's opposite, the hostile impoverishment that negates empathy and its loving correlation. In the dialogue between religions, art and the imagination may serve as a positive heuristic for transforming pathological relation into compassionate engagement.

Empathic imagining

In "The Difficulty of Imagining Other Persons," Elaine Scarry articulates the role of the imagination in shaping our behavior toward others (Scarry 1998). Arguing for both constitutional measures and "generous or spontaneous imaginings" of the other to alleviate "the inherently aversive structural position of 'foreignness'," Scarry points to both the necessity of the human imagination and its inadequacy "in picturing other persons in their full weight and solidity" (*ibid*.: 40). "The difficulty of imaging others," she writes, "is shown by the fact that one can be in the presence of another person who is in pain and not know that the person is in pain. The ease of remaining ignorant of another person's pain even permits one to inflict it and amplify it in the body of the other person while remaining immune oneself" (*ibid.*: 41).

Art – great theatre, films, poems, literature – represents efforts to critique the problem of otherness; works of art provide visibility for an otherwise invisible 'other', encourage imaginative replacement of oneself with the other, and increase human sensibility by evoking a heightened vivacity of the perceptual world (*ibid.*: 46). Advocating strategies – imaginative, linguistic, and legal – for achieving a mental equality of self and other, Scarry calls attention to the need for a material referent, a historic anchor, for art to represent "strategies such as underexposure and overexposure whose operations we can then locate at work in the material world" (*ibid.*: 49). Citing rare examples of litera- ture in which the literary representation of "others" leads to constitutional change, Scarry highlights art's potential for sensitizing and educating a public to the plight of the foreign "other." When she describes the effect of Harriet Beecher Stowe's *Uncle Tom's Cabin*, its giving blacks "the weight, solidity, injurability of their personhood," making them "imaginable to the white population in pre-Civil War United States" (*ibid.*), Scarry addresses a possibility for art to be an agent of conscience and social change.

Art offers a mirror to society and, in rare instances, a door to constitutional change. Considering its potential for inter-religious engagement, art has the capacity to create venues of visibility for inter-religious imagining, to choreograph forms of inter- religious communion that make difference real and love possible by envisioning the religious self and the religious other in their full weight, vivacity, and injurability. In its ability to bring the world nearer to us, perhaps twice as much as in the moment before, art discloses an ethical trajectory between the visible and non-visible that carries import for critical issues in the practice of inter-religious dialogue such as: representation of women, racial and ethnic minorities; the visibility of institutional power and authority; sexual difference and gender equity, among many others. In that images lend visibility to the hidden or the absent, they bring things closer to us, before our eyes, so that like Tagore we may "come to the nearer presence of the world."

Susan Sontag's *Regarding the Pain of Others* ponders similar difficulties in dialogue and representation through the art of photography (Sontag 2003). Her consideration of the problems of affect and impact in photographs of war bears meaningfully on our topic. The essay begins with a consideration of the moral outcry of Virginia Woolf's "Why War?" which inscribes a link between the imagination and empathy. "Our failure," writes Woolf, "is one of imagination, of empathy: we have failed to hold this reality in mind" (*ibid.*: 8). In Sontag's monograph, as in Scarry's essay, we are confronted with the ambivalent edge of art and representation, that a symbolic universe is an interstitial reality, harboring both blindness and insight. While a photograph makes visible and real the person or event – sometimes in a "terrible distinctness" – its shadow side ac- complishes precisely the opposite. The aesthetic distance between an image of war and its material referent in the world bears an objectifying force, making "a catastrophe that is experienced [. . .] seem eerily like its representation" (*ibid.*: 21). The mediation of an image risks a form of aesthetic disembodiment; its display and exposure can turn a face, a feeling, a place, "into something that can be possessed" (*ibid.*: 81). Jean Baudril- lard concurs, pathologizing the photographic image as a retreat from the material world.

> The intensity of the image corresponds to the extent of its denial of reality, to its invention of another stage. Making an object an image means removing dimension, one by one: weight, relief, odor, depth, time, continuity, and, of course, meaning. The image receives its power to fascinate at the expense of this disembodiment. (Baudrillard 2008: 146)

Yet this loss of weight and dimension in relation to its material referent in the world, is also the realization of the photograph's objecthood, its having an ethical bearing in the world. What on one side appears to be the removal of physicality – a flattening of difference and dimension – is on the other, the laying bare of the interstitial reality of an image – the rendering of a new form, present and existing in a shareable world. As we have seen in traditional religious icons – the icon and *murti* in particular – images limn an interstitial site between an absent referent and an imminent event of witness, a seeing and being seen by the other. Works of art are doubly disclosive; they are always more and less than themselves, revealing a presence through absence, and, more precisely, *our* absence through their presence. "Photography," Baudrillard reminds us, "accounts for the state of the world in our absence" (*ibid*.: 152). Yet this revelation of absence through presence is at least one source of art's affective power, of its ability to move us. Art silently cultivates empathic dialogues across an interstice that is within us and beyond us yet is present between us as the differential space of relation.

One remarkable instance in which art created the conditions for authentic dialogue was narrated by President Jimmy Carter in his Sadat Lecture for Peace, October 25, 1998. At the moment when the Camp David peace talks had broken down – Menachim Begin, Jimmy Carter, and Anwar Sadat had decided to leave – photographs signed by the President opened an empathic horizon for dialogue across intransigent differences. Jimmy Carter writes:

> Begin asked me to sign a photograph of the three of us for his grandchildren. My secretary brought me eight photographs, and she had also discovered the names of Begin's grandchildren. So instead of just signing Jimmy Carter, I put "With Love to" and wrote the name of every one of his grandchildren. I took them over to his cabin. He was hardly speaking to me. I knocked at the door and went in. I handed him the photographs, a stack of them. He said, "Thank you, Mr. President" and turned around, dismissing me in effect. And he looked down and he read the first photograph, and he called out the name of his granddaughter. And then one by one he read out the names of his grandchildren. Tears ran down his cheeks, and when I saw them I also cried. And he said, "Why don't we try one more time?" (Carter 1998)

By reaching into the affective, relational reality of the human heart, breaking it open to an empathic awareness of self as other, art bears the risk of creation – a continual sacrificing of endless possibility to the incarnate reality of a form, a face, a faith, a friend. Art's mimesis of the world is the labor of vision and consciousness, the tracing of a relation-through-difference that marks the source and circumference of creation itself. What is this act of creation? Probing the amazing affinity between Kurosawa's films and Dostoyevsky's novels, Gilles Deleuze asks, "How can he be in such familiar terms with Shakespeare and Dostoyevsky? Why do we need a Japanese director in order to attain such a familiarity with Shakespeare and Dostoyevsky?" (Deleuze 2006: 54). In his emi-

nently humane response, Deleuze offers us a lens, a key – to art and the creative act –
that may open a door for our thinking and practicing inter-religious dialogue anew.

> That is what a beautiful encounter is about: If Kurosawa is able to adapt Dostoyevsky it is
> precisely because he can say: *I have a deal in common with him, I have a problem in common,
> this is the one.* (*ibid.*: 55 my italics)

Notes

1   "In my early years, I did not know that my sight had become impaired. The first day when,
    by chance, I put on a pair of eyeglasses I found that I had suddenly come nearer to
    everything. I felt I had gained the world twice as much as had been given to me the
    moment before."
2   Shri Ganapati Sthapati is a sculptor-designer-builder from Mamallapuram, Tamil Nadu,
    India, who "belongs to an unbroken lineage of the designer-builder of Brihadeshwarar
    Temple of Tanjore (eleventh century CE). He is one of the few alive today who have a deep
    understanding of the Vaastu Tradition of Indian art and architecture in both its theory
    and practice."
3   Jitish Kallat continues, "possibly with the knowledge that in the future it will not 'only' be
    nations that become sole-commissioners of carnage – and overlaying these contrasting
    moments like an [sic.] palimpsest."

Bibliography

Anderson, Mary M. "On Seeing the Birth of the Heart," in *Traversing the Heart: Journeys of the Interreligious Imagination*, eds. Richard Kearney and Eileen Rizo-Patron. Leiden: Brill, 2011, 395–421.

Auden, W.H. "Musée des Beaux Arts," in *The Norton Anthology of Poetry*, 3rd Edition. New: W. W. Norton & Company, 1970.

Bakhtin, M.M. *Toward a Philosophy of the Act*, ed. and trans. Vadim Liapunov and Michael Holquist. Austin, TX: University of Texas Press, 1999.

Barnes, Michael, SJ. *Interreligious Learning: Dialogue, Spirituality and the Christian Imagination*. Cambridge: Cambridge University Press, 2012.

Baudrillard, Jean and Marc Guillaume. *Radical Alterity*, trans. Ames Hodges. Los Angeles: Semiotext(e)/MIT Press, 2008.

Berger, John. *Ways of Seeing*. London: Penguin/BBC, 1972.

de Béthune, Pierre-François. *Interreligious Hospitality: The Fulfillment of Dialogue*. Collegeville, MN: Liturgical Press. 2010.

Bhabha, Homi K. "Aura and Agora: On Negotiating Rapture and Speaking Between," in *Negotiating Rapture*. Chicago Art Institute, 1996.

Bird, Michael S. *Art and Interreligious Dialogue*. Lanham, MD: University Press of America, 1995.

Buber, Martin. *I and Thou*, trans. Ronald Gregor Smith. New York: Charles Scribner and Sons, 1958.

Carter, Jimmy. "The Sadat Lecture for Peace, in recognition of the 20th Anniversary of the Camp David Accords." October 25, 1998. Delivered at the University of Maryland, College Park. http://sadat.umd.edu/lecture/lecture/carter.htm (accessed December 23, 2012).

Chicago Art Institute website. http://www.artic.edu/exhibition/jitish-kallat-public-notice-3 (accessed December 23, 2012).

Coomaraswamy, Ananda K. "Origin and Use of Images in India," in *The Transformation of Nature in Art*. Cambridge, MA: Harvard University Press, 1934.

Cornille, Catherine. *The Im-possibility of Interreligious Dialogue*. New York: Crossroad, 2008.

Cornille, Catherine (ed.). *Criteria of Discernment in Interreligious Dialogue*. Eugene, OR: Cascade Books, 2009.

Cornille, Catherine and Christopher Conway (eds.). *Interreligious Hermeneutics*. Eugene, OR: Cascade Books, 2010.

Daney, Serge. "Montage Obligatory: The War, The Gulf, and the Small Screen," in *In the Poem About Love You Don't Write the Word Love*, ed. Tanya Leighton. Berlin/New York: Sternberg Press, 2006, 21–32.

Deleuze, Gilles. "What is the Act of Creation?," in *In the Poem About Love You Don't Write the Word Love*, ed. Tanya Leighton. Berlin/New York: Sternberg Press, 2006, 54–55.

Dillard, Annie. *The Writing Life*. New York: Harper & Row, 1989.

Dupré, Louis. *Symbols of the Sacred*. Grand Rapids, MI: William B. Eerdmans, 2000.

Eck, Diana L. *Darsan: Seeing the Divine Image in India*. New York: Columbia University Press, 1998.

Elkins, James. *Pictures and Tears*. New York and London: Routledge, 2001.

Gröning, Philip. *Into Great Silence/Die Große Stille*. Film, 52 minutes, 2005.

Hanh, Thich Nhat. *Living Buddha, Living Christ*. New York: Riverhead Books, 1995.

Illman, Ruth. *Art and Belief: Artists Engaged in Interreligious Dialogue* Oakville, CT: Equinox Publishing, 2012.

Ghose, Madhuvanti (ed.). *Jitish Kallat: Public Notice 3*. New Haven, CT: The Art Institute of Chicago and Yale University Press, 2011.

Johnson, Barbara. "Writing," in *Critical Terms for Literary Study*, eds. Frank Lentricchia and Thomas McLaughlin. Chicago: University of Chicago Press, 1995.

Levinas, Emmanuel. *Entre nous. Essais sur le penser-à-l'autre*. Paris: Bernard Grasset, 1991.

Levinas, Emmanuel. "Is Ontology Fundamental?" in *Basic Philosophical Writings*, eds. Adriaan T. Peperzak, Simon Critchley, and Robert Bernasconi. Bloomington: Indiana University Press, 1996, 1–10.

Merleau-Ponty, Maurice. "Eye and Mind," in *The Primary of Perception*, ed. James M. Edie. Northwestern University Press, 1964.

Miles-Yepez, Netanel. *The Common Heart: An Experience of Interreligious Dialogue*. New York: Lantern Books, 2006.

Novak, Philip. "Foreword," in Rabindranath Tagore, *The Religion of Man* [being the Hibbert Lectures for 1930]. Rhinebeck, NY: Monkfish Book Publishing, 1961, ix–xii.

Sashikala, Ananth. Transcript of the film, *Vaastu Marabu: The Living Tradition, A Shilpi Speaks*. Documentary Educational Resources, 52 minutes, 2004. http://anth.alexanderstreet.com.ezp-prod1.hul.harvard.edu/View/765542/.

Scarry, Elaine. "The Difficulty of Imagining Other Persons," in *The Handbook of Interethnic Coexistence*, ed. Eugene Weiner. New York: Continuum, 1998, 40–62.

Sontag, Susan. *Regarding the Pain of Others*. New York: Picador/Farrar, Straus, and Giroux, 2003.

Tagore, Rabindranath. *Thought Relics*. New York: The Macmillan Company, 1921.

Tagore, Rabindranath. *The Religion of Man* [being the Hibbert Lectures for 1930]. Rhinebeck, NY: Monkfish Book Publishing, 1961.

Tanakh: The Holy Scriptures. Philadelphia and Jerusalem: The Jewish Publication Society, 1985.

Tracy, David. "Western Hermeneutics and Interreligious Dialogue," in *Interreligious Hermeneutics*, eds. Catherine Cornille and Christopher Conway. Eugene, OR: Cascade Books, 2010, 1–43.

Truitt, Anne. *Daybook: The Journal of an Artist*. New York: Pantheon Books, 1982.

Weil, Simone. "Forms of the Implicit Love of God," in *Waiting for God*, trans. Emma Craufurd. New York: Harper & Row, 1951, 137–215.

CHAPTER 8

Inter-Religious Dialogue and Interstitial Theology

Tinu Ruparell

R eligious hybridity is simply a fact of the history of religions. Arguably there has been no time in which religious people have not expressed some degree of allegiance to a plurality of religious traditions, either simultaneously or serially. Of course, belonging to multiple traditions has been held in tension with the overarching call within all major religious traditions, to be faithful to one tradition, one god or notion of the divine, above all others.[1] The history of religions is thus marked by a dialectic of religious belonging, a tension between solidarity to an absolute, pure tradition or divinity, and a call to a view in which religious traditions are more fluid, cosmopolitan, and nonabsolute. Moreover, even within the putatively pure religious forms, there is a plurality of sects, denominations and other expressions of religion from which the adherents choose, or to which they may convert. These forms can be variously inculturated so that while they share the same name, their family resemblances may be quite slight. Hence, religious hybridity in the form of multiple religious belonging, syncretism, and serial belonging has both a broad scope and significant ubiquity. Religious hybridity does not simply mean that one belongs formally to two or more distantly related religious traditions, but also that one might "belong" to various forms of a single tradition; that one might espouse adherence to a particular tradition as expressed through formal worship or ritual, but privately practice a tradition or traditions derived from the blending of the formal, "high" tradition with indigenous and other unrelated traditions; or that one may through time move seamlessly from one tradition to another, carrying beliefs and practices from previous traditions into the present and future, producing a kind of amalgam derived from one's religious journey, while never having consciously stepped outside of a particular tradition.[2] The situation is clearly not simple. Moreover, given that all religious traditions are inculturated to some degree, religious hybridity is a salient characteristic of all religious belonging. It is in these complex senses that multiple religious identities and belonging are a simple fact of history.

The Wiley Blackwell Companion to Inter-Religious Dialogue, First Edition. Edited by Catherine Cornille.
© 2013 John Wiley & Sons Ltd. Published 2020 by John Wiley & Sons Ltd.

This does not, however, mean that the concept of religious hybridity is not contested. The category of hybridity, when it is limited merely to a description of the historical record of religion is indeed true, perhaps even obviously so. However, when the category is held to be explanatory or possibly normative, rather than merely descriptive, hybridity, and its close correlate syncretism, is the locus of much debate and strong feeling. Indeed religious syncretism, under which much of the debate around multiple religious belonging has occurred, at least in the West, has aroused a great deal of suspicion and opprobrium since the sixteenth century and continues to be a highly charged label today. In what follows, then, I will consider religious hybridity under the label of syncretism, highlighting how syncretism has become a largely pejorative and problematic term for a broader understanding of religious mixing, before proposing a model of dialogue which leverages syncretism for the purposes of continuing the conversation of religions. Before doing so, however, we should try to distinguish, as much as possible, religious hybridity and syncretism.

Syncretism and Hybridity

Religious hybridity cannot be divorced from the long history of syncretism. The terms are often used interchangeably and in general there is little to distinguish them for the lay person or indeed for many scholars of religion. Both terms clearly imply a blending or mixture which is held to cross some natural or artificial conceptual boundary. Their similarity in this regard is more important than their differences. However, some significant distinctions between the terms can be isolated. Syncretism, as we shall see below, has an indelible political and social aspect whereas hybridity tends to be associated with individual identity and also, due to its roots in biology, nineteenth century notions of race and desire (Young 1995). The term hybrid derives, of course, primarily from its biological roots: a hybrid is the offspring of two different species or varieties of plant or animal, such as the offspring of a tame sow and a wild boar (Latin: *hibrida*); and the idea of religious hybridity does not stray far from metaphors of licit or illicit interbreeding and mongrelization. Syncretism, on the other hand, is connected to communities and their common faith or beliefs, wherein the importance of purity and fidelity becomes paramount. In this context a syncretistic community has become impure or apostate due to their falling away from the "true, pure" faith into a false and dirty mixture of "foreign" beliefs. Moreover, while both terms spring from the complex negotiations of cultural encounter – hybridity carrying with it the more recent history of globalism and empire with syncretism no less the result of the clash of (admittedly older) civilizations – syncretism has been more overtly connected to religion than the modern notion of hybridity.

More recently, particularly in fields such as anthropology and sociology, hybridity seems to have shed itself of many of its overtly negative associations and has become much more useful as a descriptor of certain forms of cultural encounter (Stewart 1999: 45). In the case of postcolonial studies, largely due to the work of Homi Bhabha and others in the subaltern collective, far from being denigrated, hybridity is championed as a form of resistance against colonialism's project of domination and effacement

(Bhabha 1994: 37). Such a rapprochement is not, however, the case for the concept of syncretism, which for many still connotes nothing more than a theological muddle in need of anti-syncretistic purification (Stewart 1999: 54). The long use of the term as a pejorative has proven difficult to discharge. Not only has it indelibly marked theological discussion (as we shall see below) it has also stained nonreligious disciplines in the social sciences and humanities such that some scholars have argued that the term is no longer capable of any valuable analytic work (Baird 1991: 59–71). I would suggest, however, that a rehabilitation of syncretism is both possible and desirable. As I noted above, the historical record shows religious blending to be a straightforward fact. How we theorize such mixing is thus both crucially important as well as irrelevant: the latter because religious mixing does not depend on adequate theorization to proceed, the former because an adequate understanding of religious encounter, perhaps paradigmatically in inter-religious dialogue, will require a cogent analysis of syncretism. The promise of such a theory is that it may be leveraged to the service of inter-religious dialogue, as I will show in the second part of this chapter.

Given the complex and overlapping nature of hybridity and syncretism, and their common interchangeable usage, in what follows I propose to take a more "ecumenical" attitude towards the concept of syncretism, allowing it to encompass (at least in the area of religion) inculturation, accommodation, transformation, synthesis, absorption, amalgamation, bricolage, hybridity, and so on. The benefit of adopting this broad usage is not merely heuristic, but rather an attempt to encompass the variety of positive and negative associations of the varieties of religious blending prior to introducing a model of interstitiality aimed at moving the conversation of religions beyond any syncretistic impasse.

Much of the modern antipathy towards syncretism derives from the legacy of sixteenth-century Protestant theological controversies (Leopold and Jensen 2005). Reformed theology considered syncretism to be a capitulation to paganism, and though there are some notable exceptions, particularly in the Roman Catholic traditions, European and American Christianity has been on the whole anti-syncretistic (and thus skeptical about religious mixing and by extension inter-religious dialogue) ever since. Like the term "religion," syncretism is also a somewhat slippery term. It derives from the Greek *synkretismos* which referred to the Cretan practice of banding together despite their differences against a common enemy. Plutarch, commonly credited with the first published use of the term, writes:

> Then this further must be born in mind and guarded against when differences arise among brothers: we must be careful especially at such time to associate familiarly with our brothers' friends, but avoid and shun intimacy with their enemies, imitating in this point, at least, the practice of the Cretans, who, though they often quarreled with and warred against each other, made up their differences and united when outside enemies attacked; and this it was which they called "syncretism" (Plutarch 1939: 313).

This generally positive view of syncretism is recapitulated in the sixteenth century by Erasmus (1466–1536) and Georg Calixtus (1586–1656) in an effort to both bring conflicting Christian sects together as well as to reconcile Christian and non-Christian thought. Calixtus in particular sought to bring Aristotelian philosophy into the service of Christian theology, much as Aquinas had done centuries before. Indeed, both thinkers' pro-syncretistic stance was aimed at re-establishing a universal view of truth capable of uniting all people. But both the humanism of their project as well as its ecumenical aims engendered strongly anti-syncretistic responses. Calixtus was charged with a kind of secular opportunism in his pro-Catholic ecumenism, and Erasmus's generally positive view towards non-Christian traditions was seen as dangerously close to a validation of paganism. The post reformation hypersensitivity to anything seen as potentially undermining the strongly atomistic individuality and autonomy of Protestantism made syncretism appear to be weakness at best, and heresy at worst. The theological die was cast decisively against anything that moved in the direction of syncretism, a position which continues to reflect much of Protestant and Evangelical theology and which held sway in Roman Catholic tradition until the postcolonial period.

While theological prejudice in Europe worked against syncretism, Roman Catholicism consciously employed syncretism in their missionary efforts. Several orders of missionaries to "the new world" sought to convert the indigenous people through adapting Christianity to local cultures. Famously, the Jesuits Francis Xavier and Mateo Ricci accepted Japanese and Chinese customs, rites and ancestor worship in an effort to convert the local Japanese lords and Chinese officials. In 1622 Rome directed its missionaries, through the Congregation for the Propagation of the Faith,[3] to accept indigenous priests along with their customs and syncretized religious practices. By the eighteenth century, however, these syncretistic efforts had been thoroughly overturned. Only at the Second Vatican Council did the Roman Catholic Church officially accept the indigenization of Christian doctrine in non-European cultures, though the term syncretism in this regard is still met with suspicion.

In the academic study of religion, the idea of syncretism is no less ambivalent than in theology. Owing much to the ascendancy of Hegelian views of history, the use of the term syncretism in the history of religions began in the nineteenth century as a way to define Hellenism as a hybrid of Greek and Roman culture. In this mode, syncretism relied on the Hegelian synthetic ideal and duly took on the role of handmaid to the ascendancy of Geist. As an analytic tool, syncretism could thus interrogate the genetic traces of a mixed culture as exemplified in Hellenism, while pointing towards the transcending of these traces in history. The same power to bring to light the genealogy of a concept also allowed syncretism later to be used as an analytic tool to cast suspicion on dominant meta-narratives, highlighting their constructed nature and thus allowing their possible dissolution. However, despite the apparent analytic utility of the idea for the academic study of religion, syncretism still struggles to shake its negative, theologically derived reputation.

Syncretism has thus largely met with theological scorn and academic frustration. In the context of inter-religious dialogue as a form of religious encounter, syncretism has generally fared no better, having been influentially defined as the "incorporation by a religious tradition of beliefs and practices incompatible with its basic insights" (Vroom 1989: 26). Associating syncretism, and by extension other forms of religious mixing or blending, with incompatibility clearly prejudices its value and usefulness as an analytic category and, I suggest, greatly limits the possibilities of inter-religious dialogue. As I will show below, inter-religious dialogue leverages the dialectics of meta-phor to create new meaning and shared references. This is an ideal locus for the reha-bilitation of syncretism as inter-religious metaphors can create novel, hybrid, or syncretistic religious references. Far from being a pejorative then, syncretism/hybridity turns out to be a clear and accurate category for understanding the creation of liminal space afforded by inter-religious dialogue and thus contributes to a cogent and useful theory of religious encounter.

A New Model of Dialogue and Hybridity: Interstitial Theology

We come now to a new model for religious hybridity and inter-religious dialogue. What I have elsewhere called interstitial theology is *a mode or methodology for the comparative philosophy of religion which exploits the structure of metaphor* (as given in interactionist theories of metaphor such as Ricoeur's) *and aims at the construction of liminal, hybrid perspectives or standpoints for continuing the conversation of religions in a creative and open-ended way.* The natural hybridity of religious belonging and the dialectic of metaphor inherent in conversations across boundaries are here used to develop a new hermeneu-tic or model for inter-religious dialogue. Interstitial theology is thus a form of cross-cultural philosophy which seeks to consciously hybridize elements of disparate traditions to better articulate the religious location of many people living in pluralistic societies. Additionally, by developing a fluid and dynamic liminal space through syncretizing theological positions, interstitial theology leverages hybridity to create living bridges between religious traditions in the service of inter-religious dialogue. The model I am here proposing consciously but carefully encourages hybridization for inter-religious dialogue: it is a pluralizing program of dialogue which fosters difference but, as I will argue, does so without denigrating identity.

Interstitial theology is built on two pillars: a mitigated version of the incommensu-rability thesis and the interactionist view of metaphor afforded by Paul Ricoeur and others. To understand how interstitial theology creates liminal hybrid positions from and for inter-religious dialogue, it will be useful to briefly describe these pillars here.

The incommensurability thesis is one of the major philosophical arguments against inter-religious dialogue in general. Some critics of inter-religious dialogue argue that the lives, beliefs, and practices of adherents from different religious traditions are so different in their basic world views or conceptual schemes that there is no substantial basis on which to make any comparisons between them at all (Milbank 1990). This radical view of incommensurability is difficult to maintain in the face of the historical record of the origins of religious traditions as well as the ongoing hybrid character of new religious movements, but it also risks committing what Ben Ami Scharfstein has called the contextualist fallacy, whereby whenever two or more theories or ideas are held to be non-comparable, asking just what the decisive differences might be exempli-fies the kinds of comparisons which the incommensurabilist holds are impossible (Scharfstein 1989: 88). However the incommensurability thesis is applied, it cannot mean absolute incomparability: some more mitigated form must be used. But stipulat-ing this weaker version of incommensurability is not as easy as it might at first appear.

The thesis itself appears in various guises in various discourses, applied to all kinds of things: attitudes, beliefs, judgments, conceptions, propositions, claims, and interpretations, as well as practices and manners of behavior, have all been held to be incommensurable in some sense. The thesis seems to be both central and polymorphic. It supplies one focus for a wider movement in late twentieth-century thought in the West, corresponding to what Richard Bernstein calls a "pervasive amorphous mood . . . of deconstruction, destabilization, rupture, and fracture – of resistance to all forms of *abstract* totality, universalism, and rationalism" (Bernstein 1994: 85). However, we should be careful to note that the incommensurability thesis cannot be applied too broadly. In the context of religion it applies at the level of theoretical statements about religious beliefs and practices and not to the experienced religious lives of the adherents themselves. It is inappropriate, I suggest, to say, for instance, that the life *in toto* of a devout Muslim is incommensurable with that of a practicing Daoist. What may prove to be incommensurable are their particular beliefs as expressed in their respective "theologies," but it is difficult to see how their lives *as such* are incommensurable. Someone might make the unreflective assertion that one person's life shares no common standards of comparison with another person's, but surely whatever is *meant* by this claim it is not the experienced being-in-time-and-space of the two people. Rather, what is held to be incommensurable are the principles or beliefs which those lives are held to express. Incommensurability is a function of theories or meta-level statements, not the series of events – the phenomena – themselves. I do not wish to set up a hard or impermeable distinction between the phenomenal level of experience and the meta-level of explanation or interpretation – the two are intrinsically related – but it is nevertheless important to maintain this distinction since it keeps us from sliding into the view that modes of human existence or being-in-the-world can strictly be incommensurable, a view which too easily devolves to solipsism.

Without analyzing all of the issues surrounding the incommensurability thesis, I will propose a mitigated form of it for our purposes which, I will argue, we can accept as one basis of interstitial theology. One can describe as incommensurable:

> the aporetic situation where two or more distinct theories or sets of meta-level statements share no prima facie significant common standards by which they can be compared or judged and by which the aporia can be resolved.

How this version of the thesis applies to inter-religious dialogue and hybridity can be seen through thinking about religion as language. Thinking about religion as language could be understood as a privileged metaphorical category used to define religions, since doing so coincides with the nature of religious language as expressions of the beliefs and practices of religious adherents. Religion as language takes advantage of the nature of religious language to understand the traditions themselves. All religious knowledge is expressed in particular languages. This affords us a very useful analytic tool with which to compare and contrast religious traditions. But of course the religious languages of the various traditions differ, both in terms of the natural languages in which they are expressed and also the meta-level rules, the grammars, which they follow. This is where the notion of a mitigated incommensurability helps us understand the dynamics of inter-religious dialogue. The kinds of translational pressures arising from any cross-cultural communication reflect the mitigated incommensurability I am promoting. As Wittgenstein showed, there are no private languages and thus any strict form of the incommensurability thesis cannot be admitted, making it impossible for two languages to be mutually untranslatable in principle (Wittgenstein 2001: §243–271). The not insignificant problems of translation between languages are thus always due to failures on the part of the translator, but these failures are understandable given the holistic nature of languages and indeed religious traditions. There may be sets of state-ments which translators find very difficult to provide with a one-to-one correspondence with the translated language, just as there may be aspects of religious traditions which participants in inter-religious dialogue find difficult to square with the other and may thus consider "incompatible." The risk is often one of denuding a translated statement of its context and thus possibly denaturing it. But this difficulty does not mean that the traditions are impossible to bring into fruitful conversation with one another, or indeed that the meaning of a statement in one tradition cannot be understood by someone in another tradition. The mitigated incommensurability of languages allows for mutual translation and comparison but crucially does not give specific content to those transla-tions, that is it does not determine the nature of the translations themselves or their success. Mitigated incommensurability ensures, then, that a set of statements together defining the scope of a religious tradition must have at least some overlap with a set of statements derived from another religious tradition, but also admits that parts of these sets may not necessarily overlap. The degree of the overlap will always be contingent on the skills, purposes, and conditions of the translator working between these sets. As we shall see, the location and role of the hybrid religious adherent is thus not dissimilar to that of a skillful translator.

So the form of mitigated incommensurability expressed through the metaphor of religions as languages leaves us with one of the pillars of interstitial theology: that is a limit to the alterity between religious traditions, under-determination of the specific nature of the overlap between the traditions, and an admission of the role of the "trans-lator" in the process of inter-religious dialogue. The second pillar of interstitial theology must now provide some indication of how the specific content of the dialogue can be understood and for that I develop a version of the interactionist theory of metaphor afforded by Paul Ricoeur and others.

Ricoeur delineates his account in his influential work *La Métaphore Vive*, translated into English as *The Rule of Metaphor* (Ricoeur 1977). George Steiner commended the publication of the book as "an attempt to bring into collaborative congruence the Anglo-American tradition of linguistic philosophy and poetics . . . with the main axes of French linguistic and structural thought. The attempted conjunction leads, in turn, towards the German hermeneutic synthesis . . ." (Steiner 1975: 879). The principal concern of *The Rule of Metaphor* is with how metaphor is central to the creation of meaning in language. Indeed, the single overriding question of the eight chapters or "studies" in this work, one which theorists up until then had left unresolved, is: "that of the creation of meaning, for which newly created metaphors are the evidence" (Ricoeur 1977: 4). Ricoeur thus identifies metaphor as the central semantic generator in language. He is interested in metaphoric function rather than metaphor as a figure.

Ricoeur argues, furthermore, that metaphor not only impels us towards the creation of new meaning but also allows us to supply adequate philosophical tools to understand them (Gerhart 1995: 217). Metaphor is thus a semantic generator as well as a hermeneutic tool. This double life of metaphor is what I wish to exploit in interstitial theology. Metaphors will be used in the process of inter-religious dialogue as well as providing the philosophical tools to understand what is going on in inter-religious dialogue and the production of religious hybridity. Interstitial theology is, therefore, a mode of conversation between people of disparate religious and cultural backgrounds *as well as* a hermeneutic for these conversations.

Since Ricoeur defines metaphor in various ways throughout *The Rule of Metaphor*,[4] let us accept Janet Soskice's definition of metaphor with the understanding that it agrees with Ricoeur's but is put in a more concise way. Metaphor is thus "speaking of one thing in terms which are seen to be suggestive of another" (Soskice 1985: 49). Two things can be noted from this definition. Firstly, there is a single referent, though two "things" are involved in the metaphor. Secondly, metaphors are figures of speech which bring into constructive tension minimally two semantic units or subjects[5] in a metaphorical utterance (Ricoeur 1976: 50). This is the aspect of metaphor which is most interesting from the point of view of dialogue and hybridity. Metaphor's constructive tension is brought about by the simultaneous affirmation and denial of a resemblance which borders on identity. Ricoeur describes metaphor as "presenting in an *open* fashion, by means of a conflict *between* identity and difference, the process that, in a *covert* manner, generates semantic grids by fusion of difference *into* identity" (Ricoeur 1977: 198). Let us first consider the negative side of metaphor – the denial of resemblance resulting in what I shall term *categorial transgression*. Taking one of the many examples from the Semitic traditions, God is sometimes referred to as a shepherd (Genesis 48: 15; Psalm 23: 1). This is clearly an illogical attribution. Whatever is meant by the word "God" in the Hebrew and Christian Bibles, it is certainly not literally a shepherd. "God" and "shepherd" are terms coming from different genera. A literal interpretation would commit an error on the level of what Gilbert Ryle called a category mistake (Ricoeur 1976: 51), like saying "Wednesday is fat" to use Wittgenstein's example. But clearly, more is going on here than a mere accident of naming – a predicate is being applied to God. The impertinent predication of metaphor creates a tension between the two terms of the utterance, and out of this tension the reader is pushed towards a new meaning – making sense out of apparent nonsense. Ricoeur describes this *production out of tension* as a "self destruction" or "transformation" of the literal meanings of the terms into metaphorical ones (1976: 50). But how are the meanings of the terms transformed, and in this transformation are the literal meanings annihilated? Refining his account, Ricoeur answers that at the level of the statement, what are brought into constructive tension are the literal and metaphorical *interpretations* of the utterance:

> What we have just called the tension in a metaphorical utterance is really not something that occurs between two terms in the utterance, but rather between two opposing interpretations of the utterance. It is the conflict between these two interpretations that sustains the metaphor (Ricoeur 1976: 50).

For there to be a conflict between literal and metaphorical interpretations, both (that is both terms and both interpretations) must be simultaneously maintained – neither is subsumed by the other. The literal interpretation therefore is *not* lost. This is an important characteristic of metaphor for interstitial theology – religious hybridity or syncretism developed on the basis of interstitial theology avoids effacing its religious sources, their traces remain in the hybrid. So the denial of resemblance in metaphor, the negative pole of its dialectic, initiates a tension between two interpretations of the statement. This tension, the felt result of a contradiction or absurdity (categorial transgression), pushes the reader towards a "kind of work of meaning – which following Beardsley, we [call] a metaphorical twist – thanks to which the utterance begins to make sense" (Ricoeur 1976: 51). The metaphorical twist introduces a reconciliation which is the second, positive pole of the metaphorical dialectic: the apprehension of resemblance.

The substitution theory of metaphor, harkening back to its supposed Aristotelian pedigree, saw resemblance as a prerequisite for the substitution. One traded a metaphorical term for an ordinary one based on some previously perceived resemblance between the two. Interstitial theology, following Ricoeur's interactionist analysis, reverses this order. In the context of mitigated incommensurability and after the negative pole of the metaphorical dialectic temporarily divides the two interpretations, creating between them a gap of absurdity or incompatibility, the work of resemblance fills in this rift. A hitherto hidden similarity emerges as a result of metaphor: "two previously distant classes are here suddenly brought together and the work of resemblance consists precisely in this bringing together of what once was distant" (Ricoeur 1976: 51). So something new is disclosed in metaphor. A novel relationship is revealed: "a semantic innovation which has no status in already established language and which only exists because of the attribution of an unusual or an unexpected predicate" (Ricoeur 1976: 52). The negative–positive movement of this dialectic works in concert, sustaining the metaphor through ceaselessly moving in a hermeneutic spiral – a "spiral" rather than a circle because the dialectic is ultimately aimed at a liminal referent. When the dialectical movement stops the metaphor dies, it becomes lexicalized – that is, it becomes a commonplace, devoid of the power to shock or surprise, an accustomed part of the semantic background of a language and an accretion to the polysemy of words. Live metaphors on the other hand retain their inventiveness, they are wellsprings of new meanings, or semantic generators. Ricoeur suggests that metaphors' power to create new meanings is probably limitless (Ricoeur 1977: 95).

We now have the two pillars of interstitial theology. Mitigated incommensurability makes possible the creation of a hybrid, liminal, or interstitial position between religions while underdetermining the exact nature of their mutual translation, while the interactionist theory of metaphor explains how, in the process of mutual translation, metaphor creates novel semantic entities, giving content to the hybrid, liminal position. Let us now move on to describe, however briefly, exactly how interstitial theology creates this liminal, religiously hybrid position.

If we apply Ricoeur's interactionist structure of metaphor to the task of constructing an interstitial theology, we might begin by provisionally setting elements of the two traditions beside one another as two poles of a metaphor. But which elements? How does one decide which elements of a religious tradition can be used and whether this can be done without the elements thereby irredeemably losing their sense? On Ricoeur's interactionist view, a metaphor is realized only in the wider context of sentences or statements in contrast to the traditional, Aristotelian, substitution view of metaphor which saw it as primarily a matter of replacing one word with another, more redolent one, in order to achieve a rhetorical effect. We must look to broaden our theological contexts. This means that one cannot extract single theological ideas, word-like, out of their environments. The poles of our inter-religious metaphor must be analogous to statements, that is, they must appear within their proximate semantic contexts. There will indeed be a center or focus to each pole of the metaphor but this focus is only constituted within and through a frame – its wider context.

So our analysis dictates that the poles of the metaphor should be conglomerations made up of a more or less central idea plus the proximate notions which make up its context and by which we understand its wider meaning. Of course the interdependent nature of theological concepts makes the semantic context potentially limitless, however in practice there is, I suggest, a vanishing point where we can draw a boundary around an idea's associated notions. Following Gadamer, this extension of associated commonplaces might be called an idea's *horizon*. Some might argue that just where one draws this boundary will be too arbitrary, but this fear can be allayed if we remember that the outer limits of any horizon, semantic or otherwise, will always be indistinct and movable (Gadamer 1993: 245). Just what is included in a particular horizon will depend on the vision of its "seer." Similarly the outer limits of the semantic horizon of any given metaphor will depend on the metaphor's poet, that is the skilled, hybrid translator. This limitation is assumed in any creative product and should not overly concern us here. It reflects the particularity or locality of production and this is no grave limitation for interstitial theology. My main point here is that our inter-religious metaphor will not involve single elements of a theology but will put into a productive tension clusters of interrelated theological "conglomerates" which themselves, by virtue of their scope, will reflect an aspect, or aspects, of religious life. In this way the metaphorical model avoids the problem of destroying a notion's sense by extracting it from its context. In the process of metaphor whole contexts come into play.

The demand to supply our metaphor with clusters rather than individual elements also points to a way of overcoming the problem of choosing which theological aggregates to put into tension. When two theological horizons are combined in a metaphor there will ordinarily exist some degree of indeterminacy. By virtue of the wide scope and the interconnectedness of a theological horizon, the inter-animation between poles of the metaphor may produce metaphorical twists between components of the horizons which we could not predict. What we hope to happen in a metaphor may not. In choosing to bring together two particular theological horizons we may unwittingly bring together two *altogether different* ones. This characteristic of the interactionist view of metaphor does not provide a solution to the question of finding criteria for choosing theological horizons so much as it eludes the problem altogether. Using any theological horizon opens the doors to the others since *at some level* all the horizons are related. This interrelation constitutes living religious traditions and is one way in which traditions are defined. What the metaphorical model of interreligious theologizing does, in effect, is bring together – in the form of their associated theologies – segments, sides, or aspects of the whole complex body of religious life. The syncretism of religious traditions in metaphor involves the horizons of each tradition through the vehicle of a particular metaphor. So we begin metaphorical inter-religious theologizing, that is interstitial theology, not by choosing which doctrines or ideas to hybridize, but by tying together large sections of complete religious traditions. Syncretism here transcends its historical pejorative connotations by doing the "heavy lifting" in this new model of inter-religious dialogue.

Now that we have the poles of our metaphor, how will the process of metaphor work and what will it produce? On Ricoeur's view, metaphors are generators of meaning, and our inter-religious metaphor will produce part of a hybrid, inter-religious theology. This will not be just another evocative way of comparing religions: the creative force of metaphor will produce *de novo* a dynamic source of meaning – one which, like a change in models, opens up other new and potentially fruitful theological avenues. The metaphorical model does this, moreover, without doing violence to the traditions, since in metaphor the literal signification of the poles is required and conserved. Therefore, an inter-religiously hybrid metaphor will, if it is a real, living metaphor, maintain the particularity and distinctive nature of the religious traditions it brings together.

As I mentioned earlier, categorial transgression plays an important part in inter-religious theologizing. A tension is created when two traditions are put in a metaphorical dialectic where resemblance is simultaneously affirmed and denied. Categorial transgression will therefore obtain since each tradition exists as its own cultural linguistic class – its own distinct form of life. The boundary between the two is not impermeable, as critics of religious hybridity would have us believe, but can be breached by the dialectic of metaphor. What incommensurabilists, anti-syncretists and hybridity skeptics see as an obstacle for inter-religious theology, the metaphorical model capitalizes on and indeed requires.

The back-and-forth hermeneutic circle inherent in metaphor functions to transform its poles. Each pole is "seen as" or rather *seen through* the other. An aspect of a Hindu tradition, for example, is seen through the context of a Christian tradition and vice versa. The Hindu pole thus becomes Christian and the Christian Hindu, yet in themselves they remain the same. It is only within the relation of metaphor that the transformation is achieved. This synthetic recombination is the hybridizing power of interstitial theology.

This metaphorical interplay or "twist" also reveals resemblances which were previously hidden, and temporarily brackets or hides other aspects of each pole's horizon. Resemblance is not here a prerequisite for metaphor, but rather a result of it. This means that a great many combinations of the two traditions can be brought into metaphorical tension. One does not have to bring together analogous theories of God, or analogous doctrines of salvation. The only limitations on the metaphor will be the skills of its poet-philosopher-translator.

The transformational creativity of metaphor results in a redescription of each tradition in terms of the other. It is in this redescription that interstitial theology will gain its reference to the world and its claim to viability. The question of reference is a large one and a full discussion of it is beyond the scope of this chapter. We must, however, consider how interstitial theology is connected to the way people actually live.

Ricoeur views metaphorical redescription as the partial creation of possible worlds (Ricoeur 1977: 218). Metaphors allow us to refer beyond our own experience to a created narrative world. With this in mind, I suggest that inter-religious metaphors refer to the space in between the poles of the metaphor. This interstitial space is what Mark Kline Taylor refers to as the *liminal* world (Taylor 1986: 36–51). In the dialectic between the poles of metaphor, a shaky ground of newly created common significations is slowly built up. This ground is always being broken down, patched up, and re-examined by the force and flux created by the dialectic of metaphor. This liminal world – the collection of shared references making up Ricoeur's re-described possible world – is not a new Archimedean common ground, but a *mobile plane of intersection, a locus hibrida*, sustained by the metaphorical encounter. It is a boundary phenomenon, a shoreline, created between and at the edges of religious traditions, synthesized out of materials taken from both. It is, in effect, a bridge or framework upon which the conversation of religions can take place. But more than just conversation, since, as Homi Bhabha argues (1994), this liminal space is also the font of possible *critique* of dominant traditions which all too easily efface the subaltern. The hybrid, liminal interstice is, even in the context of overweening and brutal colonial power, always *there*, always present as a shadow reflection, a strange mimesis of the dominant power. Its role as the Other can be a powerful antidote to the excesses of domination since the hybrid is always *both-and*: it is both itself and the other, and, as we shall see, in its combination of identity-in-difference, hybridity *per se* becomes a potent foundation for inter-religious dialogue. This area of shared reference, the liminal world, will be manifested in the "body" of a hybrid religious tradition. In this way the hybrid religious tradition will be the result of interstitial theology, as well as the locus for further interstitial theological work. It thus shows a dual character: it is liminal, shifting, and dynamic with respect to its metaphorical creation out of its parent traditions, but it will also be a relatively stable ground on which people can abide and further the process of religious conversations.

"Conversation" is indeed a particularly good model for our understanding of interstitial production. Consider, for example, a conversation between a Christian and a Hindu (I will leave for now the question of what kind of Christian and Hindu). Each of them brings to the conversation their own histories, aesthetic preferences, social structures, notions of propriety, moral and epistemic commitments – in short each brings their own particular way of being in the world – a particular way of *seeing-as*. Let us further assume that they each desire to communicate with and learn from the other and that they share enough of each other's languages for their purposes. The metaphorical nature of conversation allows them to create a hybrid area of reference in the liminal world between them. The flux of question and answer, of comment and clarification, of graciousness and criticism, which takes place during the conversation constitutes the metaphorical structure of their communication. It is not difficult to imagine them coming to one or many "Aha!" experiences, when some idea has finally become clear, when the negative shaking of heads comes to a temporary end, when some understanding of the Other occurs. In this way, slowly, communication takes place and the conversants are able to extend their experience. The Hindu comes to a realization, albeit rudimentary, of how this particular Christian experiences the world and vice versa. Furthermore, the conversation can be reflective: through their dialogic encounter with the other, each participant may be alerted to aspects of his/her own self or tradition which were until then perhaps only briefly glimpsed or even undiscovered.

This sort of conversation (often quite rare in reality) is, I suggest, thoroughly metaphorical. Not only are metaphors required of each conversant in order to understand the other, but the conversation as a whole exhibits metaphorical structure. Two people are brought together and interactivate or interanimate one another. Through the conversation each person sees the world through the context of the other('s). The world of each is redescribed and reinterpreted. A mutually shared area of reference, existing necessarily and only in relation to the conversants, is built up in the interstice which separates them. This hybrid, mobile plane of intersection itself, far from achieving any "solidity" as an Archimedean foundation, nonetheless manifests a relative or subjective reality as conversants begin to inhabit this unique, shifting perspective. Over time, and further inhabitation, this liminal, hybrid area of reference becomes a quasi-reified entity as it begins to grow into the body of a recombinant religious tradition. The synthesis is complete when, on pragmatic grounds, sufficient people find a home in this newly created recombinant tradition.

This is where the viability of a recombinant religious tradition will be tested. If sufficient people settle this liminal land, the newly formed recombinant tradition will have been found to be viable. Interstitial theology thus asks pragmatic questions: does the new tradition "speak" to people, does it fill their needs, reflect their unique place between traditions? A viable tradition will retain ties to its parents yet exhibit the open-endedness and novelty which will be its hallmarks, but being pragmatically justified, the viability of a recombinant tradition can only be ascertained after the fact.

I have just described how two or more moderately incommensurable religious traditions can interact through the structure of metaphor to form a new, synthetic hybrid religious tradition existing in the liminal space – the interstice – between them. The actual mode of such production is through the metaphorical dialectic which underlies certain kinds of conversations. These conversations make up the hermeneutic I call interstitial theology. I should note that by "conversation" I do not mean strictly verbal dialogue. Conversation in this context can include other forms of communication, such as the internal dialogue which takes place in careful reading, or the inter-subjective understanding which exists when people work (or play) together harmoniously, or the structural exchange between faith communities in syncretistic inter-religious encounter. The result of these communications is a form of religious hybridity. This area of reference has two aspects: the first is the relative insubstantiality effected by the continuous flux of metaphor; the second is the relative reification which grows as the conversants, and others, choose to take up or inhabit this newly formed hybrid perspective. These two characteristics are each essential in that relative insubtantiality avoids the creation of a false Archimedean vantage point, and relative reification forms some foundation for further conversations as well as a starting point for a possible, continuing, recombinant religious tradition. The growth of a new recombinant tradition will depend on pragmatic considerations: that is, the success with which it reflects the experience of its settlers as well as how it embodies the "truth" for these "pioneers."

Furthermore, the new hybrid religious tradition is synthetic, taking elements from both its parents and thus maintaining continuity with them, as well as manifesting a unique and particular combination of these elements. On a biological model, one can understand this sort of synthesis by considering the creation of new life through (sexual) reproduction. A new entity is formed which is and is not the combination of two parent entities. Within the progeny one can perceive each parent's characteristics as they are transformed by the other's. The recombination is unique, however, so that both continuity and discontinuity are affirmed and embodied in the new cell/tradition. The nature and growth of this interstitial product provides the open-ended next step for inter-religious dialogue – one which overcomes incommensurability, eludes the charge of totalizing, because it is particular to the parent traditions and depends on the skills of its poet(s), and reflects and extends the inherent hybridity of historical religious traditions towards a greater appreciation of unity in difference.

I began this discussion by highlighting the mere factuality of religious mixing in the historical record. It hardly requires argument now to know that religious traditions have always been the result of encounter, blending, distinction, transformation, accommodation, enculturation, syncretism, identification, and the whole panoply of complex negotiations within and without the traditions under consideration. We have come to realise this fact, however, only relatively recently since for the last five hundred years the tension between singularity and diversity has been swayed towards the former. Perhaps the forces of globalism or the incredible speed and reach of communications technology have awoken us to the reality of religious diversity in a new way. However it has come to pass, the problems and promise of religious diversity can no longer be disregarded under the guise of anti-syncretism, nor can the facts of religious mixing be ignored. Inter-religious dialogue, if it is to become a force for the common goods which its proponents value, must first admit the facts of religious blending, hybridity, and syncretism, and moreover find ways to exploit these facts in the service of furthering the conversation of religions. I have argued here for a model of inter-religious dialogue which seeks to do just this. By showing dialogue to trade on the same dialectic as metaphor, room is made for the possibility of inter-religious metaphors. In this way a place is cleared for hybridity/syncretism at the heart of inter-religious dialogue, thus rehabilitating the history of this idea as well as setting loose its considerable power for creativity and discovery. I suggest that it will be only through such creativity that real progress will be made in the conversation of religions.

Notes

1 See, for instance, the Semitic insistence to absolute allegiance to one God against the gods of others in Exodus 20:3.
2 This is, of course, not an exhaustive list of the various varieties of religious hybridity, but rather just a few examples.
3 It should be noted that the impetus for the establishment of this congregation was due as much to protecting the Roman Catholic Church's economic interests as to promoting its theological doctrines against rising Protestant ambitions.

4 Ricoeur presents the various characteristics of metaphor but declines to state a single definition of it. His characteristic mode of discussing a topic is to approach it from many angles and thus build up an understanding of it. In *The Rule of Metaphor* he starts with Aristotle's definition and then successively adds qualifications and addenda as he considers the work of Benveniste, Fontanier, Black, Beardsley, Richards, and others. His use of Fontanier's definition, "to present one idea under the sign of another" (Pierre Fontanier, *Les Figures du discours* (1830) (Paris: Flammarion, 1968) p. 99. *Rule of Metaphor*: 57), as well as his statement of metaphor as, "a work on language consisting in the attribution to logical subjects . . . predicates that are incompossible with them" (from, Ricouer's "On Interpretation," in Alan Montefiore (ed.) *Philosophy in France Today*. Cambridge: Cambridge University Press, 1983: 182), and that metaphor "holds two thoughts of different things together in a simultaneous performance on the stage of a word or a simple expression, whose meaning is the result of their interaction" (*Rule of Metaphor*: 80), suggest that his (working) definition is not significantly different from Soskice's.

5 I agree with Soskice when she cautions against viewing metaphor as always involving two distinct subjects. While even her definition implies two ideas or "networks of association" (*Metaphor and Religious Language*: 49), there are metaphors in which two subjects (in the linguistic sense) are not present. For example, the phrase, "he steamed over the defence's line" does not contain two distinct subject terms but is clearly metaphorical in bringing together the associations of human and rail locomotion.

Bibliography

Baird, Robert. "Syncretism and the History of Religions," *Essays in the History of Religions*. New York: Peter Lang, 1991.

Bernstein, Richard. "Incommensurability and Otherness Revisited," in *Culture and Modernity: East-West Philosophic Perspectives*, ed. Eliot Deutsch. Delhi: Motilal Banarsidass, 1994.

Bhabha, Homi. *The Location of Culture*. London: Routledge, 1994.

Coombes, Annie C. and. Avtar Brah (eds.). *Hybridity and Its Discontents: Politics, Science, Culture*. London: Routledge, 2000.

Douglas, Mary. *Purity and Danger: An Analysis of Concepts of Pollution and Taboo*. London: Routledge Classics, 2002.

Gadamer, Hans Georg. *Truth and Method*, 2nd revised edition. New York: Continuum, 1993.

Gerhart, Mary. "The Live Metaphor," in *The Philosophy of Paul Ricoeur*, ed. Lewis E. Hahn. *The Library of Living Philosophers*, vol. XXII. Chicago and LaSalle Illinois: Open Court, 1995.

Leopold, A.M. and J.S. Jensen (eds.). *Syncretism in Religion: A Reader*. New York: Routledge, 2005.

Milbank, John. "The End of Dialogue," in *Christian Uniqueness Reconsidered: The Myth of a Pluralistic Theology of Religions*, ed. G. D'Costa. Maryknoll, NY: Orbis, 1990.

Peacock, James L. *The Anthropological Lens*. Cambridge: Cambridge University Press, 1986.

Plutarch, *Moralia* vol. 6. Loeb Classical Library edn. Cambridge, MA: Harvard University Press, 1939.

Ricoeur, Paul. *La métaphore vive*. Paris: Éditions du Seuil, 1975.

Ricoeur, Paul. *Interpretation Theory: Discourse and the Surplus of Meaning*. Fort Worth: Texas Christian University Press, 1976.

Ricoeur, Paul. *The Rule of Metaphor: Multidisciplinary Studies of the Creation of Meaning in Language*, trans. Robert Czerny, with Kathleen McLaughlin and John S.J. Costello. Toronto: University of Toronto Press, 1977.

Scharfstein, Ben Ami. "The Contextual Fallacy," in *Interpreting Across Boundaries: New Essays in Comparative Philosophy*, ed. Gerald Larson and Eliot Deutsch. Delhi: Motilal Banarsidass, 1989.

Soskice, Janet Martin. *Metaphor and Religious Language*. Oxford: Clarendon, 1985.

Steiner, George. "Metaphors on the Move," *Times Literary Supplement* 3, 829 (1 Aug, 1975): 879.

Stewart, Charles. "Syncretism and its Synonyms: Reflections on Cultural Mixture," *Diacritics*, 29.3 (1999).

Taylor, Mark Kline. "In Praise of Shaky Ground: the Liminal Christ and Cultural Pluralism," *Theology Today* XLIII (1986).

Vroom, Hendrik. "Syncretism and Dialogue: A Philosophical Analysis," in *Dialogue and Syncretism: An Interdisciplinary Approach*, eds. J.D. Gort, H. Vroom, R. Fernhout, and A. Wessels. Grand Rapids, MI: Eerdmans, 1989.

Wittgenstein, Ludwig. *Philosophical Investigations*. Oxford: Blackwells, 2001.

Young, Robert J.C. *Colonial Desire: Hybridity in Theory, Culture and Race*. London: Routledge, 1995.

CHAPTER 9

Inter-Religious Dialogue and Social Action

Paul F. Knitter

Inter-religious dialogue and social action need each other. This is a rather bold claim, so I want to lay it out as carefully and unpretentiously as possible. I am suggesting not only that inter-religious dialogue and social action have a lot to offer each other. I want to make a case that if inter-religious dialogue and social action do not really get together, something crucial will be missing in how effectively they will be able to realize their goals. They are two distinct enterprises – inter-religious conversation and social engagement; but their very different activities and ideals can be qualitatively enhanced if they would, as it were, join forces.

So first we need to clarify what we are talking about – that is, define our terms. I think the following would be a quite broadly acceptable description of inter-religious dialogue (at least, it is the description that I will be working with): To be engaged in what is called a dialogue among religious believers, one must: a) speak one's own convictions clearly and respectfully; b) listen to the convictions of others openly and generously; c) be open to learning something new and changing one's mind; and, if that happens, d) be prepared to change one's way of acting accordingly. Basically and simply, inter-religious dialogue is a particular instance of the way human beings inter-act in order to render history a movement rather than a repetition: they talk with each other, they challenge each other, they agree and disagree – and so they grow in a fuller understanding of reality, or what is called *truth*.

Social action is used in this essay very broadly. It embraces any activity by which human beings seek to resolve what obstructs and promote what advances, human and environmental flourishing. So we are taking "social" in a sweeping embrace that includes engagement with economics, politics, ecology, gender, sexual, and racial relations – any activity that seeks to do something about the suffering that results when some human beings harm other human beings or the natural world for purposes of their own gain.

The Wiley Blackwell Companion to Inter-Religious Dialogue, First Edition. Edited by Catherine Cornille.
© 2013 John Wiley & Sons Ltd. Published 2020 by John Wiley & Sons Ltd.

So I am saying that when religious people want to engage each other, they need to do so as, or together with, social activists. And social activists need to be, or collaborate with, religious practitioners if they want to effectively do the job they hope to do.

Now, to build my case that religious dialoguers and social activists need each other, I first have to contextualize and then problematize my argument.

Contextualizing: Types of Dialogue and Virtues for Dialogue

Types of inter–religious dialogue

In line with a categorization proposed by the Vatican Council for Interreligious Dialogue (Vatican 1991: 42–43), practitioners and surveyors of inter-religious dialogue generally distinguish three different types:

a) The *dialogue of theology* is based on study, the attempt to understand one another's beliefs, doctrines, and teachings. This will usually call for reading each other's sacred texts, which, to do well, requires the learning of one another's languages. This is the kind of dialogue in which we try to get our *heads* straight – that is, our concepts correct, our misunderstandings adjusted.

b) The *dialogue of spirituality* seeks to go deeper – to the experiences that give rise to, or are brought about by, the beliefs. In this dialogue we try to appreciate, maybe even share, the feelings that religious people have when they practice their rituals and tell their stories. In this dialogue, participants seek to bring their *hearts* into sync with each other. Mystics are the experts at this kind of dialogue.

c) The *dialogue of action* is where participants get their *hands* dirty – but they do so together. In this dialogue, religious people act together to confront and resolve common problems. This is the kind of dialogue that is the focus of this essay.

d) (A fourth kind of dialogue is often added: the *dialogue of life* – the interaction that takes place when people from different religions live in the same neighborhood. Since it is less intentional than the other forms, I have not included it.)

Virtues necessary for inter–religious dialogue

The editor of this volume, Catherine Cornille, recently published a book that has broadly helped to settle the dust of previous disagreement and to open new paths amid the often dead-end debates about which of the "models of theologies of religions" make the most sense: Exclusivism, Inclusivism, or Pluralism (Knitter 2002; Race 1983). In her *The Im-Possibility of Interreligious Dialogue* (2008), rather than entering the academic combat about theology and models, Cornille steps back and lists what she believes are the necessary *virtues* that anyone who wants to dialogue has to practice. She offers a kind of "virtue ethics" for dialogue. There are five such virtues, which I will try to describe as succinctly and accurately as possible:

a) *Humility:* Inter-religious dialoguers are simply not going to be able to do what
    they want to do unless they are *humble* about what they already know through
    their own religion. Dialogue is stymied before it takes off unless all participants
    admit to themselves that no matter how much they have discovered in their own
    traditions, *there is always more to know*. Cornille calls this "doctrinal humility":
    as true as any religious doctrine or belief may be, it can never be the whole truth.
    Religions deal with divine or transcendent truth. No human mind or system can
    contain the fullness of such truth. Few, if any, religions would contest this claim
    (Cornille 2008: 9–58).

b) *Commitment:* But for inter-religious dialogue to be successful, all the partici-
    pants have to hold firm to, and have to be held firm by, the truth they *do* possess
    through their religious traditions. Dialogue is not chit-chat. It is not just trading
    information. It is truth that matters, and matters not just for me, but also for
    you. So my commitment to my own beliefs will inspire and require me not just
    to *explain* them to you, but to *witness* them to you. I want to persuade you to
    share in the liberating truth that I have experienced (*ibid.*: 59–94).

c) *Trust in Interconnectedness:* Within the rooted commitments of all participants
    in inter-religious dialogue, all of them have to also trust that, despite the depth
    of their commitments and despite the often incommensurable difference between
    religious perspectives, there is "something" that makes it possible for religious
    believers to understand each other and to challenge each other. If, as is often
    heard, the religions of the world are "apples and oranges" and cannot be com-
    pared, inter-religious dialoguers insist that they are all interconnected in their
    natures as *fruit*. Being fruit, they can relate to, and understand, one another.
    This is not to say where or how to find this "fruit-fulness." But it does affirm the
    need to trust that it exists (*ibid.*: 95–136).

d) *Empathy:* This virtue signals the need for inter-religious dialogue to be personal,
    even intimate. While we are rooted in our own commitments, we also have to,
    somehow, get inside the commitments of our dialogue partners. We have to try
    to understand them not just with the clarity of our minds but also with the
    sensitivity of our hearts. That requires a goodly amount of "letting go," of allow-
    ing your imagination to lead you into new space. Empathy is the energy that
    animates what theologians of dialogue have called the process of "passing over"
    into another tradition's symbols, stories, and practices, and then "passing back"
    to see what difference this experience of the other makes for the understanding
    of one's own (*ibid.*: 137–176).

e) *Hospitality:* This virtue is pivotal among all the others. Cornille calls it "the sole
    sufficient condition for dialogue" (*ibid.*: 177). Simply, but challengingly, it means
    that if we invite other believers into our own religious home as guests, then we
    will not be good hosts, real hosts, unless we are genuinely open to the gifts that
    they bring us. We have to be *open* to receiving gifts of truth and insight that are
    new, different, and perhaps in tension with our own. Hospitality is really the
    flip-side of humility: if we realize that we can never claim the last word of God's
    truth, we have to be eagerly open to receiving more of that truth from others.
    What is *really* different from what we believe may be a needed addition to, or

correction for, what we already believe. Hospitality makes dialogue exciting, but also threatening. Unless we are truly open to being threatened, we are not going to be able to dialogue (*ibid.*: 177–210).

Problematizing: The Subjugation of the Particular by the Universal

Inter-religious dialogue – practiced in different types and requiring a check-list of virtues – is held up by many (including the contributors to this book) as urgent and promising. But it can also be dangerous and harmful – maybe even more harmful than promising. That is the warning that has come to be identified as a *fourth model* for a theological understanding of other religions. It has been dubbed with sundry names: the "postliberal" approach; or the attitude of "acceptance"; or simply and neatly, *particularism* (Knitter 2002: 173–237; Tilley 2007: 110–125; Hill-Fletcher 2008: 51–81; Hedges 2010: 146–196). Whatever the name, this is an assessment of religious plural-ism that seeks to bring theologians and dialoguers into resonance with the conscious-ness and concerns of *postmodernity*. I suggest that the postmodern critique of inter-religious dialogue boils down to this announcement: *the particular trumps the universal.* Or: *the dominance of diversity obstructs the possibility of commonality.* Again, as briefly as possible, let me try to lay out the ways this postliberal or postmodern particu-larist view problematizes, maybe even blocks, the very possibility of inter-religious dialogue.

Particularists remind all theologians of religions or practitioners of dialogue of something that should be self-evident: everything we see is determined by where we live. To look anywhere is to do so from somewhere. That "somewhere" is the culture (which includes our religion) in which we have been born. Therefore, when we appeal to "the facts, nothing but the facts," we have to remind ourselves that those facts never come naked; they are never "nothing but," for they are always dressed in, or *interpreted* by, our cultural attitudes and presuppositions. We do not first experience or know something and then try to find words or concepts to express it; rather, we start with the words or convictions of our culture, and they determine what we experience and know. This is what postmodernists would call the unavoidable "social construction" of all knowledge. Really, such an observation is nothing new. St. Thomas Aquinas was quite postmodern when he declared that "everything that is known is known according to the mode of the knower" (*Summa Theologiae*, 1a, 75,5). But inter-religious dialoguers generally forget that, and do so to their peril.

But the peril is even greater for their dialogue partners, for as the particularists go on to point out, our social conditioning is also an ideological or political conditioning. What we see is not only determined by our own perspective, but also by our inherent desire to preserve and privilege our own perspective. In affirming the truth that we see, we are concomitantly seeking to preserve the *power* that we have. Usually, we are not aware of this; but this is what is going on in all "truth claims." And if we happen to have a lot of power – whether economic or military (they usually go together) – then our truth will probably win out over others who have other truths but less power (Fou-cault 1980).

So if there is validity to the particularist claim that all our efforts to know and under-stand are socially and politically conditioned – including our efforts to know those who come from different cultures and societies – then the particularists draw a daunting conclusion: all universal truth claims, or all attempts to announce what is true always and everywhere for everyone, are inherently, incorrigibly, unavoidably *dangerous*. They are so dangerous that it is best to avoid them. Or in postmodernist jargon: all *meta-narratives* are forbidden, for every narrative that is held up as true for everyone will be formulated by someone who can see only from her own perspectives and is jealous of her own power. More pointedly, every universal truth claim is a camouflaged effort to dominate, even though the dominator is not aware of it and is full of good will to "the other." There is a lurking imperialist within every universalist.

Thus, particularists hold up and try to defend the dominance of diversity. And they do so not only out of philosophical convictions (all truth claims are socially constructed and therefore particular), but also, and especially, out of ethical concerns (to defend the right to hold particular worldviews in face of the onslaught of imperialistic universal worldviews). And the critiques that the particularists level against inter-religious dia-logue, across both its types and its virtues, are indeed devastating.

Each of the *types of dialogue* is based on the claim that there is some form of common ground or shared experience or global ethic that will sustain the dialogue of under-standing, or spirituality, or action. But religious believers, the particularists retort, really cannot be certain that such a "common something" actually exists, since each of them will see it differently. Without anything in common, or not being able to know if there is anything in common, among the religions, the beliefs and truth claims of the different religions are, in postmodern jargon, *incommensurable:* it is impossible to grasp and assess one in the light of the other. They are ships passing in the night. At the most, they can note, and perhaps signal to each other, but then pass on.

As for the different *theological models for religious pluralism*, really there is only one: some form of exclusivism. That is because there is only *one way* in which you can understand and assess another religion, and that is *your religion*. And because it is the *only* way to engage other traditions, you will necessarily hold your religion as the *best* way to determine the value of other traditions. If it is the only way to proceed, you have to consider it the preferred way to proceed.

The particularist-postmodern critique can really endorse only two of the virtues that Cornille proposes as necessary for dialogue. Unless a religious believer wants to simply abandon her own religion and culture and migrate to another, she is challenged to be fully *committed* to the religion in which she stands. And she should be *humble* about her religion, not because it is particular and, therefore, in need of help to know the Divine more adequately, but because though it is limited, it gives her all that she needs to know and "be saved or enlightened." A particularist ethic insists that we are rightly humbled by the gift we have received. As for the other virtues – trust in interconnectedness, empathy, hospitality – since there can be no universal agreement about what connects us, we can neither accurately feel that connection nor seek to generate agreement about it among other religious believers.

So just how do particularists envision the relationship of religions in our present-day world of porous boundaries and multireligious neighborhoods? Basically, they propose a kind of *good neighbor policy* among religions. Followers of differing religions should be nice to each other, respect each other, but let each religion stay in its own backyard. The religious particularist says: recognize that the fences between the religions are irremovable, and that good religious fences do make good religious neighbors. Yes, there will be opportunities, perhaps necessities, when common problems come up in the neighborhood; but these will be "ad hoc" conversations and collaborations. Meet in some common space, do what you can, but then let everyone return to their own house and backyard. Live and let live – be fully committed to your own religion, hold it up as the best, and let all the other religious neighbors do the same. The result will be, not dialogue, but a certain natural religious competition. Let each religion follow its own path; let all religions observe each other doing that. And then see what happens.

The Necessity and Priority of Socially Engaged Inter-Religious Dialogue

Having laid the foundations by naming the context and some fundamental criticisms of inter-religious dialogue, we can now begin to build the house. I hope that what follows might persuade the reader that the "and" in our title, "Inter-Religious Dialogue and Social Action," is a conjunction of both *necessity* and *priority*. I believe that inter-religious dialogue and social action not only *must* go together, but that a "dialogue of social action" has a certain *priority* over the other two forms of dialogue, that of theology and that of spirituality. (I trust that the meaning of the hedged phrase, "certain priority," will become clear as I make my case.)

The necessity of socially engaged dialogue

When I claim that a socially engaged dialogue is necessary, in no way am I denying the concomitant necessity of both a theological or spiritual dialogue. Dialogue is a multifaceted endeavor; each facet calls for the others. But the necessity for exploring, comprehending, and learning from the teachings or doctrines, as well as the spiritual or mystical practices, of other religions is evident from the very nature of a conversation between religious believers. To try to engage another religious tradition without studying its beliefs and practices would be like an anthropologist studying another culture without exploring its family systems or economic structures.

Not so with the dialogue of social action. The links between religious experience and social action are not immediately evident. They have to be, as it were, dug out and identified by looking more deeply into what happens to people when they have religious experiences in their various traditions. But also, and perhaps more importantly, we can identify why religion and social action are called to a holy union by looking more carefully at what is going on in the world around us. It is in what Catholic theologians call "the signs of the times" that we will find the matchmaker for the marriage of religion and social engagement.

In the next section, we will examine how religious experience seems to call for social engagement. In this one, we want to explore how "the signs of the time" help us answer two reciprocal questions: Why does inter-religious dialogue need social action? And, why does social action need inter-religious dialogue?

1. *Why does inter-religious dialogue need social action?* Because I believe that all religious practitioners have to take seriously the critique of Marxists and humanists that religion serves as opium for the suffering masses. When such critics look at human history and especially when they look at present "signs of the times," they witness, as we all do, an incredible amount of unnecessary human and planetary suffering. And when they identify the role of religion in this picture, it seems evident to them that, for the most part, religion has been part of the problem of such suffering. Religion has either contributed to this suffering by taking sides with the exploiting perpetrators of such suffering, or it has served as a distraction from this suffering. "If you're not now getting your share of the pie on earth, you will in the sky of heaven, by and by."

    Clearly, I take this critique, though I formulated it rather crudely, very seriously. If I cannot answer it, I would have to give up being religious. I have to be able to show to myself and to my Marxist-humanist friends, that although religion has certainly been part of the problem, it can also be part of the solution – in fact, a bigger part of the solution than it has been of the problem.

    To focus this humanist criticism of religion more directly on the way inter-religious dialogue is often carried out, I share Farid Esack's discomfort, bordering on distress, that so many of the inter-religious meetings that he has been invited to turn out to be "tea parties" (Esack 2007). They are certainly rewarding conversations which clarify divergences and similarities in beliefs, or which deepen spiritual fervor through nourishment. But so often they take place in lavish hotels or comfortable universities on the top of a mountain, as it were, while down in the valley there is rank poverty, environmental devastation, or class violence. Such mountain-top conversations of religious leaders and practitioners become either a distraction from, or an indirect support of, the economic or political realities of injustice and exploitation. This is not to say that we should not sip tea together and carry on theological or spiritual conversations between our traditions. But if that is *all* we do, if the dialogue of theology or spirituality is not in some way connected with the dialogue of action, then religion, I have to say, is being turned into a sacred canopy under which we dispense religious opium to ourselves and, worse, to others. The powers that be will happily provide generous grants for such dialogue.

2. *Why does social action need inter-religious dialogue?* Here I do not wish to tangle myself in the debate on ethics and religion – whether ethical action requires some kind of a spiritual grounding. All I would like to suggest is that if anyone sincerely committed to solving humanity's life-threatening problems ignores religion's relevance to the tasks before us, such a person is both impractical and foolish. (That, I confess, is quite a "suggestion"!)

I make this suggestion for two reasons: a) The complex problems that call for our attention and action are *global*, and the solutions therefore must be global. No one nation or race, no one solution, will be up to the task of addressing so many interconnected issues; b) The vast majority of peoples who populate this planet happen to be, for better and for worse, religious. Their lives and their responses to the world around them are based on and motivated by their religious worldviews. If you want to enlist them in the global and international, inter-cultural task of doing something about global warming, social injustice, or state or family violence, you are going to have to appeal, whether you enjoy the task or not, to their religious views and values. Secular humanists who refuse cooperation with religious believers do not qualify for the task they set for themselves.

The priority of socially engaged dialogue

To make the claim that the dialogue of action is just as necessary as the dialogue of theology or spirituality is a lot easier than what I would like to propose now: that the dialogue of action has a "certain" priority over the other two. By "certain" I mean not an essential but a practical priority. In no way am I claiming that the dialogue of social action is a more authentic kind of dialogue than that of theology or spirituality. Rather, I am suggesting that it is often a more effective place to start, or a more practical arena in which to carry on discussions about beliefs and spirituality. The practical priority I am talking about is not just *ethical* – to keep inter-religious dialogue from becoming a tea party; it is also *methodological* or *hermeneutical* – to enable inter-religious dialogue to deal with the complexities and obstacles in really understanding and empathizing with someone who comes from a totally different world.

So if in the previous section, I briefly laid out what I think inter-religious dialogue can contribute to social action, now I am investigating what social action can contribute to inter-religious dialogue. And the heart of this contribution is how socially engaged dialogue can offer a serious way of responding to important postmodern and particularist criticisms of inter-religious dialogue. By starting with, or drawing from, a socially engaged inter-religious dialogue, participants will be better able to *find or create what is common amid all their diversity.* In terms of Catherine Cornille's "virtues for dialogue," a socially engaged dialogue will be able to identify or construct what *connects* the diverse religious without minimizing or exploiting what makes them diverse.

Gathered Around the Suffering Ones of the Earth

If, as postmodernists and particularists remind us, there is no Archimedean point outside of history from which we can transcend our individual historical conditioning and see all the religions as they really are, I want to vigorously suggest that there *is* a kind of Archimedean point *within* history that can and does provide a common summons to all the religions. Or, in a shorter sentence: if we cannot be sure there is anything that all the religions have in common *within* themselves, we can be sure that they have something in common *all around* them.

I am talking about the reality of *unnecessary suffering* that surrounds and summons followers of all the religious communities. Whatever the various religions may or may not have in common in their teachings and in their experiences, they all, in differing ways and to differing degrees, feel the necessity of offering some kind of response to the sufferings that drench the human condition.

The kinds of suffering that surround or afflict religious believers in diverse traditions and that enter into human awareness in the face of a starving child, a homeless mother, a raped woman, a tortured homosexual, a dark body swaying from a lynching tree, or a polluted river – all these "faces" can summon, and are summoning, many people from all religious traditions to reach out and offer a religious response. No matter what the "social conditioning," no matter how different the views of "the Ultimate," "the Self," or "life after death" may be in each of the religious traditions, the specter of such unnecessary suffering can have the *same effect* on followers of all religions – the desire to respond, to offer something from within their religious beliefs and practices that can make a difference in the lives of those who are suffering. The analysis and response may differ, but the reaction is the same: to address, deal with, and ultimately ameliorate this suffering.

The way suffering can and does affect human beings indicates that the needless suffering of others has what we might call (challenging postmodernists) a "meta-potency" or a universal ability to touch and affect human beings prior to whatever cultural or religious conditioning they have. (I am not asserting that such suffering *always* does, but that it generally *can* so affect human consciousness.) It possesses what some have termed a *mediated immediacy* (Fiorenza 1991: 135). Mediated through the face of the suffering other, it is felt and elicits response immediately – that is, prior to or independent of conceptual awareness. The suffering of others can elicit from us a response before it is registered as a thought.

Edward Schillebeeckx describes this in his complex language, as "a negative experience of contrast": in the face of unjust, unnecessary suffering, our immediate, unprogrammed, prereflective response is "No! This should not be! I must do something" (Schillebeeckx 1990: 5–6). Mencius, long before Schillebeeckx, made the same observation: any human being witnessing a child losing its balance on the edge of a well will, without thinking or analyzing, reach out to prevent that child from falling. This, Mencius tells us, is the "human heart that cannot bear the sufferings of others." He calls this heart "the beginning [or the foundation] of humanness" (Mencius, *Book Two*, 2A6, in De Bary 1999: 129). More currently and more forcefully, Levinas calls us to be aware of how the "face of the other" (especially if that face is wracked with pain) can make absolute ethical demands on us that are loaded with the power of the Transcendent (Levinas 1999).

This, then, is what can connect many members (we can never say *all* members) in *all* religions – a call, originating not from within each of them but from around all of them, a call that summons them to join forces in responding to the faces of suffering people and the suffering planet. Such a call to *social action* is not an imperialistic imposition on religions because, as we survey the world of inter-religious dialogue over the past two decades, we can verify in such international gatherings as the Parliament of the World's Religions, that religions *are* responding to this call of suffering peoples and planet. They are doing so, evidently, because Mencius's "human heart that cannot bear the suffering of others" seems to beat all the more energetically when it is also a *religious* human heart.

But more so, we can see, in the fundamental teachings of the religions, that all of them seek to bring some kind of *betterment* – whether they call it salvation or enlightenment or moksha or harmony – to the human condition. In multifarious ways, religions address what is wrong, what is missing or missed, in the way humans understand themselves and act in this world (Knitter 1995: 97–117; Hick 2004: 21–71). They seek to change the present state of affairs; they propose ways to *transform* both individuals and society. Though, usually, they begin with spiritual practices aimed at the necessity of personal transformation (or what Thich Nhat Hanh calls *being peace*), they also propose ways of transforming the way social life is conducted (what he calls *making peace*) (Hanh 2005). Thus, scholars of religion have identified in all of the religious teachings and traditions both *mystical* and *prophetic* ideals and energies. Each religion will balance and blend mystical and prophetic practices differently, but both ingredients can be identified throughout the history of all religions. Mystical or personal transformation leads to prophetic or social engagement. Prophets who are not also mystics usually either burn out themselves, or burn up others. Both are essential to religious teachings and practice (Knitter 2003).

It is by joining their prophetic commitments in shared social action to remove suffering that religious believers from differing traditions can find not just a relevant but a propitious place to start their dialogue. If the oft-heard dictum, "We know the truth by doing the truth," is true in general, it is specifically true in the complex process of inter-religious dialogue. By acting together in addressing the needs of those who suffer, religious people who are strangers to each other can lay the *hermeneutical groundwork* for getting to know each other and understanding each other's differences. They form a *community of solidarity* with those suffering oppression which becomes a *community of conversation* with each other. The oppressed, as it were, become the go-betweens among devotees of different religious communities; the oppressed introduce religious believers to each other insofar as their suffering calls for a response from all religious believers.

This is hard to lay out clearly. But I have felt it in my own limited experiences of socially engaged dialogue with the Interreligious Peace Council, at the Parliament of Religions, and more recently, with the Occupy Wall Street movement. In all of these communities, people from markedly different religious, nonreligious, and atheistic worldviews have come together – and in working together, have understood each other, or at least wanted to know more about one another. It is as if engaging in shared social action provides people with "new ears" to hear each other, or antennas by which they can hear things in other worldviews that they could never have heard before. By working together, struggling together, being frustrated together, maybe even going to jail together, they start to feel differently toward each other.

I as a Christian marvel at your Buddhist commitment to those who are suffering. I am inspired by the firmness of your resolve as well as by the compassion with which you engage both the oppressed and the oppressors. So, I want to know more of the religious experience and teachings that so sustain and guide you. When you answer my question and start talking about strange notions of "emptiness" and "no-self" and "*dharma*," I am able to "get it," for I have seen "it" in our shared action. And I trust that Buddhists or Muslims or Hindus might find themselves reacting to me in the same way. Acting before knowing seems to make for better knowing. Trying to *do* the truth together enables us to *know* the truth together.

The "Hermeneutical Privilege" of the Oppressed Within a Socially Engaged Dialogue

A socially engaged inter-religious dialogue that begins by forming a community of solidarity with those who are suffering brings, by necessity, new voices to the conversation: the voices of those who suffer, and of those who can speak for suffering creatures and planet. A religious dialogue that addresses realities such as poverty, violence, racial or gender discrimination, and global warming cannot be just a religious dialogue. It must also include those people who are doing the actual suffering! The victims of oppression, injustice, and violence must also take their places around the table of dialogue, alongside religious practitioners, leaders, and scholars. If they are not in some way or at some point included in the dialogue, then socially engaged dialogue runs the risk of becoming another instance of "foreign aid" – of experts (in this case religious) coming to the rescue of the helpless poor. Socially engaged dialogue introduces or requires a new ingredient and dynamic in the usual way of doing inter-religious dialogue. In introducing new voices into the conversation, socially engaged dialogue is telling religious people that they cannot really understand each other unless they first listen to and try to understand those who are suffering.

And this leads to even more unsettling requirements for dialogue: these voices of the oppressed, whether or not they are religious believers themselves, have a *privileged* place in the conversation. Their voices, their experiences, their analyses of suffering must *be heard first*. Why? First of all because, intentionally or unintentionally, they have been excluded from conversations about what needs to be done, or how religious values can make a difference in the world. Or they have been neglected. They have been rendered voiceless because, although their sufferings are addressed, their opinions are not. This is what the word "marginalized" means: to be pushed violently or politely to the side. Not to be seen, or heard. Not to count. So giving the voiceless a "first voice" in the conversation is a question of *justice*, of redressing the unjustifiable neglect of the voices of the marginalized.

There is a further, even more sobering, reason why the marginalized must be given prior hearing in a socially engaged religious dialogue: because they see things and know things that those who are part of the mainstream of power simply cannot see. Despite your genuine desire to see the world from the perspective of the poor, if you are part of the dominant class, you *cannot*. This, according to James Cone's analysis of racial realities in the USA, is one of the pernicious effects of White Supremacy (Cone 2011: see esp. 152–166). In participating in that Supremacy as a white, middle-class person (especially as a male), you cannot really see it. It is like bad breath: you probably do not realize you have it, and so you need someone else to tell you that you do. Thus, the priority of the voices of victims of oppression in dialogue about that oppression. They must speak if we are going to have a clear, adequate picture of what we are all talking about. The oppressed and marginalized have "learned more about the culture of the powerful than the powerful know about those they subjugate" (Taylor 1990: 65).

Of course, to recognize that the marginalized have a prior voice in inter-religious conversation does not mean that they have the only or the exclusively normative voice. What they bring to the table is essential, but it must then be engaged by other voices – voices that bring the perspectives of mystics, scholars, and activists. While a socially engaged dialogue does and must privilege some voices, it cannot absolutize any voice.

Still, in privileging the perspectives and experience of the oppressed, a socially engaged dialogue will find that the oppressed can provide, in particular instances, a sort of "last court of appeal" for disagreements between religious truth claims. In trying to decide, for instance, whether the Asian understanding of karma, or the Christian teachings on original sin, or the Hindu view of dharma, or Jesus's notion of the "Reign of God" are more effective, and, therefore, in a particular case more true, the verdict of those who are the victims of oppression can be extremely helpful for scholarly or religious debates. If this sounds like a *pragmatic view* of truth, it is. If Jesus was right when he said that "the truth will set you free" (John 8: 32), then freedom becomes the pragmatic test of truth.

Guidelines for Socially Engaged Dialogue

To sum up, then, I would like to lay out the movements by which a socially engaged inter-religious dialogue can naturally unfold, describing first the primary characteristics of a marriage between inter-religious dialogue and social action, and then elaborating on the fruits that such dialogue can bear. Each of the names of these movements begins with the Latin preposition, *cum,* or "with"; they express growing degrees of relationship, "with-ness."

1) *Com-passion:* This, you might say, is "the condition for the possibility" of socially engaged dialogue among religious believers: the participants, from their different socially and religiously constructed viewpoints, all have to *feel* the call of Mencius' child about to fall into the well. As I have argued above, there is evidence that many religious persons from differing traditions *can feel* and actually *are feeling* a natural, spontaneous compassion for those who are suffering needlessly. This is the root meaning of the Latin *compatire* – to feel with, to suffer with. And when a Muslim and a Christian find themselves "suffering with" the marginalized, they also, perhaps to their surprise, find themselves "suffering together with" each other. Here, to somewhat improperly extend our analogy, is their first encounter, their first date: they meet in their shared compassion for the suffering.

2) *Con-version:* But if this first encounter between religious believers is going to develop into a real relationship, the feeling of compassion will have to take real,

practical effect in one's life. It will call for change, for a shift in direction, for acting differently. The feeling of compassion by which the suffering of others has touched our lives will call for a reciprocal response by which we reach back to them in the determination to touch and affect their lives. Compassion will call for *con-version;* otherwise it is not real compassion. And con-version is the resolve to, literally, *con-vertere,* to turn things around in one's own life for the sake of others. In my Christian language, I would regard such conversion to the wellbeing of others a real, but perhaps inarticulate, religious conversion, for something (the Spirit, Bodhicitta, or grace?) is calling for and enabling new directions in our life – a shift from self-centeredness to centeredness on others. But whether we call it religious experience or not, it is a conversion that turns us not only to victims of oppression but also to others who have experienced and made the "turn" or "shift" to the suffering other. It is a shared conversion felt among differing religious believers before they even begin talking about religion.

3)   *Col-laboration:* Such compassion for the suffering others and conversion to their plight naturally and necessarily leads to *acting* for them and with them on their behalf. This is where the religious participants in dialogue roll up their sleeves and get their hands dirty, together. And it is in this "co-laboring" that their shared "co-conversion" will begin to form a community of solidarity. In acting together for the sake of the suffering others, in bodily involvement with the task of alleviating suffering and restoring justice, religious believers from vastly differing traditions will bond. If "work makes free," it also makes for community. Yes, it will be an inter-religious community in which each religious perspective may have a different analysis of the cause of suffering and a different solution for it. Such differences make for the richness, indeed the possibility, of dialogue. But the overall concern or goal in such a "co-laboring" community will not be to prove that my viewpoint is better than yours. Rather, the criterion of truth will be: which analysis, which diagnosis, which response can best remove suffering. And in resolving such questions, the "religious" participants will give special hearing to the "marginalized" participants, those who are the direct victims of exploitative powers. Dirty hands will lead to closer hearts.

4)   *Com-prehension:* Here the socially engaged dialogue embodies the hermeneutical circle between praxis and theory. There is a dynamic relationship between the two – action calls for thought, thought calls back for action. But again, I am urging a certain priority to praxis. In dialogue based on social action, praxis is the entry point to the hermeneutical circle. It not only calls for thought; it enables, motivates, and clarifies thought. This has been the growing experience of socially engaged religious dialoguers. After they suffer with the suffering (compassion), after they come together in response to their plight (conversion), and especially after they feel the solidarity of acting together, religious people will feel enabled, or even compelled, to understand each other *as religious people.* The Christians in the "Base Communities" of Latin America discovered that when they read the Bible through the eyes of the poor and on the basis of a liberative praxis, they began to hear and see things in the text they had never noticed or understood before. In multireligious, socially engaged communities,

the same thing happens: Buddhists, Hindus, indigenous communities, Muslims, and Jews can hear and comprehend each other in genuinely new ways. John Gort crisply articulates the growing experience of socially engaged dialoguers:

> Joint interreligious praxis among and on behalf of the poor will yield not only the enhancement of a greater measure of justice but also an increase of communication and understanding. It is in the crucible of praxis and solidarity that religious beliefs, perceptions, experiences are tested and given deeper and broader meaning and context. (Gort 1991: 73)

5) *Com-munion:* My experience with the Interreligious Peace Council has convinced me that a further movement in a socially engaged dialogue becomes possible, even necessary, beyond what I have so far developed. In our various efforts to bring a multireligious contribution to the on-site efforts of peacemakers in different contexts of tension or violence (we have met in Chiapas, Mexico, Israel-Palestine, Northern Ireland, and on the border between South and North Korea), after spending days listening, negotiating, and acting, we found that at the end of the process we had to celebrate together in some kind of ritual. We needed something to do together that would express our solidarity and our hopes. We needed to come together, among ourselves in our different religious identities and with the people, on both sides, with whom we had been working. "Come together" is another way of translating "com-munion" – *cum-unire*: to unite, find deeper unity. Such "communions" took place in rituals in which we read from and reflected on our sacred scriptures together, prayed or expressed our intentions together, listened to our music or chanting together, and also, simply sat in silence together in the same space. These are all ways of engaging in what we have called the dialogue of spirituality; but it was a dialogue that needed some form of ritual, or in Christian language, sacramental expression – whether it be sacraments of gesture and words, or sacraments of silence.

Practical Next Steps

So how can we actually do it? How can we promote such socially engaged inter-religious dialogue? It would be a process, I suggest, that has to be both "top-down" and "bottom-up." *But especially bottom-up.* While such inter-religious engagement needs the guidance of so-called experts, while it can be planned and promoted in international gatherings, it is primarily and literally on the ground that this kind of dialogue will take root and show its possibility and promise. If such dialogue does not sink roots in the earth of local communities – *grassroots!* – all the "theory" of religious leaders or scholars will never have the opportunity to connect with the reality of "action."

So following the lead of practitioners such as Aloysius Pieris in Sri Lanka and Wilfred Felix in India (Felix 1986; Knitter 1995: 144–147, 167–180; Pieris 1989), I suggest that people who follow different religious paths but who live in the same neighborhood or nation form what might be called "*Grassroots Multi-religious Communities*" (GMCs).

Modeled after the "base Christian communities" (*Communidades cristianas de base)* of the Latin American churches, these would be neighborhood and perhaps national associations that would require two things of their members: 1) that they be committed followers of a religious tradition or community; and 2) that, on the basis of their religious beliefs, they want to do something about their neighborhood's (or city's or nation's or world's) economic problems of poverty, drug-dealing, poor schools, gang activity, or racial tensions that threaten them all.

Such "GMCs" would be organized from the bottom up, within the local community. Certainly, religious leaders – ministers, priests, imams, rabbis, elders – would generally play an important role in calling forth and coordinating such communities; but the source and the energy of these movements would be ordinary people who live and work and maybe have fun together, but who go to different religious sites on Fridays, Saturdays, or Sundays. Within my own context of the United States, such GMCs are taking shape, however they label themselves. They start as groups of differently believing people who just want to "do something" together. And they grow into communities who want to respect, cherish, learn from, and celebrate with each other.

Marriages between social action and inter-religious dialogue are happening. Their fruits, I trust, will continue to grow, and surprise us.

Bibliography

Cobb, John B. Jr. *Transforming Christianity and the World: A Way beyond Absolutism and Relativism*. Paul F. Knitter, ed. Maryknoll, NY: Orbis, 1999.

Cone, James. *The Cross and the Lynching Tree*. Maryknoll, NY: Orbis, 2011.

Cornille, Catherine. *The Im-Possibility of Interreligious Dialogue*. New York: Crossroad, 2008.

De Bary, Wm. Theodore and Irene Bloom (eds.). *Sources of Chinese Tradition*. New York: Columbia University Press, 1999.

Esack, Farid. "Is There Life after Tea? Moving from Interfaith Dialogue to Solidarity in Times of Empire." Unpublished lecture give at the Simon Fraser University, Vancouver, Canada, July 2007.

Felix, Wilfred. "Sunset in the East? The Asian Realities Challenging the Church and Its Laity Today." FABC Papers, no. 45, July (1986).

Fiorenza, Francis Schüssler. "The Crisis of Hermeneutics and Christian Theology," in *Theology at the End of Modernity*, ed. Sheila Greave

Davaney. Philadelphia: Trinity, 1991: 117–140.

Foucault, Michel. *Power/Knowledge: Selected Interviews and Other Writings, 1972–1977*. New York: Pantheon, 1980.

Gort, John. "Liberative Ecumenism: Gateway to the Sharing of Religious Experience Today," *Mission Studies* 8 (1991): 57–76.

Hanh, Thich Nhat. *Being Peace*. Berkeley, CA: Parallax, 2005.

Hedges, Paul. *Controversies in Interreligious Dialogue and the Theology of Religions*. London: SCM, 2010.

Hick, John. *An Interpretation of Religion: Human Responses to the Transcendent*. 2nd edn. New Haven, CT: Yale University Press, 2004.

Hill-Fletcher, Jeannine. *Monopoly on Salvation? A Feminist Approach to Religious Pluralism*. New York: Continuum, 2008.

Knitter, Paul F. *One Earth Many Religions: Multifaith Dialogue and Global Responsibility*. Maryknoll, NY: Orbis, 1995.

Knitter, Paul F. *Introducing Theologies of Religions*. Maryknoll, NY: Orbis, 2002.

Knitter, Paul F. "One Mysticism, Many Voices, "Interreligious Insight, Vol. 1, No. 4 (2003). http://www.interreligiousinsight.org/October2003/Oct03Knitter.html (accessed December 17, 2012).

Knitter, Paul F. and Chandra Muzaffar (eds.). Subverting Greed: Religious Perspectives on the Global Economy. Maryknoll, NY: Orbis, 2002.

Küng, Hans. A Global Ethic for Global Politics and Economics. New York: Oxford University Press, 1998.

Küng, Hans and Karl-Josef Kuschel (eds.). Global Ethic: The Declaration of the Parliament of the World's Religions. London: SCM, 1993.

Levinas, Emmanuel. "The Word I, the Word You, the Word God and the Proximity of the Other," in Alterity and Transcendence. New York: Columbia University Press, 1999: 91–110.

Marshall, K. and R. Marsh (eds.). Millennium Challenges for Development and Faith Institutions. Washington, DC: World Bank, 2003.

Min, Anselm. The Solidarity of Others in a Divided World: A Postmodern Theology after Postmodernism. New York: T & T Clark, 2004.

Pieris, Aloysius. An Asian Theology of Liberation. Maryknoll, NY: Orbis, 1988.

Pieris, Aloysius. "Faith Communities and Communalism," East Asian Pastoral Review 3 and 4 (1989): 294–309.

Race, Alan. Christian and Religious Pluralism: Patterns in Christian Theology of Religions. Maryknoll, NY: Orbis, 1983.

Schillebeeckx, Edward. The Church: The Human Story of God. New York: Crossroad, 1990.

Taylor, Mark Kline. Remembering Esperanza: A Cultural-Political Theology for North American Praxis. Maryknoll, NY: Orbis, 1990.

Tilley, Terrence W. and Others. Religious Diversity and the American Experience: A Theological Approach. Maryknoll, NY: Orbis, 2007.

Vatican Council for Interreligious Dialogue. "Dialogue and Proclamation," Bulletin of the Pontifical Council on Interreligious Dialogue, 26(2) (1991).

CHAPTER 10

Inter-Religious Dialogue and Peacebuilding

S. Ayse Kadayifci-Orellana

ethno-religious identity conflicts

> In the matter of religion, people eagerly fasten their eyes on the difference between their own creed and yours; whilst the charm of the study is in finding the agreements and identities in all the religions of humanity.
>
> Ralph Waldlo Emerson

Introduction

Just a year before the 2001 attacks on the World Trade Center in New York, on August 29, 2000, Kofi Annan addressed over a thousand religious leaders who had gathered for the Millennium Peace Summit of World Religious and Spiritual Leaders in the same city. The goal of this summit was to identify ways that worldwide religious and spiritual communities can work together as inter-religious allies with the United Nations on specific peace, poverty, and environmental initiatives. In his address, Annan recognized that "religion has often been yoked to nationalism, stoking the flames of violent conflict and setting group against group," and urged these religious leaders to set an example of inter-religious cooperation and dialogue (UN Information Service 2000). This event was a turning point in the recent history of world politics as it recognized religion as a viable tool for conflict transformation and religious leaders as important agents of peacebuilding at a time when religion is associated with violence and conflict (Little and Appleby 2004: 3).

This chapter argues that inter-religious dialogue has an important role to play in peacebuilding, especially in ethno-religious identity conflicts. Until quite recently, the field of conflict resolution did not pay sufficient attention to religious traditions as sources for resolving conflicts, and many secularists contended that it was naïve to see inter-religious dialogue as a path for resolving religiously fueled conflicts (Abu Nimer et al. 2007: xi). Influenced by the philosophical and methodological traditions of the

The Wiley Blackwell Companion to Inter-Religious Dialogue, First Edition. Edited by Catherine Cornille.
© 2013 John Wiley & Sons Ltd. Published 2020 by John Wiley & Sons Ltd.

Enlightenment, conflict resolution has viewed religion as an irrational and unquantifiable phenomenon that cannot be studied from the point of view of reason, and has expected the importance of religion to fade away as modernization and reason triumph. However, Enlightenment thinkers like Voltaire could not be further away from the truth when they predicted that religion would be eliminated from politics, and that religious superstitions and authoritarian religious order would be swept away (Appleby 1994: 7–9). Evidently, religion continues to play a significant role in political life in places as diverse as the United States, Europe, the Middle East, and southeast Asia.

Many current-day conflicts involve parties that are defined along ethno-religious lines. Religion is often a divisive factor in these conflicts, used and abused to justify violence and war. Consequently, religious fervor is associated with terrorism and violence in the minds of many today. Yet, as Arthur Schneier (2002: 105) observes, religion is rarely the cause of the conflict itself: economic or political competition over resources or unmet basic human needs such as security, identity, and food, among others, tend to be at the heart of many conflicts.

Virtually all religions incorporate values and principles promoting peace and justice, and many faith-based actors have successfully played critical roles in resolving conflicts. Different mechanisms have been employed to resolve religiously motivated conflicts including mediation, observation, education, training, advocacy, and inter-religious dialogue (Bouta et al. 2005; Sampson 1997). Each of these mechanisms has the potential to make a significant contribution to building peace in conflict-torn societies. This chapter focuses only on inter-religious dialogue as a significant peacebuilding tool.

Conceptual Framework: The Relevance of Inter-Religious Dialogue to Peacebuilding

Defining ethno–religious conflicts

The majority of conflicts in the world today are identity conflicts, in which identity is defined according to ethno-religious lines, or where religious traditions are used to justify violence and depict negative enemy images. Referred to as "ethno-religious conflicts," these conflicts often take place among communities that live in close proximity, and whose histories are filled with hostility, resentment, trauma, and violence (Kaday-ifci-Orellana 2009). In these communities, religion is a key identity marker, an integral aspect of social and cultural life, and an important source of division. At times, some religious and political leaders do not hesitate to use religious myths, symbols, and texts to fuel intolerance, hatred, create enemy images, and justify violence towards the "other," thus perpetuating a culture of violence.

Defined by Johan Galtung (1996: 11) as those religious, ideological, or linguistic symbols that legitimize direct or structural violence, cultural violence contributes to the continuation of the conflict by teaching, preaching, or condoning those acts that dehumanize and satanize the opponent, justifying discrimination, and inciting hatred. Religious texts, images, and symbols hold reservoirs of meaning that shape identities, and address the need for a sense of social, geographical, cosmological, temporal, or metaphysical locatedness (Seul 1999: 558). Religious norms and values often help to form the core of one's identity. Powerful religious rituals and symbols often give expression to collective needs and desires. Religion provides meaning to the life and death of the faithful and offers a language and symbolism through which human beings interpret reality, and through which we gain comfort for trauma and injuries. Religion answers some of the most profound questions regarding right and wrong, life and death, and good and evil (Kadayifci-Orellana 2009). Hence, religious feelings can mobilize people more efficiently than any other element of identity. Because of this unique power to mobilize populations towards spiritual and political goals, religious traditions have often been abused to legitimize violence, define group identity, and legitimate particular ethnic and national objectives.

Religion and peacebuilding

Transforming these violent conflicts requires first replacing cultural violence with cultural peace by tapping into religious, cultural, and national symbols, values, myths, and images that promote reconciliation, coexistence, and peace. Because traditional conflict resolution tools fall short of addressing and resolving ethno-religious identity conflicts, scholars and practitioners are developing new approaches and tools to address these complex and intractable conflicts. Often referred to as "peacebuilding," these new approaches are focusing on building and repairing relationships as well as addressing the root causes of conflicts.

Defined as a "whole host of activities and modalities of intervention designed to bring about a state of peaceful relations by conflicting parties" (Bercovitch and Kadayifci 2002: 22), peacebuilding is a complex and dynamic process of changing relationships, perceptions, attitudes, behaviors, interests, and underlying structures that encourage and perpetuate violent conflicts. Engaging multiple levels of society (i.e. high, mid and grass-roots), peacebuilding involves addressing the root causes of the conflict through long-term economic and social justice provisions, the reform of political structures of governance, strengthening the rule of law, and healing through reconciliation. It also refers to mechanisms and structures that can prevent a conflict, terminate it, transform it, or resolve it.

Changing behaviors and attitudes by rebuilding trust is an important aspect of peacebuilding. In deep-rooted conflicts "the parties are not simply disputing over material interests but are suffering from deeply damaged social relationships" (Notter 1995: 8). Trust "facilitates creative or integrative bargaining and cooperative solutions to the many conflicts that arise between interdependent and interacting parties" (Lindskold 1978: 777). Building trust requires clarifying misunderstandings, removing negative perceptions and stereotypes, and transforming enemy images.

When religious images, texts, and symbols are used to plant the seeds of mistrust and suspicion between groups through demonization and dehumanization, only the same religious tradition can provide the antidote. Each religious tradition holds a variety of moral and spiritual resources that can facilitate rebuilding trust, transform perceptions, and inspire a sense of engagement and commitment to the peacebuilding process (Abu-Nimer 2001: 686). Religious rituals, values, and principles can facilitate healing and trauma management (Green and Honwana 1999; Nolte-Schamm 2006). Religious texts and prophetic stories can provide examples of peacemaking, forgiveness, and compassion that can lead to a change of attitudes and behaviors.

The field of conflict resolution is increasingly focusing on religious peacebuilding, described by David Little and Scott Appleby (2004: 5) as a range of activities performed by religious actors for the purpose of resolving and transforming deadly conflict, with the goal of building social, religious, and political institutions characterized by an ethos of tolerance and nonviolence. Religious peacebuilding involves faith-based actors and religious resources such as texts, images, and myths to reduce violence, inspire peace, and build trust. One particular tool of religious peacebuilding is inter-religious dialogue.

Defining dialogue and peacebuilding

Focusing on the dynamic interpersonal and intercommunal aspects of conflict, a conflict transformation approach to peacebuilding views peace as centered and rooted in the quality of relationships. This approach aims to reduce violence and increase justice in human relations through developing a capacity for constructive, direct, face-to-face interaction, while at the same time supporting systemic and structural changes (Lederach 2003: 20). Resolving ethno-religious conflicts requires first an understanding of how religious traditions and identities contribute to a culture of violence. Second, it highlights religious values, traditions, texts, and myths that focus on justice, tolerance, coexistence, and peace to rebuild trust. Lederach (2003: 21) suggests that "a fundamental way to promote constructive change on all these levels is dialogue."

Dessel et al. (2006: 303) defines dialogue as a "public process designed to involve individuals and groups in an exploration of societal issues such as politics, racism, religion, and culture that are often flashpoints for polarization and social conflict." Dialogue involves both formal and informal discussions as well as shared educational initiatives, music performances, or art exhibitions, among other projects. In order to capture this broader meaning of dialogue, Abu-Nimer et al. (2007: 8) define it as a "safe process of interaction to verbally and non-verbally exchange ideas, thoughts, questions, information, and impressions between people from different backgrounds (race, class, gender, culture, religion and so on)." Dialogue clarifies misunderstandings and illuminates areas of both convergence and divergence through mutual sharing and listening (Abu-Nimer et al. 2007: 8). As such, it helps rebuild trust and provides a space for healing and reconciliation.

Defining inter-religious dialogue

Inspired by their religious traditions to work for peace locally and globally, many religious leaders and faith-based organizations have worked with other faith communities towards peace and justice during the past decades. What is new, however, is the consideration and use of inter-religious dialogue in the wider field of conflict resolution. With the rampant increase of ethno-religious identity conflicts, it has become virtually indispensible for the field to tap into this understudied peacebuilding tool.

David Smock (2002: 6) aptly emphasizes that "a dialogue is not a debate." Debate implies an intention to win the argument, to prove one side right, or to change the views of the opponent. Dialogue does not aim to eliminate differences of opinion and conviction, but to gain an understanding and acceptance of those differences (Shafiq and Abu-Nimer 2007). Inter-religious dialogue aims at enrichment, trust, respect, and the creation of a sense of "us/we" through increased understanding. It involves "a continuing process of learning and re-education" (Braybrooke 1993: 108) through honest, open, active communication.

Inter-religious dialogue does not aim at undermining belief, either. On the contrary, an inter-religious dialogue is more constructive when people who participate are firmly grounded in their own religious traditions, allowing them to take seriously the practices and beliefs of others (Cilliers 2002: 49). At times, the dialogue process can deepen and strengthen one's own religious identity; Boys et al. (1995: 265) affirm that "the power of encountering the deep faith of a religious person from another tradition has the potential of unleashing a search for one's own spiritual roots and yearnings" (see also Kozlovic 2003).

Inter-religious dialogue taps into the spiritual resources of the religious traditions, creating opportunities for connecting participants at a deeper spiritual level. Using spirituality as a main source of commitment to social change is what distinguishes inter-religious dialogue from other forms of dialogue (Abu-Nimer 2002: 16). Religion facilitates transformation because it tracks the deepest connections between the self, the other, and the universe. Hence, incorporating spirituality into other communication technologies makes possible "new modes of relationship, new social, economic and political structures, and thus new ways of understanding the human situation under God" (Sacks 2002: 136). This view is supported by Stalov who observes, "[w]hen we engage in deep positive interaction with each other about faith, we overcome prejudices and fears and replace them with mutual understanding, respect, trust and friendship" (2007: 131).

Inter-religious dialogue encounters often include religious symbolism and rituals. "Rituals are special contexts conducive to the symbolic transformation of identity and the framing of conflict toward sustainable, coexisting relationships"; they are "a way to celebrate and encourage transformation" (Schirch 2001: 154). Rituals can effectively communicate complex feelings and emotions in symbolic ways. Believers connect to their religious tradition and observe their values and beliefs through rituals and religious symbols (Abu-Nimer 2002: 18). During inter-religious dialogue encounters, participants get an opportunity to observe and experience the rituals of another tradition, or participants may also cocreate their own rituals. Sharing symbols and rituals opens a window to the deeper emotional and spiritual realities of those involved in conflict (Bercovitch and Kadayifci-Orellana 2009: 197) and can enthuse community action, bring support for the wider peace process, and generally transform a negative and malignant conflict into a more positive one. Religious leaders' involvement in and endorsement of inter-religious dialogue in international conflicts can also help to inspire belief, faith, and perseverance.

Especially in long standing and deep rooted conflicts, where parties have suffered significant pain and lost loved ones, it is often quite difficult for parties to acknowledge wrong-doings and ask for forgiveness. It is equally difficult for parties to let go of deep wounds and forgive the "other." Religious texts and scriptures often richly articulate values central to reconciliation and peacebuilding, including compassion, forgiveness, and accountability, among others. Rooting these values within the parameters of sacred texts provides legitimacy. Participants of inter-religious dialogue often introduce verses and passages on the designated theme or topic from their religious texts and invite other participants to have a conversation about that text. These values and texts inspire and provide guidance to the participants, especially when difficult issues are being discussed, and provide a level of "certainty" and "truth" (Abu-Nimer 2002: 19). As such, they facilitate the transformation of perceptions and help to rebuild relationships.

An important element of inter-religious dialogue is the use of religious language and vocabulary. It is important to remember that each religious tradition holds what Abu-Nimer (2002) calls a "secondary" language and a "primary" language. A "secondary" religious language emphasizes what is common between different traditions, such as tolerance, peace, and dialogue; while a "primary" language distinguishes that unique tradition from other traditions through notions such as the Holy Trinity, Jihad, the Chosen People, etc. Although it is important to address both of these aspects of religious language in inter-religious dialogue, focusing on primary language before necessary trust is built between parties can undermine the effectiveness of the process.

Objectives of inter-religious dialogue

Within the context of peacebuilding, most dialogues aim to facilitate a change from narrow, exclusionist, antagonistic, prejudiced attitudes and perceptions, to a more tolerant and open-minded attitude (Abu-Nimer 2001: 686). Inter-religious dialogue increases awareness about how to improve human interactions on multiple levels (locally, regionally, or globally) by recognizing the importance of integrating religious identities into inter-group dialogue (Merdjanova and Brodeur 2009: 13). Inter-religious dialogue fosters the (re)building of trust relations and enhances social cohesion by tapping into the numinous world of strongly experienced religious emotion. Based on the contention that violent conflict is often a consequence of mutual ignorance and the absence of meaningful interaction between parties, inter-religious dialogue aims to foster mutual learning, clarify misperceptions, and provide opportunities for constructive contact with the "other." Religious understandings become the lens through which parties recognize the irreducible dignity of all human beings, including the specific conflictual "other."

Inter-religious dialogue may bring diverse groups to break down stereotypes and images; inspire hope; build trust for dealing with tough issues; create a sense of social inclusivity; develop models of constructive engagement; transform the conflict; or solve a specific issue facing the faith communities involved. Inter-religious dialogue can be organized to share grievances, facilitate transformation of relationships, highlight similarities and differences, encourage apology and/or forgiveness, and encourage mediation. It may involve a training component on a specific area, such as conflict resolution. Whatever the particular objective, establishing and communicating a clear purpose to participants is central.

Formats of inter–religious dialogue

Based on the objectives set by the facilitators, inter-religious dialogue can take different forms. Cognitive dialogues are centered on exchange of information and aim to provide a learning opportunity about the faith of the "other." Affective dialogues focus on building relationships and concentrate on sharing stories, experiences, feelings, and thoughts. Collaborative dialogues emphasize working together to address common concerns (Abu Nimer et al. 2007: 16), such as HIV/AIDS, water sanitation, or climate change. Educational initiatives or training programs that aim to break down stereotypes through lectures, panels, and sermons at religious sites can also be considered inter-religious dialogue.

Dialogue includes more than the formal gathering of religious leaders. Spontaneous, casual interactions and gestures by religious leaders, such as sharing a meal or even shaking hands, can be quite significant (Abu-Nimer 2001: 686). Joint concerts, art exhibitions, or other performances such as plays or dances can bring communities together in a positive environment and help rehumanize the other through expressing and sharing emotions. Joint prayers or standing side by side during a funeral can also transmit important symbolic messages of peace as well as joint celebration of religious holidays.

Levels of inter–religious dialogue

Inter-religious dialogue can take place at different levels. These include: high, mid and grass-roots levels. Each of these levels have their own strengths and limitations.

High–level inter–religious dialogue   Inter-religious dialogue can take place at high leadership level, which involves religious authorities such as the Pope, the Dalai Lama, or the Chief Rabbi. As Garfinkel (2004: 2) indicates, various high-level inter-religious dialogues have taken place over the last decades to speak collectively as advocates of peace, including the Alexandria Dialogue, which led to the Alexandria Declaration. High-level religious leaders have a significant degree of authority, legitimacy, and credibility, so that their actions can send a strong message. However, these leaders often lack the necessary time to commit themselves to long-term inter-religious dialogues. In addition, their involvement tends to attract a lot of media attention, which can undermine initial dialogue efforts. Also, due to their social location as communal representatives, they may be hindered from talking openly and sincerely. For these reasons they are more effective as legitimizers of the inter-religious dialogue process.

Mid–level inter–religious dialogue   In a press conference, the Dalai Lama expressed the wish to see followers of different religious traditions interact in four distinct ways: meetings between religious leaders; pilgrimages to one another's religious sites; meetings between religious practitioners, such as monastics, regarding contemplative life; and seminars and dialogues between scholars (Mack 1997). Mid-level leaders include clergy as well as scholars, professionals, business people, and artists, among others. Although they are not as visible as the high-level leadership, they have access to both high- and grass-roots levels. As such they can influence both the grass-roots level and connect with high-level religious and political leadership. They also have relatively more time and resources to devote to inter-religious dialogue. For these reasons, middle range leaders are often the best candidates for inter-religious dialogue.

Grass–roots level inter–religious dialogue   Recognizing the importance of perceptions of the "other" at the community level, conflict transformation theory argues that in order to build sustainable peace, it is necessary to build relations first at the grass-roots level. Inter-religious dialogue at a grass-roots level includes cross-community dialogues to foster reconciliation. Participants of these dialogues, including youth groups, women's organizations, and other local organizations, come together across religious divisions to promote cross-community interaction and to develop participants into agents of reconciliation. Although building constructive relations at this level does not guarantee the resolution of conflict, it may contribute to healing and repairing of relationships, especially during the postconflict reconstruction phase. Furthermore, in democratic societies, top-level leaderships are often susceptible to the needs and demands of their constituencies. Therefore, a change among the attitudes of the population in general towards the "other" and to the conflict can lead to substantive political policy changes. So, while transforming perceptions and attitudes at the grass-roots is not an easy task, inter-religious dialogue at this level is critical to establishing lasting peace.

Conditions For Effective Inter-Religious Dialogue

It is important to note that inter-religious dialogue cannot be effective in every conflict or in every community, nor is it an alternative to official peacemaking and peacebuilding efforts. It is a complementary track that incorporates important, but often neglected, social groups: faith-based actors such as religious leaders and institutions, as well as religiously inspired individuals and nongovernmental organizations.

The effectiveness of inter-religious dialogue depends on the presence of various conditions. These include the identity of the parties and nature of the dispute, the articulation of a clear purpose, careful selection of participants, a safe environment, the balance of power, a focus on both similarities and differences, the development of collaborative tasks, intra-faith meetings prior to the inter-religious encounter, and follow-up engagements.

Identity of the parties and nature of the dispute

In order to be effective and successful, the inter-religious dialogue process must be perceived as legitimate by the participating communities. If the legitimacy of the process is questioned, IDF peacebuilding efforts will most likely fail, and this legitimacy largely depends upon the identity of the parties and the nature of the dispute (Bercovitch and Kadayifci-Orellana 2009: 194).

Faith-based actors have a unique advantage in ethno-religious conflicts where religion plays a key role in the social life and identity of the conflicted parties (Bercovitch and Kadayifci-Orellana 2009). Particularly when religious leaders themselves foment violence, using religious texts to incite hatred and intolerance, it becomes critical to engage religious peacebuilding resources to form commissions or councils, or to engage a religious group recognized by all parties as impartial, fair, and legitimate (see Kadayifci-Orellana 2009).

When the religious identities of the parties are an important dimension of the conflict, and when religious values and principles are viewed as main sources of legitimacy, religious actors can legitimately tap into religious resources such as texts, images, stories, myths, and prophetic examples to highlight values of tolerance, compassion, coexistence, and peace – resources that secular leaders often cannot access.

Clear purpose

For inter-religious dialogue to be successful, it must have clearly articulated purposes and objectives, including ultimate resolution of the conflict, solving particular problems between the communities, addressing common issues such as HIV-AIDS, rebuilding relationships, breaking down stereotypes, developing methods to effectively handle grievances, reconciling differences, and healing wounds. The objectives of the dialogue must be realistic, for unrealistic expectations can extend harm by leading to frustration and disappointment among both participants and organizers. These goals must be communicated clearly, too. Having clear and realizable objectives makes assessment possible and achieving objectives creates a sense of success, inspires hope, and develops trust. Facilitators and organizers must also carefully design and think through the dialogue process, understanding and incorporating participants' concerns through predialogue research and analysis. This will help facilitators to set realistic goals, empower the parties, and create a sense of shared ownership and responsibility.

Selection of parties

In order to build trust in a fragile environment, facilitators must make sure inter-religious dialogue participants are balanced in terms of their qualifications, numbers, education, and influence. The hierarchical position and social locations of the participants must be comparable, too. Inter-religious dialogue is often a long-term process, requiring a commitment to meet regularly over an extended period of time. Inviting well-versed clergy from one religious tradition, for example, while inviting lay-persons from the other, would create an imbalanced situation in terms of religious authority and confidence. Middle-range leaders such as clergy, educators, journalists, and business people, on the other hand, are often open, available, and capable of influence both up and down the social ladder (Steele 2002: 76). Inviting hardliners is another complicated issue. Even though resolving any conflict must eventually engage hardliners who can spoil the process, engaging them too early, immaturely, or without necessary preparation can sabotage the inter-religious dialogue process. Facilitators must understand the context, decide on the objectives of the workshop, and assess the possible synergy of potential participants very carefully. In this process, facilitators play a critical role. Facilitators bring parties together in a safe space and facilitate dialogue by a thorough process that encourages and cultivates empathy, reflection, and clarification of misunderstandings and stereotypes. They are responsible for constructively channeling the emotions of the parties (Schirch 2001: 154).

Balance of power

Selecting participants is closely linked to addressing balance-of-power issues. It is often the case in conflict situations that parties do not have equal power. Members of majority groups may have access to political, economic, and social resources that the minority might not. Structural injustices may inhibit freedom of expression, or participation in social and political life. Power asymmetry may also "express itself in the nature of the encounter, its language, structure, and cultural ethos" (Gopin 2002: 43). These power imbalances must be addressed carefully by choosing a neutral space where both parties feel comfortable; by paying attention to social and political realities; and by empowering the weaker party. In addition, the importance of flexibility cannot be overemphasized: although it is important to prepare carefully, and to have an agenda, flexibility and adaptation are critical factors for the success of inter-religious dialogue in contributing to conflict resolution. Facilitators should be aware that each group brings with it different knowledge and background. Different exercises, pace, or tempo might be required. Overly structured workshops often fail to address these different dynamics and create a sense of pressure and frustration. Facilitators must be sensitive, providing cofacilitation while also including facilitators from the religious communities themselves who can translate terms and concepts into language that is meaningful and familiar to the participants.

Creating a safe and secure environment

The success of inter-religious dialogue depends on open and sincere communication between participants, including recognizing stereotypes and wrong-doings, addressing negative self- and other-perceptions and emotions, and nurturing a willingness to learn and change. Inter-religious encounters are not easy for participants who often have suffered personally and lost dear ones during the conflict. Many participants are filled with resentment. Some of them may even be traumatized. There is often deep mistrust and apprehension. As noted by Cobb (1990: 3), even the most committed participants of dialogue may feel as if they are betraying their communities.

In this context, opening up and listening sympathetically can be extremely difficult for the participants. As Gopin observes, most enemies cannot or will not articulate their true feelings. "Either it is beyond their present capacity or what they really feel is too shameful. Examples of things too difficult to articulate may include deep envy, or shame at the collective humiliation of one's group, or an intense desire to humiliate, or to take revenge, or to see the enemy suffer" (Gopin 2002: 34). This could lead to "silence," which is also an integral aspect of dialogues, as "silence – *what is not said* – is intimately tied to the meaning of *what is said*" (Kellet 2007: 77). Lack of effective and clear communication, expressed either as silence, resistance, or anger and frustration, can become a major problem. Overcoming such a block requires building trust among the participants and facilitators.

There are various ways to ensure that safety. Keeping the dialogue rooted in specific issues, and not on individual participants, facilitators can encourage participants to share personal stories, loss, and hurt. Communicating painful memories, sharing experiences of suffering and trauma, and reflecting together on the possibility of healing can be a bonding experience (Steele 2002: 78). By rechanneling the frustrations and anger of the participants, facilitators can encourage mutual empathy and active listening techniques, while giving voice to all parties in a balanced manner. Especially at times of deep crisis and anger, religious texts, values, and prophetic examples can help to break the deadlock and invite participants to reflection. Religious rituals and texts help in this process by providing a sense of God's caring presence and acceptance. However, it is important to take care in choosing texts and rituals that will not offend or alienate participants.

Providing appropriate exercises, dividing into small groups, or giving a small break to allow participants to speak outside of the pressure of larger group interactions, can all help to assist in creating a safe space. Facilitators should pay attention to the specific needs of the participants, and address them appropriately. They should also pay attention to gestures and body-languages, which can reveal more than words. Developing an understanding of cross-cultural/religious gestures and body language can be extremely helpful in these contexts. Therefore, in addition to being trained in dialogue and negotiation, facilitators of inter-religious dialogues must be trained in the detection of other gestures of reconciliation – actions and deeds that often mean much more, and are trusted more, than words. Such training will allow facilitators to recognize and address symbolic and nonverbal opportunities, and to invent strategies to consciously align or engage the culturally and religiously familiar conciliatory paths of adversary groups (Gopin 2002: 37).

In addition to creating a psychologically and emotionally safe space, it is also important to ensure the physical safety of the participants. Often enough in conflict zones talking to the enemy is considered collaboration, a betrayal of one's own community and values. Hardliners can incite attacks on participants. If that is the case, organizers of the dialogue process must ensure the secrecy and confidentiality of the meeting, and take all the necessary precautions to provide their physical safety. Otherwise, even the slightest incident can derail the process and can do more harm than good.

Examination of similarities and differences

The examination of similarities and differences is one of the basic principles of inter-religious dialogue (Abu-Nimer 2002: 22). Religious traditions often have similar values, principles, and even practices. They envision peace and harmony, and highlight compassion, justice, love, caring for the needy, mercy, and divine benevolence as core principles. Focusing on these similarities and universal values – or secondary language (Abu-Nimer 2002: 20) – can help build bridges between communities and clarify misunderstandings. This is particularly helpful in the first stages of inter-religious dialogue, but for inter-religious dialogue to be effective in transforming the relationship it is also necessary to address differences and points of contention between the parties. If "similarity" becomes the main theme of the inter-religious dialogue, and is used to avoid dealing with inherent differences, "the dialogue may create an artificial harmony – one that does not convey the complexity of the inherent interreligious contradictions and differences . . ." (Abu-Nimer 2002: 23). Rather than serving to address the issues that cause misunderstanding in the first place, such an artificial harmony might lead to a sense of being misled, and could ferment a deepened mistrust, especially if participants encounter "religious others" who act contrary to that harmony. For that reason it is necessary to introduce the primary languages of the participants, explain the way they are understood, and discuss different interpretations and opinions about these terms within the respective religious communities.

Properly timing the introduction of primary languages can be tricky. Focusing up front on primary languages may divide the participants from one another. Focusing first on the similarities between religious traditions can help participants to draw connections between them and to create an atmosphere of trust. This helps, in turn, to create constructive communication between the participants, using a set of "generic terms" which may serve to avoid confusion over theological points (Smith 1981: 181). But such terms will not help participants develop a better understanding of each other's traditions without addressing the differences between them. Primary language, on the other hand, can be introduced once participants have developed mutual trust. If these differences create a charged environment and lead to frustration and arguments, facilitators can retract back to emphasizing similarities, and allow participants to work on building the comfort level to discuss difference. Facilitators should keep the pulse of the group to determine whether the level of trust and safety is conducive to discussing more contentious issues. In order to facilitate maximum understanding of the differences rooted in the primary languages, facilitators need to have a working knowledge of the faith traditions involved.

Collaborative task

Another critical component for effective inter-religious dialogue is the development of a collaborative task. Especially for the minority group, the end product of inter-religious dialogue is of great importance. As stressed by Abu-Nimer (2002: 23), "for the religious majority, insight and empathy may often be sufficient. But members of the religious minority tend to demand more than 'talk' and 'insights.'" Collaborative tasks create opportunities for religious communities to work together in a safe environment. Successful task-outcomes can address a significant need in the society, contribute to credibility and trust between communities, and help develop the minority community. It can also foster more interest in working with the "religious other" in general. Continuing these collaborative tasks is especially vital during times of crisis, to solidify trust and solidarity between the participants.

Nevertheless, implementing projects requires a local presence (Steele 2002: 85), time, and often financial resources. Religious leaders who have access to a vast pool of believers, and who often have international institutional support, maintain an advantage as they can reach out both to their own congregation and to religious leaders from other faith traditions. However, they are also sometimes faced with significant challenges, such as competing interpretations of motivation and intent, and campaigns of slander that depict them as traitors, etc.

Collaborative tasks may include organizing local events for the communities, environmental projects such providing safe drinking water, health projects such as establishing clinics and providing medicine, or reconstructing sites destroyed during riots or violence. The success of these efforts may contribute to inter-communal credibility, build trust, and increase wider interest in the process of resolving conflict.

Intra–faith meetings

Another critical aspect for any successful inter-religious dialogue is the organization of intra-faith meetings prior to the inter-religious dialogue. Each religious tradition hosts an array of different interpretations, understandings, and approaches. Participants in inter-religious dialogue from a single tradition or community may hold different understandings of sacred texts, religious images, and exemplars. Internal divisions are not often addressed during inter-religious dialogues, and these differences can lead to misunderstandings between and within the groups that participate in the process. Clarifying both differences and points of intra-faith agreement before inter-religious dialogue will contribute significantly to the success of the process. Organizing an intra-faith dialogue ensures that members of each religious group understand and appreciate the differences and similarities in their collective religious experience, and provides support to members who are indeed taking high risks by participating in the process (Abu-Nimer 2002: 26).

Follow–up

Although participants may experience a change in attitudes and perceptions for a while, once they go back to their communities they are faced with the challenges of conflict, violence, and a bombardment of negative messages. Often called the re-entry problem, this postdialogue situation can be quite detrimental to the ongoing process of conflict resolution. As participants are faced with enormous social pressures to change their views, or are treated as traitors, they become understandably discouraged.

One important way to address the problem of re-integration into and between communities following inter-religious dialogue is to organize follow-up measures, such as meetings or joint actions. It is also important to construct support systems to share the challenges of returning to the participants' respective communities and develop strategies to cope with them.

Limits and challenges of inter–religious dialogue

Many challenges, faced by both scholar-practitioners and religious leaders, make inter-religious dialogue an extremely difficult endeavor. These challenges also reflect some of the limitations of inter-religious dialogue.

Convincing participants   First of all, it is not easy to convince religious leaders to commit to a dialogue process. During times of conflict, mutual distrust makes any interaction with the "other" suspicious. "Inter-religious dialogue becomes almost impossible if the 'religious other' is considered a demonic force" (Mack 1997: 149), making it extremely difficult to convince invitees to join the dialogue process. Providing security to participants and their families, especially after the process, is sometimes quite difficult for inter-religious dialogue organizers.

Competing interpretations   Each religious tradition includes different interpretations and understandings, which may at times contradict each other. Based on these different interpretations, different religious leaders might recommend different courses of action. While some may encourage nonviolent methods of conflict resolution and reconciliation, others may argue in favor of continuation of conflict, and self-sacrifice for the sake of God. Those who hold extremist interpretations may attempt to spoil the process. Facilitators must be aware of these competing interpretations, and take care to involve authoritative participants who can skillfully address relevant issues and questions.

Engaging hardliners   Peacebuilding yearns to alter the attitudes and behaviors of those hardliners who oppose interaction and dialogue. However, it is a major challenge for organizers to include them in the process, and if they are included, their capacity to sabotage the process must be limited. Nevertheless, it is through more open-minded leaders, who are respected in their communities and who have ties to these extremist elements, that these more intransigent sections of the community can be influenced. Again, an intra-faith or intra-community dialogue can help to prepare and integrate a wider range of religious actors.

Time and financial challenges   Inter-religious dialogue is a long and costly process. Participants in effective dialogues often meet for several days at a time over a period of a few years. Overcoming deep-rooted hostilities and building trust and strong relationship is a hard and long process. The journey is not without obstacles: events on the ground, such as terrorist attacks, torture, and other human rights abuses, can undermine fragile relationships, and the process can break down at any time. Securing long-term financial support is also quite a challenge for the organizers, as funders give priority to immediate-term crisis situations, and would like to see results. However, demonstrating the effectiveness of long-term initiatives and complex initiatives such as inter-religious dialogue is a challenge. Losing financial support can also end the process prematurely, and create a sense of failure, betrayal, and disappointment among participants.

Gender disparity   Another limitation of inter-religious dialogue is a consistent disparity in the gender of participants. In most religious traditions, official religious leadership consists mainly of men. Quite often, women are excluded from religious education, or cannot be ordained officially. Although many women hold unofficial leadership positions, these forms of leadership are generally underrepresented in religious peace-making and inter-religious dialogue. Yet many women religious leaders are actively reaching out across religious divides, working both officially and unofficially in the area of inter-religious dialogue. These initiatives are often *ad hoc* and informal, but are no less important than more formal processes. In order to include women's perspectives and women's voices in inter-religious dialogue, it is important both to broaden our conceptions of religious leadership, and to ensure greater women's participation in formal inter-religious dialogue as well.

Conclusion

No peacebuilding effort is without challenges. Addressing conflicts where religious pre-cepts, texts, or doctrines are used to justify violence requires us to rethink our approaches to peacebuilding and conflict resolution. It requires us to develop intervention strategies that emphasize religious sources of tolerance, compassion, and cooperation, and empower religious leaders as agents of peace. This chapter argued that making use of religious and spiritual resources such as sacred texts, rituals, stories, myths, and values can be extremely beneficial in helping religious actors to address ethno-religious con-flicts. Here, it is important to re-emphasize that inter-religious dialogue is *not* an alterna-tive to other conflict resolution and peacebuilding efforts, such as official negotiations, mediation with the involvement of third-parties, or secular conflict resolution tools such as problem-solving workshops. However, while inter-religious dialogue is only one of many resources for conflict resolution, it is a very important one. As Marc Gopin (2002: 34) points out, dialogue is merely a step in the peacemaking process, and cannot be thought of as the answer to the entire conflict itself.

This chapter also analyzed conditions for inter-religious dialogue to be effective and explored its limitations. It argued that despite many challenges, there are various advantages in employing inter-religious dialogue, and that it is a particularly critical peacebuilding tool "if the opposing groups are differentiated by religious identity" (Smock 2002: 127). Inter-religious dialogue can be of great value in ameliorating conflict and advancing reconciliation even when religion is not the central cause of the conflict, for it draws on profound spiritual and emotional resources that allow a deeper human connection between opposing parties.

Inter-religious dialogue involves segments of society that are often ignored by secular approaches to conflict resolution, or are excluded by power politics and peace negotiations. Faith-based groups have unique credibility in communities where religious leaders and institutions play an important role. These actors often have access to a wide pool of people through their local congregations and international connections. Having access to both high-level leadership as well as grass-roots community members, religious leaders are in a unique position to communicate the needs and frustrations of both groups, and are well positioned to implement agreements. Engaging religious resources as part of the broader conflict-resolution process offers the possibility of changing attitudes and perceptions regarding the "other," which is as important as signing a peace agreement.

Negative images of the opponent often fuel conflict and make it possible to hurt and kill the opponent. These negative enemy images are often a result of misinformation, or lack of information. Learning about religious similarities and differences may clarify misunderstandings, reducing radicalism and the possibility of religious manipulation. Such learning helps to rehumanize the "other" and develop solidarity, and may even contribute to joint action to transform the conflict.

This chapter also argued that inter-religious dialogue helps participants to access reservoirs of meanings and practices that enrich the range of available meanings, interpretations, motivations, and strategies. It provides prophetic and moral authority. Inter-religious dialogue also marshals institutional resources and helps to articulate new roles for the religiously motivated. It especially focuses on grass-roots actors to establish cooperation, understanding, and methods of dealing with difference aimed at respecting the "other." With its focus on relationships and spirituality, inter-religious dialogue also helps participants connect at a deeper level than secular approaches to conflict resolution, and offers powerful tools for rehumanizing the "other." In any ethno-religious conflict, inter-religious dialogue is an essential complementary tool of long-term peacebuilding.

Bibliography

Abu-Nimer, Mohammed. *Dialogue, Change, Conflict Resolution and Change: Arab-Jewish Encounters in Israel*. Albany, NY: State University of New York Press, 1999.

Abu-Nimer, Mohammed. "Conflict Resolution, Culture, and Religion: Toward a Training Model of Interreligious Peacebuilding." *Peace Research* 38(6) (2001): 685–704.

Abu-Nimer, Mohammed. "The Miracles of Transformation Through Interfaith Dialogue: Are you a Believer?" in *Interfaith Dialogue and Peacebuilding*, ed. David R. Smock. Washington, DC: United States Institute of Peace Press, 2002.

Abu-Nimer, Mohammed and S. Ayse Kadayifci-Orellana. *Muslim Peace Building Actors in the Balkans, Horn of Africa and the Graet Lake Regions*. Salam Institute Report. Washington DC.: Salam Institute, 2005.

Abu-Nimer, Mohammed, Amal I. Khoury, and Emily Welty. *Unity in Diversity: Interfaith Dialogue in the Middle East*. Washington, DC: United States Institute of Peace Press, 2007.

Appleby, Scott. *Religious Fundamentalism and Global Conflict*. New York: Foreign Policy Association Headline Series #301, 1994.

Bercovitch, J. and S. Ayse Kadayifci-Orellana. "Exploring the Relevance and contribution of Mediation to Peace-Building." *Peace and Conflict Studies* 9(2) December (2002): 21–40.

Bercovitch, J. and S. Ayse Kadayifci-Orellana. "Religion and Mediation: The Role of Faith-Based Actors in International Conflict Resolution." *International Negotiation* 14(1) (2009): 175–204.

Bouta, Tsjeard, S. Ayse Kadayifci-Orellana, and Mohammed Abu-Nimer. "Faith Based Peacebuilding: Mapping and Analysis of Christian, Muslim and Multi-Faith Actors," The Hague: Netherlands Institute for International Relations "Clingandael" in cooperation with Salam Institute for Peace and Justice, 2005.

Boys, M.C., S.S. Lee, and D.C. Bass. "Protestant, Catholic, Jew: The transformative possibilities of educating across Religious Boundaries." *Religious Education* 90(2) (1995): 255–276.

Braybrooke, M. "A pilgrimage of hope," in *A Sourcebook for the Community of Religions*, ed. J.D. Beversluis. Chicago: The Council for a Parliament of the World's Religions, 1993.

Burton, John W. *Conflict and Communication: The Use of Controlled Communication in International Relations*. London: Macmillan, 1969.

CCBI Committee for Relations with People of Other Faiths. *In Good Faith: the Four Principles of Interfaith Dialogue – A Brief Guide for the Churches*. CRPOF/CCBI, 1991.

Cilliers, Jaco. "Building Bridges for Interfaith Dialogue," in *Interfaith Dialogue and Peacebuilding*, ed. David Smocks. Washington, DC: United States Institute of Peace, 2002.

Cobb, John B. Jr. "Dialogue," *Death or Dialogue? From the Age of Monologue to the Age of Dialogue*. Philadelphia: Trinity, 1990.

Dessel, Adrienne, Mary E. Rogge, and Sarah B Garlington. "Using Intergroup Dialogue to Promote Social Justice and Change." *Social Work* 51(4) (2006): 303–315.

Galtung, Johan. "Violence, Peace and Peace Research," *Journal of Peace Research* 6(3) (1996): 167–191.

Garfinkel, Renee. "What Works: Evaluating Interfaith Dialogue Programs," *Special Report #123*. Washington, DC: United States Institute of Peace Press, 2004.

Garfinkel, Renee. "Personal Transformations: Moving from Violence to Peace," *Special Report #186*. Washington, DC: United States Institute of Peace Press, 2007.

Gopin, Marc. "The Use of the Word and Its Limits: A Critical Evaluation of Religious Dialogue as Peacemaking," in *Interfaith Dialogue and Peacebuilding*, ed. David R. Smock. Washington, DC: United States Institute of Peace Press, 2002.

Green, E.C. and Honwana, A. "Indigenous healing of war-affected children in Africa." Indigenous Knowledge Notes, 10. www.worldbank.org/afr/ik/iknt10.pdf, accessed December 28, 20012

Kadayifci-Orellana, S. Ayse. "Ethno-Religious Conflicts: Exploring the Role of Religion in Conflict Resolution," in *The SAGE Handbook of Conflict Resolution*, eds. J. Bercovitch, V. Kremenyuk, and I.W. Zartman. London: Sage, 2009: 264–285.

Kellet, Peter. *Conflict Dialogue: Working with Layers of Meaning for Productive Relationships*. Thousand Oaks, CA: Sage, 2007.

Kozlovic, Anton Karl. "Seven Logical Consequences of Interreligious Dialoguing: A Taxonomy of Praxis Possibilities." *Marburg Journal of Religion* 8(1) (2003). http://web.uni-marburg.de/religionswissenschaft/journal/mjr/mjr_past.html (accessed December 12, 2012).

Kramer, Kenneth. "Silent Dialogue: The Interreligious Dimension." *Buddhist Christian Studies* 10 (1990): 127–132.

Krieger, David. "Communication Theory and Interreligious Dialogue." *Journal of Ecumenical Studies* (Summer–Fall) (1993): 331–353.

Lederach, John Paul. *The Little Book of Conflict Transformation*. Intercourse, PA.: Good Books, 2003.

Lindskold, Svenn. "Trust Development, the GRIT Proposal, and the Effects of

Conciliatory Acts on Conflict and Cooperation." *Psychological Bulletin* 85 (1978): 772–793.

Little, David (ed.). *Peacemakers in Action: Profiles of Religion and Conflict Resolution.* New York: Cambridge University Press, 2007.

Little, David and Scott Appleby. "A Moment of Opportunity? The Promise of Religious Peacebuilding in an Era of Religious and Ethnic Conflict," in *Religion and Peacebuilding*, eds. H. Coward and G.S. Smith. Albany, NY: State University of New York Press, 2004.

Mack, Terry C. "Interreligious Dialogue and Evangelism." *Buddhist-Christian Studies* 17 (1997): 139–151.

Merdjanova, Ina and Patrice Brodeur. *Religion as a Conversation Starter: Interreligious Dialogue for Peacebuilding in the Balkans.* New York: Continuum, 2009.

Mitchell, Donald W. "Report on the Parliament of World Religions," *Buddhist-Christian Studies* 14 (1994): 205–207.

Morgan, Peggy. "The Study of Religions and Interfaith Encounter," *Numen* 42(2) (1995): 156–171.

Nolte-Schamm, Claudia. "African Traditional Ritual of Cleansing the Chest of Grudges as a Ritual of Reconciliation." *Religion and Theology* 13(1) (2006): 90–106.

Notter, James. *Trust and Conflict Transformation.* Occasional Paper No. 5 Institute for Multi-Track Diplomacy, April 1995.

Panikkar, Raimundo. *The Interreligious Dialogue.* New York: Paulist, 1978.

Sacks, Jonathan. *The Dignity of Difference: How to Avoid the Clash of Civilizations.* New York: Continuum, 2002.

Sampson, Cynthia. "Religion and Peace Building," in *Peacemaking in International Conflict: Methods and Techniques*, eds. W. Zartman and L. Rasmussen. Washington, DC: United States Institute of Peace Press, 1997.

Schirch, Lisa. "Ritual Reconciliation: Transforming Identity/Reframing Conflict," in *Reconciliation, Justice and Coexistence: Theory and Practice*, ed. Mohammed Abu Nimer. Lanham, MD: Lexington Books, 145–163.

Schneier, Arthur. "Religion and Interfaith Conflict: Appeal of Conscience Foundation," in *Interfaith Dialogue and Peacebuilding*, ed. David R. Smock. Washington, DC: United States Institute of Peace Press, 2002.

Seul, Jeffrey R. "'Ours Is the Way of God': Religion, Identity, and Intergroup Conflict." *Journal of Peace Research* 36(5) (1999): 553–569.

Shafiq, Mohammed and Mohammed Abu-Nimer. *Interfaith Dialogue: A Guide for Muslims.* Washington, DC: International Institute for Islamic Thought, 2007.

Slim, Randa. "Sustained Dialogue Process in Tajikistan: 1993–2005," Presentation at the Expert Group Meeting "Dialogue in the Social Integration Process: Building Peaceful Social Relations – by, for and with people." New York, November 21–23, 2005. http://www.un.org/esa/socdev/sib/egm/paper/Randa%20Slim.pdf (accessed December 17, 2012).

Smith, Wilfred Cantwell. *Towards a World Theology.* Philadelphia: Westminster, 1981.

Smock, David. *Interfaith Dialogue and Peacebuilding.* Washington, DC: United States Institute of Peace Press, 2002.

Stalov, Yehuda "Believe It Can Happen: Interfaith Encounter Approach in to the Israeli–Palestinian Conflict," in *Beyond Bullets and Bombs: Grassroots Peace Building Between Israelis and Palestinians*, ed. Judy Kuriansky. Westport, CT: Praeger Publications, 2007, 131–137.

Steele, David. "Contributions of Interfaith Dialogue to Peacebuilding in the Former Yugoslavia," in *Interfaith Dialogue and Peacebuilding*, ed. David R. Smock. Washington, DC: United States Institute of Peace Press, 2002.

United Nations Information Service. Press Release No: UNIS/SG/2639 (August 30, 2000) http://www.unis.unvienna.org/unis/pressrels/2000/sg2639.html (accessed December 17, 2012).

USIP. "Faith-based NGOs and International Peacebuilding," *Special Report* No. 76. Washington, DC: USIP, 2001.

USIP. "Can Faith-Based NGOs Advance Interfaith Reconciliation? The case of Bosnia and

Herzegovina," *Special Report* No. 103. Washington, DC: USIP, 2003.

Walker, Carolee. "State Dept: Youth Interfaith Movement Thrives in US," *US Federal News Service, Including US State News*. Washington DC. October 27, 2006.

WCC. *Guidelines on Dialogue with People of Living Faiths and Ideologies*. World Council of Churches, 1979. http://www.oikoumene. org/en/resources/documents/wcc-program mes/interreligious-dialogue-and-coopera tion/interreligious-trust-and-respect/guide lines-on-dialogue-with-people-of-living-faiths-and-ideologies.html (accessed December 17, 2012).

CHAPTER 11

Women in Inter-Religious Dialogue

Jeannine Hill Fletcher

The question of whether the inclusion of women's voices in the dialogue setting makes any difference, or if women's voices and experiences are already present in the dialogue as such, invites us to consider a variety of forms of dialogue and women's practices within them. While obviously no volume can cover all examples of inter-religious dialogue and women's inclusion or exclusion therein, the examination of three particular forms can highlight the distinct and interrelated ways that women have been involved in inter-religious dialogue. For this, we might start with the stereotypical format that gathers esteemed religious experts, like the very public event of the 1893 World's Parliament of Religions. A newspaper account of the 1893 parliament heralds the event as a historical first:

> The Parliament of Religions that convened yesterday in Columbus Hall of the Art Institute presented a spectacle that has never been equaled in the history of the world. From the snow capped mountains of Norway, to sunny France and the German fatherland came representatives of Christianity to meet in friendly conference with the swarthy sons of India, the followers of Islam, the representatives of Confucianism from China, and the devotees of Shintoism and Buddhism from the flowery kingdom of Japan. September 12, 1893. *The Daily Inter Ocean* (Chicago)[1]

As historian Richard Seager suggests, "the global and inclusive composition of the Parliament, however limited by today's standards, made the assembly a first-of-its-kind event in the history of the world" (Seager 1993: 8). Inter-religious dialogue, in this rendering, is a modern invention, making its debut as part of the Columbian Exhibition (recalling the four hundredth anniversary of the so-called "discovery" of the New World") of the 1893 Chicago World's Fair. Within the broader Columbian Exhibition, the parliament presented itself as a showcase for the West's recent "discovery" of the "New Worlds" of the religious traditions of the globe. Only recently had information

The Wiley Blackwell Companion to Inter-Religious Dialogue, First Edition. Edited by Catherine Cornille.
© 2013 John Wiley & Sons Ltd. Published 2020 by John Wiley & Sons Ltd.

about the diverse religions of the world flowed from colonial and mission enterprises into universities and out to the wider public and the 1893 parliament brought representatives of these various traditions together for an eager audience. Given its status as a first-of-its-kind event, to be replicated in the years to come, the parliament serves as representative of the spectacled exchange characterizing inter-religious dialogue in many of its formal settings.[2]

The parliament is also an interesting point of departure for a discussion of women in inter-religious dialogue. The *Daily Inter Ocean* article continues:

> About 10 o'clock strangers from every clime began to arrive, and for the next half hour President Bonney's office was turned into a reception room, where Chinese in the mandarin's robes and pigtails; Japanese in picturesque garb of chaste colors and varicolored head-dresses, Indians in their gaudy gowns of red, orange, and green; Germans, Russians, and Scandinavians; natives of Britain and her dependencies; and half a dozen interpreters mingled and mixed in a medley of universal brotherhood. The fair sex were there, too, and they were not neglected. But sisterhood in such a gathering was superfluous. The air was full of brotherhood, and it was of the generic kind, such as fits both sexes.

In the *Daily Inter Ocean* account, attention once devoted to the "fair sex" (terminology underscoring the status of women as objects of the masculine gaze) had now turned to the exotic foreigner dressed in "mandarin's robes and pigtails," "chaste colors," and the "gaudy gowns" of the "stranger" (noting of course that the dress of European delegates was not of interest). Apparently, the masculinist gaze of mainstream religion in the late nineteenth century could hold its attention on only one "other." The non-Western, non-Christian brother had been identified as "other," shifting attention and creating the perception that the Western, Christian "sister" was no longer "other."

This newspaper account provides a transparent example of the androcentric construction that regularly frames the writing of history. When brotherhood is the norm, women are included in the generic masculine (Schüssler Fiorenza 1992: 26–29). In the words of this particular reporter, the male-centered focus of brotherhood makes "sisterhood" superfluous. This androcentric bias creates historical sources that omit the presence and experience of women, leading readers of such histories to assume that women were not actively present, unless they are explicitly mentioned. But as this account so enthusiastically shows, the erasure of women's particular voices and experiences was intentional so as to underscore the spirit of camaraderie that extended to women and men. Sisterhood in this account is superfluous in its redundancy since the brotherhood already present extended to all. In the classic conception of inter-religious dialogue represented by the parliament model, sisterhood is superfluous in the way the Daily Inter Ocean suggests – that the brotherhood of man represented by the leaders of religious traditions suffices to represent the experience of women and men.

Taking the 1893 parliament account as a frame, we might investigate women's voices in inter-religious dialogue with the question, "Is sisterhood superfluous?" That is, does the inclusion of women's voices in the dialogue setting make any difference, or are women's voices and experiences already present in the dialogue as such? In dialogue settings where women continue to function as the object of the masculinist gaze, their bodily presence may be redundant, because "women" can be taken up as the topic of discussion by men and women alike. Such constructions of women in inter-religious dialogue tend to introduce "women" only insofar as the specificity of their bodies presents a problem or challenge to male-focused traditions. The occasional introduction of "women's issues" into inter-religious dialogue betrays a reality that "the religions" in inter-religious dialogue have often been constructed androcentrically – with male experience and male participants as the implicit subjects of discussion. But, when women are introduced as subjects of inter-religious dialogue, a more textured and challenging realization is in store. As women's voices and experiences are incorporated into inter-religious dialogue, we begin to see a more dynamic construction of "the religions," which reveals that the project of dialogue stands on a slippery surface, and any gains in understanding may have an unsettling undertow when gender is in view. "The religions" at the heart of inter-religious dialogue are fluid realities, such that sisterhood is indeed superfluous, but not in the way the *Daily Inter Ocean* intended. Rooted in the more original Latin "superfluere" – to overflow – women's voices in inter-religious dialogue enact a superfluity that is the uncapturable dynamic at the heart of religions themselves. A look at three different models of inter-religious dialogue demonstrates this fluid un-capturability and why women's voices matter in the dialogue of religions.

Women and the Parliament Model of Dialogue

Among the more standard conceptualizations of inter-religious dialogue, the Parliament Model puts forth "religions" as objects available for comment, explication, and comparison. This model envisions the project as one in which expert representatives of each tradition gather for the purpose of explanation, defense, and sometimes debate. Focused primarily on doctrines or beliefs, this form of dialogue is conceived as bringing together stable "religions" for the purpose of better understanding each "religion" and undertaking a comparison among them. This way of conceptualizing the dialogue positions a knowledgeable spokesperson of the tradition to "represent" the tradition by presenting the important beliefs. This individual stands ready to explain and defend his tradition, always with the possibility that he will be called into a debate should his own religious outlook be in conflict with another's. As a contemporary philosophical text describes, the challenge of inter-religious dialogue is precisely "how rationally to convince someone from another tradition that yours is true" (Quinn and Meeker 2000: 2). In order to defend the outlook, beliefs, and doctrines of their tradition, the representative is expected to have a comprehensive scope of the tradition, a firm grasp of its logic and be trained in the explanation of its inner workings. Such representatives likely are identified by their expert status as leaders or scholars in the tradition.

For the better part of history gendered constructions within religious traditions have maintained biases against women in leadership roles. Excluded from the education and training necessary to come to be viewed as "experts," women were not considered fit

representatives for dialogue. When leadership, training, and advanced religious education is reserved to men, the Parliament Model of dialogue privileges male voices and
experiences, often to the exclusion of women. And yet, the global women's movement
emerging in the late nineteenth century enabled women to find a place at the 1893
parliament, entering the dialogue as experts. This is reflected in even a cursory glance
at the list of presenters reproduced in Seager's *The Dawn of Religious Pluralism: Voices
from the World's Parliament of Religions, 1893* (1993). Of the 186 individuals who presented papers at the parliament, 23 were women (Seager 1995: 91). Annis F.F. Eastman
spoke on "The Influence of Religion on Women," bringing to light the negative assessment of women's nature that runs through many of the religious texts around the
globe (Barrows 1893: vol 1, 752–758). Others highlighted the positive roles religion
can take in the material lives of women: Henrietta Szold addressed the question "What
has Judaism Done for Woman?" (Barrows 1893: vol 2, 1052–1056), and Fannie
Barrier Williams asked, "What Can Religion Further Do to Advance the Condition of
the American Negro?" (Barrows 1893: vol 2, 1114–1115). Demonstrating their status
as experts in the traditions of the world, women's voices were heard in the parliament
halls, for example in "The Outlook of Judaism," by Josephine Lazarus (Barrows 1893:
vol 1, 704–715). Noted American suffragettes Julia Ward Howe and Elizabeth Cady
Stanton also voiced their concerns at the parliament. Seager's list does not include the
additional women who made statements at the opening and closing of the parliament,
such as the Vice President of the Woman's Branch of the World's Congress Auxiliary
(a parallel congress to the Parliament of World's Religions) and the chair of the
Woman's Committee of the parliament itself. (In fact, from the most widely accessible
scholarly collection on the parliament, Seager's 1993 collection of 1893 parliament
addresses and introductory notes, one would not even know that there was a "Woman's
Committee" at the parliament.) None of the historical records account for the exact
number of women present in the audience gathered, further suggesting that women's
participation in this high-profile inter-religious dialogue was greater than it might
appear. In her opening address, Rev. Augusta J. Chapin remarked:

> Woman could not have had a part in [a Parliament of Religions if it had been convened
> prior to this age] for two reasons: one that her presence would not have been thought of
> or tolerated, and the other was that she herself was still too weak, too timid and too
> unschooled to avail herself of such an opportunity had it been offered . . . Now the doors
> are thrown open in our own and many other lands. Women are becoming masters of the
> languages in which the great sacred literatures of the world are written. They are winning
> the highest honors that the great universities have to bestow, and already in the field of
> Religion hundreds have been ordained and thousands are freely speaking and teaching
> this new gospel of freedom and gentleness that has come to bless mankind. (Barrows 1893:
> vol 1, 82)

Chapin's reflection on the landmark quality of women's participation in the World's
Parliament of Religions in 1893 points to the wider social changes afoot that prepared
women for such public engagement. Importantly, she recognizes that it was not only
in the Western context that women's public and political engagement had seen them

take on more social roles: "now the doors are thrown open in our own and many other lands." Jeanne Sorabji of Bombay, for example, brought with her a perspective on women in India that challenged the perceptions of her audience. She illumined the advances in women's education, introducing to her audience the "schools and colleges for women in Bombay, Poona and Guzerat; also in Calcutta, Allahabad, Missoorie and Madras" (Barrows 1893: vol 2, 1037). Identifying Indian women poets, physicians, and artists, she stirred the imagination of Western women to recognize the lead women of other countries had taken and were continuing to take. "My countrywomen have been at the head of battles, guiding their men with word and look of command. My countrywomen will soon be spoken of as the greatest scientists, artists, mathematicians and preachers of the world" (Barrows 1893: vol 2, 1038). The 1893 Parliament of the World's Religions gives evidence that the feminist movements emerging around the globe were the basis for hope that women would soon be more central to the dialogue, and increased access to education for women in the twentieth century would shift the topics of discussion, and ultimately raise challenges, when women's voices were included in dialogue.

The Challenge of Women in the Parliament Model of Dialogue

The Parliament Model of dialogue requires that one speak for the whole of the tradition and represent its features as expert, and such dialogue participants often use an androcentric lens to interpret a given tradition. That is to say, when representing "the religion," the purportedly neutral report and defense of the tradition often focuses on male experiences from which women are excluded. The outlook of "the Catholic Church," to take my own tradition as an example, has been formulated exclusively by men in its authoritative doctrines and magisterial teachings. The practices of Hinduism, if centered on the temple, are also the domain of male priests. Gendered divisions in Islam, Judaism, and Buddhism similarly take male space as the normative religious space. When representing "the tradition," spokespersons often reinscribe the "male-as-norm." Women in inter-religious dialogue may simply repeat this androcentric perspective if they have been trained in male-centered teaching and practice. But in the twentieth century, when women increasingly gained access to education and religious study, new sources of knowledge came into being. Thus, women trained in feminist methods and in the study of women in religion could bring new views to the table.

The participation of women in inter-religious dialogue may support a shift in location for what counts as "religion." Scholars of women in religion have noted repeatedly the ways in which women's experiences within religious traditions have been impacted by the gendered norms which structure our societies and our religions. This means that while experts may be able to represent the textbook outlook of a given tradition in its belief and practices, the experience of women often falls outside the purview of these authoritative texts and practices. It is from her mother that Leila Ahmed remembers learning "Islam"; but it was a different style of Islam than she would discover as an expert in commentaries and or overheard in the mosques. Ahmed's Islam infused the everydayness of life. In Ahmed's words:

For although in those days it was only Grandmother who performed all the regular formal prayers, for all the women of the house, religion was an essential part of how they made sense of and understood their own lives. [. . .] Islam, as I got it from them, was gentle, generous, pacifist, inclusive, somewhat mystical – just as they themselves were . . . Religion was above all about inner things . . . What was important was how you conducted yourself and how you were in yourself and in your attitude towards others and in your heart . . . Islam . . . was a way of being in the world. A way of holding oneself in the world – in relation to God, to existence, to other human beings. This the women passed on to us most of all through how they were and by their being and presence, by the way *they* were in the world, conveying their beliefs, ways, thoughts, and how we should be in the world by a touch, a glance, a word – prohibiting, for instance, or approving. Their mere responses in this or that situation – a word, a shrug, even just their postures – passed on to us, in the way that women (and also men) have forever passed on to their young, how we should be. And all of these ways of passing on attitudes, morals, beliefs, knowledge – through touch and the body and in words spoken in the living moment – are by their very nature subtle. They profoundly shape the next generation, but they do not leave a record in the way that someone writing leaves a text about how to live or what to believe leaves a record. Nevertheless, they leave a far more important, and literally, more vital, living record. (Ahmed 2000: 121–122)

In Hindu practice as well, the mother's role in making sacred the space of the home and punctuating a child's life with ritual goes unnoticed by many textbook descriptions of Hindu thought and practice (Stork 1992). So too in the traditions of Judaism as seen from the perspective of women's experiences. As Judith Plaskow notes:

The *tkhines* [or petitionary prayers of Eastern European Jewish women] make clear that at the same time women participated in the established cycle of the Jewish year, they also sought and discovered God in domestic routines and in the biological experiences unique to women. Women were obviously able to find great meaning in their limited number of commandments. They were deeply involved with their families, a sphere of connection that extended to the dead. They felt deeply connected to the matriarchs, whose experience and merit they invoked. The *tkhines* testify to the importance of relationship in women's spirituality. (Plaskow 1991: 49)

The gendered structure of experience means that women's engagement with a tradition is often different from the androcentric male perspective. The challenge women bring to the Parliament Model, then, is the very basic question of what "counts" as representing the tradition, its outlook, and its practices. What women contribute as formerly obscured subjects may bring into greater relief the dynamics of religion in its sheer multiplicity and the recognition that "religions" are ultimately unrepresentable in any totalizing or comprehensive sense. Dialogue itself is always partial.

But, even beyond the incomplete nature of any representation of a tradition in dialogue, women in inter-religious dialogue often point to a more sinister reality in our androcentric traditions. In the words of Tracy Sayuki Tiemeier, "religious traditions are cultural carriers that (wittingly and unwittingly) justify, sustain, and perpetuate misogynistic practices" (Tiemeier 2011: 131). As Chung Hyun Kyung concludes, inter-religious dialogue among the male leaders of religious traditions gets locked into the privileges of male power and dominance. She writes, "So-called, all higher world religions are patriarchal and are institutionalized under the patriarchal light. So we have patriarchal Buddhists and patriarchal Christians having inter-religious dialogue, and we have nice patriarchal conclusions there" (Chung 1997: 401). But, as Pamela Dickey Young and others have suggested, women's experience within their traditions brings a different perspective. Young writes, "Women, by their very presence in inter-religious discussions, often question the 'official' stances of their traditions" (Young 1995: 30). While some approaches of women in dialogue may simply report "neutrally" on the distinctive experience or perspective of women in the tradition, women trained in feminist methodologies move beyond mere reporting to insist on a structural analysis of the many factors, including the religions themselves, which compromise women's full flourishing. As Rita Nakashima Brock explains, "In examining patriarchy, feminist theories expose the structures, such as class, race, region, religion, sexuality, and nationality, that subordinate and oppress women" (Brock 1996: 117). For example, when Julia Ward Howe spoke at the 1893 World's Parliament of Religions, she extolled the virtues of the founders of the traditions in elevating humanity toward their best ends. But, she also was critical of the followers of the traditions who do not live up to the lofty expectations set forth by the founders, concluding:

> I think nothing is religion which puts one individual absolutely above others, and surely nothing is religion which puts one sex above another. . . . And any religion which will sacrifice a certain set of human beings for the enjoyment or aggrandizement or advantage of another is no religion . . . Any religion which sacrifices women to the brutality of men is no religion. (Barrows 1893: vol 2, 1251)

Such a willingness to raise a critical eye toward the ways in which religions oppress women might be the distinctive contribution of women within inter-religious dialogue settings. The willingness to raise a feminist concern in an inter-religious setting may have serious consequences within the dialogue, especially if the dialogue serves as a venue for perpetuating privileges and securing the status conferred on the expert.

Women and the Activist Model of Dialogue

The critiques voiced by Julia Ward Howe, Chung Hyun Kyung, and Pamela Dickey Young (among others) gives way to yet another model of dialogue simultaneously embedded in the Parliament Model and constituting a distinctive model of its own. The Activist Model of dialogue does not take as its point of departure a neutral exchange or comparison between religions, but actively seeks the transformation of the world *and* the transformation of religions. What is in evidence with the Activist Model is that the lines between "sacred" and "secular" are not always clear; religion is always necessarily intertwined with the social and political, and thus it is a natural vehicle to be mobilized – for better or for worse. Here, another dimension of religion's fluidity comes into view.

   The global feminist movement emerging at the end of the nineteenth century and running through the twentieth century demonstrates a concern for solidarity across religious boundaries and for the broader alleviation of oppression. An activist focus for dialogue characterized the meeting of American-Christian-feminist suffragette Elizabeth Cady Stanton and women of a local Jewish community, precisely on the intersection of women's wellbeing and the ideals of the religions (Stanton 1969: 313).[3] In the 1920s, Indian feminist Sarojini Naidu found that the secular women's movement provided a context for inter-religious dialogue and solidarity, as Naidu worked on behalf of women's education and rights standing alongside her Muslim compatriots in India (Kumar 1993: 56). In the 1970s, within the National Organization for Women, the future Episcopal priest (Pauli Murray) and Roman Catholic sister (Joel Read) followed the lead of their Jewish sister (Betty Friedan) (Braude 2004: 559); and in academic circles from the 1970s through the present, feminist theologians from across the religions have addressed the suffering rooted in the oppression of sexism, and the social conditions that acutely impact poor women and women of color, as primary foci for inter-religious dialogue (Christ and Plaskow 1989; Cooey et al. 1991).
   As women gained access to the critical study of their religious traditions, and as they demanded greater social and political rights, they almost instinctively turned their activism toward religions themselves. Like Julia Ward Howe at the 1893 Parliament of Religions, women engaged in inter-religious dialogue in the activist mode have sought the mobilization of religion both for the transformation of the world and of religions themselves. Identifying misogynistic patterns of dehumanization and exclusion within patriarchal religious traditions, women's engagement in inter-religious dialogue has often taken the form of shared struggle and mutually informing cross-fertilization of feminist strategies. The editors of one scholarly volume on feminist inter-religious dialogue envision: "we are engaged in a common project of working toward more just and humane religious and social institutions" (Christ and Plaskow 1989: 8). As Carol Christ recalls, "I vividly remember the days when the women in religion section [of the American Academy of Religion] was a place where feminists in religion engaged in dialogue across religious boundaries. I believed that we were working together to transform and recreate religious traditions" (Christ 2000: 79).
   While the Parliament Model is founded on the desire to delimit "the religions" and draw out comparisons, contrasts, and debate, the Activist Model resists this reductive strategy and recognizes instead the way that "religion" and "not religion" are always intertwined. This means that women engaged in inter-religious dialogue in the Activist Model may or may not press religion exclusively to the fore. This makes for an enriching dialogue, but it also makes the distinctiveness of the event *as inter-religious dialogue* more difficult to identify. For example, one global movement of women in the Activist Model of dialogue is the international network of "Women in Black." Established fundamentally as an anti-war network, the many independent, local expressions of the organization are committed to demonstrating against militarism and violence against women, seeing the two as intimately related. In many of the instantiations of "Women in Black," the project offers evidence of an Activist Model of inter-religious dialogue. For example, the organization's branch in Serbia was founded in 1991 as a "public nonviolent protest against the war; the Serbian regime's policy; nationalism; militarism

and all forms of hatred, discrimination and violence" (Women in Black 2011). In its ongoing workshops, the project brings together women from various regions in Serbia: "As the population in these regions is very heterogeneous – ethnically, religiously, linguistically, and culturally – the content of all the workshops focused on recognizing all these differences as a base for creative dialog and cohabitation" (Zene U Crnom 2011). What is evident in the Activist Model of dialogue is that the specific nodal point of "religion" cannot be disentangled from economic, political, social, and material realities. Such a recognition means that the "inter-religious dialogue" that takes place in the Activist Model is not simply about "religion," in its doctrine or practice, but about the role religions play in maintaining or threatening human wellbeing.

Women's involvement in inter-religious dialogue formulated on the Activist Model has begun to be documented in a wide range of locations around the globe. The Liberian Women in Peacebuilding Network (WIPNET) brought together Muslim and Christian women in 2003 (Marshall et al. 2011: 7). Many other efforts similarly bring together women across religious lines in on-the-ground encounters (Craig 2003). A brief look at just one such dialogue allows us to glimpse the distinctiveness of this style of women's inter-religious dialogue: a session of the 2004 Parliament of the World's Religions entitled, "Peace-Building for Women – Taught by Middle East Interfaith Women." The women began by telling their stories and conveying intimate details of their personal lives as a means to illuminate the challenges and lived reality of a world divided by religiously infused politics, war, and hatred. The dialogue they recounted was not focused on rationally defending the beliefs of particular religions. Rather, their conversations developed out of a keen sense of the necessity to work together to protect the bodies of their sons and daughters, their husbands and parents. They talked about how each of them was vulnerable and how neighbors of diverse religious backgrounds might share the same physical space in a way that allowed for the fullest human flourishing. In the process, they drew on their religions to envision a way forward, but their primary focus was not to compare and contrast the diverse details of doctrine, but rather, to preserve the integrity of vulnerable bodies in a location where human wellbeing was threatened daily. Such on-the-ground inter-religious dialogue among women happens in innumerable places around the globe, but as Katherine Marshall and Susan Hayward report, "Working out of the public eye, women are less likely to face resistance from detractors and hence can be more effective. But, this also makes their work harder to document" (Marshall et al. 2011: 15).

Women who have been trained in feminist methodologies will bring activist methods even to a dialogue formulated in parliament fashion. One complicating factor for women operating out of the Activist Model of dialogue may come from the clash of aims and expectations when they are invited into the Parliament Model. Women trained in a feminist approach to religions will bring to the dialogue an ambiguous outlook on the status of religion, and a willingness to raise difficult issues in the context of the inter-religious setting. I have been involved in more than one inter-religious dialogue where the raising of critical issues of gender and sexual difference has been experienced as an affront to the experts gathered. Experiencing the raising of critical issues as an "attack" in a setting "designed for understanding" and "acceptance," women trained in the Activist Model of inter-religious dialogue may not be easy conversation partners with the expectations that often frame the Parliament Model. To those trained in the Parliament Model, such activist and liberationist agendas can appear to distract participants from a more fundamental focus on a neutral description of the religion. But a feminist approach to religion is precisely concerned to insist that religion is never neutral, and that so-called "neutral" perspectives from "the religions" can buttress (or more fundamentally, serve as foundation for) unjust practices. Ignoring the critical issues of women's exclusion from religious leadership, for example, or the tendency of religious rhetoric to reinforce gender dualisms that disadvantage women and maintain heteronormativity, under the guise of a neutral exchange of ideas toward "understanding," functionally maintains an unjust status quo. Women trained in the gendered perspectives of feminist theory and theology may produce a different sort of dialogue. If the Parliament Model carves out distinctive things that are "the religions" and separates them out for comparison, it also falls prey to a pattern of privileging "religion" over and against other realities. The Activist Model sees religion intimately intertwined with other realities of our human existence, and calls religion to task for the way it can be coopted within these realities to undermine human wellbeing.

With the Activist Model, we see a further shift and complexification of "religion" from its more classic construction in dialogue settings. No longer can "the religion" stand as an artifact to be explained, described, and debated; "religion" is always necessarily entangled in the social, political, material context in which it is found. In the Activist Model, the everydayness of our human lives necessarily is included in the dialogue and religion is something that is ever-changing. The dividing line between a dialogue on "religion" and a dialogue beyond the scope of "religion" is no longer easy to draw. Women's training in feminist methodologies and women's involvement in activism for women's and human wellbeing makes it more difficult to ascertain when exactly women are involved in "inter-religious dialogue." If inter-religious dialogue is defined as more than the exchange of information about "religion," then women's activities in inter-religious dialogue are indeed overflowing in their multiplicity.

Dialogue in the Everyday – A Storytelling Model

Excluded from leadership roles that might provide access to inter-religious dialogues formulated on the Parliament Model and trained in a feminist activism that fosters a distinctive inter-religious agenda, women in inter-religious dialogue have often found alternatives to malestream inter-religious dialogues. This models what communication theorists and peace advocates have come to expect: when excluded from formal systems of communication and coalition building, those excluded have found resources in informal communication and coalition building. One strand of such informal communication has been expressly formulated as a dialogue exclusively among women. In her seminal 1990 work on women in inter-religious dialogue, Maura O'Neill advocates that women first must dialogue among themselves, before they will be heard in the public forum. This assertion was based on research suggesting that "there are very significant differences found in the way men and women communicate, both in same-sex groups and in mixed sex groups" (O'Neill 1990: 47). O'Neill points to two key findings from a published study (Kramarae 1981) that suggested that: (1) women's concerns are often considered to be of marginal importance to men; and (2) while women employ self-disclosure of personal experience as a mode of communication, "men suffer . . . from an inability or unwillingness to self-disclose, to discuss feelings, and to do interaction support work" (O'Neill 1990: 48). O'Neill concludes: "If communication styles are so very different and language is understood differently by men and women, then women need first to talk among themselves. Only then will they have the assurance of being heard, and, because their language and style of communication is understood, real dialogue can take place" (O'Neill 1990: 49). O'Neill's thesis that women will benefit from single-sex dialogues is supported by more recent studies of the way individuals benefit from the diverse networks of communication. As the work of Stacy Young has indicated, when individuals are excluded from formal networks of communication within hierarchically organized institutions (as women often are in the institutions of religion), informal networks can be empowering by allowing persons to gain knowledge, a greater sense of control, and the necessary social networks for belonging in institutions that otherwise marginalize and silence them (Young 1998). This work in communication studies suggests that dialogue beginning among women may be most empowering for women interested in having a voice in inter-religious dialogues. Projects like *Women of Faith in Dialogue*, *Womanspirit Rising*, and *After Patriarchy* further suggest that this format of "parallel projects" among women have often proven productive for academic projects.

The argument for "separate space" for women's dialogues seems to say that women's engagement *is* distinctive, and that after women have had a chance to dialogue among themselves, they will bring something unique to more mainstream dialogues. In her wide-ranging study of women's inter-religious engagements – from national and international conferences over the last several decades, to more local engagements of women across traditions, and including very particular case studies of inter-religious dialogue – Helene Egnell summarizes the findings of what might be distinctive of women's inter-religious dialogue. She highlights several components in line with feminist methodologies and insights. Among the distinctive features, she found that women's inter-religious dialogues included the integration of "traditional experience," including "telling of life stories," concluding that "women's interfaith dialogue tends to emphasise (sic) faith as lived rather than as expressed in scriptures and doctrine" (Egnell 2007: 161, 163). Practitioners of inter-religious dialogue have recognized women's interest in the everyday experiences of their dialogue partners. Just as activism blurred the lines of religion and not-religion, the approach to dialogue through everydayness does so as well. Diane D'Souza, for example, reports from her experience organizing the *Women's Interfaith Journey* program that the women involved valued not only the formal programming of dialogue, but the informal spaces around meal tables or in the kitchen, concluding that "what women offer is an unapologetic affirmation of the importance of such spaces" (D'Souza 2005: 445). As Tracy Sayuki Tiemeier writes, "A women-centric approach . . . prioritizes the informal dialogues of everyday living that build the bonds of friendship necessary for theological conversations or action plans" (Tiemeier 2011: 127).

A Storytelling Model for dialogue brings home ever more clearly the superfluity of religion itself as every participant necessarily represents her or his tradition through the filter of his or her biography – whether this is admitted or not. The expressions of any given tradition are thus irreducibly diverse, making the reality of dialogue an overflowing abundance of possibility. As Marion Grau suggests, "Even if we could perfectly understand others, each person in community only holds part of the story, sometime[s] overlapping, sometimes not" (Grau 2011: 71). Concomitant with the mode of storytelling, scholars of women in inter-religious dialogue have reported a resistance of speakers to claim authoritative, comprehensive views of their tradition (the very requisite for the Parliament Model). In Egnell's study, "none of the participants claimed to speak as a representative of her tradition, but would rather say, 'I can only speak for myself' " (Egnell 2007: 165). Rather than believing it is a liability that we now have a dialogue where no one can speak with authority about her tradition, Egnell indicates the positive realization from which this reluctance springs, namely, "acknowledgement that not only are there many strands within one religious tradition but each person has her own interpretations and emphases on what is most important within that strand" (Egnell 2007: 165). O'Neill similarly underscores the internal diversity that might characterize dialogue participants in her study of women's interfaith discussions (O'Neill 2007). A participant in a Multifaith Women's Dialogue Group in Philadelphia reflected this internal multiplicity of religious perspectives in this way:

> It was the first time I realized there isn't *a* Muslim faith, there isn't *a* Lutheran faith, it's what your personal spin of it is. The women who are Muslim, you know they don't wear the headscarf. And that *is* something that is in the Qur'an. They are very quick to say, "It's between me and God." They do their prayers, they do everything else. But that's where they draw the line. There was a Jewish woman . . . she says that her Orthodox religion says that women cover their hair. She says, "That's where I draw the line. I'm not covering my hair." And I realize that that's where the Catholic women, they had practiced birth control or whatever. The religion becomes personal with each person that you know. (Joanne 2007)

A Storytelling Model witnesses a rich and complicated approach to inter-religious dialogue as it reminds us that "religion" cannot be reduced to doctrines and scriptures, to "what I believe" or "what I do." "Religion" is always "found" embedded in and intertwined with other aspects of our lived condition: economics, gender, social relations, material conditions, life stages, family relationships, and more. Our "religious" identities are entangled in and impacted by all of these features. The particular location of the religiously identified speaker in dialogue always complexly informs the articulation of that "religion." To pretend otherwise by focusing only on what "my tradition" believes or what the tradition "teaches" ignores the way that the description of religion is always filtered through the biography of the one who articulates it. The telling of stories is not only an important foundation for building friendships, it also enables the presentation of "religion" in a way more akin to the way it is lived. In traditionally formatted dialogue, the "expert" speaks as if distanced from his actual life to describe "the religion" as if it stands somewhere apart from the messiness of actual lives. But, in sharing stories, we see that "religion" is found only in its enactment in the world, in the messiness of lives.

The recognition of the particularity of our religious articulations makes dialogue possible. That is to say, the particular emphasis a speaker calls forth will be shaped by the other stories of her life, into which her religion is woven. It is the multiplicity of our lives – and our willingness to share that multiplicity and complexity – that provides the place for weaving our lives together, for becoming an inter-religious community, and for building the friendships required to stand in solidarity in a world that divides us on the basis of religion.

The Storytelling Model has benefits not only for those engaged primarily in dialogue toward friendship, relationship, and localized understanding. The Storytelling strategy has benefits also for enhancing both Activist and Parliament Models of dialogue. Because of the richness that the Storytelling Model can provide, Tiemeier makes a strong case for recognizing this characteristic feature of women's inter-religious dialogues as essential not only for women but for *all* engaged in inter-religious activity. Tiemeier suggests that comparative theologians, scholars of religions and persons involved in inter-faith work ought to have regular inter-religious communities with whom they are in friendship. Calling these "Basic Dialogue Communities," she writes that:

> dialogue can falter if participants focus only on theological discussion or "getting things done"; and dialogue can be superficial if it is done only for strategies of action. Rather, dialogue is deepest and most enduring when solidified by the bonds of friendship. . . . Within a Basic Dialogue Community, the theologian is better positioned to understand religious traditions in their contexts and respond to the sociopolitical, cultural, and religious needs of those communities. (Tiemeier 2011: 130)

While the Storytelling Model deepens and enriches our consideration of inter-religious exchange and inter-religious friendship, this model which welcomes everydayness may further unearth the complexities of women's engagement in inter-religious dialogue.

In places where religious diversity infuses the everydayness of existence, women's on-the-ground encounters in practical exchange may constitute yet another form of dialogue that will never be fully chronicled. Mercy Amba Oduyoye, for example, theologizes from a place where Muslims and Christians are neighbors to one another, sharing space and everyday practices (Oduyoye 2004). Considerations of women in Asia demonstrate the fluidity of boundaries among religions, such that "inter-religious dialogue" is truly an everyday practice; the dialogue itself is often an internal one as persons affiliate with the dynamism of multiple religious traditions simultaneously. Considering the everyday as a site of inter-religious encounter, we may see with fresh eyes Hindu women purchasing ritual objects from Muslim neighbors at festival time in India; or we may press further the practice of dialogue as Catholic Sisters share strategies of hospital administration with their Buddhist counterparts in China (Shukla-Bhatt and Yu 2006). The everyday as a site for considering women in inter-religious dialogue promises to yield new data for further investigation. With the Storytelling Model, and the everydayness that it brings, the rich uncapturability of inter-religious dialogues is testament to the rich uncapturability of "religion" itself.

Why Women's Voices Matter in the Dialogue of Religions

This brief indication of some avenues for considering women's voices in inter-religious dialogue must end where it began – with an insistence on superfluity, and the irreducibility of women's voices in inter-religious dialogue. Just as we have not exhausted the possibilities for research into the everydayness of women's inter-religious dialogue, we have not investigated other arenas where women would have been engaged in dialogue historically – the mission fields being one notable site. This short chapter has barely scratched the surface of women in inter-religious dialogue. What it has done, I hope, is indicate some reasons why women's voices matter in inter-religious dialogue.

Sisterhood in inter-religious dialogue is indeed superfluous in the way women's presence overflows beyond any single experience, and creates a dialogue with too many experiences, too many voices, to be artificially constrained by prior assumptions about women or about "religion." It will be a messy dialogue where much is unclear, out of control, contradictory in differential experiences. But bringing in this messiness will, undoubtedly, reflect more authentically the diverse experiences of religions themselves. The challenge of looking at inter-religious dialogue through the lens of women's experience is not the sheer addition of new perspectives (although the inclusion of previously ignored insights and experiences will surely add a wide range of topics to the list of any proposed dialogue). The challenge of gender in inter-religious dialogue lies in its insistence that any given dialogue is incomplete, internally contradictory, and, at times, incoherent. The expert spokesperson in the Parliament Model of dialogue may strive to appear as if he has a comprehensive view of his religion, but the living and dynamic, shifting and contradictory impact of his religion on real bodies in real time as they are manifest in women's experience must certainly bring into relief the reality that "religion," within and beyond the dialogue of religions, is a messy thing. "Religion" in inter-religious dialogue exceeds the expert's grasp as it moves from thought and belief to lived and living experiences. "Religion" is not a category under control, nor is it easily categorized; what counts as "religion" is an uncontrollable reality with many diverse expressions.

For some, surely, this infinite diversity is precisely the draw of inter-religious dialogue: by encountering the sheer tremendous possibilities that spring forth from "religion," one may be somehow enhanced by the witnessing. For this reason, then, women's voices in inter-religious dialogue should be an essential ingredient to propelling the ongoing encounter among the faiths. The sheer introduction of new experiences and possibilities formerly foreclosed by the absence of women's insights exponentially increase the avenues for discussion in the dialogue itself. But, learning from the gendered exclusion of women's voices from dialogue, and re-engaging dialogue with activist intentions, allows us the opportunity to press even further in an unending dialogue toward ever-greater eco-human flourishing in the everydayness of lives intertwined across religious difference.

Notes

1   Cited in Richard Hughes Seager, *The Dawn of Religious Pluralism: Voices from the World's Parliament of Religions, 1893* (LaSalle, IL: Open Court Publishing, 1993) 31.
2   Using the 1893 Parliament and its colonial moment as a starting point for the discussion of dialogue also reminds us to remain attentive to the neo-colonial interests which might continue to inform dialogue today.
3   Recognizing, of course, that Stanton reflects on the fact that she and the Jewish women disagreed over whether the Biblical tradition was liberating for women.

Bibliography

Ahmed, Leila. *A Border Passage: From Cairo to America – A Woman's Journey*. New York: Penguin, 2000.

Barrows, John H. (ed.). *The World's Parliament of Religions*. 2 volumes. Chicago: Parliament, 1893.

Braude, Ann. "A Religious Feminist – Who Can Find Her? Historiographical Challenges from the National Organization for Women." *The Journal of Religion* 84(4) (2004): 555–572.

Brock, Rita Nakashima. "Feminist Theories," in *Dictionary of Feminist Theologies*, eds. Letty M. Russell and J. Shannon Clarkson. Louisville, KY: Westminster John Knox, 1996: 116–120.

Cady Stanton, Elizabeth. "Diary, 19 April 1895," in *Elizabeth Cady Stanton*, eds. Theodore Stanton and Harriot Stanton Blatch, 313. New York: Arno & The New York Times, 1969.

Christ, Carol. "Roundtable Discussion: Feminist Theology and Religious Diversity." *Journal of Feminist Studies in Religion* 16(2) (2000): 79–84.

Christ, Carol P. and Judith Plaskow (eds.). *Weaving the Visions: New Patterns in Feminist Spirituality*. San Francisco: HarperSanFrancisco, 1989.

Chung, Hyun Kyung. "Seeking the Religious Roots of Pluralism." *Journal of Ecumenical Studies* 34(3) (1997): 399–402.

Cooey, Paula M., William R. Eakin, and Jay B. McDaniel (eds.). *After Patriarchy: Feminist Transformations of the World's Religions*. Maryknoll, NY: Orbis, 1991.

Craig, Lillian Harris. "Loss and Identity: Muslim and Christian Sudanese Women in Dialogue." *Studies in World Christianity* January (2003): 154–170.

D'Souza, Diane. "Interfaith Dialogue: New Insights from Women's Perspectives," in *Ecclesia of Women in Asia: Gathering the Voices of the Silenced*, eds. Evelyn Monteiro and Antoinette Gutzler. Delhi: ISPCK, 2005. Quoted in Tiemeier: 127.

Egnell, Helene. *Other Voices: A Study of Christian Feminist Approaches to Religious Plurality East and West*. Uppsala, Sweden: Studia Missionalia Svecana C, 2007.

Grau, Marion. *Rethinking Mission in the Postcolony: Salvation, Society and Subversion*. New York: T & T Clark, 2011.

Hill Fletcher, Jeannine. "Women's Voices in Dialogue: A Look at the Parliament of the World's Religions." *Studies in Interreligious Dialogue* 16(1) (2006): 1–22.

Joanne [pesud.], Women's Interfaith Dialogue Group Participant, interview by Mara Brecht. Transcript of digital recording, December 15, 2007. Radnor, Pennsylvania.

Kramarae, Cheris. *Women and Men Speaking*. Rowley, MA: Newbury House, 1981. Quoted in Maura O'Neill, *Women Speaking, Women Listening: Women in Interreligious Dialogue*. Maryknoll, NY: Orbis, 1990: 48.

Kumar, Radha. *The History of Doing: An Illustrated Account of Movements for Women's Rights and Feminism in India 1800–1990*. London: Verso, 1993.

Marshall, Katherine and Susan Hayward, with Claudia Zambra, Esther Breger, and Sarah Jackson. *Women in religious peacebuilding.* Peaceworks (United States Institute of Peace) 71 (2011): 1–25.

Mollenkott, Virginia Ramey. *Women of Faith in Dialogue.* New York: Crossroad, 1987.

Oduyoye, Mercy Amba. *Beads and Strands: Reflections of an African Woman on Christianity in Africa.* Maryknoll, NY: Orbis, 2004.

O'Neill, Maura. *Women Speaking, Women Listening: Women in Interreligious Dialogue.* Maryknoll, NY: Orbis, 1990.

O'Neill, Maura. *To Mend the World: Women in Interreligious Dialogue.* Maryknoll, NY: Orbis, 2007.

Plaskow, Judith. *Standing Again at Sinai: Judaism from a Feminist Perspective.* San Francisco: HarperSanFrancisco, 1991.

Quinn, Philip L. and Kevin Meeker. *The Philosophical Challenge of Religious Diversity.* New York: Oxford University Press, 2000.

Schüssler Fiorenza, Elisabeth. In *Memory of Her: A Feminist Reconstruction of Early Christian Origins.* New York: Crossroad, 1992.

Shukla-Bhatt, Neelima and Chun-Fang Yu. Panel presentation, "Why Do Women's Voices Matter in the Dialogue of Religions," March 23, 2006, Fordham University, New York.

Seager, Richard Hughes. *The Dawn of Religious Pluralism: Voices from the World's Parliament of Religions, 1893.* LaSalle, IL: Open Court, 1993.

Seager, Richard Hughes. *The World's Parliament of Religions.* Bloomington, IN: Indiana University Press, 1995.

Stork, Helene. "Mothering Rituals in Tamilnadu: Some Magico-Religious Beliefs," in *Roles and Rituals for Hindu Women,* ed. Julia Leslie. Delhi: Motilal Banarsidass, 1992: 89–106.

Tiemeier, Tracy Sayuki. "Comparative Theology and the Dialogue of Life." *Japan Mission Journal,* Summer (2011): 126–137.

Women in Black. 2011. www.womeninblack. org/en/belgrade (accessed Decmeber 18, 2012).

Young, Pamela Dickey. *Christ in a Post-Christian World: How can we believe in Jesus Christ when those around us believe differently – or not at all?* Minneapolis, MN: Fortress, 1995.

Young, Stacy L. "Where Silenced Voices Speak Out: The Hidden Power of Informal Communication Networks." *Women and Language* 21(2) (1998): 21–31.

Zene U Crnom Beograd (Women in Black Belgrade). 2011. "Alternative Education: Seminar, Power and Otherness." www.ze neucrnom.org/index.php?option=com_con tent&task=blogcategory&id=20&Ite mid=11 (accessed December 18, 2012).

PART II

Case Studies

CHAPTER 12
Buddhist–Hindu Dialogue

David Peter Lawrence

At the outset, it is necessary to clarify the purview of this essay. For present purposes, I will define the two religions of Hinduism and Buddhism in broadly historical terms rather than on the basis of any criteria of doctrine, experience, or practice. At one level, the problems of defining these religions are the same as those of all others, inasmuch as any large set of cultural traditions comprises great synchronic and diachronic diversity. The problems with defining Buddhism historically may be said to be largely of this sort, and I will utilize a nearly catch-all definition of the religion as the range of traditions that view themselves as Buddhist by reason of ostensibly adhering to what are believed to be teachings of the historical, Śakyamuni Buddha – even if such traditions in actual fact derive most of their teachings from others, worship other Buddhas as gods, or what not. This essay will not be concerned with inevitable gray areas in such a definition.

The definition of Hinduism, however, is more complex, since most contemporary scholars agree that the term is a recent construction, coined by British colonialists (on the definition of Hinduism, see Lipner 1998: 1–21; Flood 2002: 5–22). Iranian invaders before the Common Era referred to the people who lived near a river called Sindhu, in what is currently Pakistan, as Sindhus. From the word Sindhu are derived the present name of the river, Indus, as well as the words Hindu and India. Muslims also later used the term Sindhu/Hindu to refer to those who followed the indigenous religious and cultural traditions of the subcontinent. The British conceived of the traditions more essentialistically as Hindu-ism, and early modern Indian/Hindu nationalists used this conception to consolidate religious and national identity. Present-day Hindu communitarian social and political movements continue to attempt to rally Indian identity around a concept of Hindutva, literally "Hinduism."

Another complication in the attempt to define Hinduism is that many who identify themselves as adherents to this religion include within it Buddhism, as well as the other indigenous religions, Jainism and Sikhism. However, it seems that most followers of

The Wiley Blackwell Companion to Inter-Religious Dialogue, First Edition. Edited by Catherine Cornille.
© 2013 John Wiley & Sons Ltd. Published 2020 by John Wiley & Sons Ltd.

those religions would not accept that classification. For the purpose of this essay Hinduism may be coherently and usefully defined as the broad stream of indigenous South Asian religious civilization that is not Buddhist, Jain or Sikh.

Some support for such a classification may be found in ancient Brahmanic philosophical authors, who described the Mīmāṃsā, Vedānta, Nyāya, Vaiśeṣika, Sāṃkhya and Yoga as orthodox (āstika, "it exists") schools, and Buddhism and Jainism as heterodox (nāstika, "it does not exist") traditions. It should be noted that there are other important Hindu philosophical traditions besides the six just mentioned, and that not all of the six will be discussed below. Also, other themes such as deference to the scriptural authority of the Vedic corpus distinguish many but not all Hindus, and even Hindus who express such deference usually rely on other oral and written religious authorities. Below we will consider some other crucial differences and similarities between Hinduism and Buddhism, as defined here.

With regard to dialogue, Mikhail Bakhtin has drawn attention to the fact that communicative exchange between diverse individuals and diverse social groups pervades all expressions of language, culture and social action (1994). Hinduism and Buddhism thus evince vast cultural exchanges and mutual influences over thousands of years. Dialogicity is evinced not only in explicit interreligious exchange and debate between Hindus and Buddhists, but also in pan-Indian and pan-Asian movements such as devotion (bhakti) and tantra, and in the multiple details of experience, belief, ritual and ethics that shape the lives of followers of both religions. Such exchange also encompasses complex dialogicity regarding South Asian castes (jāti), including efforts to eradicate caste, generated within and between the traditions throughout history.

Because I cannot survey this vast range of dialogue here, I will focus on self-conscious dialogue between the broad traditions, particularly in the form of philosophical debate. The respectful though spirited arguments between Hindus and Buddhists, developed over thousands of years, have produced some of the world's most sophisticated philosophical works, and contain valuable lessons for contemporary practitioners of inter-religious dialogue.

Doubt and Debate in Ancient South Asia, and the Challenge of Buddhism

Amartya Sen has demonstrated in his book *The Argumentative Indian* that intellectual inquiry and debate have been highly valued from the very beginning of South Asian culture (2005). The earliest work of the Vedic corpus, the *Ṛg Veda*, which probably dates from between 1200 and 1500 BCE, comprises henotheistic hymns to numerous deities, correlated with sacrificial rituals. Rudimentary philosophical speculations are already found in some of these hymns, for example, in speculations on the creation of the universe by an ineffable "One" (10.129), by the sacrificial dismemberment of a cosmic person (10.90), and by a Golden Embryo about which there is the inquiry, "What god shall we revere with the oblation" (10.121) (O'Flaherty 1981).

This philosophical tendency further developed through the parts of the Vedic corpus known as the Brāhmaṇas and Āraṇyakas. It reached an early culmination in the great speculations and dialogues, accompanying the myths and revelations of the Upaniṣads, also known as the Vedānta, the end of the Veda. In these texts, we find formulations of core Hindu concepts of the true self (ātman) and the absolute (brahman), as well as rudimentary expressions of many other ideas developed in later scholastic philosophies. Some discourses of the Upaniṣads propound a nondualism in which self and absolute are identified. Others teach a monotheistic, dualistic conception of the self as separate from the absolute, which is conceived as God. In those sections, the goal is for the self to realize only intimacy or partial identity with God.

The Upaniṣads also present the earliest expressions of the understanding of the human predicament that became common to most of later Hinduism as well as other indigenou South Asian religions: Humans and other creatures suffer due to the temporal finitude or transitoriness of things, culminating in death. This conceived unhappy condition, furthermore, is believed to obtain not only in one life, but rather (as might at first seem paradoxical to outsiders) to be repeated in a vast cycle-of- births-and-deaths, saṃsāra, as driven by action-linked-to-its-results, karma. The texts likewise advocate the pursuit of mokṣa, liberation from the cyclical predicament, through the realization of either the identity or the intimacy of the self and the absolute (on Upaniṣadic religion, see Olivelle 1996).

The earliest Pali Sūtras[1] were compiled in writing in the first century BCE based on oral traditions of discourses of the Buddha and his close disciples going back over about 400 years. Core philosophical ideas presented in these Sūtras were articulated more systematically in the first stream of Buddhist scholastic philosophy, known as Abhidharma, which developed from approximately the third century BCE. Important for our purposes is that Buddhism, beginning in its earliest texts, defined itself agonistically in relation to Vedic ritualism as well as the more metaphysical and soteriological teachings of the Upaniṣads.

Buddhism's original and continuing disagreements with Hindu traditions may be summarized under three headings:

1) Buddhists agree with most Hindus, along with other indigenous South Asian religions, regarding the predicament of temporal finitude in saṃsāra due to karma, and the goal of pursuing mokṣa from the same – which they usually call nirvāṇa, "blowing out." However, they generally radicalize the understanding of temporal finitude in claiming that there is nothing enduring whatsoever. Thus, according to the foundational Buddhist teaching of the three attributes of reality, all things are transitory, amount to suffering (duḥkha), and lack "self," in the sense of any sort of enduring or substantial nature.

    Such teachings challenge almost all otherworldly ideals and even many mundane aspects of Hindu religious life. Buddhists repudiate Hindu conceptions of liberation (mokṣa) as the attainment of an eternal condition such as the realization of an immortal self, intimacy with an eternal God, the attainment of paradise, and so on. They are generally skeptical or agnostic about any explanation of what is liberation, *nirvāṇa*. It is not immortality, not annihilation, not both, not neither.

2)   Buddhists generally deny the value of theories about the ultimate nature of things. At one level, they claim that such theories are simply a distraction from the pursuit of *nirvāṇa*. More fundamentally, according to Buddhists, theories *tend erroneously to posit enduring conditions in the world*. When faced with theoretical options such as A versus not A (such as whether or not there is immortality in *nirvāṇa*), the Buddha of the Sūtras attempts to circumvent the almost universally accepted law of the excluded middle in claiming: A is not the case. Not-A is not the case. Both A and not-A is not the case. Neither A nor not A is not the case.

3)   The Buddhist doctrine of "dependent origination" (*pratītyasamutpāda*) provides intellectuals of Buddhist traditions with a tool for supporting 1 and 2, and ostensibly refuting all Hindu and any other competing doctrines of enduring conditions of existence and nonexistence, or combinations thereof.

As explained in early Abhidharma texts, the doctrine of dependent origination is an interpretation of the path of Buddhism as a Middle Way between the two extremes of lifestyle that the Buddha is supposed to have experienced before he became enlightened – the life of pleasure or hedonism, and the life of extreme asceticism or self-torture. Both these lifestyles are said to be pursued on the basis of the fundamental moral and spiritual flaw – attachment – and lead accordingly to suffering (*duḥkha*).

    The Buddhists interpret the two extreme lifestyles as involving particular misguided views or "heresies." The pursuit of pleasure is predicated on the misconception that things have some sort of enduring or substantial existence. Thus one pursues pleasure in worldly things or even in an imagined eternal afterlife. Conversely, Buddhists view the life of extreme asceticism or self-torture as an attachment to escape from the world, correlated with the tendency towards the heresy of believing that things do not exist, or that liberation will be some sort of annihilation.

    On the one hand, Buddhists claim that the demonstration of *dependence* refutes the misconception that there is anything with an enduring substantial or *in*dependent existence. The supposed substantial existence of anything may be analyzed away by showing that the thing is dependent upon a variety of other factors. A classic example is the analysis of the chariot into material components. All one finds, in such an analysis, are parts of parts of parts. It is the same with an ostensible self or God. The earliest extant Abhidharma texts express a belief that, through the analysis of dependence, one might identify evanescent atomic facts or qualities (*dharmas*). Later schools of Buddhism, however, developed new ideas about the nature of such atomic facts, and introduced more situational and even logical factors into the analysis of dependence.

    On the other hand, the teaching of *origination* ostensibly refutes the nonexistence of things. Things cannot *not* exist, because they do originate in orderly patterns. This explains success and failure in worldly endeavors, the regularity of *karmic* consequences in *saṃsāra,* and also the efficacy of the Buddhist soteriological path. The earliest Buddhist texts thus situate suffering itself within a twelvefold chain of dependent origination, and prescribe the counteraction of that proliferation of unskillful existence with the synthesis of wisdom, morality and meditation offered in the Eightfold Path (see the selection of Pali Sūtras and Abhidharma philosophy in Radhakrishnan and Moore 1989: 172–192).

The well-known Buddhist conception of emptiness (*śūnyatā*) is found already in the Pali texts, and became predominant in later Sanskrit Mahāyāna works. It does not mean "nothing," but rather, following the reasoning of the doctrine of dependent origination, the lack of any comprehensible and enduring nature – as something, nothing, both or neither. Emptiness is an affirmation of the ultimate conceptual incomprehensibility of reality.

Buddhists of various stripes also came to frame emptiness within a doctrine of two levels of truth. At the provisional, veiled level of truth (*saṃvṛti satya*) there is ordinary existence and nonexistence, truth and falsity. At the ultimate level of truth (*paramārtha satya*), there is all-sublating emptiness. Most schools of Buddhist philosophy may be understood as various interpretations of the central teaching of dependent origination. Dependent origination ostensibly explains how things work at the provisional level while demonstrating that everything is ultimately empty.

The diverse Hindu philosophical schools that developed following the period of the Upaniṣads responded vigorously to these Buddhist challenges. The methodologies of debate that developed, and some of the particular arguments that resulted, will be described below. While there are numerous different systems of Hindu philosophy, basically they all argue against the Buddhists that there are one or more enduring, substantial realities. They also contend that dependent origination and other Buddhist teachings are also theories, and that the Buddhist claims are therefore self-contradictory.

Indian philosophy has been greatly stimulated in its development by "intertheoretic competition" of divergent religious and intellectual traditions – within and between the various schools of Hinduism, Buddhism and Jainism (see Horton 1984 on intertheoretic competition as the social requisite to scientific rationality; cf. Vernant 1982 on how democratic debate led to the development of Greek philosophy). Within these great currents of argument, the greatest impetus for the development of Indian philosophy as a whole has probably been the history of dialogue and debate between the traditions of Hinduism and those of Buddhism.

Discursive Ethics of Hindu and Buddhist Scholastic Philosophies

As Hindu and Buddhist philosophies advanced and proliferated in the millennia following the era of the Upaniṣads and Buddhist origins, they developed increasingly sophisticated protocols to regulate argumentation. We may follow contemporary theorists on public reason in interpreting such protocols as "discursive ethics" for academic dialogue and debate (see Apel 1989, 2001). South Asian discursive ethics for public debate and philosophical argument are treated in many places, such as the Hindu epic, *Mahābhārata*, various Buddhist texts such as the *Upāyahṛdaya*, the *Yogacaryābhūmiśāstra*, Vasubandhu's lost *Vādavidhi*, and Dharmakīrti's *Vādanyāya*, the Hindu *Arthaśāstra*, the medical text *Caraka*, and the texts of the Hindu Nyāya school (Solomon 1976–1978).

The discussion here will center on the most influential guidelines for discursive ethics in Sanskritic philosophy. These are the 16 categories pertaining to philosophical discussion summarized by the Hindu Nyāya realist, Gautama, in *Nyāya Sūtra* 1.1, and elaborated further in later commentaries (Gautama et al. 1985: 28; on the influence of Nyāya standards, also see Matilal 1986: 69–93.). Various other philosophical traditions of Hinduism and Buddhism (and Jainism) further modified and built upon the Nyāya scheme in their own ways (Matilal 1998). As the medieval Hindu Śaiva philosopher, Abhinavagupta explains:

> The ultimate purpose in that [a philosophical text] is nothing but [explanation in terms of] the sixteen categories, such as the means of knowledge [*pramāna*], and so on. . . When the sixteen categories are articulated, another is made to understand completely that which is to be understood. (1986: 2.3.17, 2: 140)

The 16 Nyāya categories refer to items of different orders – subject matters and proper and improper methods – and should be understood as a variety of concerns that must be addressed, more than as items that necessarily have to be considered separately. I will mention some of these concerns in my own order, as relevant to understanding the dialogue between Hindus and Buddhists, while also noting some disagreements.

Particularly important in the present context are the categories analyzing different types of philosophical argument according to their purposes and methodologies. The Nyāya analysis, which has parallels elsewhere, distinguishes between *vāda*, friendly argument in the pursuit of truth, conducted according to the highest standards; *jalpa*, argument in the pursuit of victory, and sometimes at the expense of truth, which may employ various deceptive or "Sophistic" rhetorical devices; and *vitanḍā*, argument aiming to refute the opponent"s position without establishing any doctrine of one"s own.

The *Nyāya* definition of *vāda* specifies the pragmatic ethical requirements for an honest and civil, egalitarian and truth-oriented, rather than hegemonic, philosophical discourse. Such discourse consists of a dialogue between adherents of two contrary positions (*pakṣa* and *pratipakṣa*) on a particular topic. The arguments in this dialogue must be based upon means of knowledge (*pramāna*) about the ontological knowables (*prameya*), accompanied by supportive reasoning (*tarka*). They must not contradict premises (*siddhānta*) common to the parties, and they must make use of the steps of the philosophical syllogism (*avayava*) (Gautama et al. 1985: 1.2.1; 1.1.32; 4.4.47–49).

An ancient characterization of the syllogism was developed by the Buddhist philosopher Dignāga in the fifth–sixth centuries CE and then reappropriated by the Nyāya and other Hindu schools: it was considered as an "inference for the sake of others" (*parārthānumāna*). This is distinguished from the "inference for the sake of oneself" (*svārthānumāna*) one routinely and unreflexively makes in one"s daily life. Esther Solomon observes that it was the "social need" of intellectual intercourse that led to the rigorous explication of the "inference for the sake of others" as a basic form of reasoning (1976–1978: 1: 399).

The Nyāya version of the inference in five steps includes some reiteration of key points, in order to make the proof as publicly assessable as possible. While others disputed the need for this redundancy, as well as other technical details (Solomon 1976–1978: 1: 356–357), the basic structure of argument was widely accepted by Hindu and Buddhist schools. To provide some idea what this is all about, I will briefly review the Nyāya version of the syllogism, with the common example of the inference of fire from smoke on a hill:

1) Thesis: There is fire on the hill. The hill is the subject of the inference. The fire is that which is to be established pertaining to it.
2) Reason: Because there is smoke. The smoke itself, like the inferential step which invokes it, is also designated with the word reason (*hetu*). It is a property found in the subject, and known to be concomitant with, that is, invariably to accompany, that which is to be established. As such it is the justification for the inference.
3) General principle with exemplification: Where there is smoke there is fire, like in the kitchen and unlike on the lake. This step explains the concomitance underlying the reason, and provides a positive example illustrating the concomitance, along with a negative example, showing that the property does not have concomitance with a class wider than that which is to be established.
4) Application: The hill, because it has smoke on it, has fire on it. This step explicitly asserts that the subject falls within the concomitance shown by the previous step.
5) Conclusion, which repeats the thesis as established: *therefore, there is fire on the hill* (see Potter 1977: 180–181; 1963: 60–61; Matilal 1986: 78).

It may be observed that this inference combines the induction of a relationship of classes along with a deduction based on this relationship.

Disputes Over *Jalpa* and *Vitaṇḍā*

The two other types of debate described in the Nyāya categories of philosophical argument are much more problematic and controversial. There is an understanding that they may be used for victory for the sake of personal gain. Particularly interesting in this regard is the category of *jalpa*. As Gautama explains, jalpa has some of the features of *vāda*, while also comprising "quibbling" (*chala*), "inappropriate rejoinders" (*jāti*) and the observation of "clinchers" (*nigrahasthāna*) in the opponents' arguments (Gautama et al. 1985: 1.2.1).

"Quibbling" is basically changing the meaning of expressions, improperly generalizing their meaning, and confusing literal and metaphorical meanings (Gautama et al. 1985: 1.2.10–17). For example, one might interpret the opponent"s use of *nava* in the sense of "new" improperly as meaning "nine." "Inappropriate rejoinders" identify invalid exceptions to the reasoning of the opponent, based upon superficial similarities and dissimilarities (Gautama et al. 1985: 1.2.18). One might argue that a new factory will not produce lower emissions because another new facility, of a different kind, did not do that. These tricks are used for the attainment of victory, even at the expense of truth.

With regard to "clinchers," all philosophical schools acknowledge that pointing out the flaws of opponents is an important part of a legitimate debate. My understanding is that in *jalpa*, as opposed to *vāda*, one might do this more than is necessary for the pursuit of truth. The seventh-century CE Buddhist epistemologist and logician Dharmakīrti streamlines the Nyāya list of 24 clinchers to two: not properly stating the constituent of a proof, and not properly pointing out faults of the opponent (Chinchore 1988).

Now, it must be noted that the Nyāya philosophers actually allow *jalpa* and *vitaṇḍā* when one is trying to protect adherents' confidence in the true position. If one is criticized by ignorant people, and does not readily know the proper response, they say that these devices can offer protection, like thorny bushes protecting sprouting seeds (Gautama et al. 1985: 4.2.50–51).

However, these types of argument are clearly contrary to the overarching purposes and methods of the Nyāya system, which is oriented towards the determination of veridical knowledge regarding real objects. And in fact the Nyāya philosophers offer a variety of considerations for the definitive refutation of the various strategies of both *jalpa* and *vitaṇḍā*. In this, they are joined by many other schools of Hindu and Buddhist (and Jaina) philosophy. Dharmakīrti, in his *Vādanyāya*, and the eighth-century CE Buddhist philosopher Śāntarakṣita, in his *Vipañcitārtha*, present very strict standards of debate. According to Dharmakīrti, debate with the aim of mere victory is never permitted (Dharmakīrti et al. 1972: 68–71, 107–108). Dharmakīrti"s refutations of the strategies of what the Nyāya philosophers call *jalpa* and *vitaṇḍā* further demonstrate the inadequacy of these devices.

Nyāya philosophers explain that if one is criticized for claiming a concomitance on the basis of irrelevant similarities and differences, one should answer such criticisms by showing that one's reasons are based on genuine concomitances, as supported by proper illustrations (see the discussion beginning at Gautama et al. 1985: 5.1.3). Dharmakīrti argues that quibbling through assigning different meanings to words and concepts does not establish or protect the truth, and that if one pursues victory in this way, one might as well strike the opponents with fingernails, hands or weapons, or burn them. A good person should, rather, try to aid others to understand the truth through legitimate proofs and observations of their mistakes. Dharmakīrti compares other false argumentation to singing and dancing, and offering fruits (Dharmakīrti: 65–71).

There has been a lot of debate about the viability of *vitaṇḍā*, the effort to refute others without establishing one's own position. This is the approach commonly ascribed to the second–third century CE Mādhyamaka Buddhist philosopher, Nāgārjuna, whose philosophy will be discussed below. Regardless of the tenability of Nāgārjuna's arguments, his intellectual integrity appears indisputable. There is no indication that he aimed at personal advantage, and he did not follow the tricks of *jalpa*.

In the following sections I will provide some illustrations of the mature scholastic dialogues and debates between Hindus and Buddhists over a variety of philosophical topics. I hope that this sampling of a vast range of discussions will provide an idea of the richness and depth of historical Hindu-Buddhist dialogues.

Schools of Hindu Realism versus Buddhist Idealism and Phenomenalism

Contra certain stereotypes, Hindu philosophy comprises a great deal more than doctrines of a nondual Self. Thus some philosophical schools espouse a pluralistic and direct or "naïve" realistic epistemology and ontology – which upholds our immediate perception of a real world comprising diverse enduring objects, their qualities and processes. The most influential of these are the Nyāya and the closely allied and overlapping Vaiśeṣika schools. Corresponding to the sophisticated Nyāya epistemology outlining the means of knowledge and methods of argument, these schools elaborate a complex scheme of ontological categories, comprising real objects, universals, actions, and so on, with which we have direct perceptual contact.

With regard to soteriology, later Nyāya-Vaiśeṣika traditions were variously combined with theistic devotionalism or nondual Vedānta. However, the original Nyāya claim is that, by knowing the truth about the various entities that constitute reality, one will find liberation, which is the result of the discrimination and isolation of one's individual self from all contents of worldly experience, which are not the self (Potter 1977: 18–37).

Often allied with the Nyāya and Vaiśeṣika schools in their emphasis on direct realism, but following a quite different axiology, is the school of Pūrva Mīmāṃsā, which focuses on interpreting the Veda as a set of ritual injunctions. Later Mīmāṃsā thinkers identified their traditions' understanding of the paradise attained through the Vedic sacrifice with the common South Asian objective of liberation from *karma* and *saṃsāra*. Mīmāṃsā philosophers felt it necessary to join their Nyāya and Vaiśeṣika colleagues in defending the substantive reality of the world, for it is in this world that the Vedic ritual is performed (see Arnold 2005: 57–114; Taber 2005).

Following early Buddhist Abhidharma traditions, new philosophical movements developed within Mahāyāna Buddhism. One of the main streams of Mahāyāna Buddhist philosophy is called the Yogācāra, "Yoga Practice," or Vijñānavāda, "Doctrine of Consciousness." The philosopher Vasubandhu gave this tradition its most influential early formulation in the fourth–fifth centuries CE. The evanescent atomic facts to which the early Vijñānavāda reduces things by the analysis of dependent origination are moments of consciousness. Early Vijñānavāda advocates a radical idealism of a flux consciousness that coheres on the basis of patterns of causal influence, conceived in terms of dependent origination, including that of *karma* translated moment-to-moment and between lives. Each moment of consciousness transmits its causal pattern to the next, which is similar but in no respects identical.

One of Vasubandhu's main arguments against Hindu realism is similar to Bishop Berkeley's contention that *esse est percipi*, albeit with the added specification of the transitoriness of subjective experience. Vasubandhu observes that nothing is ever known outside of momentary consciousness. Therefore, such consciousness with its integral contents is all there is. Other early Vijñānavāda arguments take their starting point from the occurrence of dreams, hallucinations and other perceptual illusions. We know that we have been experiencing such illusions only after we awake from them.

We have no proof that we are experiencing now is not such an illusion. Therefore, there is nothing but consciousness (Vasubandhu 1986).

The Hindu realists' chief response is that the correlation of what we perceive with consciousness does not mean that the former is nothing but the latter. They also question the reasonableness of the Vijñānavāda's version of the radicalization of doubt. Although illusion is always a possibility, there is normally no need to worry about that. We may be reasonably confident that our cognitions of a real external world are generally accurate (Matilal 1986).

The Vijñānavāda was greatly advanced by the philosophers Dignāga and Dharmakīrti. Their version of Vijñānavāda is sometimes called the logical and epistemological school of Buddhism because it attempts to demonstrate the superiority of the Buddhist soteriological path using forms of logic, epistemology and ontology that had been previously championed by the Nyāya and allied traditions of Hindu realism. Dignāga and Dharmakīrti's school of thought may be described as a sort of phenomenalism.

Basically, the Buddhist philosophers of this school apply the doctrine of dependent origination to analyze primitive atomic facts that are the underlying basis of veridical cognition. They claim that the only veridical cognition is cognition without conceptual construction (nirvikalpaka jñāna). This unconstructed cognition consists of temporary moments of consciousness, entirely discrete from one another and containing their own integral subjective and objective components. The objective component of each moment is called the "self-characterized particular" (svalakṣaṇa), and the subjective component is referred to as "self-consciousness" (svasaṃvedana). The latter is not an enduring substantial self, but only a momentary awareness integrally validating each consciousness episode so that one "knows that one knows."

The phenomenalists distinguish between the experience of raw atomic facts, and cognition with conceptual construction (savikalpakajñāna). Conceptual construction (vikalpa), comprising imagination as well as language, schematizes the world into entities "characterized by universals" (sāmānyalakṣana). The Buddhist understanding of the universal is more general than the understandings of Nyāya as well as Western philosophy, and comprises all sorts of identity, including those of objects, their qualities and processes. The Buddhists as well as their opponents also came to view the entire process of conceptual construction as epitomized in the experience of recognition. Recognition, as commonly understood, is the realization that an object of a present experience is the same as an object of a past experience, as retained in the memory. The same cognitive event happens in a less obvious way whenever we apply any categories from our memory to the identification of enduring entities and processes in present experience.

The Buddhist phenomenalists acknowledge that cognition with conceptual construction may be useful in ordinary life at the level of provisional, veiled truth. However, advancing the originary Buddhist skepticism about theories, they argue that conceptual constructions are in the highest perspective nonveridical. Their main contention is that there is no basis in the immediate data of present experience for the recognition of universals conceived in memory. Another Buddhist argument is that only the evanescent flashes of particulars, and not any conceptualized enduring entities, have causal efficacy (arthakriyā). It is the directly perceived fire rather than the conception of fire that heats. Furthermore, the Buddhists contend by the logic of dependent origination that it would be contradictory for entities simultaneously to comprise evanescent particulars and universals spanning different spatiotemporal situations.

Having radically divorced the conceptually unconstructed and constructed stages of perception, Dignāga, Dharmakīrti, and their followers were faced with the problem of building some form of bridge between these stages in order to explain epistemic success in the realm of veiled truth. They attempt to explain the coordination between concepts and phenomenal reality with the notion of *apoha*, "exclusion," by which a verbal designation is said not to refer to anything in reality, but only to reject contrary meanings. Cow means not non-cow.

Hindu realists, however, maintain that reality is comprised of enduring entities and processes, including objects that possess attributes such as universals in their own more restricted sense. According to them, conceptual constructions function within perception to elucidate these enduring entities and processes. This is just as, after coming from the sun, one perceives more and more as one adjusts to the light in a dimly lit room. They also explain the epistemic function of memory with the analogy of a connoisseur's appreciation of music. Nobody would suggest that the connoisseur's prior learning causes him or her to perceive less in the music. Hindu realists further argue that exclusion necessarily implies a positive meaning. "Not non-cow" can only mean cow (Stcherbatsky 1962; Shastri 1976; Matilal 1986; Dunne 2004).

Before concluding this section, mention must also be made of some arguments between Nyāya positions and Vijñānavāda Buddhism regarding the existence of God. Some Nyāya philosophers came to view the grace of God as facilitating the attainment of liberative knowledge. The eleventh-century philosopher Udayana synthesized and advanced earlier Nyāya arguments for the existence of an intelligent deity as the creator and designer of the world from preexisting atoms. Buddhists of the Dignāga-Dharmakīrti school, such as the eleventh-century CE philosopher Ratnakīrti, argued against Nyāya, somewhat along the lines of contemporary opponents of the Western theistic inferences, that an inference of an intelligent designer is not warranted by worldly experience. Inasmuch as many or most worldly things are ostensibly produced without an intelligent creator or designer, the Nyāya inference is unjustified (Patil 2009).

Universal Challenge of Mādhyamaka Buddhism

The aforementioned Nāgārjuna consolidated the other major stream of Mahāyāna Buddhist philosophy, Mādhyamaka. As with the Vijñānavāda and the older Abhidharma traditions, the starting point of the Mādhyamaka is the doctrine of dependent origination. Mādhyamaka literally means, "having to do with the middle," referring to the Middle Way interpreted as the doctrine of dependent origination. Nāgārjuna was also inspired by Mahāyāna Sūtras focusing on Prajñā Pāramitā, the Perfection of Wisdom, as the insight into emptiness.

It may be said that the Mādhyamaka has developed the most radical interpretation of the doctrine of dependent origination, inasmuch as it eschews the search for evanescent atomic facts and attempts to explicate the most skeptical logical implications of the doctrine. Using the method of *vitaṇḍā*, Nāgārjuna endeavors to refute all views about the world whatsoever without affirming any position of his own. Mādhyamaka Buddhism attacks not only virtually every Hindu category about the world, self, God, scripture, and so on, but also the Abhidharmic understanding of *dharmas*, Vijñānavāda consciousness flux and self-characterized particulars, and other Buddhist teachings – as all too substantialistic.

Nāgārjuna's overarching pattern of argument may be summarized as follows: the only way for things to function on the provisional level of truth of worldly life, as well as for the Buddhist soteriological path, is for them to be empty (*śūnya*) – that is, inexplicable (*anirvācya*) on the ultimate level of truth. If things had enduring, substantial existence, that very nature *would prevent them from functioning* as we expect them to. Thus, if the self were immutable, it could not act and interact with other selves and things. If a pot remained in a static condition as a pot it could not be used for cooking or would always be cooking. Action would always be acting, independently of all causes and concomitants. A born baby could not be born because it would always be born, and so on. Nāgārjuna sometimes shows that the analysis of dependence leads to logical problems such as regress or circularity – parent depends on child and child depends on parent, one depends on many and many on one, etc. On the other hand, it should be obvious that if things did not exist in some conventional sense, they also could not function. According to Nāgārjuna, the dependent origination or conditioned existence of constellations of factors is all we see at the provisional level, and that is the same as emptiness (1995a).

As I have said, Nāgārjuna claims not to have any position of his own. While he follows common South Asian protocols for discourse ethics, attempting to argue without deception where he believes logic leads, he also denies these standards. He refutes the Nyāya categories and even endeavors to refute the method of *vitaṇḍā*, which he uses himself (Nāgārjuna 1987, 1995b)! For Nāgārjuna, Buddhism is empty, and the teaching of emptiness is also empty. (We are reminded of the poststructualist Jacques Derrida practicing deconstruction largely through commenting on the works of others and claiming that deconstructionism itself must be deconstructed.)

Hindu realists respond to the Mādhyamaka by defending their own explanations of reality in terms of enduring substances, qualities and processes. They maintain that it is not really contradictory for something to remain the same while entering into relationships with other things and participating in processes. On the basis of their own theories, they argue, as they do against other Buddhists, that there is no need to pursue such radically skeptical doubt.

Some Hindu realists have offered transcendental arguments against Nāgārjuna's *vitaṇḍā*, similar to the observation articulated in Epimenides' paradox of the Cretan claiming that all Cretans are liars. Thus Nyāya philosophers, such as Vatsyāyana of fourth–fifth centuries CE, and Uddyotakara of the sixth century CE, claim that there are contradictions to the performance of *vitaṇḍā* even in the statement of one's purpose as demonstrating flaws in the opponent's position. The Buddhist philosopher Dharmakīrti likewise argues that there is no debate without accepting a position (Dharmakīrti and Prabhācandra 1972: 120). The controversy continues in contemporary scholarship on Mādhyamaka. Matilal defends Nāgārjuna's style of *vitaṇḍā* using Searle's notion of illocutionary negation (1986: 48).

A different sort of response to Mādhyamaka Buddhism was developed by the Hindu philosophical tradition of Advaita, or "nondualistic," Vedānta. (Nondualistic, dualistic, and other Vedānta philosophies all base their views on the teachings of the Upaniṣads.) This school of thought was consolidated by the philosopher Śaṅkara in the eighth–ninth centuries CE. According to Advaita Vedānta, only a universal self, *ātman*, is real and it is therefore identical with the source and essence of the universe, *brahman*. The world is a sort of illusion, *māyā*, projected upon the *ātman/brahman*, and that illusion disappears when one awakens to one's true identity.

I subscribe to the view, which is common but not universally accepted, that Śaṅkara followed the Mādhyamaka in his thought on the ontological status of the cosmic illusion. Because this illusion is experienced until we achieve self-realization, it cannot be nonexistent. Because it disappears once we achieve self-realization, it cannot be existent. For Śaṅkara, as for Nāgārjuna, this world is therefore inexplicable (*anirvācanīya*) (1987).

The tenth–eleventh-century Advaita Vedānta philosopher Śrīharṣa, as well as his follower Citsukha in the thirteenth century, greatly advanced Śaṅkara's appropriation and delimitation of Nāgārjuna's thought. These Advaita philosophers accepted and utilized the great bulk of Nāgārjuna's arguments demonstrating the inexplicability and emptiness of all things. However, according to the Advaita thinkers, there is one thing that cannot be refuted by the Mādhyamaka method. The Upaniṣadic *ātman/brahman* remains unsublated as the luminous consciousness and substantial existence underlying all worldly phenomena (Sarma 1974; Granoff 1978).

Hindu Philosophies of Transcendental Language

The Hindu linguistic philosopher Bhartṛhari had already in the fourth–sixth centuries CE laid the groundwork for an entirely different approach to the problems that would be debated by various schools of Hinduism and Buddhism over the next several centuries. Bhartṛhari argues, on the basis of various epistemological, linguistic and metaphysical considerations, that the source of the universe and the ground of all knowledge is the Vedic revelation, conceived in its metaphysical essence as the Word Absolute (*śabdabrahman*). While there is much specificity to his position, it has some analogies to Abrahamic philosophical theologies of Logos, as they have been articulated and developed from the Hellenistic through contemporary periods (Carpenter 1995; Lawrence 1999). According to Bhartṛhari, the Word Absolute bifurcates and emanates all separate linguistic interpretations and the universe of their referents. Thus all cognition intrinsically has the nature of the Word, and no perceptual or inferential claim can be veridical without being grounded in the Word, as accessed a priori through semantic intuition (*pratibhā*) or linguistic-recognitive apprehension (*pratyavamarśa*) (Shastri 1959; Matilal 1990).

Bhartṛhari actually influenced the Vijñānavāda Buddhist and Hindu realist schools discussed above with regard to the role of language in conceptual construction (*vikalpa*), but those schools refused to accept that cognition has a subtle, preconventionally linguistic – or, we might say, broadly semiotic – character. The Vyākaraṇa tradition of

Hindu linguistic analysis and philosophy advanced some aspects of Bhartṛhari's philosophy. However, it was the Pratyabhijñā, "Recognition," system of nondual Kashmiri Śaiva philosophy, propounded in the tenth–eleventh centuries CE by Utpaladeva and Abhinavagupta, that most fully developed Bhartṛhari's metaphysical and epistemological theories.

Nondual Śaivism, as may be gathered by its appellation, maintains that the only reality is the God Śiva. According to the predominant myth, Śiva divides himself from his integral power and consort, Śakti, and emanates and controls the universe through her. The goal of the practitioner is to realize full identity with Śiva as the cosmocratic possessor of Śakti.

Utpaladeva and Abhinavagupta formulate their main philosophical positions by subsuming Bhartṛhari's theories within a Śaiva framework, and further engaging those positions with the critiques of conceptual construction and recognition already developed in the debates between Buddhist phenomenalists and Hindu realists. The Pratyabhijñā thinkers thus identify Śiva's integral Śakti as both a principle called Supreme Speech (parāvāk), which they derive from Bhartṛhari's concept of the Word Absolute, as well as Śiva's self-recognition (pratyabhijñā, ahampratyavamarśa). Such concepts would be entirely delusory according to Buddhist phenomenalism.

In developing their arguments against the Buddhists, Utpaladeva and Abhinavagupta actually accept Vijñānavāda/Yogācāra theories that there is nothing external to consciousness. However, for the Pratyabhijñā philosophers, consciousness is not a flux of dependently originating moments. The Śaivas develop Bhartṛhari's thought in arguing that subtle language (sūkṣmaśabdana), or linguistic-recognitive apprehension (pratyavamarśa), is the very nature of consciousness. Thus they claim that recognition and speech constitute the very facts that the Buddhists say preclude them. By demonstrating the necessity and ubiquity of Śiva's speech and recognition, the Pratyabhijñā philosophers endeavor to lead their students to complete participation in Śiva's speech and recognition – that is, to liberative identity with God.

Conclusion: Hindu and Buddhist Philosophy in the Global Cosmopolis

In the early centuries of the last millennium, Buddhism disappeared from most of South Asia, outside of Nepal and small parts of north India. Since then, there has been little philosophical exchange between Buddhist and Hindu traditions. Nevertheless, the legacies of the Buddhist–Hindu debates are still studied by religious intellectuals in both streams of religious culture, and the philosophical ideas that developed therein defined the religions' central doctrinal positions. Indeed, many features of Hindu and Buddhist self-understandings would be virtually unrecognizable without the theories created in these debates. Furthermore, many of the traditions of Buddhist and Hindu philosophy that developed in the debates are still flourishing, but are now being transformed in new ways.

Over the last few centuries, the related processes of modernization and Western colonialism have provided many new challenges to Buddhism and Hinduism throughout Asia. Modern science and technology, politics, economics, and social values, have often conflicted intellectually with, and socially eroded, both Hinduism and Buddhism, just as they have done with regard to other traditional modes of knowledge and action around the world. Furthermore, early modernization was often introduced by Western colonial powers, and modernization continues to reflect Western neocolonial domination, even in ostensibly postcolonial contexts. Ironically, an insidious Western domination is often reflected even in postmodern and postcolonial cultural theories that claim to be broadly liberative.

As a result of the process of globalization, a new cosmopolitanism is emerging. While I believe that this has many positive aspects, cosmopolitanism is never neutral to power, and it is no accident that the main interlocutors of Hindu and Buddhist intellectuals have been representatives of Western religion and philosophy.[2] These new interlocutors have also brought new alignments and problematics of justification. Scholars of Hinduism have often suggested correlations between Hindu philosophies and the more metaphysical and substantialist strains of Western thought, such as Neoplatonism and later idealism (Dasgupta 1933; Deussen 1966; Harris 1981; Halbfass 1988: 69–83), Western arguments for the existence of God (Lawrence 1999; Patil 2009), as well as modern realism, empiricism and logic (Matilal 1986, 1998; Chakrabarti 2010), and phenomenological psychology (Gupta 1998).

Likewise, Buddhism has often been correlated with broadly skeptical or deconstructive developments in contemporary Western thought, including existentialist philosophies of emptiness (Abe 1989), poststructuralism (Magliola 1997), Christian apophatic theology (William 2001), and desubstantialist themes in cognitive science and systems theory (Varela et al. 1991). It remains an open question whether there will be a new flourishing of intellectual engagement directly between Hindu and Buddhist philosophy. In any event, although there will always be controversy about how the philosophies of the two religions are interpreted, the fruits of their centuries of dialogue and debate are already making great contributions to a global cosmopolis.

Another important contribution of Hinduism and Buddhism to contemporary inter-religious dialogue is the discursive ethics they developed as a practical foundation for argumentation. With regard to current categories of inter-religious dialogue, most forms of Hinduism and Buddhism, like other indigenous South Asian religions, may be viewed as varieties of inclusivism rather than exclusivism or pluralism. That is, they generally acknowledge some goodness and truth in other religious traditions, even if believing that it might take their followers further lifetimes to realize what is known more fully in their own traditions!

Exclusivism is very rare in Hinduism and Buddhism, and pluralism is in my view a de facto inclusivism of the proponent's own definition of religion, inevitably revealing the heritage of his or her own historical context. Thus recent leaders of Hindu and Buddhist traditions, such as Mohandas Gandhi and the Dalai Lama, addressing issues of globalization in their own ways, have formulated versions of religious pluralism, but their statements of faith inevitably reveal the influence of their own religious heritages.

Hierarchization is an inevitable consequence of the hermeneutic circle. In the classic dialogues and debates between Hinduism, Buddhism and other indigenous South Asian philosophies, thinkers endeavored to justify this hierarchization on the basis of criteria of fact and reason they hoped to be convincing to those who did not accept their own religious authorities. While there is certainly an elitism in Sanskritic scholastic culture, Buddhist and Hindu philosophers formulated at least as a counterfactual ideal an ethics of egalitarian discourse facilitating the establishment of truth, or even, as in the case of the Mādhyamakas, the possible demonstration that ultimately there is no truth!

While generally respectful and inclusivistic, Hindus and Buddhists did argue. And it is their arguments that enabled the traditions to achieve a great deal of sophisticated common understandings and make many enduring contributions to world culture. We should likewise understand the need not to overlook our disagreements in our laudable efforts to be tolerant and respectful of each other. Closer examination of Sanskritic discourse ethics – along with other expressions of discourse ethics of the non-West and the West – may have great value for this necessary aspect of debate between alternative religious claims in the arena of global interreligious dialogue.

Notes

1   For the sake of simplicity, in this essay I will consistently use Sanskrit rather than any Pali versions of key Buddhist terms.
2   Nevertheless, like power, dialogues are gradually becoming more polycentric. Efforts made by Rabindranath Tagore and Tan Yun-Shen in the early twentieth century to promote dialogue between Indian and Chinese cultures, have been renewed by scholars such as Chakravarthi Ram-Prasad (2005), and the new American Academy of Religion Group, Religions in Chinese and Indian Culture.

Bibliography

Abe, Masao. *Zen and Western Thought*. Honolulu: University of Hawaii Press, 1989.

Abhinavagupta. *Īśvarapratyabhijñāvimarśinī* (with *Bhāskarī*) (vols. 1–2), ed. K.A. Subramania Iyer and K.C. Pandey. Delhi: Motilal Banarsidass, 1986.

Apel, Karl Otto. "The Problem of Philosophical Foundations in Light of a Transcendental Pragmatics of Language," in *After Philosophy: End or Transformation?*, eds. Kenneth Baynes, James Bohman and Thomas McCarthy, pp. 245–290. Cambridge, MA: MIT Press, 1989.

Apel, Karl Otto. *The Response of Discourse Ethics to the Moral Challenge of the Human Situation as Such and Especially Today*. Leuven: Peeters, 2001.

Arnold, Dan. *Buddhists, Brahmins, and Belief: Epistemology in South Asian Philosophy of Religion*. New York: Columbia University Press, 2005.

Bakhtin, Mikael. *The Bakhtin Reader: Selected Writings of Bakhtin, Medvedev, and Voloshinov*, ed. Pam Morris. London: Edward Arnold, 1994.

Carpenter, David. *Revelation, History, and the Dialogue of Religions: A Study of Bhartṛhari and Bonaventure*. Maryknoll, NY: Orbis Books, 1995.

Chakrabarti, Kisor Kumar. *Classical Indian Philosophy of Induction*. Lanham, MD: Lexington Books, 2010.

Chinchore, Mangala R. *Vādanyāya: The Nyāya-Buddhist Controversy*. Delhi: Satguru, 1988.

Dasgupta, Surendranath. *Indian Idealism.* Cambridge: Cambridge University Press, 1933.

Deussen, Paul. *The Philosophy of the Upanishads.* New York: Dover Publications, 1966.

Dharmakīrti, Śāntaraksita and Prabhācandra. *Vādanyāyaprakaraṇa of Acharya Dharmakirtti with the Commentary Vipanchitārthā of Acharya Śāntaraksita and Sambandhaparīkṣā with the Commentary of Acharya Prabhachandra,* ed. Dwarikadas Shastri. Varanasi: Bauddha Bharati, 1972.

Dunne, John D. *Foundations of Dharmakīrti's Philosophy.* Boston: Wisdom Publications, 2004.

Flood, Gavin. *An Introduction to Hinduism.* Cambridge: Cambridge University Press, 2002.

Gautama et al. *Nyāyadarśana,* ed. Taranatha Nyaya-Tarkatirtha and Amarendramohan Tarkatirtha. Delhi: Munshiram Manoharlal, 1985.

Granoff, Phyllis. *Philosophy and Argument in Late Vedānta: Śrī Harṣa's Khaṇḍanakhaṇḍakhādya.* New York: Springer, 1978.

Gupta, Bina. *The Disinterested Witness: A Fragment of Advaita Vedanta Phenomenology.* Evanston, IL: Northwestern University Press, 1998.

Halbfass, Wilhelm. *India and Europe: An Essay in Understanding.* Albany: State University of New York Press, 1988.

Harris, R. Baine (ed.). 1981. *Neoplatonism and Indian Thought.* Albany: State University of New York Press.

Horton, Robin. "Tradition and Modernity Revisited," in *Rationality and Relativism,* eds. Martin Hollis and Steven Lukes. Cambridge, MA: MIT Press, 1984, 201–260.

Lawrence, David Peter. *Rediscovering God with Transcendental Argument: A Contemporary Interpretation of Monistic Kashmiri Śaiva Philosophy.* Albany: State University of New York Press, 1999.

Lipner, Julius. *Hindus: Their Religious Beliefs and Practices.* London: Routledge, 1998.

Magliola, Robert. *On Deconstructing Life Worlds: Buddhism, Christianity, Culture.* Oxford: Oxford University Press, 1997.

Matilal, Bimal Krishna. *Perception: An Essay on Classical Indian Theories of Knowledge.* Oxford: Clarendon Press, 1986.

Matilal, Bimal Krishna. *The Word and the World: India's Contribution to the Study of Language.* Oxford: Oxford University Press, 1990.

Matilal, Bimal Krishna. *The Character of Logic in India,* ed. Jonardon Ganeri and Heeraman Tiwari. Albany: State University of New York Press, 1998.

Muller, Max. *Lectures on the Origin and Growth of Religion: As Illustrated by the Religions of India.* London: Longmans, Green, 1880.

Nāgārjuna. Vigrahavyāvartanī, in *Nagarjuniana,* ed. Chr. Lindtner. Delhi: Motilal Banarsidass, 1987, 76–86.

Nāgārjuna. *The Fundamental Wisdom of the Middle Way: Nāgārjuna's Mūlamadhyamakakārikā.* Oxford: Oxford University Press, 1995a.

Nāgārjuna. *Nāgārjuna's Refutation of Logic (Nyāya): Vaidalyaprakaraṇa,* ed. and trans. Fernando Tola and Carmen Dragonetti. Delhi: Motilal Banarsidass, 1995b.

O'Flaherty, Wendy Doniger, trans. (1981) *The Rig Veda: An Anthology.* Harmondsworth: Penguin.

Olivelle, Patrick (trans.). *Upaniṣads.* Oxford, Oxford University Press, 1996.

Patil, Parimal G. *Against a Hindu God: Buddhist Philosophy of Religion in India.* New York: Columbia University Press, 2009.

Potter, Karl H. *Presuppositions of India's Philosophies.* Englewood Cliffs, NJ: Prentice-Hall, 1963.

Potter, Karl H. (ed). *Encyclopedia of Indian Philosophies,* vol. 2, *Indian Metaphysics and Epistemology: The Tradition of Nyāya-Vaiśeṣika up to Gaṅgeśa.* Delhi: Motilal Banarsidass, 1977.

Radhakrishnan, Sarvepalli and Moore, Charles A. (eds.) *A Source Book in Indian Philosophy.* Princeton, NJ: Princeton University Press, 1989.

Ram-Prasad, Chakravarthi. *Eastern Philosophy.* London: Weidenfield & Nicholson, 2005.

Śaṅkara. *Brahmasūtra Śaṅkara Bhāṣya* (Vols. 1–2), ed. K.L. Joshi. Delhi: Parimal Publications, 1987.

Sarma, V. Anjaneya. *Citsukha's Contribution to Advaita (With Special Reference to the Tattvapradīpikā)*. Mysore: Kavyalaya Publishers, 1974.

Sen, Amartya. *The Argumentative Indian: Writings on Indian History, Culture and Identity*. New York: Farrar, Straus and Giroux, 2005.

Shastri, Dharmendra Nath. *The Philosophy of Nyāya-Vaiśeṣika and its Conflict With the Buddhist Dignāga School (Critique of Indian Realism)*. Delhi: Bharatiya Vidya Prakashan, 1976.

Shastri, Gaurinath. *The Philosophy of Word and Meaning*. Calcutta: Sanskrit College, 1959.

Solomon, Esther A. *Indian Dialectics: Methods of Philosophical Discussion*, 2 vols. Ahmedabad: B.J. Institute of Learning and Research, 1976–1978.

Stcherbatsky, F. Th. *Buddhist Logic*. 2 vols., reprint. New York: Dover, 1962.

Taber, John. *A Hindu Critique of Buddhist Epistemology: Kumārila on Perception*. Abingdon: Routledge Curzon, 2005.

Varela, Francisco J., Evan T. Thompson and Elenor Rosch. *The Embodied Mind: Cognitive Science and Human Experience*. Cambridge, MA: MIT Press, 1991.

Vasubandhu. *Seven Works of Vasubandhu: The Buddhist Psychological Doctor*, ed. and trans. Stefan Anacker. Delhi: Motilal Banarsidass, 1986.

Vernant, Jean Pierre. *The Origins of Greek Thought*. Ithaca, NY: Cornell University Press, 1982.

William, J.P. *Denying Divinity: Apophasis in the Patristic Christian and Soto Zen Buddhist Traditions*. Oxford: Oxford University Press, 2001.

CHAPTER 13

Jewish–Christian Dialogue

Yaakov Ariel

On October 28 1965, Pope Paul VI, leader of the largest Christian Church, delivered an unprecedented message. *Nostra Aetate* (In Our Time) signified a new chapter in interfaith relations in general and a breakthrough in Christian–Jewish relations in particular. It included a revolutionary declaration on the proper Christian understanding of the Jews and their place in God's eyes. *Nostra Aetate* brought to fruition long decades of Christian–Jewish dialogue as well as giving an impetus to a new wave of rapprochement and reconciliation between the two faiths well beyond the boundaries of the Catholic Church.

Interfaith dialogue and systematic attempts at reconciliation between the two sister faiths have been relatively new developments. Such attempts began at the turn of the twentieth century, and while the century included historical low-peak moments in Christian–Jewish relations, it also saw the coming of age of a movement of interfaith dialogue that eventually brought about the clearing of air and rapprochement between the faiths. Interfaith dialogue made some progress in the decades between the two world wars, and advanced considerably in the years after the Second World War, reaching a "golden age" in the late 1960s and 1970s, when unprecedented momentum for reconciliation and dialogue flourished in Europe, America, Israel and other countries. Although the movement of interfaith dialogue has since witnessed setbacks and lost much of its momentum, it has nonetheless made a profound impact on the relationship between Judaism and Christianity, bringing about great improvements in the manner the different communities of faith relate to each other.

The Historical Background of the Dialogue

Organized attempts at interfaith dialogue between Christians and Jews began hesitantly in the latter decades of the nineteenth century, mostly on the initiative of liberal

The Wiley Blackwell Companion to Inter-Religious Dialogue, First Edition. Edited by Catherine Cornille.
© 2013 John Wiley & Sons Ltd. Published 2020 by John Wiley & Sons Ltd.

Protestants. A number of Jewish and Christian clergymen invited each other to give talks in their respective congregations, and personal exchanges developed between Jewish and Christian progressive leaders. Direct, systematic dialogue aimed at improving relations and promoting an atmosphere of trust has been very much a product of the late modern era and of liberal modernist thought. There have been previous social and intellectual exchanges between Christian and Jewish representatives aimed at improving cooperation. However, as a rule, Christian leaders and thinkers had not, until the late nineteenth century, shown interest in dialoguing with Jews and creating an atmosphere of greater appreciation for each other's faiths.

While some attempts at interfaith dialogue took place in Europe of the turn of the twentieth century, for the most part European Christians would join the movement of interfaith dialogue in earnest only after the Second World War, and the early attempts at dialogue took place mostly in the English-speaking world. Most significant were a number of interfaith conferences, which liberal American Protestants organized and to which religious leaders of different faiths were invited, including rabbis (Charap 2001).

The World Parliament of Religions, which convened in Chicago in 1893 in conjunction with the World Columbian Exposition, was a groundbreaking event, which many have since viewed as a new chapter in the relationship between Christianity and other faiths, including Judaism. The global interfaith meeting brought together Protestants, Catholics, and Orthodox Christians, as well as Jews, Buddhists, Hindus, Baha'i, Muslims, Native Americans, and representatives of other faiths (Braybooke 1992). It offered Jewish religious leaders, such as Alexander Kohut, Isaac M. Wise, Kaufmann Kohler, Emil G. Hirsch, and Marcus Jastrow, an opportunity to present their views to non-Jewish audiences and make a case for Judaism. While Emil G. Hirsch, a Reform rabbi from Chicago, spoke about the need to overcome parochial differences and create one world religion, other Jewish representatives used the occasion to defend Judaism against what they considered to be erroneous, and at times degrading, Christian views. In the wake of the Parliament, some liberal Jewish and Protestant religious leaders engaged in further dialogue. Hirsch and his Protestant colleague, Jenkins Lloyd Jones, a Unitarian minister and an architect of the Parliament, were particularly active in promoting interfaith dialogue (Charap 2001). However, while the World Parliament of Religions created a unique opportunity that gave Judaism a measure of legitimacy, its immediate effects on the relationship between Judaism and Christianity were more limited.

Theological exchanges and cooperation took place, however, outside formal meetings and at times in more meaningful ways. When Jewish scholars attempted to launch the Jewish Encyclopedia, a first of its kind, in the early twentieth century, they invited Protestant scholars such as Crawford Troy and George Moore to join in the writing and editing. Remarkably, the Jewish Encyclopedia was published, and partially sponsored, by Protestant publishers in New York who took special interest in improving interfaith relations (Ariel 2010).

In contrast to European academic centers, where the modernist Higher Criticism of the Bible gave little credibility to Old Testament narratives, English-speaking modernist Protestants have, for the most part, developed a critical-historical school of biblical research which has viewed those narratives more favorably. English speaking Protestants have tried to correlate events and sites narrated in the Hebrew Bible and the material evidence found in the Near East in a manner that was friendlier to the Jewish ethos about the birth of the Israelite nation. Jewish biblical scholars could find common ground with their Protestant English-speaking counterparts and join in mutual projects. Likewise, in America, universities began hiring Jewish professors of biblical studies, a historical breakthrough that took place at the same time that the first interfaith conferences took place. While European universities also hired Jewish professors to teach Semitic languages, the Protestant modernist scholars in continental European universities, such as Adolph von Harnack, remained firm in their view of Judaism as a morbid, static and redundant religious tradition. Late-nineteenth-century Jewish scholars and leaders in Germany, Britain and America defended Judaism against what they considered to be unjustified defamations resulting from the unwillingness of Christians to relate to Judaism as a legitimate faith.

At this stage, even the liberal activists in the English-speaking world who initiated interfaith meetings did not really view non-Protestant religions as equal to their faith (Marty 1987: 17–24). Influenced by theories of religious evolution which prevailed in the late nineteenth century, liberal Protestants put their faith at the top of the religious evolutionary ladder (Sharpe 1986: 47–71). In spite of their willingness to meet and dialogue with representatives of other faiths, liberal Christians before the First World War held to a triumphalist vision of Christianity, which they saw as a faith destined to become the world's all-encompassing religion, and engaged in missions on a global scale, including extensive efforts to evangelize the Jews. Missionary activity caused much resentment among Jewish leaders, who viewed the missions as a demonstration of contempt towards Judaism and Jews. Some modernist Jews responded by adopting a triumphalist Jewish stand, similar to that of their liberal Christian counterparts (Ariel 2001: 181–192).

Moreover, the Protestants who initiated the early dialogue represented only one segment of Christianity. Even within the Protestant camp they drew fire from more conservative Protestants, who strongly objected to dialogues with non-Protestants on seemingly equal terms (Gaebelein 1912). In the conservative Protestant view, only those persons who had accepted Jesus as their Savior could be justified before the Lord and could expect eternal life. Conservative Protestants, who were emerging at that time as a "fundamentalist" camp, insisted that Protestants should concentrate on spreading the Christian Gospel among non-Christians instead of wasting precious time and resources on dialogues.

Even at this early stage, certain characteristics of the dialogue were laid out. Many of the issues discussed were not spiritual or theological, yet interfaith dialogue was entrusted to clergymen. Representing Judaism and the Jewish community in dialogue with representatives of other faiths would become an important component of the rabbis' mission, including those serving as leaders or functionaries of Jewish organizations, and would add to the prestige of the rabbinate. Christian participants in the dialogue would continue to be representatives of liberal wings of their faith, while most Jewish participants were Reform rabbis or rabbis of the emerging Conservative movement. Yet, contrary to a prevailing misconception, Orthodox rabbis and communities have also taken part in the dialogued (Charap 2001). While the very attempts at dialogue during the period before the Great War should be viewed as a form of good will, it seems that both Jews and Christians were not yet ready for more transformative encounters. Matters changed in the following decades.

Stirring Times: Radical Hatred and Groundbreaking Dialogue

Following the First World War, both Christians and Jews were more open to dialogue. The horrors of the war caused a serious blow to the progressive millennial triumphalist view of liberal Christians and Jews. Liberal thinkers were more ready than before to look upon each other's faith as equal to their own. Paradoxically, the rise of more radical ethnic hatred in the 1920s–1940s stirred liberal religious activists to interfaith activity and enhanced the development of more systematic dialogue. Liberal Protestant, Catholic and Jewish thinkers offered each other a greater amount of recognition and appreciation, and there were advances in more systematic and institutionalized forms of dialogue.

In 1924, Catholic, Protestant, and Jewish activists in the United States established the Committee on Good Will. The motivation for the creation of the committee had to do with the rise of hate groups in the public life of English-speaking nations, a reality that alarmed Catholics and Jews, who were often targets of such attacks, as well as liberal Protestants who were also concerned (Kraut 1989: 133–230). The first National Council of Christians and Jews (NCCJ) was formed in Britain in 1924, even before the establishment of the American NCCJ in 1928. While the Committee on Good Will concentrated on fighting bigotry, the NCCJ concentrated its efforts on improving the relationship between Jews and Christians, and acted as a vehicle for dialogue between representatives of liberal Protestant churches and Catholic and Jewish religious leaders. While the participants were clergymen and theologians, they sensed that their conversations, openness to and concern for each other's community had an impact beyond the theoretical level and could potentially improve the relationship between Christians and Jews on social and cultural levels as well.

The avant-garde role of English-speaking nations is evident when looking at the deteriorating Christian relation to Jews in much of continental Europe during the period. While interfaith dialogue progressed, the developments in the relationships between Christians and Jews as a whole were far from being ideal. During the 1920s and 30s, virulent anti-Semitism progressed dramatically in Europe and beyond. German clergy created a Nazi-oriented organization, the German Christians, with thousands joining in, and many, including the new Reich Bishop Ludwig Mueller, served the regime and its aims wholeheartedly (Ericksen and Heschel 1999). Even in English-speaking countries, a number of Christian groups and ministers joined in attacking Jews, blaming them for their countries' problems. One of the most noted American Catholic clergymen during the period, Father Charles Coughlin, a pioneer of radio preaching, used his radio program as a vehicle to attack the Jews and blame them for the troubles of the age (Athans 1991). Coughlin was not alone. Henry Ford, Sr. financed the distribution of anti-Semitic publications, including an English translation of *The*

Protocols of the Elders of Zion, a fabricated document accusing Jews of conspiring to take over the entire world (Baldwin 2001). Protestant clergy who promoted a reactionary political agenda, such as Gerald L. K. Smith, included attacks on Jews in their rhetoric (Jeansonne 1988; Dinnerstein 1994: 48–149).

The rise of organized anti-Jewish rhetoric and policies caused Jewish communities and organizations to take an increased interest in improving interfaith relations and promoting dialogue, at least in countries in which such options were viable. Groups such as the American Jewish Committee, American Jewish Congress, Canadian Jewish Congress, World Jewish Congress, the Board of Deputies in Britain, or the Anti-Defamation League of B'nai Brith, made it their business to engage in interfaith dialogue, and their leaders served as representatives in interfaith forums. Christian participants in the dialogue were often sympathetic to Jewish feelings, although they did not necessarily represent their denominations as a whole. While opposed to bigotry and advocating for benevolent treatment of Jews, as a rule, the mainstream Christian churches at the time, not to mention more conservative churches, were far from recognizing Judaism as a faith equal to Christianity that could offer spiritual comfort, moral guidelines, or salvation. Both conservative and mainstream Christian churches continued their efforts at evangelizing Jews. Not surprisingly, such missions became a major issue of contention whenever Christians and Jews dialogued. Committed to an improvement in the relationship between Christianity and Judaism, Christian participants in the dialogue would begin distancing themselves from the efforts to evangelize Jews (Kraut 1989: 210).

An early proponent of a new attitude recognizing Judaism as a legitimate religious tradition was the Unitarian minister John Haynes Holmes of the Community Church in New York (Holmes 1928). Holmes, who advocated a progressive social and political outlook, became a close friend of Steven Wise, an independent Reform rabbi who shared Holmes's social agenda. As early as the late 1920s, Holmes had come to view Judaism as a religion that deserved respect, and as a faith able to offer its adherents spiritual content and moral guidance. A more systematic promotion of the same opinions was offered at this early stage by Reinhold Niebuhr, one of the leading Protestant theologians in the English speaking world between the 1930s and 1960s. His was a groundbreaking outlook, offering recognition and acceptance to Judaism as a religious tradition equal in worth to Christianity. Niebuhr worked for a number of years as a minister of the German-American Evangelical Church in a working-class neighborhood in Detroit. In the course of his work, he encountered socially active Jewish religious leaders and visited Jewish congregations. Rejecting the triumphalist Christian Protestant attitudes that had prevailed before the First World War, he concluded that Jews had possessed high moral standards and social consciousness, and, consequently, militated against the propagation of the Christian gospel among the Jews. This attitude, which Niebuhr expressed as early as 1926, signified a revolution in Christian Protestant thinking about Jews and Judaism. With few exceptions, mainstream Protestant, Catholic and Orthodox theologians had, until the mid-twentieth century, followed a traditional Christian line, constructed by the Church fathers in the early centuries of Christianity. Having rejected their Messiah, the Jews lost their position as the covenant people, God's first nation, and God's promises to Israel were inherited by "true Israel," the Christian church. Moving to serve as a professor at Union Theological Seminary in New York, where he advocated a neo-Orthodox theology of Christian Realism, the socially progressive Niebuhr founded *Christianity and Crisis*, a journal promoting Christian social activism. Viewing Zionism as a legitimate program for solving the political plight of the Jews, Niebuhr became a supporter of Zionism, and in the early 1940s helped found the Christian Council for Palestine, an American Protestant group that advocated the establishment of a Jewish state in what was then British Palestine (Niebuhr 1926, 1942; Rice 1977: 101–46).

During the same era Jewish thinkers also developed attitudes more in line with interfaith exchanges. In the years following the First World War, the triumphalist classical Reform Jewish theology of the nineteenth century weakened considerably, if not disappearing completely. A younger generation of Reform thinkers began to consider Christian–Jewish equality as never before. Few followed Stephen Wise when he called upon Jews to adopt Jesus as one of their own, or Mordecai Kaplan, who suggested that Jews give up on their claim to be the chosen people (Libowitz 1983; Scult 1994). But many were influenced by more mainstream Jewish liberal thinkers, such as Solomon Freehof and Abraham Joshua Heschel, who were open to mutual recognition and dialogue.

The Age of Dialogue

While Holmes's and Niebuhr's positions offered a minority opinion, matters changed after the Second World War. The spirit created by the war, including the camaraderie that developed between Jewish and non-Jewish soldiers serving in the allied armed forces during the war, as well as between Jewish, Protestant, and Catholic chaplains, helped change the relationships between the faiths. The failure of the Nazi and fascist regimes and their ideologies, and the rise of democratic nations and modes of thought, made racist anti-Semitism significantly less acceptable in Western societies. Virulent forms of anti-Jewish agitation decreased significantly in Europe and America during the post-war years.

The memory of the horrors that anti-Jewish incitements brought about in the 1930s and 1940s played an important role in enhancing the dialogue. For a number of Jewish and Christian leaders, reviving or enhancing efforts at dialogue corresponded with attempts at rehabilitating and normalizing Christian–Jewish relations at the wake of the traumas of the Holocaust. Significantly, Leo Beck, rabbi, scholar and leader of German Jewry during the Nazi era, helped initiate the first post-war interfaith meetings in Britain and Switzerland. Beck had already sought to open dialogue with Christian thinkers, and convince them of the merits of Judaism, in the early twentieth century. Sadly and somewhat ironically, the postwar era proved more congenial for such encounters, although most European Jews were now gone. There was a growing awareness among Protestant and Catholic thinkers that a theological clearing of air was necessary. In Britain, clergymen of the Church of England, such as James Parkes, were active in organizing Christian–Jewish meetings and theological exchanges, expressing recognition and approval of Judaism.

The era in general became more open to interfaith dialogue and ecumenical move-ments. In 1948, representatives of Protestant churches from numerous countries gathered in Amsterdam and established the World Council of Churches (WCC), this bringing to fruition long decades of ecumenical activity. The aim of this global institu-tion was Christian cooperation, reconciliation and, as an ideal, unity. The ecumenical spirit it promoted affected interfaith relations as well (Dirk 1969). In its early days the WCC was composed primarily of mainline, mostly national, Protestant churches, but its membership grew to include Orthodox, Middle Eastern, and third-world churches as well. While in its early years the WCC promoted missions among Jews, by the 1960s the commitment of member churches and of the wider organization to such an agenda declined sharply (Croner 1977: 72–85).

Paradoxically, the Cold War enhanced the atmosphere of interfaith reconciliation in the democratic West as it helped legitimize middle-class religious expressions in all their varieties, including Judaism. The United States and its western allies were engaged during the 1950s in an intensive global struggle and ideological debate with commu-nism. President Dwight Eisenhower expressed the new mood when he stated that he expected good Americans to be church- or synagogue-goers. In America, participation in religious life became equated with the "American way." As the sociologist and theo-logian Will Herberg pointed out, Judaism became in the 1950s one of the three "public religions" of America (Herberg 1960). The new atmosphere of greater acceptance brought about theological changes as well. More Protestant thinkers followed Niebuhr in advocating the idea that Jews were not in need of the Christian gospel and had a vital religious tradition of their own to sustain them. During the 1950s and 60s, pro-dialogue groups within mainline churches, such as the Presbyterian Church USA or the United Methodist Church, became more influential, and a growing number of Protestant denominations decided that they had no more interest in allocating money and manpower to evangelizing Jews. In New York, Presbyterian and Jewish congrega-tions shared the same architectural space, which served as both the Village Presbyte-rian Church and the Village Temple. In the atmosphere created by such an experiment there was less room for the traditional Christian Replacement Theology and the mis-sionary agenda (Merson 1951: 27, 36–37).

Catholic participation in the dialogue also intensified. In New York, Cardinal Francis Spellman, the leader of the Archdiocese, made interfaith dialogue and reconciliation between the faiths a priority. Jewish, Protestant, and Catholic clergymen operated a radio program together. The scope of participation in the dialogue also enlarged con-siderably. While at the turn of the century attempts at systematic dialogue were carried out mostly by representatives of the liberal wings of Judaism and Christianity, interfaith dialogue in the 1950s reached the mainstream of the Catholic and Protestant com-munities. On the Jewish side, Orthodox Jewish leaders were more reluctant than Reform and Conservative ones to take an active part in the dialogue, although in a number of countries, including Britain, France and South Africa, they were often major representa-tives. Influenced by the opinions of Joseph Soloveichik, a prestigious modern Orthodox thinker, many Orthodox institutions and leaders (but not all) asserted that while civic cooperation between members of different faiths was acceptable, theological give-and-take was forbidden. Ultra-Orthodox Jews would not take part in the dialogue.

In a number of countries, Christian and Jewish religious leaders also participated in mutual political activities that served, indirectly, as interfaith initiatives. A series of campaigns of that kind took place in the context of the American Civil Rights Movement (Svonkin 1997), in which black leaders and activists were sometimes supported or joined by white Protestants, Catholics, and Jews (Carson 1994: 131–143). Such mutual efforts sometimes helped to foster personal friendships and a sense of camaraderie (Heschel and Heschel 1996). The progress in interfaith dialogue began making its mark on society at large. A sociological survey conducted at the initiative of the Anti-Defamation League in the early 1960s discovered that prejudices against Jews were still prevalent among the majority of Christians in America, and were especially strong among members of the more conservative Christian groups. Perhaps not surprisingly, groups taking part in the dialogue were relatively more tolerant (Glock and Stark 1966).

Vatican II and its Aftermath

The most profound breakthrough on a global scale in interfaith relations occurred during and following Vatican II, the Catholic general council that convened intermittently between 1962 and 1965. Initiated by Pope John XXIII, the council aimed to reform the church, change its relationship to contemporary culture, and bring about an historical reconciliation between the Catholic Church and other faiths. The council attempted to put to rest some of the old hostilities between Catholic and other Christian churches, as well as with other religions, and promoted an atmosphere of forgiveness and acceptance. The activities of the council and their possible significance for Jewish–Christian relations were not lost on Jewish leaders, and a number of Jewish organizations lobbied for the inclusion of Judaism and the Jewish people in the Council's agenda for reconciliation (Gilbert 1968). The Anti-Defamation League and the American Jewish Congress, for example, sent representatives to Rome to keep in touch with the Council and its leaders. Golda Meir, Israel's minister of Foreign Affairs, also tried to send an envoy to the Council, but was rejected. A number of Catholic bishops and dignitaries who had devoted their careers to the advancement of Catholic–Jewish relations, including converts from Judaism such as Monsignor John M. Oesterreicher, were instrumental in advancing the reconciliatory agenda towards the Jews. Among other initiatives, Oesterreicher served in effect as a liaison for Jewish representatives at the Council. In its very last sessions, Vatican II issued its historic statement on the relationship between Christianity and other religions, *Nostra Aetate*. Among other things, it stated: "The Church . . . cannot forget that she received the revelation of the Old Testament through the people with whom God in His inexpressible mercy concluded the Ancient Covenant . . . the Jews should not be presented as rejected or accused by God" (Croner 1977: 1–2). Remarkably, *Nostra Aetate* also warned against the accusation of deicide, the claim that the Jews collectively and in all generations were responsible for the killing of Jesus, whom the Christian tradition has viewed as the Messiah and the Son of God. The resolution was revolutionary, opening a new phase in Jewish–Christian relationships and serving as a stepping-stone for further dialogue and additional declarations on the part of mainline Christian Churches in relation to the Jews (Croner 1985).

The Catholic declaration gave impetus to changes in the opinions of Protestant groups and, to a much lesser extent, Orthodox churches. A number of Protestant churches as well as ecumenical groups followed Vatican II in issuing statements in relation to the Jews, including retractions of the deicide charge. Some of these statements went much further theologically than that of Vatican II in their attempt to bring about reconciliation with the Jewish people. Among the first Protestant groups to issue such a statement was the Synod of Bishops of the Episcopal Church in the United States:

> The charge of deicide against the Jews is a tragic misunderstanding of the inner signifi-
> cance of the crucifixion. To be sure, Jesus was crucified by *some* soldiers at the instigation
> of *some* Jews. But, this cannot be construed as imputing corporate guilt to every Jew in
> Jesus' day, much less the Jewish people in subsequent generations. Simple justice alone
> proclaims the charge of a corporate or inherited curse on the Jewish people to be false.
> (Croner 1977: 87)

The National Council of the Churches of Christ in the USA, an ecumenical, largely liberal organization, issued the following statement: "Especially reprehensible are the notions that the Jews, rather than all mankind, are responsible for the death of Jesus Christ, and God has for this reason rejected his covenant people" (Croner 1977: 89).

Both Protestants and Catholics were motivated, at least in part, by a sense of guilt over the historical role of Christian supercessionist claims and anti-Jewish accusations. Numerous Christian thinkers concluded that Nazi hatred of Jews had been fed by ages of Christianity's adverse and hostile attitude towards Judaism and Jews (Ruether 1974; Littell 1975).

One immediate result of the new atmosphere in interfaith relationships affected missions. The Catholic Church as well as mainline Protestants churches decided to close their missionary enterprises among Jews (Gilbert 1965). They were influenced in no small measure by strong Jewish objections to Christian missionary activity. For the most part, the liberal segments of Western Christianity gave up on the claim to be the sole possessors of the road to salvation. They accepted the idea that other churches, and even non-Christian religions, could offer moral guidelines and spiritual meaning to their adherents, Judaism not excluded. However, evangelizing the Jews remained high on the agenda of conservative Protestant churches and interdenominational bodies that did not take part in the dialogue (Ariel 2000). Conservatives continued to insist that Christianity was the only viable religion, and Christians alone have truly found the path to salvation. Such has also remained the position of most Orthodox, Middle Eastern, and third-world churches; although as a rule they were not engaged in evangelizing the Jews.

However, a growing number of Protestant and Catholic thinkers came to characterize Judaism as a religious community in covenant with God. These have included Paul Ricoeur, A. Roy Eckardt, Paul M. Van Buren, and Franklin H. Littell, as well as Catholic thinkers such as David Tracy and John T. Pawlikowski (Eckardt 1967; Van Buren 1980; Pawlikowski 1982). This outlook began in English-speaking countries. While within continental European Protestantism this attitude has developed in a slower and more limited fashion, in the third-world churches it was mostly rejected (Klein 1978). However, there, too, changes have taken place. Amazingly, and perhaps unexpectedly, interfaith reconciliation took place even beyond the Iron Curtain. In East Germany, for example, Protestant theologians organized groups for interfaith dialogue with Jews, while Protestant laypersons joined synagogue choirs or initiated Jewish commemorative publications.

The new climate of interfaith dialogue embodied a greater degree of mutual recognition and legitimacy, motivating a keen Christian attempt to eradicate prejudices against the Jews. Having acquitted the Jews of the centuries-old accusation of deicide, Western liberal Protestants and Catholics went a step further to clear the atmosphere of hatred that this and similar charges had created. In the late 1960s, Protestants and Catholics examined textbooks that had been used in their religious schools and removed passages with anti-Jewish overtones. A 1972 survey found that the charge of deicide had almost disappeared from Christian textbooks in America (Strober 1972). Contrary to a common perception, the new correctness in Christian attitudes towards Jews affected a large spectrum of Christian groups. Not only liberal churches, but conservative ones as well became more sensitive to the manner in which they presented Jews in their publications or sermons. This does not mean that the old accusations against Jews disappeared in Christian popular culture. For example, Jews have continued to be portrayed as the slayers of Jesus or as the motivating cause behind his death in musical and theatrical works. In *Jesus Christ Superstar*, a popular British–American stage production of the 1970s, the Jews cry out: "Crucify him, crucify him." In the 2000s, Mel Gibson's *The Passion of the Christ* adopted the narratives and messages of traditional passion shows in presenting the Jewish crowd demanding the crucifixion of Jesus from an innocent Roman governor. Such negative presentations of Jews, which have gone on for long centuries, and have deep cultural roots, have not been easy to eradicate.

No less daring than those who undertook the project of clearing textbooks of negative images of Jews, dialogue-oriented Christian theologians have examined the corpus of Christian writings in order to amend and offer new, more reconciliatory interpretations to passages that produced the negative images of the Jews in the first place. A number of Christian theologians, historians, biblical scholars, and writers have traced the negative attitudes toward the Jews to the early centuries of Christianity, or to theologians or popular preachers in the Middle-Ages and the Reformation (Pawlikoswski 1982; Carroll 2001). Christian theologians have also dealt with the significance of the Holocaust for Christianity (Eckardt and Eckardt 1988). Such thinkers tried to find a Christian meaning to the murder of millions of innocent people, stirring at times an uneasy feeling among Jewish participants in the dialogue (Fleischner 1977; Haynes 1995; Berger et al. 2002).

Perhaps the most impressive development has been the new interest among Christian thinkers, scholars, clergymen, and students in Jewish thought, history and texts. Many Christian scholars have come to view Judaism as a tradition worthy of study, in part because it sheds light on the early history of Christianity. Contemporary scholarship on early Christianity tends to speak about rabbinical Judaism and Christianity as two traditions that developed during the same period, emerging from the same cradle (Levenson 1995). Jewish studies in different forms has become part of the curriculum at Protestant and Catholic theological seminaries and divinity schools, often taught by Jewish scholars or by Christians who have studied at Jewish or Israeli universities. The openness on the part of Christians towards the study of Judaism has affected American and European universities, and at times, Asian and African universities as well. Even conservative schools of higher learning have been affected by the change. Hundreds of Christian and secular universities all around the globe have incorporated the study of Judaism as a discipline of study during the same period.

In the atmosphere that developed following the Vatican Council, numerous regional groups of Christians and Jews organized, mostly in North America and Europe but, at times, in other regions too. Liberal and mainstream Protestants of various denominations, together with Catholics and, at times, Orthodox and Monophysite churches, have formed meeting groups with Jews, discussing issues of mutual concern, and engaging in interfaith community projects. At times, communities would invite each other to visit their sanctuaries and participate as observers in the services. Until the 1960s, synagogues had been exclusive Jewish territories, with non-Jews showing little interest in visiting Jewish houses of worship. At the turn of the twenty-first century, synagogues have become attractive to non-Jews, who, in groups or as individuals, have begun visiting synagogue services in relatively large numbers, either for such events as Bar Mitzvah services, or as part of interfaith visits, or in search of a new community of faith. Judaism has become, almost in spite of itself, an option that some spiritual seekers, most of them from educated middle-class Christian backgrounds, have seriously considered. Remarkably, tens of thousands of Christians, both liberal and conservative, have come to celebrate Passover Seders, often in communal events organized by their churches.

Although interfaith dialogue has contributed to a decrease in negative stereotypes, and has helped to improve relationships between Jews and Christians, it would be wrong to describe the attitude of mainstream Christianity toward the Jewish people as merely one of amity and friendship. Jewish observers have noted that official recognition did not necessarily equal full acceptance, and, at times, old accusations or prejudices pop up. Others have complained that old anti-Jewish sentiments have at times been replaced by anti-Israeli ones (Banki 1974; Lerner 1992). During the same years of the rapid advancement of dialogue and reconciliation, especially after the 1967 war, many Jews developed a protective attitude towards Israel, while many liberal Christians have come to criticize Israeli policies and at times the entire Israeli project. In fact, the same churches and organizations that have come to recognize Judaism as a legitimate faith, have also adopted a number of anti-Israeli stances. While many Jews, including Israeli citizens, have voiced similar criticism, some Jewish observers have claimed that Israel, being a Jewish state, has attracted much more than its fair share of Christian criticism.

In the latter decades of the twentieth century, churches in the third world gained greater influence in international church bodies, such as the World Council of Churches, and at times influenced American and European Christian opinions as well, although liberal Western church activists have come to sympathize with the Palestinian plight on their own accord (King 1981; Elkin 1985). The relations of liberal Christian churches towards Jews since the late 1960s can be summarized therefore as offering Judaism growing recognition but objecting to the Jewish state and its policies as well as to the political agenda of Jewish organizations on Middle-Eastern issues. Christian denominations, however, have often spoken with different voices. Within the same churches, there are theologians committed to dialoguing with Jews and to Christian–Jewish reconciliation, who strive to build an appreciation for Judaism in their communities. The same churches also include activists and theologians who do not necessarily take interest in improving Christian–Jewish relationships. Since the 1980s the influence of the second group has grown considerably, and since September, 2001, Christian attempts at dialogue with Arabs and Muslims have received a higher priority. For conservative Christians the Jews have remained a top priority, albeit in a very different manner than the liberal attempts at reconciliation and dialogue.

An Alternative Dialogue: Conservative Christians and Jews

The relationship between conservative Protestants and Jews developed along different lines than between liberal Christians and Jews. Conservative Christians were hesitant to join official dialogue groups, yet they too have found channels of connecting with Jews, and their attitudes towards Jews have also undergone huge transformations throughout the twentieth century.

As with liberal and mainstream Christians, the interactions of conservative evangelical Protestants with Jews have reflected the nature of this segment of Christianity, its faith, and agenda. A major component of evangelical theology is the belief that only those individuals who undergo personal religious experiences of conversion in which they accept Jesus as their savior, will be saved and granted eternal life. In their vision, all humanity should convert to Christianity in its evangelical interpretation, and granting legitimacy to the religious beliefs of others is an act of neglect towards them – a view that does not favor dialogue with representatives of other faiths. In contrast to traditional Christian supercessionist claims to be "true Israel," most evangelicals have come to view the Jews as historical Israel and the object of biblical prophecies about a restored Davidic kingdom in the land of Israel. Evangelical Christians welcomed the rise of the Zionist movement and the Jewish waves of immigration to Palestine, often interpreting them as "signs of the time," indicators that the current era was ending and that apocalyptic events were about to begin (Ariel 2006). Likewise, they have seen in the establishment of the State of Israel preparation of the ground for the eventual building of the Kingdom of God on earth. The Arab–Israeli war in 1967 had a very different effect on evangelical–Jewish relationship than on liberal Christian attitudes. For evangelicals, the war in which Israel took over the historical parts of Jerusalem served as a proof that Israel was indeed born for a purpose, that the messianic times were near and that the Jewish people would play a crucial role in the events of the End Times. Evangelical support for Israel increased throughout the last third of the twentieth century, and evangelicals have become a central component of the pro-Israel lobby in America and in other countries.

Some liberal Jewish and Christian observers have pointed to the problematic ele-ments of the conservative evangelical relationships with the Jews. Conservative Prot-estants, though not lacking in good will, are not free of negative stereotypes of Jews. Evangelical Christians believe that until Jews accept Jesus as their personal Messiah, they remain in a state of spiritual and moral deprivation. According to evangelical understanding, Judaism cannot grant salvation to its believers, nor can the observance of its precepts serve any purpose after Christ's death on the Cross (Ariel 2000). A number of evangelical authors have expressed frustration that the Jews had not accepted Jesus as the Messiah when he first appeared. Had they done so, the Kingdom of God upon Earth would already have come into being. At times, Jews were also viewed as promoters of destructive secular ideological movements, such as communism, socialism, or secular humanism, which, in the conservative view, have threatened to work against the building of Christian civilization. A primary means for conservatives to express their faith that Jews still play an important role in God's plans for humanity has been to invest time and efforts in evangelizing them, as well as engaging in acts of good will and welfare among Jews.

While, as noted above, a sociological study in the early 1960s pointed to more anti-Jewish prejudices among conservative evangelicals than among liberal Protestants or Catholics (Glock and Stark 1966), a similar study, in the mid-1980s, showed a drastic decline in the extent of such prejudices among conservatives (Ianniello 1986). This change should be accounted for, among other reasons, by an increased evangelical interest in and involvement with Jewish and Israeli affairs since the Arab–Israeli war in 1967. While evangelicals warmed up to Jews, Jewish warming up to evangelicals was slower, with many Jews viewing evangelicals suspiciously. Some Jews have con-sidered evangelicals to be a threat to an open pluralistic society, and many others resented evangelical missionary activities, but a number of Jewish leaders and activ-ists came to appreciate conservative Christian support, especially in relation to Israel and its needs.

Evangelical scholars have also joined in searching for the roots of Christianity in Second Temple Judaism. Likewise, a number of conservative institutions, such as Wheaton College, have included Judaic studies in their curriculum. Evangelical stu-dents have visited Israel, at times participating in archeological digs there, or volunteer-ing in kibbutzim. Conducted periodically by evangelical churches, colleges, Bible schools, and pro-Israel groups, visits to Israel have become common features of evan-gelical life. The messages of evangelical missions to the Jews, and the glorified role Jews play in evangelical eschatology and imagery, brought about a movement of evangelical-Jews, who have adopted the evangelical Protestant faith, yet have retained their Jewish identity (Ariel, 2000). The assertive and growing movement of Messianic Jews has become an important agent in shaping the evangelical-Jewish relationship as well as giving expression to evangelical interest in and involvement with the Jews. Ironi-cally, missions to the Jews and the Messianic-Jewish community serve as pro-Jewish interest groups within the larger evangelical community, promoting support for Israel and requesting a higher priority for evangelization efforts among the Jews.

While messianic Jews have striven for recognition as legitimate Jews, mainstream Jewish and Christian organizations have refused, as a rule, to include them in the dialogue or relate to them as legitimate Jewish groups. To some the new movement seemed bizarre. The Christian–Jewish dialogue is based on the assumption that Judaism and Christianity are two separate, completely distinct faiths, and do not lend themselves easily to in-between borderline faith. Because so much professionalized dialogue has been premised on clear distinctions between communities of faith, Messianic Jews have posed both an unwelcomed intrusion, and something of a challenge. The movement has signified an evangelical alternative to the dialogue, a different kind of easing of tension and rapprochement. Likewise, the movement gives expression to a different understanding of the relationship between religious faiths in general and Christianity and Judaism in particular. The movement is also representative of an era in which people have come to pick and choose identities, often creating hybrids and negotiating between different elements of their choices.

Although in principle conservative Protestants do not recognize the legitimacy of a religious faith not founded upon the acceptance of Jesus as a savior, and although Jews are committed to safeguarding their continued existence as a unique community, there have been some attempts at more dialogical evangelical–Jewish conversations (Rudin and Wilson 1987). As a rule, evangelical leaders who have participated in the dialogue did not represent missionary organizations, but rather voices of intellectuals and academics within evangelical Christianity. On the Jewish side, participants included institutional leaders, often coming from conservative Jewish groups, including Orthodoxy.

Among the organizations established to further understanding between conservative Christians and Jews is the Holy Land Fellowship of Christians and Jews, founded by the Orthodox Rabbi Yehiel Eckstein. Eckstein has emphasized the importance of the Holy Land and the State of Israel to Jews and evangelicals alike, and viewed support for Israel as a common basis for cooperation and understanding between the two groups. The Holy Land Fellowship has collected increasing amounts of money for helping in the immigration and absorption of Jews in Israel, as well as for social programs in the country. Right-wing Orthodox Jews have come to appreciate the conservative evangelical political agenda. In 1991, Rabbi Daniel Lapin from Seattle founded a group called Toward Tradition, "a national coalition of Jews and Christians seeking to advance the nation toward traditional, faith based, American principles of limited government, the rule of law . . . free markets, a strong military, and a moral public culture" (www. towardtradition.org). Orthodox rabbis like Lapin decided that they have more in common with conservative Christians than with liberal ones. Eckstein and Lapin have not been the only ones to establish alternative dialogue groups unaffiliated with older, more institutionalized mainstream groups.

Until the latter decades of the twentieth century, there were no systematic attempts at continued dialogue between Jews and members of non-Christian faiths. This has changed during the last half-century. In recent decades dialogue with Muslims became a major item on the interfaith agenda. Muslim–Jewish dialogue has not been an easy endeavor. For many Muslims, including those not from the Middle East, Jews have been associated with Israel and were the supporters of a country that they often resented. For liberal Christians, such a dialogue became even more urgent, in the wake of Al Qaeda's September 11, 2001 attack on the United States. Although a number of Jewish religious leaders raised their voice against the vilification of Islam and the harassment of Muslims in America, Muslim leaders have often trusted Christian representatives more than Jewish ones (Schleifer 2002).

In addition to enlarging the scope of the mainstream dialogue, during recent decades new modes and forums of what could be called alternative interfaith dialogue have developed between Jews and non-Jews. The impetus for a number of Jewish engagements in alternative avenues of dialogue with Muslims and Christians resulted from their dissenting opinions on Israeli policies and their exception to the extensive backing that the established Jewish organizations have offered Israel. A solid pro-Israeli attitude on the part of Jewish representatives in the more official dialogue groups has characterized the dialogue since the 1940s, and intensified in the late 1960s in the wake of the 1967 war. However, in the early 1980s, in the wake of the Israeli war in Lebanon, a number of Jews in Britain, the United States, and elsewhere, founded alternative forms of dialogue where Jewish, Christian and Muslim critics of Israel came together attempting to promote peace negotiations or safeguard civil rights in Israel and its occupied territories (Maduro 1991). Alternative forms of dialogue grew throughout the 1990s and 2000s, connected to larger developments within the Jewish community in America, Britain and other countries. More theological and even mystical forums of conversation and dialogue have been promoted by leaders of new and alternative Jewish communities, primarily engaging leaders of Asian religious traditions. Such encounters started in the 1970s with Zalman Schachter, founding leader of the neo-Hasidic and Renewal movements, and his associate Shlomo Carlebach, who both began befriending and exchanging ideas with Hindu gurus, Buddhist priests and Muslim mystics. Schachter was interested in learning from teachers and mystics of other faiths as well as in presenting Judaism to them (Schacter-Shalomi 1993). He believed that Judaism could enrich itself by learning from other traditions, and so make itself more viable as an option to Jewish spiritual seekers. Carlebach, however, was motivated by his sense that Judaism was now operating in an open market of religions and needs to learn from its competitors.

Conclusion

One can look back at over a century of Jewish–Christian interfaith dialogue and reach some conclusions. Essentially a liberal Christian initiative, dialogue in its early stages did not wish to immediately resolve centuries-old issues, but the early Christian participants were willing to offer a forum for Jewish–Christian engagement. Interfaith dialogue grew into a movement of Christian–Jewish reconciliation in the decades following the Second World War, partially influenced by the horrors of the war. It further developed reaching its zenith in the 1960s and 1970s, when unprecedented achievements were made in improving the relationship between Christianity and Judaism. This movement has, at least on the theoretical level, put to rest old accusations and animosities, bringing about more correct and tolerant relationships between the communities, removing unfavorable stereotypes from sermons, textbooks, and theological works. For the most part, these changes took place consciously among liberal Christians, although they influenced conservative groups as well. During the 1960s, 1970s and 1980s, a number of Christian theologians expressed appreciative understandings of Judaism and generous visions of the desired relationship between Christianity and Judaism. And a number of Christian leaders, such as Pope John-Paul II, made unprecedented gestures of recognition and good will towards Judaism and the Jews. Jewish theological responses have come about more slowly, although at the turn of the twenty-first century a group of Jewish intellectuals acknowledged the change in the Christian attitudes and the need of Jews to respond adequately in a groundbreaking declaration, *Dabru Emet* (Speak the Truth), which called upon Jews to realize that Christian attitudes toward Jews have dramatically changed and that Jews should adjust their attitudes towards their newly accepting sister religion accordingly.

While interfaith dialogue has affected the Christian and Jewish communities at large, it has also remained overwhelmingly the domain of ministers, priests and rabbis, thinkers and academicians who opted to represent their communities and traditions, leaving out, at times, more secular, countercultural, popular, conservative, or dissenting voices, and the dialogue therefore had its limitations. Paradoxically, just when the dialogue reached a historical peak, bringing an unprecedented improvement in the relationship between Christians and Jews, it also reached an impasse and not necessarily only over the Jewish enchantment with the State of Israel.

Reconciliation with Judaism, which had been a priority for mainstream Christian churches in the mid-twentieth century, has become less important at the turn of the twenty-first century, as dialogue with other faiths, especially Islam, has become a more urgent Christian concern. Interfaith dialogue with Jews is important for some but by no means to all mainstream Christian leaders. Moreover, while interfaith dialogue has had remarkable achievements, the reconciliation between Jewish and Christian groups is still fragile, with stubborn pockets of bitterness and suspicions still remaining. Not all Catholics and Protestants, even members of mainstream churches, have accepted the legitimacy of Judaism, and some Christian groups have seen no need for change from pre-twentieth century Christian attitudes toward Judaism and Jews. Likewise, not all Jewish groups have taken part in the dialogue or have come to accept its premises. While interfaith dialogue has helped bring about unprecedented improvement in the relationship between the faiths, the realities of Christian–Jewish relations have remained fragile and only time will tell how many of the older wounds have been healed.

Bibliography

Ariel, Yaakov. *Evangelizing the Chosen People: Missions to the Jews in America 1880–2000.* Chapel Hill: University of North Carolina Press, 2000.

Ariel, Yaakov. "Christianity Through Reform Eyes: Kaufmann Kohler's Scholarship on Christianity." *American Jewish History*, 89, 2 (2001) 181–192.

Ariel, Yaakov. "An Unexpected Alliance: Christian Zionism and Its Historical Significance." *Modern Judaism* 26(1) (February 2006): 74–100.

Ariel, Yaakov. "A Proud Announcement: the Jewish Encyclopedia and the Coming of Age of Jewish Scholarship in America." *Simon-Dubnow-Institut Jahrbuch* IX (2010): 381–404.

Athans, Mary Christine. *The Coughlin–Fahey Connection: Father Charles E. Coughlin, Father Denis Fahey, C.S.Sp., and Religious Anti-*

Semitism in the United States, 1938–1954. New York: Peter Lang, 1991.

Baldwin, Neil. Henry Ford and the Jews: The Mass Production of Hate. New York: Public Affairs, 2001.

Banki, Judith. Christian Responses to the Yom Kippur War: Implication for Christian–Jewish Relations. New York: American Jewish Committee, 1974.

Berger, Alan L., Harry Cargas, and Susan Nowak (eds.) The Continuing Agony: From the Carmelite Convent to the Crosses at Auschwitz. New York: Global Publications, 2002.

Braybooke, Marcus. A History of the Council of Christians and Jews. London: Vallentine Mitchell, 1991.

Braybooke, Marcus. Pilgrimage of Hope: One Hundred Years of Global Interfaith Dialogue. New York: Crossroad, 1992.

Carroll, James. Constantine's Sword: The Church and the Jews. New York: Houghton Mifflin Company, 2001.

Carson, Clayborne. "The Politics of Relations Between African-Americans and Jews." In Blacks and Jews: Alliances and Arguments, ed. Paul Berman. New York: Delacorte Press, 1994, 131–143.

Charap, Lawrence G. "Accept the Truth from Whomsoever Gives It: Jewish-Protestant Dialogue, Interfaith Alliance and Pluralism, 1880–1910." American Jewish History, 89, 3 (2001) 261–278.

Croner Helga (ed). Stepping Stones to Further Jewish–Christian Relations. New York: Stimulus Books, 1977.

Croner Helga (ed). More Stepping Stones to Jewish–Christian Relations. New York: Stimulus Books, 1985.

Croner Helga (ed). Theology of the Churches and the Jewish People: Statements by the World Council of Churches and Its Member Churches. Geneva: World Council of Churches, 1988.

Cunningham, Philip, Joseph Sievers, Mary Boys, Hans Hermann Hernix, and Jesper Svartvik (eds.). Christ Jesus and the Jewish People Today. New Explorations of Theological Interrelationships. Grand Rapids, MI: Eerdmans Publishers, 2011.

Dinnerstein, Leonard. Antisemitism in America. New York: Oxford University Press, 1994.

Dirks, Lee E. The Ecumenical Movement. New York: Public Affairs Committee, 1969.

Eckardt, A. Roy. Jews and Christians: The Contemporary Meeting. Bloomington: Indiana University Press, 1986.

Eckardt, Alice L. and A. Roy Eckardt. Long Night's Jouney into Day. Detroit, MI: Wayne State University Press, 1988.

Eckardt, Roy A. Elder and Younger Brother: The Encounter of Jews and Christians. New York: Scribner's, 1967.

Elkin, Larry. Enduring Witness: The Churches and the Palestinians. Geneva: World Council of Churches, 1985.

Ericksen, Robert P. and Heschel, Susannah, eds. Betrayal: German Churches in the Holocaust. Minneapolis: Augsburg Fortress, 1999.

Feldman, Egal. "American Protestant Theologians on the Frontier of Jewish–Christian Relations, 1922–1982," in Anti-Semitism in American History, ed. David A. Gerber. Urbana: University of Illinois Press, 1986, 363–85.

Feldman, Egal. "Reinhold Niebuhr and the Jews." Jewish Social Studies 46 (1984): 292–302.

Fleisher, Eva. Auschwitz – Beginning of a New Era: Reflections on the Holocaust. New York: Ktav, 1977.

Flusser, David. "Jewish–Christian Relations in the Past and Present," in Judaism and Early Christianity, ed. D. Flusser. Tel Aviv: Siffriat Hapoalim, 1979.

Friedman, Murray. What Went Wrong?: The Creation and Collapse of the Black–Jewish Alliance. New York: Free Press, 1995.

Gaebelein, Arno C. Christianity or Religion? New York: Our Hope, 1912.

Gilbert, Arthur. "New Trends in the Protestant Mission to the Jew." Conservative Judaism 19 (1965): 51–56.

Gilbert, Arthur. The Vatican Council and the Jews. Cleveland, OH: World Publishing Company, 1968.

Glock Charles Y. and Rodney Stark. Christian Beliefs and Anti-Semitism. New York: Harper Torchbooks, 1966.

Haynes, Stephen R. *Reluctant Witnesses: Jews and the Christian Imagination*. Louisville, KY: Westminster John Knox Press, 1995.

Herberg, Will. *Protestant, Catholic, Jew*. New York: Anchor Books, 1960.

Heschel, Susannah and Abraham Joshua Heschel. "Introduction," in *Moral Grandeur and Spiritual Audacity*, ed. Susannah Heschel. New York: Noonday Press, 1996.

Holmes, John Haynes. *Judaism and Christianity*. New York: Community Pulpit, 1928.

Ianniello, Lynne. "Release for Press," Anti-Defamation League, New York, 8 January, 1986

Jeansonne, Glen. *Gerald L. K. Smith, Minister of Hate*. New Haven, CT: Yale University Press, 1988.

King, C. M. *The Palestinians and the Church, 1: 1948–1956*. Geneva: World Council of Churches, 1981.

Klein, Charlotte. *Anti-Judaism in Christian Theology*. Philadelphia: Fortress Press, 1978.

Kraut, Benny. "A Wary Collaboration: Jews, Catholics, and the Protestant Goodwill Movement," in *Between the Times: The Travail of the Protestant Establishment in America, 1900–1960*, edited by William R. Hutchinson. Cambridge: Cambridge University Press, 1989. 193–230.

Lerner, Michael. *The Socialism of Fools: Antisemitism on the Left*. Oakland, CA: Tikkun Books, 1992.

Levenson, Jon D. *The Death and Resurrection of the Beloved Son: The Transformation of Child Sacrifice in Judaism and Christianity*. New Haven, CT:Yale University Press, 1995.

Levine, Amy-Jill and Brettler, Marc Zvi, *The Jewish Annotated New Testament*. Oxford: Oxford University Press, 2011.

Libowitz, Richard. *Mordecai M. Kaplan and the Development of Reconstructionism*. Lewiston, NY: Edwin Mellen Press, 1983.

Lindsey, Robert. *A New Approach to the Synoptic Gospels*. Jerusalem: Dugit Publishing House, 1971.

Littell, Franklin. *The Crucifixion of the Jews*. New York: Harper and Row, 1975.

Maduro, Otto. ed. *Judaism, Christianity and Liberation*. New York: Orbis Books, 1991.

Marty, Martin E. *Modern American Religion, Vol 1, The Irony of it All, 1893–1919*. Chicago: University of Chicago Press, 1986.

Merson, Ben. "The Minister, the Rabbi and Their House of God," *Collier's*, February 17, 1951, 27, 36–37.

Niebuhr, Reinhold. "Jews after the War." *Nation*, February 21, 1942, 214–16; February 28, 1942, 253–55.

Niebuhr, Reinhold. "The Rapprochement between Jews and Christians." *Christian Century*, January 7, 1926, 9–11.

Pawlikowski, John T. *Christ in the Light of the Christian Jewish Dialogue*. New York: Paulist Press, 1982.

Peck Abraham J. ed. *Jews and Christians After the Holocaust*. Philadelphia: Fortress Press, 1982.

Rice, Dan. "Reinhold Niebuhr and Judaism." *Journal of the American Academy of Religion* 45 (1977): 101–146.

Rudin A. James and Marvin R. Wilson. eds. *A Time to Speak: The Evangelical–Jewish Encounter*. Grand Rapids, MI: Eerdmans, 1987.

Ruether, Rosemary. *Faith and Fratricide: the Theological Roots of Antisemitism*. New York: Seabury Press, 1974.

Schachter-Shalomi, Zalman. *Paradigm Shift: From the Renewal Jewish Teachings of Reb Zalman Schachter-Shalomi*. Lanham, MD: Jason Aronson, 1993.

Schleifer, Yigal. "No Dialogue, Only Mutual Distrust." *The Jerusalem Report* (September 23, 2002): 16–17.

Scult, Mel. *Judaism Faces the Twentieth Century: A Biography of Mordecai M. Kaplan*. Detroit, MI: Wayne State University Press, 1994.

Sharpe, Eric J. *Comparative Religion: A History*. La Salle, IL: Open Court, 1986.

Simpson William W. and Ruth Weyl. *The International Council of Christians and Jews*. Happenheim: International Council of Christians and Jews, 1988.

Strober, Gerald. *Portrait of the Elder Brother*. New York: American Jewish Committee and the National Conference of Christians and Jews, 1972.

Svonkin, Stuart. *Jews Against Prejudice: American Jews and the Fight for Civil Liberties.* New York: Columbia University Press, 1997.

Tanenbaum, Marc, Marvin R. Wilson and A. James Rudin. *Evangelical and Jews in Conversation on Scripture, Theology, and History.* Grand Rapids, MI: Bacher Book House, 1978.

Van Buren, Paul M. *Discerning the Way: A Theology of the Jewish–Christian Realities.* New York: Seabury Press, 1980.

Van Buren, Paul. *A Theology of the Jewish–Christian Reality*, 3 vols. San Francisco: Harper and Row, 1980.

Wise, Stephen. *Challenging Years: The Autobiography of Stephen Wise.* New York: C. P. Putnam, Sons, 1948.

CHAPTER 14

Jewish–Muslim Dialogue

Reuven Firestone

Historical Background

Dialogue as conversion and the exchange of ideas and opinions has been taking place between Muslims and Jews since the emergence of Islam in the seventh century. In the case of Islam, as with early Christianity, Jews lived among those involved in the new movement and were divided among themselves over whether or not to join. Also like the case of Christianity, Islamic religious literature professes to record dialogue between oppositional Jews and new believers, thereby establishing from as early as the Qur'an itself some of the points of difference and contention between Jews and Muslims (Q 2:91, 109, 135, 145; 3:64–67, 69–72, 78; 4:150, etc.; Rubin 1999).

The canonization of contention in the early traditions of new religions can be found abundantly in Judaism, Christianity and Islam. New religions are regularly denigrated by established religions, which polemicize against them in order to prevent the emergence of religious competition. The new religions inevitably respond in kind, and in the case of scriptural religions that polemic appears in scripture. After new religions become institutionalized, however, they unsurprisingly engage in the same behavior toward new emerging religions that are perceived as religious competitors. Among Abrahamic religions, therefore, each looks both forward and backward at competing religions, and each establishes arguments to question and discredit many of the basic principles and tenets of religious competitors. This kind of argumentative dialogue is not the kind that is sought after today, but it is also important to acknowledge, because it establishes an intellectual and religious baseline around which virtually all subsequent discussion, apologetics, polemics and productive dialogue have been constructed.

From the earliest years of Islamic emergence to the present, Jews and Muslims have lived together and communicated with one another. This is dialogue in the broadest sense, and social and economic intercourse has always included discussion about personal issues such as religion. During the early centuries of Muslim rule, these discus-

The Wiley Blackwell Companion to Inter-Religious Dialogue, First Edition. Edited by Catherine Cornille.
© 2013 John Wiley & Sons Ltd. Published 2020 by John Wiley & Sons Ltd.

sions could be natural and unscripted as well as intentionally polemical, and various genres of Arabic literature incidentally mention occasions of the former (Kilpatrick 1999).

After an initial period of religious formation lasting two or three generations, relations between Muslims and the religious communities living under Muslim rule took place within parameters established officially by the Muslim law of the *dhimma* (protection/custody). Jews and Christians were *dhimmī* communities that were protected but subjugated. They held legal citizenship and were safeguarded by law, but at a secondary social status. Under the *dhimma* they were free to worship without interference as long as worship did not occur in public space, but they were forbidden to proselytize (Cahen 2012). Religious discussion, which can easily evolve into argument, could therefore become a dangerous endeavor.

Jews and Christians were protected by law as long as they accepted their subordinate status, but if they did not demonstrate subservience, then official protection could be removed, leaving them exposed to potential mistreatment. The balance between protection and inferior status was accomplished formally by requiring dhimmīs to engage in certain subservient behaviors in relation to Muslims, using specialized forms of address, and even wearing identifiable clothing (Stillman 1979). If dhimmīs were perceived as not accepting their position, they could be subject to violence directed against them individually or collectively. Sometimes accusations could be made against Jews or Christians by Muslims for personal gain or other venal reasons, which would require a collective response or campaign by the *dhimmī* community for its own protection and to ensure its rights. In sum, the *dhimma* provided legal status for Jews in the Muslim world, which was better than what obtained among Jews of the Christian world, who lost all legal rights during the High Middle Ages. But legal protection came at a price that established a clear hierarchy of status which restricted free and open discourse on religious issues to certain exceptional situations.

As is the case with law everywhere, official policies can be honored more in the breach than the observance. During the classical period of Islamic political, cultural and intellectual ascendancy from roughly the ninth through the sixteenth centuries (depending on the region), open conversation and learning between Muslims, Jews and Christians occurred at a variety of levels. Similar dialogue between traditionalists, skeptics, rationalists and sectarians also occurred within each religious community. These kinds of dialogue ranged formally from written polemics to organized discussions in courts of caliphs, sultans and other high-ranking officials, and informally through conversation between members of various religious communities living side by side in the mixed neighborhoods of city, town and village in the Muslim world (Perlmann 1974). The nature of discourse varied by location, context and period, but even during the so-called "golden age" in Spain the nature of relationships was intricate and uneven. It was so complex, in fact, that it is difficult to assess its quality and even the meaning of the terminology used to describe it (Gampel 1992; Glick 1992).

The one institution of particular interest for a discussion of dialogue in the Middle Ages is the *majlis* – a term with a wide semantic field that includes sessions or sittings of intellectuals, scientists and artists sponsored by patrons in which the arts and sciences are discussed or debated. Patrons were typically high government officials, but they could also be wealthy merchants who wished to support the arts and sciences and thereby further their own status as champions of high civilization. The quintessential *majlis* was that of the caliph, who surrounded himself with the best literati and scientists of the day in his court, which functioned in a manner reminiscent of the classic French salon of the eighteenth and nineteenth centuries. The style of discourse was often one of rivalry and competition, and the caliph would typically put poets, scientists, legal scholar and story-tellers in situations in which they would attempt to overcome their competitors in order to exult in victory and rejoice at the discomfiture of the defeated (Bosworth et al. 1996; Stroumsa 1999). Accounts or references to religious discussions or, more accurately, debates or arguments in such sessions, can be found in a variety of Muslim and Jewish sources. These debates usually took place over theological and legal differences between contending Muslims, but they also occurred between Muslims and Jews, Muslims and Christians, or between all three (Cohen and Somekh 1999; Kedar 1999; Stroumsa 1999). The sessions were not structured like inter-religious dialogues of today, and the purpose of medieval dialogue was not to better understand the religious *other* in a pluralistic environment. Instead, the participant in a medieval religious deliberation sought to demonstrate the truth of his own position, with the belief that this would bring divine reward. Sarah Stroumsa notes that "the *majlis* did not function as a study group, but rather as a debating society . . . Quite often, the debate would turn into a verbal duel . . ." (67). Despite sometimes intense competition, formal rhetoric, and hierarchical expectations, however, the participants and contenders within these *majālis* were generally protected and allowed to speak rather freely (Cohen and Somekh 1999: 130; Griffith 1999: 42f). As a result, religious scholars and intellectuals had the opportunity to learn across religious boundaries and to arrive at a better understanding of the ideals and practices of their religious neighbors, even if such understanding was developed within a contentious framework. This undoubtedly had a positive trickle-down effect among a larger body of citizens.

Societal openness and generosity toward minorities is much more prevalent when polities are stable and when economies are strong. The economic and political weakening of the Muslim world from the later Middle Ages into the early modern and modern periods corresponds with a general decline in the openness of inter-religious discourse and the status of religious and other minorities (Stillman 1979: 64–94). Because of the great expansion of the Muslim world and its political, ethnic and economic variety, these changes occurred unevenly, though the general overall trend was one of decline. During these same centuries, the West was experiencing growth in economies, populations and influence. This resulted in increased Western confidence and influence in the internal affairs of Muslim countries from the Middle East and North Africa to south and southeast Asia, resulting finally in colonization and the wresting of political control from local powers (Lapidus 1988: 268–275).

The Western colonial powers naturally privileged local Christians living in the Muslim world, with whom they could relate as religious compatriots and whom they considered more reliable than Muslims. This reversed the traditional status of dhimmī communities in general, including Jews and Zoroastrians who were likely to become part of the administrative class under colonial rule. The rise in dhimmī status naturally provoked resentment among less advantaged Muslims, and religious minorities were seen as collaborating with the foreign enemy rather than acting as loyal native citizens (Firestone 2005: 443–445; Stillman 1979: 95–107). As a result, when the colonial powers were pushed out of the Muslim world in the mid-twentieth century, minority religious communities often faced a sudden backlash involving increased discrimination and violence. Jews were especially vulnerable in many locations, and the birth of modern Israel was often considered a final oppressive colonial outpost, ruled by Jews and supported by Western Christendom and world Jewry. The history of Muslim decline and the shifting status of Jews relative to Muslims in relation to Islamic legal and social expectations have had a substantial impact on Muslim–Jewish relations historically, and that history has had a significant impact on the state of Muslim–Jewish dialogue today.

Divergent perceptions of the status of Jews under Muslim government throughout the centuries have spawned two classic opposing positions on the possibility of Jewish–Muslim dialogue in the broadest sense. On the one side are those who claim that the Muslim world was extraordinarily tolerant, and that Jews were remarkably free from persecution (Antonius 1939; Chouraqui 1968; Swartz 1970). On the other is the "dhimmitude" school maintaining that Muslims have never been tolerant of their religious minorities, that Jew-hatred (as well as hatred of Christians) is firmly rooted in Islamic theology and law, and that there is no possible way that such deeply embedded animosity can ever be overcome (Bat Ye'or 1985; Bostom 2008). Both positions are simplistic and do not stand up to scholarly historical scrutiny. The truth is neither so romantic nor disastrous, since religious minorities under Islam benefited significantly from their protected legal status, yet also experienced prejudice, violence and even massacres due to their religious identities. Medieval political systems simply did not guarantee life, liberty or the pursuit of happiness as is currently expected from enlightened democratic political systems, and careful historians today are careful to contextualize the treatment of Jews in the Muslim world with the treatment of other religious, ethnic, linguistic and sectarian minorities. Mark Cohen, for example, demonstrates indisputably that while Jews as well as other religious minorities were treated with more or less tolerance (or bigotry) in both the medieval Christian and Muslim worlds, their treatment in the Muslim world was, overall, significantly better – and measurably so – than in the Christian world (Cohen 1986, 1994, 2009). Cohen's excellent scholarship has not convinced factions on either side to abandon their constructed views, so that the rhetoric of an idealized Jewish "golden age" under Islam, and its opposite, a Jewish "disaster" in the Muslim world, continue to be promoted in ways that antagonize and serve as a hindrance to positive efforts at dialogue.

The establishment of the modern state of Israel, a Jewish state in one of the oldest and most sacred areas of the Muslim world, has further exacerbated tensions between Jews and Muslims. While the core of the Israeli–Arab/Jewish–Palestinian conflict is the competition between national communities that dispute one another's national identity and ownership of territory, the dispute itself is often articulated in religious language. The use of religious language and metaphors in this struggle is a result of a number of factors, not the least of which is the inability of either side to convince the other or the world at large that its nationalist rhetoric is fully credible and compelling.

More than that, however, is the fact that modern, secular national identity emerged in the West in large part as an antidote to disastrous religious involvement in politics and government. In many areas that did not experience an emergent modern nationalism, such sentiments and intuitions do not apply. The result is that in many counties, what Westerners might consider unacceptably religious articulations of national identity are not necessarily seen as problematic by local citizens. This is certainly the case in the dispute over Israel/Palestine. Nevertheless, religious rhetoric over the conflict has increased dramatically over the past decades. While the history and causes of this increasing "religification" remain contested, there can be no question that it has been occurring, and the increased religious identification with national struggle has negatively affected Jewish–Muslim dialogue everywhere.

Dialogue between Muslims and Jews as Conscious Community Building and Civic Engagement

Muslim–Jewish dialogue takes place in three major arenas today: Europe, Israel/Palestine and North America. Major differences in national histories, immigration patterns, and current demographic particularities between these disparate areas make it impossible to offer an adequate examination of Muslim–Jewish dialogue in all three areas here. The following, therefore, treats the American context in greatest detail, with occasional reference where appropriate to the European and Middle Eastern arenas.

It is only in the past century that inter-religious dialogue has begun to be viewed as a means for transcending historical and theological tension between religions in order to find common cause for building community and positive civic engagement. This goal remains relatively new in Muslim–Jewish dialogue. A history of these dialogues need not be rehearsed in detail here, but a few points are worthy of consideration.

Three recent historical developments that have affected all religious communities in the West have also had a profound influence on Muslim–Jewish dialogue, and a fourth event has had a great impact on the ongoing viability of such dialogue (Loskota and Firestone 2007). The first development, as noted previously, is the founding of Israel in 1948, and the subsequent wars and conflicts that have ensued. The second development was the Second Vatican Council. The third historical development was the great growth in the presence of Muslims as a demographic force in Europe and the Americas since the 1960s. And the fourth development is the sudden radical increase in mass violence committed in the name of Islam by radicals, beginning with the bombing and eventual destruction of the New York World Trade Center in 1993 and 2001, and the subsequent subway bombings in Madrid in 2004 and London in 2005.

Modern occasions of dialogue between Christians and Muslims as a means of building community and civic engagement actually began as early as the World's Parliament of Religions held in Chicago in 1893 in conjunction with the World Columbian Exposition. Two Muslims presented papers on that occasion, among the 192 presentations that were overwhelmingly dominated by English-speaking Christians (Wildman). For the next 70 years, Muslims were rarely represented in inter-religious activities in the United States. This is due to two major factors: low Muslim population and visibility, and the fact that ecumenism between Christian denominations was of much greater interest.

Noticeable interest in engaging Muslims in dialogue began only after the Second Vatican Council, the Civil Rights Movement, and the increase in Muslim immigration in the wake of the Immigration and Nationality Act (Hart–Celler Act) of 1965, which abolished the national origins formula that had for decades limited most immigration to those arriving from western and northern Europe. The establishment of modern Israel had brought Jewish–Muslim relations into global focus decades earlier, but international Jewish–Muslim conflict only became a focal point for dialogue in the United States in the 1970s.

The Second Vatican Council produced a ground-breaking document in 1965 called the "Declaration of the Relation of the Church with Non-Christian Religions," a document best known by its opening Latin phrase, *Nostra Aetate* ("In our time . . ."). This publication marked the first time in history that the Catholic Church publicly proclaimed non-Christian religions to be deserving of respect, and worthy of dialogue. One of its most famous sections recognizes "the spiritual patrimony common to Christians and Jews" and the need "to foster and recommend . . . mutual understanding and respect" through, among other acts, "fraternal dialogues" (Croner 1977: 1). The Council originally had no intention of making any statements about non-Christian religious communities other than Jews, but changed its position in response to objections from a variety of quarters (Aydin 2002: 39). In the final version of the document, a declaration regarding Muslims is positioned even before the section treating Jews: "The Church regards with esteem also the Moslems . . . Since in the course of centuries not a few quarrels and hostilities have arisen between Christians and Moslems, this sacred synod urges all to forget the past and to work sincerely for mutual understanding and to preserve as well as to promote together for the benefit of all mankind social justice and moral welfare, as well as peace and freedom." *Nostra Aetate* not only marked the beginning of serious Catholic dialogue with non-Christian religious communities, but served as a catalyst for increased Catholic–Protestant engagement as well.

Protestant dialogue with non-Christian religions had begun earlier, though primarily in a context of mission. The Edinburgh World Missionary Conference of 1910 included a discussion of religious pluralism in Commission IV, but it was ultimately set aside in the interest of evangelization. Some Protestant denominations nevertheless were more open than the Catholic Church in the 1940s and 1950s to using the term "dialogue" in their relations with non-Christian religions, and individual pastors and rabbis began to meet and even share pulpits on occasion. But interest in what we would consider true dialogical engagement with Muslims among both Protestants and Catholics only began to emerge significantly in the 1960s (Aydin 2005: 91–93).

By this time, some liberal sectors of the Western religious world had become interested in forms of inter-religious engagement that would transcend mission or polemic. Initially, that sentiment was limited principally to Jewish–Christian dialogue, which was motivated most significantly by two factors: the large demographic growth of the American Jewish community with its successful integration into virtually all sectors of American society and culture, on the one hand, and remorse and shame among many Christians after the Holocaust, on the other. While dialogue between Christians and

Jews became institutionalized in the 1960s through the formation of councils created specifically for this purpose (Braybooke 1991; Simpson and Weyl 1988), the American Muslim community at this time was still quite small, significantly less visible, and not well organized. While Muslims were sometimes invited to inter-religious events and programs, they were hardly part of the ordinary inter-religious equation because of their low demographic profile in Europe and the United States until the mid-1960s, but also because a simmering sense of anxiety in the Christian West toward members of a religious civilization that had been so threatening to Christendom and the West for many centuries in the Middle Ages (Addison 1942; Akbari 2009; Daniel 1960; Southern 1962; Tolan 1996).

American Muslim engagement in dialogue would increase with the rise in Muslim immigration after the Immigration and Nationality Act of 1965 and the subsequent rapid increase in Muslim visibility (though in retrospect it is clearly questionable whether overall anxiety toward Islam was dispelled by these developments). Muslim immigration to Europe in about the same period was made up primarily of rural workers who were willing to engage in labor-intensive working-class jobs that were unpopular with Europeans. Turks, North Africans and South Asians tended to congregate in distinct communities in Europe and experienced difficulty integrating into the larger host cultures (Manco 2004; Nielsen 1995). Muslim immigrants to the United States during this period, on the other hand, tended to be more highly educated, became part of the middle class, lived dispersed among other American communities, and integrated more smoothly into the larger population (Denny 1995; Pew 2007). Many came as university students and remained as professionals.

Beginning in the 1960s, the American Muslim community expended significant effort and resources to organize community centers, mosques and local and national organizations. Some communities had organized at the local level prior to this time and Muslim students had begun organizing groups on some US campuses in the 1950s. It was in the 1960s, however, that the Muslim Student Association (MSA) began to develop official chapters and a national presence. Other groups and organizations emerged in the same period to represent the growing communities of Muslims deriving from various national and religious origins. Students who had been active during their student days in the MSA went on to found other organizations, including, in 1982, the Islamic Society of North America, which functioned as an umbrella organization to bring all or most Muslim institutions into one network (Abdo 2007: 101, 197; Ahmed 1992; Fenton 1988: 166). Shortly thereafter, two advocacy and public policy organizations were formed, the Muslim Public Affairs Council (MPAC) in 1986, and the Council on American-Islamic Relations (CAIR) in 1994. As a result of this increased organizing, the American Muslim community positioned itself not only to support its own growth and development, but also to project a larger profile in American affairs generally. This trend naturally brought Muslims into the public arena of inter-religious discourse and dialogue.

As noted above, Jews and Christians had been engaged in dialogue at the institutional and congregational levels for some decades previously, first through clergy relationships and then between lay communities. As Muslim communities grew in many parts of the United States, and as Muslim professionals became more involved in civic and social affairs, Muslims were sometimes invited to take part in dialogues as well. This kind of dialogue was not Muslim–Jewish as such, but it brought Jews and Muslims together in dialogical environments in which they could meet one another and observe each other's behaviors in inter-religious settings. Clergy councils in some areas invited Muslim religious leaders to join or attend events. Where synagogues and mosques or Islamic centers happened to be in the same neighborhood, rabbis sometimes initiated contact with Muslim religious leaders. Connecting with Muslim religious leadership was not as straightforward as initiating contact with Christian or Jewish religious leaders because of the unique situation among many American Muslim communities at the time and even today; mosques and Islamic centers often do not have trained clergy, or their clergy are trained overseas and often struggle with English (Firestone 2012; Ukeles 2003–4: 47–50).

These congregational-level initiatives were generally ad hoc, and they were initiated by Jews. Some Muslim religious and lay leaders subsequently have become more proactive, particularly those of South Asian origin, but Jews continue to take the lead in initiating dialogue for reasons that will be discussed below. The level of bilateral contact between Jewish and Muslim leaders and laity increased during the 1980s, particularly in the wake of the Camp David Accords that were signed in 1979, which signaled a hopeful development in Israeli–Palestinian relations. Hopeful sentiments in this arena generally encourage positive developments in Muslim–Jewish relations in Europe and the United States, while negative developments tend to inhibit dialogue. Muslim–Jewish dialogues during this period were all at the congregational or grassroots level.

Activity at the university level, however, had begun earlier. The University of Denver held four consecutive annual meetings from 1981 to 1984 that brought prominent scholars of Judaism and Islam together to hear and discuss each other's research under the auspices of the Center for Judaic Studies at the University of Denver. The conference organizers subsequently published two volumes of scholarly papers that focused on Jewish–Muslim relations (Brinner and Ricks 1986, 1989). Other colleges and universities subsequently held various colloquia and conferences on Judaism, Islam and Jewish–Muslim relations, and a cadre of Muslim and Jewish scholars began to meet with one another informally to collaborate on issues of common interest in history, linguistics, philosophy, religion, etc. These efforts have resulted in a number of academic collections containing scholarly papers and studies published from the 1980s to the present time. This same informal scholarly community has organized scholarly panels on Muslim–Jewish relations at the annual meetings of the American Academy of Religion, the Society of Biblical Literature, the Association for Jewish Studies, and the Middle East Studies Association. Most recently, the University of Iowa began producing a peer-reviewed scholarly journal dedicated to the discussion of topics in Islamic and Jewish traditions, cultures and practices, particularly in areas where thematic and doctrinal aspects are common (*Mathal/Mashal*). In the middle of the first decade of the twenty-first century, centers for the study and enhancement of Muslim–Jewish relations were established at Cambridge University and the University of Southern California (CMJR; CMJE). Both have websites that provide current information about the state of Muslim–Jewish relations at the levels of scholarship and praxis.

At the congregational level both the Muslim and Jewish communities are divided internally over whether or not dialogue should be encouraged. In the Jewish community, congregations on the liberal end of the religious organizational spectrum are most active, while Orthodox congregations are the least active, though some Modern Orthodox congregations belonging to the Union of Orthodox Jewish Congregations of America engage in various ways with local Muslim communities. The Muslim community is similarly divided over dialogue in general and dialogue with Jews in particular. Because Islam has not divided into religious movements based on the same criteria and principles relating to modernity and tradition as the Jewish community, it is more difficult to categorize these internal differences institutionally. Nevertheless, the more traditional Muslim congregations tend to be less interested in reaching out to the non-Muslim community in general (Shafiq and Abu-Nimer 2007: 6–18). Additionally, Muslims of Arab descent tend to be more directly affected by the Israel/Palestine conflict and are thus somewhat less inclined to reach out to Jews than Muslims of other national backgrounds.

Congregational dialogue programs range from the relational (at a variety of levels) to community action and education. Formal dialogue groups may engage in ongoing discussion over religious ideas and practices, and social and economic justice projects bring Muslim and Jewish congregants together to join forces in community activism. Educational programs include congregational tours, religious school visits or visits of clergy or teachers to religious schools and youth programs. Other programs include voter registration drives and joint initiatives that respond to incidents of hate, or ongoing programs to combat bigotry and prejudice (CMJE 2009; Ivri 2011).

Grassroots programs are organized voluntarily by individual Jews and Muslims outside the framework of any religious congregation or organization. These tend to be less formal and are usually short-lived. They also tend to be difficult to track and analyze. Nevertheless a small survey of Muslim–Jewish initiatives was organized by the Center for Muslim–Jewish Engagement: it was sent to 44 independent organizations and groups in the United States in 2009, ranging from university dialogue groups to meetings organized over the Israel/Palestine conflict, to highly informal living-room chat-groups. The survey noted a trend of increasing interest in dialogue, with nearly all the groups founded after 2001 and nearly half founded after 2007 (CMJE 2009, 2010).

Outside of the university setting, the first significant organizational initiatives began only in the first decade of the twenty-first century. The American Jewish Committee had demonstrated an interest in beginning in the 1980s, but has not succeeded in sustaining significant ongoing working relationships with Muslim organizations (Neuwirth 2001). A particularly significant organizational initiative to promote Muslim–Jewish relations was the 2007 invitation by the Islamic Society of North America (ISNA) to Rabbi Eric Yoffie, the president of the Union for Reform Judaism (URJ), to address its 44th annual conference. This was followed by an invitation from the URJ to Dr. Ingrid Mattson, the president of ISNA, to address the URJ biennial conference later the same year. ISNA is the largest Muslim organization in the United States, an umbrella group for American Muslim associations and organizations, while the URJ is the largest Jewish membership organization. The two groups subsequently developed a series of programs ranging from pairing synagogues with mosques for dialogue programs at various levels, to developing curricula for religious schools and houses of worship (Boorstein 2007; Perelman 2007).

A second noteworthy organizational project was initiated by the New York-based Foundation For Ethnic Understanding (FFEU), which has organized an annual international campaign to join Jewish and Muslim congregations together in a "weekend of twinning." The project is designed to promote ongoing contact between Muslim and Jewish communities throughout North America and parts of Europe by joining individual congregations in one grand weekend of programs and activities suggested by the FFEU. The twinning project is continuing to expand at the time of this writing (Shamir 2012; FFEU). The most significant partnership program currently in the United States is an organization called "NewGround: A Muslim–Jewish Partnership for Change." Developed originally through a partnership in Los Angeles between the Progressive Jewish Alliance and Muslim Public Affairs Council (Ballon 2007), it has since become an independent grassroots organization organized and funded jointly by donors in the Muslim and Jewish communities (Rizwan 2012).

Some Differences and Hurdles that Affect Muslim–Jewish Dialogue

Jews already have had significant experience in dialogue with Christians prior to becoming involved in dialogue with Muslims. As noted elsewhere in this collection, Jews have been motivated to engage actively in dialogue for purposes of defense – or, to connect this more directly to the common Jewish meta-narrative of oppression and victimization, for the purpose of individual and collective survival. Good relations with non-Jews has been an institutional goal of Jewish congregations and larger Jewish organizations for over a century, and engaging with religious communities at all levels is considered an important part of Jewish communal responsibility. American Muslims, on the other hand, have been less interested and have less experience with inter-religious dialogue. The reasons for these motivational differences are significant and worthy of consideration.

One of the most obvious reasons for the different level of interest in dialogue between Muslims and Jews is the difference in their relative integration into American culture. Jews have lived in the United States and have been integrated into its social, economic and political networks for at least two or three generations more than Muslims, and this basic difference affects power relationships between the two communities vis-à-vis the larger society.

The American Muslim community today is made up of many different sub-groups that may be classified according to: nation of origin, language of origin (which often transcends national boundaries), religious trend, generation of settlement, and so forth. The three largest groups according to virtually all studies are: those immigrants and descendants deriving from Arabic-speaking countries; those immigrants and descendants from South Asia (primarily contemporary India and Pakistan); and established Americans who have converted to Islam (Pew 2007). Most American converts are African Americans who have been a part of American history since the seventeenth century, and who came to Islam primarily through the intermediary, syncretic and non-Islamic movement of the "Nation of Islam," which emphasized Black American self-reliance and separation from what was regarded as the evils of White-dominated America. While the overwhelming majority of those who were affiliated with the Nation of Islam have left that group to become mainstream Muslims, these Muslims tend to remain interested in developing their own self-reliant communities and do not feel great need to reach out to non-Muslims (Lee 1996; Tapper 2011: 87 n.27). It should be added that the particular nature of their long American experience in conjunction with their inclination toward self-sufficiency and autonomy tend to inhibit their engagement with immigrant Muslim communities as well. Those deriving from the Arab world, South Asia and elsewhere (such as Iran, Indonesia, Malaysia, the Balkans, central Asia, etc.) are largely immigrant and first-generation Americans who are still integrating into American culture. Many belong to local ethnic mosques, and these are not infrequently located in towns or neighborhoods in which Christian evangelical communities reach out to their Muslim neighbors or pester them through their local missionary work. Muslim communities in such a situation tend to be devoted to internal community cohesion, development and support, and tend to avoid interfaith relations. Many mosques are also located in larger, cosmopolitan urban communities, but they, too, tend to be particularly concerned with religious and cultural continuity in the face of power-ful forces encouraging assimilation into the larger American melting pot.

American Jews, on the other hand, have all but abandoned the ethnically defined synagogues of previous generations (German, Polish, Lithuanian, Hungarian, etc.) to form more "American" (less ethnically divided) Jewish communities, as they have inte-grated deeply into American life (Abul Rauf 2011: 61; Tapper 2011: 77, 89 n.43). Jews had already created religious, civic and advocacy bodies generations earlier, and devel-oped a complex and structured organizational presence to provide economic, social and political support to Jews both locally and abroad. While observers have remarked how the Muslim and Jewish communities of America have undergone quite similar immi-grant experiences, the fact that Jews began the immigrant and integration process some two to three generations prior to most Muslims has put them in a very different social position in America. This critical difference provides an interesting and somewhat complex aspect to dialogue, in that the common experience separated by generations has produced something less than institutional parity between the two religious com-munities (Dolev and Kazmi 2005).

The numbers of Jews and Muslims in America are roughly equivalent, though accu-rate statistics are difficult to reach because of the ways that the communities affiliate and define themselves, and because the United States Census Bureau does not ask about religious affiliation and belief when conducting censuses. Moreover, the actual results of studies have become controversial because the size of each community relative to the other is viewed in the American public arena as a declaration of power and influ-ence (Ivri 2011; Tapper 2011: 74–75). The rough figure of five to six million for both communities seems as accurate an estimate as any, which puts Muslims and Jews in rough demographic parity. Their level of education is also equivalent, and both are very highly represented in the middle and professional classes. Jews, however, are far more established in the American system. Many more Jews hold offices in local, state and national governments, sit on the boards of large corporations, and are represented in the media and the arts. While Jews have experienced significant discrimination in America, since the Second World War they have become integrated into virtually all levels and areas of society and culture and project a sense of cultural confidence. Muslims, on the other hand, remain victims of very considerable prejudice in American society and culture, and have not yet achieved the kind of social and political success that Jews enjoy.

These parallel but different levels of involvement in the American immigrant experience, among other factors, have resulted in different levels of comfort and fluency as Americans. Comfort and competence contribute to a sense of security and power. This is felt and expressed in non-conscious ways that can present a barrier to ongoing dialogue. For example, Jews have a much more developed institutional infrastructure and, because they are generally comfortable in American social situations, have tended to reach out more to Muslims and invite Muslims to their own "space." Hosts inviting guests into their own space immediately introduces a power relationship into the sphere of dialogue. The host sets the agenda for the event, while the guest enters someone else's space and anticipates what will happen there. When the power and comfort relationship is not balanced, true dialogue is unsustainable (Forward 2001: 108–114). Whereas an individual event may work and contact may be established between two parties, ongoing programs die out when they are not developed through equal planning and sharing of space and agendas (Loskota and Firestone 2007).

While there can be no doubt about the relative power relationship between Jews and Muslims within the United States, American Muslims are part of a world community that is three hundred times the size of the global Jewish community. Another way of conveying the difference is that while Muslims make up some 20–25 percent of the world population, Jews make up approximately two tenths of one percent (Tapper 2011: 78, 89 n.46). An intuitive sense of relative numbers in the American and global contexts has an impact on both communities' relative confidence at the deepest level, a topic that has not yet been adequately explored. Muslims, for example, sometimes marvel when they hear Jews complain that they are a tiny and weak minority while it appears to them that Jews have a tremendous amount of power and influence in America. Something similar was observed in the Israeli context by the Arab Israeli Professor Sami Ma'ri, who is reported to have articulated the following in the mid-1970s: "In Israel, there is an Arab minority with a mentality of a majority, living within a Jewish majority with a mentality of a minority." The imbalance between relative power and perceived power can also adversely affect positive dialogue. One of the reasons that some Jewish advocacy organizations are adverse to improving relations with their Muslim counterparts, for example, may be anxiety at the growing power and influence of the American Muslim community. Support and assistance to Muslim organizations that are likely to support Palestinian over Jewish positions on Israel/Palestine may lie behind some Jewish organizations' criticism of Muslim organizations for alleged ties with terrorism.

Anti-Semitism and Islamophobia have had a major negative impact on dialogue between Muslims and Jews, and these are both affected greatly by the ongoing struggle over Israel/Palestine. As noted at the beginning of this essay, antipathy between Jews and Muslims derives from natural polemics related to the competitive emergence of new religions. Such antipathy is neither anti-Semitism nor Islamophobia, which are racist forms of irrational hatred directed against Jews or Muslims as individuals or as groups that can be expressed rhetorically or physically against their persons, property and institutions (USDS, EUMC1, EUMC2). Notwithstanding the relatively benign relations between Muslims and Jews in the pre-modern period, vile and virulent anti-Semitism has become culturally embedded in many layers of contemporary Muslim religious culture since the nineteenth century. This has had a powerfully adverse impact on the ability of Muslims to view Jews open-mindedly (Berenbaum 2008; Bodansky 1999; Kotek 2009; Küntzel 2007).

Islamophobia has been embedded in Western culture for centuries (Shryock 2010). As Jews have absorbed Western values and standards, particularly in the last two centuries, they have integrated Islamophobia into the natural Jewish antipathy toward Islam as a competing and sometimes threatening religious civilization. As an often latent Western Islamophobia has become more thoroughly activated in the past decade, Jews have been included among the vanguard of extremist activists who articulate an Islamophobic perspective in their hateful attacks (Shryock 2010: 104; Islamophobia Today). Their militancy has had a negative impact on the Jewish community's views of Muslims and of Islam in general. The escalation of prejudice within both religious communities is a product of a number of forces ranging from frustration over the lack of resolution to the Israel/Palestine conflict, to postmodern and post-colonial developments, and competition over influence and authority in national and trans-national politics (Brenner and Ramzy 2007; Bunzl 2007; Firestone 2010; Schenker and Abu-Zayyad 2006). Muslim–Jewish dialogue outside of the conflict zones has suffered as a result.

Positive engagement between Muslims and Jews declines when bloodshed flairs in Israel/Palestine during wars, bombings, incursions and other forms of violence, while positive engagement increases when positive events occur, such as President Sadat's visit to Jerusalem, or the signing of the Camp David Accords (Ivri 2011; Loskota and Firestone 2007). The complexity of the Israel/Palestine situation has more often hindered positive Muslim–Jewish dialogue than helped it, but the conflict also sometimes stimulates positive dialogue in the Middle East, as well as in the United States and Europe. For example, the ongoing conflict has stimulated investment in many programs and projects in Israel, the West Bank and Palestine that bring Muslims and Jews together in dialogical environments there and abroad. These are sponsored by a variety of local and international agencies.

The events of September 11, 2001 and the ensuring "war on terror" motivated Jews and Muslims to reach out and engage one another. For example, mosques that had little prior interest in outreach outside their communities were motivated to open their doors and engage with the larger American population, and specifically with Jews. After the backlash against Muslims following September 11, 2001, many synagogues (as well as churches) reached out to local Muslim communities, held positive educational programs on Islam and took adults and children to local Islamic institutions in an effort to better understand their neighbors and forestall the rise in Islamophobia (Loskota and Firestone 2007).

Some Shared Attributes and their Impact on Dialogue

A number of factors serve as positive influences on dialogue between Muslims and Jews. In the United States and Europe, Jews and Muslims share a common status within countries made up of overwhelmingly Christian populations with a history of antipathy toward both monotheist minorities. As non-Christian religious minorities in Christian environments, they share a common status as religious outsiders that is reinforced in myriad ways, from the institutionalization of religious holidays to public assumptions and negative comments in the media. This contemporary experience is coupled with a common history of suffering as victims of prejudice in the West. In fact, Jews and Muslims were commonly considered allies of one another in pre-modern times (Cutler and Cutler 1986). Such perspectives tend to remain operative in one way or another over generations when they are embedded in cultural forms such as literature, the arts and music.

Related to the common status of religious *other*, Muslims and Jews have common advocacy issues to which the larger Western culture and society is not naturally receptive, such as the need for religious circumcision, religious animal slaughter (kosher/hallal), and issues of personal status such as marriage and inheritance. Other mutual interests include advocacy to establish and enforce hate-crimes legislation, as well as support for faith-based education. These shared and material existential benefits have provided an impetus for establishing initiatives that highlight commonalities and common religious and cultural heritage (Ivri 2011).

Such coalition building requires bilateral dialogue that is separate from the larger dialogue of religious perspectives. Bilateral dialogue establishes a special relationship between allies relative to a third community (or more communities) to which the two allied communities may be in joint opposition on particular issues. Positive outcomes from such dialogue are less feasible without prior coordination between the bilateral partners. Bilateral dialogue must therefore occur among subgroups within the larger amalgam of religious communities. Just as Muslims and Jews need to dialogue periodically without Christians, so Muslims and Christians need to dialogue periodically without Jews, and Jews and Christians need to dialogue periodically without Muslims. There are, of course, many occasions in which all religious communities, Abrahamic and non-Abrahamic, may and should dialogue together.

Note that the commonalities between Muslims and Jews listed here arise from a shared experience of living as outsiders within larger cultures and societies. While deriving from a common negative experience, the result can be positive not only for the two communities adversely affected, but also for the larger community, which can learn to be more accommodating and accepting of difference.

Jews who are in favor of dialogue with Muslims usually perceive a benefit in breaking down stereotypes and being understood or accepted by Muslims as fellow citizens. This is consistent with the general Jewish interest in "dialogue for survival." Jews who engage with Muslims in dialogue also tend to believe that the effort will help bring understanding about the aspirations of Jews for a homeland in Israel and a reduction in anti-Semitic attitudes among Muslims. They also wish to cultivate ties with a community that will inevitably have increasing political and institutional clout in the coming generations.

Muslims in favor of dialogue with Jews usually perceive a benefit in breaking down negative stereotypes of Muslims and bringing greater understanding among Jews for the aspiration of Palestinians for a national homeland in Palestine. Many also hope that outcomes of dialogue will include greater trust with an influential Jewish minority and knowledge about successful strategies for lobbying and institution building (Abdul Rauf 2011; Dolev and Kazm 2005; Ivri 2011; Loskota and Firestone 2007).

Current Trends and Observations in Muslim–Jewish Relations in North America

Muslim–Jewish dialogue remains weak and underdeveloped, particularly when compared to Christian ecumenical dialogue and Jewish–Christian dialogue, and increasingly to Christian–Muslim dialogue. The Council of Centers on Jewish–Christian Relations lists 35 regular member institutions and four affiliate members (CCJR). An internet search reveals seven centers for Christian–Muslim relations, and only three centers for Jewish–Muslim relations. While Christians and Muslims have generated formal platforms for dialogue (*Nostra Aetate*, "A Common Word") and Christians and Jews have generated similar documents (*Nostra Aetate*, *Dabru Emet*), no such document has been developed as a foundation for dialogue between Muslims and Jews.

Aside from the ongoing association between the Islamic Society of North America and the Union for Reform Judaism, there is currently little cooperation between Muslim and Jewish organizations. Core tensions revolve around different perspectives on Israel/Palestine and different views regarding the causes and definition of terrorism. Jewish organizations object vociferously when Muslim organizations define Israeli incursions and bombings of neighboring areas such as Gaza and Lebanon as acts of state terror, and when Muslim organizations voice support for Islamist groups such as Hamas. Muslim organizations strenuously object to American Jewish organizational lobbying for Israel that will benefit Israeli government policies, such as the building of settlements and retention of land in the West Bank, or the tendency of Jewish organizational leaders to define certain militant acts among Muslims as terrorism. The anger and tension has prevented dialogue for all intents and purposes at the organizational level.

At the grassroots, level, however, there appears to be a surge in interest since 2001 in dialogue and learning among Muslims and Jews. Anecdotally, we have observed a significant increase in the study of Arabic among Jews in colleges and universities, and a somewhat lesser increase among Muslims interested in learning about Judaism. Grassroots groups appear to transcend age and gender differences, ranging from women who meet to bake and talk, salon discussions, the comparative textual study of religious sources, and initiatives on college campuses to prepare and eat kosher/hallal food (CMJE 2009, 2010). The college campus can also serve as a focus for contention, particularly over Israel/Palestine and the causes and definitions of terrorism.

Muslim–Jewish dialogue at the congregational level is increasing as well, particularly with the publicity and the organizational activity of the Foundation for Ethnic

Understanding in its congregational twinning program. Muslim congregations are reaching out increasingly to other communities through visitation programs and invitations to break the Ramadan fasts through communal *iftars*. If grassroots and congregational efforts continue to expand at the current rate, such efforts may influence the revision of official institutional stances, and may foster further support for dialogue itself. But everything can change quickly with a shift in the situation in Israel/Palestine or in the politics of the larger global arena.

Bibliography

A Common Word. Official Website: http://www.acommonword.com/ (accessed December 10, 2012).

Abdo, Geneive. *Mecca and Main Street: Muslim Life in America After 9/11*. Oxford: Oxford University Press, 2007.

Abdul Rauf, Feisal. "Evolving from Muslims in America to American Muslims: A Shared Trajectory with the American Jewish Community" in *Muslims and Jews in America: Commonalities, Contentions, and Complexities*, eds. Reza Aslan and Aaron Tapper. Basingstoke: Palgrave Macmillan, 2011, 57–70.

Addison, James. *The Christian Approach to the Moslem*. New York: Columbia University Press, 1942.

Ahmed, Gutbi Mahdi. "Muslim Organizations in the United States," in *The Muslims of America*, ed. Yvonne Yazbeck Haddad. Oxford: Oxford University Press. 1992, 11–24.

Akbari, Suzanne. *Idols in the East: European Representations of Islam and the Orient, 1100–1450*. Ithaca, NY: Cornell University Press, 2009.

Antonius, George. *The Arab Awakening*. Philadelphia: Lippincott, 1939.

Aydin, Mahmut. *Modern Western Christian Theological Understandings of Muslims since the Second Vatican Council*. Washington, DC: Council for Research in Values and Philosophy, 2002.

Aydin, Mahmut. "The Catholic Church's Teaching on Non-Christians with Special Reference to the Second Vatican Council," in *Multiple Paths to God: Nostra Aetate 40 Years Later*, ed. John Hogan and George McLean.

Washington, DC: Council for Research in Values and Philosophy, 2005, 23–65.

Ballon, Marc. "Breaking New Ground: Jewish, Muslim Groups' Program Encourages Leaders to See the 'Other' as Friend." *Jewish Journal*, January 18, 2007. http://www.jewishjournal.com/articles/item/breaking_new_ground_jewish_muslim_groups_program_encourages_leaders/ (accessed 10 December 2012).

Bat Ye'or. *Islam and Dhimmitude: Where Civilizations Collide*. Rutherford, NJ: Fairleigh Dickinson University Press, 2001.

Bat Ye'or. *The Dhimmi: Jews and Christians under Islam*. Rutherford, NJ: Fairleigh Dickinson University Press, 1985.

Berenbaum, Michael (ed.). *Not Your Father's Antisemitism: Hatred of the Jews in the 21st Century*. St. Paul: Paragon House, 2008.

Bodansky, Yossef. *Islamic Anti-Semitism as a Political Instrument*. Houston: Freeman Center for Strategic Studies, 1999.

Boorstein, Michelle. "Jews and Muslims Set Up Big Interfaith Effort." *Washington Post*. December 16, 2007.

Bostom, Andrew (ed.). *The Legacy of Islamic Antisemitism*. Amherst, NY: Prometheus, 2008.

Bosworth, C. E., E. Van Donzel, B. Lewis and C. Pellat. "Madjlis," in *The Encyclopedia of Islam* (new edition 1986), Vol. 5, 1031–1033.

Braybooke, Marcus. *Children of One God: A History of the Council of Christians and Jews*. London: Vallentine Mitchell, 1991; and www.ccj.org.uk.

Brenner, Ira and Nadia Ramzy, (eds.). "Anti-Semitism in Muslim Cutlures." *International*

Journal of Applied Psychoanalytic Studies Special Issue 4(3) (2007): 187–254.

Brinner, William, and Stephen Ricks, *Studies in Islamic and Judaic Traditions*. Atlanta: Scholars' Press, 1986.

Brinner, William, and Stephen Ricks, *Studies in Islamic and Judaic Traditions II*. Atlanta: Scholars' Press, 1989.

Bunzl, Matti, *Anti-Semitism and Islamophobia: Hatreds Old and New in Europe*. Chicago: Prickly Paradigm, 2007.

Cahen, Claude. "Dhimma," *Encyclopedia of Islam*. Leiden: Brill, 2012. http://www.pauly online.brill.nl/entries/encyclopaedia-of-islam-2/dhimma-SIM_1823?s.num=3 (accessed December 10, 2012).

CCJR (Council of Centers on Jewish–Christian Relations): http://www.ccjr.us/ (accessed December 10, 2012).

Chouraqui André. *Between East and West: A History of the Jews of North Africa*, trans. Michael Bernet. Philadelphia: JPS, 1968.

CMJE (Center for Muslim–Jewish Engagement (CMJE). http://cmje.org/ (accessed December 10, 2012).

CMJE (Center for Muslim–Jewish Engagement). "Survey Released of Muslim/Jewish Engagement," May 19, 2010. http://www.wnrf. org/cms/muslim_jewish_dialogue.shtml (accessed December 10, 2012).

CMJE (Center for Muslim–Jewish Engagement) *The Field of Muslim–Jewish Engagement*. Los Angeles: CMJE, 2009: http://www.usc.edu/ schools/college/crcc/private/cmje/Final_ Publication.pdf (accessed December 10, 2012).

CMJR (Center for the Study of Muslim–Jewish Relations (CMJR):. http://www.woolfin stitute.cam.ac.uk/cmjr/ (accessed December 10, 2012).

Cohen, Mark. "Islam and the Jews: Myth, Counter-Myth, History." *Jerusalem Quarterly* 38 (1986): 125–37.

Cohen, Mark. *Under Crescent and Cross: The Jews in the Middle Ages*. Princeton, NJ: Princeton University Press, 1994.

Cohen, Mark. "The 'Convivencia' of Jews and Muslims in the High Middle Ages," *The Meeting of Civilizations: Muslim, Christian,* and Jewish, ed. Moshe Ma'oz. Brighton: Sussex Academic Press, 2009, 54–65.

Cohen, Mark and Sasson Somekh. "In the Court of Ya`qub bin Killis: A Fragment from the Cairo Geniza." *Jewish Quarterly Review* 80 (1990): 283–314.

Cohen, Mark and Sasson Somekh. "Interreligious Majālis in Early Fatimid Egypt," in *The Majlis: Interreligious Encounters in Medieval Islam*, eds. Havah Lazarus-Yafeh et al. Wiesbaden: Harrassowitz, 1999, 128–136.

Croner, Helga. *Stepping Stones to Further Jewish–Christian Relations: An Unabridged Collection of Christian Documents*. London: Stimulus Books, 1977.

Cutler, Allan, and Helen Cutler. *The Jew as Ally of the Muslim*. Notre Dame, IN: University of Notre Dame, 1986.

Dabru Emet: A Jewish Statement on Christians and Christianity. http://www.jnjr.div.ed. ac.uk/Primary%20Sources/contemporary/ holtschneider_dabruemet.html (accessed December 10, 2012).

Daniel, Norman. *Islam and the West: The Making of an Image*. Oxford: One World, 1960.

Denny, Frederick. "The *Umma* in North America: Muslim 'Melting Pot' or Ethnic 'Mosaic'?" in *Christian–Muslim Encounters*, eds. Yvonne Yzbeck Haddad and Wadi Zaidan Haddad. Gainesville: University of Florida Press, 1995, 342–356.

Dolev, David, and Salma Kazmi. "Jewish–Muslim Dialogue in America; Challenges and Opportunities." *Shma: A Journal of Jewish Ideas*, 2005. http://www.shma.com/ 2005/05/jewish-muslim-dialogue-in-amer ica-challenges-and-opportunities/ (accessed December 10, 2012).

Elkin, Larry. *Enduring Witness: The Churches and the Palestinians*. Geneva: World Council of Churches, 1985.

EUMC 1. European Monitoring Centre on Racism and Islamophobia. "Working Definition of Antisemitism." http://fra.europa.eu/ en/publication/2011/working-definition-antisemitism (accessed December 10, 2012).

EUMC 2. European Monitoring Centre on Racism and Islamophobia. "Muslims in the

European Union: Dicrimination and Islamophobia." http://fra.europa.eu/fraWebsite/attachments/EUMC-highlights-EN.pdf (accessed December 10, 2012).

Fenton, John. *Transplanting Traditions: Asian Indians in America*. Westport, CT: Greenwood, 1988.

Firestone, Reuven. "Jewish–Muslim Relations," in *Modern Judaism: An Oxford Guide*, eds. Nicholas de Lange and Miri Freud-Kandel. Oxford: Oxford University Press, 2005.

Firestone, Reuven. "Contextualizing Anti-semitism in Islam: Chosenness, choosing, and the Emergence of New Religion." *International Journal of Applied Psychoanalytic Studies* 4.3 (2007): 235–254.

Firestone, Reuven. "Islamophobia and Antisemitism." *Arches Quarterly* 4: 7 Thematic Issue: "Islamophobia and AntiMuslim Hatred: Causes and Remedies." (Winter, 2010): 4–13.

Firestone, Reuven. "Islamic Clerics: Tradition and Transition," in *Rabbi – Pastor- Priest: Their Roles and Profiles through the Ages*, ed. Walter Homolka and Heinz-Günther Schöttler. Berlin: Walter de Gruyter, 2012, 257–276.

FFEU (Foundation for Ethnic Understanding (FFEU). "Twinning." http://www.ffeu.org/twinning.html (accessed December 10, 2012).

Forward, Martin. *A Short Introduction to Inter-Religious Dialogue*. Oxford: Oneworld, 2001.

Gampel, Benjamin. "Jews, Christians, and Muslims in Medieval Iberia: *Convivencia* through the Eyes of Sephardic Jews," in *Convivencia: Jews, Muslims, and Christians in Medieval Spain*, ed. George Braziller. New York: The Jewish Museum, 1992,11–37.

Gilbert, Arthur. *The Vatican Council and the Jews*. Cleveland: World Publishing Company, 1968.

Glick, Thomas. "Convivencia: An Introductory Note," in *Convivencia: Jews, Muslims, and Christians in Medieval Spain*, ed. George Braziller. New York: The Jewish Museum, 1992, 1–9.

Griffith, Sidney. "The Monk in the Emir's *Majlis*: Reflections on a Popular Genre of Christian Literary Apologetics in Arabic in the Early Abbasid Period," in *The Majlis: Interreligious Encounters in Medieval Islam*, eds. Havah Lazarus-Yafeh et al. Wiesbaden: Harrassowitz, 1999, 13–65.

Hick, John and Edmund Meltzer. *Three Faiths One God: A Jewish, Christian, Muslim Encounter*. Albany: State University of New York, 1989.

Hinze, Bradford and Irfan Omar (eds.). *Heirs of Abraham: The Future of Muslim, Jewish, and Christian Reliations*. Maryknoll, NY: Orbis, 2005.

Islamophobia Today (IT). August 5, 2012. http://www.islamophobiatoday.com/tag/jewish-community/ (accessed December 10, 2012).

Ivri, Noam. "American Muslims: The Community and Their Relations with Jews," Jerusalem Center for Public Affairs electronic publication No. 64. January 18, 2011: http://jcpa.org/article/american-muslims-the-community-and-their-relations-with-jews/ (accessed December 10, 2012).

Kedar, Menjamin. "Multilateral Disputation at the Court of the Grand Qan Möngke, 1254," in *The Majlis: Interreligious Encounters in Medieval Islam*, ed. Havah Lazarus-Yafeh et al. Wiesbaden: Harrassowitz, 1999, 162–183.

Kilpatrick, Hilary, "Representations of Social Intercourse between Muslims and Non-Muslims in Some Medieval *Adab* Works," in *Muslim Perceptions of Other Religions: A Historical Survey*, ed. Jacques Waardenburg. New York: Oxford, 1999, 213–224.

King, C. M. *The Palestinians and the Church, 1: 1948–1956*. Geneva: World Council of Churches, 1981.

Kotek, Joël. *Cartoons and Extremism: Israel and the Jews in Arab and Western Media*. Portland, OR: Vallentine, 2009.

Küntzel, Matthias. *Jihad and Jew-Hatred*. New York: Telos, 2007.

Lapidus, Ira. *A History of Islamic Societies*. Cambridge: Cambridge University Press, 1988.

Lazarus-Yafeh, Yaffah, et al. *The Majlis: Interreligious Encounters in Medieval Islam*. Wiesbaden: Harrassowitz, 1999.

Lee, Martha. *The Nation of Islam: An American Millenarian Movement*. Syracuse, NY: Syracuse University Press, 1996.

Loskota, Brie, and Reuven Firestone. "Challenges in Jewish-Muslim Dialogue: The American Context," in *Muslim–Jewish Dialogue in a 21st-Century World*, ed. Humayun Ansari and David Cesarani. London: Royal Holloway College, 2007, 135–150.

Magonet, Jonathan. *Talking to the Other: Jewish Interfaith Dialogue with Christians and Muslims*. London: I.B. Taurus, 2003.

Manco, Ural. "The Turks in Europe: From a Garbled Image to the Complexity of Migrant Social Reality," Brussels: Centre E'Etudes Sociologiques, 2004: http://www.flw.ugent.be/cie/umanco/umanco5.htm (accessed December 10, 2012).

Mathal/Mashal: a Journal of Islamic and Judaic Multidisciplinary Studies. http://ir.uiowa.edu/mathal/ (accessed December 10, 2012).

Neuwirth, Rebecca. "AJC Global Jewish Advocacy: Seeking to Advance Muslim–Jewish Relations." October 11, 2001. http://www.ajc.org/site/apps/nlnet/content3.aspx?c=ijITI2PHKoG&b=1530705&ct=1083361 (accessed December 10, 2012).

Nielsen, Jorgen. "Muslims in Europe in the Late Twentieth Century," in *Christian–Muslim Encounters*, ed. Yvonne Yzbeck Haddad and Wadi Zaidan Haddad. Gainesville: University of Florida Press, 1995, 314–327.

Peace, Jennifer, Or Rose, Gregory Mobley (eds.). *My Neighbor's Faith*. Maryknoll, NY: Orbis, 2012.

Perelman, Marc. "Top Reform Rabbi Gives Watershed Address to Largest U.S. Muslim Group," *The Jewish Daily Forward*, September 7, 2007. http://forward.com/articles/11554/top-reform-rabbi-gives-watershed-address-to-larges-/ (accessed December 10, 2012).

Perlmann, Moshe. "The Medieval Polemics between Islam and Judaism," in *Religion in a Religious Age*, ed. S. D. Goitein. Cambridge, MA: Association for Jewish Studies, 1974, 103–138.

Pew Forum on Religion and Public Life. "Muslim Americans: Middle Class and Mostly Mainstream," 2007. http://www.pewforum.org/Muslim/Muslim-Americans-Middle-Class-and-Mostly-Mainstream(2).aspx (accessed December 10, 2012).

Reedijk, Rachel. *Roots and Routes: Identity Construction and the Jewish–Christian Muslim Dialogue*. Amsterdam: Rodopi, 2010.

Rizwan, Fatima. "Diversity Group Breaks 'New-Ground' for L.A. Muslims and Jews." USC Annenberg School, University of Southern California. May 6, 2012. http://www.neontommy.com/news/2012/05/newground-jews-and-muslims-los-angele (accessed December 10, 2012).

Roggema, Barbara, Marcel Poorthuis, and Pim Valkenberg (eds.). *The Three Rings: Textual Studies in the Historical Trialogue of Judaism, Christianity and Islam*. Leuven: Peeters, 2005.

Rubin, Uri. *Between Bible and Qur'an: The Children of Israel and the Islamic Self-Image*. Princeton, NJ: Darwin Press, 1999.

Schenker, Hillel and Ziad Abu-Zyyad (eds.). *Islamophobia and Anti-Semitism*. Princeton, NJ: Markus Wiener, 2006.

Schleifer, Yigal. "No Dialogue, Only Mutual Distrust." *The Jerusalem Report* (September 23, 2002): 16–17.

Shafiq, Muhammad and Mohammed Abu-Nimer. *Interfaith Dialogue: A Guide for Muslims*. Herndon, VA: International Institute of Islamic Thought, 2007.

Shamir, Shlomo. "Jews and Muslims Gather Around the World for a 'Weekend of Twinning,'" *Haaretz*, August 7, 2012.

Sharpe, Eric J. *Comparative Religion: A History*. La Salle, IL: Open Court, 1986.

Shryock, Andrew. *Islamophobia/Islamophilia: Beyond the Politics of Enemy and Friend*. Bloomington, IN: Indiana University, 2010.

Simpson William W. and Ruth Weyl. *The International Council of Christians and Jews*. Heppenheim: International Council of Christians and Jews, 1988; and www.iccj.org.

Social Welfare History Archives. University of Minnesota, National Conference of Christians and Jews records, http://special.lib.umn.edu/findaid/xml/sw0092.xml (accessed December 10, 2012).

Southern, R. W. *Western Views of Islam in the Middle Ages*. Cambridge, MA: Harvard University Press, 1962.

Stern, Kenneth. *Antisemitism Today*. New York: American Jewish Committee, 2006.

Stillman, Norman. *The Jews of Arab Lands*. Philadelphia: Jewish Publication Society, 1979.

Stroumsa, Sarah. "Ibn al-Rāwandī's *sū' adab al-mujādala*: the Role of Bad Manners in Medieval Disputations," in *The Majlis: Interreligious Encounters in Medieval Islam*, eds. Havah Lazarus-Yafeh et al. Wiesbaden: Harrassowitz, 1999, 66–83.

Swartz, Merlin. "The Position of Jews in Arab Lands Following the Rise of Islam." *Muslim World* 60 (1970): 6–24.

Tapper, Aaron. "The War of Words: Jews, Muslims, and the Israeli-Palestinian Conflict on American University Campuses," in *Muslims and Jews in America: Commonalities, Contentions, and Complexities*, eds. Reza Aslan and Aaron Tapper. New York: Palgrave Macmillan, 2011, 71–92.

Tolan, John. *Medieval Christian Perceptions of Islam*. New York: Routledge, 1996.

Ukeles, Raquel. *The Evolving Muslim Community in America: The Impact of 9/11*. New York: Mosaica, 2003–4.

USDS. "Report on Global Anti-Semitism." 2005. http://www.state.gov/j/drl/rls/40258.htm (accessed December 10, 2012).

Wildman, Wesley (ed.). *Boston Collaborative Encyclopedia of Western Theology*. Boston. N.D. http://people.bu.edu/wwildman/bce/worldparliamentofreligions1893.htm (accessed December 10, 2012).

CHAPTER 15

Christian–Muslim Dialogue

Daniel Madigan, SJ

Though one would surely want to avoid the exaggerated, albeit often expressed, notion that the greatest problem facing our world is the relationship between Islam and Christianity, there is little doubt that an attitude of constructive dialogue between Muslims and Christians would contribute a great deal to the world, if only because of the sheer numbers or people involved and the resources, both human and natural, at stake. Yet at the same time, for reasons both historical and theological, this is among the most challenging of dialogues.

To the Christian in particular, the Muslim is, to use a term often employed to understand the complexity of Jewish–Christian relations, the "proximate other" – the other who is problematic because too-much-like-us, or perhaps even claiming-to-be-us. The Qur'an does not present the submission (*islām*) it preaches as something new, but rather as the perennial religion taught by all the prophets, both those known to the biblical tradition and those not. In some respects Islam presents the same quandary to the Christian as Christianity does to the Jew: it clearly grows out of the same matrix, and yet it proposes an alternative reading of the same figures and the same history of God's engagement with humanity, a reading it claims is more valid, and definitive. Indeed Islam resembles nothing so much as a reform – God's reform, Muslims might say – of the interconnected Jewish and Christian traditions.

Certainly the Qur'an does not relate to the New Testament the way the New Testament relates to *its* scriptural antecedents; it does not embrace the earlier texts as its own. Yet at the same time it does address its hearers as though they are familiar with the Biblical tradition and what developed from it and around it in the intervening centuries. The Qur'an presents itself not only as confirming that tradition, but also as safeguarding it from the human heedlessness or malice that may have distorted its true meaning. As the New Testament proposes to offer the most insightful reading of the sacred texts of the Jewish tradition – a reading Jews themselves do not recog-

The Wiley Blackwell Companion to Inter-Religious Dialogue, First Edition. Edited by Catherine Cornille.
© 2013 John Wiley & Sons Ltd. Published 2020 by John Wiley & Sons Ltd.

nize – so the Qur'an sees itself as God's definitive word on how to read prophetic history from Adam to Jesus and beyond. This has been called a kind of "divine exegesis" (Bertaina 2011, 45–72). Just as the New Testament claims the inheritance of Abraham on behalf of those who recognize Jesus, so the Qur'an pointedly asks both Christians and Jews why they argue with each other over the Abrahamic heritage, when the patriarch belonged to neither of their religions, but rather was a *ḥanīf* (Q 3:67), a term which seems to mean that he was a faithful monotheist. Those most entitled to claim the heritage are the Prophet and the believers who follow him (Q 2:135; 3:68).

Unlike the New Testament, however, the Qur'an does not see itself as the *fulfillment* of the earlier scriptural tradition within which and to which it speaks. If it sees itself as the end of the story, then it is so only in the sense that it is a return to the purity of the original and perennial message, rather than the culmination of a process that had been leading up to this revelation. Still, as Christians for so long held Jews culpable for their failure to recognize God's revelation in Christ, so much of the Islamic tradition has taken it for granted that any Christian refusal to acknowledge the Qur'an and its prophet can be explained only by hardness of heart; after all, the Qur'an itself testifies that, when they hear the recitations, one sees Christians' eyes fill with tears because, being already schooled in divine revelation, they recognize it anew in what this prophet brings (Q 5:83).

Thus, Islam is born and develops, it could be said, in dialogue with Christianity; and that has always made the engagement of Muslims and Christians a most particular dialogue. It has certainly been a more robust dialogue than the kind of irenic exchange which is often sought under that title today. Even when political realities have dictated a certain circumspection and a careful choice of words, the participants have rarely been slow to challenge one another's theological commitments, as well as ethical practice and norms.

Mixed Messages

The authoritative sources of neither tradition really offer believers univocal advice about dealing with this particular other. For obvious chronological reasons, there is no comparison between what the Qur'an knows of Christians and what the New Testament could furnish by way of guidance for understanding Muslims and their faith. Though many Muslims have seen in the promised Paraclete of John 14: 16 a reference to Muhammad, a Christian reading of the New Testament knows nothing of Muhammad or Islam – or at least nothing positive. Many Christian interpreters continue to read the New Testament's warnings against "false prophets" (e.g., Matthew 7: 15; 24: 11, 24 and parallels; also 2 Peter 2: 1 and 1 John 4: 1) and those who "preach a different gospel" (2 Corinthians 11: 4) as referring to the Prophet of Islam, and some have seen in him the "Antichrist" spoken of in the letters of John (1 John 2: 18, 22; 4: 3; 2 John 1: 7).

The Qur'an's attitude towards Christians is at best ambiguous, offering both to those in favor of dialogue and to those against it ample scriptural support. In the midst of what is otherwise a rather strong critique of Christians and Jews, we find the assurance that "those who believe, and those who are Jews, and Sabaeans, and Christians – whoever believes in God and the Last Day and does good – there is no fear for them, nor shall they grieve" (Q 5:69). Muslims are told they will find Christians "nearest in affection" to them, not least because among them are priests and monks who are not arrogant (Q 5:82). Yet in other places the role of the monk is much more controversial: monasticism (so characteristic of Near Eastern Christianity at the time) was an innovation, a self-imposed ideal that, even so, was not lived up to (Q 57:27); monks are rapacious and send people astray (Q 9:34). Most damning of all is the fact that, like Jesus and Mary, they are "taken as lords apart from God" (Q 9:31) – leading people into the fundamental sin of *shirk*, associating others with the One God, just as earlier generations of pagan polytheists had done (Q 5:77). The Qur'an has little doubt that the claims made for Jesus and his mother are exaggerated, and find no foundation in his teaching (Q 5:116–7). It is also adamant that any use of "three" with regard to God is unbelief, because that too constitutes *shirk* (Q 4:171; 5:73). No less insistent is the rejection of any notion of God's having a son (e.g., Q 2:116; 6:101; 10:68). It may be that the Qur'an's repeated preference (23 times) for calling Jesus "Son of Mary" is a pointed denial of the Christian affirmation of him as "Son of God."

Though Christian commentators have often enough claimed that the Qur'an does not condemn actual Christian faith but only some misunderstood or heretical versions of it, that is a difficult argument to sustain. It seems quite likely that the Qur'an knows well enough what it is condemning with regard to the Trinity and the Incarnation (Q 4:171; 5:17, 72–73, 116–117), and it is certainly the case that many of the Muslim thinkers who further developed the Qur'an's critique in the ensuing centuries had a not unsophisticated knowledge of the range of Christian doctrinal positions on these issues.

One sees already in the Qur'an (Q 9:29) the political institutionalization of Christians' inferior position within the burgeoning Muslim polity by means of a tax (the *jizya*), to say nothing of the command to fight those who do not believe or who do not subscribe to the commands and prohibitions of the new religion.

At the same time, the Qur'an is often interpreted as treating the varieties of belief and belonging as a divinely willed pluralism which should give rise not to conflict but to trying to outdo one another in good works: ". . . To each among you, We have prescribed a law and a clear way. If God had so willed, He would have made you one nation, but you are to be tested in what He has given you; so seek to outdo one another in good deeds. You are all destined to return to God; then He will inform you about the things over which you used to differ" (Q 5:48; see also Q 10:99). In this context, the Prophet is urged to argue with the People of the Scripture only in "the best of ways;" he is told to say to Jews and Christians, "We believe in what has been revealed to us and revealed to you, and our God and your God is One, and to Him do we submit" (Q 29:46; see also Q 16:125).

Given these observations about the scriptural bases for understanding the Muslim–Christian relationship, it should perhaps be more surprising that there has been any dialogue at all rather than that it has not always been easy.

Perennial Issues

Although the issues raised by the Qur'an are primarily theological – Christians' belief in God as Trinity, in the divinity of Christ, in the significance (and even the historical reality) of his crucifixion, and their refusal to accept the mission of Muhammad as God's prophet – there has probably never been a time when the engagement of Muslims and Christians did not also involve elements of politics and culture. Indeed, the context of the first Christian writings about Islam was the Arab conquests of the seventh century, which were initially interpreted in apocalyptic terms (Hoyland 1997: 257–335; Thomas et al. 2009).

One of the earliest sustained Christian engagements with Islamic thought comes from the pen of a man who, like his father before him, held high office at the court of the Umayyad Caliphs. John of Damascus' (ca. 655–750) treatise *De Haeresibus* includes a final chapter on "The Heresy of the Ishmaelites," which shows evidence of direct engagement with the Qur'an, with Muslims and their beliefs. Although much of John's take on Islam is quite polemical, it is also clear that he pays close attention to it. His ability and willingness to distinguish those aspects of Islam with which he is in agreement from what is clearly unacceptable to him makes him "one of the most serious originators of the Muslim–Christian dialogue" (Sahas 1972: xiii). The Iconoclast controversy that raged around John in the first half of the eighth century CE dramatically demonstrates how Islam and Christianity are acting upon each other in the early centuries of their co-existence in the broader Middle East even as they do within the pages of the Qur'an. John lists Islam among the heresies that have affected Christianity, and one way of reading the Qur'anic approach to Christian faith is that it sees Christianity as a heresy. In the Qur'an's understanding, after all, there is only one religion, submission, preached from the beginning by all the prophets. Like most heresies, the claims of Christian faith are "exaggerations" (see Q 4:171; 5:77) of certain elements of true faith. Although involving a clearly negative judgment, the identification of something as a heresy has its positive aspect: the recognition of a common religious matrix. From the beginning it is not at all clear the extent to which Christians or Muslims perceived the other's faith as what we might nowadays call a separate religion. Rather, the perennial issues of Muslim–Christian engagement, whether discussed irenically or tipping over into polemic, should probably be seen as the outworking of this mutual definition as heresy.

In the decades and centuries after John of Damascus' first serious venture into the field, both Christians and Muslims developed several genres of theological work in this vein, many of them in the form of dialogues, question-and-answer manuals, or epistolary exchanges (Griffith 2008, 75–105; Bertaina, 2011). These literary products no doubt reflect to some extent actual encounters, though one has to remember that the final author always has control, and therefore the better, of the argument. These works served both communities in their formation of an identity-in-relation-with-the-other, and for an education in apologetics. Particularly for the Christians, they also served to elaborate the image of a new kind of religious hero (Bertaina 2010, 167–191), whose prowess had less to do with the spectacular penances of the monastic tradition than with the calm ability to defend the faith through appeal both to revelation and to reason – an ability, however, that could still be vindicated by the miraculous if necessary.

It is important to note the difference between the approaches evident in, on the one hand, the Syriac and Arabic texts produced by Christians under Islamic rule, who are engaged in a genuine attempt to express and defend their faith within a new linguistic and religious milieu, and, on the other hand, the much more polemical and vituperative material from Latin- and Greek-speaking writers (Griffith 2008, 105). For them these apologetic and polemic exercises, while no doubt made more acerbic by political conflict, were less personally engaging than for the Church which lived (to use Sidney Griffith's evocative phrase) "in the shadow of the mosque."

One is struck, reading the medieval dialogues and debates, by how little progress seems to have been made in the centuries since. Even today the dialogues no less than the polemics follow the same well-worn paths that we find broached in the Apology of the Christian al-Kindi, written probably early in the ninth century (Newman 1993). Many contemporary Christian responses to Muhammad do not even succeed in going as far in their estimation of the prophet as did the East Syriac Patriarch Timothy I (d. 823) in his celebrated dialogue with the 'Abbāsid Caliph al-Mahdi in the late eighth century (Mingana 1928). Timothy is prepared to say that Muhammad "walked in the way of the prophets," and he seems to have much less difficulty than Christians do nowadays with the Prophet of Islam's military campaigns; after all, he observes, this is one of the roles of the genuine prophet – to wield the sword, as Moses did, in defense and propagation of the truth (Mingana 1928: 59–60).

After the period of the Crusades, there seems to have been relatively little development of this dialogical form, though texts recounting the more famous dialogues, such as Timothy's, continued to be elaborated and copied. This reflects two developments: first, the changing demographics of the Islamic empire, where Christians were now much less numerous and influential (Bertaina 2010, 247); and second, the maturation within Islamic theology. Though some would see a failure by Christian thinkers to compete successfully within that highly developed system (Thomas 2008, 1–18), others would credit their achievement in developing an internally coherent theological synthesis in a new language and conceptual system largely shaped by Islam. Whereas in the ninth century Muslim writers seem to have engaged with Christian positions as a serious challenge, by the following century such engagement seems more pro forma.

Renewed Christian attempts in the fourteenth century to express and defend their faith in an Islamic style and context, and at a time of weakness for the Islamic empire because of the Mongol invasions, elicited one of the more famous responses of the genre, Ibn Taymiyya's (d. 1328) *al-Jawāb al-ṣaḥīḥ li man baddala dīn al-Masīḥ* ("The correct response to those who have altered the religion of Christ") (Ibn Taymiyya 1984). It is clear that Ibn Taymiyya and his contemporary Ibn Abī Ṭālib al-Dimashqī (d. 1327), who also reacted strongly and at great length to the provocations of Paul of Antioch (fl. ca. 1200) and the Cypriot editor who revised and expanded Paul's work a century later (Ebied 2005), saw Christian ideas as just examples of the kind of errors into which Muslims, particularly Shi'ites and Sufis, were also falling. Indeed, for Ibn Taymiyya, Sufis who push to extremes the notion of God's union with and indwelling of all reality are in fact worse than the Christians; at least the Christians only believe God is united with Christ, who is a human being higher in rank even than the majority of other prophets and messengers – though for this they are still considered unbelievers. How much more blameworthy, then, are the Sufis who maintain that God indwells persons much inferior to Christ (Ibn Taymiyya 1984: 344–5).

If in these theological engagements we see clearly the interconnectedness of the two traditions as they gradually refine their distinct positions, it is in philosophical discourse that the mutuality of these two communities of faith is even more evident. Perhaps the greatest Christian philosopher (though he was also a theologian) writing in Arabic was Yaḥyà ibn 'Adī (d. 974) – known as al-Manṭiqī, the Logician. He had both Muslim as well as Christian students who went on to be eminent scholars, and he was himself the student of the renowned Muslim philosopher al-Farābī (Yaḥyà ibn 'Adī 2002, xiii–xxv). The Greco-Arabic translation movement in ninth and tenth century Baghdad, in which ibn 'Adī was an active participant, brought about a renaissance in which Greek thought came to be woven into the fabric of Islamic intellectual life. The logic of the Aristotelians did not sit easily with the methods that had been developed by the speculative theologians (mutakallimūn), which were based primarily on the rules of grammar, and which took as their starting point the revealed texts rather than philosophical first principles. Nor did Baghdad's custom of inter-religious debate appealing only to reason rather than to scriptures sit well with more traditionalist mindsets from other parts of the Islamic world (Griffith 2008: 64). However, even in this period when Islam was gradually achieving demographic dominance in addition to its political hegemony, Christian and Muslim thinkers were engaged together in the new philosophical developments.

This Baghdad renaissance had profound results, as we know, for theological development in Western Christianity: the recovery of Aristotelian thought as developed by the Arab thinkers gave rise to a new theological synthesis developed by Thomas Aquinas, one that holds a distinctive position in Christian theology even today. Negative aspects of Muslim–Christian relations also had their positive effects in the West: some developments in the theology of religions were provoked by the experience of conflict between Muslims and Christians. Nicholas of Cusa's search in his De Pace Fidei (1453–4) for a theological settlement based on the notion of a single religion in various rites still attracts attention from those concerned to account for and manage religious pluralism.

This is not the place for a full treatment of the history of Muslim–Christian relations over the centuries. The early centuries have been dealt with in some detail in order to demonstrate that from the time of its emergence Islam was in close dialogue particularly with Christianity, and that they continued to engage one another as each developed. The history of our relations is replete not only with thinkers and leaders in both traditions who saw only a threat that would have to be dealt with militarily, but also with others who emphasized what was common and who hoped to find, if not resolution, then at least accommodation of differences.

The Twentieth Century

It is in the twentieth century that profound changes begin to take place in the dialogical relationship between Islam and Christianity, changes that may herald further development in our own time, but which have not always repaid the optimism of those responsible for them. While certain innovative thinkers and bold initiatives have emerged in the last century, other factors have rendered the whole relationship much more problematic. The most obvious is the Israeli-Palestinian issue, which is constantly in the background in inter-religious relations and renders them difficult, at times impossible.

It is perhaps worth beginning with *Nostra Aetate*, the 1965 Vatican Council Declaration on the relationship of the Catholic Church to non-Christian religions. Although the Council avoided any mention of Muhammad or the Qur'an, it affirmed the faith and piety of Muslims, and encouraged Christians and Muslims to overcome the conflicts of the centuries and work together for human flourishing. In an epochal shift, the Council affirmed, in words that are still being carefully parsed and disputed nearly half a century later, that Muslims "professing to hold the faith of Abraham, along with us adore the one, merciful God, mankind's judge on the last day" (*Lumen Gentium* 16). This change towards a positive affirmation of Muslim faith, even to the point of hesitantly asserting a commonality with Christian faith and worship, was long in preparation among some fascinating figures of French colonial experience, most particularly the scholar of Islamic mysticism, Louis Massignon (1883–1962) and his spiritual mentor Charles de Foucauld (1858–1916). Indeed, even today there is in evidence in many places a very characteristic strand of French religiosity committed to being present to Muslims. One thinks of the Little Brothers and Little Sisters of Jesus, of the Trappist communities in Algeria and Morocco, and of many others. Massignon had returned to the practice of his native Catholic faith after a dramatic experience of moral and religious conversion while working in Iraq in 1908, and in his 40s and 50s he sought to develop a positive Christian theology of Islam. This was focused ultimately on the figure of Abraham (Griffith 1997), and Massignon affirmed, against the consensus of historians, that Muhammad was indeed a descendent of Abraham through Ishmael. Though Muhammad's religion may have grown in inauthentic ways after his death, it was the mystics of the Islamic tradition, Massignon believed, who with their Abrahamic spirituality could rescue it from error and bring it to the profession of the full truth.

Other Christian figures too in the last century were sharpening their appreciation of the spiritual richness of Muslim life and moving away from the polemics and public disputations that characterized many nineteenth-century colonial situations: Anglican missionaries W. H. T. Gairdner and Constance Padwick, then later the hugely prolific Bishop Kenneth Cragg, whose sympathy for Muslims and insight into Islam, coupled with a keen theological mind have nourished generations of Christian readers. The major shift in attitude expressed by *Nostra Aetate* certainly had its effect among Christians beyond the Roman Catholic Church, and the structures set up by the churches singly and together – for example the World Council of Churches' Programme on Inter-religious Dialogue and Cooperation – have elicited responses and commitment from individual Muslims and Muslim organizations (Pratt 2010). Centers originally equipped for the training of missionaries to the Muslims – such as the D. B. MacDonald Center in Hartford, the Selly Oak Colleges in Birmingham, the Henry Martyn Institute in Hyderabad, Deccan – recalibrated their approaches to promote dialogue rather than proselytism.

Among Arab Christians one of the main figures in both the preparation and carrying forward of the new approach to engagement with Muslims was the Dominican friar George Anawati (1905–1994). A renowned scholar of Islamic philosophy and theology, Anawati dedicated his life to building bridges with Muslims through culture. As early as 1944 the Vatican had asked the Dominicans to create a center in Cairo for the serious study of Islam, without any intention of proselytism: L'Institut Dominicain d'Études Orientales (IDEO). Anawati was the first member appointed to its team of scholars. Another significant aspect of this renewal of relations between Muslims and Christians was the recovery and making available of the Arab Christian literary and theological patrimony, some of which we have already sketched. A major figure in this effort has been the Egyptian Jesuit Samir Khalil Samir at the Université Saint-Joseph, Beirut.

Muslim scholars, too, have been active in the renewed dialogue. Among the more senior figures have been Seyyed Hossein Nasr, Mahmoud Ayoub and Ismail Raji al-Faruqi (d. 1986) in the US, Ataullah Siddiqui and Zaki Badawi (d. 2006) in the UK, Prince Hassan bin Talāl of Jordan, and Mustafa Ceric in Bosnia. A more recent important force in this area is the very broadly dispersed movement that takes its inspiration from the Turkish reformer Bediuzzaman Said Nursi (1878–1960), in particular the branch of that movement that looks to the leadership of Fethullah Gülen. This latter group, known often as the Hizmet (Service) Movement is very active in multi-faith education, with hundreds of schools and colleges throughout the world, as well as very active institutes for inter-religious dialogue in many cities.

Following this change of tack with regard to other religions at the Second Vatican Council, the Vatican set up a department to develop policy, to encourage local churches to take dialogue seriously, and to handle formal international dialogues, such as those with Al-Azhar University, the Muslim World League and the World Islamic Call Society. Although it has a broad brief covering all religions except Judaism, the Pontifical Council for Interreligious Dialogue (PCID) has understandably devoted much of its energy since its founding (as the Secretariat for Non-Christians) in 1964 to relations with Muslims. It has numbered among its leadership, staff and consultants some of the most important Catholic figures in the field, among them Michael Fitzgerald M. Afr., and Thomas Michel SJ. The Missionaries of Africa (known also as the Pères Blancs) have been central figures in the dialogue with Muslims and are responsible for the Pontifical Institute for the Study of Arabic and Islamics (PISAI) in Rome, and the Institut des Belles Lettres Arabes (IBLA) in Tunis.

Under the long pontificate of John Paul II (1978–2005) Muslim–Christian dialogue thrived, in part because the pope had an ability to use gestures and personal contact to cement relationships without getting into discussions of doctrine. Since the election of Benedict XVI, there have been a few missteps that have soured relations, and there seems to have been less energy in the Vatican and, perhaps in the Roman Catholic Church generally, for dialogue with Muslims. The political situation of the last decade has also no doubt contributed to a loss of enthusiasm. Even so, it is important to acknowledge the efforts made by a group of scholars animated by Prince Ghazi bin Muhammad of Jordan. This is the group behind the initiative that produced the open letter to Christian leaders entitled "A Common Word," referring to a Qur'anic invitation to the People of the Scripture to come to a common statement of faith with Muslims (Q 3:64). This group has brought a focused energy to interfaith relations in spite of their disappointments with Pope Benedict's statements. It is new and slightly discomfiting for the PCID to recognize that its Muslim partners are now taking some control of the dialogical process.

If the events of the last decade have made dialogue more difficult, they also seem to have strengthened people's resolve to engage in it. A fine example of a sustained scholarly dialogue, which has cultivated growing networks of respect and affection, is the series of "Building Bridges" Seminars convened annually by the Archbishop of Canterbury beginning in 2002 (http: //berkleycenter.georgetown.edu/resources/networks/building_bridges).

However, it is neither these scholarly dialogues, nor the formal institutional dialogues, that have been most significant in the development of strong relations between Christians and Muslims in recent decades. It is the more local, less ceremonious encounters of smaller groups in many countries that create the kind of friendships that can sustain relationships when at the official religious or political level relations are in crisis.

Theological Dialogue

When it comes to the question of theological dialogue between Muslims and Christians, the sheer length of time that has been spent in rehashing the same questions without success might be enough to make one abandon hope of making any progress in this area. It is not uncommon to hear a Christian ask how one can possibly engage in dialogue with a person who believes the Qur'an is God's Word. A Muslim might very well respond by asking whether it is any more possible to engage seriously with some who believes that Jesus Christ is God's Word. The very commitments that are at the heart of our faith are considered obstacles to dialogue. To each of us, our confession of the Word seems more or less self-evident, while the other's confession seems preposterous.

However, what we fail to realize is that neither confession is self-evident. We both, of course, believe that God addresses us in history. Christians are claiming that the place where that word is most eloquently and definitively spoken is in Jesus. The one who, to many people, even most of those who knew him, might just seem like a first-century Jewish carpenter-turned-rabbi, is to others God's eternal Word expressed in the flesh. Muslims on the other hand believe God's Word to have been expressed definitively and most eloquently in the Qur'an. Though to many, even those that originally heard it, it is simply a seventh-century Arabic text with strong biblical echoes, to others it is God's very Word expressed in Arabic. It is only when we take full account of how extraordinary is the claim we ourselves are making that we are in a position to listen to someone else with an analogous claim.

Christians have often allowed the terms of theological engagement to be dictated by the Qur'anic categories of 'prophet' and 'scripture,' yet this structure leads to category mistakes that leave each side at best puzzled, at worst scandalized by the theology of the other. Christians think Muslims have too high an estimation of the Qur'anic scripture as God's actual word, whereas Muslims believe Christians have exaggerated the importance of Jesus in raising him from the level of prophet to that of divine Word or Son. There is no satisfactory way out of such mutual miscomprehensions, and it is essential to recognize that they result from using the same terms in very different ways. We have each been trying to convince the other of the truth of our position, but the language we are using almost guarantees we will never do so. We might have to be satisfied in the first place with making clear the structural parallels of our respective faith positions, even if we do not at the same time make them entirely convincing.

The fundamental point we have in common is that we both believe the divine Word to have been addressed to us in the concreteness of our history. The Word, which both of us claim is an eternal attribute of God, is the common term which can ground our mutual theological understanding, even if it cannot guarantee our agreement. We both experience the Word as being given "from above" and yet at the same time as having a resonance with what has already been expressed by God in creation and in the divine activity in history. Neither Christians nor Muslims believe that what we are doing in our profession of faith is elevating without any justification a merely human Word to a divine status it has no right to occupy. Rather we both perceive that Word as having been sent down to us (as witness the many Qur'anic uses of the verb *nazzala* "send down," and in John's Gospel the uses of *pempo* "send" and *katabaino* "come down").

Whether for a Muslim or a Christian, the only appropriate response to what is perceived as a divine Word is obedience and a readiness to follow – for a Muslim this would be called *islam*, for a Christian, perhaps, discipleship. The Word addressed to us clearly has human aspects – in the case of the Qur'an the fact that it is in Arabic and is clearly rooted in the historical circumstances of the prophet who is its primary addressee; in the case of Jesus, his bodily human nature, having been born, having lived and having died in a particular historical situation. If the divine Word did not have these human aspects, how could it be comprehensible to its human hearers? Still, neither community believes that this undoubted humanity compromises the divine nature of the Word.

The Islamic tradition no less than the Christian has grappled with the questions posed to divine unity by the affirmation of a divine word. Many of the Christological issues disputed during the patristic era were, *mutatis mutandis*, discussed by Muslim theologians in their attempts to understand the nature of the Qur'an and its relation to God's eternal speech. Experience suggests that there may be new possibilities available now for mutual understanding of our respective theological positions as long as we find the appropriate structure within which to conceive our commonalities.

Abrahamic Dialogue

Dialogue among Jews, Muslims and Christians now appeals increasingly to Abraham in the hope that this figure of faith, who holds an important place in each of our traditions, will provide us with a way forward in mutual understanding and honest dialogue with one another. Abraham is made the cornerstone of a strategy for leaving behind past polemics and moving ahead in mutual respect. We like to say that he is the father of all those who believe in the one God.

The difficulty with this is that what we might call the "Abraham Strategy" has most often been a strategy of polemic; this patriarch has been used repeatedly in our traditions to dispossess, as it were, the previous claimants to his inheritance. Over the centuries in claiming Abraham as our father, we have tried to take him away from his other children, only to find that another group comes along later and claim to be the *real* children of Abraham. Recovering Abraham as an asset to dialogue in our own day would require first acknowledging the negative and polemical elements within our prior presentations of him. Only then can this figure be re-appropriated in a more positive way.

In the New Testament, the appeal to the figure of Abraham by Paul in Romans and Galatians, and by John in his gospel (John 8: 31–59), seems to necessarily involve the dispossession of the Jewish people. Although there is no reason why the Abraham of Romans (4: 16) could not equally remain the father of the Jews as well as of those not under the Law, in Galatians Paul makes quite explicit the disinheritance of the Jews. In an extraordinary image he turns his attention to the mothers of Abraham's two sons. He refers to the Jews as the children of Hagar the slave woman, because he interprets them as being still enslaved to the Law. His own community, on the other hand, he considers to be the children of Sarah the free woman. Scripture tells us, Paul says, "Get rid of the slave woman and her son, for the slave woman's son will never share in the inheritance with the free woman's son" (Galatians 4: 30 citing Genesis 21: 10).

In the Qur'an too, a similar strategy is used, invoking Abraham to establish a connection with the original covenant of God without having to accept either Torah or Gospel – or membership in Judaism or Christianity: "O People of the Scripture! Why do you argue about Abraham, when the Torah and the Gospel were not revealed till after him? Have you no sense?" (Q 3:65) As we have seen in the earlier examples with Christians, there is an implicit claim to be the "true heirs" of Abraham: "Lo! those people who are most worthy of Abraham are those who followed him, and this prophet and those who believe; and God is the guardian of the believers" (Q 3:68). We *can* read this text in an inclusive way, understanding it to mean all believers. However, Muslim tradition has usually preferred to interpret it exclusively, that is to say as implying that it is only the followers of the *sunna* of Muḥammad, those who perform the Ka'aba rituals that go back to Abraham, who are his true heirs.

If we add to these two observations about the New Testament and the Qur'an how in the Torah God's promise of the Land then belonging to other peoples is projected back to Abraham, we see how the patriarch is pressed into service across all three traditions that take their name from him. The claim to the land and the justification for the dispossession of its various tribes is seen to originate with the divine promise to Abraham in Genesis 12, and this is geographically further specified at the time of the enactment of the covenant in Genesis 15: 18–21. This is a justification appealed to by both Christians and Jews in our own day.

Once the negative use of Abraham has been acknowledged, there are elements of the patriarch's story which make him an ideal model. It is Abraham the *pilgrim* who offers us a way forward together – not Abraham the father, whom we may try to claim as our own and nobody else's, but rather the one who is called "God's friend" (Isaiah 41: 8; James 2: 23; Q 4:125). The life of Abraham, as we know it from our scriptures and traditions holds some particular lessons for all of us on the way of the pilgrim. To be a pilgrim is to allow God to show you his world. It means learning from God to see the world and its people with the same loving and compassionate regard that God has for them. In one sense this means leaving the world we ordinarily inhabit – a world divided into family and outsiders, friends and enemies, compatriots and foreigners, black and white, male and female, believer and unbeliever. It means allowing God to show us God's world with new eyes. God promises to show us a new land – but it is not necessarily a land we have not seen before. It may be the same land with the same people, but we have never seen them with God's eyes before. This is a lifetime's journey. It is a particular way of being in the world. It is the way of the pilgrim, the person God takes by the hand day by day.

Once God had called him to go on this pilgrimage in which he would be shown the world as God sees it, Abraham never really had a home, even in death. He was constantly on the move and finally had to purchase a plot of ground and a cave in someone else's territory to bury his wife, and in that plot in Hebron he would eventually be buried himself. Nevertheless Abraham was able to be hospitable. He did not *own* the land where he lived, but was able still to welcome people into it. Though we differ among our traditions in how we understand Abraham and Sarah's three guests (Genesis 18: 1–15; Q 11:69–73; 15:51–60), we all recognize that this act of willing hospitality was somehow an encounter with the divine.

Abraham said to the people where he was living when Sarah died, "I am a stranger and sojourner among you." In Hebrew, *ger wa-toshav*. This is the model for those who claim to be followers of Abraham's tradition; a model for our being in the world. We are always tempted to mark out our territory and either exclude the other, or at least welcome the other on our own terms.

Detachment from anything less than God is an essential aspect of monotheism. Abraham was more attached to God's self than to what he took to be the embodiment of God's promise. He had thought that his son (whether it was Isaac or Ishmael is immaterial here) was to be the fulfillment of God's promise. But when God asked for the sacrifice of that son, Abraham was still willing to believe in God's promise and to sacrifice the security he thought he had. We all have things that we take to be the embodiments of God's promise, blessings we think of as God-given, and indeed sometimes they are: our land, our law, our cultures, our doctrines and rituals; all good things. However, we have always to be attentive that these things do not become, in effect, idols that separate us from God. God, as the acclamation *Allahu akbar* reminds us, is always greater – greater than our images of God, greater than our religious systems, just 'greater'. We can settle for nothing less.

For all traditions, Abraham is not identified with a scriptural tradition, with only one particular set of laws and customs, or with only one particular manifestation of the divine will. He is not given a book of instructions, but rather he is led towards the truth and must constantly be attentive to God's will drawing him in unexpected directions. Abraham's relationship with God indicates to us the real meaning of scripture for us. The Word of God constitutes us in a constantly growing, ever-changing relationship of guidance, a relationship in which God gradually reveals to us his knowledge and will.

Yet there is also something very intriguing about how that relationship played itself out. Abraham learned from others and he challenged God. Twice, Genesis tells us, Abraham hid the fact that Sarah was his wife, and he let the ambiguity of their relationship work to his temporal advantage. In Genesis 12 he traps Pharaoh, and in Genesis 20 he traps Abimelech the same way. Each of them explains to him that what he did was wrong, though of course he should have known it himself.

What is perhaps more intriguing is his negotiating with God over the fate of Sodom and Gomorrah. Abraham and Sarah's three visitors went toward Sodom, but Abraham, Genesis tells us, "remained standing before the Lord. Then Abraham approached [God] and said: 'Will you sweep away the righteous with the wicked? What if there are fifty righteous people in the city? Will you really sweep it away and not spare the place for the fifty righteous people in it? Far be it from you to do such a thing – to kill the righteous with the wicked, treating the righteous and the wicked alike. Far be it from you! Will not the Judge of all the earth himself do justice?" We know the rest of the story – Abraham keeps bargaining. Abraham seems to have a sense of justice that does not allow him to simply accept that a decision that claims to come from God must automatically be just. He knows that to do such a thing as to punish the innocent along with the guilty is incompatible with the divine justice. So he takes the risk of speaking up to God. Are not we, like Abraham, obliged to speak up against manifest injustices that claim to be God's will or to be done by God's command?

Dynamics for the Future

Reciprocity?

Much has been made in recent times of reciprocity as an important principle in Muslim–Christian dialogue. To a Christian engaged in dialogue this seems a very dubious development indeed and one that requires some clarification. There is a world of difference between reciprocity as a *condition* for dialogue, and reciprocity as a hoped-for *outcome* of dialogue. However, that distinction tends to be blurred, even among theologians. Although it seems at first sight self-evidently good and rational, reciprocity cannot be said to be a Christian value. The Gospel teaches not a *quid pro quo* reciprocity but rather an exaggerated generosity that calculates no return, a disarmed forbearance that risks even annihilation, a willingness to lose one's life rather than take another's, a determination to respond to hatred with love and to curses with blessings in the conviction that all this is transformative (Matthew 5: 39–47). It is difficult to see how a dialogue that sets prior conditions can really be considered Christian.

Muslims in dialogue take seriously for themselves the Qur'an's command to the Prophet to dialogue only "in the best of ways" (Q 29:46), yet in the Islamic tradition the kind of humble, turn-the-other-cheek generosity taught by Jesus has long been criticized as being hopelessly idealistic and so no reliable guide to action in the real world. It should, perhaps, be acknowledged that that is how much of Christian history has seen Jesus's teaching too.

Reciprocity in relation to laws, rights, and freedoms is sometimes set as a condition for dialogue, or as an element for the negotiation of the civil rights of minorities. There are many calls in Europe to restrict the rights of Muslim citizens and immigrants until full and equal rights are accorded to Christians in Muslim-majority countries – Saudi Arabia is the case usually cited because it is the most flagrant violator of the rights and freedoms of non-Muslims. Some commentators have wanted to see in the Vatican's references to reciprocity a concern and a demand for reciprocal rights as a condition of further dialogue, or at least an encouragement for using Muslim citizens' rights and freedoms in the West as leverage for promoting reform in Muslim countries.

Such a strategy can be reconciled neither with the gospel, nor with explicit Catholic teaching about the basis of religious freedom in the dignity of each person. That principle, enshrined authoritatively in the Second Vatican Council's declaration on religious freedom, *Dignitatis Humanae* (1965), would require equal rights and freedoms for Muslims in the West, even if such recognition of minority rights is not reciprocated by the governments of Muslim-majority countries. One may not repay one wrong with another. In any case, if the concern for the fate of the oppressed were genuine, then Christian-majority countries might refuse to trade with oppressor countries – refuse, for example, to sell arms to Saudi Arabia or to buy oil from it, until it reforms its laws to recognize the human rights of non-Muslims. However, this would require more sacrifice than most people are prepared to make, and so some propose to force the poor Muslim citizen or immigrant to pay the price. This is tantamount to hostage-taking: we will oppress "theirs" until they stop oppressing "ours."

Only when we examine this discourse carefully do we notice the too-easy slippage between the notions of Muslim–West dialogue and Muslim–Christian dialogue. Of course, the West is not defined any longer by Christianity, even in name, and is not obliged to respect the Gospel injunctions of self-emptying generosity. However, Christians in dialogue cannot allow the power calculus of the post-Christian West, or its enlightened self-interest to substitute for those injunctions.

There is sometimes also an expectation that a reciprocal recognition of the legitimacy of each one's religion is an essential starting point for dialogue. Yet, if such a mutual recognition were ever to come about, it would surely be the result of dialogue, rather than the pre-condition for it. One often hears an expectation or a demand for a Christian recognition of the prophethood of Muhammad as the just reciprocation of Muslim recognition of Jesus. Yet Muslims affirm about Jesus only what the Qur'an maintains about him, not what Christians hold. A Christian might argue that in failing to acknowledge Muhammad she is doing precisely the same thing – she affirms about Muhammad only what the New Testament says about him. Dialogue begins in earnest not from a premature equiparation of one other's beliefs, but from a fundamental rec-ognition of each person's equal dignity.

Asymmetries

The Gospel injunctions that bind the Christian partners – and, if we are honest, shame us – are not the only elements of asymmetry in Muslim–Christian dialogue. Nor are the theological differences already discussed with regard to the nature of scripture, revelation and prophecy.

Many social and political factors also make this dialogue particularly complex, no less today than they did in the early centuries of our history together. Professional religious leaders in the West, some of whom also have training in Islamic studies, very often lament that they have searched in vain for a true counterpart among the minority, often immigrant Muslim population. Christians are sometimes scandalized that local Muslim communities are not always ready for a frank and open dialogue of the kind that is commonplace in Western culture, in which those Muslims do not yet feel them-selves at home. These asymmetries will not be resolved quickly, yet with the passing of time and the further integration of Muslims into what were once largely Christian cultures, the difficulties to which those social asymmetries give rise are gradually lessening.

However, geopolitical asymmetries are becoming, if anything, more pronounced as the Islam–West polarization deepens, and this takes its toll not only on Muslim minori-ties in the West, but also on Christian minorities in predominantly Muslim countries. The minority community in either case is seen as client of or proxy for the perceived enemy, and bears the brunt of the global conflict.

None of these elements is extraneous to dialogue. The adjective "inter-religious" can be misleading in two ways: it can suggest that dialogue takes place between religions rather than among believers; and it can give the impression that what those believers should be dialoguing about is religion. If social and political factors are rendering the encounter of believers difficult or impossible, then it is those factors that need to be the focus of dialogue. This is, perhaps, what is implied in the call for an "inter-cultural" rather than an "inter-religious" dialogue – a dialogue about the concrete political and cultural forms to which each faith gives rise, and the shared cultural and political space within which believers of different traditions function. In most cases, such cultural and political dialogue is more urgent and often more satisfying than theological dialogue. However, it does not in the end substitute for it, since our theologies – our understand-ings of God and of how things are between the world and God – very much affect our politics and the cultures we build.

Repentance

Whereas we saw that the early dialogical encounters between Muslims and Christians were quite robust and forthright examinations of each other's positions, in which the theological terrain no less than the political was contested, our own time privileges the polite inspection of one another's texts, artifacts, customs and beliefs as though they were museum pieces – to be admired but not touched. We demonstrate for each other the beauties of our tradition and the exquisite ideals to which we aspire, and express surprised pleasure at how much we have in common. Yet behind the politeness we remain sceptical that our dialogue partners have any practical commitment to these ideals they are holding up for admiration. At the same time we are hardly aware of how we ourselves have failed to uphold those we claim to espouse. We compare our high ideals with their much less edifying reality, and of course they do the same. The result is profoundly unsatisfying. Sometimes in situations like this there will escape from a participant an exasperated demand to know how all this talk of peace is to be squared with the savagery of terrorism or of military occupation and torture, or what all this talk of love can mean when children are not safe from abuse by the very clergy who preach it. Moments of bitter truth that are all too often seen as the breakdown of dialogue rather than possibilities to break through to a more honest one.

The alternative to this superficial and unsatisfying mutual admiration is much more demanding, yet also more fruitful. It requires a preparedness to acknowledge failures, and not just because we have been caught out or backed into a corner and forced to it. To enter into such honest dialogue requires great humility, and such humility is always risky, because it can easily be misinterpreted as weakness. Yet this is a risk Christians cannot avoid, if they claim to be followers of the Christ who made himself "humbler yet, even to accepting death, death on a cross" (Philippians 2: 8). There is no other choice for Christians in dialogue but to trust that the way of the humble Christ is the way to the truth. Pope Paul VI put this elegantly in his encyclical *Ecclesiam Suam* (1964): "Our dialogue must be accompanied by that meekness which Christ bade us learn from Himself. . . . Our dialogue . . . makes no demands. It is peaceful, has no use for extreme methods, is patient under contradiction and inclines towards generosity."

Bibliography

'Abd al-Jabbār ibn Aḥmad al-Asadābādī. *Critique of Christian Origins: a Parallel English–Arabic Text*. Trans. Gabriel Said Reynolds and Samir Khalil Samir. Provo, UT: Brigham Young University Press, 2010.

Ayoub, Mahmoud, and Irfan A. Omar. *A Muslim View of Christianity: Essays on Dialogue*. Maryknoll, NY: Orbis Books, 2007.

Bertaina, David. *Christian and Muslim Dialogues: The Religious Uses of a Literary Form in the Early Islamic Middle East*. Piscataway, NJ: Gorgias Press, 2011.

Board of Missionary Preparation. *Presentation of Christianity to Muslims: The Report [1917] of a Committee approved by the Board of Missionary Preparation*. Piscataway, NJ: Gorgias Press, 2010.

Ebied, R.Y. and David Thomas. *Muslim–Christian Polemic during the Crusades: The Letter from the People of Cyprus and Ibn Abī Ṭālib al-Dimashqī's response*. Leiden: Brill, 2005.

al-Faruqi, Isma'il R. *Islam and Other Faiths*, ed. Ataullah Siddiqui. Leicester: Islamic Foundation and International Institute for Islamic Thought, 1998.

Gaudeul, Jean-Marie. *Encounters and Clashes: Islam and Christianity in History*. Roma: Pontificio Istituto di Studi Arabi e d'Islamistica, 2000.

Griffith, Sidney Harrison. *The Church in the Shadow of the Mosque: Christians and Muslims in the World of Islam*. Princeton, NJ: Princeton University Press, 2008.

Griffith, Sidney Harrison. "Sharing the faith of Abraham: The 'Credo' of Louis Massignon." *Islam and Christian–Muslim Relations*, 8(2): 193–210.

Goddard, Hugh. *Christians and Muslims: From Double Standards to Mutual Understanding*. Surrey: Curzon Press, 1995.

Haddad, Yvonne Yazbeck and Wadi Zaidan Haddad. *Christian–Muslim Encounters*. Gainesville: University Press of Florida, 1995.

Hoyland, Robert G. *Seeing Islam as Others Saw it: A Survey and Evaluation of Christian, Jewish, and Zoroastrian Writings on Early Islam*. Princeton, NJ: Darwin Press, 1997.

Ibn Taymiyya, Taqī al-Dīn. *Al-Jawāb al-ṣaḥīḥ li-man baddala din al-masīḥ (The Correct Answer to the One Who Changed the Religion of the Messiah)*, trans. T. F. Michel, *A Muslim Theologian's Response to Christianity*. Delmar, NY: Caravan Books, 1984.

Kairanvi, M. Rahmatullah. *Izhar al-Haqq* (4 vols). London, Ta-Ha Publishers, 1989.

Levenson, Jon D. *Inheriting Abraham: The Legacy of the Patriarch in Judaism, Christianity, and Islam*. Princeton, NJ : Princeton University Press, 2012.

Madigan, Daniel A. and Diego Sarrio Cucarella. "Islam and Christianity," in *Oxford Bibliographies Online*. New York: Oxford University Press, 2010.

Michel, Thomas F. and Irfan A. Omar (ed.). *A Christian View of Islam: Essays on Dialogue*. Maryknoll, NY: Orbis Books, 2010.

Mingana, Alphonse. "The Apology of Timothy the Patriarch before the Caliph Mahdī." *Bulletin of the John Rylands Library*, 12 (1928), 137–298; reprinted in *Woodbrooke Studies*, vol. II, Cambridge: W. Heffer, 1928, 1–162.

Newman, N. A. *The Early Christian–Muslim Dialogue: A Collection of Documents from the First Three Islamic Centuries, 632–900 A.D.: Translations with Commentary*. Hatfield, PA: Interdisciplinary Biblical Research Institute, 1993.

Pratt, Douglas. *The Church and other Faiths: The World Council of Churches, the Vatican, and Interreligious Dialogue*. Bern: Peter Lang, 2010.

Renard, John. *Islam and Christianity: Theological Themes in Comparative Perspective*. Berkeley, University of California Press, 2011.

Sahas, Daniel J. *John of Damascus on Islam: The "Heresy of the Ishmaelites."* Leiden: Brill, 1972.

Siddiqui, Ataullah. *Christian–Muslim Dialogue in the Twentieth Century*. New York: St. Martin's Press, 1997.

Smith, Jane I. *Muslims, Christians, and the Challenge of Interfaith Dialogue*. Oxford: Oxford University Press.

Thomas, David. *Christian Doctrines in Islamic Theology*. Leiden: Brill, 2008.

Thomas, David, Barbara Roggema, Juan Pedro Monferrer Sala and Alex Mallett. *Christian Muslim Relations: A Bibliographical History*. Leiden, Boston: Brill, 2009.

al-Warrāq, Muḥammad ibn Hārūn. *Early Muslim Polemic Against Christianity: Abū ʿĪsá al-Warrāq's 'Against the Incarnation'*, trans. David Thomas. Cambridge: Cambridge University Press, 2002.

Volf, Miroslav. *Allah: a Christian Response*. New York, HarperOne, 2011.

Watt, W. Montgomery. *Muslim–Christian Encounters: Perceptions and Misperceptions*. London, Routledge, 1991.

Yaḥyà ibn ʿAdī. *The Reformation of Morals. A Parallel Arabic–English text*. Trans. and Introduced by Sidney H. Griffith. Provo UT: Brigham Young University Press, 2002.

CHAPTER 16
Shinto–Buddhist Dialogue

Aasulv Lande

Shinto–Buddhist dialogue (神道仏教対話 *shintobukkyo taiwa*) is rooted in the history of Japan from its dawn as a state in the sixth century, and Japanese identity has been thoroughly shaped by the encounter between these two traditions. Their relationship thus poses far-reaching questions to contemporary inter-religious dialogue – in Japan and beyond. In exploring dialogue between these two religious traditions, I wish to suggest that a concern with the concept of "harmony" is crucial.

Harmony in Shinto–Buddhist History

Shinto–Buddhist relationship focuses on harmony in tension. In this section, after introducing the concept of "harmony," I look at Shinto–Buddhist history up until the Meiji restoration in 1868, the breakthrough to modernity. The roots of Shinto are conventionally traced back to the rice cultivating Yayoi era, which spanned 600 years from around 300 BCE. During the next period, *kofun* (tumulus, from 300 to 550 CE) Shinto rites became more elaborate. Tutelary deities (氏神 *uji-gami*) played a central role in the life of the different clans. Due to increasing contacts with the Asian continent in the *kofun* period, Buddhism, Taoism, and Confucianism trickled into Japan. According to official sources, Buddhist images, sutras and other cultic items were introduced from Korea in the middle of the sixth century CE. The importation of Buddhist views and practices was met with skepticism and even direct opposition from the Mononobe and Nakatomi clans, who carried indigenous priestly responsibilities and warned of divine punishment and national disasters if traditional Shinto rites were neglected. However, the clan of the ruling house (Soga) supported the new Buddhist cult enthusiastically, and the Shinto opposition shortly gave way to cooperation. By the end of the sixth century, Buddhism dominated the court. Buddhist influence

The Wiley Blackwell Companion to Inter-Religious Dialogue, First Edition. Edited by Catherine Cornille.
© 2013 John Wiley & Sons Ltd. Published 2020 by John Wiley & Sons Ltd.

increased particularly during the reign of Prince Shotoku (574–622). His *Seventeen-article Constitution* of 604, prominently featuring the term harmony (和 *wa*), was instrumental in softening conflicts between Buddhism and indigenous cults. Let me quote two paragraphs from the constitution.

> § 1:Take harmony to be the highest value and take cooperation to be what is most honored. All persons are partisan, and few indeed are sufficiently broadminded. It is for this reason that some offend against lord and father and some transgress wantonly against neighboring villagers. But when those above are harmonious and those below live congenially with one another, and when mutual accord prevails in resolving the affairs of the day, then all matters without exception will be properly and effectively dispatched.
>
> § 2 Revere in earnest the three treasures: the Buddha, the "dharma" and the clergy, for these are the final refuge for all sentient beings and are the most sacred and honored objects in the faith of all nations. What persons in what age would fail to cherish this dharma? There are few persons who are truly wicked. Most can be instructed and brought into the fold. Revere in earnest the three treasures: the Buddha, the "dharma" and the clergy, for these are the final refuge for all sentient beings and are the most sacred and honored objects in the faith of all nations. Without repairing to these three treasures, wherein can the crooked be made straight? (See Heisig et al. 2011: 36–39)

The concept of "harmony" in a context of conflict appears paradigmatic for Shinto–Buddhist relations in Japan. Disharmony arose on occasions in overt or covert forms during the centuries. The two paragraphs above aptly illustrate how "harmony" became a decisive political concern in Japanese inter-religious encounter. I will at certain points below consider whether a politically promoted "inter-religious harmony" has left any lasting legacy in the Japanese religious world.

Shinto–Buddhist Dialogue before Modernization

It is commonly assumed that a Shinto–Buddhist amalgamation (神仏習合 *shinbutsu-shûgô*) occurred during the Nara and Heian periods (710–1185). Zennosuke Tsuji, a Meiji-period scholar (1868–1912), convincingly divides the process of integration into four stages (Zennosuke Tsuji 1955 in Teeuwen and Rambelli 2003: 7–31). The final stage envisaged Buddhist reality emanating into the Shinto world.

Buddha a foreign kami, *552–700*

During the first period of the amalgamation process, significant Buddhas and *kami* (Shinto divinities) stood apart. Buddhas were venerated as foreign kami (*adashikuni no kami*). Although the rituals were different, the character of veneration was similar. The foreign kami caused diseases and calamities when angered, but empowered clans who conducted their cult properly. Amalgamation did not occur at this stage of early coexistence.

Buddha leads kami to enlightenment, 700–900

In this period, a number of shrine temples (*jingûji*) were established. More than twenty shrine temples can be identified by sources, and presumably there were others as well. An illustration of motivations can be found in an oracle from the kami of Tado at Ise: "At this time (763) a certain person was possessed by the kami and said: 'I am the kami of Tado. Because I have committed grave offences over many kalpas, I have received the karmic retribution of being born as a kami (*jindô*). Now I wish to escape from my kami state once and for all, and take refuge in the Three Treasures of Buddhism'" (Teeuwen and Rambelli 2003: 10). A small chapel was erected and dedicated to the great Bodhisattva of Tado. The temple compound grew over the years to a leading temple for regional ascetics. The praxis of erecting shrine temples is seen by some scholars as a feature of Buddhist mission-policy.

Dharma–protecting kami

The Shinto cult of the kami Hachiman(八幡) had an early center at Usa in Buzen region, North-eastern Kyushu, and shows the early Shinto integration of Buddhist veneration practices. The cult of Hachiman was awarded a prominent status when Emperor Shomu started the work on the great Buddha Vairochana in Nara (completed 749). Copper and expertise from Buzen were essential for the completion of the image. During this process, Hachiman presented an oracle to the court promising the safe completion of the project (Grapard 2003: 77–94). Hachiman thus acted as a powerful protector of Buddhist dharma. Tutelary shrines for Hachiman were established at Todaiji (where the large Buddha image was erected) as well as Yakushiji in Nara, Tôji in Kyoto and elsewhere in the eighth and ninth centuries CE. Hachiman was a supreme guardian of the dharma, but other kami as well took on this task. The founder of Japanese Tendai Buddhism, Saichô (767–822), adopted the Hiei Mountain King (originally two in number) as a guardian of the Enryaku Temple at Hiei Mountain.

Kami as emanations of Buddhist entities, 900–1185

A deepened level of Shinto–Buddhist integration followed in the latter part of the Heian period (794–1185). The expression "essence emanation" (本地垂迹 honji suijaku) offered an overarching concept for Shinto–Buddhist relations. Buddhas and bodhisattvas (*honji* = original sources) were not isolated in their realms. Temporarily they could appear as *suijaku* (traces, footprints) in the shape of Shinto gods. Honji suijaku is indeed no particularly Japanese theory, but common to religious thought worldwide, particularly in Hinduism and Buddhism. The Lotus Sutra which is foundational for many schools of Japanese Buddhism, portrays Gautama Siddharta as the "*suijaku*" of the eternal Buddha. This Buddhist understanding was then extended to indigenous faiths, such as Shinto, and the two religions could now be related to each other in a simple and meaningful way.

As early as the ninth century, in a document from Enryakuji, Zennosuke Tsuji identified kami as *suijaku*. (Teeuwen and Rambelli 2003: 16). From the Kamakura period until the Meiji restoration (1868), Shinto–Buddhist relations were stable. *Kenmitsu* Buddhism (a Tendai Shingon superstructure) was the religious apex of a socio-religious structure with political legitimacy.

Honji suijaku: *The Shinto–Buddhist norm, 1185–1867*

In the model of honji suijaku, the original position, essence (本地 *honji*), was mostly given to Buddhism, whereas emanation (垂迹 *suijaku*) was related to Shinto. The honji suijaku model culminated during the Kamakura period (1185–1333), but continued to determine the Japanese religious establishment until 1867. Powerful versions of the model were developed by Shingon and Tendai, the dominant branches of Buddhism from the ninth century. Shingon Buddhism developed Double Shinto (両部神道 *Ryôbu Shinto*) and Tendai fostered Three Kings One Essence Shinto (山王一実神道 *Sannô ichijitsu Shinto*), also called Sannô Shinto (山王神道 *Sannô Shinto*). As the logic of these two Shinto theories are closely related, I will below concentrate on one of them, *Ryôbu Shinto*. (For an introduction to Sannô Shinto, I refer to Breen and Teeuwen 2010: 93, 97; Ito 1998/2003: 88–93; Matsunaga and Matsunaga1974/1976 II: 294–296).

Ryôbu Shinto

According to Shingon, Buddha Mahavairochana, Great Sun Buddha, (大日如来 *Dainichi nyorai*) penetrates all phenomena. *Dainichi* appeared in two aspects: the cosmic Buddha and the Buddha of the physical world. The cosmic Buddha was illustrated by a mandala showing the universal and static "diamond world" (*kongokai* in Japanese, *vajradhatu* in Sanskrit), with the cosmic Buddha sitting in the center of assemblies of Buddhas. The other aspect of Dainichi's appearance is as the Buddha of the physical "womb world" (*taizôkai* in Japanese, *garbhadhatu* in Sanskrit). Here the Buddha sits in the center of the mandala surrounded by his physical manifestations. Versions of the double mandala are found in Shingon temples all over Japan. The double mandala was used to illustrate the work of Buddha for devotional purposes. It was also used to illustrate Shinto–Buddhist relations (Ito 1998/2003: 68).

The mandala was also related to the Shinto sanctuary at Ise, devoted to the Sun goddess, *Amaterasu*. Shingon Buddhists saw the sun as a symbol of Dainichi, so that the Buddhist solar symbol provided a connection to the Sun goddess at Ise. Another Shinto–Buddhist point of contact was the duality of ultimate reality. The Shinto sanctuary in Ise consisted of two shrines, an inner shrine devoted to the Sun goddess Amaterasu and an outer shrine devoted to her mother *Toyouke* (god of food and shelter). A structural parallel to the two-dimensional character of Dainichi thus was visible in the Ise Shinto compound. Like the Great Sun Buddha, Shinto divinity was twofold.

Based on this parallelism, Ryôbu Shinto related Shinto to Buddhism according to the model of honji suijaku. Dainichi was accordingly seen as a honji of Amaterasu. The double character of Buddhist reality furthermore provided a honji for the double char-acter of Ise Shinto, mediated by the double mandala of Dainichi. But the usage of Ryôbu Shinto symbols might at times favor the Shinto position. The mandala-symbolism was for instance used in Shinto thought to illustrate Shinto–Buddhist equality, even framing understandings of Shinto as the dominant or primary faith. Although the concept Ryôbu Shinto originally expressed Buddhist Shinto, it has later been interpreted ambig-uously as "Shinto rites and theories that have strong links with the esoteric Buddhist Shingon School" (Ito 1998/2003: 69). The Buddhist origin of the terminology does not necessarily imply Buddhist preeminence.

Pure Land and Nichiren Buddhism

Tendai and Shingon, jointly called exo-esoteric (kenmitsu) Buddhism, were the domi-nant Buddhist traditions in shaping Shinto–Buddhist relationships for almost one thousand years (800–1800 CE). Pure Land and Nichiren traditions from the Kamakura period (1185–1333) onwards focused on "single praxis," which at first glance appears to differ from Shingon and Tendai praxis. The founder of True Pure Land Buddhism (Jodo Shinshu), Shinran (1173–1262), emphasized the exclusive necessity of trusting in the grace of Amida. He taught the need for refuge in the Three Treasures and warned against belief in devas or gods such as the kami (Matsunaga and Matsunaga 1974/1976: II: 107). A thorough study of True Pure Land scriptures such as Shinran's Kyôgyôshin-shô reveals, however, that Shinran's trust in the grace of Amida might imply an accept-ance of other religious practices. After all, elements of faith in Amida's grace were included in other religious cults (Matsunaga and Matsunaga 1974/1976: II: 111).

The exclusive devotion to the Lotus Sutra by Nichiren (1222–1282) frequently led to harsh verbal attacks on other traditions (Matsunaga and Matsunaga 1974/1976: II, 165–169). Nichiren was sharply critical of competing Buddhist sects. But to native gods (Shinto) he displayed a more tolerant attitude. Applying the Buddhist honji suijaku thinking of his time, he considered Shinto gods, particularly the Sun goddess Amat-erasu, to be suijaku of the eternal Buddha Shakamuni of the Lotus Sutra. Expecting the native gods to support his "true Buddhism," he believed that their absence meant that they had returned to the heavenly abode. When Mongols attacked Japan in 1281, Nichiren held that the kami Hachiman had returned to heaven and had thus failed to revenge his followers.

Shinto Challenges Buddhist Dominance, 1185–1867

Beginning with the Watarai family serving at the outer Ise sanctuary, and with Kyoto priests of the Yoshida family, a new Shinto perspective on Buddhism appeared in the Kamakura period (1185–1333). One may well see this development as a continuation of the initial Shinto opposition to Buddhism from the sixth century CE.

Ise Shinto (Watarai Shinto) used the esoteric dialectic of Ryôbu Shinto to express its essence, particularly in the dynamics and relations between the outer and the inner shrines of Ise. Two prominent figures should be mentioned: the priest of Ise outer shrine, Ieyuki Watarai (1256–1356) and his close ally Chikafusa Kitabatake (1293–1354). By the end of the fourteenth century, associates and priests of the Watarai School had developed a coherent system of Ise Shinto based on texts, later to be termed *Shinto Gobusho* (The Five Books of Shinto, cf. Ito 1998/2003: 84–88 and Teeuwen 1996 and 2000). A change of focus was in the making. Initially, Buddhist enlightenment was retained as the goal of Shinto rites. Different gods of Ise were, however, considered the essential source of individual purification and progress towards enlightenment. Later, Buddhist terminology was marginalized and replaced by Confucian idioms. The Watarai school identified Shinto gods with the Confucian *ri*, 理 the cosmic principle which supports the ordered society (Bocking 1996: 218). Shinto thought thereby stepped further toward independence from Buddhism. Dating back to the tenth century, the purpose of Ise pilgrimages had been to obtain Buddhist enlightenment. The Watarai School reconsidered the purpose of the Ise pilgrimages, and Buddhist "enlightenment" became "obtaining a close union of one's inner nature with *ri*." Although the Buddhist flavor of Shinto continued to weaken, the double mandala remained in Shinto usage. Kanetomo Yoshida (1435–1511), the founder of *Yoshida Shinto* or *Yui-itsu Shinto* (Unique Shinto) (Bocking 1996: 228) used images of the double mandala to distinguish exoteric Shinto of the textbooks *Kojiki* 古事記 and *Nihonshoki* 日本書紀 from esoteric Shinto, transmitted in the Yoshida family.

A further step away from Buddhism came with the neo-Confucian, anti-Buddhist school of *Suiga Shinto* スイカ神道 (Descent of divine blessing Shinto), founded by Anzai Yamazaki (1616–1682), (Bocking 1996: 189). Continuing the Confucian tendency of Watarai Shinto, he promoted a Confucian social order. Traditionally, filial piety had been promoted as the foundational social relationship. In the work of Yamazaki, the ruler–subject relation attained precedence. He identified the ruler as the emperor and regarded Japan as a divine country. He was devoted to worship of kami, particularly the supreme kami for the Imperial lineage, the Sun Goddess, Amaterasu. From Amaterasu flowed all divine blessings (*suiga*). Yamazaki further emphasized the virtue of *tsutsushimi*, humble and honest service to kami and superiors, and questioned contemporary kenmitsu Buddhism. Challenging an interreligious harmony founded on Buddhist terms, Yamazaki pointed to the Imperial system as the proper ground for harmonious relations in the country.

Emerging Shinto Dominance

Watarai-, Yoshida- and Suiga Shinto schools had initiated the development of a self-confident Shinto. None of these schools were, however, "pure" Shinto movements. Watarai Shinto was involved with esoteric Buddhism, and Yoshida had developed an inclusive Shinto in which Buddhas played prominent roles. And although Suiga Shinto was critical of Buddhism, it embraced Confucian principles. A leading scholar in the tradition of "nativism" (*kokugaku*, national learning), Norinaga Motoori (1730–1801), promoted the idea of a pure Shinto. Strongly attracted by Japanese classical literature such as *The Genji Monogatari*, he developed the aesthetic concept *mono no aware*, to describe Japanese intimate and inner awareness. He favored the study of the classical Japanese chronicle *Kojiki*, which had appeared in 712. *Kojikiden*, a treatise on Japanese thought, folklore and culture, became his life's work. Among his disciples, the radical nativist Atsutane Hirata advanced the Motoori legacy in the fields of religion and ethics. I therefore focus on him as a representative of the influential kokugaku, which also is termed Shinto nativism (Endo 2003: 152–156).

Atsutane Hirata (1776–1843)

Following Suiga Shinto, Hirata focused on the Ancient Way of the Emperor (古道大意 *kodôtaii*). He considered this doctrine to be based on the classical Japanese chronicle Kojiki (古事記), favored also by his master Motoori. This original and old Japanese teaching he regarded to be far above the level of Buddhist or Confucian ideas (Hirata 1976: 14f). Denouncing Buddhist-Shinto syncretism, he argued vigorously for a global perspective. In that capacity he wanted to integrate wisdom from various origins, Asian and European, Buddhist and Christian, into a strong Shinto perspective. Classical Japanese literature provided the norm for this Shinto-based cosmology. He preferred Buddhist writings to Confucian works, but none of them matched in his view the rich and profound heritage of classical Japanese literature.

Interestingly, Hirata sought acceptable foreign contributions from any continent within periods parallel to the age of the gods in Japan. In the selection process, there was basically no room for spiritual pluralism: "Good and evil are dimensions of the work of kami." Hirata sought in particular to accommodate Buddhism in his system. Essentially, Buddhism was seen as a branch of the activity of kami, and was understood to function within a Shinto framework (仏教も神道の大きな枠の中で考えられること になる. *Bukkyo mo Shinto no okina waku no naka de kangaerareru koto ni naru*). This inclusivity, however, involved criticism of Buddhist schools, in particular Pure Land Buddhism and Nichiren Buddhism. Hirata found the Buddhist traditions doctrinally poor as he saw in them only four simple teachings: (*tendô*/heaven, *jikoku*/hell, *rinne*/samsara, *jishin*/self control). He also criticized the personality of Gautama Siddhartha (Kishinshinron/ Sueki 1995).

In *The Meaning of Present Shinto* (俗神道大意 *Zokushintôdaii*; Sueki 1995) he differentiates between five types of Shinto: (1) pure Shinto – based on the reverence towards the Sun Goddess; (2) involvement in divine veneration: worship, prayer, purification and devotion to kami; (3) divine guidance; (4) Ryôbu Shinto; and (5) Yuiitsu Shinto (Yoshida Shinto). In light of his reading of Shinto classics, Hirata finds the first three categories acceptable. The two last categories he marks as premature stages. He sees the Buddhist–Shinto amalgamations, "shinbutsu shûgô" and the dynamic of "honji suijaku" in the last two categories and finds them unacceptable. In a sophisticated analysis he explores the Chinese Buddhist background of these two categories and their transmission to Japan, identifying the founder of Shingon, Kukai, as the one who introduced them to Japan. In spite of his high regard for Kukai, Hirata questions the character of Chinese Buddhism. He was convinced that Kukai had committed mistakes and was furthermore misunderstood. Hirata's distrust of the accuracy of the Japanese

Buddhist traditions allowed him to select what he considered more adequate Buddhist insights. In popular tradition, the truth of Kukai's doctrines were confirmed by miraculous events. Doubts about such events helped to authorize Hirata's Buddhist re-interpretations and their integration into his Shinto system (Sueki 1995: 28–39).

In response to the Buddhist-dominated Ryôbu Shinto of Shingon, a new national focus emerged among Shinto intellectual leaders. Any parallel structure between Shinto and Buddhism was of minor interest to nativists like Atsutane Hirata. His new Shinto "theology" of Shinto–Buddhist relationships remained, however, inclusivist. Although particular Buddhist concepts were held up for criticism, "Buddhism" was considered a part of Shinto, included within the Shinto concept of reality. One might term Hirata's Shinto perspective on Buddhism "critical inclusivism."

Shinto–Buddhist Dialogue under State-Shinto

By the Meiji restoration (1868), the kenmitsu Buddhist system was dissolved – and the honji-suijaku theory which constituted its backbone, lost its political significance. Shinto now became institutionally divorced from its longstanding Buddhist partner.

The separation was accompanied by violent actions against Buddhism, the so called *haibutsu kishaku* (destroy Buddhism, subdue Buddha). Temples were set on fire and Buddhist images destroyed. A continued suppression of Buddhism proved untenable, however as it was too strongly rooted in common Japanese spirituality.

But, even within Shinto an internal separation emerged. Around 1877 an awareness of difference between rite and religion appeared in Japanese discourses. In 1882 the awareness matured into an administrative policy. A web of rites and patriotism came to cluster around the emperor, considered religiously neutral and different from religious Shinto. The constitution of 1889 and the Imperial Rescript of Education enforced the differentiation. In 1909, a governmental office for State Shinto was established in the Department of Justice. It encompassed a national network of shrines and contained traditional rites for veneration of the Imperial House. The Department of Education similarly included a governmental office for religious matters. It supervised 13 organizations of "religious Shinto," together with recognized Buddhist and Christian institutions. Within limits prescribed by State Shinto, adherents of any recognized religion were granted freedom of religion. Originally there was no forced veneration at Shinto shrines (Nitta in Breen and Teeuwen 2000: 252–271). The freedom was, however, precarious. During the period of Showa imperialism in the early twentieth century, Buddhists and believers of other faiths were compelled to participate in a number of local and national Shinto rites. Formally separated, Buddhism and Shinto became politically united in an increasing battle for the Imperial-nationalist cause. The Japanese annexation of Taiwan (1895) and subsequent expansion on the Asian Continent climaxed in the Pacific War (1941–1945). Such imperial aggression demanded total support from the Japanese religious world, leading to Shinto Buddhist cooperation, guided by State Shinto.

The differentiation of State Shinto and Religious Shinto, promoted during the aggravating political situation, produced new conditions for Shinto–Buddhist dialogue. Religious harmony of kenmitsu Buddhism ceased to exist in the political realm. Social and inter-religious harmony was, however, transformed and conceived in new terms.

There are reasons to believe that the 700-year-long tradition of "honji suijaku" still remained, promoting "harmony" on local, unofficial levels. On the national political level, however, a new "harmony" took shape. Buddhist communities were expected to support and participate in State Shinto rites, performed in local and national Shinto shrines. This enforced Shinto–Buddhist harmony was basically a union in support of the Japanese Imperial cause. One might even identify a honji suijaku structure in the political world: The emperor-system provided the new "honji." As the emperor-system was accepted and actually included in Japan, traces, "suijaku," of the emperor-system could appear in any Japanese religion. While the Buddhist word "suijaku" was not used, when unreserved service for the emperor during war years was considered in terms of, for example,compassion or even enlightenment, we probably see a trans-formed "suijaku" of the Imperial "honji." This honji suijaku structure reflected the new, political "harmony" between Shinto and Buddhism.

For the concrete dialogue between the two religious traditions, this politically con-ditioned harmony partly implied a cooperation between different religious traditions for the sake of Japan's imperial policies. Conferences were held where terms of the cooperation were considered, and where practical steps of support for the emperor at home and overseas were discussed. The sharing of experience was a longstanding tradi-tion of Buddhist Shinto coexistence in Japan, where people shared in rites of Buddhist or Shinto origin. With the official split between the two faith traditions which was enforced during the Meiji period until 1945 (Showa 20) this sharing was downplayed. However, as participation in (State Shinto) shrine rites became a common feature and on certain political occasions, a harmony-based dialogue between Buddhism and Shinto again became commonplace. While the official sharing of rituals became founded on a political structure, I permit myself to forward the qualified guess that a traditional Buddhist-centered honji suijaku remained alive on private and local levels.

Toshio Kuroda and Kenmitsu Buddhism

Toshio Kuroda (1926–1993) came from a Buddhist family. He graduated from Kyoto University in 1948. After a few more years in Kyoto, he taught at Kobe University beginning in 1955, and then at Osaka University from 1961 to 1989. He then trans-ferred to Buddhist Otani university in Kyoto. His Marxist methodology inspired a socially oriented concept of religion and promoted a critical approach to the Meiji Shinto legacy.

In 1963, he published a study of the Buddhist–Shinto relationship (Kuroda 1963). In this book he described a comprehensive socio-religious system of authority, criticiz-ing contemporary Japanese historiography. Kuroda questioned substantially the pre-vailing idea of a religiously plural Tokugawa period (1600–1868), holding that Japanese medieval society was religiously, economically and politically integrated within a dominant Shingon–Tendai power structure, the above-mentioned kenmitsu system. Moreover, he criticized the widespread view of Japanese medieval history as featuring two independent religious traditions (Shinto and Buddhism). He argued that this misinterpretation was caused by the disturbing effect of the Meiji separation of Buddhism and Shinto. According to him, the misguided concept of Shinto and Buddhism in Japanese history thus originated in the governmental religious policy of the Meiji era (Dobbins 1996: 220).

Kuroda's research in Japanese medieval history offered a new, multi-dimensional concept of religion, and a normative methodology for the critical study of religion in history. His new concept of religion was particularly related to religio-political relationships. In early medieval Japan he identified the interplay of Imperial Law (王法 ôbô) and Buddhist dharma (仏法 buppô), whereby the two power-factors supported each other. Imperial Law promoted the spread of Buddhism, whereas Buddhist dharma, buppô, brought out Imperial prosperity. He saw this inter-relationship in the light of Shinto–Buddhist mutuality, apparent in the honji suijaku model (Kuroda 1996b). Kuroda saw pre-Meiji Shinto as subordinated to this socio-religious superstructure (kenmitsu taisei), dominated by Shingon–Tendai power (Kuroda 1996a).

Kuroda's insights are decisive for the understanding of Shinto–Buddhist dialogue. He consistently argued for the view that pre-Meiji Shinto was no independent religion, and this perspective has incited deep debate among historians of religion about the Shinto–Buddhist relationship prior to Meiji (Kuroda 1981).

His methodological approach implied descriptive as well as normative perspectives. His method might be termed "mythological suspicion," whereby he sought for untenable historical projections in modern politics. Projecting modernity into past history and projecting premodernity into modernity were repeated charges against Shinto-based Meiji and postwar policy. Kuroda thus held that Shinto was a religion constructed by Meiji leaders for the purpose of nation-building.

Kuroda pointed at numerous examples of misguided, historical projections. One recurring issue of this kind has been the war memorial of the Yasukuni Shrine in central Tokyo. The shrine was constructed after the Meiji restoration to enshrine spirits of Imperial loyalists who had died during battles related to the restoration. Later more than two and a half million war dead up to 1945 have been enshrined there. A political movement to make the shrine a national war memorial has led to one of the sharpest debates in Japanese postwar democracy, and the bill to create a formal memorial has repeatedly been rejected. Several Japanese prime ministers have, however, since 1974 paid homage at the shrine (Breen 2007).

Kuroda argued that the Yasukuni Shrine functionally followed the early Japanese practice of pacifying the spirits of persons who died unfortunate deaths (Kuroda 1996c). Many researchers (Umehara 1986) have identified the pacification of onryô (unsatisfied spirits) as a central policy of the Japanese state from the early stages of its history. One way of pacifying them is to enshrine them as kami. These insights have been crucial for the conduct of Buddhist–Shinto dialogue over contemporary political issues.

Through his critical suspicion of politicized historical "projection," Kuroda has managed to raise radical questions for contemporary Shinto–Buddhist dialogue. His medieval research has questioned traditional understanding of "religion" and "religious identity." Should religions, for example Buddhism and Shinto as they have evolved in Japanese history, be considered parts of a complex socio-religious interplay of forces?

When and how did Shinto attain religious identity? The contemporary, academic dialogue on these questions dominates the Shinto–Buddhist world.

Shinto–Buddhist Dialogue in Democratic Japan

In the Shinto Directive promulgated by the Allied Forces in December 1945, State Shinto was demolished and Shinto shrines were redefined as religious bodies. Most of these shrines joined under a national Shinto office, *Jinja Honchô*. Furthermore, the new constitution of Japan guaranteed religious freedom and defined the state as secular and democratic. But, the separation between Shinto and Buddhism has basically remained from the Meiji period onwards. In one area, however, integrated Shinto–Buddhist devotional traditions have been revived. I refer to *shugendô* 修験道 (mountain ascetism). The *shugendô* praxis was ruled out as unacceptable by the Meiji government in 1872. Now, vital centers of *shugendô* have begun to reappear.

Revived Shugendô

This religious praxis presents an intricate blending of indigenous Japanese faith, Taoism and Buddhism. Shugendô, rooted in prehistoric mountain worship, literally means "the way of *gen*-practice." Gen 験 means experience, in this context more properly rendered as "magico-religious power." Traditionally shugendô is traced back to a legendary founder, En no Gyoja (En no Ozuno) from the sixth century CE (Earhart 1970: 18–19). Rooted in a complex of rites, myths and practices related to mountains, shugendô included new dimensions after encountering Buddhism in the sixth century. The faith is connected to numerous Japanese mountains, among which are Aso in Kyushu, the Kumano–Yoshino area in Wakayama, Hiei in Kyoto, and Haguro in north Honshu. En no Gyoja is supposed to have initiated the Kumano shugendô. Shingon and Tendai traditions have left a strong influence as well. But during the years 1868–72 the Shinto–Buddhist amalgamation of shugendô became suspicious. Finally, shugendô itself was forbidden by the Meiji government in 1872, and subsequently disintegrated. In the context of religious freedom following the Second World War, however, shugendô has experienced a revival. Several mountains are presently home to shugendô ascetics.

In this tradition, the Shinto–Buddhist interaction is vital. Buddhist temples (*yama dera*), Shinto shrines (*yama miya*), *torii* (Shinto gates), and Buddhist guides accompany practitioners along standard pilgrimage routes. The practice actually originated as veneration of sacred mountains, far back in Japanese prehistory. The mountain gods (*yama no kami*) are traditional, local deities, frequently understood as female kami. During the historical development of shugendô, such indigenous elements were interwoven with Buddhist sutra reading, the use of magical formulas, and the adoption of Buddhist dress. Mandalas were assimilated into almost all dimensions of shugendô (Earhart 1970: 28). The twofold mandala of Shingon consisting of a "womb mandala" and a "diamond mandala" is frequently used. The iconographic mandala is projected into a "landscape mandala," so that Buddhist doctrines on one hand, and the concrete reality of landscapes and ascetic practices on the other, correspond intimately with one another.

The cosmic character of The Sun Buddha (Dainichi) in Shingon is also prominent in shugendô, signifying the practitioner's participation in universal Buddha nature. The Shingon doctrine of becoming Buddha in your present body, *sokushin jobutsu*, 即身成仏 is equally central to the shugendô ideal of attaining Buddhahood through ascetic mountain training.

In shugendô, Buddha and kami are on equal footing. The interpretation of "the other reality," Shinto or Buddhist, is radically inclusivist. It means that Buddhist as well as Shinto traditions include the other faith. One might talk of a reciprocal honji–suijaku relationship. "Harmony" is in this case based on a mutual integration of the two traditions. In shugendô, we see a Shinto–Buddhist process of integration, rather than a dialectical interaction of separate entities. The ensuing dialogue is basically of an experiential character, and shows growing popularity. The attainment of spiritual power, one of the claims of shugendô, apparently offers special attraction. To this should be added that the inter-relationship between these two traditions are frequently the topic of conferences or lecture seminars, which often accompany participation in popular events of shugendô. Religious study-centers such as the Nanzan Institute for Religion and Culture (Nagoya) or temples and shrines connected to shugendô practice in, for example, Kumano or Kyoto provide theoretical instruction and dialogue on these relationships, frequently with international participation.

Harmony in Interreligious Dialogue in Japan

In this section I approach contemporary concepts of inter-religious dialogue in Japan, exploring ideas of a young scholar, Emi Mase Hasegawa and the postwar thought of a leading Shinto scholar, the late Kenji Ueda(1927–2003). He studied under dialectical theologian Paul Tillich in USA. Both of these scholars hold and recommend a Shinto-informed "harmony" for inter-religious relations in Japan.

In her work on Endo Shusaku's theology of religion, Emi Mase-Hasegawa addresses the issue of harmony in Japanese inter-religious relations (Mase-Hasegawa 2008: 35–37). In order to address present modes of Japanese inter-religious dialogue, she discusses the views of three scholars. Two of the scholars are Roman Catholic, Jan van Bragt (1928–2007) and Jan Swyngedow (1935–), both previously connected to the Nanzan Institute for Religion and Culture in Nagoya. She also takes into account the views of Shinto scholar Kenji Ueda from Kokugakuin University in Tokyo.

Mase-Hasegawa appreciates that professor Jan van Bragt has confirmed the existence of a peaceful coexistence between religions in Japan, but criticizes his claim that "each (Japanese) religion has an absolute lack of interest in the other religion" (Nanzan Institute for Religion and Culture 1984: 51). Van Bragt's colleague Jan Swyngedouw also observes a lack of interest in other faiths among Japanese religions, and perceives an absence of "common responsibility" in the Japanese religious world (Nanzan Institute for Religion and Culture 1984: 74; Mase-Hasegawa 2008: 35). Mase-Hasegawa interprets the interreligious silence of Japanese religions otherwise. She finds the views of van Bragt and Swyngedouw disturbingly conditioned by a "dual value system of the West, based on the Platonic-Judeo-Christian tradition of thinking." She favors on her part the Eastern value system of the Shinto scholar Kenji Ueda, who interprets Japanese "religious coexistence by harmony" in a framework of Shinto polytheism. Ueda holds that ". . . people who stand on pluralism . . . consider that coexistence is possible even among those who have different opinions or ideas because each individual has a truth in its individuality, so they have to give tribute to each other. It is coexistence by harmony. Shinto based on pluralism takes up the plural-value orientation. It can be said that Shinto – in this case the Japanese – has accepted foreign religions such as Buddhism, Confucianism and Yin–Yang thought – as the Japanese have always followed this pluralistic value orientation" (Ueda 1999, quoted in Mase-Hasegawa 2008: 36).

From a pluralist standpoint, Mase-Hasegawa questions the construction of any "common responsibility" and criticizes what she sees as a Western tendency to search for one religious truth: "But who can be so sure that we may find only one truth or only one responsibility? There might be many truths, or we might find nothing at all. There may be one common responsibility, but there might (also) be many. In reality, we are all on a spiritual pilgrimage and we might not find a common goal, aim or responsibility. The experience of a radical plurality in Japanese religiosity opens up the possibility of seeing a plurality of responsibilities as well" (Mase-Hasegawa 2008: 37). The careful and apparently passive inter-relationship between Japanese religions should not be seen as a "lack" of interest or responsibility. She understands the relationship instead as a mode of mutual respect and tolerance. It does not show "lack" of concern, but rather "pluralist" concern.

Shinto–Buddhist Harmony Revisited

In this section I offer concluding ideas on the character of Shinto–Buddhist dialogue, basically a Japanese phenomenon. I focus on "harmony," a concept which decisively influenced Shinto–Buddhist interaction from the time of Prince Shōtoku about 600 CE. Although the content of "harmony" has varied according to circumstances, this very concept continues to inform the Japanese religious world, not at least Shinto Buddhist dialogue. First, I point to three categories of dialogue between the two traditions.

The *dialogue on social issues* appears as one of the three categories. To some extent this category contains conference encounters. Buddhist as well as Shinto agencies are represented in multi-religious forums, such as World Parliament of Religions and World Conference of Religion and Peace, the latter forum actually pioneered by the Buddhist community Rissho Kosei Kai. The above mentioned two global organizations first and foremost provide focus on peace issues, human rights and ecological concerns. Interreligious conflicts hardly occur in these forums which promote positive cooperation between participants. The character of this dialogue changes radically, however, when sensitive, national issues are at stake.

For more than five decades, representatives of Shinto and Japan Buddhist Federation (JBF) have participated in discussions on the nationalization of Yasukuni Shrine.

Especially sensitive is its enshrinement of spirits who sacrificed their lives for the emperor during the Pacific War. Shinto leaders support plans of establishing Yasukuni as an official War Memorial. JBF has remained critical (Breen 2007). Any official status of this memorial nourishes a deep, national conflict after the 1945 Japanese military surrender. The Yasukuni issue furthermore colors a continuing, broad dialogue on Japanese modernity, which is commonplace at Japanese universities. The dialogue on modernization is not necessarily conducted in multi-religious contexts. It rather emerges in educational programs and courses on Japanese religious history. The research of historian Toshio Kuroda has played an important role in promoting a dialogue between religions on modernization in contemporary Japan. Shinto–Buddhist relationship is a major concern of Kuroda. In itself, his political interpretation of Meiji Shinto is not remarkable, the national establishment of State Shinto as a political creation during Meiji, Taisho and early Showa periods is universally accepted. But, his implied understanding of Shinto as integrated in kenmitsu Buddhism, until artificially constructed as a national religion in the Meiji era, has challenged academic and religious identities. Calling any view of Shinto as an established medieval religion a historical misunderstanding, manipulated by Meiji political projections, he stirred a major discussion on Shinto–Buddhist relations. Not only did his claims about misleading and overlooked nationalist presuppositions disturb historians. His research also disturbed religious convictions by questioning the religious identity of pre-Meiji Shinto. His research continues to invoke sensitive Shinto–Buddhist dialogue on religious identities and social roles.

Another category of Shinto–Buddhist dialogue might be termed *dialogue of experience*. Whereas the dialogue on social issues largely effects the religious elites, ordinary people are the main agents in the dialogue of experience. In this dialogue, two aspects appear: a popular experience of combining Buddhist and Shinto rites and special arrangements of Buddhist–Shinto experience.

Japanese religious history is a thoroughly integrated affair. It is common for Japanese citizens to attend Buddhist as well as Shinto rites. One and a half millennia of Shinto–Buddhist coexistence in the country has promoted longstanding exchanges of such experiences. The split between Buddhist and Shinto establishments in the wake of Meiji restoration never substantially disturbed the ongoing process of double religious experience among ordinary Japanese people. The double religious experience is vital, deep and normal in Japan, flowing from the widespread Shinto–Buddhist dialogue of experience. Within this huge field of broad and continued interaction, however, one special kind of event might be singled out: the shugendô praxis. This praxis, implying varying degrees of austerities, offers a highly attractive Buddhist–Shinto experience to practitioners. Its growing popularity, even internationally, adds to its contemporary significance. In the shugendô connected to cultic centers in central, Japanese mountainous areas such as Kumano, Aso and Hakusan, the dialogue of experience climaxes as personal empowerment. Due to its commonality, long tradition and emotional fascination, the dialogue of experience contends for primacy in contemporary Shinto–Buddhist dialogue.

It is, however, appropriate to single out a third category of dialogue, the *dialogue of personal truth*. It applies to individuals, but not to the religious elite only. It is a particular category within the social and experiential categories, containing a search for personal or existential truth. There are numerous individuals who consider themselves religious pilgrims. Practitioners stroll along multi-religious paths, searching for an answer to existential questions. Frequently they consider themselves on the road to a deeper understanding of life or proceeding towards solution of a personal problem. Shinto people in the tradition of kokugaku (nativism), for example Atsutane Hirata and others already reflect this category. They have made use of alternative faiths to build up their own understanding of truth. Interesting examples might also be discovered in the Buddhist-centered Kyoto School of philosophy, where philosophers considered themselves moving towards a deeper understanding by encountering other faith traditions. Other faiths are seen to contribute to one's deeper understanding of the truth. In Japan, the dominating inter-religious pilgrimages for obvious reasons have taken and do take place in the dual, Shinto Buddhist world.

One feature is common to all these three categories of Shinto–Buddhist dialogue: the ideal of harmony. In early Japanese history – illustrated by the Prince Shotoku Constitution,'harmony' was defined within the realms of society and family. It was, furthermore, described as cooperation. In spite of an overt relation to Buddhism expressed in Section 2 of the Constitution, any specific religious base of the harmony is ambiguous. The term of harmony (wa) itself, with its character of cooperation and focus on concrete social contexts, indicates a Confucian background. However, adaption to the spirituality of existing Japanese communities should not be ruled out. In the end, this notion of harmony always contained a political dimension.

From the early medieval period until breakthrough of modernity (Meiji) the harmony apparently became substantially founded on kenmitsu Buddhism. Honji suijaku thought constituted its generally accepted theoretical base. A redefinition of harmony took place after Meiji Restoration. Harmony was still defined as cooperation, but now with an explicit national accent: the imperial cause. A partly inverted honji suijaku structure was installed. The emperor-system constituted the honji. As Buddhism, Shinto and other religious communities integrated State Shinto in their cultic identity, they radiated suijaku of the emperor-system. However, one has to keep in mind the existence of different levels of harmony. The honji suijaku idea adapted to the emperor-system confirmed a superstructure securing political harmony in the country. But on the popular level, in local communities, a harmonious relationship between different religious communities was formed by historical traditions of kenmitsu Buddhism. The Shinto–Buddhist relationships after Meiji thus developed in a twofold way – a traditional continuity of kenmitsu Buddhism in local communities under a superstructure of political harmony conditioned by the emperor-system. The traditionally fostered inter-religious harmony became, in the Meiji era, subordinated to actual, political priorities. This situation lasted from late Meiji until a democratic era dawned in 1945.

After 1945, the politically enforced harmony disappeared. Does, then, the idea of harmony govern Shinto–Buddhist relations in new ways? The debate featuring Protestant scholar Emi Mase-Hasegawa, Catholic fathers Jan van Bragt and Jan Swyngedow, and Shinto scholar Kenji Ueda, might illustrate a mood of Shinto–Buddhist harmony in contemporary, democratic Japan. The four participants in this exchange of ideas agree on the existence of an apparent passivity in Japanese inter-religious dialogue. Swyngedow regrets this passivity and believes that it comes from a "lack of common concern," whereas Mase-Hasegawa, supported by Shinto scholar Ueda, sees it as reflecting a pluralist commitment. The apparent passivity indicates, in her interpretation, active concern, but subject to an inner, pluralist orientation.

My present study of religious relations in medieval Japan as well as in modern Japan prior to 1945 has confirmed that Shinto–Buddhist harmony has strong political roots. However, the powerful political superstructure of the emperor-system which officially carried Japanese inter-religious harmony after Meiji restoration was lost in 1945. There is no reason to question that there is a lack of a common responsibility in the postwar Japanese religious world. But does this "lack" demonstrate a pluralist respect for "the other"? Emi Mase-Hasegawa and Kenji Ueda may have a point when identifying a "pluralist" concern rather than a "lack" of concern.

I will, however, suggest a different explanation for the apparent lack of common responsibility. Rather than revealing a respect for plurality, it might indicate a consensus: "We are the same! We do not necessarily have to work together because we are already together in what we do. One works for the same goal anyhow!" To this comes another decisive factor: the lack of a political dictate. As a democratic state has no authoritarian leadership, Shintoists and Buddhists see no compelling reasons to formulate overarching, common responsibilities. Therefore, Shinto and Buddhism in Japan presently find themselves in a void, created by a democratic system of religious freedom. Conditioned by this freedom, they go for religious harmony – in the shape of silent consensus. This state of affairs points in my view at a surprising, concluding insight: The legacy of medieval Shinto-Buddhist integration preeminently conditions contemporary Shinto–Buddhist dialogue.

Bibliography

Breen, John and Teeuwen, Mark (eds). *Shinto in History: Ways of the Kami*. London: Curzon, 2000.

Breen, John (ed.). *Yasukuni, the War Dead and the Struggle for Japan's Past*. London: Hurst and Company, 2007.

Bocking, Brian. *A Popular Dictionary of Shinto*. London: Curzon, 1996.

Bukkyo Times Weekly, May 2010. "Kindai Bukkyôshi kenkyû ni isseki tôzuru" ("Laying down a Stone for the Study of Modern Buddhist History").

Dobbins, James C. "Editor's Introduction: Kuroda Toshio and His Scholarship." *Japanese Journal of Religious Studies*, 23(3–4) (1996): 217–232.

Earhart, Byron H. *A Religious Study of The Mount Haguro Sect of Shugendô. An Example of Japanese Mountain Religion*. Tokyo: Sophia University, 1970.

Endo, Jun. "The Early Modern Period, In search of a Shinto Identity," in *Shinto – A Short History*. Mark Teeuwen and John Breen (trans., ed. and adapt.). London: Routledge-Curzon, 2003, 108–158.

Grapard, Allen."The source of oracular speech: absence? presence? or plain treachery? The Cases of Hachiman Usa-gu gotakusenshu," in *Buddhas and Kami in Japan. Honji Suijaku as a Combinatory Paradigm*, eds. Mark Teeuwen and Fasbio Rambelli. London: Routledge Curzon, 2003, 77–94.

Mase-Hasegawa, Emi. *Christ in Japanese Culture, Theological Themes in Shusaku Endo's Literary Works*. Leiden: Brill, 2008.

Heisig, James W., Kasulis, Thomas P. and Maraldo, John C. (eds.). *Japanese Philosophy, A Sourcebook*. Honolulu : University of Hawai'i Press, 2011.

Hirata, Atsutane. *Zenshu*, Vol. 8. Tokyo: Meicho, 1976.

Inoue, Nobutaka (ed.). *Kami*. Institute for Japanese Culture and Classics. Tokyo: Kokugakuin University Press.

Ito, Satoshi. "The Medieval Period: The Kami Merge with Buddhism," in *Shinto – A Short History*, trans., adapt., Mark Teeuwen and John Breen, ed. Nobutaka Inoue. London: RoutledgeCurzon, 2003, 63–107.

Kobayashi, Bigen. *Ko-shintô nyûmon (Introduction to Koshinto)*. Tokyo: Hyôgensha, 1998/2000.

Kuroda, Toshio. *Chûsei no kokka to Tennô (The Medieval State and Emperor)*. Tokyo: Iwanami Shoten, 1963.

Kuroda, Toshio. "Shinto in the History of Japanese Religion." *Journal of Japanese Studies* 7(1)(1981): 1–21.

Kuroda, Toshio. "The Development of the Kenmitsu System as Japan's Medieval Orthodoxy." *Japanese Journal of Religious Studies*, 23 (1996a): 234–269.

Kuroda, Toshio. "The Imperial Law and the Buddhist Law." *Japanese Journal of Religious Studies*, 23 (1996b): 271–285.

Kuroda, Toshio. "The World of Spirit Pacification." *Japanese Journal of Religious Studies*, 23 (1996c): 321–351.

Kuroda, Toshio. "The Discourse on the 'Land of Kami' (*Shinkoku*) in Medieval Japan." *Japanese Journal of Religious Studies*, 23 (1996d): 353–385.

Matsunaga, Daigan and Alicia Matsunaga. *Foundation of Japanese Buddhism*. Tokyo: Buddhist Books International, Eikyôji Foundation, 1974 (Vol. 1)/1976 (Vol. 2).

Murayama, Shuichi. *Henbô suru kami to hotoketachi (Changing Kami and Buddhas)*. Tokyo: Jinbun Shoin, 1990.

Nanzan Institute for Religion and Culture (ed.). *Shintô to kiristukyô (Shinto and Christianity)*. Tokyo: Shunjûsha, 1984.

Nanzan Institute for Religion and Culture (ed.). *Shûkyô to bunka (Religion and Culture)*. Tokyo: Jinbun Shoin, 1991.

Nitta, Hitoshi. "Shinto as a 'Non-Religion': The Origins and Development of an Idea," in *Shinto in History: Ways of the Kami*, eds. John Breen and Mark Teeuwen. London: Curzon, 2000, 252–271.

Niwano, Nikkei, *Hokkekyô no atarashii kaishaku (A New Interpretation of The Lotus Sutra)*. Tokyo: Kosei Shuppan, 1989.

Okuyama, Michiaki and Mark MacWilliams (eds.). *Defining Shinto*. Sheffield: Equinox, 2013.

Shinto Kokusai Yukokai. *Dai 39 kai Shinto Kaigai Koryu. Isuraeru shûkyô jijô shisatsu kenkyû kiroku*, (Shinto Overseas Contact no 39. *Study-Report on the Observed Religious Situation in Israel*). Tokyo, 2010.

Sonoda, Minoru. *Shinto Nihon no minzoku shûkyô (Shinto, The Folk Religion of Japan)*. Tokyo: Kôbundô, 1988.

Sueki, Bummishi (末木文美士). "Shinbutsu-ron Josetsu (神仏論序説)," in *Kami to Hotoke no Kosmorojii*, ed. Nippon Bukkyô Kenkyûkai. Kyoto: No III Nihon no Bukkyô, Hôzôkan, 1995, 23–43.

Swanson, Paul and Clark Chilson (eds.). *Nanzan Guide to Japanese Religions*. Honolulu: University of Hawai'i Press, 2006.

Teeuwen, Mark. *Watarai Shintô: An Intellectual History of the Outer Shrine of Ise*. Leiden: CNWS Publications, 1996.

Teeuwen, Mark. "The Kami in Esoteric Buddhist Thought and Practice," in *Shinto in History: Ways of the Kami*, eds. John Breen and Mark Teeuwen. London: Curzon, 2000.

Teeuwen, Mark and John Breen (trans. and adapt.), Nobutaka Inoue (ed.). *Shinto – A Short History*. London: RoutledgeCurzon, 2003.

Teeuwen, Mark and Rambelli, Fabio (eds.). *Buddhas and Kami in Japan. Honji Suijaku as a Combinatory Paradigm*. London: RoutledgeCurzon, 2003.

Tsuji, Zennosuke. "Honji suijaku setsu no kigen ni tsuite," in *Nihon Bukkyôshi*, Vol. 10. Tokyo: Iwanami Shoten, 1955.

Ueda, Kenji. *Shinto*. Tokyo: Jinja Honcho, 1999.

Ueshima, Keiji, Kuki Ietaka and Tanaka Riten Kumano. *Kami to Hotoke (Gods and Buddhas)*. Tokyo: Hara Shôbô, 2009.

Ueshima, Keiji. "Kumano Kô" ("Kumano Revisited"), in *Kami to Hotoke (Gods and Buddhas)*, eds. Keiji Ueshima, Kuki Ietaka and Tanaka Riten Kumano. Tokyo: Hara Shôbô, 2009, 2–39.

Umehara, Takeshi. *Kakusareta jujika*. Tokyo: Shinkosha, 1986.

CHAPTER 17
Muslim–Hindu Dialogue

Anna Bigelow

Inter-religious dialogue between Muslims and Hindus in India is not a recent product of neoliberal efforts at social integration or post-Partition cultural reconciliation. Muslims and Hindus have been in dialogue since the arrival of Muslim traders in the seventh and eighth centuries. Indeed the earliest accounts of encounters between Arab Muslims and South Asian Hindus depict a wide range of interactions and mutual perceptions. Far from being perpetually antagonistic groups, Muslims and Hindus in many places and times formed communities in which there were intermarriages, places of collective worship, shared political and economic institutions, and other forms of exchange. Certainly there also been times and places where the interactions have been contentious and violent, but without understanding the full range of encounters, it is difficult to make sense of either the conflict or the cooperation that make up the fullness of history. To understand these interactions through a framework of interreligious dialogue, as this volume suggests we might, it is important to recognize the very different contexts and conversations that have taken place and those that continue to this day. This essay will provide a survey of Hindu–Muslim encounters and of the various scholarly efforts to understand the nature of these mutual engagements and their meaning.

Dialogue, of course, takes many forms – several of which will be described in what follows. Theologians, activists, and religious actors define dialogue in various ways. For some it is a preamble to proselytization – one must converse with and understand the religious other in order to most effectively impress upon them the superiority of one's own faith. For others, dialogue provides new insights into their own religion by rendering apparent that which is similar, and that which is distinctive. Such efforts may facilitate the view that the other religion is a less evolved or less precise version of the analyst's tradition – making a certain kind of space for the other, but without acknowledging the validity, and sometimes desirability, of difference. The dialogue that promotes what Indologist and pluralism scholar Diana Eck calls engaged pluralism is

The Wiley Blackwell Companion to Inter-Religious Dialogue, First Edition. Edited by Catherine Cornille.
© 2013 John Wiley & Sons Ltd. Published 2020 by John Wiley & Sons Ltd.

one that seeks understanding and accepts difference. "The encounter of a pluralistic society is not premised on achieving agreement, but achieving relationship" (Eck 1993). Her view of dialogue as primarily oriented towards the forging of relationships between religiously committed people also echoes the work of Martin Buber, who described "genuine dialogue" as that dialogue "where each of the participants really has in mind the other or others in their present and particular being and turns to them with the intention of establishing a living mutual relation between himself and them" (Buber 1947: 19). Of course, relationships take many forms, and in the case of inter-religious dialogue, those relationships may help to solidify differences, facilitate cooperative engagement, improve mutual understanding, or bolster oppositional identities. India's history of inter-religious exchanges has witnessed all of these possible conformations and more. Given over a thousand years of such complexity, it is important to bracket contemporary assumptions about what dialogue looks like now and what it looked like historically.

Traders and Raiders

The earliest contact between South Asia and the Middle East came even before the advent of Islam in the early seventh century CE, through trade across the Indian Ocean in the south and along the Silk Road in the north. South Asia was a highly desirable trading partner, possessing valuable natural resources in the form of spices, textiles, and precious metals and jewels. In the south, along the Malabar Coast, cities flourished due to the ocean trade through the region, and in some cases, Arab traders established long term residences in these areas and were allowed by the Hindu rulers to intermarry with the local population (Wink 1990: 80). With the emergence of Islam, these unions developed into the Mappila Muslim community, which exists to this day. In the north of India, trading relationships existed, but raiding parties from Afghan and Turkic tribes and dynasties were also common from the early eighth century forward. Initially, few of these warlords attempted to establish permanent territories, the brief rule of Muhammad bin Qasim in Sindh, established in 711, being an exception. However, even profit-seeking invasions provided some opportunities for dialogue. Many of these engagements were pragmatic, geared towards the adoption and adaptation of new ideas, technologies, and crafts. Indeed as Carl Ernst has pointed out, during the Abbasid period (ca. 750–1258), the main thrust of Arab interest in Hindu knowledge focused on mathematics, astronomy, medicine, and other "practical" sciences (Ernst 2003: 175). These knowledge systems, developed in India, helped to fuel the institutions of intellectual inquiry in the Middle East such as the Dar al Hikma, or House of Wisdom, in Baghdad in which scholars translated materials from all over the world and produced an enormous body of new scholarship that spread throughout the Islamicate world.

In this period, one of the most sustained examples of one Muslim scholar's efforts to understand the nuances of Hindu theology, philosophy, and science came in the person of al-Biruni. Al-Biruni was in the employ of the famous warlord Mahmud of Ghazni, who invaded north India seventeen times in the early eleventh century. Al-

Biruni was a polymath and a reluctant member of Ghazni's retinue, but he took advantage of his post on the frontier to explore the knowledge of the subcontinent. Like many Muslim scholars, he took seriously the Prophet Muhammad's directive to the faithful that they should "Seek knowledge, even unto China." He studied Indian languages and employed pundits and priests to instruct him. His *Book of India* (*Kitab al Hind*) touches on a wide range of topics, though it draws mostly from elite brahmanical Hindu sources, and thus gives little idea of how the majority of the population lived and worshiped (Al-Biruni, trans. Sachau [1888] 1971). Still, it remains an important record of a scholar's effort to understand a distinct religious system. Al-Biruni was particularly impressed by certain elements of philosophical Hinduism that adhere to a monist view of the godhead, which to him is close to monotheism and opposes the idolatry practiced by the masses. Indeed he is quite dismissive of popular religion among both Hindus and Muslims as being superstitious and essentially idolatrous. He describes Hindu idols in detail only to warn his reader "Our object in mentioning all this mad raving was to teach the reader the accurate description of an idol if he happens to see one, and to illustrate what we have said before, that such idols are erected only for uneducated low-class people of little understanding; that the Hindus never made an idol of any supernatural being much less of God; and lastly, to show how the crowd is kept in thralldom by all kinds of priestly tricks and deceits" (Al-Biruni trans. Sachau [1888] 1971: 122). He also spends a great deal of time drawing connections between certain elements of Hindu thought, philosophical Sufism, and Greek philosophy, especially neo-Platonism. Al-Biruni was intrigued by the mathematical and astronomical sciences developed by the South Asians, and wrote extensively on them. However, he also recognized the limits of the conversations in which he was involved, perceiving among the upper-caste Hindus with whom he largely interacted a profound prejudice against foreigners and those of other faiths, marked by, for example, their views against sharing food or beverage with non-Hindus or lower castes. Although these negative mutual perceptions are sometimes deployed as evidence of perpetual antipathy between Muslims and Hindus, such a characterization is both overdrawn and requires the neglect of the far more substantial portions of the text that al-Biruni devotes to his fascination with Hindu metaphysics, mysticism, metempsychosis, mathematics, astronomy, astrology, and theology.

Islamic Empires, Plural Populations

From the time of Mahmud of Ghazni in the eleventh century until the establishment of British direct rule in 1857, much, but not all, of the Indian subcontinent was under the control of Muslims. Whether in the form of imperial dynasties such as the Lodhis (1456–1526) and Mughals (1526–1857) or of regional powers such as that of the Nizams of Hyderabad or Mysore State under Haider Ali and Tipu Sultan, Muslim authority was widespread. However, even at the territorial height of Mughal power in the early eighteenth century, scholars estimate that only about 25 percent of the population ever accepted Islam, countering the common perception that Muslim rulers forced their subjects to convert. The work of Richard Eaton in particular has helped to distinguish truth from fiction in evaluating the degree to which South Asia Islamicized, and the means by which Islamicization may (or may not) have occurred.

These great debates center on the question of forced conversions and temple desecrations – issues that continue to fuel communal conflict in South Asia to this day. In two probing essays, Eaton explores both issues. In "Temple Desecration and Indo-Muslim States," Eaton points out that "much misunderstanding over the place of temple desecration in Indian history results from a failure to distinguish the rhetoric from the practice of Indo-Muslim state-formation" (Eaton 2000: 124). He argues that while mutual destruction of sacred sites was indeed a strategy of conquest employed by Muslims, it was also practiced by Hindus, both in battles between Hindu forces and in conflicts with Muslims. Yet in many cases, the recorded histories seem to exaggerate some or all of the damage that was inflicted upon their enemies. Comparing these records to epigraphic and archeological evidence, Eaton debunks many of the claims made both by present-day partisans as well as by the court chroniclers during the periods in question. Another important result of the expectation of Muslim–Hindu antagonism is the effect of these histories on both sectarian discourses in India and on the British colonial state and its perception of the incommensurability of the two religions under their control. Projects like the eight-volume collection of partial translations from Indian historians done by Elliot and Dowson in 1849, seemed to offer evidence of the necessity of British mediation and mastery to prevent all-out war between their Hindu and Muslim subjects. *The History of India as Told by Their Own Historians* edited, redacted, and selected in order to demonstrate primordial antipathies. The effects of such orientalist projects in service of colonial power has continued to feed communalist sentiment in the minds of many who have access to these English translations, but not their Persian and Arabic originals.

In another essay, "Approaches to the Study of Conversion to Islam in India," Eaton systematically undermines three common theories of Muslim attitudes towards the Hindu majority during the period of Muslim rule. These theories are the "religion of the sword theory," the "political advantage theory," and the "religion of social liberation theory" (Eaton 1987: 107–109). Eaton argues that there is little evidence that any of these three resulted in much conversion. By examining records of names, mosque-building, and other measures, he proves that Islam spread gradually and in greater numbers in areas peripheral to brahmanical Hinduism. He characterizes the spread of Islam as the "religion of the plough," since the rise of Islam accompanied the conversion of territory into arable land. In the Punjab, for example, this process was facilitated by the introduction of well and canal technologies that enabled cultivation of lands that had hitherto been agriculturally unproductive. Eaton's work helps to break down the myths of Muslim expansion that persist to this day.

It is important, however, to acknowledge the power of these imaginings that characterize the Muslim expansion as essentially violent and destructive. The eminent historian Romila Thapar, for example, has done fascinating work on the vast chasm between fact and fiction regarding Muslim treatment of Hindu holy sites such as the great Shiva temple at Somnath, Gujarat and the place identified as the birthplace of the Hindu God Rama in Ayodhya, Uttar Pradesh (Thapar 2005). The former site was legendarily destroyed by Mahmud of Ghazni in one of his many eleventh-century raids.

The latter site is believed by many to have been destroyed at the direction of the Mughal Emperor Babur in the early sixteenth century, to give way for a mosque known as the Babri Masjid. Hindu nationalists tore down that mosque on December 6, 1992, leading to riots, deaths, and a controversy that continues to trouble India to this day. Thapar's work, however, illustrates that the absence of historical evidence in both cases has not prevented Somnath and Ayodhya from being flashpoints of conflict between Indians of all faiths and none. Indeed contemporary inter-religious relations are often organized around managing the continued grievances of both communities. However, Babur's conquest of north India brought and expanded Turko-Afghan and Persianate culture to the region as well, resulting in new cultural and imperial structures that shaped Indian society profoundly and in many positive ways.

During the Mughal period (1526–1857), Muslim–Hindu relations took many forms. At both the imperial and regional levels, certain rulers and courts were quite open not only to employing and strategically allying with one another – which was common – but also to pursuing deeper engagement and understanding. To some extent this can be understood as relevant to the pragmatics of statecraft, but there are many examples of sincere interest and genuine curiosity. The most famous example of such fascination about other religions is the Mughal emperor Akbar, who not only spoke local languages, but was a patron of Hindu poets writing in the Indic language of Brajbhasha, which was, along with Persian, the literary language of north India during his period (Busch 2010). Recent scholarship by Allison Busch reveals much about the fascinating nexus of language, religion, and the arts in the imperial and regional Mughal courts. Although language is often linked to religious identity – Persian for Muslims and Sanskrit and its offshoots for Hindus – Busch and others effectively demonstrate how oversimplified and impoverished such characterizations are. For example, the poets Gang and Keshavdas Mishra wrote in Brajbhasha in praise of Akbar and other Mughal notables, indicating a close association between the poets and the princes and their advisors. Akbar is also well known for having commissioned art, music, and literature from a wide range of sources. He had the Hindu epics and other key texts translated into Persian, as had other rulers and powerful figures before. But as Carl Ernst has pointed out, the zeal for translation and patronage of the arts under Akbar must be seen as part of his imperial policy "designed to reduce intellectual provincialism and linguistic divisiveness within the empire" (Ernst, 2003: 180). However, the continued patronage of Brajbhasha and Sanskrit literary endeavors, as discussed by Busch, adds nuance to this pragmatic assessment of Mughal patronage of non-Muslim literary and creative arts.

One particularly interesting example of a sustained inquiry into Hindu and Muslim concepts and practices was produced by Akbar's great-grandson, Dara Shikoh (1615–1659). A committed Sufi, Dara Shikoh authored a Persian text called the *Meeting of the Two Oceans (Majma' al Bahrain)*, which is often mistaken as an effort to reconcile Hinduism and Islam. Instead, the text is a comparative project, digging into the esoteric truths unveiled by the elite practitioners of monist Hinduism and Sufism (Ernst 2003). He was also interested in the epics, texts on yoga, and philosophical materials, many of which he had translated. Like many Sufis and yogis, Dara Shikoh believed that certain kinds of knowledge may be shared by adepts from various traditions, but these ideas are quite distinct from those held by the masses and should remain the provenance of an elite few. Indeed many texts belonging to esoteric and mystical paths within Islam and Hinduism are clearly not meant to initiate a large-scale inter-faith dialogue, have little to do with the kind of popular religion that is common to South Asia, and defy religious categorization. These were traditions for those few who were initiated into their highly complex practices by teachers trained in lineages that went back generations.

Often times devotional (*bhakti*) Hinduism and Sufi Islam, both of which are wide-spread throughout the subcontinent, are depicted as converging streams within their respective religions, which in some cases certainly is true. While it is important to avoid overgeneralizing, many important figures within the Bhakti and Sufi movements in South Asia were primarily concerned with attaining direct experience and knowledge of the divine and less interested in doctrinal or ritual orthodoxy. In some cases, these figures actively explored the traditions and spiritual technologies of a variety of faiths. For example, the great poet-saint Kabir was born into a Muslim household but came to reject sectarian identification and devoted himself to the praise of an abstract (*nirguna* – without form) divine essence he referred to as Ram. The Baul movement in Eastern India is grounded in highly esoteric practices that involve manipulation of the mind and body, employing concepts, images, and themes that resonate with Hinduism and Islam, among other systems (Roy 1983; Salomon 1995).

Discussions of mutual Bhakti and Sufi influence are often infused with the social and political agendas of the interlocutors. It is easy to find points of intersection and diver-gence, origin and expansion, adaptation and translation. Recent scholarly work on the popular and devotional traditions that emerge around charismatic holy people associ-ated with Bhakti and Sufi religion has helpfully introduced a regional scope of analysis that avoids the largely obscurantist label of syncretism that is too often employed (Ernst and Stewart 2003). Ernst, Stewart, and others argue convincingly that implicit in the term syncretism is the idea of combined religion traditions that existed in some pure and unadulterated form prior to their combination into a synthetic form. That synthe-sized faith is by implication a more obviously manipulated entity that does not merit the same degree of legitimacy as the traditions from which it derived. As an analytical category, therefore, syncretism does little to help us understand how all religions develop and are maintained, nor how they are understood and practiced by their communities of faith. In a useful effort to avoid the trap of originalism and stigma of corruption, Tony K. Stewart introduced a theoretical framework of translation (Stewart 2001). In this approach, it becomes apparent that when communicating principles and practices in local idioms, environments, and socio-political contexts, religious actors engaged one another through familiar languages, tropes, themes, and rituals. In such a complex situation, labels such as Hindu or Muslim may be over-determining, limiting the true range of meaning for practitioners. Historian Farina Mir illustrates a similar turn towards the shared pietistic sensibilities of diverse people who inhabit a shared linguis-tic, cultural, and natural environment in her work on colonial Punjab, to be discussed below.

Shared religious landscapes do not, of course, always result in shared ideas about the nature of the places that animate those regions. Indeed, much dialogue between

Hindus and Muslims in South Asia has involved competition to control the symbolic and spiritual identities of places and people important to both traditions. Simon Digby has written extensively about folklore featuring spiritual competitions between yogis and Sufis in which one's victory over the other in the performance of miracles revealed the ideological orientation of the story's source. (Digby 1970, 2000). In the Deccan, Nile Green reveals the ways in which local interlocutors represented a key fortress – Deogiri or Daulatabad – imbuing it with spiritual histories to reflect the site's identity as military and political power shifted (Green 2012). Examining three different narratives composed from the mid-eighteenth to the early nineteenth centuries, Green illustrates shared rhetorical structures between the two Muslim and one Hindu versions of the site's history and etiology. Given the centrality of this fortress in terms of political control of the region, it provides a compelling example of narrative competition over its symbolic meaning.

Colonial India

Mughal authority declined steadily from the early eighteenth century onwards, with the rise of regional Hindu kingdoms, such as the Marathas in the west, and the emergence of British trading centers mostly in the south and east. The victory of the British East India Company in 1757 and the advent of direct British rule in 1857 changed the dynamics between Hindus and Muslims profoundly. Politically, Muslims had dominated much of the north from the Ghaznavid period in the beginning of the eleventh century until the demise of the Mughal dynasty in the mid-nineteenth. In the central and southern regions, Muslim principalities emerged in the Deccan in particular, with successive dynasties such as the Asif Jahis in Hyderabad controlling parts of that territory even throughout the period of British colonialism. Hindu princely states such as Jaipur, Udaipur, and Gwalior continued in semi-autonomy as well. At no time was the entirety of South Asia under Muslim rule, and although Muslims did dominate much of the territory until the consolidation of British rule in 1857, at no time was Islam the majority faith for the whole subcontinent. Indeed, as stated previously, at the moment of Indian independence in 1947, only 25 percent of the population was estimated to be Muslim. Most Muslims were concentrated in urban areas and in the northwest and northeast of the subcontinent, a distribution largely attributable to the lesser presence of brahmanical Hinduism in those regions. Certainly the decline and fall of Muslim imperial patronage changed the landscape for Muslim scholars, clerics, and artists. The British tended to employ Hindus in greater numbers as bureaucratic functionaries and to identify certain ethnic and religious groups as bearing particular moral characteristics – such as the martial Sikhs and the scoundrel Thugs.

British colonialism in part derived its legitimacy from a claim that without the British, Muslims and Hindus would be immediately in conflict with one another, a claim even some Indians espoused. Sometimes referred to as a divide and conquer policy, the British attitude towards the religions of their subjects often had the effect (and possibly the intention) of demarcating differences between religious communities. Though it is overstating it to say that the British invented Hinduism and other religious identities through their enumerative policies of census taking, ethnographic data-gathering, and taxation, these practices certainly had profound effects upon the population and required a good deal of social organization to effectively respond to their demands.

In the late nineteenth and early twentieth centuries, resistance to British rule began to grow. During the Indian independence movement, dialogue between Muslims and Hindus that more closely resembles contemporary understandings of interfaith dialogue became an important strategy of some of the key actors – most especially Mohandas K. Gandhi. Gandhi, of course, was a devout Hindu as well as a canny political strategist. One of his greatest interests and challenges during his years working to unite Indians against British colonial authority was to bring Hindus and Muslims together for the cause. He pursued this goal both through political action and devotional practice. One of the first political efforts Gandhi and his followers pursued in order to strengthen their support among Muslim Indians was known as the Khilafat movement from 1919 to 1924 (Minault 1982). The movement began after the First World War, in the aftermath of the demise of the Ottoman Empire and the end of the Caliphate, which had ruled much of the Middle East, including the holy places of Mecca, Medina, and Jerusalem. Although the Ottoman Caliphs had had little influence in South Asia, the loss of Ottoman authority represented more than just the end of that empire, but also meant the end of an Islamic global power and the end of one of the last competitors with the Europeans for dominance as the Ottoman territories were broken up. As such, within the context of a South Asia controlled by Britain, the nominal, essentially ineffective support for the movement to re-establish the caliphate was a gesture that both fostered Muslim support for the broader Indian independence movement, and spoke to indigenous rights of self-governance. Of course, not all South Asian Muslims felt any particular connection to the Khilafat movement, and it was short-lived, leaving some freedom-minded Muslims inclined towards Gandhi's Congress Party and others preferring Muslim-oriented groups such as the Muslim League.

Another group that emerged during the independence movement was known as the Khudai Khidmatgar, also known as the Red Shirts. Under the leadership of Abdul Ghaffar Khan, a Pathan tribal leader from the northwest of India (present day Pakistan and Afghanistan), the Khudai Khidmatgar advocated nonviolent resistance to British colonialism. Though Khan worked closely with Gandhi (and is sometimes rather derivatively called the Frontier Gandhi), he also developed tactics, mobilization strategies, and a language of resistance that was autochthonous to the Pashtun culture of the northwest. He told his followers that his methods were not new, but were the same methods and values that the Prophet Muhammad had taught – "*amal, yakeen, muhabbat* – work, faith, and love" – which no enemy could stand against (Easwaran 1999: 13). By putting nonviolent resistance into the language of Islam and making it part of the Pashtun code of honor, Khan was able to gather more than 100,000 activists to the cause of nonviolent resistance and spent many years in jail himself. In a similar fashion, Gandhi also deployed religious language and culturally resonant concepts, framing resistance as *satyagraha* – holding fast to the truth, and evoking the ideal of *Ramrajya* – the perfectly righteous time when the god Rama ruled on earth – as a goal for the movement. The two men spent time at Gandhi's ashram together in prayer and consultation and also went out together on tour of the country (Easwaran 1999).

The idealism of Khan and Gandhi did not, however, win the day. Ultimately, the independence movement gathered steam even as it became more fractious, and it became clear after the Second World War that the British were going to leave the subcontinent. As the inevitable approached, the Muslim League under the leadership of Muhammad Ali Jinnah pressed for a more regionally federated nation than was acceptable to the leadership of Congress under Jawaharlal Nehru. Partition of India and Pakistan emerged from the negotiations as the expedient option, and so 1947 saw the devastating violence and mass transfer of population that accompanied the independence of India and Pakistan. The communal violence that occurred during this period was particularly horrifying in the regions of Punjab in the northwest and Bengal in the northeast. Scholars estimate that a million or more people died and approximately fifteen million moved from one side of the new borders to the other.

Yet even in those extremely dark times, there were places where relations between Muslims and Hindus – as well as Sikhs, Jains, Buddhists, Christians, and others – were strong enough to preserve certain communities from the worst of the crisis. One particularly interesting case is that of the former princely state of Malerkotla, ruled by a Muslim nawab in the eastern part of Punjab – the side that remained with India. Few Muslims left for Pakistan from that small state and many Punjabi Muslims sought refuge and remained in the area. Today the town is regionally famous as a place where no one died in partition and where communal relations are overall very congenial. Several studies of the town by myself, Pippa Virdee, and others have sought to understand how the legend of peace has become a kind of reality (Bigelow 2010; Virdee 2007). This question takes us into the territory of grassroots peacemaking and coalition building that occurs on a daily basis in Malerkotla. Indeed, much of the interreligious dialogue that occurs in this town, as in many others, is not of the formal or institutional variety. Rather it is the outgrowth of relationships that have developed organically over time and generations, but continue to be cultivated as a matter of a shared local ethos. Thus in this town Muslims and non-Muslims exchange visits and food around one another's holy days, and attend shared public gatherings (such as the annual burning of the demon king Ravana from the Hindu epic Ramayana, or the public procession for the Shi'i observation of the martyrdom of Imam Hussain). Wedding receptions are large, multi-religious, and have provision for vegetarian and non-vegetarian guests, as well as areas for women only. There are numerous shrines, usually dedicated to Sufi saints, which are attended by Hindus and Sikhs, as well as Muslims. Many local businesses are joint ventures or at least employ people from various religions, clans, and castes. Politics are particularly complicated and integrated, especially since the family of the former nawab's lineage has dwindled and, as their former dominance ebbed, others have stepped into municipal and regional political positions. However, even typically sectarian parties like the Sikh Shiromani Akali Dal have forwarded Muslim candidates for their slates from Malerkotla. In a similar fashion, religious organizations such as the local Jama'at-i Islami and Rashtriya Swayamsevak Sangh have typically enjoyed leadership that seeks to build relationships with one another, rather than foster enmity. In separate conversations with the author, past presidents of both organizations spoke warmly of the "family relations" they had with one another.

Such informal networks of association are foundational to sustainable multireligious communities in India. Many recent scholars have sought to understand why ethnic or communal violence does not occur in some places, yet seems almost endemic in others (Brass 2003; Kakar 1996; Nandy et al., 1995; Talbot 2007; Tambiah 1996; Varshney 2002; Wilkinson 2001). These studies take various views on the causes of religious conflict, ranging from psychic trauma to electoral competition to elite opportunism to political manipulation. Yet the study of ways in which religiously diverse communities connect with one another, formally and informally, is just beginning to take shape. Varshney, for example, while interested primarily in the causes of conflict between communities, also highlights the role of interethnic associational links at the civil societal level in reducing the likelihood of violent conflict in several urban areas of India. Wilkinson explores the ways in which inter-religious riots are instigated and organized by politicians who believe they may gain traction with the electorate by fomenting religious division. Nandy documents the steady increase of alienation between communities that occurs under the confluence of economic and political change accompanied by urbanization and the breakdown of traditional networks.

Other recent studies reveal in close detail how religious communities have connected with one another in various cultural and historical contexts. Already mentioned is the important work of Allison Busch on Mughal patronage of Brajbhasha literature produced by non-Muslims and that of Carl Ernst on the translations of Hindu texts and interpretations of Hindu traditions undertaken in Persian and Arabic in the same period. These studies greatly expand our grasp of the social and cultural milieus of both inter-religious interaction and the production of knowledge. Another study that adds profoundly to our understanding of the circulation of knowledge through a literary culture is that of Farina Mir and her work on the romance ballads of the Punjab (Mir 2010). Her book *The Social Space of Language* is a richly textured history of the thriving vernacular language literary market in colonial Punjab that appealed across religious and ethnic communities and defies conventional wisdom about the role of the British in reifying, or even generating, communal division through language policy and other bureaucratic systems. Mir demonstrates how the romantic ballad *Hir-Ranjha* was told and retold by poets from every walk of life, and found audiences even more diverse. This speaks to a shared cultural ethos in which Hindus, Muslims, and Sikhs all resonated with the tragic romance of the star-crossed lovers, and were drawn together through the telling. Similarly, Sufia Uddin's study *Constructing Bangladesh* shows how Bengali language and shared cultural formations helped to shape Bangla identity (Uddin 2006). Chief among these shared traditions is the devotion to Sufi saints who draw people of all religions, classes, and ethnicities into their orbit.

"Dialogue of Life"

From the perspective of daily coexistence, Hindus and Muslims have long been engaged in what Riffat Hassan calls a "dialogue of life." She points out that the "dialogue of life which emerges out of the processes of life is not a contrived matter. It arises 'naturally' as it were from the interaction, positive and negative, obvious and subtle, verbal and nonverbal, between various peoples or persons" (Hassan 1992: 405). While not over-looking the value of formal dialogue between officials, Hassan argues that scholars and observers should pay attention to the "dialogue from below," just as we look to theology from below and so on. A generation of scholars has begun to take on this task, not under the rubric of inter-religious dialogue, but in finely grained ethnographies of communities wherein religious identities are entwined and often reflect positive, proso-cial engagement. For example, Peter Gottschalk's book *Beyond Hindu and Muslim* explores the shared memory systems that draw together a diverse population in a network of Bihari villages (Gottschalk 2000). In these places, local identities are more salient in some cases than religious difference. Not only does this study invite more careful thinking of the ways in which caste and class intersect with religion, but it also serves as a corrective to assumptions that religious identities always supercede any other affiliations.

Similarly, Joyce Burkhalter Flueckiger's book *In Amma's Healing Room* provides a window into the life of a Muslim woman healer in Hyderabad and her religiously mixed clientele (Flueckiger 2006). Having known Amma for many years, Flueck-iger's study is richly detailed and the healing room comes to life in her narrative. She points out that Hindu and Muslim clients share a "ritual grammar" with Amma and one another. This shared grammar determines the structure of the healing, how it is performed and how it is deemed effective. Though some of this grammar derives from particular religious systems – such as the Arabic writing Amma employs in writing amulets – its efficacy and authority are not exclusive. Furthermore, Flueck-iger acknowledges that while "differences between Hindus and Muslims matter very much" in relation to some issues or concerns (marriage, employment, admissions, elections), in other contexts, such as the healing room, "these differences are over-ridden by what is shared" (Flueckiger 2006: 168–9). Participation in that healing tradition does not require conversion or suspension of religious identity. In many other life arenas, the participants' salient identities may indeed be religious (or caste, or gender, etc), but the choice to engage in the multireligious context of the healing room has its own authenticity and centrality in the lives of its denizens. Flueckiger describes it as a "crossroads," a place where a multitude of lifeways converge, but do not remain confined. The dialogues that take place within that healing room did facilitate profound interpersonal relationships and a recognition of shared humanity. While not formal dialogue of the kind that religious institutions and their representa-tives promote, in many ways these autochthonous exchanges are more indicative of the actual quality of relations between Hindus and Muslims in that particular community.

This kind of "dialogue of life," as Hassan calls it, is also pervasive in my own research at shared shrines throughout the Indian subcontinent. At these places, often the tombs of Sufi saints, Muslims and non-Muslims join together in acts of devotion and prag-matic exchanges between one another and with the object of their devotion. Pilgrims in attendance will at times mimetically adopt one another's modes of prayer, repeat each other's stories and testimonials about the site and its sacrality, and engage one another in conversations attesting to their shared concerns and giving one another comfort and advice. In some places these shared sites serve as ad hoc community centers at which and through which residents and visitors imagine and enact idealized forms of citizenship in a plural India.

Another scholar who has assiduously researched interfaith relations, particularly as they relate to the status of the large Muslim minority in India, is Yoginder Sikand. An avid blogger and author of many articles and books, Sikand has documented a wide range of sustained, living multifaith traditions across South Asia. In his book *Sacred Spaces*, twelve sites shared between Muslims, Hindus, Christians, Sikhs, and others come to life, demonstrating the vibrancy and normalcy of these everyday spaces of local devotion throughout the subcontinent (Sikand 2003). In other work he explores the interfaith practices of a group typically thought of as zealously communitarian – the Jama'at-i-Islami (JI) (Sikand 2001). The JI was founded in 1941 by Maulana Maududi, an autodidact who became an extremely influential ideologue in shaping contemporary Islamist thought both in South Asia and beyond. However, Sikand points out that after the Partition of India and Pakistan, the Indian branch of the JI focused out of necessity on improving the overall condition of Muslims in India rather than on Islamizing the state, as the Pakistani branch did. Indeed, even as JI activists in India believe in the perfection of Islam as a way of life, they also reject religious chauvinism and isolationism, promoting dialogue and understanding between Hindus and Muslims as the best way to lift up the entirety of the Indian society they share. Sikand demonstrates that even this extremely conservative Muslim organization is committed to improving communal relations and has organized conferences, published books and pamphlets, and participated in dialogues in order to achieve that goal (Sikand 2001: 57). Anecdotally, the local JI leader in Malerkotla during the time of my research there (1999–2004), Maulana Abdul Rauf, was an excellent example of Sikand's observations. Rauf not only had good relations with the local leader of the Hindu nationalist outfit, the Rashtriya Swayamsevak Sangh (RSS), but he also worked with many non-Muslim village leaders to ensure the protection and development of mosques and religious education for Muslim residents. He participated in the Malerkotla Peace Committee that convened to mitigate communal conflicts in town. Though his commitment to his faith was unquestionable, Maulana Rauf was also committed to building a strong community free of religious prejudice.

Interfaith Activists

Today in South Asia many organizations approach human rights and social justice through the lens of religion. For some groups this involves caste, class, and tribal rights, while for others activism is framed in terms of a struggle against communalism. Communalism refers to extreme religious chauvinism and antagonism towards the religious other, often accompanied by exclusivist political mobilization. A wide range of activists and organizations are striving to counter communalism, some working from within religious traditions and others as secularist activists. Secularism in South Asia refers not just to the separation of religion and state, but also to the constitutionally mandated public embrace of a plural religious culture. This entails, according to the Indian constitution, the guarantee of rights of groups to organize, educate, observe customs, and propagate their faith.

The organization Sabrang ("all colors") is a human rights advocacy organization founded in 1993 to:

> provide information on, analyse and expose the machinations of communal politics in India, on the subcontinent and abroad and to publicise the attempt of secular individuals, groups and organisations engaged in fighting them. We stand for equal respect to all religions but are opposed to the cynical manipulation of faith in the pursuit of power. Therefore we are opposed to both majority and minority communalism.

Sabrang Communications provides a framework for several interconnected advocacy organizations, including the journal Communalism Combat, and is also connected to watchdog groups Citizens for Justice and Peace (CJP) and Muslims for Secular Democracy. Sabrang works to inform the public about activism and news relating to religious intolerance, violence, human rights violations, caste, women's rights, and a myriad of social issues. Communalism Combat is a monthly journal reporting on the activities of communalist and anti-communalist activists. Citizens for Justice and Peace has gone on factfinding missions after incidents of communal violence, such as 2002's riots in Gujarat.

The Centre for the Study of Society and Secularism was founded in 1993 by Muslim scholar and activist, Asghar Ali Engineer. Engineer has developed a strong reputation as a voice for inter-religious tolerance, producing numerous essays and books on India's secular tradition and Islamic teachings on inter-religious relations, many of which can be found on the centre's website (http://www.csss-isla.com/). The centre's objectives are "To spread the spirit of Secularism and communal harmony and social peace; to study problems relating to Communalism and Secularism; to organize inter-faith and ethnic dialogue and justice." To achieve these ends, the centre engages in research, seminars, publishing, training programs, youth camps, and dialogue events. In addition to Engineer, the centre's board is made up of prominent intellectuals and activists from a variety of religious backgrounds and perspectives.

A similar group is Aman Panchayat (http://www.amanpanchayat.org/), which came together in response to the rise of communal and sectarian activism in the mid-1980s. Also spearheaded by a group of scholars, artists, and activists, the main concern of Aman Panchayat is to counter various forms of oppression and violence, including that which is fueled by intolerance and communalism. Their particular concern is "the social and psychological rehabilitation of people made invisible by conflict, especially orphans, refugees and widows. The group's networking, sensitisation and legal-aid programmes strengthen democratic institutions and develop society's resources for non-violent conflict resolution." Aman Panchayat's activities center on education, advocacy, and sponsorship of local organizations and activists. These are just two of many NGOs in India whose goals, either principally or in part, seek to improve relations between religious and ethnic communities. Many of those involved are committed to India's secular ideals, and while they work for inter-religious harmony and tolerance, they do so from an NGO and activist perspective, which is often non-religious.

However, there are also many prominent religious actors within the Hindu and Muslim communities who reach out to one another in order to promote deeper understanding and spiritual dialogue. One such person is Maulana Wahiduddin Khan. Khan is the spiritual leader of the International Centre for Peace and Spirituality (http://www.cpsglobal.org/), founded in 2001. The centre has many activities, ranging from Islamic education to combatting terrorism to interfaith dialogue:

> At CPS we believe that we are living in a world of multi-religious, multi-cultural, multi-ethnic societies – a world of differences. A reformer has rightly said that nature abhors uniformity. This means that 'difference' is a part of nature and it exists in every aspect of life. The art of difference management is only possible through meaningful and positive 'inter-faith dialogue' between people on all aspects of life including religions. The aim of dialogue being to seek peaceful solutions to controversial matters, in spite of differences. By giving people respect and honour, these difference will become blessings. The result will be dialogue, sharing of views – that will result in intellectual development, which is a boon for everyone concerned. (http://cpsglobal.org/content/interfaith-efforts)

The dialogue Khan describes is one that does not seek to eliminate or overcome difference, but to embrace it as part of a divine plan. Indeed a well-known Qur'anic verse 49: 13 is invoked often – "O humankind, God has created you from male and female and made you into diverse nations and tribes so that you may come to know each other." To support his interpretation of the Islamic basis for inter-religious dialogue and peace activism, Khan has written many books and pamphlets available in several South Asian languages (Hindi, Urdu, Telugu, Marathi, English), and uses the organization's website as a resource center with video lectures in English and Urdu. In his lecture "The Concept of Harmony in Islam," Khan gives an exegesis of the Qur'an chapter 109, verse 6 "For you, your religion, and for me, mine," calling it the "most beautiful formula of coexistence. . . . Follow one and respect all. This is the formula of coexistence. In a multireligious, multicultural society there is no other feasible formula, no other formula can be practiced in such a society." Widely known throughout South Asia, Khan is an excellent example of a religious leader who views interfaith dialogue as essential to the practice of his faith as an Indian Muslim.

A prominent Hindu activist for human rights is Swami Agnivesh. This leader of the Arya Samaj is oriented principally towards the most vulnerable among the poor, focusing particularly on the issue of bonded labor, but he has also made combatting communalism one of his chief concerns. He engages in political activism and education, founded the Bandua Mukti Morcha to work against bonded labor, and organizes rallies against Hindu nationalist initiatives to polarize local communities. For Swami Agnivesh, the goal of religious dialogue is to bring together people of good will in the common cause of fighting injustice and lifting up the poor. Although a renunciant, his work is not focused on personal salvation: "[T]he task of the spiritually enlightened is not to promote one particular religion; much less to pit one religion against another. He repeatedly calls for identifying the good and the common factors that exist within all religions. He dreams of a world where religions interact in an integrative model as against the present conflictual and competitive model" (http://www.swamiagnivesh.

com/aboutswamiji2.htm). Like Maulana Wahiduddin Khan, Swami Agnivesh is a frequent speaker at interfaith gatherings and often champions the rights of India's minorities. Religious nationalism and communal politics have made inter-religious dialogue a matter of paramount concern to human rights activists as well as religious professionals like Khan and Agnivesh.

Conclusion

High-profile and well-publicized conflicts between religious groups in South Asia have made it easy to lose sight of the many positive forms of dialogue between Hindus and Muslims that have occurred in South Asian history. It is certainly true that the partition of India and Pakistan that accompanied independence in 1947 deeply challenged the capacity of the two religious communities to live together. The terrible violence and lasting mistrust that ensued cast a long shadow across the subcontinent. But it would be a mistake to allow that trauma to obscure other, equally important, realities. Since the first arrival of Muslims in the region, there have been many arenas of exchange, cooperation, and positive coexistence. Though the term "inter-religious dialogue" is a modern convention, our earliest records of the Hindu–Muslim encounter indicate enormous curiosity and lively interchange between religions in matters of technology, arts, and sciences, as well as spirituality. From the investigations of al-Biruni, to the translation projects in the Mughal period, to the Bhakti and Sufi devotional movements, to the daily pious practice at countless shared sites, to the social and political activism of human rights advocates, inter-religious dialogue between Muslims and Hindus is rich, complex, and ongoing.

Bibliography

Al-Biruni (trans. Edward C. Sachau). *Alberuni's India*. New York: W.W. Norton and Company, 1971.

Assayag, Jackie. *At the Confluence of Two Rivers: Muslims and Hindus in South India*. Delhi: Manohar, 2004.

Bigelow, Anna. *Sharing the Sacred: Practicing Pluralism in Muslim North India*. Oxford: Oxford University Press, 2010.

Brass, Paul. *The Production of Hindu–Muslim Violence in Contemporary India*. Seattle: University of Washington Press, 2003.

Buber, Martin. "Dialogue," in *Between Man and Man*. London: Kegan Paul, 1947.

Busch, Allison. "Hidden in Plain View: Brajbhasha Poets at the Mughal Court," *Modern Asian Studies* 44(2) (2010): 267–309.

Digby, Simon. "Encounters with Jogis in Indian Sufi Hagiography." Unpublished lecture, School for Oriental and African Studies, 1970.

Digby, Simon. "Medieval Sufi Tales of Jogis and Tales from the Afghan Sultanates in India," in *Wonder Tales of South Asia*. New Delhi: Manohar, 2000, 221–40.

Easwaran, Eknath. *Nonviolent Soldier of Islam : Badshah Khan, a Man to Match His Mountains*. Tomales, CA: Nilgiri Press, 1999.

Eaton, Richard M. "Sufi Folk Literature and the Expansion of Indian Islam." *History of Religions* 14(2) (1974): 117–127.

Eaton, Richard M. *Sufis of Bijapur, 1300–1700: Social Roles of Sufis in Medieval India*. Delhi: Munshiram Manoharlal, 1996 (1978).

Eaton, Richard M. "Approaches to the Study of Conversion to Islam in India," in *Approaches to Islam in Religious Studies*, ed. Richard C. Martin. New York: One World Press, 1987.

Eaton, Richard M. *The Rise of Islam and the Bengal Frontier: 1204–1760*. Berkeley: University of California Press, 1993.

Eaton, Richard M. "Temple Desecration and Indo-Muslim States," in *Essays on Islam and Indian History*. New Delhi: Oxford University Press, 2000.

Eck, Diana. "The Challenge of Pluralism," *Nieman Reports* XLVII(2), 1993 http://pluralism.org/articles/eck_1993_challenge_of_pluralism (accessed May 16, 2012).

Elliot, H. M. and John Dowson. *The History Of India As Told By Its Own Historians*. Delhi: Low Price Publications, 1990 (1867–1877).

Ernst, Carl. "Muslim Studies of Hinduism? A Reconsideration of Arabic and Persian Translations from Indian Languages." *Iranian Studies* 36(2) (2003): 173–195.

Ernst, Carl and Tony K. Stewart. "Syncretism," in *South Asian Folklore*, eds.Peter J. Claus and Margaret Mills. London: Routledge, 2003.

Flueckiger, Joyce Burkhalter. *In Amma's Healing Room: Gender and Vernacular Islam in South India*. Bloomington: Indiana University Press, 2006.

Gilmartin, David. "A Magnificent Gift: Muslim Nationalism and the Election Process in Colonial Punjab," *Comparative Studies in Society and History* 40(3) (1998): 415–436.

Gilmartin, David. "Religious Leadership and the Pakistan Movement in the Punjab," *Modern Asian Studies*, 13(3) (1979): 485–517. Reprinted in *Beyond Turk and Hindu: Rethinking Religious Identities in Islamicate South Asia*, eds. David Gilmartin and Bruce Lawrence. Gainesville: University Press of Florida, 2000.

Gilmartin, David and Bruce Lawrence (eds.). *Beyond Turk and Hindu: Rethinking Religious Identities in Islamicate South Asia*. Gainesville: University Press of Florida, 2000.

Gottschalk, Peter. *Beyond Hindu and Muslim: Multiple Identity in Village Narratives in India*. Oxford: Oxford University Press, 2000.

Green, Nile. *Making Space: Sufis and Settlers in Early Modern India*. New Delhi: Oxford University Press, 2012.

Hassan, Riffat. "The Basis for a Hindu–Muslim Dialogue and Steps in That Direction," in *Muslims in Dialogue: The Evolution of a Dialogue*, ed. Leonard Swidler. Lewiston, NY: Edwin Mellen Press, 1992.

Kakar, Sudhir. *The Colors of Violence: Cultural Identities, Religion, and Conflict*. Chicago: University of Chicago Press, 1996.

Khan, Dominique-Sila. *Conversions and Shifting Identities: Ramdev Pir and the Ismailis in Rajasthan*. New Delhi: Manohar, 1997.

Minault, Gail. *The Khilafat Movement: Religious Symbolism and Political Mobilization in India*. New York: Columbia University Press, 1982.

Mir, Farina. *The Social Space of Language: Vernacular Culture in British Colonial Punjab*. Berkeley: University of California Press, 2010.

Nandy, Ashis, Shikha Trivedy, Shail Mayaram and Achyut Yagnik. *Creating a Nationality: The Ramjanmabhumi Movement and Fear of the Self*. New Delhi: Oxford University Press, 1995.

Oberoi, Harjot. *The Construction of Religious Boundaries: Culture, Identity, and Diversity in the Sikh Tradition*. Chicago: University of Chicago Press, 1994.

Pandey, Gyanendra. *The Construction of Communalism in Colonial North India*. New Delhi: Oxford University Press, 1990.

Pandey, Gyanendra. *Remembering Partition*. Cambridge: Cambridge University Press, 2001.

Roy, Asim. *The Islamic Syncretistic Tradition in Bengal*. Princeton, NJ: Princeton University Press, 1983.

Salomon, Carol. "Baul Songs," in *Religions of India in Practice*, ed. Donald Lopez. Princeton, NJ: Princeton University Press, 1995.

Sikand, Yoginder. "Islamic Mission and Inter-Religious Dialogue in a Minority Context: the Jama'at-i-Islami of India." *Islam and Christian–Muslim Relations* 13(1) (2001): 50–64.

Sikand, Yoginder. *Sacred Spaces: Exploring Traditions of Shared Faith in India*. New Delhi: Penguin India, 2003.

Stewart, Tony. "In Search of Equivalence: Conceiving the Hindu–Muslim Encounter through Translation Theory." *History of Religions* 40(3) (2001): 260–287.

Tambiah, Stanley J. *Leveling Crowds: Ethnonationalist Conflicts and Collective Violence in South Asia.* New Delhi: Vistaar Publications, 1996.

Thapar, Romila. "Communalism and the Historical Legacy: Some Facets." *Social Scientist* 18(6/7) 1990: 4–20.

Thapar, Romila. *Narratives and the Making of History.* New Delhi: Oxford University Press, 2000.

Thapar, Romila. *Somnatha: The Many Voices of a History.* London: Verso, 2005.

Troll, Christian W. (ed.). *Muslim Shrines in India: Their Character, History and Significance.* Delhi: Oxford University Press, 1989.

Uddin, Sufia. *Constructing Bangladesh: Religion, Ethnicity, and Language in an Islamic Nation.* Chapel Hill: University of North Carolina Press, 2006.

Van der Veer, Peter. *Religious Nationalism: Hindus and Muslims in India.* Berkeley: University of California Press, 1994.

Varshney, Ashutosh. *Ethnic Conflict and Civic Life: Hindus and Muslims in India.* New Haven, CT: Yale University Press, 2002.

Virdee, Pippa. "Partition and the Absence of Communal Violence in Malerkotla," in *The Deadly Embrace: Religion, Politics, and Violence in India and Pakistan, 1947–2002,* ed. Ian Talbot. Karachi: Oxford University Press, 2007.

Werbner, Pnina and Helene Basu (eds.). *Embodying Charisma: Modernity, Locality, and Performance of Emotion in Sufi Cults.* London: Routledge, 1998.

Wilkinson, Steven. *Votes and Violence: Electoral Competition and Ethnic Riots in India.* Cambridge: Cambridge University Press, 2004.

Wink, Andre. *Al-Hind: The Making of the Indo-Islamic World,* Vol. I *Early Medieval India and the Expansion of Islam, 7th to 11th Centuries.* Leiden: Brill, 1990.

Wink, Andre. Al-Hind: The Making of the Indo-Islamic World, Vol. II The Slave Kings and the Islamic Conquest, 11th to 13th Centuries. Leiden: Brill, 1990.

CHAPTER 18

Christian–Confucian Dialogue

John Berthrong

Transmitting the Confucian Dao 道: The Chinese Prelude

What follows is a summary introduction to certain features of the historical development of the Confucian Way in China.

While the most common way to describe the history of Confucianism is to break it into three major periods – the classical era (ca. 1700 BCE–221 BCE); neo-Confucianism (Song-Qing, 960–1911); and the modern encounter with the West (ca. 1840 onward) – a more nuanced division recognizes six distinct eras. In order to understand the development of Confucian–Christian Dialogue it will be necessary to examine the various stages of the Confucian Way, and this in turn will help us to better understand the historical complexities of this dialogue. It is not only important to keep in mind, for instance, that the world of the Tang dynasty (618–906) is dramatically different from life in modern Beijing or Shanghai, but also that neo-Confucianism dominated east Asian intellectual life beyond China itself from at least the fourteenth century, and had a major impact of the lives of Korean, Japanese and Vietnamese intellectuals. The following six-fold typology, therefore, challenges the hypothesis that the Confucian tradition has been a perpetually rigid moral formalism of ritual and social domination – a philosophical tradition without transformation after the initial work of Kongzi (Master Kong), or Confucius, and his classical followers.

The first or classical period (ca. 1700–221 BCE) begins with Kongzi; is reshaped by Mencius or Mengzi (Master Meng) (371–289 BCE.); and is concluded by Xunzi (fl. 298–238 BCE). In framing his vision of the Dao, Kongzi relied on a number of early traditions, including historical documents, governmental decrees, poetry and ritual texts that were later given the title "classics." In terms of philosophy, Confucius, Mencius/Mengzi and Xunzi are commemorated as the foundational masters, and in fact they do indeed provide the basic structure for Confucian thought down throughout its long development in East Asia in one form or another.

The Wiley Blackwell Companion to Inter-Religious Dialogue, First Edition. Edited by Catherine Cornille.
© 2013 John Wiley & Sons Ltd. Published 2020 by John Wiley & Sons Ltd.

The great Han dynasty (206 BCE–220 CE) encompasses the second epoch or transformation, which was marked by the formulation of a state-supported imperial Confucian ideology to replace the discredited Legalism of the Qin dynasty (221–209 BCE). This is also the grand era of commentary as the preferred technique for understanding the words and meanings of the sages. In one form or another, this Han mixture of Legalist *realpolitik*, Confucian ethics, and Yin–Yang and Five Phases cosmology dominated the Chinese political, social and intellectual world right up to the end of the imperial state and the founding of the Chinese republic in 1911. Three of the most representative of the Han Confucians were Dong Zongshu (ca. 179–104 BCE), Yang Xiong (53 BCE–18 CE), and Xun Yue (148–209).

The third era (221–907) begins with the Wei-Qin period (220–420 CE) and the revival of a form of elite Daoist speculation called Neo-Daoism or *xuanxue* 玄學, "abstruse learning." Many of the greatest intellectuals of this era, such as the precocious Wang Bi (226–249), mixed their Confucian reflections with Daoist cosmology and metaphysics. Even more momentous during this period was the arrival of Buddhism in China. The Chinese intellectual world was never the same after the impact of the Buddha's *dharma*. Although Confucianism never lost its pride of place in the Chinese state or family, it is accurate to say that the most acute religious, artistic and philosophical mind–hearts in China from the third to the tenth centuries devoted themselves to the appropriation and Chinese transformation of the Buddhist dharma. The rise and flourishing of this great Chinese Buddhist world formed the background for new transformations of the Confucian Way.

The fourth epoch (960–1644) of the development of the Confucian Dao is the justly celebrated revival of Confucian thought known in the West as the neo-Confucianism of the Northern and Southern Song (960–1279). The Song scholars of the neo-Confucian revival invented a new name for their teachings, calling it the Learning of the Way, or *daoxue* 道學. The revival itself began in the Northern Song period and reached its great conclusion with the synthesis of Zhu Xi 朱喜 (1130–1200). Regarding the scope and influence of his work, Zhu has been likened to St. Thomas Aquinas in the West, and there is little doubt that except for Confucius, no one has been more important in defining the course of the Confucian tradition. The most important challenge to Zhu Xi's summation of the Way came during the Ming dynasty in the form of Wang Yangming's 王陽明 (1472–1529) epic struggle to come to terms with Zhu Xi's rationalistic study of principle. Wang held that pattern or coherent principle, the rationale of Dao in human nature, was found in the mind–heart of the sincere student of the Way. He further taught a doctrine of the unity of thought and action based on this understanding of true principle being in the mind–heart.

This grand debate about the nature and the moral cultivation of the mind–heart between the followers of Zhu Xi and Wang Yangming has framed the internal deliberations between Confucians concerning the ordering of the personal, social and even spiritual dimensions of the Confucian Way. These differing neo-Confucian conceptual and moral frameworks are still very much at play as the background for modern Christian–Confucian dialogue. Interestingly, both of the these major forms of neo-Confucian thought have a significant place for the spiritual dimensions of the Confucian Way.

The fifth epoch (1644–1911) of Confucian learning is itself a reaction and transformation of the great neo-Confucian achievement of the fourth phase of the Song and Ming dynasties. The great Qing dynasty scholars, as well as colleagues in Korea and Japan, believed that Confucianism must be of some concrete, practical use for the people, often stressing strict, accurate and empirical historical research. Likewise, they argued that much Song and Ming thought was infected with an unhealthy Buddhist and Daoist love of meditation without proper attention to what ought to be Confucian self-cultivation, namely, the practice of service to self and others in practical ways.

The sixth epoch (1911–) of the Confucian Way is dramatically different from the first five. With the arrival of the expansive and aggressive Western powers, the Confucian tradition, like every other aspect of Chinese culture, was disrupted. This agitation continues today as Chinese intellectuals, along with their Korean, Japanese and Vietnamese colleagues, struggle to come to grips with the interruption of the West and the modern question of "globalization." East Asian Confucian intellectuals have responded to this great challenge from the West by searching for a modern identity for the Confucian Way. This modern movement is called "New Confucianism" in order to distinguish it from the earlier neo-Confucian synthesis.

The First Phases of Confucian–Christian Dialogue

No one really knows when the dialogue between Confucianism and Christianity (hereafter CCD) began. Our earliest reliable records date from the Tang Dynasty (618–906), a period often considered one of most glorious epochs in Chinese history. The first Christian group we can reliably locate in China is the Syriac Church, who are sometimes called "Nestorian," but who called themselves the Church of the East. In China this influential church was given the official name of the Syrian Church in 745 through an imperial edict of the Emperor Zuanzong. It was also known as *Jingjiao* 景教, the Luminous Religion. While the Church of the East has not flourished in later times, it is important to remember that in the Tang period it was far and away the most geographically expansive of Christian churches, extending from modern day Iraq to Tang China, with thriving communities all along the Silk Road. There is a famous semi-official stele erected in 781 CE in Ji'an during the Tang dynasty marking the arrival of the Bishop Alouben (Alopen) in 635 CE.

We have some records of the contact of the Syriac Church of the East in Chinese to accompany the various official and semi-official Chinese memorials and stele. Martin Palmer (2001) has edited and produced a contemporary translation of what he calls the Jesus Sutras. He makes the very excited claim that these texts represent a form of Daoist Christianity. Other scholars dispute Palmer's enthusiasm for connecting the Church of the East with the flourishing Daoist religions of the Tang period. Most scholars, while not discounting Daoist influence, believe that we can see Buddhist influence on the language of these texts much more readily than Daoist inspiration. Be this as it may, it is clear that the texts of the Church of the East (East Syriac Christianity) mark a moment of significant intercultural exchange, as evidenced by the use of classical Chinese to describe this Syriac Christian church. Hence, there was a well-defined exchange going on among Christians, Buddhists, Daoists – and, no doubt, Confucians.

It is important to remember that in the Tang period any educated person, including learned Buddhist and Daoist scholar-monks, would know their Confucianism as well as their own Buddhist and Daoist teachings. There was never such a strict separation of philosophical and religious traditions in China as there was in West Asia. Later in the Ming period, though Christians were not included, there was even a strong movement claiming *sanjiao heyi* 三教 合一, namely, that the three religions of Buddhism, Daoism and Confucianism were one. The Luminous Religion, which by the late Ming period had disappeared from China, never joined the three great religio-ethical traditions of China as part of the club.

The story does not end with even this very important record of the life of the Luminous Religion and its relation to the Chinese state, but extends into the complex and interconnected world of religion in Tang. The Tang period has often been considered the high point of Buddhist influence in China. It was also the time of massive translation projects. In 782 the famous Central Asian missionary Prajña reached the Chinese capital to join a major translation project taking place there (Moffett 1998–2005: 1, 298–302), and was joined by a "Persian" (Syriac) priest named Adam to work with the various Buddhist languages of the time. Adam, as a Syriac Christian, seems to have been a scholar with command of all the relevant languages, including literary Chinese, and Prajña and Adam worked on at least seven volumes together. Moreover, and although we have no complete proof, the great Japanese pilgrim monk Kukai, founder of the Japanese Shingon tradition, took back with him one of the translations of Prajña and Adam. So this early Christian participation in the open world of Chinese religion might have even helped the seeds of the Buddha dharma flourish in Japan.

The disappearance of the Luminous Religion from China remains a mystery, but it is clear that by the time of the rise of the Song dynasty and the great neo-Confucian revival, it had disappeared. Moffett speculates, probably for sound reasons, that since both the Church of the East and the Zoroastrians were caught in the great 845 persecution of Buddhism, they too suffered so much that they never recovered from the blow. As Moffett notes, later Protestant scholars such as James Legge argued that the demise of the Church of the East could also be linked to its too easy accommodation to the powerful gravitational pull of sinification. Not being as robust as Buddhism, and caught up in the various civil wars and persecutions of the late Tang period, the Church of the East disappeared from the Chinese scene until the Jesuit missionaries discovered that there had once been a recognized Christian church in Tang China.

The second, much better documented phase of CCD was the Roman Catholic mission to China, beginning at the end of the Ming period (sixteenth century) and extending until the demise of the mission caused by the Rites Controversy in the seventeenth and eighteenth centuries. But for a number of centuries this was a vibrant encounter between Confucians, ordinary Chinese people, and the learned scholar-missionaries of the Jesuit order. Other missionary orders, such as the Dominicans and Franciscans were also interested in the China mission. But, unlike the Jesuits, who learned to appreciate their conversations with the Confucians, most of the members of the other orders took a different approach. They were almost completely committed to primary evangelism and apologetics aimed at the conversion of the Chinese people. Dialogue in anything resembling the modern understanding of the term as respectful conversation was not part of their vision. It was also partly a battle between these orders and the Jesuits that led to the disastrous unfolding of the Rites Controversy and the expulsion of almost all Catholic missionaries from China in the eighteenth century. This is an often-told story and we do not need to rehearse the details. For the Dominican side of the story see Menegon (2010). For a general description of the Jesuit mission and the Rites Controversy (1636–1742) see Moffett (2005 II, 105–142). For a good general history of this exchange see Mungello (2009).

It is also a story that has been often repeated in modern scholarly discussion, and many of the issues that perplexed the early Jesuit dialogues with Confucians have remained a staple of the ongoing CCD over the centuries. We will return to a number of these dialogical points when we discuss the emergence of contemporary CCD in the twentieth and twenty-first centuries. For the moment we will explore some of the less well-known episodes of CCD from the sixteenth to the eighteenth centuries. One of the most interesting of these interlocking encounters is chronicled in Mungello's *Curious Land* (1985). This work is not only a learned account of CCD from Ricci to Le Comte and Le Gobien, it also discusses how knowledge of Confucianism became a part of European intellectual debates. It demonstrates that even in this early modern period, CCD was a two-way street.

Mungello's metaphor for the Jesuit approach is that of accommodation. Along with the theological charge of Jesuit accommodation to Confucian *theoria*, and with Jesuit adherence to Chinese cultural expressions such as *li* 禮 (rites, ritual or personal and social civility), there was an even broader attempt, as European intellectuals learned more about Confucianism, to find both philosophical and religious accommodation between Europe and China, including a search for a universal language in Kircher's famous *China illustrata* (Mungello 1985). It is actually rather easy to see how these European scholars would be fascinated by the nature of the written Chinese language: could it be an example of a universal language?

It was at this point that Leibniz (Cook and Rosemont 1994) entered the discussion on Chinese language and philosophy. As Leibniz searched for elements of universal signification as the basis of human thought, the early accounts of the Chinese language and philosophy intrigued the great German philosopher. Mungello provides a fascinating account of how Leibniz interrogated his Jesuit sources of Chinese wisdom. This kind of trail did not end with Leibniz, but continued on with the work of Couplet and Bouvet. Each of these Jesuits followed Ricci's attempt to find an accommodation between Confucianism and Christian theology.

A later example of CCD summarizes the Jesuit desire to find accommodation. James Legge (1815–1897), the Victorian English translator of a vast collection of Confucian texts chose to call the Confucian texts (the Chinese *jing* 經) "Classics." He selected classic (rather than scripture) for a dialogical reason, since in so doing, they could be treated in the same fashion as the Greco-Roman canon. That is, while not revealed scripture, they are still works that could be read for profit by Christians. To translate jing as "scripture," would signal that the texts in question were religious in nature and in need of complete refutation.

But to return now to Leibniz and Wolff's (neither of whom ever visited China) work on understanding Confucian thought, it is clear that both German scholars favored the Jesuit approach (Ching and Oxtoby 1992a, b). For instance, addressing the central problems involved in what became the great Rites Controversy, Leibniz sided with Ricci in believing that, for the best-educated Confucians, Confucian rites were civil and not religious in nature. Therefore Leibniz saw no reason for the Confucians to reject ancestor veneration. This actually made a great deal of sense given Leibniz's desire to seek religious and political accommodation wherever possible. He dreamed of a time when the theological divides of Europe could be dealt with in a civilized and ecumenically tolerant manner. Hence it is also not surprising that Leibniz would likewise be inclined to charity in his readings about and estimation of Confucianism.

What is truly fascinating is how well Leibniz was able to reason out what the neo-Confucian philosophical position actually was. Contrary, for instance, to Longobardi, who thought that the classical Confucians and neo-Confucians were materialists and atheists, Leibniz held what we now realize is a much more nuanced and sophisticated interpretation. Many of the Jesuits considered that the classical Confucians retained at least a vestigial understanding of the divine reality via the Shang and Zhou doctrines of *shangdi* 上帝 and *tian* 天. This was a form of Confucian wisdom about supernal matters that (unfortunately, from the Jesuit position) waned over time. In fact, we know that some of the most famous of the elite Christian converts made by the Jesuits were impressed with how the Jesuit fathers helped them to reconstruct the theistic import of some the early Confucian classics.

Leibniz wrote:

I would think that many philosophers from the Orient, no less than the Platonists and Stoics, regarded God as the World-soul or as the universal nature immanent in things; that other spirits also assumed bodies; and that some even considered the soul as a divine particle of the divine aura, which would return to the Ocean of souls with the body's death. (Cook and Rosemont 1994: 72)

While this is not the way Confucians would normally deal with such matters, it would not be impossible to find analogies to the Leibnizian train of thought in neo-Confucian writings. Moreover, as we shall see, many of these questions of divine–world relations have become a perennial aspect of CCD.

What is even more fascinating is how well Leibniz actually deduces the neo-Confucian interpretation of what he calls spiritual substances. We must remember here that Leibniz is working from materials sent to him by the Jesuits, and they often held that the neo-Confucians were atheistic materialists. Leibniz wrote: "Initially, one may doubt whether the Chinese recognize, or have recognized, spiritual substances. But after thinking hard about it, I judge that they did, although perhaps they did not recognize these substances as separate, that is, existing quite apart from matter" (Ching and Oxtoby 1992a: 87ff). Leibniz then goes on to give an account of how he understands the neo-Confucian philosophical discussion of the *li–qi* 理氣 dyad, no doubt the signature cosmological and axiological theory driving conceptual debate in the neo-Confucian world of discourse. *Li* is often translated as pattern, order, cosmic principle, or coherent principle, and *qi* (which almost defies translation into even multiple English terms) as vital energy or configurational force in terms of the neo-Confucian philosophical debates. Leibniz seems to have almost intuitively understood the importance and profundity of the neo-Confucian debate that swirled for centuries (and continues today) around the correct understanding of the li–qi dyad. This attitude of imaginative generosity is precisely what strikes a modern reader about the genius of Leibniz's perceptive interpretation of Zhu Xi's neo-Confucian synthesis. Perhaps because of his detachment from the China mission itself, he was able to more dispassionately analyze the neo-Confucian worldview of Zhu Xi. It is probably not an exaggeration to state that no European thinker gave his readers a better or more sophisticated reading of the Confucian and neo-Confucian philosophical world than did Leibniz, until well into the twentieth century. It took hundreds of years for European scholars to catch up with Leibniz's brilliant engagement with the Confucians of Ming-Qing China.

While it is now clear that the general early modern European enthusiasm for Confucianism waned by the turn of the nineteenth century, as witnessed by the negative opinions of great philosophers such as Kant and Hegel, in the early part of the eighteenth century, Christian Wolff continued the work of Leibniz in two fascinating short essays, *Discourse on the Practical Philosophy of the Chinese* (1721–1726), and *On the Philosopher King and Ruling Philosopher*. As Wolff explained, these two texts caused him a number of problems in the republic of letters of his day. What Wolff took to be the just appreciation of Confucian philosophy did not sit well with more conservative Protestant and Roman Catholic thinkers.

Whereas Leibniz was especially famous for his interpretation of the philosophy and philosophical theology of the Confucians and neo-Confucians, Wolff chose to write about the practical and ethical aspects of the Confucian Way. In this regard Wolff demonstrated as much foresight as his older colleague Leibniz (Ching and Oxtoby 1992a, b). Whatever else Confucianism may be, it is certainly a form of personal and social ethics as well as an extended reflection on statecraft. In Chinese this is summarized by the formula of *neisheng waiwang* 內聖 外王, or the sage within, the king without. This means that an authentic Confucian must cultivate the sagely mind–heart as a person and share this learning with the larger social world. As Wolff noted, this meant that ultimately there should be a conjunction of the philosopher and the ruler, the dream of the philosopher king that was as old in the European tradition as it was in the Confucian Way.

The Modern Renewal of Confucian–Christian Dialogue

Many of these earlier themes are still very much at play in contemporary Christian–Confucian exchange. The story, drawn from the author's personal experience, of the beginning of contemporary ecumenical CCD is intriguing. During the 1980s there were a series of international Buddhist–Christian dialogues held at the University of Hawai'i. At one of the early meetings, a question was raised about why east Asian Buddhism, while obviously socially active in many settings, did not seem to play a major role in the governance of China, nor did it have sophisticated plans for the improvement of society as whole. It was explained that, for the most part, there was a division of such intellectual, social and educational labor in imperial China from the Tang dynasty to the end of the Qing dynasty in 1911. It was the Confucians who were in charge of local and national education, family life, ritual, and the staffing of the imperial civil service. In fact it was a well-known fact that Confucianism has functioned as the official state ideology of the Chinese empire ever since the Han dynasty. So if one wanted to ask certain kinds of questions about the relationship of Buddhism to Chinese society and culture on both macro and micro levels, the Confucians needed to be encouraged to enter into dialogue.

As it turns out, this was a timely discussion because, by the late 1980s and early 1990s, Confucianism, like Buddhism and Daoism, was undergoing a revival in the People's Republic of China. Confucianism was already a lively participant in the debates over the modernization of South Korea, Japan, Hong Kong, and Singapore, but now it was also feasible to invite colleagues from the PRC to join the conversation. The outcome of the early discussions in Hawai'i in the mid-1980s led to two international Confucian–Christian Dialogues held in Hong Kong in 1988 and Berkeley in 1991 (Lee 1991; Berthrong 1994). These two meetings, and the dialogues that flowed from them, represent the revival and now flourishing of CCD in the modern world.

The published papers from the 1988 meeting in Hong Kong establish, first, that there always needs to be an awareness of the changing historical dynamics between Confucians and Christians. As we saw, the early dialogues were conducted during a period of great strength on the Chinese side. This changes dramatically in the nineteenth century, when China came under persistent attack by Western imperial powers. The situation was so dire that the Chinese often consider the period between the first Opium War (ca. 1839–42) and the victory of the Chinese Communist Party and the founding of the People's Republic of China in 1949 as a semi-colonial period. It was only in 1949 that, as Mao said, the Chinese people stood up, and have ever since moved to reclaim China's place as a great world power and culture. Moreover it is important to remember that all religions and traditional forms of Chinese culture suffered greatly in the period from 1949 to the dramatic transformation of China's approach to the world in the 1980s. Both Confucianism and Christianity suffered grievous harm during the infamous Cultural Revolution. Both have also risen like the phoenix from the ashes of twentieth century turmoil to renew the dialogue.

Along with a robust interest in historical reflections – and one would expect this from two of the world's religio-ethical traditions most concerned with history per se – three other linked sets of theological themes emerged in 1988, and these have reappeared in all the subsequent CCD. The first theme is the nature of what Christians would call God–World relations, and Confucians would often name as reflections on human beings *ren* 人 and *tian* 天 or the *dao* 道. This, of course, has its Confucian counterpart in Confucian discussions of the relations of *tian* 天, *di* 地, and *ren* 人 – often translated as heaven (the supernal), earth, and humanity. Of course, these dialogues focused primarily on how differently Christians and Confucians understand these terms. For instance, it is never clear that "Heaven" is really a good translation of tian, depending on the Confucian context.

The second cluster of questions related to ethics, both personal and social, and the issues of lived human experience in the world. This clearly was a set of topics that was and is near and dear to the Confucians. Whatever else Confucianism has been deemed to be over its long history, no one has ever doubted its ethical convictions and praxis. Confucians for more than 2500 years have asked the question about how we are to conduct ourselves in relation to other people, society, the state, the environment, and the world at large. If Confucianism has spiritual or religious dimensions, they are all tinged with an unquenchable commitment to proper human relations and forms of conduct. The last of the great classical Confucians, Xunzi, always stressed that we need to understand and practice *yili* 義禮, or appropriate ritual and civility. While Xunzi quarreled with the Second Sage of the Confucian Way, Mengzi/Mencius, they were both committed to the embodiment of *ren* 仁 (humanity) as the cardinal Confucian virtue. And as Kongzi/Confucius taught, virtue always has a neighbor (*Analects* 4.25). Our first neighbors, if you like, are our families and hence our ethical self-cultivation and social realization always begins with *xiao* 孝, filial piety, or, as some modern translators put it, family reverence.

The third set of themes has to do with the relationship of the natural world and human society. While Confucians have traditionally focused their attention on issues of statecraft, contemporary ethical thought includes questions of science, technology, modernization, and globalization. For instance, the New Confucians have become, as has been the case for so many other religious communities, interested in ecology (Tucker and Berthrong 1998). Here, again, the authors address a range of issues, from the nature of the cosmological context of ecological thought, to more practical-historical questions, such as how Confucian ecological insights have been applied or misapplied over the centuries.

In terms of the spiritual dimension of the Confucian Way, one of the most commonly quoted passages from the Northern Song is Zhang Zai's (1020–1077) "Western Inscription" (de Bary et al. 1999: 1, 683–684):

> Heaven is my father and Earth is my mother, and even such a small creature as I finds an intimate place in their midst. Therefore that which extends throughout the universe I regard as my body and that which directs the universe I consider my mind. All people are my brothers and sisters, and all things are my companions. . . . In life I follow and serve [Heaven and Earth]. In death I will be at peace.

New Confucians and most other Chinese intellectuals take this to be both a profound statement of an ecological cosmology, and an equally rich reaffirmation of Confucian social ethics. It is also reminiscent of Kongzi's reflection that, if he could hear the Dao in the morning, he could die at peace in the evening.

A further perennial issue of CCD encounters is the question regarding the religious nature of the Confucian Way. There is clearly no consensus on this question. As Wilfred Cantwell Smith (1991: 69) wrote decades ago ". . . we may simply observe once again that the question, 'Is Confucianism a religion?' is one that the West has never been able to answer, and China never able to ask." But now scholars on both sides of the Pacific are asking this question and also exploring the case that can be made for or against assigning other Western religio-philosophical labels to Confucian discourse. For instance, no one has ever doubted that Confucianism is a form of personal and social ethics. And going another step into the discussion, many scholars would argue that Confucianism is a form of virtue ethics. But is it a religion? (Richey 2008; Tu and Tucker 2003–2004).

Tu Wei-ming, a renowned New Confucian scholar and public intellectual, and a participant in many CCDs over the last three decades, has provided a very important definition of what it means to be religious in a Confucian modality (Tu 1989). As Tu has argued, rather than trying to define Confucianism as a religion, it is better to ask: what does being religious mean for a Confucian?

> Being religious, in the Confucian perspective, informed by sacred texts such as the *Zhongyong*, means being engaged in the process of learning to be fully human. We can define the Confucian way of being religious as *ultimate self-transformation as a communal act and as a faithful dialogical response to the transcendent"* (Tu 1989: 94).

Frederick Streng (1985: 2) provides a definition of religion that is broad enough to include the religious dimensions of the Confucian Way as defined by Tu. Streng writes:

> The definition of religion . . . focuses on the role of *processes of change* through which people bring into their lives what they consider life's highest values. In this analysis of religious life, our formal definition is as follows: Religion is a *means to ultimate transformation* [italics in original].

As a student of Buddhism involved in interfaith dialogue, Streng's definition is supple enough to encompass both Buddhism and Confucianism, especially if we provisionally accept Tu's definition. In the Confucian case, the ultimate transformation is that of the self in conforming to the Dao, by becoming fully human. As with so many Confucian thinkers, Tu retains a sense of Confucian spirituality in tune with the insight of his great teacher Mou Zongsan (1909–1995), who called Confucianism a religion of immanent transcendence.

Actually, a number of scholars, including Tu Weiming, Rodney Taylor, Julia Ching, Peng Guoxiang, Robert Neville and John Berthrong, have tried to nuance this discussion of the religious nature of Confucianism. Clearly if we use a West Asian definition of religion, a definition that would have to assume a notion of God as a personal (and usually a transcendent one at that) and intentional force in the universe, Confucianism never seems to come into focus as a religious tradition. There is just too much immanence, and too much focus on the human, even if the human should conform human nature to *tiandao* 天道, the Way of Heaven. The revised definition includes the hypotheses that there are "religious dimensions" to the Confucian Way even if we do not want to define it as a religion in the West Asian sense of the term. What this means is that for many Confucians the *Rudao* 儒道, the Confucian Way, has spiritual elements, traits, teachings and dimensions, but also that one can be a perfectly good Confucian, that is, one can be devoted to the teachings of the First Sage and the Confucian classics, without being overly concerned about the spiritual dimensions of the tradition. Hence it would never have occurred to someone like the great neo-Confucian Zhu Xi to place a Confucian astronomer, who had no interest whatsoever in spiritual self-cultivation, outside of the tradition. What this comes down to is that the religious dimensions or contours of the Confucian Way are different from west Asian religious prototypes.

Discussion of all three themes – (1) God–World relations, (2) ethics and self-cultivation, and (3) the natural and social world – have been prominent in various formal dialogues, such as those taking place in Hong Kong in 1988, Berkeley in 1991, and more recently, Nishan Forum, Shandong, 2010. One of the most interesting ongoing discussions revolves around the question of God–World relations. While this may seem a topic more germane to the Christian partners in the exchange, it is often raised by the Confucians for reasons internal to the structure of Confucian philosophy and religious sensibilities. Confucians often have the impression, warranted in some respects for segments of the Christian theological world, that Christians hold a doctrine of God's complete transcendence of the world. This is understood as meaning that although the world depends utterly on God for its creation, flourishing and ultimate salvation, God in no way depends on the world. This is a very strong version of *creatio ex nihilo* in which God creates the world, but the world does not actually mutually influence the divine reality. Confucians note that this is not how they understand the religious dimensions of their tradition. Building on the immense philosophical and religious thought of foundational New Confucian scholars such as Tang Junyi (1909–1978) and Mou Zongsan (1909–1995), Confucians defend what they call immanent transcendence or transcendent immanence.

Current Confucians participating in CCD, such as Tu Weiming or Liu Shuxian, follow the line of reasoning of both Tang and Mou in terms of immanent transcendence – and many Christian scholars such a Julia Ching, Peter K. H. Lee, Philip Shen and Chung Chai Sik, would agree with this assessment of the Confucian religious sensibility. Even Xunzi had a deeply spiritual side, but one focused on the human domain for the triad of *tian* – heaven, *di* – earth, and *ren* – humanity. In terms of the development of CCD, it is important to remember what an important role the great early New Confucians play as teachers for the new generations. For instance, Tang and Mou (and others as well) were very clear in recognizing the religious dimensions of Confucianism, and this, although not unique in the history of Confucianism, was highly significant for many New Confucians in terms of their engagement with other cultures and religious traditions. So, along with more general kinds of intercultural dialogue, it makes internal sense to New Confucians to engage in CCD. As the *Zhongyong* taught so long ago, tian, di, and ren form a union wherein each element must play its role for the betterment of all. It is often called the Confucian doctrine of co-creativity.

It is at this point that the discussion becomes a dialogue, because many Christian theologians have attempted to explain that not all Christians hold such an extreme view of divine transcendence as Confucians take to be the case. For instance, the doctrine of the incarnation and of the *imago dei* in every human being can be taken to express the immanent dimension of God for Christians. While it is no doubt true that Confucians do hold a stronger theory of immanence than do many Christians, the divide is not as stark as some Confucians have come to believe.

In fact it is equally difficult for Confucians to explain to Christians just what the Confucian sense of transcendence really means and how it can be expressed, without any dominant doctrine of God per se in the Confucian tradition. For instance, Tu Weiming has written extensively about the religious dimensions of Confucian humanism. Tu points out that humanism can be restrictive or inclusive in scope. Confucian humanism is deemed inclusive rather than restrictive because it is open to all forms of human experience, be it empirical, rational, ethically normative, spiritual or even transcendent. The restrictive form of humanism, as understood by contemporary Confucians, denies any reference to a religious or spiritual dimension to human existence. Rather, Tu, here building on the insights of his teachers such as Tang and Mou, and concurring with colleagues such as Liu Shuxian, rather prefers to understand Confucian humanism as inclusive not only of the human and natural orders, but also of a spiritual dimension.

Roger Ames (2011: 69–71) has offered an interesting discussion of the spiritual dimensions of the Confucian Way. He argues that Confucian spirituality results from the tremendous sense of reciprocity that arises from the foundational elements of the correlative classical Confucian cosmology, a cosmological vision that continues to inform the entire Confucian tradition. It is this sense of interdependent reciprocity that gives Confucianism its spiritual goals. Every exemplary person, a worthy or sage, inherits achievements from the past and passes on new achievements to future generations. As Ames puts it, the sense of correlative reciprocity gives rise to a spiritual sense that is based on the interdependence and reciprocity of human beings as creatures embedded in the vast dynamic matrix of the ever-creative Dao. So there is never a sense of final discreteness about the Confucian cosmos. It configures and reconfigures itself without end, and each one of us, as Zhang Zai wrote in the "Western Inscription," finds our place in it. Sometimes this sense of spirituality is as simple as recognizing the difference between what is and what ought to be, the right from the wrong, and is expanded to that sense of spiritual insight that allowed Kongzi to hear the Dao in the morning and die at peace in the evening, or Zhang Zai to follow heaven and earth and die at peace – a peace with profound spiritual vitality.

In recent CCD exchanges, the distinction between religion and spirituality has also become a topic for discussion. In Chinese the term for religion is relatively modern, *zongjiao* 宗教, and usages for spirituality build on the equally venerable term *shen* 神, a word that has always meant the spirits and the spirit alike. The terms spiritual and spirituality provide useful designations, perhaps because they are such wonderfully vague general terms, for an analysis of the New Confucianism which has emerged in China in the last two decades and which, in various forms, has also flourished throughout East Asia, and even as Boston Confucianism. (The term was coined by Robert Neville and arose, in part, because of his three-decade-long engagement in CCD. See Berthrong 1994; (Chinese revised edition 2006) and Neville 2000, 2008).

Sadly not all goes smoothly in contemporary CCD. A stark example has arisen in the case of Christians from a small town very close to Qufu who sought permission to build a new church to serve the local Christian community. The whole question of the design of such a large structure near the old Confucian Temple and graveyard raised the ire and concern of many local and national Confucian scholars and spokespersons. The

Qufu Church controversy, as it has now been come to be known on the Internet, will provide yet another chapter in CCD now and into the future. A simple Google search just in English brings up a range of sites commenting, pro and con, on the debate about the proposed new Christian church.

In closing we should also note the founding of the Nishan Forum on World Civilization. It is a gathering co-sponsored by various agencies of the Chinese national and provincial governments, and by a diverse group of academic institutions. The statement of the objectives for the first Nishan Forum held in Nishan, Shandong Province, in the birthplace of Kongzi, spells out what the organizers hoped to achieve in this large example of formal CCD.

> As an international cultural and academic exchange event, *Nishan Forum on World Civilizations* (the "Nishan Forum") is to be held in Nishan, birthplace of Confucius, the great ancient Chinese thinker and educator. With the theme of carrying out dialogues among world civilizations, the forum aims to promote the Chinese culture, cultural exchanges between China and the rest of the world and to build a harmonious world. It is academic, non-governmental, international and open.

What was striking at the opening plenary of the Nishan Forum was a short speech by a senior government official wherein, for the first time in a public forum, the speaker called for a dialogue between Confucianism, which was labeled a form of spirituality, with representatives of the Christian churches. The aim was to promote dialogue between religions as an important component of the ongoing dialogue among civilizations. Considering the intensely anti-religious convulsions of the Chinese Cultural Revolution of the 1960s and 1970s, the transformation was dramatic, and the explicit call for such a CCD was most welcomed. At the end of the forum, all members, Confucian, Christian and non-religious, signed the following *Declaration of Harmony* which states in part:

> Troubled over the present state of world affairs;
> Anxious about our common human future; . . .
> We advocate harmony;
> We advocate loving-kindness;
> We advocate tolerance;
> We advocate decorum and civility;
> We advocate faithfulness and reliability;
> We advocate "never doing to others what you would not have done to yourself";
> We advocate "loving all creatures as we would love ourselves" and "the unity of Heaven and humanity";
> We advocate the principle that "while we enjoy the beauty of our own culture, we also appreciate the beauty of other civilizations";
> We advocate the belief that within the four seas, all people are brothers and sisters;
> We advocate for a harmonious world and for the principle of "harmony with diversity". . . .
> We appeal for solidarity and collaboration to build our future together.
> We hope and pray that –

Our advocacies and appeals will be echoed and embraced by the entire world.
We hope and pray that –
Our advocacies and appeals will be transformed into common practices for all human beings.

The Confucian tone and sentiments are obvious, just as it is equally clear that such a document could never have happened without the patient work of CCD in the traditional and modern world. The declaration alludes to profound religious and spiritual convictions, a call for finding peace in the world, and, beyond the human realm, a healing of our shared and common world. In many ways the First Nishan Forum's contemporary declaration expresses the perceived commonalities affirmed by Confucians and Christians in modern CCD. Moreover, it states a hope for what might be achieved by such ongoing CCD. In a world so transfixed by what seem like endless and horrific conflicts, the dream of respectful dialogues based on harmony and mutual learning is an aspiration well worth embracing.

Bibliography

Ames, Roger T. *Confucian Role Ethics: A Vocabulary*. Hong Kong: Chinese University of Hong Kong Press, 2011.

Berthrong, John H. *All Under Heaven: Transforming Paradigms in Confucian–Christian Dialogue*. Albany: State University of New York Press, 1994. *Pu tian zhi xia* 普天之下: *Ru Yeh dui hua zhong de tianfan zhuanhua* 儒耶對話中得典范轉化. Revised and Expanded Edition of *All Under Heaven* (1994). Translated and edited by Peng Guoxiang 彭國翔 for Hebei: Renmin Chupanshe 河北: 河北人民出版社, 2006.

Berthrong, John H. *Concerning Creativity: A Comparison of Chu Hsi, Whitehead, and Neville*. Albany, NY: State University of New York Press, 1998.

Berthrong, John H. "Boston Confucianism: The Third Wave of Global Confucianism," in *Confucianism in Dialogue Today: West, Christianity and Judaism*, eds. Liu Shu-Hsien, John Berthrong and Leonard Swidler. Philadelphia: Ecumenical Press, 2004.

Berthrong, John H. *Expanding Process: Exploring Philosophical and Theological Transformations in China and the West*. Albany: State University of New York Press 2008.

Ching, Julia, and Willard Oxtoby (eds.). *Discovering China: European Interpretations in the Enlightenment*. Rochester, NH: University of Rochester Press, 1992a.

Ching, Julia, and Willard Oxtoby (eds.). *Moral Enlightenment: Leibniz and Wolff on China*. Nettetal: Steyler Verlag, 1992b.

Collins, Randall. *The Sociology of Philosophies: A Global Theory of Intellectual Change*. Cambridge: Harvard University Press, 1998.

Cook, Daniel J. and Henry Rosemont, Jr. (trans. and intro.). *Gottfried Wilhelm Leibniz: Writings on China*. La Salle, IL: Open Court, 1994.

Cornille, Catherine. *The Im-possibility of Inter-religious Dialogue*. New York: The Crossroad Publishing Company, 2008.

de Bary, W. Theodore, Irene Bloom and Richard Lufrano (eds.). *Sources of Chinese Tradition*. 2 Vols, 2nd edn. New York: Columbia University Press, 1999–2000.

Elvin, Mark. *The Retreat of the Elephant: An Environmental History of China*. New Haven, CT: Yale University Press, 2004.

Foltz, Richard. *Religions of the Silk Road: Premodern Patterns of Globalization*. Basingstoke: Palgrave Macmillan, 2010.

Hansen, Valerie. *The Open Empire: A History of China to 1600*. New York: W. W. Norton, 2000.

Iorio, Dominick A. *Nicolas Malenbranche: Dialogue Between a Christian Philosopher and a Chinese Philosopher on the Existence and Nature of God*. Washington, DC: University Press of America, 1980.

Jenkins, John Philip. *The Lost History of Christianity*. New York: HarperOne, 2008.

Lach, Donald F. (trans. and ed.). *The Preface to Leibniz's Novissima Sinica*. Honolulu: University of Hawaii Press, 1957.

Lach, Donald F. *Asia in the Making of Europe*. 3 Vols. Chicago: University of Chicago Press, 1965.

Lee, Peter K. H. (ed.). *Confucian–Christian Encounters in Historical and Contemporary Perspective*. Lewiston, NY: The Edwin Mellen Press, 1991.

Menegon, Eugenio. *Ancestors, Virgins, and Friars: Christianity as a Local Religion in Late Imperial China*. Cambridge, MA: Harvard University Asia Center, 2010.

Moffett, Samuel Hugh. *A History of Christianity in Asia*. Vol. I, *Beginnings to 1500*; Vol. II: *1500–1900*. Maryknoll, NY: Orbis Books, 1998–2005.

Mote, Frederick W. *Imperial China 900–1800*. Cambridge, MA: Harvard University Press, 1999.

Mungello, David E. *Leibniz and Confucianism: The Search for Accord*. Honolulu: The University of Hawaii Press, 1977.

Mungello, David E. *Curious Land: Jesuit Accommodation and the Origins of Sinology*. Stuttgart: Franz Steiner Verlag, 1985.

Mungello, David E. *The Great Encounter of China and the West, 1500–1800*, 3rd edn. Lanham, MD: Rowman & Littlefield, 2009.

Neville, Robert C. *Boston Confucianism: Portable Tradition in the Late-Modern World*. Albany: State University of New York Press, 2000.

Neville, Robert C. *Ritual and Deference: Extending Chinese Philosophy in a Comparative Context*. Albany: State University of New York Press, 2008.

Palmer, Martin. *The Jesus Sutras: Rediscovering the Lost Scrolls of Taoist Christianity*. New York: Ballantine Wellspring, 2001.

Richey, Jeffery (ed.). *Teaching Confucianism*. Oxford: Oxford University Press, 2008.

Smith, Wilfred Cantwell. *The Meaning and End of Religion*. Minneapolis: Fortress Press, 1991.

Streng, Frederick. *Understanding Religious Life*, 3rd edn. Belmont, CA: Wadsworth, 1985.

Tu, Wei-ming (Du Weiming). *Humanity and Self-Cultivation: Essays in Confucian Thought*. Berkeley, CA: Asian Humanities Press, 1979.

Tu, Wei-ming (Du Weiming). *Confucian Thought: Self-hood as Creative Transformation*. Albany: State University of New York Press, 1985.

Tu, Wei-ming (Du Weiming). *Centrality and Commonality: An Essay on Confucian Religiousness*. Albany: State University of New York Press, 1989.

Tu, Weiming and Mary Evelyn Tucker (eds.). *Confucian Spirituality*. 2 Vols. New York: The Crossroad Publishing Company, 2003–04.

Tucker, Mary Evelyn and John Berthrong (eds.). *Confucianism and Ecology: The Interrelation of Heaven, Earth, and Humans*. Cambridge, MA: Harvard University Press, 1998.

Winkler, Dietmar W. and Li Tang (eds.). *Hidden Treasures and Intercultural Encounters: Studies on East Syriac Christianity in China and Central Asia*. New Brunswick, NJ: Transaction Publishers, 2009.

Yang, Fenggang and Joseph Tammey (eds.). *Confucianism and Spiritual Transformation in Modern China and Beyond*. Leiden: Brill, 2012.

CHAPTER 19

Dialogue between Islam and African Religions

John Azumah

The encounters between the Islamic and indigenous African religions need much more careful analysis than they have hitherto received. Explorations of the encounters between these traditions have been vitiated by a number of factors. These include the fact that discourse about the encounters has been carried out in the shadow of Western Christian missionary and colonial encounters with traditional African religions. The resultant received wisdom has been that Islam has been more sympathetic and accommodating to traditional African religions and culture than its Christian rivals. Another prevailing assumption of previous scholarship has been that the incoming traditions of Islam and Christianity have functioned as the main determinant agents in religious change in Africa, according traditional religions the position of passive recipients. In the specific case of Islam, another crucial factor is that many observers simply wrote as if there is one monolithic phenomenon called "Islam" interacting with traditional African religions.

The comparative–competitive approach to understanding Islamic–African religious encounters had its most eloquent proponent in E.W. Blyden (d. 1912). A Presbyterian African-American educationist, Blyden became quite understandably critical of the Christian tradition as it had been used to undermine African traditional religions and cultures, sowing the seeds of an inferiority complex in the African psyche. Looking at the psychological and physical effects of colonialism and the slave trade on the traditional African heritage and psyche, Blyden makes a strong point in his assessment of the effects of Western Christian legacy in Africa and on Africans. This is the more so when viewed against the background from which Blyden wrote, a time when colonialism and a white superiority complex were the order of the day. Against that backdrop, Blyden contrasted the effects of the Western–Christian legacy in Africa – which, he argued, had instilled servility, docility and dependence in the African in order to perpetuate white domination – against that of the Arab-Islamic tradition. The effects of Arab–Islam upon the African, he argued, inspired new "spiritual feelings to which they

The Wiley Blackwell Companion to Inter-Religious Dialogue, First Edition. Edited by Catherine Cornille.
© 2013 John Wiley & Sons Ltd. Published 2020 by John Wiley & Sons Ltd.

had before been utter strangers" and "strengthened and hastened certain tendencies to independence and self-reliance which were already at work." Blyden contends further that where Islam came into contact with Africa:

> Local institutions were not destroyed by the Arab influence introduced. They only assumed new forms, and adapted themselves to the new teachings. In all thriving Mohammedan communities, in West and Central Africa, it may be noticed that the Arab superstructure has been superimposed on a permanent indigenous substructure; so that what took place, when the Arab met the Negro in his own home, was a healthy amalgamation, and not an absorption or undue repression. (Blyden 1967 [first edition 1887]: 11–12)

A good number of Western and African scholars have made similar claims on behalf of Islam. Writing on the coincidences and convergences between Islam and traditional African religions, I.M. Lewis characterizes Muslim theology as "tolerant in its attitude towards divination, magic, witchcraft, and sorcery," and notes how in these areas "Islamic ideas share a large measure of agreement with those of traditional religion" (1980: 60–65). Lewis talks about "the generous catholicity of Islam" towards traditional religious elements, while R. Horton, on his part, compares the "catalytic role" of both Islam and Christianity in religious change in Africa and concludes that Islam allows "the individual [African] to make his own particular selection from official doctrines," and, in contrast to Christianity, "does not nag excessively at those who lie towards the pagan end of the continuum" (1971: 105). The assessments of both of these eminent scholars beg the question: which Islam?

A. Mazrui, a leading contemporary African Muslim scholar, makes similar claims in comparing Islamic and Christian encounters with African religion: "On the wider spectrum of comparison, it remains true that Islam has been more accommodating to indigenous African custom and traditions than European Christianity has been" (1986: 142–3). An All-Africa Conference of Churches (AACC) report of its 1969 Assembly in Abidjan observed that Islam, unlike Christianity, "tolerates African traditions" (AACC 1969: 117). The implication of these claims is that Islam by its nature is favorably disposed towards dialogue with traditional African religions.

It is indisputable that exchanges have taken place at the very deepest level between Islam and African religions. In many significant ways, Ahmadou Hampâté Bâ is right that "en Afrique, l'Islam n'a pas plus de couleur que l'eau; c'est ce qui explique son succès: elle se colore aux teintes des terroirs et des pierres' (Monteil 1964: 41). In other words, in Africa, Islam, like water, has no color of its own except that of the soil and stones it flows over. The difficulties of such claims on behalf of Islam, however, include the fact that these are ensuing from largely postcolonial scholarship in Africa, where scholars have advanced such claims in order "to grant to Islam in Africa the capacity for tolerance and adaptation which they refuse to a begrudged Christianity" (Sanneh 1980: 1). But what is even more problematic is the tendency to grant the primary initiative of exchange to the incoming traditions and its agents. It is by this procedure that Islam is spoken of as "tolerant," "catholic," "flexible," and "accommodating" towards traditional elements. However, as Sanneh rightly points out, "it seems incontestable that more often than not Islam was absorbed into pre-existing notions of flexibility and tolerance rather than introducing these for the first time" (1997: 14). The past procedure upon which:

> Islam has achieved the double victory of successful conversion and of generosity towards African values [is] a contradictory state of affairs that clearly discredits that procedure. The imputing to Islam of a wide degree of flexibility in its interaction with African societies completes the process by robbing traditional societies of a crucial element of their heritage: [namely] the tradition of "enclavement" (which accords protection and guarantee to stranger and non-kin groups) on the one hand, and on the other the inclusive and tenacious nature of local religions. (Sanneh 1980: 6)

In other words, for a satisfactory assessment of the dialogue between African religions and the incoming tradition of Islam (and Christianity), it has to be recognized that in most cases the initiative of exchange lay with the former. J.S. Trimingham notes that, "when assimilation took place between African and Islamic institutions, the basic institution into which the other was assimilated might be either, but was generally the African." African Muslims, Trimingham argues, "did not so much adapt Islam, a legalistic religion, as secure the acceptance of certain Islamic customs in such a way that the customary framework of society remained intact" (1968: 44–46). Throughout tropical Africa, Muslim immigrant groups were accommodated as non-kin minorities within well-organized traditional political systems, in which traditional religions predominated. The ruling classes, who in most instances were the first to come into contact with Islam, appropriated Islamic elements from a position of strength (Azumah 2001: 34–62). This important point needs to be borne in mind as we proceed to explore engagements between Islam and traditional religions in Africa.

When talking about dialogue or engagement between Islam and African religions, it is important to identify two main streams of Islam. For the purposes of this paper I will differentiate between Islam in its scriptural and theological formulations – which tend to be iconoclastic and puritanical, and therefore less tolerant of non-Islamic elements – from Islam in its historical and cultural expressions, or lived Islam, which, as we shall demonstrate, has found a home in many indigenous African cultures. Commenting on this phenomenon, Hampâté Bâ notes that "the empire of Islam in Africa established itself, I shall not say upon the ruins of animism, for it survives still . . . but upon the foundations of animism" (Asfar 1994: 149). Failure to distinguish between Islamic orthodoxy and orthopraxy, or normative Islam from lived Islam or what some have called "folk Islam," has obfuscated the assessment of the interactions between traditional African religions and the Islamic tradition.

Normative Islam and African Religions

Islam emerged in the context of seventh-century Arabia, a deeply polytheistic society with a religious worldview similar in many ways to that of traditional Africa. Muhammad, the prophet of Islam, directed significant portions of his preaching against idol worship, which was pervasive in Arabia. After the fall of Mecca in 630, the prophet of

Islam is said to have ordered the destruction of all idols in the sanctuary, the Ka'ba. Islamic teaching depicts pre-Islamic Arabia as *jahiliyya*, or bound within an age of ignorance, and the Qur'an is categorical in its condemnation of polytheistic practices and idolatry, which it categorizes as *shirk* (associating created objects and beings with the Creator) – the only unforgivable sin in Islam. In classical Islamic jurisprudence, while "people of the book" – i.e., Christians, Jews, Zoroastrians, etc. – are given a special, albeit second-class status within an Islamic state, the only fates prescribed for idol worshippers are conversion to Islam, enslavement, or death. It is therefore fair to say that, for Islamic orthodoxy, there is hardly any room for dialogue with traditional African religions, which must be deemed polytheistic by Qur'anic standards.

This was the position taken by the nineteenth century Islamic jihadists/reformists, who have been widely acclaimed as representatives of orthodox or normative Islam in Africa, towards traditional religions in Africa (Azumah 2001: 94–100). Uthman dan Fodio, the most celebrated of the jihadists, quotes Islamic authorities to support his view that indigenous African religions, customs, arts, values, music, drumming and dancing are forbidden in Islam, and dan Fodio declared everything of the "ignorant" as *'ajam* – a derogatory term originally used to refer to non-Arabs, but later adopted by some Muslim groups to anathematise all non-Muslims (Fudi 1978: 90). One of the many accusations leveled against West African Hausa rulers by dan Fodio is that "they will not abandon the custom which they found their forebears practising, even though it is evil" (Hiskett 1960: 569). The people of Bambara, along with many others in the Senegambian region, "were caused to sacrifice the memorials of their cultural past to the mercilessness of al-Hajj 'Umar," another of the leading jihadists (Willis 1989: 145). Dan Fodio's grandson, Sa'idu dan Bello, exclaimed, "Let us thank God, the Lord of the office, the Unique/King who shows no mercy to the unbeliever," and went on to declare that "a man who has no knowledge [of Islam], he is a mere creature of the bush/He can have no wish to live among men" (Hiskett 1973, 166).

Lamin Sanneh therefore correctly observes that "the Islamic regime explicitly forbids, quite apart from refusing to recognize, involvement in African traditional religious customs. It consigns these customs to the sphere of unclean things. Doctrinally they qualify for jihad" (1980: 2). Therefore, notes Shehu Umar Abdullahi, "wherever they [the jihadists] went, their central theme was one and their target was one; that is the total destruction of all customs and traditions that were in conflict with the Sharia" (1984: 30). Indeed, the nineteenth-century jihad campaigns in the Western Sudan have been generally characterized as reform or renewal movements aimed at purging Islam of the contamination from traditional religious and customary elements. Sanneh makes the point that "reform in Islam has always been on the basis of an uncompromising repudiation of the African religious heritage without any attempt to allow a margin of interface" (1980: 11). Responding to Hampâté Bâ's claim that, like water, Islam has no colour of its own, H.J. Fisher notes that jihadist policies

> involved sometimes sharp and even cruel insistence upon proper standards, and an equally sharp break with local traditions. No one who has read of the stern law-enforcement of the theocracies . . . will ever think of that kind of Islam as coloured no more than water. It was dyed with blood. (Fisher 1973: 37)

On the one hand, it is fair to say that orthodox or normative Islam does not tolerate, let alone encourage, dialogue with traditional African religions. Unlike Christianity, which has all but severed itself from its Semitic cultural cradle, the Arabic language and cultural milieu remains the reference point for normative Islam. As one Muslim scholar put it, "Islam is the spiritual base of Arab culture" (Haseeb 1985: 56). In the words of one of the leading Muslim scholars of the last century, "Islam did not come into existential being *ex nihilo*; nor did it ever create for itself a consciousness or spirit that was not Arab" (Al-Faruqi 1962: 202). Normative Islam has often remained uncompromising in its refusal to translate or use local vernacular languages. The Qur'an was revealed in Arabic, which Muslims have come to view as "the language of God" (Mazrui 1986: 141). From this perspective, translated versions of the Qur'an have no spiritual, liturgical or devotional value. The Qur'an can only be recited in Arabic. The Call to Prayer (*adhan*) has to be said in Arabic, and all Muslims have to pray in the direction of the *qibla*, i.e., towards Mecca, which remains Islam's holiest City and centre of religious orientation. The annual pilgrimage cements the status of Mecca in particular and Saudi Arabia in general as the undisputed geographical centre of Islam. Al-Faruqi spells out the full implications of this Arab emphasis in Islam for non-Arab converts:

> Converts to Islam [have] to learn an Arabic Qur'an; that is, ethically and religiously think in Arabic, and to think in terms of ideas of Arab consciousness. They [have] to emulate Arab conduct; that is to realize values whose ought-to-be's and ought-to-do's have been constructed as particulars of Arab personal and social life. (1962, 204)

To translate or seek to detach Islam from its Arab orientation would only lead in one direction, namely, decline and degeneration. To quote al-Faruqi once more, "a Pakistani, a Nigerian or Croatian may possess [Islam] in a degree as high or higher than any Meccan, Syrian or Egyptian. But commitment to [Islam] of the many communities within this stream on the whole varies in one direction only: It becomes progressively weaker, just as the stream water becomes progressively shallower, the further it is removed from the principal bed of the stream" (199). Thus, Islam, in effect, can only be found in its normative, orthodox form in its original Arab cultural clothing. All non-Arab cultures are potential sources of corruption, and have to be relegated to the realm of hopeless *kufr*, standing in need of not just Islamization but also Arabization. That is why:

> the Prophet's requirement was that the non-Arab converts ought to be Arabicized and the divine dispensation that the Qur'an – the main fount of Islam – is divine in its Arabic and hence untranslatable, thus establishing once and for all that the ideal values can be reached only through the medium of Arab consciousness. (Al-Faruqi 1962: 204–5)

Lamin Sanneh has made the most persuasive argument throughout his works that Islamic missions in Africa are properly identified with "cultural diffusion," as compared to Christian missions, which are best identified with translation (1989). For instance, in thoroughly Islamized societies in Africa, the vernacular names for God are completely lost, replaced with the Arabic Allah. Indeed, in Africa as in other parts of the non-Arab Muslim world, there remains a latent and sometimes explicit suggestion that the degree of one's Islamic commitment depends on the level of one's connectedness to the Arabic cultural milieu. Writing on the Jakhanke, a pacifist Islamic group in West Africa, Sanneh notes that even though due to their particular clerical orientation, Jakhanke Islam inevitably has a high degree of tolerance for appropriating local elements:

> Yet both in the traditions concerning the founder of the [Jakhanke] tradition as well as in the detailed work of the clerical center . . . Mecca remains the unwavering point of religious orientation, reinforced by observance of the *salât*, the standing reminder of the *hâjj* obligation, and the use of Arabic in study, teaching, and counseling. (Sanneh 1989: 228)

Sufism and African Religions

At the same time, others have pointed to the fact that, from its inception, Islam was pragmatic and accommodating, contrary to the claims of normative Islam itself. Citing many instances in which the prophet of Islam demonstrated pragmatic attitudes toward traditional Arab religions, Hasan al-Karmi writes that "this spirit of compromise pervaded many of the teachings of Islam. Think of the rules of marriage, the prohibition of wine, slavery, and others: they were all examples of compromise" (1964: 94). Similarly, Mohamed El-Awa points out that "Islam was not a legislative revolution directed against all that was known and practised by the Arabs before its emergence," and goes on to state that "the Prophet, in his capacity as Islam's legislator, made innumerable rulings legalizing Arabian customary law." Examples given by El-Awa include the laws on marriage and divorce, retaliation and the payment of blood-money, and the concept of *shûra*, consultation (1973: 177). There is, on such accounts, an abundance of precedent in prophetic practice or Islamic orthopraxy for fruitful and dynamic engagements with indigenous cultures and religions. N. Levtzion writes, "the Islamization of Africa became more successful because of the Africanization of Islam" (1979: 208). Muslims across sub-Saharan Africa engaged in concurrent participation in traditional religions, a blending of Islam and local practice, or a substitution of one in place of the other. Commenting on the "syncretizing reality" of Islam in Africa, C.F. Molla writes:

> Sacrifices are made in the name of Allah, but one is surprised to note that the former gestures have undergone no change whatsoever. Circumcisions are performed but other rites lead up to them and follow them. The new taboos join ranks with old ones. (Molla 1967: 467)

It is generally accepted by scholars of Islam in Africa that the Sufi Orders, and the extra-liturgical practices of divination and the production of charms and amulets, account for the spread of Islam in much of tropical Africa. Sufism is to Islam in Africa what Pentecostalism has become for Christianity in Africa since the second half of the twentieth century. Sufism offered to African Muslims the charismatic force that Pentecostalism offers to African Christians, and it was through Sufi Islam that Africans rose to leadership positions in Islam as founding masters and revered clerics. Their extra-liturgical practices in turn put an African imprint on Islam through the appropriation of indigenous cultural and religious elements. Many of the supernatural phenomena which Pentecostal and charismatic African Christians associate with "charismatic gifts" can be found in Sufi Islam – healings, visions, interpretation of dreams, miracles, etc. All of these have very strong resonances with traditional African cosmology.

In Africa, Sufism is dominated by indigenous religious figures, and has produced local saints, incorporated local rituals, and created local shrines. In Hampâté Bâ's view, "Africa has always been a land rich in *walys* [Islamic saints]" (Asfar 1991: 143). In most cases these local saints, rituals and shrines form a more immediate focus of devotion for ordinary Muslims than the Prophet of Islam or the *hijaz*. For instance, in West Africa the shrines of the Mouride founder Ahmadu Bamba at Touba, and that of Tiva-ouane of the Hafid Tijaniyya, attract large crowds of pilgrims on a scale comparable to the pilgrimage to Mecca. Similarly, the cult of Shaykh Hussayn Baliale in Ethiopia and the Somali veneration of Sharif Yusuf al-Kawneyn are important devotional foci for the faithful, and are in some cases considered more meritorious and rewarding orientations for practice and pilgrimage than the annual pilgrimage to Mecca (Lewis 1980: 74).

Indigenous Movements

Islam in Africa has also produced equivalents of Christian AICs (African-Initiated Churches). The AICs – called "Zionist" in Southern Africa, "Roho" in East Africa, and "Aladura" in West Africa – were founded by indigenous Africans dissatisfied with mission-founded churches. These African Protestant Churches arose to satisfy the spiritual hunger and thirst which the mission-founded churches failed to meet. They did this by "more self-consciously seeking to be African than the churches of missionary origin" (Bediako 1995: 63). The AICs employed local lyrics, and incorporated indigenous forms of rituals in their worship. AIC leadership used traditional religious designations and costumes, and, in contrast to missionary Christianity's emphasis on argumentation and rationalism, placed emphasis on prayer, healing, exorcism, prophecy, the interpretation of dreams, etc. The appeal and success of the AICs, in the words of one observer, were due to the fact that "their approach was nearer the African ethos whereas the churches of European origin are often so distressingly European and dull" (E.W. Smith, cited in Parrinder 1961: 43).

African Muslims also expressed their dissatisfaction with the Arab cultural and liturgical mediums of normative Sunni Islam by initiating African-oriented Islamic movements (Azumah 2001: 185–9). An example of this trend is the teaching of Seydina Mouhamoudou Limamou Laye (1845–1909), a native of Yoff, a small village north of Dakar, capital of modern-day Senegal, who claimed in 1884 that he was a re-incarnation of the Prophet of Islam. This was in the wake of a succession of mahdist claims made by numerous Muslim clerics, and a corresponding zeal to "reform" Islam within the central and western Sudan region. Limamou founded a religious confraternity, the Layennes, but unlike most mahdist claimants in the region, preached not a military jihad, but the fear of God, respect for the lawful authority of rulers and parents, purity, and conjugal fidelity. Limamou encouraged the use of Wolof instead of Arabic in recitals and chanting, a practice still common amongst Layennes in modern-day Senegal. Biographers, who are mainly Layennes themselves, depict Limamou variously as a hero, an inspired leader, a sage, and a very good patriot for the Wolof, the Senegalese, and the Black race.

He is reported to have castigated those who doubted his Mahdi claims: "Is it the colour of my skin which prevents you from believing? You would not have hesitated had I been white." At one point, he also told others, whom he felt were overly impressed with the prestige of the Arabic language, that "on the day of the resurrection I will speak to you in Wolof" (Singleton 1990: 5). One biographer maintains that Limamou:

> consciously or unconsciously, accomplished a genuine spiritual revolution. In fact, at that time, Senegalese, indeed Africans as such, especially the Wolof and Lebou were convinced of the inferiority of the black race. In their eyes the negro would not be a divine envoy, was not even worthy to be one, as it seemed to them he was not much more than one of the damned of this earth. Limamou showed the opposite and proved that the black race was as worthy if not more so than any other, that God created men differently and did not privilege some races more than others. One can ask oneself today if the apostle of God, Limamou Laye, was not also one of the first pioneers of negritude, albeit a misunderstood one. (Singleton: 8–9)

To his followers, therefore, Limamou was someone who held high the flag of Wolof, Senegalese and Black African dignity and identity, within the context of Arab racial and religious chauvinism. Hence some, like the biographer quoted above, called for Limamou's mission to be recognized and placed within the wider context of African self-assertion and self-determination.

A further example of the assertion of indigenous African Muslim identity is the controversial Maitatsine movement of Northern Nigeria. This sect was founded by Mohammadu Marwa (d. 1980), a Cameroonian national who lived for a long time in northern Nigeria. He was patronized by politicians and businessmen and widely respected by the masses of Kano State. Marwa went on *hajj* in 1971, and subsequently proclaimed himself a prophet in 1980 with the mission of cleansing and purifying Islam. He decried materialism, the possession of bicycles and wristwatches, and the use of tobacco – all traits of the affluent Muslim elite of Kano.

Marwa is said to have prohibited his followers from mentioning the name of the Prophet of Islam, calling him "an Arab," and he rejected the Sunna as a source for Muslim faith and behavior, insisting that the Qur'an was the only valid guide for Muslims (*sola scriptura*). Marwa reportedly ordered his followers to pray three times a day instead of the traditional five, and prohibited them from facing Mecca during prayers – a practice he insisted arose from the Sunna, rather than from the Qur'an, though he based his argument on the Qur'an itself: "And unto Allah belongs East and West, so whatever way you turn, there is the Face of God" (Sura 2: 115).

Marwa's teaching was understandably seen as a threat not only to Islamic orthodoxy, but to the local status quo as well. (This resulted in bloody conflicts in

Kano and other parts of Northern Nigeria in the early 1980s, during which Marwa himself apparently died from injuries sustained in one such riot.) What seemed evident was the "remarkable appeal" of Marwa's preaching, which can be attributed to the fact that:

> he angled his interpretations to accommodate a largely non-literate congregation for whom the classical exegesis, based on classical Arabic, and on a Middle Eastern environmental frame of reference, was a closed book. Instead, the Maitatsine related his tafsir to the local West African scene with which the perceptions of such a congregation could readily cope. (Hiskett 1987: 217–18)

A. Mazrui observes that "the most distinctive yearning within [Marwa's] sect was a burning desire for the Africanization of Islam, which later became a burning desire for an African prophet" (1986: 36). Indeed, newspaper reports during the riots at Kaduna in 1980 suggested that Marwa's followers regarded him as a prophet for African Islam. Hence, even though Marwa was killed, the appeal of his teaching did not necessarily die with him and, as noted by one observer, that teaching might have gone into "a sort of *hijra* underground" (Christelow 1985: 389).

Less dramatically, but still directly related to longstanding African challenges to the Arabicity of Islam in Africa, is the widely reported early twentieth-century controversy involving Shaykh Muhammad Ramiya (son and successor of Shaykh Ramiya, former slave and founder of the Qadariyya order in East Africa). Shaykh Muhammad explicitly questioned the ethnicity of the Prophet Muhammad, as a letter written in 1938 by the acting district commissioner reporting the controversy to his provincial superior makes clear. The letter reveals:

> an unfortunate internal dissension . . . that has sprung up in Bagamoyo township among the local Moslem leaders. A short time ago Sheikh Mohamed Ramia (son of a former liwali, and a Manyema by tribe) pronounced twice in a local Mosque that the Prophet was not an Arab. Other Sheikhs and local Arabs were incensed at this heretical statement, while many adherents of the religion took a keen interest in the matter. (Nimtz 1980: 138–9)

Shaykh Muhammad, who himself described the incident as "an enormous controversy," contended that even though Muhammad was physically born of Arab parentage, he was man of all races: "He was a personage of Arabs, Swahilis and other peoples." In the Shaykh's opinion, the universal reach of Muhammad's prophethood overrides any specific ethnic affiliation. Although the Shaykh did not declare himself *mahdi* or prophet, as did Limamou and Marwa, respectively, the Shaykh's stance was nonetheless seen as heretical. His statement on the universality of Muhammad's ethnicity was largely taken by his Arab protagonists as an anti-Arab position, determined by the Shaykh's personal experience of Arab enslavement and discrimination. The most important point that needs to be borne in mind, at this point, is that the Qadiriyya and other Sufi orders came to be known for their appropriation of indigenous African elements into Islamic ritual practice. In this general historical context, it is interesting to note that a number of leading African Muslim scholars have been advocating Kiswahili, rather than Arabic, as the Islamic language of education in East Africa (Balda 1993: 231–7).

Ceremonies in African Islam

The appeal of the above trends and movements had more to do with the continued sway of traditional African cosmology, and the positive quest for an African Islam, rather than a merely negative set of anti-Arab sentiments. In turn, African Muslim clerics seem to be fully aware of the futility of fighting traditional religious elements, and recognize the ongoing opportunity to appropriate those elements to advance Islam. Across Muslim Africa, various traditional spirit-possession cults became the wineskins for Islamic ceremonial and ritual practice. These include the Swahili *pepo*-possession cults; the zar cults of Eritrea, Ethiopia, Somalia and Sudan; Songhay *holey*, Mossi *kinkirsi*, Hausa *bori*; the *homtu* or *homturu*, *hirsi*, *dando*, seasonal ceremonies of the Wodaabe Fulani of northern Nigeria, and a host of others (Lewis 1980: 64). Singing, drumming and dancing, all condemned by jihadist reformists, persist as part of African Sufi rituals. One observer notes that among the Yao of Malawi, the Sufi ritual of *dhikr* (mystical incantations involving invocations of the attributes of Allah, the prophet of Islam, or some prominent saint, and/or the use of specific qur'anic passages), or *sikiri* as the Yao call it, "was swiftly incorporated by the Yao and replaced the performance of pre-Islamic dances at marriages, funerals and other ceremonies" (Thorold 1993: 84).

Across sub-Saharan Africa, ordinary Muslims (like their Christian counterparts) continue to seek out traditional priests and priestesses, diviners, witchdoctors, and healers in times of personal and family crisis. As far back as the late fifteenth or early sixteenth century, Askia Mohammed, the ruler of the Songhay Empire, complained of subjects who, despite professing the *shahada*:

> Believe that there are beings who can bring them benefit or do them harm other than God, Mighty and Exalted is He. They have idols and they say: "The fox has said so and so and thus it will be," and "if the thing is thus then it will be so and so." They venerate certain trees and make sacrifices to them. They have their shrines and they do not appoint or undertake any matter either great or small except at the command of the custodians of their shrines. So I admonish them to give up all that and they refused to do so without the use of force. (Hunwick 1985: 77)

Writing on various forms of *sadaqa* (extra-liturgical alms) given to beggars, people with physical handicaps, religious figures, strangers, and children as a form of sacrifice amongst the Dyula of West Africa, Robert Launay identifies four meanings of these pious donations, which 1) confer religious merit on believers; 2) offer a ritualized opportunity to obtain a specific, this-worldly material and spiritual benefit for the giver; 3) ceremonially distribute food or money by individuals and families on the occasion of life crises; and 4) promote or maintain harmony and general well-being within kin groups. *Saraka*, as the Dyula call it, is a way of asking God for "well-being," but "well-being," like *saraka* itself, means not one but many things. It is the material well-being of individuals, not only health and long life for themselves and their dependents, but material possessions, worldly success, even political power. It is also their spiritual well-being, particularly in the next life (Launay 1992: 217–18).

The meal served following the ceremonial burial of Yao Muslims is called *sadaqa*, and the same term is used for ritual meals commemorating lineage ancestors (Thorold 1993: 85). In all of these cases, we see African Muslims replacing indigenous forms of blood sacrifice and ritual meals with extra-liturgical Islamic alms, for the well-being of individual believers, families and communities.

The muezzin's call to prayer is an invitation to worship/prayer (*salat*) but also to well-being/success (*falah*). For African Muslims, the pursuit of physical, material and spiritual well-being calls for a serious engagement with, and control or manipulation of, the Supreme Being, lesser spirits, and a host of supernatural beings that are also acknowledged by normative Islam.

Critical Questions

Such integrations, however, have limits. Writing on the interactions and tensions between Songhay and Islamic beliefs, Thomas Hale asks a rhetorical question in the form of a Songhay proverb; "Can a single foot follow two paths" and concludes with another proverb that, "if a log spends 100 years in the water, it will not become a crocodile" (1991: 131–9). In other words, while it may not be possible for a single foot to follow two paths, no amount of pressure from Islam (or Christianity) can radically change, let alone completely eradicate, traditional religions and their appeal amongst the African faithful. Patrick J. Ryan has given an extremely illuminating account of how for centuries Yoruba Muslim clerics in south-western Nigeria have been following two paths with a single foot i.e. participation in both traditional and Islamic religious traditions. Ryan observes that:

despite half a century of Modernizing Reform and perhaps a century and a half of Conservative Reform, most of the Muslim Yoruba today are under the leadership of clerics who would most accurately be characterized as Accommodating [i.e., attempting to harmonize traditional and Islamic religious elements]. (1978: 147)

In a 2010 survey, the Pew Forum noted that, along with high levels of commitment to Islam (and Christianity), many Africans retain beliefs and rituals that are characteristic of traditional African religions. Twenty-six percent of Muslims exhibited a "high level of belief and practice" in traditional religions, with Senegalese scoring the highest (75 percent) in the belief in the protective powers of traditional charms and sacrifices (Pew Forum 2010: 33). The harmonization of indigenous and Islamic practices includes the use of amulets made of Qur'anic verses and herbal concoctions from a traditional priest-herbalist. Among the Fulani, who are "among the most thoroughly Islamized peoples of sub-Saharan Africa," narratives of initiation "provide strong evidence of the confluence of Islam and traditional African religion" (Asfar 1991: 153).

It is clear that lived Islam is in daily interaction with traditional African religions, in many places at a very deep level. The point at issue, however, is the "surprising hiatus" between what pertains amongst the Muslim faithful of Africa, and a real African Muslim intellectual appreciation of the vitality of African traditional religions as they relate to Islam (Sanneh 1997: 21). African Muslim scholarship in general consistently regards the pre-Islamic past of Africa as *jahiliya* (a period of ignorance). A leading African Muslim scholar, while decrying Western Christian cultural chauvinism, writes approvingly of the two-pronged "de-traditionalization and Islamization" of the nineteenth-century jihadists, in which the "successes of Muslims in many areas of the West Sudan led to the gradual destruction of the traditional cults and the emasculation of the old aristocracy." This writer then bemoans the European colonial intervention and wonders "what would have happened had Europe's expansion into other areas of the world been delayed for a century or more" (Nyang 1990: 40). Still, some regard the revival of indigenous African culture as "a threat to Islam" comparable to secularism, albeit less immediately serious (Mazrui 1986: 19). Others refer more bluntly to African religions and customs as "reprehensible and evil." The same Muslim writer goes on to declare that "Islam does not accept that people should have customs or traditions other than religious ones; for if Allah's way is a comprehensive way of life, what is there for custom and tradition?" (Sulaiman 1986: 48–49).

Sanneh draws an insightful contrast between patterns of reform in African Islam and Christianity. Reform in Islam, he argues, tends to press "for a choice between the old and the new, and although there were gaps, the pressure was towards the 'orient' in terms of orientation toward Mecca and Medina. The 'reform' tradition in Christian Africa moved in the opposite direction and espoused greater identification with the African setting" (1989: 229). The gaps to which Sanneh refers are important, for, as we have pointed out above, there have also been African Muslim reform or protest movements that actively promote African identifications. The main thrust of Sanneh's argument, however, remains valid: reform Islam in Africa tends to be oriented primarily toward Mecca and Medina. From the 1980s onward, a number of anti-Sufi groups arose across Muslim Africa, challenging what they dismiss as the superstitions of local clerics and non-liturgical practices. These reform groups include the *sukuti* movement in Malawi, the *Jama'at izalat al-bida' wa iqamat al-sunna* (Movement for Suppressing Innovations and Restoring the Sunna) of Nigeria, and other Wahhabiyya-inspired groups across Muslim Africa. In the words of one such reformer, "We must fight animism and those who interpret the Qur'an improperly and do not practise it as it was written by the Prophet. We must get rid of the additions and of the intermediaries between God, the Prophet and mankind" (Grégoire 1993: 111).

Ahmadou Hampâté Bâ seems to be a fresh voice in these discussions, writing appreciatively of Islam's interactions with traditional Bambara and Fulani religions as very rare exceptions to the general norm of Islamic relations with indigenous African religious traditions. Bâ celebrates the fact that "Islam took hold and grew in sub-Saharan Africa upon the foundations of traditional religion." Bâ points out at length that traditional religions have been hospitable to Islam in Africa, a hospitality that accounts for the amalgamation of the two traditions in many African Muslim societies. For Bâ, traditional religion forms a crucial substructure for Islam in Africa, and he writes of several "great principles" shared in common between African traditions and Islam: the integral relationship between the profane and sacred; a single-tiered worldview; and "the existence of a supreme being, transcendent yet immanent by its force in all things and in all places" (Asfar 1991: 147–9). Bâ is a highly respected leader of the Tijaniyya Sufi Order, and is a representative voice of lived Islam rather than normative Islam in Africa.

Even so, the ongoing relationships between Islam and African religions remain largely hidden to many scholars, for whom the process of Islamic "indigenization" in Africa has taken place "through blind social forces" (Mazrui 1986: 150). In a similar vein, Sanneh describes the results of historical interaction between Islamic and African religious traditions as "a patchwork quilt" (1997: 21). As demonstrated in this essay, however, quite deep (if bittersweet) engagements between Islam and African traditions have also occurred in a number of instances, with clear signs of inter-religious intentionality and creativity.

Bibliography

Abdullahi, S.U. *On the Search for a Viable Political Culture: Reflections on the Political Thought of Shaikh 'Abdullahi Dan-Fodio.* Kaduna: Commercial Printing Dept., 1984.

Al-Faruqi, I. *On Arabism; 'Urubah and Religion: A Study of the Fundamental Ideas of Arabism and Islam as its Highest Moment of Consciousness,* Amsterdam: Djambatan N.V., 1962.

Al-Karmi, H. "The Prophet Muhammad and the Spirit of Compromise." *Islamic Quarterly,* 8(3 & 4) (1964): 84–98.

Asfar, G. "Amadou Hampâté Bâ and the Islamic Dimension of West African Oral Literature," in *Faces of Islam in African Literature,* ed. K.W. Harrow. Portsmount: Heinemann Educational Books, 1994.

Balda, J.L. "The Role of Kiswahili in East African Islam," in *Muslim Identity and Social Change in sub-Saharan Africa,* ed. L. Brenner. London: C. Hurst, 1993.

Blyden, E.W. *Christianity, Islam and the Negro Race.* Edinburgh: Edinburgh University Press,1967.

Christelow, A. "Religious Protest and Dissent in Northern Nigeria: From Mahdism to Qur'ânic Integralism." *Journal of the Insti-* tute of Muslim Minority Affairs, 6(2) (1985): 375–88.

El-Awa, Mohamed "The Place of Custom ('Urf) in Islamic Legal Theory." *Islamic Quarterly.* 17(3 & 4) (1973): 177–82.

Fisher, H.J. "Conversion Reconsidered: Some Historical Aspects of Religious Conversion in Black Africa." *Africa* 43(2) (1973): 27–40.

Fudi, Uthman Ibn. *Bayân Wujûb al-Hijrah 'Ala 'l-'Ibad,* ed. and trans. F. H. El Masri. Oxford: Oxford University Press, 1978.

Grégoire, E. "Islam and Identity in Maradi (Niger)," in *Muslim Identity and Social Change in sub-Saharan Africa,* ed. L. Brenner. London: C. Hurst, 1993.

Hale, T.A. "Can a Single Foot Follow Two Paths? Islamic and Songhay Belief Systems in the Timbuktu Chronicles and the Epic of Askia Mohammed," in *Faces of Islam in African Literature,* ed. K.W. Harrow. London: James Currey, 1991, 131–140.

Haseeb, K. El-Din (ed.). *The Arabs and Africa.* London: Croom Helm, 1985.

Hiskett, M. "Kitab al-Farq: A work on the Habe Kingdoms Attributed to 'Uthman dan Fodio." *Bulletin of School of Oriental and African Studies* 23 (1960): 558–79.

Hiskett, M. *The Sword of Truth: The life and Times of the Shehu Usuman Dan Fodio*. Evanston, IL: Northwestern University Press, 1973.

Hiskett, M. "The Maitatsine Riots in Kano, 1980: An Assessment." *Journal of Religion in Africa* 17(3) (1987): 209–22.

Horton, R. "African Conversion." *Africa* 41(2) (1971): 85–107.

Hunwick, J.O. (ed. and trans.). *Shari'a in Songhay: The Replies of Al-Maghîlî to the Questions of Askia Al-Hâjj Muhammad*. New York: Oxford University Press, 1985.

Launay, R. *Beyond the Stream: Islam and Society in a West African Town*. Berkeley: University of California Press, 1992.

Levtzion, N. (ed.). *Conversion to Islam*. New York: Holmes and Meier, 1979.

Lewis, I.M. *Islam in Tropical Africa*, 2nd edn. London: Hutchinson University Library, 1980.

Mazrui, A.A. *The Africans: A Triple Heritage*. London: BBC Publication, 1986.

Molla, C.F. "Some Aspects of Islam in Africa – South of the Sahara." *International Review of Missions* 56 (1967): 459–68.

Monteil, V. *L'Islam Noir*. Paris: Éditions de Seuil, 1964.

Nimtz, A.H. *Islam and Politics in East Africa: The Sufi Order in Tanzania*. Minneapolis: University of Minnesota Press, 1980.

Ryan, P.J. *Imale: Yoruba Participation in the Muslim Tradition. A Study of Clerical Piety*. Missioula, MT: Scholars' Press, 1978.

Sanneh, L. "The Domestication of Islam and Christianity in African Societies: A Methodological Exploration." *Journal of Religion in Africa* 11(1) (1980): 1–12.

Sanneh, L. *Translating the Message: The Missionary Impact on Culture*. Maryknoll, NY: Orbis, 1989.

Sanneh, L. *The Crown and the Turban: Muslims and West African Pluralism*. Oxford: West View Press, 1997.

Singleton, M. "Seydina Mouhamoudou Limamou Laye (1845–1909) – The Black Mahdi of Senegal." *CSIC Occasional Papers* 2 (1990).

Sulaiman, I. *A Revolution in History: The Jihad of Usman Dan Fodio*. London: G. Mansell, 1986.

Thorold, A. "Metamorphoses of the Yao Muslims," in *Muslim Identity and Social Change in sub-Saharan Africa*, ed. L. Brenner. London: C. Hurst, 1993.

Trimingham, J.S. *The Influence of Islam upon Africa*. London: Longman, 1968.

Willis, J.R. *In the Path of Allah: The Passion of Al-Hajj 'Umar: An Essay into the Nature of Charisma in Islam*. London: Frank Cass, 1989.

CHAPTER 20
Hindu–Christian Dialogue

Anantanand Rambachan

Although there are traditions that connect the apostle St. Thomas with India, and evidence of a Christian presence in south India from the seventh or eighth centuries CE, we have no records of Hindu–Christian interaction prior to the colonial period (Coward 1989).

The European quest for products and trade routes in the seventeenth century brought merchants from Portugal and Britain to India, and Christian missionaries were not long in following. The British East India Company, which exercised control of significant portions of Indian territory from the 1750s, was initially reluctant to allow missionaries to proselytize in India. Company officials were concerned that the work of missionaries would stir hostility among Hindus and impede business prospects. The Company's charter, however, was revised in 1813 and again in 1833, removing obstacles to missionary work in its territories.

From its earliest days, the Christian tradition in India was diverse and distinguished by national origin, theology, liturgy and culture. The oldest community, the Thomas Christians, traced by some Indian Christian traditions to the arrival of the Apostle Thomas in the first century, was concentrated in the region of Kerala and maintained generally cordial relations with Hindu neighbors (Amaldass 1989). These communities were not active proselytizers. Roman Catholic communities (ca. fifteenth century) were concentrated in the Portuguese enclaves, but present in smaller numbers elsewhere. Beginning in the eighteenth century, Protestant missionaries commenced work in India and by the nineteenth century the largest and most influential Christian communities comprised European and American Protestant denominations. These groups had the more significant dialogical encounters with the Hindu tradition. Although Hindus did not always distinguish among the various Christian communities, they were aware of the relationship between the Protestant denomination and the British colonial power. English-educated Hindus were most familiar with the latter forms of Christianity.

The Wiley Blackwell Companion to Inter-Religious Dialogue, First Edition. Edited by Catherine Cornille.
© 2013 John Wiley & Sons Ltd. Published 2020 by John Wiley & Sons Ltd.

It was in the region of Bengal, in the eighteenth and nineteenth centuries, where the Christian tradition made its greatest impact in India, coinciding with the establishment of British control in the same area. There were many influential missionaries whose work had reverberations in the Hindu community and contributed to the development of Hindu–Christian interactions. One of these was William Carey (1761–1834). Carey, a pioneer in the foundation of the Baptist Missionary Society, operated first from a Danish enclave near Calcutta. He enlisted the help of traditional Hindu scholars to assist him with the work of translating the Bible into Indian languages. The publication of a Bengali version of the New Testament in 1801 was followed by the translation of large parts of the Bible into the languages of India. Carey's methods for the spread of Christianity in India included traditional preaching, education and the above-mentioned translation and distribution of Christian literature in local languages.

The use of education as an instrument for preparing Hindus for Christianity is seen particularly in the work of Alexander Duff (1806–1878). Duff, a missionary of the Church of Scotland, was convinced that "the highest form of education is Christian education, namely a thoroughly sound intellectual and scientific training, built on the moral and religious principles of Christ" (Farquhar 1914: 19). Duff attracted wealthy and promising Indian students, hoping that exposure to Western learning and Christianity would loosen the grip of Hindu ideas and lead to conversion. According to Farquhar, "a stream of fine young fellows began to pass out of Hinduism into the Christian Church and Duff's work and Christianity became the most absorbing topic of conversation throughout the Hindu community" (Farquhar 1914: 20). Missionaries undertook similar work in other cities.

Although missionaries successfully converted many educated Hindus to Christianity, it is likely that they did not anticipate perhaps the most important outcome of exposure to Christianity and Western education. Education had the effect also of turning Hindus back to their own tradition, seeking a clearer and deeper understanding of its insights. These Hindus were among the principal agents for the renewal and reinvigoration of the Hindu tradition. They engaged in vigorous debates with their Christian contemporaries and are among the earliest participants and shapers of Hindu–Christian dialogue. The lives of these pioneers of Hindu–Christian dialogue exemplify the profound way in which an encounter with another tradition can transform and enrich one's understanding of his or her home tradition.

Hindu Reform Movements and Dialogue with Christianity

The earliest and one of the most influential Hindus in this regard was Rammohan Roy (1772–1833) and it is helpful to begin our account of Hindu–Christian dialogue with him. Farquhar describes him as "the pioneer of all living advance, religious, social and educational, in the Hindu community" (1914: 29). Roy was born in an orthodox Brahmin Hindu family in the village of Radhanagar, Bengal, in 1772. He studied Islam at Patna and Hinduism in Varanasi, but became disenchanted with his ancestral tradition. Service in the East India Company and the Bengal Civil Service gave Roy exposure to the English language and to British politics, administration, culture and religion. In

1829, Roy founded the Brahmo Sabha (subsequently called the Brahmo Samaj), for the reform and regeneration of Hindu society. Between the years 1829 and 1884, the Brahmo Samaj, though numerically small, was the center of all progressive religious and social movements and exerted considerable influence. The movement produced a series of charismatic leaders who determined its doctrine and direction.

Roy enjoyed cordial relations with the missionaries at Serampore. He attended worship, participated in discussions and took keen interest in their educational efforts. On their side, the missionaries certainly saw the opportunity to convert one of the best-educated Hindus in the nineteenth century. Roy's study of the New Testament, like Gandhi later in the same century, profoundly affected his religious views, but also resulted, again like Gandhi, in disillusionment with institutional Christianity, its rituals, the rivalries of Christian denominations and the intricate theologies associated with Jesus. Significant in Roy's dialogue with his Christian counterparts was the fact that missionary denunciation of Hinduism, and the missionary alliance with British coloni-alism, did not deter his interest in Jesus. Roy was the first Hindu to make the effort to disconnect Jesus from institutional Christianity, and all the major Hindu figures in the nineteenth and early twentieth centuries followed his lead. He identified some of the salient concerns that would dominate the dialogue between Hindus and Christians.

In 1820, Roy published *The Precepts of Jesus*, a collection of what he considered to be Jesus's ethical teachings. Roy clarified his intention in words that are often quoted:

> These precepts separated from the mysterious dogmas and historical records, appear, on the contrary, to the compiler to contain not only the essence of all that is necessary to instruct mankind in their civil duties, but also the best and only means of obtaining for-giveness of sins, the favor of God and strength to overcome our passions and to keep his commandments. (Thomas 1970: 10)

Roy believed that the ethical teachings of Jesus offered resources for the reform of Hindu society and that these teachings could be distinguished from the doctrines of the Church about Jesus. What Roy included in his selection from the Gospel is as significant as what he chose to omit. He omitted biographical passages and references to the mira-cles of Jesus, in large part because the historical does not have the same significance for liberation (*moksha*) in the Hindu tradition as it does for Christians. The differing valuation of the historical, here underlined by Roy through exclusion, is a continuing thread in Hindu–Christian dialogue, as we will see again later. Roy's interpretation of the Christian tradition, as Kopf (1979) so ably demonstrates, was also deeply influenced by Unitarianism.

It is not certain what response Roy expected from his Christian missionary friends. Perhaps he anticipated support for his commendation of Jesus's teaching to Hindus, or an invitation to continuing dialogue. The response, in any case, was one of condemna-tion and hostility. Joshua Marshman described Roy as an "intelligent heathen," and a danger to the cause of truth. At the heart of the Christian response to Roy was the accusation that he focused on the ethical teachings of Jesus to the exclusion of the central claim of these texts that salvation is possible only through the atoning sacrifice of Jesus on the cross.

Although it is beyond the scope of this chapter to detail in full the fascinating exchange between Roy and the Christian missionaries, it will be helpful to highlight the importance of a few particular issues for the continuing dialogue between Hindus and Christians. First, Roy defended his theocentric approach, and questioned how one affirming the unity of God and the ethics of Jesus could be labeled a "heathen." Second, admitting his selective use of Gospel texts, he justified this practice by calling attention to long-standing patterns of Christian exegesis. Finally, Roy explained that his understanding of morality was not limited to the ethical, but included also the love of God (Samartha 1974).

Though holding Jesus in high esteem, "superior even to the angels in heaven," Roy did not share the traditional Christian understanding of Jesus as identical with God. He argued that Jesus himself had a theocentric understanding of his relationship with God. On this issue Roy differs from later Hindus who are more willing to consider the divinity of Jesus, but reject the exclusivity of such claims. In rejecting the divinity of Jesus, Roy was consistent, since he also disclaimed the Hindu doctrine of divine descent (*avatar*).

Although Roy was the earliest Hindu to engage in sustained dialogue with Christians in India, the concerns of his conversation were limited. He was interested primarily in refuting Trinitarian Christianity and in arguing for the subordination if Jesus to God. Doctrines derived from Hinduism did not feature prominently in this dialogue. His Christian missionary interlocutors were responsible also for the narrow focus of the dialogue; their concern was to refute all salvific possibility in the Hindu traditions and to affirm Jesus as the only way of salvation. Though much of Roy's work was concerned with religious and social reform, such matters did not feature prominently in his dialogue with missionaries. At the same time, it is Roy who called Hindu attention to Jesus, who sought to offer an interpretation of Jesus independent of the doctrines of the Christian church, and who opened the doors for other Hindus to contribute to this discussion.

Keshub Chunder Sen inherited the mantle of Brahmo Samaj leadership from Rammohun Roy. As his own career as a religious leader developed, Keshub adopted a highly eclectic terminology and religious practice that made it very difficult to identify him with any particular tradition. Perhaps his distinctive contribution to Hindu–Christian dialogue is his introduction of the idea of the Asiatic Christ. This idea resonated later in the exposition of leading Hindu voices like Swami Vivekananda and Mahatma Gandhi. This idea was first enunciated in an eloquent and wide-ranging lecture delivered on May 5, 1866 in Calcutta (Collet 1870). Sen began his lecture with a description of Jesus as "the greatest and truest benefactor of mankind." He painted a dismal picture of human civilization prior to the birth of Jesus, describing the world as "deep in the gloom of ignorance and corruption."

> Jesus Christ was thus a necessity of the age: he appeared in the fullness of time. And, certainly, no great man ever rose in the world but his birth was necessitated by surrounding circumstances, and his life was a necessary response to the demands of the age. (Collett 1870)

Sen traced the history of the Church from its periods of early persecution and martyrdom to the time of Constantine, when Christianity became the religion of the empire.
Political power, he argued, resulted in corruption and created the conditions for the
work of Luther. He sketched the history of Christianity in India, building his speech to
a rhetorical question that was greeted with applause:

> Is there a single soul in this large assembly who would scruple to ascribe extraordinary
> moral heroism to Jesus Christ and him crucified? (Collett 1870)

He spoke of the gratitude of India for Christianity and of British political control as the
expression of divine will, while lamenting the rancor, hatred and mutual stereotyping
that characterized relationships between Indians and Englishmen. After calling European attention to their oppression of natives, he spoke of their "muscular Christianity,"
which caused Indians to identify the tradition with power, privilege and injustice.

> Behold Christ crucified in the lives of those who profess to be his followers! Had it not been
> for them, the name of Jesus Christ would have been ten times more glorified than it seems
> to have been. (Collett 1870)

It is at this point in his lecture that Sen introduced his idea of the Asiatic Christ, using
it to affirm his dignity and self-worth as an Indian.

> I rejoice, yea, I am proud, that I am an Asiatic. And was not Jesus Christ an Asiatic? Yes
> and his disciples were Asiatics, and in Asia. When I reflect on this, my love for Jesus
> becomes a hundredfold intensified; I feel him nearer to my heart, and deeper in my national
> sympathies. Why should I then feel ashamed to acknowledge that nationality which he
> acknowledged? Shall I not rather say, he is more congenial and akin to my oriental nature,
> more agreeable to my Oriental habits of thought and feeling? And is it not true that an
> Asiatic can read the imageries and allegories of the Gospel, and its descriptions of natural
> sceneries, of customs and manners, with greater interest, and a fuller perception of their
> force and beauty, than Europeans? (Collet 1870)

Like Roy before him, Sen claimed that his understanding of Jesus was independent of
the Church, derived directly from his reading of the Biblical texts. He also followed Roy
in giving emphasis to the so-called ethical teachings of Jesus, especially those having
to do with forgiveness and self-sacrifice.

After Sen, there is no figure, either in the Brahmo Samaj or any other Hindu reform
organization, who was not a Christian convert and who spoke in such exalted terms
about Jesus. Sen influenced Swami Vivekananda, but Vivekananda saw the nondual
(*Advaita*) tradition as the fulfillment of Christian dualism, and interpreted Jesus as a
teacher of nondual truth.

A radical change in Hindu–Christian dialogue is best exemplified in the approach of
Swami Dayananda Saraswati (1824–1883), founder of the reformist Arya Samaj
organization. Dayananda was quite different from Brahmo Samaj leaders. He rejected
entirely any claims to truth in Christianity or other religions and asserted the sole truth

of his exposition of the teachings of the Vedas. He did not speak English and was not educated in Western institutions. He spoke Sanskrit and was unapologetic in his defense of the authority of the Vedas.

Dayananda Saraswati was much clearer than both Roy and Sen about his authoritative ground for entering into dialogue with other religions, as well as the normative doctrines by with the claims of other traditions are to be evaluated. In this regard, there are four critical elements of his engagement in dialogue (Jordens 1978: 171–172). First, he affirmed the Vedas to be the repository of eternal and universal truth. The concern of Hindu scripture is not to inform us of history, but to provide truths valid for all times and places. The Bible's emphasis on history was thus a deviation. Second, Dayananda affirmed that the Vedas taught monotheism and that the many names used in the Vedas refer to many aspects of the One God, not multiple gods. Third, like Gandhi later on, Dayananda emphasized that revelation does not contradict morality or reason. Fourth, since the Vedas contained all truth, they also embodied the later discoveries of science. Dayananda introduced a quite different tone and content into the Hindu encounter with Christians and Christianity, contrasting sharply with Brahmo Samaj figures like Roy and Sen. Dayananda's treatment of Hindu traditions with which he disagreed was no different. His treatment of all religions was informed by his belief that the Vedas contained all truth, religious and scientific. He understood the claims of Christianity as standing or falling on the authority of the Bible and developed his critique of the Christian tradition in his magnum opus, *Satyartha Prakash* (Light of Truth). The Bible, in Dayananda's view, ought not to be considered divine revelation, because its teachings are irrational, immoral and untrue. "The Christian Bible," according to Dayananda, "contains hundreds of thousands of things that are condemnable. . . . Truth adulterated with untruth can never remain pure and hence the works that contain it can never be acceptable. Besides, in the acceptance of the Vedas the whole truth is accepted" (Saraswati 1975: 648). Unlike the Vedas, the Bible does not propound eternal truths since its teachings are rooted in historical events. Saraswati was also critical of the image of God emerging from the Biblical texts: bound by time and space, violent, jealous, and relying on miracles that are inconsistent with scientific truths. On the Christian doctrine of the virgin birth of Jesus, Dayananda is sarcastic, but includes similar Hindu narratives in his critique: "If the story of the birth of Christ were held to be true, any unmarried girl that happens to conceive could say that she was with child of the Holy Ghost. . . . This story is as possible as that recorded in the Puranas about Kunti being conceived of the Sun" (Saraswati 1975: 618).

In Dayananda, there is none of the esteem and respect for Jesus that we encountered earlier. He challenges the Christian understanding of Jesus as the Son of God, the truth of the miracles ascribed to Jesus, Jesus's resurrection from the grave, and atonement as a core Christian doctrine. "God would indeed be unjust if good or bad deeds done by one man should affect another, or if the judge should take on himself the crimes of the criminal" (Saraswati 1975: 622). Christians, according to Dayananda, were inconsistent in arguing for the miracles of Jesus while denying such claims in the Hindu tradition. Jesus, in Dayananda's view, is not a person who offers valuable religious teachings to Hindus, and cannot serve as an exemplar of ethics.

Dayananda read Christian texts in ways that were similar to missionary readings of Hindu texts – literal, dogmatic, and uncharitable. The sympathetic reading that Gandhi would later apply to the New Testament is entirely absent. Dayananda's theological stand is exclusive, and he engages in dialogue from a critical normative perspective, based on his understanding of the Vedas as the sole ahistorical and therefore eternal authority in matters religious. He is cognizant also of the many places where Christian teachings about sin and salvation cannot be reconciled with Hindu claims. He seeks to highlight rather than downplay such divergences, while arguing for the truth of Hindu claims. His apologetic orientation toward Christianity was thus closer in method to the Christian adversaries than to Roy and Sen, although he was influenced as well by ancient Hindu traditions of religious debate and argument.

The legacy of Dayananda Saraswati's approach to Hindu–Christian dialogue continues through the Arya Samaj and other Hindu organizations that came under his influence. His legacy continues in a vigorous Hindu challenge to Christianity based on the authority of the Vedas, as well as in efforts, through *shuddhi* (purification) ceremonies, to reconvert Hindus who have joined Christian denominations. Through programs aimed at the reform of Hindu society and rooted in defense against missionary criticism, Dayananda boosted Hindu self-confidence. He was much clearer than his predecessors that inter-religious encounters are predicated on commitment and location in a specific tradition, and such encounters cannot exclude normative claims. Although his tone and manner were combative and often derogatory, he reminds us that Hindu–Christian dialogue must not overlook core theological differences. He offers clarity about the source for his engagement with other traditions. For Dayananda, the Vedas are primary, the normative source for his evaluation of other traditions. Roy and Sen embraced the ethics and theocentric devotion of Jesus, while disassociating themselves from institutional Christianity. But Dayananda Saraswati rejected both Jesus and Christianity. Roy and Sen were also much less clear than was Dayananda about the authoritative Hindu sources for their engagement with Christians.

Vivekananda in Dialogue with Christianity

Swami Vivekananda (1863–1902), disciple of Sri Ramakrishna (1836–1902) and founder of the Ramakrishna Mission, locates the normative source for Hindu–Christian dialogue in nondual religious experience, and adopts a model that many contemporary typologies will regard as inclusive, or one of fulfillment (Knitter 2002). Vivekananda's approach to dialogue with Christianity was consistent with his approach to intra-religious dialogue. Movement in religion, according to Vivekananda, is not a growth from falsehood to truth, but one from a lower to a higher truth. The world of religions is, as he puts it, "only a travelling, a coming up of different men and women, thorough various conditions and circumstances to the same goal" (Rambachan 1989: 11). For Vivekananda, the climax of this journey is the awakening to the nondual reality underlying the universe and constituting the self (*atman*) of all. This awakening is available in all the religions of the world. Paths may be different, but the goal (nonduality) is one and the same. Vivekananda positions religions at various evolutionary locations on the road to nondualism:

> All religions are so many stages. Each of them represents the stage through which the human soul passes to realize God. Therefore not one of them should be neglected. None of these stages are dangerous or bad. They are good. Just as a child becomes a young man, and a young man becomes an old man, so these are travelling from truth to truth, they become dangerous only when they become rigid, and will not move further, when they cease to grow. (Swami Vivekananda CW2: 500)

Vivekananda traces three stages in the development of all religions. In the first stage, God is an extra-cosmic being, both omnipotent and omniscient. There is little human intimacy with God at this stage, and an emphasis on divine transcendence. The second stage builds on the doctrine of omniscience, and emphasizes panentheism. God is not only in the heavens, but also present in our world and, most importantly, in the human being. In the final stage of religious evolution, the human being discovers unity and identity with the all-pervasive, nondual truth of the universe. "The gulf between God and man is thus bridged. Thus we find, by knowing God, the kingdom of heaven within us" (Swami Vivekananda CW1: 323). All religions, according to Vivekananda, reflect all three phases, since the evolution to a higher stage does not imply the discarding of any earlier phase.

Vivekananda applied this evolutionary theology to his understanding of Christianity and his to dialogue with Christians. He saw no difference between what he understood to be the religion of Jesus and the teaching of nondual Hinduism (*Advaita Vedanta*). Employing the same principle that he used to reconcile the dualistic and non-dualistic traditions in Hinduism, Vivekananda claimed that Jesus taught at different levels to disciples of varying religious aptitudes.

> To the masses who could not conceive of anything higher than a personal God, he said, "Pray to your father in heaven." To others who could grasp a higher idea, he said, "I am the vine, ye are the branches," but to his disciples to whom he revealed himself more fully, he proclaimed the highest truth, "I and my Father are One." (Swami Vivekananda CW2: 143)

> Where goest thou to seek for the Kingdom of God? Asks Jesus of Nazareth, when it is there within you. Cleanse the spirit and it is there. It is already yours. How can you get what is not yours? It is yours by right. You are the heirs of immortality, sons of the Eternal Father. (Swami Vivekananda CW4: 145)

Unlike Swami Dayananda Saraswati and the Brahmo Samaj, who rejected the Hindu doctrine of divine descent (*avatara*) into the human world, Vivekananda interpreted the meaning of Jesus through this Hindu affirmation of multiple divine manifestations. Vivekananda, however, like Hindu interpreters following him, disagreed with Christian claims for the uniqueness of Jesus. "Christ was a manifestation of God, so was the Buddha, so were some others, and there will be hundreds of others. Do not limit God anywhere" (Swami Vivekananda CW4: 29). It seemed to contradict God's love and infinity to claim that divine revelation has occurred only once, and Vivekananda appealed to Christians to acknowledge the many incarnations of God, both in the past and yet to come.

> Let us, therefore, find God not only in Jesus of Nazareth but in all the great ones that have preceded him, in all that came after him, and that are yet to come. Our worship is unbounded and free. (Swami Vivekananda CW4: 148)

Swami Vivekananda introduced a novel interpretation of nondualism (*Advaita*) as the culmination of the human religious quest and employed this as a norm with which to evaluate Christianity. He rejects the patronizing attitude that one religion is the fulfillment of all others (Swami Vivekananda CW4: 182), proposing instead not mere tolerance, but universal acceptance. He claims that he is making an argument that all religions are true, and that religious growth proceeds not from error to truth, but from lower to higher truth. It is important, however, to note that Vivekananda takes his stand on a definite view of truth, and advances a specific religious commitment. Advaita is the highest truth and the goal towards which all religions are moving – these religions representing, as it were, different points along the way. This needs to be emphasized in order to counteract impressions that the Hindu dialogue with Christianity lacks firm claims about truth.

At the same time, it is clear that Vivekananda does not see nondualism as exclusive to the Hindu tradition, or as a "truth" over which the tradition has proprietary rights or control. As already noted, he contends that all traditions and individuals, by a process of evolution, are moving towards nondualism. Each one in time will come to this truth.

> If it be true that God is the center of all religions, and that each of us is moving towards Him along one of these radii, then it is certain that all of us *must* reach that center. And at the center where all radii meet, all our differences will cease; but until we reach there, differences there must be. (Swami Vivekananda CW2: 384–5)

In other aspects of his dialogue with Christianity, Vivekananda reflects the influence of the Brahmo Samaj, even though his own impact was much greater in shaping contemporary dialogue with other traditions. He inherited the generally positive attitude toward Jesus from the Brahmo Samaj. His earliest known views about Jesus were expressed in the preface to his Bengali translation of *The Imitation of Christ*, a work attributed to the medieval Catholic monk, Thomas à Kempis. Vivekananda translated six chapters of this work, added quotations from Hindu texts, and published these collections in a monthly Bengali journal (Swami Vivekananda CW8: 159–61). *The Imitation of Christ* fascinated Vivekananda, and it was the only text, other than the *Bhagavadgita*, that he kept during his travels through India following the death of his teacher, Ramakrishna. He explained that his intention in translating this text was to present the true spirit of Christianity to his fellow Hindus, since this spirit was lacking in the Christians they encountered. It was a remarkable effort by a Hindu interpreter to save Christianity from Christians.

> Look where we may, a true Christian nowhere do we see. The ugly impression left on our
> mind by the ultra-luxurious, insolent, despotic, barouche-and-brougham-driving Chris-
> tians of the Protestant sects will be completely removed if we but once read this great book
> with the attention that it deserves. (Swami Vivekananda CW8: 160)

In support of his call to take this Christian text seriously, Vivekananda cited an aphorism from one of the orthodox Hindu traditions (*Vaiseshika*): *aptopadeshavakyam shabdah*,
which suggests that the words of a spiritually accomplished person are authoritative.
Vivekananda is clearly commending Thomas à Kempis to be such a person (*apta*).

As a Hindu renunciant (*sanyasin*), Vivekananda found it easy to identify with the
aspirations of a Christian monk. He is the earliest Hindu monk to turn to a Christian
monastic text for inspiration, anticipating later interest in these traditions. He admires
the Christian's radical renunciation, his thirst for purity, and his ardent spiritual effort
(*sadhana*). He likened *The Imitation of Christ* to the *Bhagavadgita*, and spoke of the author
as one embodying the Hindu ideal of devotion to God as a servant to master (*dasya
bhakti*). Here, in his preface, we find, for the first time, his later often-repeated reference
to the divergence between Christian ideals and Christian practice. The importance of
renunciation in the religious life is an idea to which he returned repeatedly in his dialogue with Christians.

> If you can join these two, this wonderful prosperity with the ideal of Christ, it is well. But
> if you cannot, better go back to him and give this up. Better be ready to live in rags with
> Christ than to live in palaces without him. (Swami Vivekananda CW8: 213)

Vivekananda commented, more than did earlier Hindu exegetes, on specific Christian
doctrines. In his apologetic method, he was closer to Swami Dayananda Saraswati of
the Arya Samaj than he was to the Brahmo Samaj, and his normative standpoint was
nondual Advaita. Vivekananda questioned Christian eschatological doctrine, especially
those that represented heaven or hell as eternal. Any effect is commensurate with its
cause, and if the cause is finite, the effect, of necessity, will be finite. Any number of
good works, therefore, cannot produce an infinite or permanent result. By the same
reasoning, hell cannot be a place of eternal suffering. Vivekananda is, of course,
drawing on Hindu notions of heavenly or hellish worlds as temporary postmortem
destinations before rebirth.

Vivekananda also questioned the Christian doctrine of original sin and compared
this with the Advaita understanding of the inherent purity of the *atman*. He felt, on the
whole, that the Christian tradition as he encountered it emphasized, too much, human
depravity and sinfulness.

> Be not deluded by your religion teaching original sin, for the same religion teaches original
> purity. When Adam fell, he fell from purity. Purity is our real nature and to regain that is
> the object of all religion. (Swami Vivekananda CW7: 418)

He expressed abhorrence at the idea of salvation gained through the shedding of blood.
The Hindu understood sacrifice to mean the receiving of that which is offered to God.

Vivekananda also marshaled Advaita nonduality to evaluate the Christian understanding of the soul's eternal nature. In the Advaita tradition, the doctrine of the eternal nature of the atman implies that it is also without beginning. Claiming immortality for anything that is created, for Vivekananda, is irrational.

> Sometimes people get frightened at the idea, and superstition is so strong that thinking men even believe that they are the outcome of nothing, and then, with the grandest logic, try to deduce the theory that although they have come out of zero, they will be eternal afterwards. . . . Neither you nor I nor anyone present, has come out of zero, nor will go back to zero. (Swami Vivekananda CW2: 217)

Swami Vivekananda has much less to say about Jesus than he does about Christianity. Following the Brahmo Samaj leader, Keshub Chandra Sen, Vivekananda made a sharp distinction between the Asiatic and European approaches to life and emphasized the oriental features of Jesus. Vivekananda made sweeping generalizations, characterizing the Asian attitude as one of detachment from worldly concerns. He saw Jesus as a true oriental in his unworldliness.

> He never talks of this world and of this life. He has nothing to do with it, except that he wants to get hold of the world as it is, give it a push and drive it forward and onward until the whole world has reached to the effulgent Light of God, until everyone has realized his spiritual nature, until death is vanished and misery banished. (Swami Vivekananda CW4: 146)

Vivekananda's emphasis on Jesus's disinterest in the world offers a useful point of transition to Mahatma Gandhi, who contributed significantly to Hindu–Christian dialogue, but who also brought new concerns to this conversation. Gandhi's engagement with the Christian tradition, which occurred in the context of his leadership of a nationalist struggle for Indian independence and for religious and social reform, reflects both continuities and discontinuities with earlier participants. Of all the Hindus we have considered, Gandhi had the most extensive contacts and dialogue with Christians, and became close friends with several.

Gandhi and Christianity

Gandhi's first encounters with Christianity were not positive. He heard Christian missionaries near the street corner of his high school "pouring abuse on Hindus and their gods" (Gandhi 1963: 1). He had also heard that conversion to Christianity required cultural renunciation and Europeanization.

> I heard of a well-known Hindu having been converted to Christianity. It was the talk of the town that, when he was baptized, he had to eat beef and drink liquor, that he also had to change his clothes, and that thenceforth he began to go about in European costume including a hat. (Gandhi 1963: 1)

His deeper encounter with Christians and Christianity occurred when he was a law student in England. He conversed with Christians and read parts of the Bible. He had much difficulty getting through the Hebrew texts, but the *Sermon on the Mount* went "straight to my heart." His contacts with Christians in South Africa (1893–1915) were more extensive. He engaged in dialogue with evangelical Protestants, and attended prayer services. Here also, he encountered the writings of Leo Tolstoy and was deeply attracted to Tolstoy's Christian pacifism and commitment to a life of simplicity. Tolstoy also reinforced Gandhi's efforts to distinguish Jesus from institutional Christianity, a theme already noted in our discussions of Roy and Vivekananda. By the time of his return to India, the principal elements of Gandhi's dialogue with Christianity were in place, and varied little during his life. At the same time, Gandhi's contacts in India were principally with foreign Christian missionaries who sought him out for dialogue on Jesus, Christianity and conversion.

Gandhi, like Hindu interpreters before and after him, was very selective in his use of Christian scriptures, and saw the message of Jesus as articulated almost exclusively in the Sermon on the Mount.

> When I read in the *Sermon on the Mount* such passages as "Resist not him that is evil; but whosoever smiteth thee on thy right cheek, turn to him the other also," and "Love your enemies and pray for them that persecute you, that ye may be sons of your Father which is in Heaven," I was simply overjoyed and found my own opinion confirmed where I least expected it. The *Bhagavadgita* deepened the impression, and Tolstoy's *The Kingdom of God is within You* gave it permanent form. (Gandhi 1963: 4–5)

What Gandhi found in Jesus's teaching and example was a practical method for resisting evil through nonviolence. Jesus, in other words, is one of our finest examples of *satygraha* (truth force). Gandhi disagreed strongly with Christians who interpreted the Sermon on the Mount as irrelevant to the conduct of human affairs in the world. Jesus, for him, embodied suffering, sacrifice and martyrdom. Gandhi was not hesitant to acknowledge his indebtedness to Jesus.

> Though I cannot claim to be a Christian in the sectarian sense, the example of Jesus's suffering is a factor in the composition of my underlying faith in non-violence, which rules all my actions, worldly and temporal. Jesus lived and died in vain if he did not teach us to regulate the whole of life by the eternal law of Love. (Cited in Thomas 1970: 205)

Gandhi's importance for Hindu–Christian dialogue is rooted in his interpretation of the nonviolent meaning of Jesus, which has had the greatest impact on the Christian tradition. His example has influenced nonviolent movements in various parts of the world (United States, South Africa, Philippines, Poland), but also leading Christian thinkers and activists (Rynne 2008: 26–27). Martin Luther King Jr. is an outstanding example of a Christian whose understanding of Jesus was transformed by Gandhi. King makes an extraordinary claim about the significance of Gandhi's understanding of Jesus:

Gandhi was probably the first person in history to lift the love ethic of Jesus above mere interaction between individuals to a powerful and effective social force on a large scale. Love for Gandhi was a potent instrument for social and collective transformation. (King 1958: 97)

John Thatamanil contends that the significance of this familiar King statement is yet to be fully appreciated. King may be read as asserting that Gandhi offered more than a novel method of nonviolent resistance. Gandhi, according to Thatamanil, is offering Christians a new Jesus, a new Christology. Gandhi's new Jesus is one "whose redemptive work lies not just in the generation of the private atonement of individual persons from their sin but in the collective redemption of the social order itself" (Thatamanil 2011: 7).

Gandhi's interest in working for justice, in the transformation of the social order, and in the quality of life in this world, gave special character to his dialogue with Christians and his learning from the Christian tradition. This distinguished Gandhi from many of his Hindu predecessors, and drew many Christians to Gandhi. In other respects, however, Gandhi followed his Hindu predecessors, but deepened and clarified some of issues they introduced into Hindu–Christian dialogue. Like Vivekananda, Gandhi had minimal interest in institutional Christianity and sought to separate Christ from Christianity, a move prompted for many Hindu thinkers by their recognition of the contradictions between the teachings of Jesus, on the one hand, and the behavior of those nations who claimed allegiance to him, on the other. "I consider Western Christianity," wrote Gandhi, "in its practical working a negation of Christ's Christianity" (Gandhi 1963: 33). Gandhi's concern with Western Christianity is also related to his concerns about the loss of cultural identity as a consequence of conversion. He was troubled by his encounters with "Christian Indians almost ashamed of their birth, certainly of their ancestral religion, and of their ancestral dress. The aping of Europeans on the part of Anglo-Indians is bad enough, but the aping of them by Indian converts is a violence done to their country and, shall I say, even to their new religion" (Gandhi 1963: 25–26).

Gandhi did not grant to Jesus any unique incarnational status. He regarded Jesus as "one of the greatest teachers of mankind," as an embodiment of sacrificial love, but not as the only son of God. In often-quoted words, Gandhi summarized his views on Jesus:

It was more than I could believe that Jesus was the only incarnate son of God, and that only he who believed in him would have everlasting life. If God could have sons, all of us were his sons. If Jesus was like God, or God Himself, then all men were like God and could be God Himself. (Gandhi 1963: 11–12)

Gandhi interpreted the language of Jesus as the "son of God" metaphorically, indicating Jesus's obedience to the will of God and his closeness to perfection.

It is not surprising that Gandhi had little interest in Christian arguments for the historical Jesus: "I may say," wrote Gandhi, "that I have never been interested in a historical Jesus. I should not care if it was proved by someone that the man called Jesus never lived, and that what was narrated in the Gospels was a figment of the writer's imagination. For, the *Sermon on the Mount* will still be true" (Gandhi 1963: 65–66). Gandhi's indifference to the historical Jesus meant also that he rejected doctrines of atonement and forgiveness rooted in the crucifixion of Jesus. Gandhi contended that the birth and death of Jesus are ongoing events in the life of humanity. One cannot think of birth without death on the cross; the living Christ implies the living cross. In a fascinating twist of argument, Gandhi advances the argument that the world still awaits the birth of Christ. As long as the hunger for peace remains unsatisfied, "Christ is not yet born . . . When real peace is established, we will not need demonstrations, but it will be echoed in our life, not only in individual life but in corporate life. Then we shall say, Christ is born" (Gandhi 1963: 66–67). Gandhi challenged his Christian friends to realize the meaning of the life and death of Jesus each day in their lives of sacrificial love.

> God did not bear the Cross only 1900 years ago, but He bears it today, and He dies and is resurrected from day to day. It would be poor comfort to the world if it had to depend upon a historical God who died 2,000 years ago. Do not preach the God of history, but show Him as he lives today through you. (Gandhi 1963: 37–38)

Gandhi's remarks about his preference for living examples over preaching are appropriate for commenting on an issue that was of particular importance to him in Hindu–Christian dialogue, that of conversion. Gandhi was not the first to highlight this issue. Vivekananda and Dayananda Saraswati, for example, had done so before him. The matter of conversion came up again and again in Gandhi's dialogue with Christian missionaries, and conversion remains an issue of deep controversy in Hindu–Christian dialogue. Gandhi occasionally said that he was not against conversion, but only opposed to missionaries' businesslike methods and their impersonal metaphors of "harvest." The preponderance of his writings and statements on the subject suggest that he saw no need for conversion, and advanced many arguments against it. Many of these arguments continue to be advanced in contemporary Hindu–Christian dialogue. In addition, Gandhi recognized in his Christian interlocutors a reluctance to receive from Hindus, and he challenged Christians on this issue:

> You are here to find out the distress of the people of India and remove it. But I hope you are here also in a receptive mood, and if there is anything that India has to give, you will not stop your ears, you will not close your eyes, and steel your hearts, but open your ears, eyes, and most of all, your hearts to receive all that may be good in this land. (Gandhi 1963: 17–18)

Gandhi reminds his Christian partners that we cannot give without receiving and of the mutuality of sharing that is necessary in dialogue.

His attitude to conversion was deeply informed by his commitment to the principle of *swadeshi* (one's own community/nation). In terms of religion, it meant, for Gandhi, loyalty to one's ancestral religion and commitment to working for its reform, where necessary (Thomas 1970). One can learn from and assimilate the truths of other traditions without abandoning one's own. In Gandhi's view, we do not commit ourselves to our tradition because we think it's the best in the world, but because commitment offers the ongoing possibility of transformation, both for the individual and for the tradition. He compared his loyalty to Hinduism to his feelings for his wife.

Gandhi's attitude to conversion reflects also his commitment to the doctrine of the equality of all religions: *sarva dharma samanatva* (Samartha 1974). His advocacy of this principle is clearly motivated by his political concern for religious harmony in India and his awareness of the potential for violence among the traditions of India. When Gandhi unpacks this doctrine theologically we get the general idea of a belief in the common-source of all religions, an underlying unity, and the concomitant notion of the diversity of religions as necessary for meeting various human religious needs.

> I believe in the fundamental truth of all great religions of the world. I believe that they are all God-given, and I believe that they were necessary for the people to whom these religions were revealed. (Gandhi 2001: 55)

Gandhi's doctrine of the equality of religions affirmed also their shared fallibility. Although all traditions were true, "everything that the human hand touches, by reason of the very fact that human beings are imperfect, becomes imperfect" (Gandhi 2001: 56). Awareness of the errors in our traditions should dispose us to humility in dialogue. On the whole, Gandhi's doctrine of the equality of all religions appears to be concerned primarily with cultivating a relationship among religions characterized by tolerance, respect, cooperation and learning. The equality of religions is not a closely argued theological claim, and Gandhi certainly does not think that all religious doctrines make an equal claim on him. We have already noted the many ways in which he dissents from traditional Christology. It is only in the context of his distinctive understanding of the equality of religions that we can understand why there is no need for Gandhi to become Christian in order to appreciate the wisdom of Jesus, and to be his disciple.

Although Gandhi, more than any other Hindu in his day, engaged in theological exchanges with Christians, he expressed a clear preference for what has been characterized as the dialogue of life, allowing our own living embodiment of tradition to communicate its meanings for us. Gandhi returns again and again to the analogy of the rose emitting its fragrance as a metaphor for the manner in which faiths should be shared in dialogue:

> A rose does not need to preach. It simply spreads its fragrance. The fragrance is its own sermon. If it had human understanding and if it could engage a number of preachers, the preachers would not be able to sell more roses than the fragrance itself could do. The fragrance of religious and spiritual life is much finer and subtler than that of the rose. (Gandhi 1963: 69)

Christians often pressed Gandhi about the necessity of preaching as a medium for transmitting Christian teachings. Gandhi did not relent and urged his Christian friends to step out of the way and allow God to work as God chooses. Gandhi was also deeply troubled by aid-evangelism, or proselytization that accompanied humanitarian work. He felt that such work was its own end and satisfaction. This is a matter that continues to be a source of tension between Hindus and Christians in India and elsewhere.

We have already noted Gandhi's discomfort with Indian converts' adoptions of western culinary and dress habits. Conversion engendered shame about one's ancestral religion and heritage and became synonymous, in Gandhi's eyes, with westernization. Gandhi did not believe that being Christian and Indian were so mutually exclusive.

> Conversion must not mean denationalization. Conversion should mean a definite giving up of the evil of the old, adoption of all the good for the new and a scrupulous avoidance of everything evil in the new. Conversion, therefore should mean a life of greater dedication to one's country, greater surrender to God, greater self-purification. (Gandhi 1963: 26)

He commended the example of Indian Christians like Kali Charan Bannerjee and S.K. Rudra, who simultaneously affirmed an Indian way of life and a serious Christian religious commitment.

Gandhi was concerned about the relationship between religion and national identity, an issue that found distinctive articulation in the writings of the Hindu nationalist, Vinayak Damodar Savarkar (1883–1966). In the works of Sarvarkar, Hindu identity and Indian national identity were fused with implications that would have troubled Gandhi. Savarkar's definition of Indian identity engendered tensions between Hindus and Christians, and made Hindu–Christian dialogue more difficult. Savarkar's *Hindutva* became the source of the Hindu nationalist movement in the 1920s and the term is widely used today to describe various expressions of the Hindu nationalist movement.

Savarkar and Christianity

In the *Essentials of Hindutva*, Savarkar seeks to describe the characteristics of Hindu identity. His work is an attempt to answer the question "Who is a Hindu?" by providing a definition of *Hindutva* or "Hinduness." Savarkar's criteria of Hindu identity consist of three inter-related attributes. The first is geographical: India, or Hindusthan, as Savarkar would prefer to call it, constitutes a distinct geographical entity demarcated by mountains, oceans and rivers, and a Hindu is "primarily a citizen, either in himself or through his forefathers of 'Hindusthan'" (Savarkar 1989: 82). The second and perhaps most important requirement of Hinduness is what Savarkar refers to as "common blood" or *jati*. A Hindu is a descendant of Hindu parents and shares with other Hindus a common blood traceable to the Vedic fathers or Sindhus. This argument rests essentially on an intuitive or affective claim. The third criterion of Hinduness for Savarkar is the tie of homage to Hindu culture or civilization, called Sanskriti, on the basis of the claim that Sanskrit is the language that expresses and preserves all that is worthy in the history of the Hindus. This includes a shared history, literature, art, law festivals, rites, rituals and heroes.

This third criterion was the basis for the exclusion, not only of Indian Muslims, but also of Indian Christians. Despite sharing territory and blood, they had, in Savarkar's words, "ceased to own Hindu civilization (Sanskriti) as a whole. They belong, or feel that they belong to a cultural unit altogether different from the Hindu one" (Savarkar 1989: 100–101). Savarkar was well aware of the existence of certain syncretistic communities in India, such the Muslim Bohras and Khojas of Gujarat who incorporated many elements of Sanskriti culture into their daily life. In order to exclude such groups from his definition, he turned quite late in his work to a consideration of the religious dimension of Hinduness. Hinduism or Hindu *dharma* includes all of the religious traditions, Vedic and non-Vedic, that originate from the soil of India. While the majority of Hindus subscribe to what is denoted as Sanatana Dharma or Vaidik Dharma, other traditions originating in India, such as Jainism, Sikhism, and Buddhism, must be included in the generic category of Hinduism or Hindu dharma. It is very important to note that, as the religion of the Hindus, Hindu dharma, for Savarkar, partakes of all the essentials that characterize a Hindu, such as common territory, race and culture. In addition (and, given its importance for Savarkar, this may even be regarded as a fourth attribute of Hinduness), all traditions included under the umbrella of Hindu dharma look upon India, not only as fatherland (*Pitrbhu*), but also as holyland (*Punyabhu*). In spite of its late appearance in his analysis, Savarkar gives considerable significance to this requisite of *Hindutva* and uses it as the ultimate reason for the exclusion of Christians:

> For though Hindusthan to them is Fatherland as to any other Hindu yet it is not to them a Holyland too. Their Holyland is far off in Arabia or Palestine. Their mythology and Godmen, ideas and heroes are not the children of this soil. Consequently their names and their outlook smack of foreign origin. (Savarkar 1989: 113)

Swami Vivekananda and Mahatma Gandhi were nationalists, but their nationalism was not anti-Christian. Savarkar's ideology of *Hindutva*, on the other hand, is essentially an ideology of religious nationalism. *Hindutva* makes and thrives upon a sharp distinction between Hindus and non-Hindus. It is a definition of the meaning of Hindu identity based on exclusion and otherness. In Savarkar's view, Christians are essentially an alien community in India. A contemporary exponent of the *Hindutva* perspective expressed it in the following way:

> Non-Hindus can join to create a Hindustani unity, but first they must agree to adhere to the minimum requirement: that they recognize and accept that their cultural legacy is Hindu, or that they revere their Hindu origins, that they are as equal before the law as any other but no more, and that they will make sacrifices to defend their Hindu legacy just as any good Hindu would his own. (Swamy 2006: 41)

Hindu nationalists, inspired by the thinking of Savarkar, have successfully moved the issue of conversion to the center of Hindu–Christian dialogue in India, and public dialogue is often characterized by mistrust and suspicion.

Present Hindu–Christian Dialogue

Our survey of over 150 years of Hindu–Christian dialogue, particular through the eyes of leading Hindu practitioners, reveals important trends and future challenges. Swami Dayananda Saraswati, the Arya Samaj founder, is the exception to these trends. Swami Dayananda Saraswati rejected both Christ and Christianity, and did not think that there was anything of value that Hindus may learn from Christians. He was the clearest about the authoritative Hindu sources for his engagement with Christians, developing his theological judgments about Christianity on the basis of his reading of the Vedas. He wrote about Christianity and engaged Christians with the single aim of demonstrating the irrationality and falsity of the tradition. On the other hand, Roy, Sen, Vivekananda, and Gandhi, in their different ways, embraced Jesus, but turned away from the institution of the Church and its doctrines. In affirming the significance of Jesus, each Hindu thinker gave importance to a different facet of Jesus's life and teaching. All commended the centrality of Jesus's ethics but Vivekananda spoke of Jesus's renunciation and his non-dual experience, while Gandhi saw Jesus as the embodiment of *satyagraha* or non-violent resistance and focused exclusively on the Sermon on the Mount.

One serious consequence of Hindu uninterest in institutional Christianity is the absence of any sustained engagement with Christian theology and the major Christian interpreters of Christian tradition. The analogous approach would be Christian engagement with the Hindu tradition that ignored theological giants such as Shankara, Ramanuja, Madhav or more recent voices like Vivekananda, Gandhi or Radhakrishnan. Disengagement from the rich theological traditions of Christianity and Hinduism leads to selective readings of religious texts and practices, readings that suit one's own purposes and allow one to ignore dimensions of the other tradition that are valued by its practitioners. The result is a superficial and limited dialogue. There are, for example, very few Hindus with expertise in Christian theology, and who therefore continue to rely on Hindu interpreters like Gandhi and Vivekananda for their understanding of Christianity and Christ. This remains an impediment to deep dialogue between the traditions.

It is clear also that Hindus engaged in dialogue with Christians during the colonial period adopted a defensive stance in the face of missionary attacks on Hindu teaching and practice. Each of the figures we have reviewed was concerned to defend the Hindu tradition against such attacks; each sought to call attention to the gaps between Christian ideals and practice; and each questioned the truth of Christian doctrines. The positive Hindu response to the person of Jesus, though divorced from Christianity, found no similar echo in the Christian attitude toward basic Hindu teachings, and dialogue was reduced largely to verbal attacks and counterattacks, so that opportunities for interreligious dialogue on issues of justice and socio-economic realities were also lost. Missionary onslaught in a colonial political context did not allow the self-critical space and vulnerability that makes dialogue on such issues possible and fruitful. The character of Hindu involvement in dialogue was influenced considerably by anxieties about missionary intentions and programs. Most Hindus today believe that proselytization remains the principal concern of Christians, and suspect that Christian interest in dialogue is still part of a larger evangelical agenda.

One of the important ways in which Hindu practitioners of dialogue sought, under the conditions of Christian proselytization, to distinguish their own tradition from Christianity was by making the claim that Hinduism, unlike Christianity, does not claim to be a singularly true religion. In different ways, they argued that Hinduism affirmed the validity of all religions. We see this claim particularly in the writings of Gandhi and Vivekananda. This claim, however, is quite misleading. Both Gandhi and Vivekananda unambiguously rejected specific Christian truth claims, and advanced alternatives. Gandhi disagreed with Christian doctrines arguing for the uniqueness of Jesus, as well as the atoning significance of his crucifixion. Vivekananda contested Christian eschatological teachings and emphases on human sinfulness, and highlighted what he saw as a contradiction in the argument for the eternity of a created soul. With the exception of Dayananda Saraswati, however, Hindus in dialogue were not explicit enough about the distinctive authoritative sources and norms of their truth claims. Christians were not the only ones making specific truth claims, but Hindus did so with a less explicit self-consciousness. This legacy, with rare exceptions, continues today, and works as an impediment to constructive dialogue.

Political considerations, especially in colonial India, were never absent from dialogical encounters between Hindus and Christians. Such political considerations took a new turn with the rise of Hindu nationalism, inspired by Savarkar's ideology of *Hindutva*. Fusing religious, cultural and national identity, this ideology heightened suspicions about Christian commitments to the Indian nation, and strongly critiqued conversion missions as divisive efforts to destroy the unique religio-cultural heritage of India. Even on this issue, however, the dialogue between Hindus and Christians remains stuck in mutual stereotyping. Christians see Hindu concerns about conversion as disguised efforts to preserve the privileges and power relationships inherent in the caste system, reflecting a monolithic view of Hindu tradition, and thereby failing to recognize the controversial nature of caste within Hinduism, and the challenges to that system from distinguished Hindu leaders and reformers. Hindus, in turn, see Christianity as a tradition concerned only with increasing power through conversion, with the aim of overcoming all other traditions. It appears to me that there are few serious attempts on the Hindu side to understand the meaning and attraction of Christianity to the convert. It must be instructive that the largest numbers of converts from Hindu traditions to Christianity come from the so-called untouchable castes. They experience their home tradition as oppressive and as negating their dignity and self-worth. For such persons, the Christian messages of the inclusive love of God, and acceptance in a community affirming human equality and value, are liberating. There needs to be an acknowledgment by Christians that even the Christian Church in India has not been able to free itself from the social inequities and expressions of caste, pointing to caste as phenomenon that transcends any specific religious doctrine.

The future of Hindu–Christian dialogue is uncertain. I concur with Klostermaier (1989) that the Hindu–Christian dialogue must emphasize wisdom (*jnana*), while confessing my own sadness at the absence of sustained theological engagement between these traditions. The reasons for this current absence are complex, and lay beyond the scope of this discussion. There are anti-intellectual trends in both traditions that lead to disinterest in theology, and which distinguish theology from spirituality. In many contemporary Hindu movements, there is greater interest in the political, and less involvement in religious reflection. In calling for renewed theological engagement between Hinduism and Christianity, I have in mind the rich history of rational reflection by persons of deep religious commitment, exemplified in the works of saintly scholars such as Shankara, Ramanuja, Aquinas and Augustine. Along with a focus on theological depths of each tradition, Hindu–Christian dialogue must be concerned also with justice and with the role and responsibility of religion in overcoming systems of oppression and domination. Hindu–Christian dialogue needs a new infusion of interest and energy. It is quite likely that such an infusion, contrary to the belief of Klostermaier (1989) will come from Hindu and Christian communities outside of India. In many of the these communities, the United States for example, the impediments to dialogue, such as tensions engendered by the politics of nationalism and proselytization, are not as prominent. The conditions are more conducive for mutual learning and cooperation.

Bibliography

Abhishiktananda (Henri le Saux). *The Hindu–Christian Meeting Point*. Bombay: The Institute of Indian Culture, 1969.

Abhishiktananda (Henri le Saux). *Saccidananda: A Christian Approach to Advaitic Experience*. Delhi: ISPCK, 1974.

Amaladass, Anand. "Dialogue between the Hindus and the St. Thomas Christians," in *Hindu–Christian Dialogue*, ed. Harold Coward. Maryknoll, NY: Orbis, 1989.

Ariarajah, S. Wesley. *Hindus and Christians: A Century of Protestant Ecumenical Thought*. Grand Rapids, MI: Eerdmans, 1991.

Clooney, Francis X. *Theology After Vedanta: An Experiment in Comparative Theology*. Albany: State University of New York Press, 1993.

Clooney, Francis X. *Seeing Through Texts: Doing Theology Among the Srivaisanavas of South India*. Albany: State University of New York Press, 1996.

Collett, S.D. (ed.). *Lectures and Tracts by Keshub Chunder Sen*. London: Strahan, 1870.

Coward, Harold. "Introduction," in *Hindu–Christian Dialogue*, ed. Harold Coward. Maryknoll, NY: Orbis, 1989.

Eck, Diana. *Encountering God*. Boston: Beacon Press, 1993.

Farquhar, J.N. *Modern Religious Movements in India*. Delhi: Manorharlal, 1914.

Gandhi, Mahatma. *The Message of Jesus Christ*, ed. Anand T. Hingorani. Bombay: Bharatiya Vidya Bhavan, 1963.

Gandhi, Mahatma. *All Men Are Brothers*, ed. Krishna Kripalani. New York: Continuum, 2011.

Griffiths, Bede. *Christ in India: Essays towards a Hindu–Christian Dialogue*. Springfield: Templegate Publishers, 1966.

Griffiths, Bede. *Vedanta and Christian Faith*. Los Angeles: The Dawn Horse Press, 1973.

Jordens, J.T. *Dayananda Sarasvati: His Life and Ideas*. Delhi: Oxford University Press, 1978.

King, Martin Luther, Jr. *Stride Towards Freedom: The Montgomery Story*. New York: Harper, 1958.

Klostermaier, Klaus. "The Future of Hindu–Christian Dialogue," in *Hindu–Christian Dialogue*, ed. Harold Coward. Maryknoll, NY: Orbis, 1989.

Knitter, Paul. *Theologies of Religion*. Maryknoll, NY: Orbis, 2002.

Kopf, David. *The Brahmo Samaj and the Shaping of the Modern Indian Mind*. Princeton, NJ: Princeton University Press, 1979.

Panikkar, Raimundo. *The Vedic Experience: Mantramanjari: An Anthology of the Vedas for Modern Man and Contemporary Celebration.* Berkeley: University of California Press, 1977.

Panikkar, Raimundo. *The Unknown Christ of Hinduism: Towards and Ecumenical Christophany.* Maryknoll, NY: Orbis, 1981.

Rambachan, Anantanand. "Swami Vivekananda: A Hindu Model for Interreligious Dialogue," in *Interreligious Dialogue,* ed. M. Darrol Bryant and Frank Flinn. New York: Paragon House, 1989.

Rynne, J. Terrence. *Gandhi and Jesus: The Saving Power of Nonviolence.* Maryknoll, NY: Orbis, 2008.

Samartha, Stanley. *The Hindu Response to the Unbound Christ.* Madras: Christian Literature Society, 1974.

Saraswati, Dayananda. *Light of Truth,* trans. C. Bharadwaja. Delhi: Arya Pratinidhi Sabha, 1975.

Savarkar, V.D. *Hindutva.* Delhi: Bharti Sahitya Sadan, 1989.

Swami Vivekananda. *The Collected Works,* abbreviated CW. 8 Vols. Kolkata: Advaita Ashrama. 1964–1971.

Swamy Subramanian. *Hindus Under Siege.* New Delhi: Har-Anand Publications, 2006.

Thomas, M.M. *The Acknowledged Christ of the Indian Renaissance.* Madras: Christian Literature Society, 1970.

Thatamanil, John. "The Hospitality of Receiving: Mission and Conversion In an Interreligious Age." Unpublished Lecture delivered at Louisville Presbyterian Seminary, October 20, 2011.

CHAPTER 21

Native American Spirituality and Christianity

Achiel Peelman

Inter-religious dialogue has often been restricted to participants from the so-called major "world religions": Judaism, Christianity, Islam, Hinduism and Buddhism. The inclusion of native, aboriginal, tribal or "traditional religions" in such dialogue, though still limited, is nonetheless highly significant because it includes also many Native persons who have become Christian without abandoning their traditional beliefs. We will examine how this unique situation affects both the future of aboriginal spirituality and Christianity in the North American context with a particular focus on the First Nations peoples in Canada. My reflections on this topic are inspired by personal initiation into the traditional spirituality of the Cree people in Northern Alberta and by regular meetings with aboriginal persons in the Anishinabe Spiritual Centre in Anderson Lake, Ontario. I will first present a brief picture of aboriginal spirituality and then reflect on the different types of dialogue between traditional spirituality and Christianity.

Native American Religions: A Way of Life

The Native American religions figure among the oldest in the world. They are excellent examples of the so-called primitive, primal or tribal religions that are still very much alive today, and deserve their distinctive place among the great spiritual traditions of humankind. Their inclusion in inter-religious dialogue may contribute to a deeper appreciation of their uniqueness and contribution to humankind, especially because of the holistic nature and the ritual dimension of their spirituality.

A millennial experience

Archaeologists and anthropologists continue to study the mysterious (probably) Asian origins of Native American peoples, while showing how they developed and diversified

The Wiley Blackwell Companion to Inter-Religious Dialogue, First Edition. Edited by Catherine Cornille.
© 2013 John Wiley & Sons Ltd. Published 2020 by John Wiley & Sons Ltd.

in adapting to the various geographical and ecological conditions of the Americas. We are dealing here with a wide spectrum of religious and spiritual traditions, which clearly demonstrate Native peoples' remarkable ability to cope with cultural changes and the deprivations provoked by intertribal contacts and conflicts, and by confrontation with the Western world. It should come as no surprise that these religions continue to play an important role in many Native communities across Canada.

Contemporary archaeological research tends to situate the arrival of the first Paleo-Siberians around 15,000 BCE, perhaps even earlier. By 8,000 these first "Native" peoples can be found in all parts of the Americas, from Alaska to Tierra del Fuego (Dickason 1994: 20–50). All these peoples shared a common circumpolar culture, with more or less similar characteristics: hunting taboos, animal ceremonialism, belief in spirits and shamanism. At the end of a very long period of migration, this common religious stratum gradually diversified into two contrasting religious systems: the old hunting religions and the new horticultural religions. Each "system" developed its own myths, beliefs, symbols and rituals by being faithful to its own origins (cultural continuity) and by adapting to new geographical and historical conditions (cultural discontinuity and acculturation).

Basic characteristics of Native American spirituality

Cornelius Peter Tiele's influential 1876 monograph, *Outline of the History of Religions to the Spread of Universal Religions*, established a clear distinction between the "world religions" and the religions of the traditional peoples around the world. "World religions" are often presented as "universalistic religions" or book religions. But there seems to be no unanimity around the presentation of the religious experience of traditional peoples. Some Native authors avoid the term "religion" because of its institutional overtones. Others avoid "spirituality" because of its New Age connections. Some African theologians, like Laurenti Magesa, are not at ease with the term "African Traditional Religion" (ATR) to designate what many Africans simply call their "way of life." The qualifier *traditional* is therefore redundant. They prefer to use the terms African spirituality or African religiosity. Contemporary scholarship has expressed itself in favor of the parity of African religiosity with the other "world religions" (Magesa 1997: 1–34). Speaking out of his own initiation into the spirituality of aboriginal peoples in Australia, David Turner vigorously challenges the academic dichotomy between aboriginal and world religions. When we focus on mystical experiences, we may discover that aboriginal religions have more things in common with the world religions than we are ready to accept (Turner 1996).

These observations also apply to North America. Whether we refer to Native American "religions" or "spiritualities," they present themselves from time immemorial primarily as an all-embracing "lifeway" and not as a "belief system." Because of the Native person's intimate experience of the Great Mystery (God – the Supreme Being) and his/her connection with the universe as a spiritual or animated environment, Native American religions are both profoundly sacramental and mystical. These religions present themselves as an ongoing spiritual journey or religious process which is first experienced on the level of tribe, clan, extended family or nation (Peelman 1995: 39–60). Further, Native authors like Sam Gill point to the *performative* or *practical/ritual* dimension of the Native American religious experience (Gill 1987: 81–101). The survival of this experience depends directly on the transmission of the oral traditions and ritual practice. The fact that we have today more published studies by Native authors like Vine Deloria Jr, Jace Weaver, George Tinker, Stan McKay, William Baldridge, Robert Allen Warrior, Marie Therese Archambault and many others on Native American spirituality does not change this (Treat 1996). The development of Native American spirituality depends directly on the people's willingness to participate in its ongoing realization. Significantly, in many Native communities elders and spiritual leaders are concerned about the lack of interest in traditional Native spirituality among Indian youth. We will see further how this situation profoundly affects the contemporary relationship between Native American spirituality and Christianity.

The fact that Native American spirituality gives high priority to experiential learning, practice and ritual does not mean that it is less "theological" or "philosophical" than the institutionalized world religions. In his posthumous work, *The World's Rim*, published in 1953, Hartley Burr Alexander was able to demonstrate that over the centuries the aboriginal peoples of the Americas have developed an extraordinary awareness of the sacred, and that many rituals like the Sun Dance represent complex symbolic forms of thinking (Alexander 1953). Joseph Epes Brown speaks of a "metaphysics of nature" spelled out by each Native group in detail and in close relationship with its environment, notwithstanding the pressures of modern technological cultures (Brown 1982). Contemporary Native theologians like George Tinker (Osage/Cherokee), and Jace Weaver (Cherokee) insist on the priority of symbolic thinking and ritual practices when they study the relationship between the Native American and Christian traditions (Tinker 2008; Weaver 1998). Inter-religious symbolism has come to full expression in the *Stations of the Cross* of Leland Bell (Anishinabe) and in the *Tree of Life* of Blake Debassige (Anishnabe) (Peelman 1995: 195–226).

A contemporary reality with deep historical roots

The survival of aboriginal spirituality is one of the most fascinating aspects of the multicultural American landscape. Traditional spirituality is still very much alive. This represents a formidable challenge for many Christian churches because of the historical link between colonialism and their missionary enterprise. Aboriginal spirituality continues to color the religious and cultural identity of many contemporary Native Americans, not only of those who consider themselves "traditionalists," but also of those who became Christian and want to remain Christian. From the very beginning, the historical encounter between aboriginal spirituality and Christianity has been highly confrontational. The Catholic and Protestant churches came to the Americas with a double missionary agenda: to civilize and to save (Grant 1984). Indians were pagans in need of a double conversion (Pagden 1982). To explain the astonishing survival and contemporary vitality of aboriginal spirituality I would like to make two important observations.

My first observation concerns dialogue as a fundamental dimension of the aboriginal ethos. One of the first things that the "newcomers" discovered when they came to America was the importance of the exchange of gifts among the aboriginal tribes or nations, often during elaborate ceremonies and in situations of both conflict and cooperation (Dickason 1992: 176–179). It is important to note that this exchange of gifts was not limited to material commodities but also included important religious objects like the sacred drums and the sacred pipe, often called the "pipe of peace," by which the aboriginal peoples communicated with the Great Mystery. The exchange of these prayer instruments strengthened inter-tribal relationships and can be considered as a form of inter-religious dialogue. Moreover, for the aboriginal peoples this "dialogue as exchange of gifts" was not limited to humans alone but extended itself to all vital forces in their spiritual world as many of their legends and rituals illustrate. The sacred pipe stands central in many contemporary efforts to foster a ritual and theological context for dialogue between aboriginal spirituality and Christianity (Peelman 1995: 133–162; Steinmetz 1990).

My second observation concerns the Native American reception of Christianity. Many Native Americans welcomed the missionaries as prayerful women and men and adopted Christianity but without abandoning their traditional worldview or spirituality. This forces us to recognize that their initial response to Christianity cannot be reduced to a simple yes or no. Their yes was indeed also a no! Modern historiography, in particular ethnohistory, helps us to understand that Christianity had a tremendous impact on the aboriginal peoples but that it was unable to change drastically their religious worldview (Trigger 1985). John Webster Grant summarizes this situation by stating: "If the measure of success [of the missionary epoch in Canada] is that most Indians have become Christian, the measure of failure is that Christianity has not become Indian" (Grant 1984: 262). I have explained elsewhere that all this resulted in the development of a great variety of syncretic and prophetic movements (Peelman 1995: 61–98). But what we need to remember here is that, throughout North America, many Native persons and communities continue to struggle with the question: "Can I be both Christian and Indian, or must I choose?" This question stands at the center of our contemporary efforts to move from confrontation to dialogue between Christianity and the Native American spiritual traditions.

A Dialogue in the Making

Since the famous first "Day of Prayer for Peace," which took place at Assisi in October 1986, we have become more aware of the vital importance of aboriginal spiritualities for humankind and of the urgency to include them in the inter-religious dialogue process. The symbolic significance of this event was truly enhanced by the participation of two traditional Elders: Togbui Assenou, representing the traditional African religions of Togo, and John Pretty On Top, member of the Crow Nation in the United States. The Sacred Pipe Ceremony, presided by John Pretty On Top, was considered one of the highlights of this encounter. The Sacred Pipe, used during the Native American prayer ceremony, and the olive plants which were given by young people to the participants at the end of this ceremony, were the only two "material" symbols used during the entire day. Yet, we must also recognize the limits of this event. In Assisi, people came together to pray but they did not pray together. By all means, the organizers wanted to avoid the danger of syncretism. We will see further that syncretism remains a major preoccupation in the dialogue between traditional spiritualities and Christianity.

An invitation to dialogue

During the Synod of Bishops for America (Rome 1991), two Native American participants, Bishop Donald Pelotte and Chief Harry Lafond, launched a strong appeal to dialogue. Pelotte, born of an Abenaki father and French-Canadian mother, was bishop of the diocese of Gallup (New Mexico) from 1986 till his death in 2010. Gallup is one of the poorest dioceses in the United States, with a very diversified Native population (Zunis, Lagunas, Acomas, Navajos, Apaches), and Pelotte's career as bishop was marked in part by his emphasis on the vital link between solidarity and inter-religious dialogue. The Church must support the efforts of the aboriginal peoples to obtain justice regarding treaties, land and water rights, education, housing, health care and other social services. He spoke of two forms of dialogue: on the one hand, dialogue among the aboriginal Christians regarding the future of their own communities, and, on the other hand, dialogue between these aboriginal Christians and those who either never became Christian or who have left the Church to return to their own traditions. Personal and communal healing is a major issue in these two forms of dialogue (Pelotte 1997). Chief Harry Lafond (Meskeg Lake Indian Band in Saskatchewan) was the only lay-person invited to address the Synod and to share with the pope and the bishops the background of his bi-cultural Native and Christian education and his concern for the future of the Catholic Church among Canada's aboriginal peoples. Addressing the pope as *Nimosom kitatamiskatinan* (Grandfather) and as *kitchi katayino* (a true spiritual leader), he referred to the historically troubled relationship between the Catholic Church and the aboriginal peoples. For more than 100 years, Native elders prayed secretly and kept their own spiritual traditions alive despite all forms of oppression and suppression by the Government and the Church. But these same elders, who as "Christlike" figures can be compared to the early leaders in the New Testament Church, are now ready to share openly their teachings about the Creator, Mother Earth, healing and reconciliation with the young. The Church, he said, must continue to "walk with the aboriginal peoples," which means in his Cree language *sitoskatowin*, to lean on another as we journey together. But in this journey, he concluded:

> We must become risk takers and dialogue on subjects leading to tremendous change. We must openly dialogue about the ordination of elders, the role of elders, organized structures, ceremonies and rites. As we sit down in that circle to plan our spiritual goals, we begin a journey that will change both of us. In the context of Jesus Christ's message, we can experience evangelization together. (Lafond 1997)

Chief Lafond reminds us that Native-American dialogue cannot be limited to a conversation on pre-established topics but that it is a social process inviting the participants to become "risk-takers" in view of real and mutual transformations.

Four types of dialogue

Many contemporary Christians may be inclined to believe that inter-religious dialogue is almost the exclusive affaire of scholars and experts, symposia and intellectual conversations among Church leaders. Yet, a joint document of the Congregation for the Evangelization of Peoples and the Pontifical Council for Inter-Religious Dialogue (two important Roman Catholic organizations), published in 1991, reminds us that this type of intellectual exchange presupposes three other types of dialogue; (a) a "dialogue of life," in which people engage with others in their community to share their daily joys and sorrows, their human problem and expectations; (b) the "dialogue of action," a call for Christians to cooperate with those of other faiths in projects for the integral development and the liberation of people; and (c) the "dialogue of religious experience," where persons well rooted in their own tradition share their prayers, spiritual experiences and rituals with others of different faiths (Arinze 1997). How does this reflect the North American context of Native-Christian dialogue?

The "dialogue of life" and the "dialogue of action" are personal and community-based forms of dialogue. They constitute the basis for a real transformation of our social and human environment. They lay the foundations for the development of culture of peace. They must become an essential dimension of the education of each child or young person if we want to avoid conflicts based on religious differences. In the Canadian multicultural context, this education must focus on the special needs and expectations of the First Nations as well as on their cultural uniqueness. This may help to reverse once and for all the assimilation ideology (Canada's "original sin") which dominated politics from the beginning of the European settlement.

Since the publication of *God is Red. A Native View of Religion* in 1972 by the great Native American Scholar Vine Deloria Jr., the "theological dialogue of intellectual exchange" has also progressed (Deloria 2003). We see more Native theologians seizing responsibility for their own spiritual well-being and generating their own interpretive theologies – whether Christian or traditional. Their reflections cover all fields of theology; they are often dialogical, sometimes openly confrontational, as they seek to move beyond the colonial perspectives of the past (Treat 1996). On the non-Native side, only a limited number of theologians, including myself, have ventured on to Indian Territory. Jesuit theologians like Paul Steinmetz and Carl Starkloff, are truly interested in Native American dialogue, but their major concern is "inculturation": the dynamic relationship between Native cultures, the Christian message, and the building of truly Native-Christian communities (Starkloff 2002; Steinmetz 1990). Christopher Vecsey offers an overview of this approach in his presentation of the evolution of American Catholic mission studies (Vecsey 1999). We will come back to the relationship between inter-religious dialogue and inculturation.

The most challenging of all forms of inter-religious dialogue is the "dialogue of religious experience" in which Christians and members of other living faiths come together to pray, meditate, contemplate and celebrate. This type of spiritual hospitality cannot develop without the mutual readiness to share the most precious dimension of one's existence: one's personal relationship with the Great Mystery (God – the Absolute), something that words alone cannot adequately express. I was offered this type of spiritual hospitality soon after I set out (in the mid-1980s) to study the future of the Catholic Church in Indian Territory. Some elders told me very delicately: "Your research is too Church-centered, not sufficiently people-centered. We are a 'spiritual people.' No one is going to take our spirituality away from us and we have many spiritual things to offer you if you are ready to receive." During my personal journey, I welcomed every opportunity that was offered to me to participate in the spiritual life of my Native guides: praying with the Sacred Pipe for peace and reconciliation, suffering and praying for purification and healing in the Sweat Lodge, celebrating the New Creation in the early Sun Rise Ceremony, sharing the pristine joy of a young Native girl and boy during their Name Giving Ceremony, and a long but beautiful journey leading to my own Vision Quests in Northern Alberta in the mid-1980s. Cardinal Frances Arinze, former president of the Pontifical Council for Inter-Religious Dialogue, considered the "dialogue of religious experience" as the basis of all forms of dialogue (Arinze 1997), and Christian monastics such as the French Benedictines Henri Le Saux, also known as Swami Abhishikananda (1910–1973), and Jules Monchanin, also known as Swami Paramarubyananda (1895–1973), German-Japanese Jesuit Enomiya-Lassale (1898–1990), American Cistercian Thomas Merton (1915–1968), and English Benedictine Bede Griffiths (1906–1993), have been pioneers in this dialogue (Blée 2011).

Reconciliation and dialogue

In the Canadian context, the dialogue between aboriginal spirituality and Christianity remains a difficult process. After the war of 1812, the early relationship of "mutual cooperation" and "creative symbiosis" between the Natives and the "newcomers" rapidly developed into a colonial relationship of total dependency (Dickason 1990: 273–289). Notwithstanding their cultural renaissance, Canada's Native peoples continue to figure among the most dispossessed peoples of the earth (York 1990). Their social situation remains extremely fragile. Contemporary Native leaders seem to focus more on community and personal healing than on political solutions (Morrisseau 1998). This has become a major theme during the many hearings organized by the Canadian Truth and Reconciliation Commission, established by the Canadian Government in 2008, to reflect on the experience of the aboriginal children in Residential Schools between 1870 and 1996. The historical role of these schools is complex, but they continue to be viewed as the very symbol of the cultural oppression experienced by Canada's First Nations. Reconciliation between the aboriginal peoples, the Christian Churches and Canadian society is one of the fundamental objectives of the Commission. This objective cannot be achieved without renewed efforts of dialogue between

Christianity and Native American spirituality. But is there any future for this type of dialogue in North America?

The Meeting of the Rivers

In 1983, when participating in an Arapaho Sun Dance Ritual, theologian Carl Starkloff was told by one of the ceremonial chiefs that one day the Native Peoples' traditional religion and Christianity will come together like the Wind River and the Little Wind River in Wyoming (Starkloff 2002). A similar prophecy was made by Peter Otcheese, one of the most respected Cree Elders, during a gathering involving Elders from Guatemala, Mexico and the United States which took place in Assumption Alberta in 1979 (Peelman 1995: 118). The image of the "two rivers" evokes the dynamic and enigmatic character of the Aboriginal–Christian dialogue as it unfolds today with all its cultural and religious implications.

The syncretic process

The fear of syncretism has been one of the main causes for the exclusion of the traditional religions from the inter-religious dialogue process. "Syncretophobia" has dominated Protestant and Catholic mission studies and ecclesiology since the Second World War, very much because of Hendrik Kraemer's total rejection of the phenomenon (Starkloff 2002: 146). Syncretism was often associated with relativism, indifferentism, confusion, and deviation. It was accused of disrupting the purity or the perfection of the Christian faith and of producing decadent forms of Christianity. Bad syncretism was often opposed to good inculturation. But the opponents of syncretism seemed to ignore the fact that Christianity, with its Jewish and Hellenistic roots, has always been culturally syncretic, like most of the World Religions.

With the rapid development of Christianity outside the Western world during the second half of the twentieth century, a more positive understanding of syncretism has developed. Christian Churches are recruiting the large majority of their members among the traditional peoples and must allow them to respond to the Gospel message in new and creative ways in order to become a "world religion." Syncretism allows Christianity to develop new links between the global and the local (Schreiter 1997: 62–83). Syncretism is therefore not opposed to Catholicity, understood as "universality"; it is its generative force.

Contemporary scholars like Carl Starkloff and myself, long involved in inter-religious dialogue and inculturation in the North American context, are convinced that syncretism is a fundamental aspect of the historical encounter of the Gospel with the aboriginal peoples. Borrowing insights from Bernard Lonergan and Eric Voegelin (the metaxy concept,) Starkloff views syncretism not as a "system" but as an ongoing process or even as a symbol, not a symbol of distortion or disorder, but of the enduring quest for unity (Starkloff 2002). In my own research on the mysterious presence of Christ among Canada's Native peoples, following the famous statement made by Pope

John Paul II in 1984 that "in the members of his own Body Christ is himself Indian," I was able to appreciate their unique contribution to the development of a contextual Amerindian/Christian theology at the grassroots level. Only Native people could give the answer to the question concerning the "Indian" Christ: Who do you say I am? (Peelman 1995: 99–132). This question has received a large variety of answers throughout the Americas (and elsewhere), illustrating the fact, according to Brazilian theologian Alfonso Soares, that syncretism is the pluralistic revelation of God in action. Syncretism is above all a practice (a process) that precedes all our theological options and ideological colors; making us attentive to how God interacts with human beings in their specific cultural context (Vigil 2010: 154–169). Other Latin American theologians have examined the images that Native Americans have of God after half a millennium of contact with Christianity. Peruvian theologian Manual Marzal argues that these Indian faces of God are not the result of the missionaries' pastoral efforts but of the Native Peoples' syncretism; they arise from their efforts to make the Christian message more comprehensible while conserving the basic elements of their aboriginal religion. They call for new forms of dialogue between aboriginal religion and Christianity (Marzal 1996).

Religious identity and religious mobility

During many Native rituals across Canada, I have often heard the statement, "God wrote two books: the Book of Life (our life) and the Bible. The Bible, God's second book, was given to us by the Christian missionaries to enrich or enlighten our life experience but it did not replace the worldview that supported this experience from time immemorial." Indigenous peoples have their own way of understanding divine revelation as a dialogue: the ongoing dialogue between God and all the peoples God created, each with their own cultural and religious traditions. Some have developed a significant synthesis between the two books of revelation, but for most the dialogue between the two books remains an arduous process. Many Native persons are still wondering where they belong. For them, "To be or not to be Christian/Indian" is still a real question.

Double or multiple religious identity is a widespread phenomenon when traditional peoples "converted" to a meta-cosmic or "world religion." In many Asian countries multiple religious belonging is a rule rather than an exception, at least on the popular level. It is not perceived as a problem as long as religions are considered as inclusive systems which help people to cope with their basic needs and questions in the course of life. Double religious belonging becomes a theological problem only in the "religions of the book" (Judaism, Christianity and Islam) because of their exclusive claim to divine revelation (Phan 2003). All over Africa, the dialogue between Christianity and the African Traditional Religions is profoundly affected by the fact that African Christians continue to cross the boundaries between traditional lifeways and Christian practice. This phenomenon remains a major concern for the large majority of contemporary Church leaders.

In North America the astonishing survival of aboriginal religion has long been viewed as a failure of the Church's mission enterprise. Missionary Churches have welcomed the renaissance of Native religion or attempted to help their Native members find a balance or harmony between their traditional spirituality and their new Christian faith. Many Native persons experience some version of "double religious belonging" and cross boundaries between Christianity and their traditional spirituality, especially on the ritual level. Asian theologian Michael Amaladoss views this religious mobility as a fundamental right: the right to search for meaning outside the boundaries of one's socio-religious group or system. But he is well aware of the implications of this phenomenon for the maintenance or the development of one's religious identity (Amaladoss 2008: 148–153). It should therefore not come as a surprise that in many Native communities this religious mobility can be a source of profound tensions. And for many Native persons, inter-religious dialogue has indeed become an "internal" dialogue regarding their identities and practices as aboriginal persons and as Christians (Starkloff 2002: 103). Peter Phan describes this "internal" dialogue as the encounter or interaction between two or more religious traditions sometimes leading to unexpected and unforeseeable personal "transformations," while Starkloff uses the term "internal conversions" (Phan 2003: 511).

It seems clear that this "internal" dialogue, as well as the future of the dialogue between the traditional Native religion and Christianity, will involve persons who have a "bi-cultural" formation and who are deeply rooted in their Native and Christian traditions. Amaladoss refers to them as "liminal persons" but also notes that ordinary people know to "integrate traditional rituals into a new faith framework." But these phenomena of symbiosis are not official and the elite in the community often look down on them (Amaladoss 2002, 149–150). In his remarkable study of Aymara Catholicism in Bolivia, based on the groundbreaking research of Canadian missionary Jacques Monast, Andrew Orta calls Aymara "syncretic subjects," persons (Native catechists) deeply involved in the making and remaking of entangled social orders (Orta 2004, 147–181).

Inter–religious dialogue and Inculturation

Because Native American cultures are fundamentally religious cultures, inter-religious dialogue remains closely connected with inculturation. Inculturation emerged as a new theological concept in the second half of the twentieth century to express the dynamic relationship between the Gospel message and the culture or the way of life of those to whom the Gospel is proposed as a source of life. Today there is a growing tendency to replace the term "inculturation" with the term "contextualization." Both concepts continue to turn the contemporary theological imagination toward the complex cultural implications of the Church's evangelizing mission. Some Native American theologians like Jace Weaver and George Tinker continue to view inculturation as a basic form of domination. Christianity, with its universal and exclusive truth claims, dominates and assimilates all the local cultures it meets during its missionary journey across the world (Tinker 1993: 84–111; Weaver 1998: 1–25). Because of the Christian Churches' negative attitudes toward Native American cultures in the past, new efforts to inculturate the Gospel in aboriginal communities are often met with skepticism, distrust and even opposition. It is not unusual to meet Native persons, especially those who are familiar with the history of the Indian-White relations in North America, who interpret inculturation as a new form of colonization supporting Church control over Native members, especially those who embrace traditional spirituality. Therefore, inculturations of the Gospel will always remain a tremendous challenge in traditional societies where religion and culture are closely connected.

To keep things in an historical perspective, we have to remember that the North American missionary epoch was never a "one way" experience, but always involved cultural transfers and interactions between the teachers and the receivers of the Gospel message. These interactions set in motion important prophetic and revitalization movements. The most important example of these cultural and religious interactions is the Peyote Religion, a new religious movement that emerged among the Plains Indians near the end of the nineteenth century. As the most significant and widespread pan-Indian religion of the twentieth century, Peyotism became in 1950 the Native American Church of the United States, and later, so as to include the Canadian Peyotists, the Native American Church of North America (NAC of NA).

In his famous study on Oglala Lakota religious identity, Paul Steinmetz demonstrates convincingly that interaction between Peyote, Sacred Pipe and Christianity on the Pine Ridge Reservation in South Dakota has produced at least six types of composite religious groups. These religious identities are very ambivalent and flexible, based on both continuity and discontinuity, and are influenced by the basic human needs for security, strength and vulnerability. Steinmetz concludes his study by stating that both the missionary and the anthropologist have often misunderstood the religious situation of the Native Americans: "The Native Americans did not embrace Christianity divorced from their traditional religion, as the missionary assumed, nor did they practice a traditional religion unaffected by their Christianity, as the anthropologist assumed" (Steinmetz 1990: 199). His study, and many others, illustrate that the theological reality of "inculturation" is inseparable from the anthropological phenomenon of "acculturation," as well as the often devastating impact of one (dominating) culture on another (minority) culture.

In many Native communities, "inculturation" remains an important theological and pastoral preoccupation as I could personally witness in the Anishinabe Spiritual Centre in Anderson Lake, Ontario, where Native persons meet to reflect on the future of their Christian communities. They are very much preoccupied with the adaptation of the Christian liturgy to their traditional spirituality. Several Christian Churches in Canada (the Catholic Church, the Anglican Church and the United Church of Canada) have incorporated indigenous symbols and rituals in their public worship. One of the reasons given for this openness is that Native traditions are interpreted as spiritualities and not as religions. But this has nothing to do with the authentic inculturation and inter-religious dialogue. Inculturation is often, and wrongly, understood as a missionary strategy to bring the Native cultures into the Western Church. Authentic inculturation is exactly the contrary. It is not a program imposed by Church leaders or outsiders, but rather the result of the Native communities' creative response to the Gospel message. Their task and challenge is to create new ways of being a Church community, and to become authentic followers of Christ while being faithful both to their own Native traditions and to the Gospel message they have welcomed. The challenge of inculturation is linked to the challenge of inter-religious dialogue.

In her remarkable study of the Sioux Lakota and the Rio Grande Pueblo, Joëlle Rostkowski uses the concept of "unachieved conversion" to capture the historical relationship between Christianity and traditional Native religions (Rostkowski 1998). She refers mainly to the dialogue that involved Native Elders and Catholic missionaries. This dialogue must go on now that both aboriginal spirituality and Christianity are experiencing tremendous transformations. Since Vatican II, Catholicism is more ready to recognize the elements of truth in other religious traditions. But this development is often opposed by fundamentalist movements within the Christian Churches. Aboriginal spirituality is enjoying a significant renaissance but many Elders are concerned about the transmission of this tradition to the younger members of their community. They also express concerns about the exploitation of their traditional religion by followers of the New Age movement or by "wannabe" Indians who claim Native ancestry for personal interests.

Conclusion

All this leads to the conclusion that the Aboriginal–Christian dialogue will affect not only the future of the Christian Churches which have implanted themselves in Native American territory, but North American society as a whole. Both inter-religious dialogue between Native American religions and Christianity, and the more general process of inculturation, draw our attention to the vital significance of traditional spiritualities for humankind as a whole. This was often stressed by Pope John Paul II, starting with his often-quoted speech to the aboriginal peoples of Australia in Alice Springs, November 1986:

> Your culture, which shows the lasting genius and dignity of your race, must not be allowed to disappear. Do you think that your gifts are worth so little that you should no longer bother to maintain them? Share them with each other and teach them to your children. Your songs, your stories, your paintings, your dances, your languages, must never be lost. (John-Paul II, 2006)

In a similar fashion, African philosopher Aimé Césaire declared at UNESCO: "If the voice of the African cultures, the voice of the Indian cultures, and the voice of the Asian cultures are silenced, this will be a true loss for human civilization" (Rostkowski 1998: 356). But why is the survival of these traditional cultures and spiritualities so important?

Michael Amaladoss insists that every religious experience is symbolic and at the same time fundamentally apophatic (Amaladoss 2008: 240). No religion or spirituality has a direct experience of the Great Mystery. The survival of the traditional spiritualities may help Western Christianity to rediscover its own symbolic and ritual dimensions in dialogue with other living faiths. Traditional spiritualities or religions point to the most profound and mystical dimension of human existence or to what we may call the truly "primitive" or "aboriginal" in all of us. Therefore we welcome the fact that contemporary Native Americans are more and more assuming responsibility of keeping their traditional spiritualities alive. Their inclusion in the process of inter-religious dialogue enriches humanity as a whole and may contribute to the development of a much needed universal culture of peace.

Bibliography

Alexander, Hartley Burr. *The World's Rim. Great Mysteries of the North American Indians.* Lincoln: University of Nebraska Press, 1953.

Amaladoss, Michael. *Beyond Dialogue. Pilgrims to the Absolute.* Bangalore: Asian Trading Corporation, 2008.

Arinze, Francis. *Meeting Other Believers.* Herefordshire: Gracewing, 1997.

Blée, Fabrice. *The Third Desert. The Story of Monastic Dialogue.* Collegeville, MN: Liturgical Press, 2011.

Brown, Joseph Epes. *The Spiritual Legacy of the American Indian.* New York: Crossroad, 1982.

Deloria, Vine Jr. *God is Red. A Native View of Religion.* 30th Anniversary Edition. Golden, CO: Fulcrum Publishing, 2003.

Dickason, Olive Patricia. *Canada's First Nations. A History of Founding Peoples from the Earliest Times.* Toronto: McClelland & Stewart, 1992.

Gill, Sam. *Native American Religious Action. A Performance Approach to Religion.* Columbia: University of South Dakota Press, 1987.

Grant, John Webster. *Moon of Wintertime. Missionaries and the Indians of Canada in Encounter Since 1543.* Toronto: University of Toronto Press, 1984.

John Paul II. "Address to the Aborigines and Torres Strait Islanders in Alice Springs, 29 November 1986." *The Australian Catholic Record* 3(38) (2006).

Lafond, Harry. "The Church and the Indigenous Peoples of Canada." *Origins* 5(1) (1997).

Magesa, Lorenti. *African Religions. The Moral Traditions of Abundant Life.* Maryknoll, NY: Orbis Press, 1997.

Marzal, Manual. *The Indian Face of God in Latin America.* Maryknoll, NY: Orbis Books, 1996.

Morriseau, Calvin. *Into the Daylight. A Wholistic Approach to Healing.* Toronto: University of Toronto Press, 1998.

Orta, Andrew. *Catechizing Culture. Missionaries, Aymara, and the New Evangelization.* New York: Columbia University Press, 2004.

Pagden, Anthony. *The Fall of Natural Man. The American Indian and the Origins of Contemporary Ethnology.* Cambridge: Cambridge University Press, 1982.

Peelman, Achiel. *Christ is a Native American.* Maryknoll, NY: Orbis Books; reprinted 2006 Eugene, OR: Wipfl & Stock, 1995.

Pelotte, Donald. "The Gospel and the Fate of Indigenous peoples." *Origins* 5(1) (1997).

Phan, Peter. "Multiple Religious Belonging: Opportunities and Challenges for Theology and the Church." *Theological Studies* 64 (2003).

Rostkowski, Joëlle. *La conversion inachevée. Les Indiens et le Christianisme.* Paris: Albin Michel, 1998.

Schreiter, Robert. *The New Catholicity. Between the Global and the Local.* Maryknoll, NY: Orbis Books, 1997.

Starkloff, Carl. *The Theology of the In-Between.* Milwaukee, WI: Marquette University Press, 2002.

Steinmetz, Paul. *Pipe, Bible and Peyote Among the Oglala Lakota. A Study in Religious Identity.* Knoxville: The University of Tennessee Press, 1990.

Tinker, George. *Missionary Conquest. The Gospel and Native AmericanCultural Genocide.* Minneapolis: Fortres Press, 1993.

Tinker, George. *American Indian Liberation.* Maryknoll, NY: Orbis Press, 2008.

Treat, James (ed.). *Native and Christian. Indigenous Voices on Religious Identity in the United States and Canada.* London: Routledge, 1996.

Trigger, Bruce. *Natives and Newcomers. Canada's "Heroic Age" Reconsidered.* Manchester: Manchester University Press; Kingston/ Montreal: McGill Queen's University Press, 1985.

Turner, David. "Aboriginal Religion as World Religion. An Assessment." *Studies in World Christianity* 2(1) (1996).

Vecsey, Christopher. *Where the Two Roads Meet. American Indian Catholics III.* Notre Dame, IN: University of Notre Dame Press. 1999.

Vigil, José Maria (ed.). *Toward a Planetary Theology.* Montreal: Dunamis Publishers, 2010.

Weaver, Jace (ed.). *Native American Religious Identity.* Maryknoll, NY: Orbis Books, 1998.

York, Geoffrey. *The Dispossessed. Life and Death in Native Canada.* Toronto: Lester & Orpen Dennys, 1990.

CHAPTER 22

Islam and Buddhism

Imtiyaz Yusuf

> On truth's path, wise is mad, insane is wise.
> In love's way, self and other are the same.
> Having drunk the wine, my love, of being one with you,
> I find the way to Mecca and Bodhgaya are the same.
>
> Rumi, *Kulliyat-e Shams-e Tabrizi* 302

Historically and theologically, the Qur'an and the Muslims have engaged primarily in discussion and dialogue with other Semitic religions. This is understandable, considering those religions' interconnections and relationships. Muslim engagements with the Asian religions of Hinduism, Buddhism, and Taoism are largely the result of commercial relations, immigration, and political interactions between the worlds of Islam and Asia.

This paper examines Islam's view of Buddhism as a non-theistic tradition, the history of relations between these two traditions, themes and issues in Muslim–Buddhist dialogue, and the implications of such dialogue for the contemporary religious scene. While Muslims and Buddhists have coexisted in different parts of the world, their exchange has been largely political, military and economic, instead of doctrinal, and only a few scholars have studied the relations between the two traditions in any detail (Berzin 2007: 225, 251).

Islam and Buddhism first came into contact in central Asia (Foltz 1999) and later in south and southeast Asia (al-Attas 1963). These early encounters were followed, in some instances, by the conversion of Buddhists to Islam, as happened in central and maritime southeast Asia. Yet there were also other regions where Buddhists and Muslims continued to exist side by side, as in India, Tibet, and parts of mainland southeast Asia.

Despite the long record of Muslim–Buddhist interaction, such contact is at the present either nonexistent or rare, largely due to the strong trend of reified interpretations of religion in the contemporary world – interpretations which in turn overlook the historical exchanges that took place between these religions during the Age of the Silk Road (400 BCE–1400 CE) and the Age of Commerce (1450–1680 CE).

Buddhism and Islam in History

Encounters between Islam and Buddhism are as old as Islam itself (Yusuf 2003). The first encounter between Islam and Buddhist communities took place in the middle of the seventh century CE in East Persia, Transoxiana, Afghanistan and Sindh (Fyre 2012). Historical evidence indicates that early Muslims extended the Qur'anic category of *ahl al-Kitab* ("people of the book" or revealed religion) to Hindus and Buddhists (Ikram 1965: 11; MacLean 1997: 40–41; Vajda 2012; Wink 1990 1: 193–194).

During the second half of the eighth century CE, central-Asian Muslims translated many Buddhist works into Arabic. Arabic titles such as *Bilawhar wa Budhasaf* and *Kitab al-Budd* are clear evidence of Muslim learning about Buddhism (Goldziher and Lewis 1981: 141) Significantly, in spite of his awareness that idols of the Buddha were objects of reverence and worship, Ibn al-Nadim (d. 995 CE), the author of *al-Firhist*, observes that:

> These people [Buddhists of Khurasan] are the most generous of all the inhabitants of the earth and of all the religionists. This is because their prophet *Budhasf* [Bodhisattva] has taught them that the greatest sin, which should never be thought of or committed, is the utterance of "No." Hence they act upon this advice; they regard the uttering of "No" as an act of Satan. And it is their very religion to banish Satan. (Muhammad ibn Abi Yaqub Ishaq Ibn al-Nadim 1971: 407; see also Yusuf 1955: 28)

There is also evidence of central-Asian Buddhist influence on Muslims in the succeeding period. One possible source of this may lie in the Barmak family, who were descendants of Buddhist monks and governors in the non-Muslim regions during the early Abbasid caliphate, which ruled the greater part of the Islamic world for five centuries (750–1258 CE). It is noteworthy that the Buddhist monastery of Naw Bahar near Balkh, in addition to other Iranian monasteries, remained under the supervision of the Barmak family (Bulliet 1976: 140–145; Foltz 1999: 100; Xinru Liu 2011: 55–81).

We find vestiges of several Buddhist beliefs and practices among the Muslims of central Asia. For example, during the Samanid dynasty, which ruled Persia during the ninth and tenth centuries CE, the madrasahs devoted to Islamic learning were modeled after Buddhist schools in eastern Iran. (Foltz 1999: 100). The *pondoks* or *pasenterens*, Muslim religious schools of southeast Asia, seem also to have been influenced by the Hindu and Buddhist temple schools of the region.

The celebrated historian and Qur'anic exegete, Abu Ja'far Muhammad ibn Jarir al-Tabari (d. 923 CE), who was born in northern Persia, mentions that Buddhist idols were brought from Kabul to Baghdad in the ninth century CE. It is also reported that Buddhist idols were sold in a Buddhist temple next to the Makh mosque in the market of the city of Bukhara in modern Uzbekistan (Foltz 1999: 100).

There is a common misunderstanding that Islam wiped out Buddhism by means of conversion and persecution. Marshall Hodgson comments:

> Probably Buddhism did not yield to Islam so much by direct conversion as by a more insidious route: the sources of recruitment to the relatively unaristocratic Buddhism – for instance, villagers coming to the cities and adopting a new allegiance to accord to their new status – turned now rather to Islam than to an outdated Buddhism. The record of the massacre of one monastery in Bengal, combined with the inherited Christian conception of Muslims as the devotees of the sword has yielded the widely repeated statement that the Muslims violently "destroyed" Buddhism in India. Muslims were not friendly to it, but there is no evidence that they simply killed off all the Buddhists, or even all the monks. It will take much active revision before such assessments of the role of Islam, based largely on unexamined preconceptions, are eliminated even from educated mentalities. (Hodgson 1977: 557)

Further encounters between Islam and Hindu-Buddhist civilization took place in Indonesia, Malaysia and Thailand. The Islam of this region had a conspicuously mystic orientation, and the Muslims who first brought Islam to Indonesia and then to Malaysia and southern Thailand during the twelfth–fifteenth centuries CE were largely Sufi mystics. In religious terms, this led to a meeting between the Hindu view of *moksha* (liberation) through the Hindu notion of monism, the Buddhist notion of *Dhamma* (Truth) through the realization *sunyata* (emptiness), and the Islamic concept of *fana'* (the passing away of one's identity by its merging into the Universal Being) as expounded in the monotheistic pantheism of the Sufis. Gradually there emerged a syncretic culture, particularly in Java and other parts of southeast Asia, giving rise to a version of Islam that was mystical, fluid and soft (Gordon 2001; Shih 2002).

The attitudes of Muslims and Buddhists toward one another in the course of history involves both positive and negative experiences and perceptions. Johan Elsverkog has recently commented that Buddhist views that Muslims destroyed Nalanda University in 1202, and that Islam caused the general demise of Buddhism in India, is an invented myth. Nalanda University continued to function until the thirteenth century CE, Buddhist rulers remained in power after making deals with Muslim leaders, and the Buddhadhamma survived in India until the seventeenth century CE. He believes that the Dhamma declined because of its own failings (Elverskog 2010: 2).

Another negative Buddhist image of Muslims is contained in the Kalacakra Tantra, a text containing passages that may be construed as demonizing Muslims, including a prophecy about a holy war between Buddhists and *mleccha* – barbarians in general, but commonly interpreted as Muslim invaders of central Asia and India (Berzin 2012). The Kalacakra narrative continues to shape the Buddhist view of Islam and Muslims.

Shiite Persians settled in the Siamese kingdom of Ayutthaya and at the court of King Phra Narai (r. 1656–88), whose reign witnessed great commercial and diplomatic activities. Several Persians served as Prime Ministers and ambassadors at the court of King Phra Narai (Marcinkowski 2005: 6) and there was close diplomatic communication between Safavid Iran and Ayutthaya between 1660s and 1680s, including an exchange of embassies. The primary account of the state of the Persian community in

Ayutthaya is contained in Ibn Muhammad Ibrahim's *Safinai Sulaimani*, or *Ship of Sulaiman*, where the author suggests that Buddhism should be understood as idolatrous (Alam and Subrahmanyam 2010: 159–171; O'Kane 1972).

In Siam and in modern Thailand, Muslims are often viewed as a threat toward Buddhism, and as violent toward the Thai Buddhist state. The roots of this image lie in the history of political relations between premodern Siam and its Malay Muslim vassal states, Patani and Trengganu, at the southern cultural border between the ethno-religious worlds of Thai Buddhism and Malay Islam (Baker and Pasuk Phongpaichit 2005; Ibrahim Syukri 1985; Milner 2008; Teeuw 1970). At Wat Matchimawat in the southern Thai city of Songkla, a mural depicting the Buddha's defeat of Mara during the night of the Buddha's enlightenment shows a bearded Muslim figure embedded in Mara's retinue (Keyes, 2008/2009).

Besides suspicion and rejection, the relationships between Muslims and Buddhists have also included numerous positive expressions of respect and receptivity. The classical Muslim scholar of comparative religion 'Abd al-Karim al-Shahrastani (1086–1153 CE), in a section called *Ara' al-Hind* (The Views of the Indians) within his magnum opus, *Kitab al-Milal wa 'l-Nihal* (*Book of Religious and Philosophical Sects*), shows a high regard for Buddhism and its spiritual richness, identifying the Buddha with the Qur'anic figure of al-Khidr as a seeker of enlightenment (al-Shahrastani 1910: 1275; Lawrence 1976: 113–114; for al Khidr see Qur'an 18: 64).

Rashid al-Din (1247–1318 CE) who was attached to the Persian Il-khanid court, wrote a detailed introduction to Buddhism in his monumental *Jami al-tawarikh* (*Compendium of Chronicles*), aiming to make Buddhism accessible to Muslims (Canby 1993: 299–310 Elverskog 2010: 149–162).

Today Islam and Buddhism coexist in South Asia, southeast Asia, east Asia and the West. The state of this relationship is varied and diverse, a diversity that can be appreciated only in the context of the local histories of each region. Recently, the late Professor Muhammad Hamidullah (d. 2002) promoted a view of the Buddha as a Prophet. He refers in particular to the mention of a fig tree in the Qur'an (95: 1), which, according to several old and new commentators of the Qur'an, "may refer to the Bodhi tree of the revelation of Buddha; and his birth place Kapila-Vastu is supposed to have given the name of the prophet Dhu 'l-Kifl" (Hamidullah 1974: 54). Hamidullah concludes that because the Buddha attained *nirvana* under a wild fig tree (*Ficus religiosa*) – and because that tree does not figure prominently in the life of any of the Qur'anic Prophets – the Qur'anic verse itself must refer to Gautama Buddha (Hamidullah 1974: 54 and 160 f; Scott 1995 141–155).

The general contemporary Thai Muslim attitude towards Buddhism is that of "live and let live": "Unto you, your religion (moral law), and unto me mine" (Qur'an 109: 6). Educated Thai Muslims tend to view Buddhist understandings of *dukkha*, or suffering, and the search for nirvana, as a philosophical and methodical approach to life, while more popular Thai religious beliefs in spirits and demons appear strange and unwise.

At this popular level, Thai Muslims see Buddhism as a religion of *kufr* (disbelief in God) and *shirk* (idolatory/polytheism). They view Thai Buddhists as *kafirs* (unbelievers) and infidels and *mushrikeen* (polytheists). These two categories of religionists are scorned by the Qur'an and opposed vehemently by Prophet Muhammad. As a result, they adopt and apply a literal understanding of Qur'anic passages to their Thai context, without applying interpretive tools of historical criticism. Hence, in charged or conflicted political situations, Thai Muslims view many Thai Buddhists as *najis* (unclean, immoral and faithless) engaged in kufr and shirk, which are to be opposed by engaging in jihad. Such a view, of course, remains ignorant regarding classical Muslim views of Buddhism, and thereby contributes to intensifying conflict.

Buddha and Muhammad – Prophetic Dimensions

From a Muslim perspective on the history of religions, God has from time immemorial raised prophets among all nations, only some of whom are mentioned by name in the Qur'an. The Qur'an mentions 25 prophets, including Muhammad, all of them belonging to semitic religious traditions. However, there is no ambiguity about the fact that the Qur'an affirms prophethood as a universal phenomenon:

> And indeed, [O Muhammad], We have sent forth apostles before your time; some of them We have mentioned to thee, and some of them We have not mentioned to thee (40: 78; cf. 4: 164).

> And never have We sent forth any apostle otherwise than [with a message] in people's own tongue . . . (14: 4).

> To each among you have We prescribed a Law and an Open Way. If Allah had so willed He would have made you a single people but (His plan is) to test you in what He hath given you: so strive as in a race in all virtues. The goal of you all is to God; it is He that will show you the truth of the matters in which ye dispute. (5: 48)

The Qur'anic concept of *risalah*, or prophethood, offers an analogue with the Buddhist concept of "Buddha" in certain ways. Buddha is not a personal name, but a designation which may be considered, if not identical with, then somewhat similar to, the designations of *nabi* or *rasul* (prophet). Buddhas appear in different epochs to teach the path to nirvana, and Buddhist sources mention that 27 Buddhas have appeared over a period of 5,000 years (Fozdar 1973: 13; Griffiths 1994: 87–119).

Both Muhammad and the Buddha sought answers to age-old questions about the human predicament: What does it mean to be human? Why is there anguish and suffering? The Buddha called this phenomenon dukkha (suffering), whereas the Qur'an refers to man as being created in *kabad*, or affliction (Qur'an 90):

> NAY! I call to witness this land –
> this land in which thou art free to dwell –
> and [I call to witness] parent and offspring:
> Verily, We have created man into [a life of] *kabad* – pain, toil and trial.
> Does he, then, think that no one has power over him?
> He boasts, "I have spent wealth abundant!"

Does he, then, think that no one sees him?
Have We not given him two eyes,
and a tongue, and a pair of lips,
and shown him the two highways [of good and evil]?
But he would not try to ascend the steep uphill road . . .
And what could make thee conceive what it is, that steep uphill road?
[It is] the freeing of one's neck [from the burden of sin/bondage],
or the feeding, upon a day of [one's own] hunger,
of an orphan near of kin,
or of a needy [stranger] lying in the dust –
and being, withal, of those who have attained to faith, and who enjoin upon one another
patience in adversity, and enjoin upon one another compassion.
Such are they that have attained to righteousness;
whereas those who are bent on denying the truth of Our messages – they are such as have
lost themselves in evil,
[with] fire closing in upon them.
(Qur'an 90: 1–20)

Through the achievement of nirvana, the Buddha was liberated from the fetters of suffering (dukkha) and entered a state of relief, peace, and rest. He was freed from confusion, turmoil, anguish and distress, and entered a state of bliss (detachment). Similarly, the Prophet's experience of *wahy* (revelation) liberated him from the suffering caused by religious ignorance obtaining in his milieu, including *shirk* (polytheism, that is, attribution of divine qualities to aught but God) and kufr (rejection/denial of the existence of One Unseen God). Thus, Muhammad entered the state of *salam* (peace). The Buddha realized the state of being an *arahant* (an enlightened human being), Muhammad the state of being *rasul* (the Messenger of God). Each of them defeated the antagonistic forces of evil, called *mara* in Buddhism and Shaytan in Islam. A *hadith* states: "*aslama shaytana*" – my *shaytan* has become a Muslim, and does whatever I order him – meaning that through internal *jihad*, the Prophet had turned his lower faculties and instincts to the service and obedience of God. The Prophet thereby became *al-insan al-kamil* (the perfect man), with full control over the Shaytan (Schimmel and Ernst 2011: 113, 196).

The Buddha's experience of nirvana (enlightenment) and the Prophet Muhammad's wahy (revelation) became important sources of their essential religious message. The significance of these two prophets is rooted in their achievements as message-bearers of enlightened and humane worldviews to overcome ignorance. In the case of the Buddha, the ignorance he targeted is the cause of the cycles of *samsara* (endless rebirth and re-death) and dukkha (suffering). In the case of Muhammad, ignorance stems from the illusions of kufr (human rebelliousness or human rejection/denial of the existence of God) and shirk (polytheism or attribution of divine qualities to aught but God) as the cause of *khusr* (loss) (Qur'an 103: 1–3).

To have a better appreciation of the matter it would be pertinent to bear in mind that the Buddha was born and lived in a world full of belief in magic, petty gods, nature spirits (trees, mountains, rain, rivers and sky), and a world wherein priests had a vested interest in conducting prayers and rituals to appease these gods and spirits. All this, however, did not bring an end to the mental anguish or social suffering of birth, sickness, old age and death, which were the Buddha's primary concerns.

In seeking to dispel belief in the superstitions prevalent in his time, the Buddha offered what might be termed a rational approach to salvation, based on humanist values of compassion and merit. The Buddha's main goal was to show the way to the end of human suffering. It was presumably for this reason that he remained silent on questions about God and gods. This does not mean that he was an atheist.

Moreover, the Buddha distinguished between the mundane and supramundane worlds, identifying the supramundane world with enlightenment, peace, and freedom from suffering. In the Buddhist scripture of the Udāna (Inspired Utterances), the Buddha describes the supramundane realm as eternal:

> There is, O Bhikkhus, an unborn, unoriginated, uncreated, unformed. Were there not, O Bhikkhus, this unborn, unoriginated, uncreated, unformed, there would be no escape from the world of the born, originated, created, formed. Since, O Bhikkhus, there is an unborn, unoriginated, uncreated, unformed, therefore is there an escape from the born, originated, created, formed. (Strong 2010: 112)

Nonetheless, a significant difference should be highlighted again: the Buddha obtained nirvana from within himself, on the basis of self-effort, whereas Muhammad was given his spiritual stature through wahy (revelation), from outside himself, while seeking to comprehend the meaning of being *insan* (human) within God's creation.

Islamic–Buddhist dialogue need not stumble in any final way over fundamental differences in theistic perspective, particularly if the broader and more flexible concept of ultimate reality, interpreted as personal or non-personal, is used. It may also be possible to use a concept of God as *in precipe*, or a principle of axiological value, rather than *in esse*, an essential nature or creator God. (Al-Faruqi 1962: 219; Fletcher 2011: 92–112). Such flexibility allows in turn for discourse between the concepts of *Tawhid* (transcendence) and Dhamma (truth), whereby Islam and Buddhism can both be understood as religious systems directed towards easing the kabad (affliction) and dukkha (suffering) through *rahma* (mercy) and *metta-karuna* (loving compassion).

The Buddha and Muhammad as Founders of Traditions

The Buddha and Muhammad each left intriguingly similar instructions to their communities about how to proceed religiously following their deaths. The *Mahaparinibbana Sutta* (Digha Nikaya 16) records:
Then the Blessed One addressed the venerable Ananda:

> "Ananda, it may be that you would think:
> 'Gone is the Teacher's word! We have no teacher.'
> It should not be seen thus, Ananda, for the *Dharma* and the *Vinaya* [the Teaching and the Discipline] that I have taught and explained to you, will, at my passing, be your teacher. (Gopaka Moggallana Sutta 2012)

For the twentieth-century Thai master Buddhadasa, "The real teacher, the *dhamma-vinaya*, is still with us,"(Buddhadasa and Swearer 1991: 51–52) working towards the extinction of suffering (Swearer 1996: 331).

Similarly, the prophet Muhammad noted in his Last Sermon:

O People, no prophet or apostle will come after me and no new faith will be born. Reason well, therefore, O People, and understand my words which I convey to you. I leave behind me two things, the Qur'an and my example, the Sunnah, and if you follow these you will never go astray (Prophet Muhammad's Last Sermon).

The Qur'an comments:

Say: If you do love Allah, follow me: Allah will love you and forgive you your sins, for Allah is Oft-Forgiving, Most Merciful. (Qur'an 3: 31)

And the Buddha says the following:

Enough, Vakkali! What is there to see in this vile body? He who sees Dhamma, Vakkali, sees me; he who sees me sees Dhamma. Truly seeing Dhamma, one sees me; seeing me one sees Dhamma. (Samyutta Nikaya 22. 87)

The Buddha as Enlightened *Bodhisattva* and Muhammad as *Insan al–Kamil*

Muslims often employ the concept of *al-insan al-kamil*, which refers to the idea of the perfect human being, and in particular to the personality of the Prophet Muhammad. In practical Islamic life, reference to the Prophet as an al-insan al-kamil is intended to invoke imitation of Muhammad. Similarly, the Buddhist bodhisattva refers to one on the path of liberation, but who compassionately refrains from entering *nibbana*, in order to remain as a compassionate presence for those who suffer. Just as the Buddha was a bodhisattva before his enlightenment, so everyone is encouraged to become a bodhisattva in imitation of the Buddha. The concepts of al-insan al-kamil and the bodhisattva are active and practical encouragements toward emulation for religious adherents, in their aspiration to become similarly perfect human beings.

The concept of al-insan al-kamil is based in the prophetic hadith reported by Ibn Hanbal that, "God created Adam in His image ['ala suratih]": the one who has realized his original nature has realized that he was made in the image of God, thereby becoming an essential man and not an accidental one.

Here his every act is in accordance with the Divine Will, with which it is in fact identical; he is in perfect activity but 'motionless,' because he is identified with the First Cause but not with effects . . . When man has realized all the states of being, he contains the whole universe and has effectively returned to the state of Adam as he was before the Fall: his will and knowledge are in no way contradictory to God's, he is the master of garden, the perfect 'slave' (*'abd*) of God and thus the "perfect man" *(al-insan al-kamil.")* (Glasse and Smith 2001: 216–217)

Sufis such as Ibn al-'Arabī (1165–1240 CE), Mahmud al-Shabistari (d. 1320 CE) and Abdul Karim al-Jili (1365–1417 CE) have commented at length on the term al insan al-kamil. Ibn al-Arabi's use of the term al insan al-kamil expresses a pantheistic monism, in which all Being is essentially one, and different religions are equivalent. In his view al insan al-kamil means that man "unites in himself both the form of God and the form of the universe. He alone manifests the divine Essence together with all its names and attributes. He is the mirror by which God is revealed to Himself, and therefore the final cause of creation" (quoted by Gibb 1997 170–171).

For Ibn al-'Arabī, the Prophet "is the total theophany of the divine names, the whole of the universe in its oneness as seen by the divine essence. Muhammad is the proto-type of the universe as well as of man, since he is like a mirror in which each sees the other. The Perfect Man is necessary to God as the medium through which He is known and manifested" (Schimmel and Ernst 2011: 272).

Abdul Karim al-Jili comments that the state of perception of sublime essence is obtained by the perfect man through mystical revelation (*kashf*). It is a state in which one knows that "thou art He and that He is thou and that this is not *hulul* (substantial union) nor *ittihad* (becoming one), and that the slave is slave and the Lord a lord, and that the slave does not become a lord nor the Lord a slave" (quoted by Gibb 1997: 171).

Ayatollah Murtaza Motahhari (1920–1979) comments that the al insan al-kamil is one who has developed the values of love, intellect, justice, freedom, service and devo-tion in a harmonious way. He is of pure heart, and does not engage in mere talk or proffer empty knowledge. He is one in whose heart the devil is replaced by an angel, he is benevolent, and he is interested in serving and loving humanity (Mutahhari, n.d.: 70).

In moral terms, the al-insan al-kamil represents the highest type of human being. He acts in accordance with the precepts of the moral divine will, free from all attach-ment to results. With a heart full of love, kindness and compassion toward everyone and every being, he acts in a selfless spirit, and becomes a moral guide worthy of emulation.

This spiritually enlightened and morally active concept of the human being in Sufism is fully compatible with the concept of the bodhisattva. Gautama Siddhartha as Buddha was a bodhisattva for many lives prior to his enlightenment. For a bodhisattva, "salvation of one entails the salvation of all beings. Bodhisattvas vow to postpone their own liberation and to remain in the world as Sakyamuni did following his enlighten-ment, exercising compassionate concern for others until all beings have been saved" (Jones 2004: 996–1000). The bodhisattva seeks the liberation of others before that of oneself, through selfless compassion (karuna). Hence, bodhisattvas postpone their own enlightenment, choosing to remain in the world practicing compassion for others until all beings have been saved: "the fundamental feature of the ideal of the Bodhisattva is compassion and self-giving. "*Mahakaruna*" ("the great compassionate Heart of the Buddha") becomes the actuating principle of his life" (Spencer 1963: 89). The Bodhisat-tva path requires the practitioner to become perfect, over many lifetimes, in ten virtues, or *paramitas*: generosity, morality, patience or forbearance, effort/endeavor, contemplation/meditation, transcendental insight/wisdom, skill in means, resolution, strength, and knowledge.

Prior to the coming of Islam to Asia, the concept of the Bodhisattva had passed from India and East Asia to southeast Asia, where it gained wide socio-political acceptance. Many southeast Asian Buddhist kings understood themselves as practicing Bodhisatt-vas (Samuels 1997). The Buddhist concept of Bodhisattva had been employed by the Hindu–Buddhist rajas of southeast Asia to identify themselves with the idealized per-sonage of Buddha. However, following the arrival of Islam, Indonesian and Malay kings appropriated the title of al-insan al-kamil in order to legitimize their royal positions politically and religiously. The Hindu and Buddhist kings of Java, Sumatra, and Celebes, who had previously presented themselves as *dev rajas* (incarnations of Shiva) or *dham-marajas* (kings of Buddhist law), also adopted titles such as al-insan al-kamil, or Arabic–Persian royal titles such as sultan, shah, or zillullah fil alam (God's Shadow on Earth). The Hindu kings of Patani were particularly interested in the Sufi doctrine of the al-insan al-kamil, and, upon conversion to Islam, used it as a way to hold together their complicated socio-cultural structures. The sultans of Patani claimed that they were al-insan al-kamil – one with God and blessed by Him. The concept of al-insan al-kamil was thus easily integrated with previous beliefs as Islam came to be adopted across southeast Asia, where Muslim sultans sought to represent themselves as saints worthy of emulation, to further support the conversion of their communities to Islam (Bruines-sen 1994: 121–145; Hooker 1983: 12–13; Mansurnoor, 1999). The sultans also came to be seen as endowed with special powers capable of performing *karamat* (miracles) and possessing *berkah* – spiritual gifts that they could pass on to others during their lifetime or after death. Such notions were not far from those of local Hindu and Bud-dhist traditions.

The history of southeast Asia shows that the two mystically oriented concepts of the al-insan al-kamil and the bodhisattva became the ground for dialogue between Islam and Hinduism–Buddhism. During the Islamic phase of southeast Asian history the concept of al-insan al-kamil replaced that of the bodhisattva at the religious, political, and social levels, leading to the formation of inter-religious communities marked by the moral value of religious tolerance. As a result of this phenomenon, the mystical dimen-sion of Islam and the tolerant aspect of Buddhism played a significant role in forming the character of religious coexistence in southeast Asia.

Thus the encounter between Islam and Hindu–Buddhist civilization that took place in Indonesia, Malaysia, and Thailand was a sort of dialogue between a monotheistic and pantheistic form of Islam, and the monistic and non-theistic religious traditions of Hinduism and Buddhism. Sufi mystical approaches fit well with local populations' pre-viously inherited world views from Hinduism and Buddhism (Bougas 1994: 28–40).

Contemporary Issues and Themes of Dialogue

There is a theoretical, historical and regional variety in the character of Muslim–Buddhist relations and dialogue shaped by the dominant form of religious practice and national identities of their followers.

Muslim minorities in majority Theravada Buddhist countries such as Sri Lanka and those of southeast Asia where both Islam and Buddhism have taken strongly ritualistic and ethno-nationalistic identities are concerned about maintaining their ethno-religious identities and protecting and preserving their political status as citizens in face of rising conservative Buddhism (Satha-Anand, 2003: 193–213). Similarly, Buddhist minorities in Pakistan, Malaysia and Indonesia are concerned about protecting their status and freedoms in face of the rise of Islamic puritanism, exclusivism and religious intolerance (Andree Feillard 2010). For example, Thai and Chinese Buddhists in Malaysia are grappling with the challenges of maintaining their ethno-religious identities and claiming their political rights as non-Malay citizens in a Muslim-majority country (Johnson 2012), and in Indonesia, Buddhists of the native and immigrant Chinese communities are also engaged in safeguarding their constitutional rights and civil liberties as Indonesian citizens. In these Buddhist and Muslim countries there is strong link between state and religion. Thus dialogue is centered around matters of Halal/non-Halal, Hijab, linguistic, cultural and religious identities and freedom of religion such as permission to build mosques and temples, teaching of religion in public schools, inclusion of the minority's history in national historical narratives, etc. In predominantly Mahayana Buddhist countries like Taiwan, Korea and Japan, where Buddhism assumes a more philosophical orientation, the space for dialogue between Buddhism and Islam and other religions is more open. Muslim–Buddhist relations in the Indo-Tibetan-Mongolian cultural spheres of Kashmir, Ladakh and Tibet which in the past have seen wars and political tensions today experience more peaceful co-existence and the tensions between their communities are largely economic rather than religious.

The contemporary dialogue between Buddhism and Islam takes many forms. Some converts to Buddhism attempt to overcome the ethnic divides between Buddhists and Muslims and attempt to engage in a purely spiritual dialogue, leaving aside the historical and political relations between the two traditions. While some Muslims have recognized the Buddha as prophet from within the Islamic notion of prophet hood, others do not see him as prophet since he did not preach *Tauhid* – the oneness of God. Muslim minorities in Buddhist countries often recognize the Buddha as a sage for the purpose of building harmonious relations between Muslims and Buddhists (Obuse 2010: 21–232). Traditional Buddhists, of course, assert that the Buddha was more than a prophet.

Shifting the focus somewhat, Maria Habito has suggested that the notions of *tathagata-garba*, or Buddha-Nature, and *Haqiqah Muhammadiyah*, or Muhammadan reality, can serve as a ground for dialogue between Islam and Buddhism (Habito 2010: 233–246). Somparn Promta has called for the need to distinguish between Buddha's open-mindedness towards other religions and the views or interpretations of later Buddhist scholars and writers. (Promta 2010: 302–320). I have written about how the Qur'anic concept of *ummatan wasatan* (the Middle Nation) in Islam and *majjhima-patipada* (the Middle Way) in Buddhism can serve as a models worthy of emulation by both Muslims (or other monotheists) and Buddhists (Yusuf 2009: 367–394). I have also pointed to the Buddha and Muhammad as bearers of charisma, achieved through contact with supernatural realms of being, and as religious leaders embodying moral values worthy of imitation by their followers. The Buddhist and Muslims concepts of *Tathagata* – "one who has gone thus" – and *Nur Muhammadi* – light of Muhammad – offer religious paradigms for the development of a new humanism which emphasizes the moral dimension of coexistence in harmony with the Ultimate Reality or moral law. Without seeking to Buddhicize Islam or Islamize Buddhism, I argue that paradigms drawn from religious phenomena can serve as mediums for understanding and dialogue between these two religions and their societies. The Buddha and Muhammad are charismatic personalities, enlightened and blessed in religious ways, and worthy models for their communities thus offering a bridge for Muslim–Buddhist dialogue (Yusuf 2005: 103–114).

Reza Shah Kazemi has called for a dialogue of spiritual affinities between Islam and Buddhism, rooted in the concepts of Allah as *al-Haqq* and dharma as ultimate reality or truth (Kazemi 2010). And Chandra Muzaffar and Sulak Sivaraksa, Muslim and Buddhist activists from Malaysia and Thailand respectively, have discussed the role of Islam and Buddhism as a basis for political transformation, social reconstruction and civil society for Asian Buddhist and Muslim societies. They believe that mutual appreciation and exchange may help to find common solutions to national and global issues facing the two religions (Sivaraksa 1999).

The most devastating event in recent Islamic–Buddhist relations was the Taliban's destruction of the Bamiyan Buddha statues in March, 2001. That act of destruction has left a lasting negative impression of Islam and Muslims among many Buddhists, though this is not expressed publicly in Buddhist countries. And although relations between these two religious communities are often constituted by mutual tolerance and peaceful relations, there are ongoing areas of conflict, such as the simmering ethno-religious conflict in southern Thailand, (Jerryson 2011; Pitsuwan 1985; Yusuf 2006) the expulsion of Rohingaya Muslims from Myanmar, (Berlie 2008; Yegar 2002) and the political impacts of the ethnic conflict in Sri Lanka on the Tamil Muslims in that country (Ali 2004 372–383; Iqbal et al. 2011: 375–389; Mcgilvray 2011: 45–64).

Among intellectuals, an example of significant recent contact between Islamic and Buddhist scholars occurred on 29–30 May, 2009, at a conference titled "Buddhism and Islam: Encounters, Histories, Dialogue and Representation," jointly organized by the Faculty of Religious Studies, the Institute of Islamic Studies, and the Centre for Research on Religion at McGill University in Montreal, Canada.

At the level of local religious community initiatives, the Islamic Center in Bangkok, Thailand holds occasional dialogues with Thai Buddhist monks, scholars and layperersons about issues of common national and international concern. Similar initiatives are undertaken by both Muslims and Buddhists in Sri Lanka, Malaysia and Indonesia.

Muslims and Buddhists have jointly engaged in relief and social work in face of natural disasters, such as the 2004 Tsunami in Indonesia, Thailand and Sri Lanka, and other local disasters, such as floods or other national hardships. At the international level, in the wake of the destruction of the Bamiyan Buddha statues and the 9/11 tragedy in the United States, the Taiwanese Dharma Master Hsin Tao, Chief Executive Officer of the Museum of World Religions, initiated a series of dialogues between Buddhists and Muslims in many parts of the world. The first of these dialogues took place at Columbia University in New York City on March 7, 2002, followed by dialogues in Kuala-Lumpur in May, 2002, and in Jakarta in July, 2002. These dialogues were designed to foster new awareness between the Muslim and Buddhist communities, and to find effective ways of educating both communities about shared commonalities.

On May 5–7, 2003, a Buddhist–Muslim Dialogue Conference on Global Ethics and Good Governance took place at UNESCO headquarters in Paris, and similar symposia were held in November, 2005 in Morocco, in China in 2006, and at the United Nations Headquarters in New York in September, 2008. Attended by Muslim and Buddhist scholars, activists and community leaders, these meetings discussed topics such as: Global Ethics and Good Governance; Religious Responses to Violence; Interfaith Peace Education and Community Partnership Building; Poverty and Social Inequality; and Ecological Healing and Earth Rights. Though Islam and Buddhism appear externally different they can find common ground through mutual dialogue and mutual engagement concerning topics mentioned above by recognizing of interdependence between religious claims and lifestyles in the pluralistic age through cooperation not confrontation (Yi 2012: Yi and Habito: 2005).

The coming formation of the ASEAN community in 2015 made up of southeast Asian group of nations highlights the urgent need for religions of southeast Asia to move from co-existence to dialogue. In the ASEAN community Islam and Buddhism will make up the two largest religions, with Muslims making up 42 percent and Buddhists making 40 percent of the total ASEAN population, along with Christians and others. As the ASEAN region continues to gain economic and political importance, Muslim–Buddhist relations will become an increasingly significant issue for building harmonious socio-cultural relations in southeast Asia. In light of this developing situation, the Center of Asian Studies (CENAS), Jakarta, Indonesia in collaboration with Museum of World Religions (MWR), Taiwan, the Global Family for Love and Peace (GFLP) – a UN-affiliated NGO – with support from the Fetzer Institute of USA, organized the Buddhist–Muslim Youth Camp in Yogyakarta, Indonesia on May 7–14, 2012 on the theme of "Love and Forgiveness." The goals of the youth camp were: to provide opportunities for Buddhist and Muslim youth to develop friendships through shared tasks and dialogical encounters, in ways that will influence their lives as individuals, and in their respective communities and organization; to foster harmonious life between Buddhists and Muslims in Indonesia; to promote religious pluralism, protect minority groups and build constructive relationships between Buddhist and Muslim youth leaders, as future leaders of the nation (Buddhist– Muslim Youth Camp 2012).

On July 17–18, 2012, CENAS organized a national conference on the theme, "Love and Forgiveness in Asian Religions" also in Jakarta, Indonesia, with the aim to build harmonious relations between Buddhists and Muslims in Asia. The conference discussed following topics: history of Islam and Buddhism in southeast Asia; concepts of love, forgiveness and compassion in Islam and Buddhism; inter-religious dialogue in southeast Asia; peace in southeast Asia; ecological issue from the perspectives of Islam and Buddhism. The participants also practiced meditation session led by Dharma Master Hsin Tao and visited the Istiqlal mosque in Jakarta to observe Muslim prayer ritual (Buddhist–Muslim National Conference 2012).

The history and state of Islam–Buddhism relations and dialogues around the world is subject to different factors of doctrinal, ethnic and political nature. As such it has a multifaceted appearance and needs a multipronged approach.

Bibliography

Ali, A. "The Muslims Of Sri Lanka: An Ethnic Minority Trapped in a Political Quagmire." *Inter-Asia Cultural Studies* (2004): 372–383.

Andree Feillard, R.M. *The End of Innocence?: Indonesian Islam and the Temptation of Radicalism.* Honolulu: University of Hawaii Press, 2010.

Alam, Muzaffar and Sanjay Subrahmanyam. *Indo-Persian Travels in the Age of Discoveries, 1400–1800.* Cambridge University Press, 2010.

Al-Attas, S.M. *Some Aspects of Sufism as Understood and Practised among the Malays.* Singapore: Malaysian Sociological Research Institute, 1963.

Al-Faruqi, I.R. *On Arabism. I. 'Urubah an Religion: A Study of the Fundamental Ideas of Arabism and of Islam as its highest Moment of Consciousness.* Amsterdam: Djambatan, 1962.

al-Shahrastani, M.b.-K. *Kitab al-Milal wa 'l-Nihal – The Book of Sects and Creeds.* Cairo: Matbat al-Azhar, 1910.

Baker, C.J. and Pasuk Phongpaichit. *A History of Thailand.* Cambridge: Cambridge University Press, 2005.

Berlie, J.A. *The Burmanization of Myanmar's Muslims.* Bangkok: White Lotus Press, 2008.

Berzin, A. "A Buddhist View of Islam," in *Islam and Inter-Faith Relations: The Gerald Weisfeld Lectures,* eds. Perry Schmidt-Leukel and Lloyd Ridgeon. Norwich: SCM Press, 2007, 225–251.

Berzin, A. Holy Wars in Buddhism and Islam: The Myth of Shambhala (2012) http://www.berzinarchives.com/web/en/archives/study/islam/kalachakra_islam/holy_wars_buddhism_islam_myth_shamb/holy_war_buddhism_islam_shambhala_long.html Accessed 26 December 2012.

Bougas, W.A. *The Kingdom of Pattani: Between Thai and Malay Mandalas.* Bangi: Institut Alam dan Tamadun Melayu, 1994.

Bruinessen, M.v. "Pesantren And Kitab Kuning: Maintenance and Continuation of a Tradition of Religious Learning," in *Texts From The Islands. Oral And Written Traditions Of Indonesia And The Malay World,* ed. Wolfgang Marschall. Berne: University of Berne, 1994, 121–145.

Buddhadasa, B. and D.K. Swearer. *Me and Mine: Selected Essays of Bhikkhu Buddhadasa* 1st edn. India: Sri Satguru Publications, 1991.

Buddhism. Retrieved July 14, 2012, from *Encyclopaedia Iranica*: http://www.iranicaonline.org/articles/buddhism-index

Buddhist–Muslim Youth Camp. 2012 Narrative Report. Retrieved August 9, 2012, from http://cenasofindonesia.org/buddhist-muslim-youthcamp-2012-narrative-report/

Buddhist–Muslim National Conference. 17–18 July 2012. Retrieved August 10, 2012, from http://cenasofindonesia.org/agenda-buddhist-muslim-national-conference-17-18-july-2012/

Bulliet, R. "Naw Bahar and the Survival of Iranian Buddhism." *Iran,* (1976): 140–145.

Canby, S.R. "Depictions of Buddha Sakyamuni in the Jami' al–Tavarikh and the Majma' al–Tavarikh." *Muqarnas* 10 (1993): 299–310.

Elverskog, J. *Buddhism and Islam on the Silk Road.* Philadelphia: University of Pennsylvania Press, 2010.

Fletcher, C. "Ismail al Faruqi's Interfaith Dialogue and Asian Religions with Special Reference to Buddhism." *American Journal of Islamic Social Sciences* 28(3) (2011): 92–112.

Foltz, R. *Religions of the Silk Road.* New York: St. Martin's Press, 1999.

Fozdar, Jamshed K. *The God of Buddha.* New York: Asia Publishing House, 1973.

Fyre, R.N. *"Balkh . . ."* Retrieved August 4, 2012, from *Encyclopaedia of Islam,* Second Edition, Brill Online Reference: http://reference works.brillonline.com/entries/encyclopaedia–of–islam–2/balkh–SIM_1153.

Gibb, H.A.R. *Shorter Encyclopaedia of Islam.* Leiden: Brill, 1997.

Glasse, C. and Smith, H. *New Encyclopedia of Islam: A Revised Edition of the Concise Encyclopedia of Islam* (Revised.. Lanham, MD: AltaMira Press, 2001.

Goldziher, I., and Lewis, B. *Introduction to Islamic Theology and Law*. Princeton, NJ: Princeton University Press, 1981.

Gopaka Moggallana Sutta. Retrieved July 12, 2012, from http://dharmafarer.org/wordpress/wp–content/uploads/2010/02/33.5–Gopaka–Moggallana–m108–piya.pdf

Gordon, A. and Malaysian Sociological Research Institute. *The Propagation of Islam in the Indonesian–Malay Archipelago*. Kuala Lumpur: Malaysian Sociological Research Institute, 2001.

Griffiths, P.J. *On Being Buddha*. Albany: State University of New York Press, 1994.

Habito, M.R. "The Notion of Buddha-Nature: An Approach to Buddhist–Muslim Dialogue." *The Muslim World: A Special Issue on Islam and Buddhism* (April/July 2010): 233–246.

Hamidullah, M. *Muhammad Rasulullah*. Lahore: Idara-e-Islamiat, 1974.

Hodgson, M.G.S. *The Venture of Islam*, Volume 2: *The Expansion of Islam in the Middle Periods*. Chicago: University of Chicago Press, 1977.

Hooker, M.B. "Introduction: The Translation of Islam into Southeast Asia," in *Islam in South–East Asia*, ed. M.B. Hooker. Leiden: Brill, 1983, 12–13.

Ibn al-Nadim. Muhammad ibn Abi Yaqub Ishaq. *Kitab al-Fihrist*. Tehran: Raza-Tajaddud, 1971.

Ibrahim Syukri. *History of the Malay Kingdom of Patani*. Athens: Ohio University, Center for International Studies, 1985.

Ikram, S.M.E. and T. Ainslie (eds.). *Muslim Civilization in India*. New York: Columbia University Press, 1965.

Iqbal, A.R.M. and M.C.M. Imtiyaz. "The Displaced Northern Muslims of Sri Lanka: Special Problems and the Future." *Journal of Asian and African Studies* (2011): 375–389.

Jerryson, Michael K. *Buddhist Fury: Religion and Violence in southern Thailand*. Oxford: Oxford University Press, 2011.

Johnson, Irving Chan. *The Buddha on Mecca's Verandah: Encounters, Mobilities, and Histories along the Malaysian–Thai Border*. Seattle, WA: University of Washington Press, 2012.

Jones, L. (ed.). *Encyclopedia of Religion*, 15 Vols (2nd edn). New York: Macmillan Reference USA, 2004.

Kazemi, R.S., H.H. Lama et al. *Common Ground Between Islam and Buddhism: Spiritual and Ethical Affinities*. Louisville, KY: Fons Vitae, 2010.

Keyes, C. "Muslim 'Others' in Buddhist Thailand." *Thammasat Review* 13 (2008/2009): 19–42.

Lawrence, B.B. *Shahrastani on the Indian Religions*. Paris: Mouton, 1976.

MacLean, D.N. *Religion and Society in Arab Sind*. Leiden: Brill, 1997.

Mcgilvray, D.B. "Sri Lankan Muslims: Between Ethno-Nationalism and the Global Ummah." *Nations and Nationalism* (2011): 45–64.

Mansurnoor, I.A. "*Territorial Expansion and Contraction in the Malay Traditional Polity as Reflected in Contemporary Thought and Administration*." Retrieved December 28, 2008, from http://www.l.u-tokyo.ac.jp/IAS/HP-e2/eventreports/mansurnoor.html

Marcinkowski, M.I. *From Isfahan to Ayutthaya: Contacts between Iran and Siam in the 17th Century*. Singapore: Pustaka Nasional, 2005.

Milner, A. *The Malays*. Oxford: Wiley-Blackwell, 2008.

Mutahhari, M. *Perfect Man*. Tehran: Foreign Department of Bonyad Bethat, n.d.

O'Kane, J. (ed.). *Ship of Sulaiman*. London: Routledge, 1972.

Obuse, K. "The Muslim Doctrine of Prophethood in the Context of Buddhist–Muslim Relations in Japan: Is the Buddha a Prophet?" *The Muslim World: A Special Issue on Islam and Buddhism*, 100 (April/July 2010): 215–232.

Pitsuwan, S. *Islam and Malay nationalism: A case Study of Malay-Muslims of Southern Thailand*. Thai Khadi Research Institute, Thammasat University, 1985.

Promta, S. "The View of Buddhism on Other Religions: With Special Reference to Islam." *The Muslim World: A Special Issue on Islam and Buddhism* (April/July 2010): 302–320.

Prophet Muhammad's Last Sermon. Retrieved July 10, 2012, from http://www.alim.org/library/hadith/prophet

Samuels, J. "The Bodhisattva Ideal in Theravada Buddhist Theory and Practice; A Reevaluation of the Bodhisattva–Sravaka Opposition." *Philosophy East and West* (1997): 399–415.

Satha–Anand, S. "Buddhist Pluralism and Religious Tolerance in Democratizing Thailand," in *Philosophy, Democracy and Education*, ed. P Cam. Seoul: The Korean National Commission for UNESCO, 2003, 193–213.

Schimmel, A. and C.W. Ernst. *Mystical Dimensions of Islam*. Chapel Hill: University of North Carolina Press, 2011.

Scott, D. "Buddhism and Islam: Past to Present Encounters and Interfaith Lessons." *Numen* (1995): 141–155.

Shih, A. "The Roots and Societal Impact of Islam in Southeast Asia." *Stanford Journal of East Asian Affairs* (Spring 2002): 114.

Sivaraksa, S.M., Chandra. *Alternative Politics for Asia: A Buddhist–Muslim Dialogue* (1st edn). *International Movement for a Just World*. Brooklyn, NY: Lantern Books (1999).

Spencer, Sidney. *Mysticism in World Religion*. Harmondsworth: Penguin, 1963.

Strong, D.M. *The Udana; Or, The Solemn Utterances of the Buddha*. Charleston, NC: Nabu Press, 2010.

Swearer, D.K. "Bhikkhu Buddhadasa's Interpretation of the Buddha." *Journal of the American Academy of Religion* 331, 1996.

Teeuw, A. *Hikayat Patani: The Story of Patani*. Leiden: Martinus Nijhoff, 1970.

Vakkali Sutta: Vakkali. Retrieved August 6, 2012, from http://www.accesstoinsight.org/tipitaka/sn/sn22/sn22.087x.wlsh.html

Vajda, G. *Ahl al-Kitāb*. Retrieved August 5, 2012 from *Encyclopaedia of Islam*, Second Edition. Brill Online: http://referenceworks.brillonline.com/entries/encyclopaedia-of-islam-2/ahl-al-kitab-SIM_0383.

Wink, A. *Al-Hind: The Making of the Indo–Islamic World*. Leiden: Brill, 1990.

Xinru Liu. "A Silk Road Legacy; The Spread of Buddhism and Islam." *Journal of World History* 22(1) (2011): 55–81.

Yegar, M. *Between Integration and Secession: the Muslim Communities of the Southern Philippines, Southern Thailand, and Western Burma/Myanmar*. Lanham, MD: Lexington Books, 2002.

Yi, B.L. 2012. *Heart to Heart: Buddhist–Muslim Encounters in Ladakh; Buddhist–Muslim Dialogue 2010*. New Taipei City: Museum of World Religions Development Foundation.

Yi, B.L. and Habito, M.R. Museum of World Religions Development Foundation, and Buddhist–Muslim Dialogue. *Listening: Buddist–Muslim Dialogues 2002–04*. Taiwan: Museum of World Religions Development Foundation, 2005.

Yusuf, I. "Religious Diversity in a Buddhist Majority Country: The Case of Islam in Thailand." *International Journal of Buddhist Thought and Culture* 3, (2003): 131–143.

Yusuf, I. "Dialogue between Islam and Buddhism Through The Concepts of Tathagata and Nur Muhammadi." *International Journal of Buddhist Thought and Culture* 5 (2005): 103–114.

Yusuf, I., Lars Peter Schmidt, and Konrad-Adenauer-Stiftung. *Understanding Conflict and Approaching Peace in Southern Thailand*. Bangkok: Konrad Adenauer Stiftung, 2006.

Yusuf, I. "Dialogue Between Islam and Buddhism through the Concepts Ummatan Wasatan (The Middle Nation) and Majjhima–Patipada (The Middle Way)." *Islamic Studies* (2009): 367–394.

Yusuf, S.M. "The Early Contacts Between Islam and Buddhism." *Ceylon Review* (2013): 1955.

CHAPTER 23

Christian–Buddhist Dialogue

Paul O. Ingram

The first mention of the Buddha in Christian sources dates from around the year 200 CE in the *Miscellany* (*Stromateis*) of Clement of Alexandria, in which he argued that Christian *gnosis* ("knowledge") is superior to every other kind of knowledge. In reference to Gautama the Buddha, Clement wrote: "And there are in India those who follow the commandments of the Buddha, whom they revere as God because of his immense holiness"(Küng 1989: 307).One hears little else about Buddhism from this period, and we are also little informed about details of the contact between Christian tradition and Buddhism in the Middle Ages. It was not until Francis Xavier and Mattaeo Ricci's Jesuit missions to Japan and China in the late sixteenth century that Christians began to receive information about Buddhist traditions and practices. As knowledge of Buddhism gradually made its way into the West, Christian encounter with Buddhism was more monological than dialogical, for cultural and historical reasons peculiar to both traditions. Sustained Western attempts to understand Buddhism on its own terms did not begin until the emergence of scholarly research in the field of history of religions (*Religionswissenschaft*) in the mid-nineteenth century, a field which provided the contemporary foundation for Christian dialogical encounter with the world religions in general, and dialogue with Buddhism in particular.

Until recently, the agenda of most Christian theological reflection on other traditions focused on demonstrating the exclusive superiority of Christian faith and practice as the sole vehicle of humanity's salvation. However, since the first "East–West Religions in Encounter" conference, organized by David Chappell in the summer of 1980 at the University of Hawaii, the structure of Christian encounter with Buddhism has slowly changed from theological monologue to theological dialogue, at least in liberal circles of contemporary Catholic and Protestant thought. In the fall of 1987 at the National Meeting of the American Academy of Religion, the initial East–West Religions in

The Wiley Blackwell Companion to Inter-Religious Dialogue, First Edition. Edited by Catherine Cornille.
© 2013 John Wiley & Sons Ltd. Published 2020 by John Wiley & Sons Ltd.

Encounter Group was permanently organized into the Society for Buddhist–Christian Studies (SBCS). This society and its journal, *Buddhist–Christian Studies*, has evolved into an important international forum for world-wide support of the continuing dialogue now occurring between Christians and Buddhists in North America, Europe, South Asia, Korea, Japan and China, including Tibetan Buddhist exiles living in India, North America and Europe.

Three interdependent forms of Buddhist–Christian dialogue have emerged to this date: conceptual dialogue, socially engaged dialogue, and interior dialogue. The focus of conceptual dialogue is doctrinal, theological, and philosophical, because it is concerned primarily with a religious community's collective self-understanding and worldview. In conceptual dialogue, Buddhists and Christians compare and contrast theological and philosophical formulations on such questions as ultimate reality, human nature, suffering and evil, the role of the historical Jesus in Christian faith and practice, the role of the Buddha in Buddhist faith and practice, and what Buddhists and Christians might appropriate from one another, and how. Recently, I have argued that the natural sciences should be included in conceptual Buddhist–Christian dialogue as a "third partner" in the creation of a Buddhist–Christian "trilogue" (Ingram 2008: 2009).

"Socially engaged Dialogue" was first used as a description of Buddhist traditions of social activism by Sallie B. King in her analysis of Thich Nhat Hahn's notion that "inner work," or meditation, must engender non-violent "outer work," or "social engagement" with the systemic structures of injustice (Hahn 1987; King 1996: chapters 9 and 11). Buddhist–Christian conceptual dialogue has generated deep interest in the relevance of dialogue for issues of social, environmental, economic, and gender justice. Because these issues are systemic, global, interconnected, and interdependent, they are neither religion-specific nor culture-specific. Accordingly, socially engaged dialogue is concerned with how Buddhists and Christians have mutually apprehended common experiences and resources for working together to help human beings liberate themselves and nature from the global forces of systemic oppression (Hahn 1987).

It was Thomas Merton who over forty years ago coined the term "monastic dialogue" to refer to what is now called "interior dialogue" (Burton 1975: 309–17). Buddhist–Christian interior dialogue is concerned with how in the human struggle for liberation Buddhists and Christians share an experiential "common ground" that enables them to hear one another and be mutually transformed in the process. Hence interior dialogue emphasizes Buddhist and Christian practice traditions – for example, meditation and centering prayer – with Christians participating in Buddhist meditational techniques and Buddhists participating in Christian techniques of centering and contemplative prayer.

While conceptual, socially engaged, and interior dialogue each have unique emphases, in fact they are interdependent. This is because conceptual dialogue is foundational to social justice issues, and vice versa, while conceptual and socially engaged dialogue is experientially grounded in Buddhist and Christian practice traditions. Accordingly, what follows is a descriptive account of the defining features of each particular form of dialogue that assumes interrelatedness with the other two.

Conceptual Dialogue

Contemporary Christian encounters with Buddhism reflect the pluralism of postmodern, and some would argue, post-Christian cultural and religious diversity because Christian encounters with Buddhism, as well as Buddhist encounters with Christianity, are diverse. This pluralism is rooted in the history of Christian encounters with the world's religions since the first century CE, a history in which there have existed limited theological options for considering non-Christian religious traditions. But by the second half of the twentieth century Christian theologies of religions within some liberal circles had taken a new direction as many theologians recognized the truth and validity of non-Christian traditions. Partly as a negative reaction to this trend, neo-orthodox writers reasserted theological exclusivism by claiming that Christian faith is not one religion among others, but is not "religion" at all. For example, Karl Barth, Emile Brunner, and Dietrich Bonhoeffer defined "religion," including Christian "religion," as a human activity, while Christian "faith" is trust in God's decisive action in the world through the historical Jesus as the Christ. Such trust does not result from the human will to believe, but is an absolute gift originating in God's grace. Neither Protestant neo-orthodoxy nor pre-Vatican II Catholic theology took the world's religious traditions seriously as objects of theological reflection.

Two important transitional Protestant figures emerged in the mid-twentieth century: Paul Tillich and Jürgen Moltmann, both of whom set important theological precedents for Christian conceptual dialogue with Buddhism. After Tillich's encounter with important Buddhist philosophers in Japan that resulted in the publication of his *Christianity and the Encounter with the World's Religions*, he concluded that his "method of correlation" was inadequate for judging the truth of non-Christian religions. (Tillich 1963). This method was deeply influenced by Søren Kierkegaard's existentialist philosophy and asserted that the universal questions all human beings have about the meaning of existence are most completely answered by Christian revelation. Until his encounter with Zen Buddhism, he did not seriously entertain the possibility that there might exist more adequate Buddhist, Hindu, Jewish, or Islamic answers to these universal questions. Accordingly, Tillich began reflecting on how Christian encounter with the world's religions might creatively transform both Christian theology and Christian experience. Unfortunately, he died before he could develop his evolving insights into a systematic theology of religions.

Moltmann wrote of the necessity for Christian encounter with the world's religions as a means, in an increasingly secularizing world, not only of Christian renewal, but also of the renewal of non-Christian religions. He believed that before Christians can enter into fruitful dialogue with non-Christians, two Christian prejudices must be renounced: the absolutism of the church and the absolutism of Christianity. Moltmann's theology of religions is intentionally inclusivist. For him, faith as trust in God's actions for humanity and the entirety of existence – past, present, and future – makes dialogue with non-Christians not only possible, but a theological necessity. This is so because the reality that faithful Christians encounter in the life, death, and resurrection of the historical Jesus as the Christ has also encountered human beings through non-Christian experience and practice (Moltmann 1977: 157ff).

A number of important Christian and Buddhist voices extend Tillich's and Moltmann's views by devoting attention to Buddhist–Christian conceptual dialogue as an important element in their theologies (Ingram 2009: 42–8n). For purposes of illustration, three writers, two Protestants and one Roman Catholic, will serve as an illustration: John B. Cobb, Jr., John P. Keenan, and Hans Küng.

According to Cobb, the practice of Buddhist–Christian dialogue entails a process he calls "passing beyond dialogue" (Cobb 1982: 89–116). Since theological reflection is itself a dialogical process, "passing beyond dialogue" names the process of continual theological engagement *in* dialogue as a contributive factor of one's growth in Christian faith. He assumes the same process will occur for Buddhists as well, who, faithful to Buddhist tradition, go beyond dialogue with Christian tradition. In his understanding, dialogue is a theological practice involving two interdependent movements: (1) in dialogue with Buddhists, Christians should intentionally leave the conventional boundaries of Christian tradition and enter into Buddhist thought and practice, (2) followed by a return to Christian faith enriched, renewed, and "creatively transformed," which is the goal of "passing beyond dialogue." "Creative transformation" names the process of critically appropriating whatever one has learned from dialogue into one's own faith, whereby one's faith is challenged, enriched, and renewed. For Christians, the image of creative transformation is the historical Jesus, who explicitly provides a focal point of unity in which the many centers of meaning that characterize the present "post-Christian" age of religious pluralism are harmonized. Because Cobb thinks that no truth can be contradictory if really true, Christians can and should be open to the "structures of existence" of the other "religious ways" of humanity (Cobb 1975: 21 and 58).

For example, Cobb thinks that there are remarkable affinities between the Mahayana Buddhist notion of "emptying" (*śūñyatā*) and Whitehead's doctrine of the "primordial nature of God," as well as biblical portrayals of God and human selfhood. According to Buddhist teaching, since "non-self" constitutes all events because all things are "empty" of "self-existence" (*svabhāva*), there are no permanent "things" or "events." Since according to process theology, God aims at the concrete realization of all possibilities in their proper season, God is "empty" of substantial selfhood insofar as "self" is understood as an essence that can be preserved by excluding "other" things and events. It is here that Cobb and other process theologians separate themselves from classical Christian theism. In his view, theology should reject notions of God as an unchanging substance as well as the immortality of the human soul by reappropriating biblical, especially Pauline, teaching. In other words, dialogue with Buddhism, mediated through Whiteheadian process philosophy, brings Christian faith and practice into closer alignment with its particular reading of the biblical tradition, since classical Christian teaching that God is an unchanging substance and the doctrine of an immortal soul are in harmony with neither biblical tradition nor the "structure" of Christian existence (Cobb 1975: 28ff).

Perhaps the most radical attempt to reinterpret Christian theology through the categories of Buddhist doctrine is John Keenan's reading of Christian tradition through the lenses of the metaphysics of Yogacāra ("Way of Yoga") and the Mādhyamika ("Middle Way") epistemology of Nagarjuna as a means of clarifying New Testament understandings of the historical Jesus as the Christ (Keenan 1995, 1989). Keenan sees his theological task as developing new forms of Christological thought capable of expressing faith in ways relevant to a postmodern experience of the relativity of all normative claims about reality. Accordingly, Keenan's theological construction of a "Mahayana Christology" focuses on demonstrating how the Christ incarnated in the historical Jesus is also the "heart of wisdom" attested to in the Gospel of John, the Synoptic Gospels, the Pauline Epistles, and the Epistle of James.

By "heart of wisdom" Keenan means experiential apprehension of the structures of existence as interdependent, an apprehension he believes is at the core of both Buddhist thought and biblical tradition. Keenan's primary motivation is to regain contact with biblical meanings as a way of reinterpreting classical christological doctrines that will be spiritually relevant in a postmodern, post-Christian age characterized by religious pluralism. The Christian textual sources of his Mahayana theology lie in the wisdom traditions of the Hebrew Bible and Christian experience of God as the wisdom incarnate in the historical Jesus, as well as all things and events in space-time (John 1: 1–14). He believes that the Mahayana Buddhist name for this wisdom is "Emptying" or *śūñyatā*, which, Keenan acknowledges, has no theistic connotations in Buddhist tradition whatsoever. Nevertheless, he argues that what Yogacara philosophy and Madhyamika epistemology describe as "wisdom," meaning the experiential apprehension of all things and events as empty of independent and permanent self-existence or "own being" (*śvabhāva*), is similar to biblical teaching regarding Christ as the Wisdom (Logos) through which God creates and sustains the universe. Accordingly, Keenan argues that Wisdom is incarnated not only in the historical Jesus, but also in all things and events at every moment of space-time. In this way, Buddhist teachings about interdependence and emptying are thought to clarify Christian experience.

In place of thinking of the historical Jesus as the Christ in terms of an identifiable metaphysical substance, as was affirmed in the Nicene and Chalcedonian Creeds, Keenan argues that Christian theology should shed all essentialist metaphysics by concentrating on the themes of emptying and non-self. Nowhere did Jesus as portrayed in the Gospel of John and the Synoptic Gospels, the Pauline Epistles, and the Epistle of James cling to permanent selfhood. Rather, these texts specifically identify the historical Jesus with wisdom, meaning in its New Testament context, an immediate awareness of God as Father (Abba). Or, as Keenan writes, in the heart of Christian Wisdom, the historical Jesus "disappears in the reality he proclaims. In Ch'an (Zen) Buddhist terms, he is a finger pointing at the moon" (1989: 228).

Unlike Cobb and Keenan, Roman Catholic theologians have not sought to creatively transform Catholic doctrine through the appropriation of Buddhist doctrines. Contemporary Catholic dialogue with the world's religions assumes, in several forms, Karl Rahner's theology of religions, the center of which is his notion of "anonymous Christianity." Stated simply, Rahner concluded that to the degree that non-Catholics are living creatively according to their specific religious traditions, non-Christians are in touch with the same realities most fully revealed in the theology and sacraments of Catholic Christianity. Hence faithful non-Christians are "anonymous Christians" who need conversion to the more fully revealed truths of Roman Catholic faith and practice. For this reason, contemporary Roman Catholic dialogue with the world's religions assumes an inclusivist theology of religions.

Among the best-known Roman Catholic theologians engaged in conceptual dialogue with Buddhism is Hans Küng. While Küng does not explicitly employ Rahner's notion of anonymous Christianity, he draws similar conclusions to Rahner's. For Küng, Catholic Christianity is the "ordinary way of salvation," while persons living at the depths of non-Christian traditions are in touch with less fully revealed truths similar to Catholic teachings and practices. This means that non-Christian traditions are "extraordinary ways of salvation," since God's grace has not been without witnesses. But like Rahner, he asserts that non-Christians need to be brought into a fuller relation with the full truth of Roman Catholicism.

Specifically, Küng's dialogue with Buddhism employs a comparative methodology. Relying on scholarship in Buddhist studies, he is concerned with pointing out the similarities between Buddhist and Christian doctrines and practices, along with incommensurable differences. His theological goal is the clarification of differences in order to help Christians gain accurate comprehension of Christian tradition while simultaneously helping Buddhists obtain accurate understanding of Buddhism. His starting point is a comparison of the historical Jesus with the historical Buddha and the roles of Jesus and the Buddha in Christian and Buddhist traditions. He notes "a fundamental similarity not only in Jesus' and the Buddha's conduct, but also in their message": both were teachers whose authority lay in their experience of ultimate reality; both had urgent messages, although the content of each differed, which demanded of people fundamental changes of attitude and conduct; neither intended to give philosophical explanations of the world nor did they aim to change existing legal and social structures; both worked from the assumption that all human beings are in need of redemption and transformation; both saw the root of humanity's unredeemed state in human egoism, self-seeking, and self-centeredness; both taught ways of redemption (Küng 1986: 322).

For Küng, it is the differences between Jesus and the Buddha that are most profound and important, which he characterizes as the "smiling Buddha" and the "suffering Christ." It is here, according to him, that the incommensurable differences between Christian and Buddhist tradition are found. The two traditions have fundamentally different attitudes toward suffering. Suffering (*dukkha*) is the First Noble Truth of Buddhism. Release from suffering is possible through self discipline in the practice of meditation, which is the sole means of achieving Awakening, the attainment of which leads to leads to no further rebirth in the realm of samsaric suffering. Awakened Ones, that is "Buddhas," are eventually "extinct," no longer involved in the cycles of rebirth that constitute existence. This means that Buddhas show the way to Awakening, but they are not "saviors" or "redeemers."

But for Christians, the historical Jesus as the Christ *is* the Way. That is, Jesus *became* the way of salvation, meaning eternal life in the kingdom of God made manifest in his life, death, and resurrection. Salvation comes only through trust (faith) in the historical Jesus as the Christ expressed through social engagement with the world in the struggle to create a human community based on love and justice. Accordingly, "awakening" in Buddhist tradition and "salvation" in Christian tradition are not identical concepts or experiences, even though Christians can learn much from the practice of Buddhist traditions of meditation. Küng concludes that Buddhists indeed experience what Christians experience as "salvation" through Christ's "extraordinary" working through the traditions of faithful Buddhists, some of whom have attained awakening. Therefore, while Christians can and should be open to Buddhist experience and can learn much from Buddhist insights regarding interdependence, non-self, and suffering and its causes, the "ordinary" way of salvation is through faith in the historical Jesus as the Christ.

Unlike liberal Christian conceptual dialogue with Buddhism, Buddhist conceptual dialogue with Christianity has not sought the creative transformation of Buddhist doctrines through the appropriation of aspects of Christian theological tradition into Buddhism. This is so because Buddhist teaching and practice is hardwired to a non-theistic worldview. Change or delete any item from this worldview, and Buddhism ceases to be "Buddhist." All schools of Buddhism, in their own distinctive ways, are theoretical interpretations of this worldview.

Foundational to Buddhist doctrine is the Buddha's teaching that all existence is implicated in suffering and impermanence (dukkha and *anitya*); that we cause suffering for ourselves and others by clinging (*taṇha*) to permanence in an impermanent universe; that release from suffering is possible; that the Noble Eightfold Path is the ethical and meditative practice that leads to the cessation of suffering and the achievement of awakening (*nirvāṇa*). Crucial to the Buddha's teaching about the structure of impermanent existence are the doctrines of interdependence (*pratītya-samutpāda*) and non-self (*anātman*). "Non-self" means that all things and events at every moment of space-time are constituted by ceaselessly changing interrelationships. Accordingly, awakening is achieved through self-disciplined ethical and meditational practice, not through reliance on the grace of God. For most Buddhist teachers, worship of a deity is merely another form of clinging to a non-existent permanent entity, the result of which can only lead to individual and communal suffering. In other words, a difference exists between the structure of Buddhist existence and the structure of Christian existence which makes it difficult for Buddhists to engage in conceptual dialogue with non-Buddhists. However, this is not to assert that no Buddhists have conceptually engaged in dialogue with Christianity. In fact, it can be argued that the first contemporary Buddhist–Christian conceptual dialogue began in Japan in 1957.

This dialogue has its origins in the early twentieth century in the work of Nishida Kitaro (1879–1945). Under his leadership, the philosophy department of Kyoto University began a conceptual dialogue with Christianity. Several disciples of Nishida – Tanabe Hajime (1885–1962), Hisamatsu Shin'ichi (1899–1980), and Masao Abe (1915–2006) – formed what is now called the "Kyoto School." The Buddhist tradition espoused by the Kyoto school was Zen Buddhism, coupled with an interest in Western Continental philosophy, particularly Kantian idealism. While utilizing Western idealist philosophy, the Kyoto School also employed Buddhist philosophy, particularly Madhyamika epistemology and Zen traditions of meditation, to seek the absolute truth, identified as "emptying," that is beyond all rational discourse. Perhaps the clearest expression of the Kyoto School's philosophical methods and goals is Hisamatsu's *Tōyo-teki Mu* or *Oriental Nothingness*, written in 1939.

Following World War II, Hisamatsu sent his student Abe Masao to Union Theological Seminary to study Christianity under Paul Tillich and Reinhold Niebuhr. Then, in 1957, Hisamatsu traveled to Harvard for the fall semester and engaged Tillich in several meetings that mark the beginning of Buddhist Conceptual dialogue with Christianity (Di Martino 1971, 1972, 1973). Hisamatsu was particularly interested in Tillich's notion of "God beyond God" and his understanding of human nature. Specifically, Hisamatsu's focus was on what Zen calls the "Formless Self," rather than on what is doctrinally unique in Buddhist or Christian teaching. Following his teacher's lead, Abe transformed Nagarjuna's epistemological understanding of emptying into a metaphysically absolute ultimate reality which is the ground of all religious experience, but which manifests itself most clearly in Buddhist, particularly Zen, teachings and practices. Thus Christians who realize the experiential depth of their particular doctrines partially glimpse emptying even if they think they are experiencing God.

An eminent Thai Buddhist, Bhikkhu Buddhadasa (1906–1993), further refined Buddhist conceptual dialogue with Christianity with his "two languages theory;" (1) dharma language and (2) conventional language. The teachings of all religious traditions, Buddhism included, is "conventional language," while "dharma language" refers to the language that expresses awakening, which is only achieved through the practice of meditation. Thus while the conceptual differences between religious traditions are real, all religions are united in the higher truth concerning reality, to which Buddhists and non-Buddhists refer in the paradoxes of "dharma language." But there exists a deeper level of religious experience in which all conceptual distinctions melt away with the attainment of awakening. Buddhadasa's inclusivist viewpoint is also an ingredient in the Dalai Lama's philosophy of religious pluralism: different religious traditions share a common religious goal that each seeks in their own distinctive ways. But the truth of awakening transcends all religious distinctions, including Buddhist distinctions.

Socially Engaged Dialogue

Although Buddhists tended to be more interested in socially engaged dialogue than conceptual dialogue, Christian conceptual dialogue with Buddhists has also generated interest in the relevance of Buddhism to issues of social, environmental, economic, and gender justice. As previously noted, since these issues are systemic, global, interconnected, and interdependent, they are neither religion-specific nor culture-specific. Accordingly, Buddhists and Christians have mutually apprehended common experiences and resources for working together to liberate human beings and nature from the global forces of systemic oppression.

The Vietnamese Zen monk, Thich Nhat Hahn is given credit for coining the term "socially engaged Buddhism" in 1963 as a description of the Buddhist anti-war movement in Vietnam. But in fact, the Buddhist Renewal Movement in Vietnam first coined this term as *nham gian Phat Giao* in the 1930s (Rawlins-Way 2008: 56). Nevertheless, because of Thich Nhat Hahn's leadership of the Buddhist anti-war

movement in the 1960s, "social engagement" is now the most common term desig-
nating Buddhist social activism. No current scholar has written on Buddhist social
engagement more clearly than Sallie B. King (1996: 401–436). She describes Buddhist and Christian social activism as "spiritual social activism." She notes that
socially engaged dialogue has been ongoing since the end of the nineteenth century
and further notes that, although he was not a Buddhist, Mahatma Gandhi was a
model for social engagement for Buddhists like Thich Nhat Hahn and for Christians
like Martin Luther King, Jr.

Three elements define Buddhist social engagement. First, Buddhist social activism
in all of its forms must, in the words of Thich Nhat Hahn, "be peace" in order to "make
peace." Or as the Dalai Lama phrases the same principle, "Everyone loves to talk about
calm and peace, whether in family, national or international contexts, but without *inner
peace*, how can we make peace real? (Tenzen Gyatso 1995), Since all things and events
are interdependent, working for peaceful social change through compassionate nonviolence requires the practice of meditation, the point of Thich Nhat Hahn's formula,
"outer work involves inner work." That is, one who has experienced interdependence
through meditation simultaneously sees through the delusion of separate selfhood. The
result is that things and events, including forms of injustice, are apprehended truly
without illusion, so that one's social activism actually reflects the realities of particular
situations of injustice. One's self is never separate from another human or non-human
being; the oppressed is never separated from the oppressor.

Second, this means that Buddhist understandings of compassion are not only
grounded in the doctrine of interdependence, but also in the doctrine of non-self. Cultivating experiential awareness of selflessness is the core of Buddhist spirituality and
the center of Buddhist social activism. The practice of meditation is the "skillful means"
(*upāya*) through which one seeks to eradicate preoccupation with oneself in order to
cultivate recognition of the sameness of one's own and others' value, and one's wish
for the well-being of those others. One works for the well-being of another because one
literally *is* the other.

Finally, the doctrine of *karma* plays an important role in Buddhist practice of social
engagement in two ways: (1) the role karma plays in the construction of one's present
and future identity, and (2) violent reaction against a person who does injury, that is,
returning violence with violence, always causes negative results for both the receiver
of violence and the perpetrator of violence. Violent actions, even in violent self-defense
against an aggressor, merely add to the spiraling cycle of violence.

The structure of Buddhist social engagement is a primary interest of Christian
socially engaged dialogue with Buddhists. Contemporary Christian social activism is
deeply rooted in liberation theology. While the word "liberation" is not often used
in Buddhist social activism, examples of Buddhist struggle for what Christians call
"liberation" abound: Dr. B Ambedkar, who led millions of ex-untouchable Hindus to
Buddhism; Dr. A.T. Ariyaratne, the founder of the Sarvodya Sramadana movement in
Sri Lanka, whose goal is to establish new social structures that embody Buddhist values
so that both individuals and society can achieve awakening; the Dalai Lama's nonviolent Tibetan liberation movement; Sulak Sivaraksa's "gadfly" attempts to lead the
Thai government away from participation in drug trafficking and the sex trade in South

Asia; the Won Buddhist movement of South Korea; the Nichiren Buddhist movements of Rissho Koseikai and Soka Gakkai in Japan; and the Fo Huang Shan movements in Taiwan (Queen and King 1996: chapters 2, 4, 6, 8, and 10).

The term "liberation" in Christian theology, according to Gustavo Gutierrez, has two meanings (Guiterrez 1973: 36). First, "liberation" refers to the worldwide aspirations of oppressed human beings. In this sense, "liberation" names a struggle that places oppressed human beings and nature at odds with oppressive national, social, economic systems. "Liberation practice" is active engagement with these oppressive systemic forces. Second, "liberation" assumes a particular understanding of history. Christian liberation theologians, for example, tend to see history as a process in which human beings gradually assume conscious responsibility for their own individual and collective global future. Of course, what liberation practice means will be nuanced differently in Buddhist social engagement and Christian social activism. For Christians, the central image of liberation is the historical Jesus as the Christ who brings liberation to human beings not only from the bondage of sin and death, but also from the social, economic, and political sins of oppression. The model for liberation for Theravada Buddhists is the enlightened practice of Gautama the Buddha, and for Mahayana Buddhists, all Buddhas and bodhisattvas. Awakening engenders compassionate action skillfully applied to help liberate all sentient beings from suffering. For Christian thinkers like Paul F. Knitter, the quest for liberation provides a common ground for Buddhist–Christian dialogue in particular, and inter-religious dialogue in general (Knitter, 1995).

One of the most important forms of Buddhist–Christian socially engaged dialogue focuses on the liberation of women from patriarchal oppression and androcentrism. Androcentrism and patriarchy usually go hand in hand in Buddhist and Christian feminist writing. Androcentrism names a mode of consciousness, a thought-form, and a method of gathering information and classifying women's place in a male-defined metaphysical view of reality. Andocentric thought asserts that the structure of humanity has one defining center, so that masculinity is the sole norm for measuring what is human. As a worldview, androcentrism occurs in both masculine and feminine heads, with patriarchy being the institutionalized expression of androcentrism. This means that patriarchy always expresses itself as a gender hierarchy that places men over women.

Here, Buddhist and Christian feminists in socially engaged dialogue agree on four points. First, a male-centered set of values dictates which texts to keep and which experiences to preserve in the historical records of a tradition. Stories about men and the thought and practices of men are far more likely to be recorded than stories about what women did or said. Second, even when a religious tradition preserves significant records about what women said or did, later developments tend to ignore these stories and stress male stories as authoritative for faith and practice. Third, Western and non-Western scholarship on the world's religions still largely agrees with these male-centered biases. Finally, all contemporary forms of the world's religions continue to maintain an unrelenting, ongoing androcentrism.

Consequently, Buddhists and Christian feminists like Rita M. Gross and Nancy R. Howell, seek to reconstruct Buddhist and Christian tradition through recovering an accurate and usable past that focuses on the pluralism of Buddhist and Christian women's experience. "Accuracy" has to do with feminism as an academic methodology of historical investigation, while "usability" refers to the feminist goal of liberating both women and men from patriarchy (Gross 1993: 31–48; Howell 2006: chapter 5). But as important as accurate and usable history is, the liberation of women is interdependent with humanity's liberation from social, political, and economic oppression, because women are generally the most socially, politically, and economically exploited human beings in every culture and religious context. The liberation of women from oppression is also interdependent with the liberation of the environment from human exploitation. Accordingly, the lesson of Buddhist–Christian socially engaged dialogue is this: to the degree that women achieve liberation from patriarchal oppression, to that degree do all human beings achieve social, political, and economic liberation; to that degree does the earth achieve liberation from human oppression; to that degree is life itself liberated from the threat of human-caused environmental destruction.

Interior Dialogue

If the participants in Buddhist–Christian interior dialogue are to be believed, in the common struggle for liberation Christians and Buddhists share an experiential referent that enables them to hear one another and to be mutually transformed in the process. In interior dialogue Buddhists and Christians participate in each other's practice and reflect on the resulting experiences. Since spiritual and monastic disciplines continue to energize Roman Catholic experience, while monastic disciplines like centering prayer and contemplative prayer have, since Luther's time, been viewed as forms of "works of righteousness" and therefore de-emphasized in Protestant tradition, Roman Catholics have generally paid more attention to Buddhist–Christian interior dialogue that Protestants. In this regard, Thomas Merton's encounter with the Dalai Lama and other Tibetan monks, Thai Buddhist monks, and Zen teachers still serves as a paradigm for Christian interior dialogue with Buddhism (Merton 1975: 309–25).

Merton's frustration with the state of Trappist monasticism as he had experienced it was the motivating force of his engagement with Buddhism in general and the world's religions in particular. Towards the end of his life he had reached the conclusion that Christian monasticism should be reformed through dialogue with Buddhist monks and nuns, in particular through the mutual participation and sharing of Christian and Buddhist meditative techniques and experiences. The purpose of "contemplative dialogue," as he referred to what is now called "interior dialogue," is to discover whether there exist similarities and analogies in Christian and Buddhist experience in spite of the doctrinal differences in Christian and Buddhist thought. He concluded that while doctrinal differences will always differentiate Christian and Buddhist tradition, doctrinal differences do not invalidate the existential similarities of the experiences engendered by Christian and Buddhist monastic practices like and meditation, centering prayer, and contemplative prayer. He grew to believe that the reality experientially encountered by both Buddhists and Christians is beyond the power of doctrine to delimit (Cunningham 1999: 155–82).

Somewhat inspired by Merton, Raimundo Panikkar, in *The Silence of God, the Answer of the Buddha*, explored the conceptual incommensurability between Christian theism and Buddhist non-theism as a means of helping Christians search for new meanings of God beyond the limits of the traditional categories of Euro-American theological tradition. Unlike Cobb's primarily conceptual dialogue with Buddhism, Panikkar combined interior dialogue with conceptual dialogue. His intention was to help Christians experience, as well as rationally comprehend, that the object of Christian faith is a reality beyond the boundaries of theological language. Thus Christians needed to hear "the answer of the Buddha": the ultimate reality to which the Buddha awoke as nonpersonal and beyond the limits of language. Appropriating the Buddha's "answer" became for Panikkar a method of "entering the silence," as Merton phrased it, beyond the limitations of doctrinal description, even those of Christian theology (Panikkar 1989: chapter 10).

"Entering the silence" has always been the goal of Christian and Buddhist contemplative and monastic training. Among Catholic Christians engaged in interior dialogue with Buddhism, Ruben Habito is unique in that as a Jesuit he trained in Zen meditation under Yamada Koun Roshi (1907–1989), receiving Yamada Roshi's *inko* or "seal of approval," and became interested in the implications of interior dialogue for conceptual and socially engaged dialogue. The central theological question he brings to his interior dialogue with Buddhism centers on liberation.

In an essay entitled "The Resurrection of the Dead and the Life Everlasting: From a Futuristic to a Realized Christianity," Habito points to the tension between the "future outlook" and, borrowing a phrase from Zen Buddhism, the "realized outlook" of Christian experience. While both outlooks are interdependent and presuppose faith as trust in the promises of eternal life made manifest in the historical Jesus's resurrection (the future outlook), he argues that the resurrection is simultaneously a present reality open to anyone who accepts Christ here-and-now (the realized aspect). Accordingly, Christian faith's realized aspect manifests the experience of eternal life and resurrection in the here-and-now moment of the experience of faith. In this way, Zen's stress on experiencing the here-and-now moment of experience can help Christians appreciate the realized aspect of the Christian experience of liberation more fully (Habito 1999: 223–238; 1983).

Perhaps the most important collective example of interior dialogue is The Gethsemani Encounter. In 1978, ten years after Merton's death, two Catholic dialogue commissions were created: the Monastic Interreligious Dialogue (MID) in North America and the Dialogue Inter-Monastique (DIM) in Europe. From these two commissions evolved the Spiritual Exchange in Europe and the Hospitality Program in North America, programs in which Buddhist monks and nuns spent time living in Catholic monasteries in the West, while Christian monastics were guests in Zen and Tibetan monasteries in the East. Prior to the 1993 Parliament of World Religions, Fr. Julian von Duerbeck, OSB, and Br. Wayne Teasdale proposed that the MID host an interfaith dialogue session at the Parliament with the Dalai Lama and other Buddhist leaders. It was the Dalai Lama who suggested that the monastic dialogue be continued at Thomas Merton's Trappist monastery, Gethsemani Abby, in Kentucky. The encounter lasted five days and included 25 invited Buddhist monks and nuns and 25 Catholic monks and nuns, plus several Protestants.

The topic of the Gethsemani Encounter was the "spiritual unity" underlying the doctrinal plurality of Buddhist and Christian spiritual practices. As summarized by the Dalai Lama:

> Now, it is also quite clear that different religious traditions – in spite of having different philosophies and viewpoints – all have great potential to help humanity by promoting human happiness and satisfaction. As a matter of fact, it is quite clear that given the vast array of humanity – of so many different kinds of people with different mental dispositions – we need, and so it is far better to have, a variety of religious traditions. Religions are like medicine in that the important thing is to cure human suffering. . . . Here, too, it is not a question of which religion is superior as such. The question is, which will better cure a particular person. (Mitchell and Wiseman 1998: 47)

Similarly, in his description of contemplative prayer as a form of "mindfulness," Pierre-François de Béthune, OSB, observed that:

> . . . with a heart enlarged by love of God that embraces all of creation, he or she is spontaneously in communion with all those who suffer and all those who follow the spiritual life, *whatever their religion*. Ultimately, the prayer of the Holy Spirit that brings us into communion with all of humanity and even the whole creation which, as St. Paul says, groans and travails in pain (Rom 8: 26). Conversely, the opportunity to meet other fellow pilgrims stimulates us to deepen our prayer. (Mitchell and Wiseman 1998: 82)

According to the participants at Gethsemani, specific meditative and contemplative prayer techniques lead Buddhist and Christian practitioners to a unitive experience of an Absolute Reality named differently by Buddhists and Christians that both transcends as it is simultaneously immanent within all things and events at every moment of spacetime. This experience, known in Christian mystical theology as "apophatic" experience, is unitary in structure for both Buddhists and Christians. During such experiences, subject–object differentiations and conceptual differences utterly drop away from consciousness so that reality, "the way things really are in contrast to the way our egos wish or desire things to be," is apprehended without doctrinal boundaries. In other words, Buddhist meditation in its plurality of forms and Christian centering and contemplative prayer in its plurality of forms engender structurally similar experiences for Buddhists and Christians in spite of the conceptual differences in the Buddhist and Christian doctrines that guide practices of meditation, and centering and contemplative prayer.

Still, Buddhist participants at Gethsemani agreed that five doctrinal assumptions guide the practice of meditation in its various specific disciplines.

- Since the development of mindfulness requires the avoidance of negative activities, ethical self-discipline is the foundation of the specific techniques of meditation.
- Meditation can be practiced by concentrating on just one object, called "calming" or "stabilizing" meditation (*samatha*).

- Meditation can be "analytical," as in "insight" (*vipassanā*) meditation, through which reason and emotions, both positive and negative, can be replaced by non-egoistic responses like compassion that flow from the apprehension of universal interdependence.
- Meditation may also be a reflection on the various levels of a spiritual path.
- Meditation may involve visualization techniques, chanting mantras, or simply focusing on one's breathing rhythm or a *koan*.

"Meditation" names a collection of mental techniques meant to experimentally confirm the truth of Buddhism's worldview and defining doctrines (Ingram 2009: 112).

Likewise, the goal of Christian contemplative practices – *lectio divina* ("divine reading"), centering prayer, and contemplative prayer – offer experiential confirmation of the truth of Christian doctrines about God as incarnated in the life, death, and resurrection of the historical Jesus as the Christ. Comparing the goals of Buddhist meditation with Christian contemplative practices, Donald Mitchell writes that:

> . . . in reading the description of the qualities of a person who abides in *Nibbana*, namely compassion, loving kindness, sympathetic joy, and equanimity – one recognizes the qualities of a person who abides in the Kingdom of God. On the other hand, while *Nibbana* is primarily a state of consciousness, when *we* Christians gaze into the heart of our supreme refuge with the "mind of Christ," we find a personal God who is love. (Mitchell and Wiseman 1998: 28)

Concluding Observations

Christian theologians in conceptual dialogue with Buddhists testify that Christian theology is positively affected by this encounter. Furthermore they deeply respect and admire Buddhist faith and practice. Nor is there a hidden missionary agenda in most Christian dialogue with Buddhism. Yet the very openness of Christians and Buddhists to the possibilities of mutual creative transformation through dialogue has brought to light issues and questions that are now setting the agenda for continuing Buddhist–Christian encounter. Four issues and an emerging consensus merit special comment.

First, Christians have tended to be more open to creative transformation through conceptual dialogue with Buddhism than have Buddhists in conceptual dialogue with Christianity. In fact, Buddhist conceptual engagement with Christian theology has had little positive or negative impact on the development of contemporary Buddhist thought. The reason for this may be that the Christian worldview contains more flexibility. That is, a Christian can appropriate the worldviews of Marx, existentialism, Plato, Aristotle, or Neo-Platonism; one can be a Thomist or Neo-Thomist, a scientist, or even "a Buddhist, too," according to John Cobb, and still be a Christian (Cobb 1978). But non-theism and the doctrines of impermanence, no-self, and dependent co-arising are so necessary to the structure of Buddhist faith and practice that Buddhism is not open to creative transformation through conceptual dialogue with Christianity. Accordingly, it does not seem appropriate to think of creative transformation of these defining

Buddhist doctrines because they have been indispensable to Buddhist faith and practice for 2500 years. Without these defining doctrines, Buddhism ceases to be "Buddhist." Thus Christian theology as "faith seeking understanding" does not have a correlate in Buddhist experience. Buddhism also attaches less importance to doctrines. According to Buddhist self-understanding, doctrines are "vehicles" or "pointers" that guide the practice of meditation in the hope of awakening to an ultimate reality beyond all conceptualities and symbols.

This fact has pushed current Christian–Buddhist conceptual dialogue to evolve beyond its earlier search for common doctrines and experiences to focus more on the "hard" issues of what appear to be incommensurable differences between Christian and Buddhist doctrines: Buddhist non-theism and Christian theism; the role of Jesus in Christianity and the role of the Buddha in Buddhism; Christian emphasis on faith and grace and Buddhist focus on the practice of meditation; the place of contemplative prayer in Christianity compared with the role of meditation in Buddhism. The main question behind this form of current conceptual dialogue is whether the doctrinal differences between Christianity and Buddhism are contradictory or complementary concepts that point to an ultimate reality underlying Christian and Buddhist experience. So far, a consensus has not emerged among Christians and Buddhist interested in this question (Gross and Muck 2000).

The second issue concerns how to prevent Christian–Buddhist encounter from remaining an elitist intellectual enterprise of interest only to professional academic theologians, philosophers, ministers, priests, monks, and nuns. The solution lies in expanding the dialogue by including interested non-academic and lay Christian and Buddhist persons active in their religious communities into the discussion, both as listeners and teachers of intellectuals who may not have adequate perceptions of the actual religions experiences of ordinary Christians and Buddhists. For Christians, the goal is the Church's creative transformation. For Buddhists, the question is what "creative transformation" means given the specific doctrinal content that defines Buddhism's worldview. But the Christian community as a whole (the Church) and the Buddhist community as a whole (the Samgha) need to brought into this discussion. Exactly how to do so is a matter on ongoing conversation between Christian theologians and Buddhists teachers.

Third, interior dialogue has brought a number of difficult and unresolved questions to consciousness that are now energizing much Christian-Buddhist discussion. What is the connection between theological-philosophical conceptualities and specific experiences engendered by Christian contemplative prayer or Buddhist meditative discipline? How does theological expectation influence contemplative prayer or Buddhist meditation? Carmelite nuns practicing contemplative prayer do not ordinarily interpret their contemplative experience as oneness with the Buddha Nature that constitutes all existence at every moment of spacetime. Nor do Zen Buddhist nuns practicing meditation normally interpret their experiences as union with Christ the Bridegroom. Do Christians practicing a Buddhist discipline of meditation guided by Christian theological assumptions obtain experiences a Buddhist could recognize as "Buddhist"? Do Buddhists practicing Christian contemplative prayer guided by the Buddhist worldview obtain "Christian" experiences? Are conceptual commitments inherently part of Christian and Buddhist spiritual disciplines? Does one not receive from a religious discipline what one's tradition conceptually trains one to expect to receive? What *are* the connections between conceptual dialogue and interior dialogue?

Fourth, some Christians and Buddhists are now reflecting on the possibility of including the natural sciences and the social sciences as a "third partner" in their conceptual dialogue. What the natural sciences are revealing about the physical processes at play in the universe certainly has a bearing on Christian and Buddhist self-understanding and practice. All of the natural sciences and the social sciences – big bang cosmology, relativity theory, quantum mechanics, evolutionary biology, the cognitive sciences, economics – have relevance for the central doctrines of Christian and Buddhist tradition. For example, what are the implications of scientific cosmology, relativity theory, and quantum mechanics for Buddhism's and Christianity's worldviews and doctrines? What are the implications of the biological and ecological sciences for Christian and Buddhist doctrines? What do the cognitive sciences imply about the practice of Christian and Buddhist contemplative-meditative disciplines? How can the environmental sciences and economics be brought to bear on Buddhist–Christian socially engaged dialogue with issues of poverty and environmental injustice (Loy 2011)?

Finally, an important consensus seems to have emerged from contemporary Christian–Buddhist encounter. Conceptual, socially engaged, and interior dialogue are interdependent. Or to paraphrase the Epistle of James, conceptual dialogue and interior dialogue apart from socially engaged dialogue is dead for the same reasons that "faith without works" is dead. That is, the central point of Christian and Buddhist practice, in separation or in dialogue, is the liberation of human beings and all creatures in nature from forces of oppression and injustice and the mutual creative transformation of persons in community with nature. Buddhist wisdom implicated in awakening and Christian doctrines of creation and incarnation point to the utter interdependency of all things and events at every moment of space-time – a notion also affirmed by contemporary physics and biology in distinctively scientific terms (Ingram 2008; Peacocke 1993). Awareness of interdependency, in turn, engenders social engagement, because awareness of interdependence and social engagement are themselves interdependent. Thus we experience the suffering of others as our suffering, the oppression of others as our oppression, the oppression of nature as our oppression, and the liberation of others as our liberation – and thereby we become empowered for social engagement.

Bibliography

Abe, Masao and John B. Cob, Jr. "Buddhist–Christian Dialogue: Past, Present, Future." *Buddhist–Christian Studies* 1 (1981): 13–20.

Burton, Naomi, Patrick Hart, and James Laughlin (eds.). *The Asian Journal of Thomas Merton*. New York: New Directions Books, 1975.

Cobb, John B., Jr. *Christ in a Pluralistic Age*. Philadelphia: Westminster Press, 1975.

Cobb, John B., Jr. "Can a Christian be a Buddhist, Too?" *Japanese Religions* 10 (December 1978): 1–20.

Cobb, John B., Jr. *Beyond Dialogue: Toward the Mutual Transformation of Christianity and Buddhism*. Philadelphia: Fortress Press, 1982.

Cunningham, Lawrence C. *Thomas Merton and the Monastic Vision*. Grand Rapids, MI: Eerdmans, 1999.

Cunningham, Lawrence C. *Christ in a Pluralistic Age*. Philadelphia: Westminster Press, 1975.

D'Costa, Gavin D. *Christian Uniqueness Reconsidered: The Myth of a Pluralistic Theology of Religions*. Maryknoll, NY: Orbis, 1990.

De Martino, Richard D. (trans.). "Dialogue East and West: Paul Tillich and Hisamatsu Shin'ichi." *The Eastern Buddhist* 4 (October 1971): 39–107; 5 (October 1972): 108–128; and 6 (October 1973) 87–114.

Gross, Rita M. *Buddhism After Patriarchy: A Feminist History, Analysis, and Reconstruction of Buddhism*. Albany, NY: State University of New York Press: 1993.

Gross, Rita M. and Muck, Terry C. (eds.). *Buddhists Talk About Jesus, Christians Talk About the Buddha*. New York: Continuum, 2000.

Gutierrez, Gustavo. *A Theology of Liberation: History, Politics, and Salvation*. Trans. Sister Caridad Inda and John Eagleson. Maryknoll, NY: Orbis, 1973.

Habito, Rubin L.F. *Healing Breath: Zen Spirituality for a Wounded World*. Maryknoll, NY: Orbis, 1993.

Habito, Rubin L.F. "The Resurrection of the Dead and Life Everlasting: From a Futuristic to a Realized Christianity," in *The Sound of Liberating Truth*, eds. Sallie B. King and Paul O. Ingram. Surrey: Curzon Press, 1999, 223–238.

Hahn, Thich Nhat. *Interbeing: Fourteen Guidelines for Engaged Buddhism*. Berkeley, CA: Parallax Press, 1987.

Hick, John and Knitter, Paul F. (eds.) *The Myth of Christian Uniqueness: Toward a Pluralistic Theology of Religions*. Maryknoll, NY: Orbis, 1990.

Howell, Nancy R. "Beyond a Feminist Cosmology," in *Constructing a Relational Cosmology*, ed. Paul O. Ingram. Princeton Theological Monograph Series 62. Eugene, OR: Pickwick, 2006, 104–16.

Ingram, Paul O. *Buddhist–Christian Dialogue in an Age of Science*. Lanham, ML: Rowman and Littlefield, 2008.

Ingram, Paul O. "Interfaith Dialogue as a Source of Buddhist–Christian Creative Transformation," in *Buddhist–Christian Dialogue: Mutual Renewal and Transformation*, edited by Paul O Ingram and Frederick J. Streng, 77-66. 1986. Reprint, Eugene, OR: Wipf and Stock, 2007.

Ingram, Paul O. *The Process of Buddhist–Christian Dialogue*. Eugene, OR: Cascade Books, 2009.

Ingram, Paul O. *Wrestling With the Ox: A Theology of Religious Experience*. New York: Continuum, 1997.

Keenan, John B. *The Gospel of Mark: A Mahayana Reading*. Maryknoll, NY: Orbis, 1995.

Keenan, John B. *The Meaning of Christ: A Mahayana Christology*. Maryknoll, NY: Orbis, 1989.

King, Sallie B. "Thich Nhat Hahn and the Unified Buddhist Church: Non-dualism in Action," in *Engaged Buddhism: Buddhist Liberation Movements in Asia*, edited by Christopher S. Queen and Sallie B. King. Albany, NY: State University of New York Press, 1996, chapters 9 and 11.

King, Winston L. *Buddhism and Christianity: Some Bridges of Understanding*. Philadelphia: Westminster Press, 1972.

Knitter, Paul. *One Earth, Many Religions: Multifaith Dialogue and Global Responsibility*. Maryknoll, NY: Orbis Books, 1995.

Küng, Hans. *Christianity and the World Religions*. Garden City, NY: Doubleday and Company, 1986.

Loy, David. "The Poverty of Economic Development," in *The World Market and Interreligious Dialogue*, eds. C. Cornille and G. Willis. Eugene, OR: Wipf and Stock, 2011, pp. 91–106.

Merton, Thomas. "Monastic Experience and East–West Dialogue," in *The Asian Journal of Thomas Merton*, eds. Naomi Burton et al. New York: New Directions, 1975.

Mitchell, Donald W. and Wiseman, James (eds.) *The Gethsemani Encounter*. New York: Continuum, 1998.

Moltmann, Jürgen, *The Church in the Power of the Spirit: A Contribution to Messianic Eschatology*. New York: Harper and Row, 1977.

Panikkar, Raimundo. *The Silence of God, the Answer of the Buddha*. Maryknoll, NY: Orbis, 1989.

Peacocke, Arthur. *Theology for a Scientific Age*. Minneapolis: Fortress Press, 1993.

Queen, Christopher S. and Sallie B. King (eds.). *Engaged Buddhism: Buddhist Liberation Movements in Asia*. Albany, NY: State University of New York Press, 1996,

Rawlins-Way, Olivia M. F. "Religious Interbeing: Buddhist Pluralism and Thich Nhat Hahn." Unpublished Ph.D. dissertation, University of Sydney, 2008.

Tenzen Gyatso [The Fourteenth Dalai Lama]. *The World of Tibetan Buddhism: An Overview of its Philosophy and Practice*. Trans. ed. Geshe Thupten Jinpa. Boston: Wisdom Books, 1995.

Tillich, Paul. *Christianity and the Encounter with the World's Religions*. New York: Columbia University Press, 1963.

CHAPTER 24

Buddhist–Jewish Relations

Nathan Katz

From King Solomon to the Dalai Lama, from Marco Polo to Chaim Potok, from medieval Kabbalists to contemporary JuBus, there have been encounters between Buddhists and Jews for millennia. Ancient interactions are hinted at in sacred texts of both religions, and medieval links are often tantalizingly disguised. It has been only since the middle of the twentieth century – the era of the Holocaust and nuclear weapons – that the Buddhist–Jewish encounter has emerged from the shadows.

Ancient Times

There is no shortage of evidence for commercial and cultural links between India and Israel in even the most ancient strata of history. From the days of Sumer and the Indus Valley civilization, both archaeological evidence and textual references provide evidence of links between these two civilizations (Katz 1999). Sanskrit and Tamil loan words are found in the Hebrew Bible (Rabin 1971), obscure biblical place names have been identified in India (Chakravarty 2007), and first-century CE Hellenized Jewish authors Josephus Flauvius and Philo of Alexandria wrote admiringly of Indian culture and religion (Katz 1999: 20–22).

The evidence for ancient Indo-Israel links is clear. But what of specific Buddhist–Jewish materials? We can find one such connection. A Buddhist Jataka story connects the Buddha, the wisest man of India, with King Solomon, the wisest man of Israel. In the *Mahoshadha Jataka* a *yakshini*, or demoness, stole a baby from his mother, intending to eat him. The mother confronted the *yakshini*, but was rebuked by the demoness who claimed the baby as her own. They happened to pass by the judgment hall of the Maharaja of Benares, who was none other than the Buddha in a previous birth. The text reads:

This chapter was first published in Perry Schmidt-Leukel (ed.), *Buddhist Attitudes to Other Religions*, St. Ottilien/Germany: EOS-Verlag 2008. We thank EOS for the kind permission to reuse it here.

He heard the noise, sent for them, inquired into the matter, and asked them whether they would abide by his decision. And they agreed. Then he had a line drawn on the ground; and told the yakshini to take hold of the child's arms, and the mother to take hold of its legs; and said: "The child shall be hers who drags him over the line."

But soon as they pulled at him, the mother, seeing how he suffered, grieved as if her heart would break. And letting him go, she stood there weeping. Then the future Buddha asked the bystanders, "Whose hearts are tender to babes? Those who have borne children, or those who have not?" And they answered, "O Sire! The hearts of mothers are tender." Then he said, "Whom do you think is the mother? She who has the child in her arms, or she who has let go?" And they answered, "She who has let go is the mother."

The tale concludes happily. The child is returned to its mother, and the remorseful *yakshini* vowed to follow the five fundamental ethical precepts of Buddhism. (Rhys-Davids 1880: xxii–xxvi).

This legend of the Buddha is strikingly similar to the judgment tale of King Solomon (I Kings 3: 16–28). It impossible to say who is borrowing from whom, or whether both Jews and Buddhists were borrowing from a yet older, common source, or whether this striking similarity was simply coincidental.

Medieval Times

One of the inherent difficulties in discerning Jewish–Buddhist relations in the ancient and medieval eras is terminological. In Indian literature, all foreigners are called "Yavanas," – "Greeks." Mirroring this conflation, in Jewish literature all things Indian are called "Hindu'a."

As we move into medieval times, the documentation of links between Jews and India become increasingly clear (Katz and Goldberg 1993: 35–61). Physical evidence places Jewish communities in India since the ninth century; Goitein's analysis of early medieval documents from the *genizah* at Fustart, Cairo, is replete with numerous letters of Jewish merchants who plied "the India trade" (Goitein 1973); and medieval travelers, from al-Beruni to Benjamin of Tudela to Marco Polo, have described a Jewish presence in and interactions with Indian culture. (Sachau 1964: I: 206).

Medieval cultural interactions between Jews and India have been detailed in two recent, significant studies (Marks 2007; Weinstein 2007), but contain only two indications of a specifically Jewish–Buddhist medieval interaction. One is found in the travel diaries of "the greatest medieval Jewish traveler" (Levanon 1980: 20), Rabbi Benjamin of Tudela (twelfth century CE). Benjamin described a Jewish community of some 23,000 in Lanka which, of course, is predominantly a Buddhist country (Levanon 1980). Benjamin's report is corroborated by the great Muslim geographer, Abu 'Abdallah Muhammad ibn Idris, known as Idrisi (1099–1154), who wrote: "The king of this island has sixteen ministers, of whom one-quarter are native to that nation, a quarter are Christians, a quarter Muslims, and a quarter Jews." (Asher n.d.: 188) These sources indeed suggest of Buddhist–Jewish encounters of nearly a thousand years ago, but Benjamin's and Idrisi's accounts are not very reliable. There is no real evidence that Benjamin actually traveled beyond the Middle East and he mostly relied on traveler's tales; and Idrisi likely confused the Hindu-centered town of Chendamangalam, near Kochi, with Ceylon. In medieval times, the capital of the area around Kochi was known to Jewish and Arab travelers as Shingly, easily confused with one of the names of Ceylon, Singhala Dipa, or "Singoli" as Idrisi called it (Katz and Goldberg 1993: 37).

A most suggestive discovery regarding the early history of Judaism in China was first reported in 1901 by the British-Jewish archaeologist, Sir Marc Auriel Stein (1862; Weinstein 2007). Excavating Dandan-Uiliq, near Khotan in Turkestan, he found a manuscript written in Judeo-Persian and dated 718 CE. Stein also excavated the "Cave of the Thousand Buddhas" at the Silk Road oasis of Tun-huang, Kansu Province, in which his colleague, Paul Pelliot (1876–1945), found one page of a Hebrew penitential prayer book with verses from the Psalms and the Prophets, also dating from the eighth or perhaps the ninth century (Leslie 1972: 5). One can only speculate about the implications of the fact that the oldest Hebrew fragment on paper ever discovered was found in a Chinese Buddhist library. Not so long after, Marco Polo (thirteenth century) described Jewish advisors to the Chinese Emperor (Marco Polo 1985: 301).

Perhaps in Lanka or China at the turn of the millennium, traces of a Buddhist–Jewish encounter can be inferred.

Mysticism

Ideas, of course, travel east to west as much as from west to east, and in Tudela a century after Benjamin, the seminal Kabbalist Abraham Abulafia (1240–1291) adapted Indian mystical practices, symbols and ideas into his system (Idel 2000). While I was in residence at Jerusalem's Shalom Hartman Institute, where Hebrew University Professor Moshe Idel is a fixture, Idel described to me numerous kabbalistic manuscripts in his personal library that clearly demonstrate Indian mystical influences and direct borrowings: meditation techniques and even sacred diagrams known as mandalas, all Judaized and incorporated as part and parcel of Abulafia's "ecstatic Kabbalah."

Jewish mystical concepts of reincarnation (gilgul) and angelology seem to carry an Indian stamp, and centuries later a nineteenth century Kabbalist named Asher Halevi (1849–1912) left behind very difficult writings that discuss parallels between his Kabbalah and specifically Tibetan Tantra. In his "Book of Visions," for example, he discusses the Judaic golem, a teaching of Rabbi Judah Loew ben Bezalel (1525–1609), better known as the Maharal of Prague, about constructing a zombie from body parts to serve as a defender of the beleaguered Jews. Significantly, he calls it not golem, but uses the Tibetan word ro-langs, a teaching for revivifying a corpse (Hallevy n.d.). Asher was a cobbler and mohel (ritual circumsizer) who lived in Darjeeling, a Himalayan summer resort for heat-weary Calcuttans. He left behind at least three manuscripts, including an autobiography or book of visions, a treatise on the circumcision ritual, and an essay on the psychology of religion. His works await analysis (Sassoon 1932: 574 and 999).

Modern Europe

Jews, like all many European intellectuals, became enamored of "eastern" thought somewhere in the mid-eighteenth century. As a matter of fact, many of the pioneering German and British orientalists were Jews, who may have been motivated in part by a search for non-Christian paradigms.

From the other side, ever since Aristotle, Jews have been viewed as Orientals, an ascription alternately welcomed and disdained by Jews. This ambivalence was manifested in two of the twentieth century's most influential European Jewish theologians: Franz Rosenzweig (1886–1926), who disdained "eastern" thought (Samuelson 1998: 7–12), and Martin Buber (1878–1965), who relished it (Friedman 1981: 149–171).

Specifically Buddhist ideas entered into secular Yiddish culture with the publication of a translation of the *Dhammapada* (Kliger 1958). As was the nature of the era, this phase of the Buddhist–Jewish encounter remained textual.

The Buddhist–Jewish encounter was also a subtext of a remarkable novel by Chaim Potok, *The Book of Lights*. Potok, one of the twentieth century's leading Jewish novelists, juxtaposes Gershon Loran, a rabbinical student who becomes an Army chaplain during the Korean War, with Arthur Leiden, son of one of the developers of the atomic bomb. Loran seeks meaning in studying Kabbalah, the Zohar's theology of lights in particular, while Leiden tries to find solace for the destruction wrought by his father's invention by taking up residence in Kyoto, flirting with Buddhism. The two types of lights – the Zohar's light of mysticism and Hiroshima's lights of destruction – make for a richly symbolic encounter between Jewish and Buddhist consciousness.

The same Jewish ambivalence about things eastern also found its way into the Zionist movement. Mainstream Zionist leaders sought to establish a European-style socialist utopia in Palestine, while others such as Moshe Sharett (1894–1965), who became Foreign Minister of Israel, envisioned a Jewish return to their Asian, oriental home, removing themselves from the destruction that was Europe. Israel's first Prime Minister, David Ben-Gurion (1886–1973), although firmly secular, was more than a dabbler in Buddhism. He developed an especially close personal bond with the Prime Minister of newly independent Burma, U Nu (1907–1995), and spent time learning *vispassana* meditation in Burma's monasteries. U Nu was the first Asian leader to visit Israel (Avimor 1989: 1). Even the generally unsentimental Foreign Ministry of Israel characterized early Burmese-Israeli relations as having a "chemistry of mutual affection," (Avimor 1989: 4) no doubt reflecting the closeness of the two leaders.

Asian Nationalisms and the Jews

While Jews and Judaism played a significant role in the discourse known as "the Hindu Renaissance" in India, there was only scant parallel in the language of "the Buddhist Revival."

The Hindu Renaissance began in mid-nineteenth century Bengal. To characterize it very broadly, this was an attempt to counteract the supposed supremacy of British culture and the Christian religion, as well as to "reform" Hinduism. In this discourse, Jews were seen, on one hand, as an Asian people like themselves. Moreover, Judaism is non-missionizing, like Hinduism. Also like Hindus, Jews have a history of oppression. One Tamil leader, Arumuga Navallar, used the "Old Testament" to counter the arguments of the missionaries (Hudson 1994: 55–84). And for good measure, Jesus the Jew was spiritual, like Hindus, who recognized him as the Jewish *avatara* (incarnation of G-d). But on the other hand, Judaism was seen as the source of the very western civilization that they claimed to detest, the mother of the despised Christianity and Islam, the very source of monotheistic intolerance and exclusivism. Borrowing from a well-known Christian characterization, Judaism was reviled as "materialistic," contrasted against Hinduism, which of course was "spiritual." (On the portrayal of Jews in western occultist appropriations of Hinduism and Buddhism, such as Blavatsky's Theosophical Society, or of the complicity of a number of Sanskritists and Tibetologists in Nazi occultism, see Levenda 2002, and cf. Goodrick-Clarke 1998).

Although there had been very small Jewish communities in such Buddhist countries as Thailand and Sri Lanka, they are absent in the discourse of the "Buddhist Revival." Among the leaders of the "Buddhist Revivals" in colonial Ceylon, Anagarika Dharmapala was scathing in his comments about the G-d of the "Old Testament." For example, reflecting on the story of Abraham's readiness to sacrifice his son Isaac, he wrote that "Every savage race has its own totem deity" (Dharmapala 1965: 409). As this essay demonstrates, Buddhists could employ sharply polemical language in their encounters with Christian missionaries, the Panadura debates are the most notable example (Katz 1987: 157–176), but their real targets were not actually Jews. In this, they mimicked Hindu Renaissance rhetoric in the style of Swami Dayanand Saraswati.

Two twentieth-century Buddhist pamphlets – one in Thai and one in Tibetan – did focus on Jews. King Rama IV of Thailand (1881–1925) wrote the first. He understood Jews as a parasitic commercial class, self-satisfied and disloyal, a fifth column to be extirpated from his Thailand. In fact, in his work "Jews" was a code word for "Chinese," who tended to dominate Bangkok's commercial and economic life.

This kind of view remains. Just two years ago I was channel surfing in my hotel in New Delhi when I heard someone comparing Jews with Brahmins. I smiled, thinking this was a reflection of Aristotle, and expected to hear how Jews, like Brahmins, live a life of special purity, pray in an ancient, sacred language, and serve as priests to the world. It was jarring as I focused on the speaker's words to hear sentiments similar to the former King of Thailand's: I heard that the Brahmins were like the Jews, unscrupulous bloodsuckers and usurers who sought to enslave the Dalits ("the oppressed").

Educated according to missionary and British standards, most Asian elites knew Jews through their syllabi rather than through normal social interactions. They learned that Jews killed Christ and demanded their "pound of flesh" as repayment for a loan. These same elites also imbibed Marx's screed "On the Jewish Question" (1844). So from their point of view, Jews were simply paradigms for whatever group whom they saw as their oppressors – whether the Chinese of Thailand or the Brahmins of Tamil Nadu.

Jamyang Norbu, the fiery president of the highly politicized Tibetan Youth Congress and editor of *Rangzen*, "Independence," published "An Outline of the History of Israel" in 1973, on the purported 2100th anniversary of the Tibetan state, drawing inspiration from Jewish experience. His central narrative is Jewish steadfastness in the face of two millennia of oppression, and a sense of unity that led to the re-establishment of the State of Israel in 1948. He is lavish in praising Jewish morality, intelligence, industry, and bravery. It is interesting to note that among Zionist groups, he has the highest regard for the most militant, the "Lehi" party, whom the British called "the Stern Gang" (Norbu 1973, translated by Katz 1998: 81–90).

The perception of Jews in Asian nationalist discourses is diverse, including a mixed perception among Hindu nationalists, an absence of engagement in the Buddhist Revival, a negative image of Jews in early-twentieth-century Thai nationalism, and an idealized portrait in Norbu's Tibetan treatise.

The Holocaust and the Genesis of JuBu

Paradoxically, it was the Holocaust era when the first significant, non-mediated – which is to say not merely textual – encounters between Western Jews and Buddhists took place.

The first important figure of the era was Sigmund Feninger (1901–1994), a secular Jew from Hanau, Germany, who converted to Buddhism, took the dharma-name Nyanaponika, and joined a monastery in Ceylon in 1936. Three years later, he brought his mother and other relatives to escape the Nazis. Ironically, because Nyanaponika was a German national, he was interred by the British as an "enemy alien" at Dehru Dun. Resident in the same detention center were the eminent historian of Buddhist art and later professor at Halle, Dr. Heinz Mode, who once related to me his experiences there with Nyanapomnika and Lama Anagarika Govinda (born Ernst Lothat Hofgman), a prolific author and tantric adept.

After the war, Nyanaponika returned to Ceylon, eventually taking up residence at the Forest Hermitage near Kandy, where he co-founded the Buddhist Publication Society, which published a number of his authoritative scholarly works. A "monk's monk," Nyanaponika was revered by Theravada Buddhists around the world.

Nyanaponika never mentioned his Jewish background, and his analyses of the Buddha's teachings find the dharma (or dhamma) to be incompatible with a belief in G-d (Nyanaponika 1960).

To complete the circle, Nyanaponika's preeminent disciple is Ven. Bhikkhu Bodhi, né Jeffrey Block. Bodhi has continued his teacher's scholarly interests, offering some of the finest translations ever of Pali texts, and heading the BPS until his return to the United States in 2002.

As I wanted to review Nyanaponika's influential article about G-d, I unsuccessfully tried to find my copy of his pamphlet—it is "somewhere in my office." I searched and found that it had been reprinted in a recent book(Nyanaponika 2000). The book was edited and introduced by his disciple, Bhikkhu Bodhi. The eminent Swiss psychiatrist Dr. Erich Fromm, another Jew, also introduced it, and the back cover featured testimonials by Sharon Salzberg, Sylvia Boorstein and Joseph Goldstein – all highly regarded Jewish–Buddhist meditation teachers!

Another refugee from Nazism became one of the leaders of the contemporary Buddhist nuns' movement: Ayya Khema (1923–1997). Her life became emblematic of the quest of contemporary Jews who pursue spirituality through Buddhism. Born in prewar Berlin into an upper class, highly assimilated Jewish family, she attended the best schools and avidly enjoyed German culture. She grew up with servants and soirees, music and poetry, but very little Jewishness.

Her father had the perspicacity to get his family out of Germany while it was still possible. They found their way to Shanghai where they waited out Germany's madness and where he continued his business amidst a cosmopolitan Jewish community. It was here that Ayya Khema first encountered Jewish mysticism. One war followed another. Mao's revolution forced them out of China, and they made their circuitous way to California where she eventually married and raised children and grandchildren.

Whether from innate inclination, or because of her remarkable experiences, Ayya Khema's interest in mysticism grew. Having read Gershom Scholem's studies of Kabbalah, she wrote the professor in Jerusalem, asking for advice as to how to set about studying Kabbalah experientially. She now knows how naive that letter was. Some months later, she received a curt reply. "He told me to forget about it, that a woman – especially one who lacked extensive background in Torah and Talmud – was prohibited from ever approaching these mystical treasures of Jewish tradition," she told me. "So I continued to read and study on my own."

Her readings were eclectic and included spiritual masterpieces from the East. She was especially impressed with Buddhist literature. Its directness, its freedom from metaphysical and ritual embellishment, was naturally attractive, especially considering her frustration at the traditional barriers safeguarding Jewish mysticism from the hoi polloi. More important than these theoretical concerns, however, was the openness of Buddhist teachers. One did not have to be of a certain age, ethnicity, or gender, or be especially learned or observant, as prerequisites to mystical practice. She jumped at the opportunity. Her study of Buddhism and practice of meditation grew, and after the death of her husband she took ordination as a Buddhist nun in the early 1970s.

"Of course I'm still Jewish. What else could I be?" she replied to my unasked question. "Jewish is something you *are*, and I am proud of our heritage." Apparently she did not share Nyanaponika's diffidence, either about discussing her past, about her Jewishness, or even about G-d, an idea she found compatible with her own Buddhist practice. Our conversation was punctuated with words from both Yiddish and Pali. Her manner was suffused with Buddhist compassion and Jewish warmth. I reflected that it was too bad she had not been born 20 years later, at a time when Kabbalah could be approached without quite so many barriers. How contemporary Judaism needs powerful, spiritual, female teachers! I felt that the loss was Judaism's, not Ayya Khema's, since it was evident that her life was so very rich, that her spirit had grown so strong.

Many leading Buddhist teachers in the west are Jews: Zen teachers Philip Kaplau Roshi and Roshi Bernie Glassman; Jodo priest Rev. Alfred Bloom, Theravada teachers Sylvia Boorstein, Harvey Aronson, Sharon Salzberg, Joseph Goldstein, and Jack Kornfield; and Tibetan teachers Alexander Berzin, Lama Surya Das, Lama John Makransky, Geshe George Dreyfus, and the nun Ven. Thubten Chödron.

When considering Jews who adopt Buddhist practice, it is useful to distinguish between two general types: those who, like Nyanaponika, sever ties with Jewish life, and those who, like Ayya Khema (especially during the last years of her life), affirm their Jewishness. I would suggest that the term "JuBu" be reserved for the latter group; for the former we need no special term; they are simply Buddhists of Jewish background.

Some JuBus go so far as to seek to combine the practices of Buddhism and Judaism, attempting to affirm both. For example, Ven. Thubten Chödron has written about the influence of the JuBus' Jewish social consciousness in their roles in the Buddhist women's movement (Chodron 1999), and journalist Ellen Goldberg has commented on Ayya Khema's role in the nun's movement in Sri Lanka (http://www.csmonitor. com/1984/0402/040236.html). Roshi Bernie Glassman founded the Zen Peacemakers Sangha (www.zenpeacemakers.org), a prime example of socially engaged Buddhism that draws at least some inspiration from the Jewish background of its leaders. Glassman created the "Bearing Witness at Auschwitz Birkenau" annual retreat, which is described on his webpage:

> We will gather as a multi-faith assembly of practitioners of many cultures . . . in Oswiecim, Poland, on the grounds of Auschwitz-Birkenau, the place of personal and universal human tragedy during World War II. There, we will be offered many opportunities to bear witness to the diverse aspects of ourselves and others. The retreat will be guided by an experienced group of international leaders representing diverse cultures and religious traditions. Participants will spend most of the daylight hours each day at the Birkenau camp, practicing periods of silence and meditation, offering prayers, chanting the names of the dead, offering Kaddish (the Jewish Memorial Prayer) and religious services in many traditions.

There are many other examples of how JuBus have brought their social consciousness with them into the worlds of Buddhism.

Of course, the relationship is reciprocal, and many practicing Jews have brought their Buddhist meditation with them as they returned to their synagogues. A prime example is the so-called "Zen Rabbi" of San Francisco, the late Alan Lew(Lew and Jaffe 1999).

It is not surprising that many in the Jewish Renewal Movement (JRM) have backgrounds in Dharma centers and/ or Hindu ashrams. In a nutshell, JRM is a mixture of the neo-Hasidism of Rabbi Zalman M. Schachter-Shalomi, Eastern practices of yoga and meditation, the new left social consciousness of Rabbi Arthur O. Waskow, feminism, environmentalism, and the "paradigm shift" of the new age movements. What is less well documented, but none the less vibrant, is a Buddhist influence on the Ba'al Teshuva Movement (BTM), the "return" to Orthodox Jewish practice by secular Jews, many via Dharma centers and ashrams. Interestingly, here one can discern the impact of Buddhism on both the Judaically-left JRM and the Judaically-right BTM. This phenomenon has also led rabbis and Jewish thinkers to engage Buddhists and Buddhism dialogically, perhaps for the first time (for example, Tatz and Gottlieb 2004).

In short, the same process of inter-religious encounter has supported both the export of Jewish social consciousness into the worlds of Buddhism, as well as the transfer of Buddhist (and Hindu) practice into Judaism via JRM and BTM, and from there into mainstream Conservative and Reform Judaisms in America and elsewhere (Katz 2007: 123–124).

It is not easy to interpret today's globalized spirituality, which allows for such easy movement between and within religious worlds. At times I have mused that there is a mysterious hand behind it. One day I was discussing all of these mysterious matters with one of the world's greatest Kabbalists. I had just told him about Ayya Khema, the Buddhist nun who wanted to study Jewish esotericism but was rebuffed by Professor Scholem. I had commented that it was her loss. "Maybe not," he replied. "Maybe this is what was best for her." I backtracked. Perhaps it was not her loss, but surely her adopting Buddhism was a loss to the Jewish people. "Maybe not," he replied again. "From what you have told me about these Jews who have gone east, I suspect they may be participating in some very deep *tikkun*. They are mending the fissure between East and West, but this is deeper than politics. They may be mending the souls of the Jewish people."

The Contemporary Jewish–Buddhist Encounter

The first time that a group of Jews met for a formal dialogue with a group of Buddhists occurred in 1990, when a delegation of eight rabbis and Jewish scholars accepted an invitation from His Holiness the Dalai Lama to be his guests for an intensive series of dialogues with himself, Tibetan religious and secular leaders, educators, and – yes – JuBus residing in Dharamsala. The Dalai Lama's manifest interest was in the "Jewish secret" about how a people can preserve their religion and culture while living in exile, a question of obvious existential import to Tibetans. The historically significant event was the subject of a very popular and excellent book (Kamenetz 1994) and a number of articles, including my own reflections (Katz 1991: 33–46).

Each of the delegates presented a partial response to the Dalai Lama's question. As these responses have been described fully in print, a tabular summary (Table 24.1) is sufficient: it identifies each speaker, her or his topic, the Tibetans' level of interest in the topic, whether the topic points to Buddhist–Judaic similarities or to Judaic uniqueness, and the impact of this topic for the Tibetans.

Assuming that the reader is familiar with the content of the presentations from other sources, it can readily be seen that several issues were of great interest to the Tibetans. Foremost among these is the role of the Jewish home in transmitting religious practice and identity. In Jewish practice, especially traditional Judaism, the home is more central than the synagogue, which follows the Talmudic paradigm that the dining table in the home replaced the altar in the destroyed Temple (Babylonian Talmud, Tractate Berachot 55a and Tractate Chagigah 27a). For a monastery-centered faith, as most of Buddhism is, Rebbetzin Greenberg's presentation was startling. As I noted at the time, "Perhaps this is the most fruitful of all exchanges, especially from a Tibetan point of view. The Dalai Lama's fascination with our home-centered observances makes me appreciate the singularity of Jewish traditions" (Katz 1991: 43).

Table 24.1 Responses to the Dalai Lama's question about the "Jewish secret" – how a people can preserve their religion and culture while living in exile.

Name	Topic	Interest	Similarity/ Uniqueness	Impact
Nathan Katz	Historical background	Moderate	Similarities (historical contacts)	Little
Rabbi Zalman M. Schachter-Shalomi	Mystical theology, Kabbalah	High	Similarities	Little
Rabbi Irving Greenberg	Implications of destruction of Second Temple and development of rabbinic Judaism	Moderate	Unique to Judaism	Little
Paul Mendes Flohr	Jewish modernism and secularism	High	Uniqueness	Some, especially Jewish summer youth camps
Rabbi Jonathan Omer-Man	Jewish meditation	High	Similarity	Little
Moshe Waldoks	Jewish hermeneutics	Moderate	Similarity	Little
Rebbetzin Blu Greenberg	Home-centered nature of Diasporic Judaism	High	Uniqueness	Highest
Rabbi Joy Levitt	Jewish communal institutions in America	High	Uniqueness	High

Also of high interest were Rabbi Levitt's description of Jewish communal organizations, from free loan societies that assist Jewish immigrants getting started in a new country to political lobbying organizations, day schools, federations, old age homes and burial societies: Mendes-Flohr's description of his formative experiences at a summer youth camp in America was immediately applicable to the Tibetans' situation in India, and in fact just a few years later Rabbi and Rebbetzin Greenberg were able to facilitate six-month internships for three Tibetan educators in the New York offices of several such camps, capped off with visits over the summer. Today, Tibetan summer youth camps based on the American Jewish model have been established in India.

In the areas of the greatest overlap – mystical theology, meditation, hermeneutics, and the like – there was mutual interest but little subsequent impact on the Tibetan community. This ought to surprise no one: discovering religious similarities is pleasant but not particularly meaningful.

But Tibetans are not the only Buddhists in the world. While there have been no corporate dialogues on the level of the one in Dharamsala with Sri Lankan, or Thai, or Japanese Buddhists, nevertheless smaller scale encounters have been taking place around the world. In America, Asian-Americans of many ethnicities have encountered Jewish-Americans, both formally and informally. Here the issues of modernization and diasporization rise to the fore.

Today we see two kinds of diasporas: the forced exile of the Tibetans, Vietnamese and Cambodians, and the voluntary exile of most Hindus, Japanese, Korean or Sri Lankan Buddhists for examples. Jews experienced the first variety until 1948, but since the establishment of Israel, *galut* has become home voluntarily. Jewish struggles over nearly 2000 years may inspire Tibetans and Vietnamese, but many Asian-Americans rightly or wrongly see American Jews as role models for their gentle exile: Jews are taken as fully participating in American life while simultaneously maintaining religio-cultural traditions. Hebrew day schools, federations, newspapers, self-defense organizations such as the Anti-Defamation League (ADL), youth summer camps and lobbying organizations for both domestic and international issues, are serving as models for other minority peoples who fear assimilation and the loss of traditions.

For many newly diasporized peoples – such as Tibetans and Indochinese-Americans – diasporization and modernization are simultaneous. In some senses, the two phenomena are interrelated. Diasporization shatters the premodern sense of a nation as a confluence of land–people–language–religion. If one is landless, then the fusion of these four separable factors unravels. Similarly, the essence of modernization is pluralism, wherein one's sacred canopy is seen as a human cultural product rather than as a fabric of sacred, eternal meanings. Diasporization confronts one with the cultural other, with a pluralism of meanings. So does modernization, and in this sense the two phenomena are related. Jews are seen as the first diasporized *and* the first modernized people, even if in the Jewish case the former preceded the latter by 1600 years. Peoples who are just now becoming diasporized and/or modernized tend to look to Jews for guidance, and this topic has risen to the forefront of contemporary Buddhist–Jewish encounters, especially in America.

Idolatry?

I have reserved the thorniest issue for the last: the question of idolatry. For an observant Jew, idolatry has been the biggest stumbling block to serious encounters with Buddhism, if not with Buddhists themselves. However, a very recent, precedent-setting event may have removed this difficulty.

The Judaic concept that is approximated by the English "idolatry" is *avodah zarah*, or "foreign worship." In the Torah, the Talmud and legal codifications, *avodah zarah* is among the most heinous of sins, and layers of strictures have been rabbinically established to limit, if not prevent, any association with not only the practice, but also the people who perform the practice. It has seemed obvious that Buddhists, most of whom bow down before a statue of the Buddha or other figure, are practicing idolatry.

There has, however, been a counter-current in Judaic legal thinking about idolatry. Rabbi Menachem Meiri (1249–1316), for example, held that contemporary practices are not the same thing as the idolatry described in the Torah, and that people of his day were merely following ancestral custom, not actually performing idolatry. This has been a minority opinion, but it has been significant.

On February 5–6, 2007, Rabbi Yona Metzger, the Chief Ashkenazic Rabbi of Israel, led a delegation of distinguished Orthodox rabbis to India for a meeting with Hindu leaders from a wide variety of sects who had been convened by Swami Dayanand Saraswati of the Hindu Dharma Acharya Sabha. This was a much higher-level and more official encounter than the Dharamsala dialogue, as in a significant sense the Chief Rabbinate of Israel can speak for Judaism in a way that a pluralistic collection of eight scholars and rabbis cannot.

The rabbis and swamis concluded their meetings with a nine-point "Declaration of Mutual Understanding and Cooperation from the First Jewish-Hindu Leadership Summit." The very first point in the declaration stunningly removed the idolatry issue from the dialogical table. "Their respective Traditions [hold] that there is One Supreme Being who is the Ultimate Reality, who has created this world in its blessed diversity and who has communicated Divine ways of action for humanity, for different peoples in different times and places" (http://www.wfn.org/2007/02/msg00073.html).

As bold as this point is theologically, one cannot but wonder whether it would apply to Buddhists as well, whose beliefs are quite different from those of Hindus, especially regarding a Creator G-d. Some thinkers have tried to identify *shunyata* with a mystically understood G-d (for examples of this view, see Abe and Borowitz 1992; Rubenstein and Abe 1995; and cf. Teshima 1995) and others have even taken *nirvana* in this light as a kind of negative theology (Altizer 1981: 18–19). But when one leaves the domain of mysticism and tries to reconcile a Creator G-d with Buddhist philosophy, the issues become murky at best. It is intriguing to note that for years, many JuBus have argued that Buddhism's nontheism make it more palatable Judaically than Hinduism, for example, which could be understood as positing "another" G-d than the G-d of Israel; yet if we correctly apply the principles articulated at this Jewish-Hindu encounter, precisely this nontheism might be a greater stumbling block than the purported polytheism that had for long been ascribed to Hinduism.

But perhaps Buddhist–Jewish understanding would be best left to emerge out of a future dialogical encounter rather than our speculation of the moment. After all, who could have imagined that Orthodox rabbis would affirm the identification of the G-d of Israel with the G-d of the Hindus?

Trajectories

What trends can be discerned from the modern Buddhist–Jewish encounter, and what trajectories can we anticipate for the future?

As in many inter-religious encounters, boundary-drawing seems to be a starting point. Areas of overlap are mapped, and at the same time boundaries are drawn. In the Buddhist–Jewish dialogues of recent years, overlaps have been found in mystical theologies and practices, as well as in ethical principles.

Boundaries follow traditional demarcations. The Buddha taught that anywhere the noble eightfold path is found, there his dharma is to be found (Digha Nikaya, sutta 16).

But would a Jewish viewpoint in which the Creator G-d is so central be counted as "right understanding"? Similarly, Judaism has taught that "the righteous of all nations have a share in the world to come," (Babylonian Talmud, Tractate Sanhedrin, 105a, citing Tosefta Sanhedrin 13: 2), but that leaves us to ask who might be counted among the righteous? Tradition has held that whoever observes the seven Noahide command-ments merits the same ultimate reward as the observant Jew. It must be noted, however, that the first of the Noahide laws is a prohibition against idolatry, and this issue must be honestly considered. Nevertheless, at least some authoritative rabbinic texts have described "Hindu'a" people as bnai Noach and therefore may be counted among the righteous (See R. 'Abdallah Sameah 1891).

So in the case of Hinduism and Buddhism, there is neither so much similarity nor a clear breach of boundaries, and it is at the intersection of neither clear similarity nor well defined boundaries that is precisely the most fruitful arena for mutual edification and growth.

There are trends and streams within modern Judaism that have absorbed and appro-priated Buddhist meditation and spiritual practices. This phenomenon, we have argued above, can be detected on both the right (BTM) and left (JRM) branches of Judaism, and one may also observe the influence filtering into the mainstream.

In the domain of ethics one can posit a complementary relationship. Judaism's ethic of action has found its way, largely via JuBus, into socially engaged Buddhism and the Buddhist women's movement. At the same time, the Buddhist ethic of restraint has influenced Jewish environmentalism. Although the point has yet to be explored, such Buddhist virtues as patience (*ksanti*) have echoes in Judaism's nineteenth-century Mussar movement, a spiritual path based on active reflection and the cultivation of virtues, and the recent upsurge of interest in Mussar may become a ground for inter-religious fertilization.

Buddhists have taken Judaism's home-centeredness seriously, as this is one of the most divergent themes in the two religions, seriously. Judaism's long experience with diasporization and modernization are significant themes for many Buddhists, as are Jewish social and communal responses to these forces – communal institutions, politi-cal activism, and emphasis on education, for example.

But I would be remiss if I did not note one other contribution Jews have made to Buddhism, and a silent contribution at that. I will close with this story.

Some years ago I participated in a public Buddhist–Jewish dialogue in Atlanta, Georgia, with my good friend, Ven. Geshe Lobsang Tenzin, and on that occasion Geshe-la reminded me about the traditional Judaic self-understanding as a "nation of priests, a light unto the nations" in a novel way. As I wrote of that encounter:

Hearing about the heartless silence of the United Nations to the Tibetan plight, one man in the audience could stand it no longer. He rose to his feet, red-eyed, pained. He asked Geshe-la, "What can we Jews do to help you Tibetans? Should we try to lobby the U.N. to take up your cause? Ought we work through the U. S. Congress?" He reminded Geshe-la about American Jewry's political strength, suggesting we commence a lobbying effort on behalf of the Tibetans. "Just tell us what we can do to help," he implored.

Geshe-la's response was immediate. "Nothing," he said. "You don't have to do anything. Just be who you are, just be Jews." I smiled a deep smile as the interlocutor turned left and right in bafflement. The geshe deigned to elaborate. "You cannot imagine how much encouragement we take from you, just for being who you are. The fact that you are still here, the fact that you still worship in your way – this means more to us than anything you could possibly do. You are a great source of strength to us, and we are grateful to you." Just like that, Geshe-la revealed our own wisdom to us. (Katz 2001: 16)

Bibliography

Classical Primary Sources

Aryasura. *The Gatakamala or Garland of Birth Stories*. J. B. Speyer, trans. 1900; reprinted Kessinger Publishing, 2006.
Babylonian Talmud, *Tractate Berachot*.
Babylonian Talmud, *Tractate Chagigah*.
Babylonian Talmud, *Tractate Sanhedrin*.
Buddhist Birth Stories; or, Jataka Tales. 1880. T.W. Rhys-Davids, ed. and trans. London: Trübner.

Digha Nikaya. T.W. Rhys-Davids and J. Estlin Carpenter, eds. 3 vols. London: Pali Text Society, 1911, 1938, 1949.
Tanakh (the Hebrew Bible).

Medieval Primary Sources

Asher, A. (trans. and ed.). *The Itinerary of Rabbi Benjamin of Tudela*. New York: Hakesheth, n.d.
'Jam-dbyangs Nor-bu. *I-si-ral gyi-rabs snying-bsdud bsgrig-pa*. Dharamsala: Tibetan Information and International Relations Office, 1973.
Hallevy, Asher. *Sefer Hayasher v'hu Sefer Hachtom*. (Sassoon no. 848)
Meir, Rabbi Menachem. *Beit Ha-Bechirah*.

Polo, Marco. *The Travels of Marco Polo*. New York, Orion Press, 1985.
Sachau, Edward C. (trans.). *Alberuni's India: An Account of the Religion, Philosophy, Literature, Geography, Chronology, Astronomy, Customs, Laws and Astrology of India about A.D. 1030*. Delhi, S. Chand, 1964.
Sameah, Rabbi. Abdullah. *Zevchi Tsedeq Halakha*. Baghdad, 1891.

Modern Works

Abe, Masao, with Christoper Ives. *Divine Emptiness and Historical Fullness: A Buddhist–Jewish–Christian Conversation with Masao Abe*. Philadelphia: Trinity Press International, 1995.
Abe, Masao, and Eugene Borowitz. *A Jewish–Buddhist Dialogue with Prof. Masao Abe and Eugene Borowitz*. New York: Sh'ma, 1992.
Altizer, Thomas J.J. "Nirvana as a Negative Image of God," in *Buddhist and Western Philosophy*, ed. Nathan Katz. New Delhi: Sterling, 1981, 18–29.
Avimor, Shimon. *Relations between Israel and Asian and African States: A Guide to Selected Documentation – No. 5, Union of Burma*. Jerusalem: The Hebrew University, 1989.
Charkaravti, Ranabir. "Reraching Out to Distant Shores: Indo-Judaic Trade Contacts (Up to CE 1300)," in *Indo-Judaic Studies in the Twenty-First Century*, eds. Nathan Katz

et al. New York: Palgrave Macmillan, 2007, 19–43.

Chodron, Thubten. "Finding Our Way," in *Blossoms of Dharma: Living as a Buddhist Nun*, eds. Sylvia Boorstein and Thubten Chodron. Berkeley: North AtlanticPress, 1999.

Dharmapala, Anagarika. "The Repenting God of Horeb," in *Anagarika Dharmapala, Return to Righteousness*, ed. Anange Guruge. Colombo: The Anagarika Dharmapala Birth Centenary Committee, Ministry of Education and Cultural Affairs, 1965, 401–425.

Friedman, Maurice S. "Martin Buber and Oriental Religions," in *Buddhist and Western Philosophy*, ed. Nathan Katz. New Delhi: Sterling, 1981, 149–171.

Goitein, Solomon D. *Letters of Medieval Jewish Traders*. Princeton, NJ: Princeton University Press, 1973.

Goldberg, Ellen S. "Buddhist nuns make comeback in Sri Lanka – to monks' dislike." *Christian Science Monitor*, April 2, 1984. http://www.csmonitor.com/1984/0402/040236.html (accessed December 30, 2012).

Goodrick-Clarke, Nicholas. *Hitler's Priestess: Savitri Devi, the Hindu–Aryan Myth, and Neo-Nazism*. New York: New York University Press, 1998.

Hudson, D. Dennis. "A Hindu Response to the Written Torah," in *Between Jerusalem and Benares: Comparative Studies in Judaism and Hinduism*, ed. Hananya Goodman. Albany: State University of New York Press, 1994, 55–84.

Idel, Moshe. *Abraham Abulafia: An Ecstatic Kabbalist*. Benfleet, Essex: Labyrinthos, 2002.

Katz, Nathan. "Buddhism and Poltiics in Sri Lanka and Other Theravada Nations Since 1945," in *Movements and Issues in World Religions: A Sourcebook and Analysis of Developments Since 1945*, eds. Charles Wei-hsun Fu and Gerhard Spiegler. New York: Greenwood Press, 1987, 157–176.

Katz, Nathan. "The Jewish Secret and the Dalai Lama: A Dharamsala Diary." *Conservative Judaism* 43(3) (1991): 33–46.

Katz, Nathan (trans.). "A Tibetan Language History of Israel by Jamyang Norbu." *Journal of Indo-Judaic Studies* 1, 81–89.

Katz, Nathan. "India and Israel in the Ancient World." *Shofar* 17(3) (1999): 7–22.

Katz, Nathan. "What we are could be more vital than what we do." *Jewish Star Times*, Miami, October 3, 2001, 16.

Katz, Nathan. "The State of the Art of Hindu-Jewish Dialogue," in *Indo-Judaic Studies in the Twenty-First Century*, eds. Nathan Katz, et. al. New York: Palgrave Macmillan, 2007, 113–126.

Katz, Nathan, and Ellen S. Goldberg. *The Last Jews of Cochin: Jewish Identity in Hindu India*. Columbia: University of South Carolina Press, 1993.

Kamenetz, Rodger. *The Jew in the Lotus*. San Francisco: Harper, 1994.

Kliger, Aba (trans.). *Der weg tsu layterung: Budha lernt*. New York: Shlusinger Bros., 1958.

Leslie, Donald Daniel. *The Survival of the Chinese Jews*. Leiden: Brill, 1972.

Levanon, Yosef. *The Jewish Travellers in the Twelfth Century*. Lanham, MD: University Press of America, 1980.

Levenda, Peter. *Unholy Alliance: A History of Nazi Involvement with the Occult*. 2nd edn. New York: Continuum, 2002.

Lew, Alan, with Sherril Jaffe. *One God Clapping: The Spiritual Path of a Zen Rabbi*. Woodstock, VT: Jewish Lights Publishing, 1999.

Marks, Richard G. "Hindus and Hinduism in Medieval Jewish Literature," in *Indo-Judaic Studies in the Twenty-First Century*, eds. Nathan Katz et al. New York: Palgrave Macmillan, 2007, 57–73.

Nyanaponika Mahathera. *Buddhism and the God-Idea*. Wheel Series No. 18, Kandy: Buddhist Publication Society, 1960.

Nyanaponika Mahathera, Bhikkhu Bodhi (ed.). *The Vision of Dhamma: Buddhist Writings of Nyanapokika Thera*. 2nd edn. Seattle: BPS Pariyatti Editions, 2000.

Pollak, Michael. *Mandarins, Jews, and Missionaries: The Jewish Experience in the Chinese Empire*. Philadelphia: Jewish Publication Society, 1980.

Potok, Chaim. *The Book of Lights*. New York: Ballantine, 1982.

Rabin, Chaim. "Loanword Evidence in Biblical Hebrew for Trade between Tamilnad and

Palestine in the First Millennium B.C.," in *Proceedings of the Second International Seminar of Tamil Studies*. Madras: International Association of Tamil Research, 1971, 432–440.

Samuelson, Norbert M. "Rosenzweig's Philosophy of Buddhism." *Journal of Indo-Judaic Studies* 1 (1998): 7–12.

Sassoon, David Solomon. *Ohel Dawid; Descriptive Catalogue of the Hebrew and Samaritan Manuscripts in the Sassoon Library, London*. London: Humphrey Milford, 1932.

Tatz, Akiva and David Gottlieb. *Letters to a Buddhist Jew*. New York: Targum/Feldheim, 2004.

Teshima, Jacob Yuroh. *Zen Buddhism and Hasidism: A Comparative Study*. Lanham, MD: University Press of America, 1995.

Weinstein, Brian. "Traders and Ideas: Indians and Jews," in *Indo-Judaic Studies in the Twenty-First Century*, eds. Nathan Katz et al. New York: Palgrave Macmillan, 44–56, 2007.

CHAPTER 25

Hindu–Jewish Encounters

Barbara A. Holdrege

When reflecting on the nature and forms of inter-religious dialogue, I can think of a number of specific forms of dialogue in which Jews are one of the principal partners – for example, Jewish–Christian dialogue or Jewish–Muslim dialogue – or in which Hindus are one of the principal partners – for example, Hindu–Christian dialogue or Hindu–Muslim dialogue. However, I would wager that up until recently few religious leaders or scholars would expect to find Jews and Hindus actively engaging with one another in some form of "Hindu–Jewish dialogue" or other form of Hindu–Jewish encounter. This is due in part to two commonly held assumptions. First, Hindu and Jewish traditions have often been characterized as representing opposite ends of the spectrum of the world's religions. "Polytheistic," iconocentric Hindu traditions, with their panoply of deities enshrined in images, have generally been considered anti-thetical to "monotheistic," iconoclastic Jewish traditions, with their emphasis on the unity and transcendence of God and abhorrence of image-making practices. Second, in contrast to religious traditions that have had longstanding genealogical and histori-cal connections, such as Jewish and Christian traditions or Hindu and Buddhist tradi-tions, Hindu and Jewish communities have generally been deemed to have had little historical contact and hence there has been little impetus for these communities to enter into sustained mutual engagements prior to the modern period. However, in recent decades both of these assumptions have been challenged from a variety of dis-ciplinary perspectives, and there has been an upsurge of interest among scholars in the comparative study of Hindu and Jewish traditions and of Indic and Judaic cultures more broadly. The first assumption has been debunked because it perpetuates mislead-ing stereotypical characterizations and fails to take into account the rich diversity of perspectives within each tradition as well as the significant structural affinities among the array of Hindu and Jewish traditions. The second assumption has been shown to be mistaken by recent studies that have brought to light evidence that Hindus and Jews

The Wiley Blackwell Companion to Inter-Religious Dialogue, First Edition. Edited by Catherine Cornille.
© 2013 John Wiley & Sons Ltd. Published 2020 by John Wiley & Sons Ltd.

have engaged in economic, cultural, and religious interactions for over two millennia within the broader matrices of Indic and Judaic cultures.

In this essay I will begin by highlighting a number of landmark collaborative initiatives that have served to catalyze and sustain the burgeoning interest in Hindu–Jewish encounters both within and beyond the academy. I will then consider three kinds of encounters: (1) historical encounters between Indic and Judaic worlds within the broader context of South Asian and Middle Eastern cultures; (2) collaborative scholarly encounters between specialists in South Asia and Judaica engaging in comparative studies of Hindu and Jewish traditions; and (3) contemporary inter-religious encounters between Hindu and Jewish leaders that – in contrast to the first two forms of encounter – conform more closely to prevailing notions of "inter-religious dialogue."

Mapping Hindu–Jewish Encounters: Landmark Collaborative Initiatives

A number of landmark collaborative initiatives in the past two decades have sought to map different forms of Hindu–Jewish encounters. One of the pioneering initiatives arose in the religious studies arena and has focused on comparative studies of Hindu and Jewish traditions. A second type of initiative developed around the same time in the arena of cross-cultural area studies and has focused on comparative studies of the cultures of South Asia and the Middle East. A third form of initiative emerged soon thereafter and narrowed the focus to explorations of the historical interactions and structural affinities between Indic and Judaic worlds within the broader context of South Asian and Middle Eastern cultures. Finally, a fourth type of initiative has found expression in recent years in a series of formal inter-religious dialogues between Hindu and Jewish leaders designated as "Hindu–Jewish Leadership Summits."

With respect to comparative studies of Hindu and Jewish traditions, a pioneering volume in this area was the 1994 collection of essays edited by Hananya Goodman, *Between Jerusalem and Benares: Comparative Studies in Judaism and Hinduism*, which represents one of the first serious efforts by a group of scholars of Judaica and South Asia to explore the historical connections and cross-cultural resonances between these religious traditions.[1] Another major milestone was the formation in 1995 of the Comparative Studies in Hinduisms and Judaisms Consultation, which my colleague Paul Morris and I co-founded as an experimental program unit in the American Academy of Religion (AAR), the flagship professional organization of scholars of religion. The Consultation provided the basis for the establishment in 1998 of the Comparative Studies in Hinduisms and Judaisms Group as a regular program unit of the American Academy of Religion, which has as its mandate "to bring together specialists in South Asia and Judaica to discuss topics within Hindu and Jewish traditions, with the intention of re-visioning categories and developing alternative models to the Protestant-based paradigms that have tended to dominate the academic study of religion" (Comparative Studies in Hinduisms and Judaisms Group 2012). This scholarly forum continues to flourish to the present day and has found fruition in the establishment of a new sub-field within religious studies dedicated to comparative studies of Hindu and Jewish traditions. This ongoing collaboration between scholars of South Asia and

Judaica has inspired the publication of a number of volumes, including *Judaism and Asian Religions*, edited by Harold Kasimow, which was published in 1999 as a special issue of *Shofar: An Interdisciplinary Journal of Jewish Studies*. Such wide-ranging collections are complemented by monographs and edited volumes that interrogate and re-vision important analytical categories in the study of religion through sustained comparative historical studies of Hindu and Jewish traditions – for example, scripture (Holdrege 1996), sacrifice (McClymond 2008; Holdrege and McClymond forthcoming), hospitality (Bornet 2010), and food (Gross and Whitmore 2013).[2]

In addition to the establishment of comparative studies of Hindu and Jewish traditions as a sub-field within religious studies, a second type of multidisciplinary initiative has arisen in the past two decades in the human sciences that seeks to foster a new form of *cross-cultural* area studies that goes beyond the traditional area studies approach and engages in comparative studies of the broader network of cultures in which Hindu and Jewish traditions are rooted: South Asia and the Middle East. A major milestone in this broader comparative project was the establishment in 1995, under the leadership of Gordon Newby, of the Department of Middle Eastern and South Asian Studies (MESAS) at Emory University, which is one of the few institutions in the United States to offer an undergraduate degree in Middle Eastern and South Asian Studies. MESAS, as a multidisciplinary department, "approaches the study of the region integrally, focusing on historical, cultural, linguistic, and religious continuities from the Ancient Mediterranean and Indo-Pakistani sub-continent, through the Islamic period up to the present day" (MESAS: Department of Middle Eastern and South Asian Studies 2012). More recently, in 2001, my colleagues and I at the University of California, Santa Barbara (UCSB), inaugurated the Middle East and South Asia Comparative Studies Project in order to foster sustained comparative studies of the multifaceted connections between the cultures of the Middle East and South Asia without privileging Europe as a partner in the comparison. These multidisciplinary collaborations have generated a number of publications, including the forthcoming *Encyclopedia of the Middle East and South Asia* edited by Gordon Newby.

Within the network of South Asian and Middle Eastern cultures, a third form of initiative has arisen in the past fifteen years that is concerned more specifically with mapping the connections between Indic and Judaic worlds. A pivotal event was the inauguration in 1998 of the *Journal of Indo-Judaic Studies*, edited by Nathan Katz and Braj Sinha, as an interdisciplinary journal dedicated to "analyzing the affinities and interactions between Indic and Judaic civilizations from ancient through contemporary times" (Katz and Sinha 1998). The journal includes comparative studies of Jewish and Indian religious and philosophical traditions; historical studies of economic and socio-cultural links between Jewish and Indian communities; ethnographic studies of Jewish communities in India and Indian Jewish communities in Israel; theoretical analyses of images of Jews and Jewish religious traditions in Indian literature and images of Indians and Indian religious traditions in Jewish literature; studies of political and cultural connections between contemporary India and Israel; and explorations of issues in inter-religious dialogue between Jewish and Indian religious communities. Building on the momentum of earlier initiatives, an international conference was convened at the Oxford Centre for Hebrew and Jewish Studies in 2002, which inspired the 2007 collection of essays *Indo-Judaic Studies in the Twenty-First Century*, edited by Nathan Katz, Ranabir Chakravarti, Braj Sinha, and Shalva Weil, all of whom have assumed central roles in the development of Indo-Judaic studies. This collection advanced the emerging field of Indo-Judaic studies in significant ways by providing the first single-volume multidisciplinary investigation of the economic, cultural, religious, and political connections between Indic and Judaic cultures from ancient times to the present day. Another landmark study was the 2008 collection of essays *Karmic Passages: Israeli Scholarship on India*, edited by David Shulman and Shalva Weil. This volume, whose publication coincided with the fifteenth anniversary of the establishment of full diplomatic relations between India and Israel in 1992, provides a brief historical overview of Israeli scholarship on South Asia and then charts three types of Israeli encounters with India: philological and literary excursions by Israeli scholars into Indic languages and texts; Israeli scholars' explorations of Buddhist traditions from multiple perspectives; and sojourns in India by Israeli travelers and backpackers on a quest for spiritual transformation.[3]

A fourth type of initiative, inspired in part by these earlier initiatives, has involved a series of formal inter-religious dialogues between appointed delegations of Hindu and Jewish religious leaders, beginning in 2007. These Hindu–Jewish Leadership Summits are described as "an initiative of the World Council of Religious Leaders in partnership with the Chief Rabbinate of Israel and the Hindu Dharma Acharya Sabha" (Report of the Hindu–Jewish Leadership Summit 2007). The first Hindu–Jewish Leadership Summit was convened on February 5–7, 2007, in New Delhi, India, and was followed by a second summit on February 17–20, 2008, in Jerusalem, Israel. The stated goal of these summits was to "promote understanding and mutual respect between the Rabbinic leadership and the major religious leaders of the Hindu Dharma Acharya Sabha," and each summit produced a formal declaration affirming the theological principles, value systems and practices, and social visions shared by Hindu and Jewish traditions (Declaration of the Second Hindu–Jewish Leadership Summit 2008).

Historical Encounters: South Asian and Middle Eastern Cultures, Indic and Judaic Worlds

Wilhelm Halbfass, in his study *India and Europe* (1988), explores the history of intellectual encounters between India and Europe from classical antiquity to the twentieth century. He concludes his study with a discussion of the "global predicament of Westernization" in the contemporary period, reflecting more specifically on the problems that the so-called "Europeanization of the earth" presents for both European and Indian partners in the "dialogue."

> Will the "Europeanization" of the earth be reversed? Are other cultures and traditions . . . ready to provide alternatives? In the modern planetary situation, Eastern and Western "cultures" . . . meet *in* a Westernized world, under conditions shaped by Western ways of thinking. The medium, the framework of any "dialogue" seems to be an irreducibly Western one. But is this factually inescapable "universality" the true *telos* of mankind?

Could it be that the global openness of modernity is still a parochially Western, European horizon?[4] (Halbfass 1988: 440)

Halbfass's question lays bare the European – and more broadly, European-American – presumption that history's direction is towards a modern, universal, and essentially "Western" global culture – a presumption that is certainly not shared by all the players in the global drama of ideological, cultural, and political conflicts that is currently unfolding on the world's stage. In order to go beyond the "parochially Western, European horizon" of the "dialogue" among the world's cultures, we need to foster alternative forms of cross-cultural encounter in which Europe is not the privileged partner. Indeed, what if we were to remove Europe as a principal partner in the encounter and to shift the dialogue from "India and Europe" to "South Asia and the Middle East," investigating the longstanding connections between these ancient cultural networks whose distinctive histories have unfolded outside of, inside of, and in spite of the West? In my work as a founding member of the UCSB Middle East and South Asia Comparative Studies Project, I have suggested that this type of comparative enterprise can serve as an important antidote to the epistemological hegemony of "Europeanization" – and its more recent counterpart, "Americanization" – by providing a multiplicity of different imaginaries that do not privilege "Western" idioms associated with the modernist project but are rather grounded in the indigenous idioms of the cultures of South Asia and the Middle East.

As a comparative historian of religions, I have emphasized the role of comparative study as a method of critical interrogation that can serve as a means to challenge and dismantle the tyranny of prevailing paradigms in the academy and to explore a range of alternative epistemologies. I have been concerned in particular with interrogating two related sets of paradigms that have assumed the status of dominant discourses in the human sciences in Europe and North America since the nineteenth century as part of the process of the "Europeanization of the earth": the *Eurocentric paradigms* that have dominated scholarship in the social sciences and humanities, including history, anthropology, sociology, political science, economics, geography, psychology, philosophy, religious studies, and literary studies; and the *Protestant Christian paradigms* that have dominated scholarship in religious studies more specifically. One of the important tasks of comparative study in this context is to challenge scholars to become critically self-conscious of the legacy of these dominant paradigms that lingers in our categories and taxonomies and to reconfigure our scholarly discourses to include a multiplicity of epistemic perspectives. Comparative studies of South Asian and Middle Eastern cultures – and of Indic and Judaic worlds within these cultural networks – can provide the basis for developing alternative epistemologies to the Eurocentric paradigms that have dominated scholarship in the human sciences. Moreover, as I will discuss in the following section, comparative studies of Hindu and Jewish traditions can provide the basis for developing alternative epistemologies to the Protestant-based paradigms that have dominated the academic study of religion.

Eurocentrism has its counterpart in orientalism and Christian missionizing projects, in which "Europe" or "the West" provides the implicit standard against which the "Rest of the World" and the "Rest of the Religions" are compared and evaluated. Thus,

Western studies of South Asia and the Middle East have generally been undertaken, explicitly or implicitly, within a comparative framework in which European conceptual categories provide the standard of comparison. This "European epistemological hegemony"[5] has served to legitimate and perpetuate colonial and neocolonial projects. Long after the period of decolonization, the "postcolonial predicament" of scholars in the human sciences has involved coming to terms with the legacy of this hegemonic discourse, which still prevails as an "internal Eurocentrism" and "internal orientalism" that operate – albeit unconsciously – in the representational strategies, categories, and practices of many scholars (see Breckenridge and van der Veer 1993).

Following the seminal critiques of Eurocentric ideology in Edward Said's *Orientalism* (1978) and Samir Amin's *Eurocentrism* (1989), scholarship in the areas of world economic and social history and world-system analysis has challenged the dominant discourse of Eurocentrism on two fronts: first, through sustained critiques of prevailing social, economic, and geographic theories and the Eurocentric historiographies on which they are based; and, second, through extended analyses of the contributions of the "Rest of the World" – and in particular Asia and the Middle East – to the world-system before, during, and after the "European hegemony" that characterizes the modern period.[6] One possible approach to generating new epistemologies, suggested by the work of Janet Abu-Lughod (1989), J.M. Blaut (1993), Andre Gunder Frank (1998), and other world-system theorists as well as global studies advocates, is to adopt a global perspective and to develop new categories and models through a comparative macro-history of the contributions of the key players in the world-system in various historical periods. A global studies approach provides an attractive alternative to the traditional area studies approach, with its orientalist legacy and historical roots in cold war strategic concerns.

The UCSB Middle East and South Asia Comparative Studies Project fosters an approach that can serve to mediate between a global studies approach and the traditional area studies approach by engaging in a more circumscribed form of comparative study focused on two of the key players in the world-system before, during, and after European hegemony: South Asia and the Middle East. Moreover, rather than viewing South Asia and the Middle East from the perspective of these regions' precolonial, colonial, and postcolonial encounters with Europe, this comparative approach removes the European optic and gives priority instead to studying the historical connections and structural affinities between the cultures of South Asia and the Middle East directly, without privileging Europe as an explicit or implicit partner in the comparison. Comparative studies of the cultures of South Asia and the Middle East – including a consideration of economic, political, social, cultural, and religious connections – can contribute to our scholarly discourse in the human sciences by generating a rich array of new categories and models that are grounded in the distinctive idioms of cultures that shared complexly interwoven histories long before the "rise of the West." My colleague Dwight Reynolds remarks concerning the significance of such comparative studies:

Western scholarship on the Middle East and South Asia has been dominated almost entirely by discussions of the bilateral relationship of each of these regions to the West while ignoring questions about their relationship to each other. . . . The emergence of critical schools of thought such as subaltern studies, postcolonial studies, and the overall critique of orientalism, have all attempted to rectify this dominant view, but even these schools of thought have generally restricted their focus to critiquing the "vertical" or "center-periphery" relationship between colonized and colonizers. They have for the most part ignored the potential for radically resituating that discourse through scrutiny of the "lateral" relationships that obtain among regions of the globe without triangulating that inquiry through Europe. . . . [T]here is a complex web of multifaceted historical connections linking these two regions [the Middle East and South Asia] that remains virtually ignored in western scholarship due to the overriding interest in studying how each of these regions has interacted with the West. To study the Middle East and South Asia without constant reference to the West is thus not only to study these regions from a perspective much closer to their own historical worldview, but also to explore territory almost untouched by western scholarship. (Reynolds 2001)

Abu-Lughod, as the keynote speaker at the inaugural symposium of the UCSB Middle East and South Asia Project in March 2001, emphasized the need for sustained comparative studies of the longstanding economic, social, cultural, and religious connections between the Middle East and South Asia. She also highlighted the potential contributions of such comparative studies in "de-center[ing] both traditional area studies and the ostensibly new field of globalization studies."

The persistent connections between the Middle East and Asia cannot be overemphasized. Anyone with a deeper historical perspective would take these connections as an assumed "fact," since the existence of mini-world-systems, prior to the achievement of "western" dominance over both regions during the colonial period, is hardly a problematic to be explained. . . . [H]istory is written by the victor, [and therefore] for too long not only the world, but the description of it has been shaped by the dominant. This has led not only to distortions, but to a sad neglect of the study of ongoing connections between the Middle East and Asia . . . . (Abu-Lughod 2001)

Within the broader domain of Middle Eastern and South Asian studies, the mandate of Indo-Judaic studies, as a distinct multidisciplinary field of scholarly inquiry, is to investigate more specifically the historical connections between Indic and Judaic worlds. I will briefly survey the recent fruits of this scholarly inquiry in two areas: (1) trade contacts; and (2) cultural and religious encounters.

Trade contacts

Ranabir Chakravarti (2001, 2007a, 2007b), an economic and social historian who specializes in the maritime trade of ancient and early medieval India, notes that studies of commercial and cultural exchanges between Indic and Judaic cultures have focused primarily on the early modern and modern periods and have not given sufficient attention to excavating the history of contacts between these ancient cultures prior to 1300 CE. In order to remedy this problem, he presents a historical reconstruction of Indo-

Judaic trade contacts that spans more than two millennia, from 1000 BCE to 1300 CE, and highlights key moments that forged significant connections between Indian and Jewish communities (Chakravarti 2007b). He presents this historical reconstruction as part of the broader history of trade between South Asia and the Middle East, or West Asia, in which both Indian and Jewish merchants assumed pivotal roles.

> That India . . . has a cherished history of long-distance trade with West Asia, and the Near and the Middle East, is well known. The arterial routes of overland commerce through the northwestern borderlands of the subcontinent and the almost central position of the subcontinent in the Indian Ocean immensely facilitated India's overseas trade and contacts. The Land of Israel, in its turn, was a bridge between Asia and Africa. Egypt, which was well known for its Jewish population, acted as a hinge between the Indian Ocean and the Mediterranean. (Chakravarti 2007b: 20)

Chakravarti, in his efforts to reconstruct the early history of trade contacts between Indian communities in South Asia and Jewish communities in Israel, Egypt, Babylonia, and other parts of the Middle East, builds on and extends the work of earlier scholars who have made significant contributions to Indo-Judaic studies in this arena, including Chaim Rabin (1971, 1994), Katz (1999), and Brian Weinstein (2000, 2001). In their respective contributions to this history, these scholars draw on philological, literary, historiographic, archival, epigraphic, and archaeological evidence from a diverse array of Indian, Jewish, Persian, Greek, Roman, Chinese, and Arabic sources. It is not possible within the scope of the present essay to provide a full account of the evidence assembled by these scholars. I will rather limit my discussion to select examples of the evidence from Indian and Jewish sources.

Although Chakravarti presents some evidence from early Indian sources, he emphasizes that there is a major problem with these sources in that they employ the encompassing terms *Yavana* or *mleccha* to designate foreigners, irrespective of their ethno-cultural identities, and they do not use any specific designation to refer to the Jews as a distinct ethno-cultural community.

> The historian here faces a major problem: India occasionally figures in early Jewish sources, but no ancient Indian source categorically refers to the Jews. The Jews must have come under the encapsulating category of *Yavanas*, a term indiscriminately employed by early Indian writers, to denote the Greeks, Iranians, Scythians, Parthians, Huns, and Muslim communities alike. The Jews could also have been brought under the category of *mlecchas* (impure outsiders) in early Indian normative literature. In other words, it is difficult to establish a person's Jewish identity on the basis of Indian documentation which did not use any religious/ethnic label to refer to a Jew. (Chakravarti 2007b: 20)

The evidence from Indian sources includes references from early Buddhist texts such as the Bāveru Jātaka, which mentions periodic sea voyages by Indian merchants to the land of Bāveru, or Babylonia (Katz 1999: 14), a well-established center of Jewish life. The Indian evidence also includes seven Aramaic edicts from Afghanistan promulgated in the name of Aśoka (ca. 272–233 BCE), the acclaimed Buddhist ruler of the Maurya dynasty, which indicate that, as part of his mission to spread the Dhamma, the teachings of the Buddha, beyond the Indian subcontinent to the Yavana rulers in Syria, Egypt, Macedonia, and elsewhere in the Middle East and the Mediterranean, he intended to extend his message to the speakers of Aramaic. Chakravarti suggests that "Asoka's messages of *Dhamma* and his use of Aramaic in the northwestern extremities of his empire could have reached the Hebrew-speaking Jewish communities of West Asia, especially those in Babylon, though at this moment that is only a plausible conjecture" (Chakravarti 2007b: 24).

With the rise of the Roman empire from the late first century BCE onwards, the Roman world became connected to India via the celebrated Red Sea route, which, together with the discovery of the south-western monsoon wind system, made it possible for merchants to travel from Berenike, a Red Sea port in Egypt, to Muziris (Cranganore), a port in Kerala on the Malabar Coast, in forty days (Chakravarti 2007b: 27). The Romans subsequently established a colony at Muziris, which, as Katz notes, was a momentous event in the history of Indian Jewish communities in India.

> Having secured both the sea lanes of the spice trade, as well as the overland silk route, the Romans went on to establish their first permanent colony in India at Muziris, "the nearest mart in India" [according to the Roman scholar Pliny]. This is of particular interest to Jewish India, because Muziris was also the earliest Jewish settlement in India, known in the Jewish world as Shingly. (Katz 1999: 18)

Tamil works from South India provide corroborating evidence concerning the flourishing trade networks between Indian communities in South India and Yavanas from the Roman world. For example, the Tamil *caṅkam* anthology *Akanāṉūṟu* (ca. first to second century CE) speaks of the Yavanas arriving at the port of Muziris in large ships carrying gold and returning with shipments of pepper to their homelands. The Tamil national epic *Cilappatikāram* (ca. fifth century CE) describes wealthy Yavana merchants who spoke with strange tongues and who, having brought great ships filled with precious goods, left their homelands behind and settled in the capital city of the Cēras (Katz 1999: 19; Weinstein 2000: 26). Although the Tamil works do not specify the ethnocultural identity of these Yavana merchants, a number of later inscriptions, including two inscriptions on copper plates, indicate that by the tenth and eleventh centuries CE there were established networks of Jewish merchants along the western seaboard of India who were accorded important roles in the commercial and socio-cultural life of port towns – in particular, Sanjan north of present-day Mumbai on the Konkan coast and Kottayam and Cochin in Kerala on the Malabar Coast (Chakravarti 2007b: 31–32).

In addition to the evidence from Indian sources, a number of Jewish sources point to early trade connections between India – termed *Hōdû* in Hebrew[7] – and Jewish communities in the Middle East. The earliest source is the Hebrew Bible, which includes several verses, I Kings 9.26–28 and 10.22 (cf. II Chron. 8.17–18; 9.21), that refer to "the famous voyages of Solomon [tenth century BCE] to reach the land of Ophir from where gold, silver, ivory, peacocks, and apes were brought in Tarshish ships" (Chakravarti 2007b: 22). A number of scholars have suggested that Ophir, or Sophir, is a designation for an ancient center of commerce in India – more specifically, the well-known port of Suppara near present-day Mumbai, or Sauvira in the lower Indus Valley in the north-western region of the Indian subcontinent. This suggestion coincides with that of the Jewish historian Josephus (ca. 37–100 CE), who identifies "the land that was of old called Ophir" with India.[8] Moreover, philological evidence indicates that the Hebrew terms for ivory, apes, and peacocks in I Kings 10.22 (cf. II Chron. 9.21), along with terms for other articles of trade in the Hebrew Bible, are loanwords derived from Sanskrit or Tamil (Rabin 1994: 28–29; 1971). Further evidence of commercial transactions between Jewish and Indian communities is suggested by the numerous references in the Hebrew Bible and the Babylonian Talmud to certain spices and other commodities of Indian origin, indicating a demand for Indian products that could only be procured through trade (Weinstein 2000: 18–24; Chakravarti 2007b: 29).[9]

The evidence from Jewish sources also includes references to India and Indian philosophers in the works of the Alexandrian Jewish philosopher Philo Judaeus (ca. 20 BCE–50 CE), who belonged to an influential family of merchants and administrators that included his well-known nephew Marcus Julius Alexander, a wealthy merchant who appears to have been directly involved in the Roman empire's trade with India in the first century CE (see Chakravarti 2007b: 28–29; Weinstein 2000: 14). Although Philo's idealized representations of Indian philosophers may have been influenced in part by the Greek historian Megasthenes's account of Alexander of Macedon's encounter with Indian gymnosophists in the fourth century BCE, as Frances Schmidt (1994) has suggested, it is likely that he also learned about India and its sages directly from his own family members who were involved in commerce with India.

A critical source of evidence that demonstrates the pivotal role of Jewish merchants in the maritime trade with India in the eleventh to thirteenth centuries CE is the treasure trove of documents from the Cairo Geniza brought to light through the groundbreaking studies of S.D. Goiten (1967–1993, 1973; Goiten and Friedman 2007). Goiten's final work, *India Traders of the Middle Ages: Documents from the Cairo Geniza* (Goiten and Friedman 2007), which was completed in collaboration with Mordechai Friedman and published posthumously, contains translations of over 450 documents comprising letters written by medieval Jewish merchants engaged in trade with India along with other records such as commercial bills and shipping manifests. Many of these merchants lived in India for extended periods of time and formed alliances with Hindu and Muslim merchants, and this archive of letters is thus an invaluable resource for understanding the commercial, cultural, and religious exchanges between these Jewish "India traders" and their Hindu and Muslim counterparts.[10]

Cultural and religious encounters

This brief survey of Indian and Jewish sources provides tantalizing glimpses of key historical moments in which connections were forged between ancient and medieval Indic and Judaic worlds as part of the broader commercial networks that connected South Asia and the Middle East over the course of two millennia prior to 1300 CE. Moreover, the connections that were forged involved not only commercial transactions but also cultural and religious exchanges. The Jewish and Indian merchants who plied the sea lanes and overland routes between South Asia and the Middle East were not only the transporters of material goods, they were also the transmitters of cultural and religious ideologies and practices.

> The very transactional nature of commerce would always foster the exchange of ideas, cultural norms, practices, and belief systems among the participants in that trade. Herein lies one of the most significant messages of the long history of Indo-Judaic contacts. . . . Merchants were not merely carriers of commodities, but were purveyors of cultural traits and ideas across long distances. (Chakravarti 2007b: 37, 38)

I would like to briefly consider three types of cultural and religious encounters between Jewish and Indian communities that were catalyzed in part by cross-cultural trade networks in ancient and medieval times: (1) cross-fertilization of knowledge systems; (2) perceptions of the other; and (3) settling of Jewish communities in India.

The first type of encounter between Jews and Hindus involves cross-fertilization of knowledge systems. As a result of the burgeoning interest in Indo-Judaic studies in recent years, a number of scholars, such as Weinstein (2007), have sought to illuminate the extent to which medieval Jewish discourses may have been directly or indirectly influenced by Hindu śāstras, specialized knowledge systems, in the areas of mathematics, astronomy and astrology, medicine, linguistics, and other domains. However, there is a need for more in-depth inquiries into these and other areas of Hindu influence, as well as into the other side of this intellectual intercourse: the influence of Jewish discourses on Hindu śāstras in various areas prior to the modern period.

The second type of encounter involves perceptions of the other – Jewish images of Hindus and Hindu images of Jews. In a recent essay Richard Marks (2007) provides a preliminary "history" of medieval Jewish perceptions of Hindus and Hindu traditions based on an examination of 19 Jewish works from the tenth to fourteenth centuries representing a range of genres, including "a biblical commentary, a legal work, philosophy books, scientific treatises, histories and story collections, a Kabbalistic work, a travelogue, and alchemy texts" (Marks 2007: 58). He then raises important questions regarding the various sources of these Jewish images of Hindus as well as the implications of such images for constructions of Jewish identity. There are no comparable studies, to my knowledge, of Hindu perceptions of Jews and Jewish traditions in the medieval period. However, Yulia Egorova's recent studies (2006, 2007) provide illuminating analyses of Indian perceptions of Jews in the modern period in which she suggests that "it was due to the advance of British rule that the Indian discourse about the Jews first came into being" (Egorova 2006: 2). The Indian sources that she examines include discourses of neo-Hindu reformers, such as Ram Mohan Roy (1772–1833), Dayananda Saraswati (1824–1883), and Vivekananda (1863–1902), and discourses of Indian nationalists, such as Bankimchandra Chattopadhyay (1838–1894) and M.K. Gandhi (1869–1948).

Egorova's analyses suggest that these neo-Hindu reformers and nationalists developed their perspectives on Jewish traditions as part of their distinctive reformulations of Hindu tradition-identity that were designed to counter European constructions of "religion" and more specifically Christian missionaries' critiques of Hindu traditions. For example, Vivekananda, as part of his response to Christian critiques, provides both positive and negative evaluations of Jewish traditions. On the one hand, he praises Hindus and Jews as both Asian peoples who are "the two races from which have originated all the great religions of the world" (Egorova 2007: 199). He affirms certain common features that Jewish and Hindu traditions share – in particular, their nonmissionizing character and consequent lack of interest in converting others, their basis in scriptures, and their systems of dietary regulations – and through this comparative venture he clearly intends to distinguish these *Ur* religions from their Christian and Buddhist offspring. On the other hand, as part of his response to Christian critiques of Hindu image worship, he criticizes the Jews as the ultimate source of this iconoclastic perspective and claims that they themselves practiced their own form of image worship by revering God's presence in the Ark (Egorova 2007: 199–200). In reflecting on Vivekananda's possible motivations for constructing Jewish traditions in this way, Egorova comments:

> Vivekananda's comparisons involving Judaism appear to have served two main purposes. The first one was to deflect the arguments of his Christian opponents. When Vivekananda finds some positive features in Judaism, he argues that Hinduism shares those features and stresses that Judaism and Christianity – which grew out of Judaism and was founded by a Jew – are Asian religions, like Hinduism, as only Asia could give birth to great prophets. . . . When he denounces Judaism, his critique seems to serve the purpose of showing the superiority of Indian religious culture. This way of constructing Judaism appears to stem from his general argument that Europeans – who were now practicing a religion that was an offshoot of Judaism – were spiritually inferior to the Indians despite the fact that their religion is Asian. (Egorova 2007: 201)

The third type of encounter between Jews and Hindus is the deepest and most transformative, for it involved transplanting Jewish cultural and religious traditions on Indian soil through the establishment of Jewish communities in India beginning in the first millennium CE. The study of Indian Jewish communities is central to Indo-Judaic studies, as evidenced in the proliferation of an extensive literature that focuses primarily on the three principal communities: (1) the Cochin Jews of Kerala; (2) the Bene Israel of Maharashtra; and (3) the Baghdadi Jews of Calcutta (Kolkata) and Bombay (Mumbai).[11] "[T]hese two great and ancient civilizations, Indic and Judaic, interact within the very being of India's Jews," as Katz (2000: 3) has observed, and the study of Indian Jewish communities can thus serve as a means of understanding the distinctive strategies that they each have deployed in negotiating the Jewish and Indian poles of their respective identities. In his extended study of the three principal Indian Jewish communities, Katz (2000) emphasizes that, in contrast to Jews in other parts of the diaspora, Jews in India have experienced the benefits of acculturation in the larger Indian society without compromising their cultural and religious integrity through assimilation.

> A crucial distinction between India and the rest of the Diaspora . . . is that in India acculturation is not paid for in the currency of assimilation. By *acculturation* I mean fitting comfortably into a society while retaining one's own identity, whereas by *assimilation* I mean that the loss of that identity is a perceived condition for acceptance. The study of

Indian Jewish communities demonstrates that in Indian culture an immigrant group gains status precisely by maintaining its own identity. (Katz 2000: 3)

This process of acculturation – as distinct from assimilation – is perhaps best exemplified by the case of the Cochin Jews. The oldest Jewish community in India, they claim to have arrived in Cranganore, a port in Kerala on the Malabar Coast – which, as discussed earlier, was known in the Roman world as Muziris and in the Jewish world as Shingly – in 72 CE, two years after the Roman sack of Jerusalem and destruction of the Second Temple.[12] The community later moved to Cochin, where they were integrated into the socio-cultural fabric of Indian life while at the same maintaining their distinctive ethno-cultural and religious identity as Jews. One of the two copper plates with inscriptions mentioned earlier is from Cochin ca. 1000 CE, and the inscriptions indicate that the Jewish merchants of Cochin were granted major economic concessions and other privileges by the local king, which suggests that they were accorded a high social status in the broader Indian hierarchy. "Various privileges granted to them signal the status and prestige of the Jewish merchants at Cochin; the Jewish settlers appear to have been considered among the elite groups in the coastal society" (Chakravarti 2007b: 32).

In their ethnographic studies of the Cochin Jews, Katz and Ellen Goldberg (1990; 1993) use the concept of "foregrounding" in order to illuminate the mechanisms of acculturation through which the Cochin Jews successfully adapted to the dominant Hindu culture in Kerala. The Jewish community secured a high place for themselves in the caste hierarchy of Kerala by aligning themselves with the lifestyles and practices of the two highest castes: the Nambudiri brahmins, the religious elite, and the Nāyars, the dominant caste politically and economically. This process of creative adaptation involved "foregrounding" certain aspects of Jewish practice – such as purity practices and liturgical symbols of royalty – that resonated with the Hindu symbol systems and practices of the Brahmins and Nāyars.

> In their *minhagim* [local customs] the Cochin Jews have foregrounded the symbols of purity and nobility inherent in Judaism at the same time as they have adapted some of the priestly and royal symbols of Hinduism, making for one of the most exotic systems of Jewish observance found anywhere in the Diaspora. On the one hand, they have appropriated certain Brahmanical symbols of purity in their unique Passover observances. On the other hand, they have adapted aspects of the Nāyars' symbols of royalty and prosperity in their unique Simchat Torah observances as well as in their marriage customs. Moreover, they managed this syncretism judiciously so as not to contravene *halacha*.[13] (Katz and Goldberg 1990: 200–201)

Collaborative Scholarly Encounters: Comparative Studies of Hindu and Jewish Traditions

Studies of the intersections of Indic and Judaic worlds within the broader cultural networks of South Asia and the Middle East can thus serve to illuminate the neglected histories that have interconnected these ancient worlds and can also provide the basis

for developing alternative epistemologies to the Eurocentric paradigms that have dominated scholarship in the social sciences and humanities. In addition to studies of the
historical connections between Indic and Judaic worlds, another type of cross-cultural
enterprise involves collaborative inquiries between scholars of South Asia and Judaica
engaging in comparative studies of Hindu and Jewish traditions within a religious
studies framework. Such studies can play an important role in dismantling European
epistemological hegemony by providing alternative epistemologies to the Protestant-
based paradigms that have dominated the academic study of religion and served to
perpetuate the ideals of Enlightenment discourse and colonialist projects. Indeed, one
of the express purposes of the AAR Comparative Studies in Hinduisms and Judaisms
Consultation (1995 to 1997) and its successor, the AAR Comparative Studies in Hinduisms and Judaisms Group (1998 to present), has been to bring together specialists in
South Asia and Judaica to engage in a series of sustained reflections on topics within
Hinduisms and Judaisms, with the intention of challenging scholars of religion to critically reassess the prevailing paradigms and to reconfigure our scholarly discourses to
include a range of analytical models and categories arising out of case studies of Hindu
and Jewish traditions.

The prevailing paradigms originated from a predominantly Protestant Christian elite
in the European academy in the nineteenth century. The Christian – and more specifically Protestant – legacy of the academic study of religion is evident in the way in which
these paradigms tend to privilege certain categories while marginalizing others, emphasizing a series of hierarchical dichotomies in which categories that accord with the
Protestant ethos are given priority. This hierarchizing of categories can be seen in a
number of persistent trends in religious studies scholarship: first, the tendency to emphasize the distinction between sacred and profane and, as a corollary of the separation
of church and state, to compartmentalize religion as something distinct from culture;
second, the tendency to define religion as a "belief system" and to give priority to categories such as faith, belief, doctrine, and theology while under-privileging the role of
practice, ritual, and law; third, the tendency to give precedence to the individual over
the community as the locus of religious life and consequently to give less emphasis to
the social and cultural dimensions of religion; and, fourth, the tendency to define religious identity in terms that privilege universalism over particularism and hence reflect
a missionizing model of religious tradition. While recent developments in the fields of
ritual studies and cultural studies have provided important correctives to such tendencies, the Protestant legacy still lingers – albeit unconsciously – in the practices of many
scholars of religion.[14]

The Protestant subtext of the dominant paradigms provides the implicit standard
against which other religious traditions are compared and evaluated. While perhaps
appropriate for the study of some religious traditions, such paradigms, together with
the hierarchical taxonomies they perpetuate, become straitjackets when applied to
other traditions. One of the tasks of the comparative study of Hindu and Jewish
traditions – as articulated in our founding vision for the AAR Comparative Studies in
Hinduisms and Judaisms Consultation and for the AAR Group that succeeded it – is to
test and critique the Protestant-based paradigms by showing how two of the world's
major religious traditions defy the classificatory schemas associated with the dominant

paradigms. These traditions construct other categories and taxonomies that bring to light different sets of relationships, such as those between religion and culture, ethnic identity and religious adherence, observance and nonobservance, and purity and impurity. Such relationships are obscured by the application of the prevailing models. In contrast to the Protestant-based paradigms, in which precedence is given to belief, doctrine, and theology, and tradition-identity is rooted in the universalizing values of missionizing traditions, Hindu and Jewish traditions provide alternative models of religious tradition, in which priority is given to issues of practice, observance, and law, and tradition-identity is defined primarily in terms of particular ethnic and cultural categories that are tied to notions of blood descent.

The sessions sponsored annually by the AAR Comparative Studies in Hinduisms and Judaisms program units since 1995 have engaged a wide spectrum of Hindu and Jewish traditions in a diverse array of configurations: Biblical and Vedic traditions, Brahmanical and Rabbinic traditions, the esoteric traditions of Tantra and Kabbalah, *bhakti* and Ḥasidic movements, women's traditions, religious nationalisms in India and Israel, Hindu and Jewish diaspora communities, and so on.[15] Through our annual program of AAR sessions we have sought to test, reassess, refine, deconstruct, and reconstitute a range of analytical categories that are critical to our scholarly inquiries in the study of religion. Two exempla will serve to illustrate the types of analytical categories and issues addressed by the Comparative Studies in Hinduisms and Judaisms Group and its predecessor, the Consultation. I will first consider a cluster of issues brought to light by the distinctive nature of Hindu and Jewish traditions as "embodied communities." I will then focus on the category of sacrifice in order to illustrate how analytical categories can be fruitfully reimagined through a comparative analysis of Hindu and Jewish instantiations of the category.

Embodied communities

In my work as a comparative historian of religions, I have suggested that one way of rethinking what constitutes a religious tradition is to posit a spectrum in which religious traditions are mapped according to different degrees of ethno-cultural specificity, with what I term "embodied communities" on one end of the spectrum and missionizing traditions on the other end. Among the array of Hinduisms and Judaisms, Brahmanical Hinduism and Rabbinic Judaism are paradigmatic embodied communities in that their notions of tradition-identity, in contrast to the universalizing tendencies of missionizing traditions, are embodied in the particularities of ethno-cultural categories defined in relation to a particular people (Indo-Āryans, Jews), a particular sacred language (Sanskrit, Hebrew), a particular sacred land (India, Israel), a particular corpus of sacred texts (Veda, Torah), and a particular set of socio-cultural practices. Missionizing traditions such as Christian and Buddhist traditions, in contrast, construct their tradition-identities primarily in terms of universalizing teachings that are intended for potentially all peoples and cultures. In their early formative periods such missionizing traditions are generally concerned to disassociate themselves from identification with a particular people–language–land–culture so that they can spread their teachings across ethnic, linguistic, geographic, and cultural boundaries, beyond a single constituency.[16]

My work suggests that – contrary to stereotypical characterizations of Hindu and Jewish traditions as representing opposite ends of the spectrum of the world's religions – Brahmanical Hinduism and Rabbinic Judaism constitute two species of the same genus of religious tradition: as *ethno-cultural systems* concerned with issues of family, ethnic and cultural integrity, blood lineages, and the inter-generational transmission of traditions; as *elite textual communities* that have codified their norms in the form of scriptural canons transmitted in their respective sacred languages; and as *religions of orthopraxy* characterized by hereditary priesthoods and sacrificial traditions, comprehensive legal systems, complex dietary laws, and elaborate regulations concerning purity and impurity. The feature that underlies these shared characteristics is that of *embodiment*: embodiment in the particularities of ethno-cultural identity tied to a specific people, language, and land and to an authorized set of sacred texts and socio-cultural practices. These embodied communities share an abiding concern for the body as a site of central significance that is the vehicle for the maintenance of the social, cosmic, and divine orders. The body is the instrument of biological and socio-cultural reproduction that is to be regulated through ritual and social duties, maintained in purity, sustained through proper diet, and reproduced through appropriate sexual relations. In their roles as "peoples of the body"[17] the Brahmanical and Rabbinic traditions provide the basis for constructing alternative models of religious tradition to the prevailing Protestant-based paradigms.

The AAR Comparative Studies in Hinduisms and Judaisms program units have devoted a number of sessions to mapping Hindu and Jewish discourses of the body and associated regimens of bodily practices. We have explored the multiform ways in which the human body has been represented, disciplined, regulated, and cultivated in the discursive representations and practices of a range of Hindu and Jewish traditions (1998). We have also examined various constructions of divine embodiment along with the ritual and meditative technologies through which human bodies are refashioned in the likeness of divine bodies (1998, 2012).

Our collaborative investigations have included an examination of the modes of bodily practice – such as purity codes (1995), sexual disciplines (1996), dietary regulations and transactions (1996, 2004, 2012), and hair practices and polemics (2007) – through which the Rabbinic and Brahmanical traditions construct and maintain the particularized ethno-cultural identities of their communities, circumscribing external boundaries that distinguish them from gentiles and Yavanas, respectively, while at the same time delineating internal boundaries that establish socio-religious hierarchies within their own communities. Through these regimens of bodily practice, the biological bodies of those whose *ascribed identity* is Jewish or Hindu, by virtue of birth into a community that defines itself in terms of blood descent, are reconstituted as "religiously informed bodies" that are *inscribed* with the socio-religious taxonomies of their respective communities.[18]

Within the householder ideals upheld by Rabbinic and Brahmanical authorities, these bodily regimens assume the status of a domesticized form of asceticism, which challenges us to re-vision theories of asceticism from the perspective of these embodied communities. In accordance with this mandate, the AAR Comparative Studies in Hinduisms and Judaisms Consultation, in conjunction with the Ascetic Impulse in Religious Life and Thought Group, co-sponsored a session interrogating the analytical category of asceticism (1996). The session participants argued that the category of asceticism needs to be expanded beyond the confines of renunciant and monastic traditions to take into account disciplines of "domestic asceticism" promulgated by Rabbinic and Brahmanical authorities, including sexual disciplines, dietary restrictions, periodic fasting, purity practices, vows, and other forms of householder austerities. Through such regimens of domestic asceticism these "peoples of the body" ensure the biological and socio-cultural reproduction of disciplined bodies adept at maintaining the distinctive ethno-cultural identities and religious norms of their respective communities.

One of our most recent AAR sessions explored the ways in which Jews and Hindus in North America have reimagined their notions of ethno-cultural identity in relation to modern discourses pertaining to the freighted categories "race" and "ethnicity" in the changing American landscape in the twentieth and twenty-first centuries (2012). Although scholars such as the historian David Hollinger (2006, 2011) have characterized contemporary American culture as "post-racial" and "post-ethnic," the session participants challenged such characterizations and raised critical issues regarding the persistent constitutive role of embodied notions of ethno-cultural identity in shaping the social formations of Jews and Hindus in North America over against normative constructions of "Americanness" defined by Protestant religiosity and whiteness.

Sacrifice

The AAR Comparative Studies in Hinduisms and Judaisms program units have sponsored a number of sessions that have critically reassessed the analytical category of sacrifice through a cross-cultural examination of Hindu and Jewish instantiations of this category (1997, 2000, 2008). One of our AAR sessions interrogated the prevailing theories of sacrifice in the academy (2000), with particular emphasis on the ways in which Vedic and Jewish sacrificial traditions – as two of the most extensive, sophisticated, and well-documented sacrificial systems in the world – challenge the models of sacrifice proposed by theorists such as Henri Hubert and Marcel Mauss (1964), René Girard (1977), and Walter Burkert (1983). The session began with a critical analysis of the manner in which the scholarly projects of nineteenth- and twentieth-century interpreters of sacrifice in Indology and Judaica have perpetuated classificatory schemas that tend to privilege certain characterizations of sacrifice while relegating others to the periphery. The session centered on the work of Kathryn McClymond (2000), who, on the basis of her sustained studies of Vedic and Jewish sacrificial traditions, has challenged the dominant theories that represent sacrifice as a violent, bloody act and has proposed an alternative polythetic model of sacrifice that more adequately reflects the Vedic and Jewish cases.

One of the central contributions of this comparative investigation of Vedic and Jewish constructions of sacrifice – particularly as represented in the ongoing work of McClymond (2002, 2008) and my own work on Vedic ritual (1998b, 2001) – has been to call into question a number of assumptions that underlie the dominant theories. The first assumption is that animal sacrifice is the paradigmatic form of sacrifice, which is recast in a Christian discursive framework as finding fruition in the consummate atoning sacrifice: the immolation of Jesus Christ on the cross. The second assumption is that sacrifice involves the destruction of the offering – or the killing of the victim – and that the act of killing is the defining element of sacrifice. The third assumption, which follows from the first two, is that sacrifice can be equated with ritual violence. Ivan Strenski, in his review of studies of sacrifice in the 1990s, observes that "these days, the very concept of ritual violence seems to have been folded into that of sacrifice, making the two virtually identical. . . . This obsession with violence in studies of sacrifice shows little sign of diminishing" (Strenski 1996: 11).

The first phase of this comparative inquiry involves interrogating these assumptions and demonstrating that theories that characterize sacrifice as ritual violence, which are based on Western exempla in which bloody animal sacrifices are paradigmatic, are inadequate to account for the Vedic ritual tradition. First, animal sacrifices are not paradigmatic in the case of the Vedic *yajña*. Although the term *yajña* is generally translated as "sacrifice" by Western scholars, it is defined by the Vedic tradition itself as an offering (from the root *yaj*, "to offer, worship") of an oblation (*dravya*) to a deity (*devatā*). The Vedic *yajña* in its public form comprises the classical *śrauta* rituals that are traditionally divided into three principal classes, which are distinguished primarily by the material substances that are used as oblations or offerings: the *iṣṭi*, which centers on rice or barley offerings; the *paśubandha*, which is characterized by animal offerings; and the Soma ritual, which centers on offerings of juice from the Soma plant. It is the Soma ritual – not the *paśubandha*, or animal sacrifice – that is given precedence in the Vedic tradition as the paradigmatic sacrifice that is the apex of the sacrificial hierarchy. Second, the destruction of the offering is not the defining characteristic of *śrauta* sacrifices but rather must be understood as only one among a number of interdependent activities that together constitute the syntax of Vedic ritual. Third, the destruction of the offering is framed in classical Vedic ritual texts as part of a carefully ordered ritual system that relegates the messy actualities of violence and blood to the world beyond the ritual enclosure.[19] In the case of the *paśubandha*, the destruction of the animal is characterized as "quietening" (root *śam*) and not as "killing" (root *han*), and the actual immolation is marginalized and domesticated in that it is performed outside the ritual enclosure and the animal is suffocated or strangled rather than decapitated, thus avoiding the inauspicious act of bloodletting. In the case of the Soma ritual, the paradigmatic Vedic sacrifice, the act of destruction involves the crushing and pressing of the Soma plant in order to extract the Soma juice that will be used as an oblation.

The first phase of this comparative inquiry thus leads to the conclusion that theories that imagine sacrifice as ritual violence involving the bloody slaying of a victim are not adequate to account for the multilayered significations of Vedic *śrauta* sacrifices. The second phase of the inquiry focuses on the Jewish sacrificial tradition and reimagines sacrifice, opening up hitherto unexplored dimensions, by juxtaposing Jewish constructions of sacrifice with Vedic constructions. In the Jewish sacrificial tradition, in contrast to the Vedic tradition, animals are the preferred offering substance in four of the five classes of offerings delineated in Biblical and Rabbinic texts: the *'ōlāh* (burnt offering), the *ḥaṭṭā't* (sin offering or purification offering), the *šᵉlāmîm* (peace offering or well-being offering), and the *'āšām* (guilt offering or transgression offering). The fifth class of offerings comprises grain offerings, or *minḥāh*. As McClymond's work has emphasized, an investigation of the Jewish sacrificial tradition within a broader comparative framework that includes the Vedic sacrificial tradition brings to light a number of elements in the Jewish case that have previously received insufficient attention. First, as in Vedic *śrauta* sacrifices, vegetal offerings play a significant role in the Jewish sacrificial tradition – not only as a distinct class of offerings but also as an important component of animal sacrifices. Second, in the various classes of animal sacrifice, the killing of the animal is not the defining element of the sacrifice. As in the Vedic case, the destruction of the offering is not the *sine qua non* of the sacrifice but is rather one among a number of interrelated activities that together constitute the sacrificial matrix. Moreover, within the matrix of animal sacrifice the critical elements that distinguish one class of animal sacrifice from the other are the procedures for manipulating the blood and the methods of dividing and distributing the portions of the animal – not the slaughtering procedures. Third, although the central importance of blood in the Jewish sacrificial tradition provides a counterpoint to the Vedic sacrificial tradition's abhorrence of blood, the juxtaposition of the two cases provides an opportunity for us to re-evaluate the significance of blood in the Jewish case. If we shift our attention from the blood as a counterpart of the violent death of the animal to the blood as the "life-essence" of the animal, we open up fruitful avenues of comparative inquiry that point to the role of sacrificial rituals in providing access to various types of life-essence: the blood that is extracted from the animal in Jewish animal sacrifices, the breath that is extracted from the animal in the Vedic *paśubandha*, and the juice that is extracted from the Soma plant in Vedic Soma rituals (see McClymond 2002, 2008).

In addition to reimagining sacrifice through comparative investigations of Vedic and Jewish sacrificial traditions, in other AAR sessions (2000, 2008) the Comparative Studies in Hinduisms and Judaisms Group has explored the discursive strategies through which the category of sacrifice has been re-inscribed in Hindu traditions and Jewish traditions following the decline of the Vedic *śrauta* rituals after 200 BCE and the discontinuation of the Jewish sacrificial rituals in 70 CE as a result of the destruction of the Second Temple in Jerusalem. Sacrifice has functioned in both Hindu and Jewish traditions as a "canonical category" – to use Brian K. Smith's term – "a category that acts to provide explanatory power, traditional legitimacy, and canonical authority" (1989: 202, 216–218). The category of sacrifice has operated in both traditions as an authoritative network of signifiers that, once divested of its delimited significations tied to a particular complex of ritual practices, has been mapped onto a variety of discursive domains, becoming invested with distinctive new significations in each domain. Through the discursive strategies of re-signification sacrifice, as a canonical category, has been expanded beyond the circumscribed boundaries of the ancient Vedic and Jewish sacrificial rituals and has been used to valorize a diverse range of practices as legitimate new forms of sacrifice. For example, sacrifice has been variously re-signified as internalized practices of meditation and fasting in the ascetic regimens of renunciants and householders, as scriptural recitation and study in Brahmanical and

Rabbinic hermeneutics, as prayer and ritual worship in temple and synagogue liturgies, as hospitality rites and other domestic rituals in householder domains, and as esoteric meditative practices in Tantric and Kabbalistic traditions.[20]

One of the important tasks of the comparative study of Hindu and Jewish traditions, and of Indic and Judaic worlds more broadly, is thus to challenge scholars to critically interrogate the theories, models, and categories that perpetuate the legacy of hegemonic paradigms in the academy – whether Eurocentric paradigms, Protestant Christian paradigms, or other dominant paradigms – and to reconstitute our scholarly discourse to allow for a multiplicity of epistemologies. Comparative analysis is not only intrinsic to the process through which categories and models are constructed and applied, but it can also serve as an important corrective to the scholarly practices through which certain categories and models are privileged over others in the human sciences, and in religious studies more specifically.

Inter-Religious Encounters: Hindu–Jewish Dialogue

The two Hindu–Jewish Leadership Summits that met on February 5–7, 2007, in Delhi, and on February 17–20, 2008, in Jerusalem were historic events in that they were the first occasions on which appointed delegations of Hindu and Jewish religious leaders have come together to engage in formal inter-religious dialogue. The Hindu delegations to the two summits were convened under the auspices of the Hindu Dharma Acharya Sabha, an official group of Hindu leaders headed by Swami Dayananda Saraswati, while the Jewish delegations were convened under the auspices of the Chief Rabbinate of Israel led by Ashkenazi Chief Rabbi Yona Metzger, the first Chief Rabbi of Israel to visit India.[21]

As initiatives of the World Council of Religious Leaders, the central goal of the two Hindu–Jewish Leadership Summits was to promote mutual understanding, respect, and cooperation between Hindu and Jewish leaders and their respective religious communities. The more specific objectives of the summits, as noted by Yudit Greenberg (2009), included both abstract long-term goals, such as promoting education, social justice, a healthy environment, and world peace, and more pragmatic immediate goals, such as combating religious violence and terrorism, countering the missionizing efforts of Christians and other religious groups, and fostering political, economic, and cultural ties between India and Israel.

> [O]bjectives included addressing the relevance of their respective spiritual teachings for contemporary society, focusing on justice, compassion, and humility; recognizing commonalities in values and social and religious conduct; working together to preserve tradition in an increasingly global and secular society; implementing both strong secular as well as religious education; and carrying out their mutual responsibility to those who suffer, to the environment, and to world peace. These spiritual and philosophical goals are long-term in nature. Participation in the Summit was also driven by more immediate and pragmatic considerations. The threat of terrorism and the challenge of missionary activity are common concerns of both groups. . . . Another mutually beneficial objective for the dialogues was the potential expansion of cultural and diplomatic ties between India and Israel. (Greenberg 2009: 28)

The participants in the Hindu–Jewish Leadership Summits, as reflected in the reports and formal declarations associated with the two summits, emphasized the significant affinities between Hindu and Jewish traditions in terms of their notions of religious identity, value systems, scriptural traditions, and practices. With respect to Hindu and Jewish constructions of religious identity, the Declaration of the First Hindu–Jewish Leadership Summit (2007) states:

- The religious identities of both Jewish and Hindu communities are related to components of Faith, Scripture, Peoplehood, Culture, Religious Practices, Land, and Language.
- Hindus and Jews seek to maintain their respective heritage and pass it on to succeeding generations, while living in respectful relations with other communities.
- Neither seek to proselytize, nor undermine or replace in any way the religious identities of other faith communities.

These statements succinctly encapsulate the constitutive components of what I have termed the embodied nature of Hindu and Jewish communities: a notion of peoplehood that is defined in relation to a particular land, language, scriptural tradition, and system of religio-cultural practices. In contrast to missionizing traditions, these communities do not engage in proselytizing, but rather they maintain their distinctive ethno-cultural and religious heritages by transmitting their traditions across generations through blood lineages. The participants in both summits expressed concern over the persistent missionizing efforts of other religious communities and emphasized that "they expect other communities to respect their religious identities and commitments, and condemn all activities that go against the sanctity of this mutual respect" (Declaration of the First Hindu–Jewish Leadership Summit 2007). In this context Chief Rabbi Metzger, speaking of the long history of Jewish communities in India, thanked Hindu leaders for allowing Jews to live in peace in India for 2,000 years and for respecting their right to maintain their distinctive religio-cultural practices without fear of persecution or forced conversion (Report of the Hindu–Jewish Leadership Summit 2007).

A number of the participants in the Hindu–Jewish Leadership Summits discussed more specific affinities between the constitutive components of their respective Hindu and Jewish religious identities: (1) their notions of peoplehood tied to a sacred land, India or Israel, that has found fruition in the modern period in the establishment of independent nation-states; (2) their revealed scriptures, Veda or Torah, that are preserved in their sacred languages, Sanskrit or Hebrew, and are interpreted through hermeneutics; and (3) their dharmic and halakhic injunctions pertaining to purity, diet, ritual observances, and ethical conduct (Report of the Hindu–Jewish Leadership Summit 2007).

In addition to highlighting the affinities between the value systems and practices of their respective communities, Hindu and Jewish leaders at both summits grappled with freighted theological issues concerning whether Hindu notions of divinity are "polytheistic" and whether their forms of worship constitute "idolatry." After serious and sustained discussions, the Declaration of the First Hindu–Jewish Leadership Summit (2007) concluded that both Hindu and Jewish traditions "teach Faith in One Supreme

Being who is the Ultimate Reality . . . and who has communicated Divine ways of action for different peoples in different times and places." The Declaration of the Second Hindu–Jewish Leadership Summit (2008) went even further and asserted, "It is recognized that the One Supreme Being, both in its formless and manifest aspects, has been worshipped by Hindus over the millennia. This does not mean that Hindus worship 'gods' and 'idols.' The Hindu relates to only the One Supreme Being when he/she prays to a particular manifestation."[22]

These two historic Hindu–Jewish Leadership Summits have resulted in the creation of a Standing Committee on Hindu–Jewish Relations and a Hindu–Jewish Scholars Group and have been followed by a series of other meetings, including the International Hindu–Jewish Leadership Dialogue, which convened on June 14, 2009, in New York and was co-hosted by the American Jewish Committee, the Hindu American Foundation, and the Hindu Dharma Acharya Sabha. The most significant fruit of these interreligious encounters between Hindu and Jewish leaders is eloquently framed by Rabbi David Rosen, International Director of Interreligious Affairs of the American Jewish Committee:

> Above all this meeting provided the opportunity . . . to shatter distorted stereotypes and misconceptions that all too often have contributed to keeping the Hindu and Jewish worlds apart. . . . [W]e were part of the beginning of a new historic era of understanding and cooperation between our two faith communities. (Cited in Greenberg 2009: 32)

Notes

1   Goodman's introduction provides a brief survey of previous studies that have attempted to delineate connections between Hindu and Jewish traditions.
2   See also Chatterjee 1997 for an illuminating analysis of a range of socio-political and religious issues addressed by modern Jewish and Hindu thinkers.
3   See also Weil 2004–2005. For an annotated bibliography of publications pertaining to the comparative study of Hindu and Jewish traditions and to the broader field of Indo-Judaic studies, see McClymond forthcoming.
4   In his use of the expression "Europeanization of the earth," Halbfass invokes both Husserl's discussion of the "Europeanization of all foreign parts of mankind" and Heidegger's reflections on the "complete Europeanization of the earth and of mankind." See Halbfass 1988: 167–170, 437, 439–442.
5   This expression derives from Pollock 1993: 114–115.
6   For an analysis of the contributions of Abu-Lughod 1989, Blaut 1993, Hodgson 1993, and Frank 1998, see Holdrege 2010.
7   The term *Hōdû* is derived from the Old Persian *Hind'u*, which in turn derives from *Sindhu*, the Sanskrit designation for the Indus River in the north-western region of the Indian subcontinent.
8   For relevant references, see Chakravarti 2007b: 22; Weinstein 2000: 17–18.
9   In addition to these Biblical and Talmudic references to commodities of Indian origin, the Hebrew Bible explicitly mentions India (Hōdû) once, in Esther 1.1, while the Babylonian Talmud contains six explicit references to India (Weinstein 2000: 16–17).

10   For discussions of the critical importance of the Cairo Geniza archive of letters of Jewish merchants in illuminating "the stellar role of Jewish 'India traders' in commerce with India, especially sea-borne commerce," see Chakravarti 2007b: 33–38; Weinstein 2001. Both scholars wrote their respective articles before Goiten's final work, *India Traders of the Middle Ages: Documents from the Cairo Geniza* (Goiten and Friedman 2007), was available in published form.

11   For an extended study of the three principal Indian Jewish communities, see Katz 2000. For reviews of scholarship on the Cochin Jews, Bene Israel, and Baghdadi Jews, respectively, see Johnson 2007, Weil 2007, and Roland 2007. For a five-part bibliography of publications on Indian Jewry from 1993 to 2001, see Katz and Shulman 1999–2005.

12   For a discussion of the origin narrative of the Cochin Jews, see Katz 1999. After surveying the evidence regarding historical links between India and Israel in the ancient world, Katz concludes that "the Cochin Jews' legend is entirely plausible" (1999: 7).

13   Once numbering around 2,500, most of the Cochin Jews emigrated to Israel after 1950, with only a few remaining on the Malabar Coast today.

14   A number of scholars have raised issues concerning the persistence of Protestant presuppositions and categories in the academic study of religion. See, for example, Neusner 1986: 13–17; Schopen 1991. See also Staal's (1989: 387–419) more general critique of Western paradigms of religious tradition, which he argues are inappropriate for the study of Asian traditions.

15   The format for the sessions of the AAR Comparative Studies in Hinduisms and Judaisms program units has generally included presentations by South Asia specialists and by Judaica specialists, followed by a response that serves to highlight the broader comparative implications of the presentations, especially with respect to their contributions to the re-visioning of certain analytical categories in the study of religion. We have experimented with different formats, all of which are designed to foster collaborative research, including sessions with four complementary papers by specialists in the two traditions, sessions with two papers providing in-depth analyses of a particular theme, and sessions with a mix of comparative papers and joint presentations.

16   For a discussion of the distinctions between embodied communities and missionizing traditions, including a consideration of intermediary cases such as Islamic traditions, see Holdrege 1999. It is important to emphasize that in differentiating between embodied communities and missionizing traditions, I do not mean to suggest a hard dichotomy between mutually exclusive paradigms but rather a *spectrum*, with the ideal types "embodied particularism" and "disembodied universalism" at either end of the spectrum and a range of possible expressions of ethno-cultural specificity in between. On the one hand, as the universalizing teachings of missionizing traditions are appropriated and adapted by different cultures, they of course become embedded in specific ethno-cultural complexes and assume distinctive forms. Hence, among the varieties of "Christianities" and "Buddhisms," we find Spanish Catholics, Irish Catholics, Russian Orthodox, Romanian Orthodox, Chinese Buddhists, Japanese Buddhists, Tibetan Buddhists, and so on. On the other hand, in the course of their history members of embodied communities may move from their homeland – whether through forced exile or voluntary emigration – and, while attempting to maintain their distinctive ethno-cultural identity and their connection with the sacred language and sacred land of their people, at the same time adapt to their host cultures in a variety of different ways. Hence in the long history of the Jewish diaspora, Jewish traditions have assumed variant forms as they have adapted to the local customs of

different gentile cultures – as seen, for example, in the medieval period in the divergent traditions of the Sephardi communities of Spain and the Ashkenazi communities of France and Germany.

17   Howard Eilberg-Schwartz uses this designation for the Jews in his edited collection *People of the Body: Jews and Judaism from an Embodied Perspective* (1992). See also Boyarin 1993. For a brief analysis of Hindu discourses of the body, see Holdrege 1998a. For an extended study, see Holdrege forthcoming.

18   My notion of a "religiously informed body" draws on Bourdieu's (1977, 1990) notion of a "socially informed body" in which the socio-cultural taxonomies of a community are inscribed in the bodies of its constituent members through practice.

19   Heesterman (1993), in his theory of Vedic ritual, posits a "pre-classical" Indo-Aryan sacrifice that preceded the establishment of the "classical" Vedic *śrauta* ritual described in the Brāhmaṇas and Śrauta Sūtras. He is particularly concerned to elucidate the mechanisms through which the "agonistic" pre-classical sacrifice, which was characterized by conflict, violence, and uncertainty, was transformed into the carefully regulated world of Vedic ritualism, which sought to establish an absolute order of perfect peace and stability within the ritual enclosure.

20   For a brief survey of the post-Vedic history of *yajña* as a canonical category in Hindu traditions, see Smith 1989: 202–218. Among relevant papers from our AAR sessions, see in particular Spinner 2000, Lubin 2000, Swartz 2000, and Bornet 2008, which examine a range of discursive strategies through which sacrifice has been re-signified and "re-packaged" in Rabbinic and Brahmanical traditions. The collective fruits of our AAR sessions on sacrifice are presented, along with a number of additional essays, in *Beyond Hubert and Mauss: Reimagining Sacrifice in Hindu and Jewish Traditions*, a forthcoming collection of essays that I am co-editing with Kathryn McClymond.

21   For the reports and declarations of the two summits, see Report of the Hindu–Jewish Leadership Summit 2007; Declaration of the First Hindu–Jewish Leadership Summit 2007; Report of the Second Hindu–Jewish Leadership Summit 2008; Declaration of the Second Hindu–Jewish Leadership Summit 2008. For an illuminating analysis of how encounters between Hindus and Jews reconfigure the phenomenon of inter-religious dialogue in distinctive ways, see Katz 2007.

22   For an analysis of the significance and implications of the two Hindu–Jewish Leadership Summits, particularly with reference to issues of idolatry, see Greenberg 2009.

References

Abu-Lughod, Janet L. *Before European Hegemony: The World System A.D. 1250–1350.* New York: Oxford University Press, 1989.

Abu-Lughod, Janet L. "Middle East–Asian Connections: Before, During, and After European Hegemony." Paper delivered at the Symposium on the Middle East and South Asia: Comparative Perspectives, University of California, Santa Barbara, 2001.

Amin, Samir. *Eurocentrism.* Trans. Russell Moore. New York: Monthly Review Press, 1989.

Blaut, J.M. *The Colonizer's Model of the World: Geographical Diffusionism and Eurocentric History.* New York: Guilford Press, 1993.

Bornet, Philippe. "Comparing Normative Discourses: On Hospitality in Brahmanic and Rabbinical Texts." Paper delivered at the Annual Meeting of the American Academy of Religion, Chicago, Illinois, 2008.

Bornet, Philippe. *Rites et pratiques de l'hospitalité: Mondes juifs et indiens anciens.* Stuttgart: Franz Steiner Verlag, 2010.

Bourdieu, Pierre. *Outline of a Theory of Practice.* Trans. Richard Nice. Cambridge: Cambridge University Press, 1977 [1972].

Bourdieu, Pierre. *The Logic of Practice.* Trans. Richard Nice. Stanford, CA: Stanford University Press, 1990 [1980].

Boyarin, Daniel. *Carnal Israel: Reading Sex in Talmudic Culture.* Berkeley, CA: University of California Press, 1993.

Breckenridge, Carol A., and Peter van der Veer. "Orientalism and the Postcolonial Predicament," in *Orientalism and the Postcolonial Predicament: Perspectives on South Asia,* ed. Carol A. Breckenridge and Peter van der Veer. Philadelphia, PA: University of Pennsylvania Press, 1993: 1–19.

Burkert, Walter. *Homo Necans: The Anthropology of Ancient Greek Sacrificial Ritual and Myth.* Trans. Peter Bing. Berkeley, CA: University of California Press, 1983 [1972].

Chakravarti, Ranabir (ed.). *Trade in Early India.* New Delhi: Oxford University Press, 2001.

Chakravarti, Ranabir. *Trade and Traders in Early Indian Society.* 2nd edn. New Delhi: Manohar, 2007a [2002].

Chakravarti, Ranabir. "Reaching out to Distant Shores: Indo-Judaic Trade Contacts (Up to CE 1300)," in *Indo-Judaic Studies in the Twenty-First Century: A View from the Margin,* ed. Nathan Katz, Ranabir Chakravarti, Braj M. Sinha, and Shalva Weil. New York: Palgrave Macmillan, 2007b: 19–43.

Chatterjee, Margaret. *Studies in Modern Jewish and Hindu Thought.* London: Macmillan, 1997.

Comparative Studies in Hinduisms and Judaisms Group. *American Academy of Religion,* 2012. http://www.aarweb.org/meetings/annual_meeting/Program_Units/PUinformation.asp?PUNum=AARPU117 (accessed January 4, 2013).

Declaration of the First Hindu–Jewish Leadership Summit. *The World Council of Religious Leaders,* 2007. http://www.millenniumpeacesummit.com/1st_Hindu-Jewish_Leadership_Summit_Declaration.pdf (accessed January 4, 2013).

Declaration of the Second Hindu–Jewish Leadership Summit. *The World Council of Religious Leaders,* 2008. http://www.millenniumpeacesummit.com/2nd_Hindu-Jewish_Leadership_Summit_Declaration.pdf (accessed January 4, 2013).

Egorova, Yulia. *Jews and India: Perceptions and Image.* New York: Routledge, 2006.

Egorova, Yulia. "Describing the 'Other,' Describing the 'Self': Jews, Hindu Reformers, and Indian Nationalists," in *Indo-Judaic Studies in the Twenty-First Century: A View from the Margin,* ed. Nathan Katz, Ranabir Chakravarti, Braj M. Sinha, and Shalva Weil. New York: Palgrave Macmillan, 2007: 197–211.

Eilberg-Schwartz, Howard (ed.). *People of the Body: Jews and Judaism from an Embodied Perspective.* Albany: State University of New York Press, 1992.

Frank, Andre Gunder. *ReOrient: Global Economy in the Asian Age.* Berkeley, CA: University of California Press, 1998.

Girard, René. *Violence and the Sacred.* Trans. Patrick Gregory. Baltimore, MD: Johns Hopkins University Press, 1977 [1972].

Goiten, S.D. *A Mediterranean Society: The Jewish Communities of the Arab World as Portrayed in the Documents of the Cairo Geniza.* 6 vols. Berkeley, CA: University of California Press, 1967–1993.

Goiten, S.D. *Letters of Medieval Jewish Traders.* Princeton, NJ: Princeton University Press, 1973.

Goiten, S.D., and Mordechai A. Friedman. *India Traders of the Middle Ages: Documents from the Cairo Geniza.* Leiden: Brill, 2007.

Goodman, Hananya (ed.). *Between Jerusalem and Benares: Comparative Studies in Judaism and Hinduism.* Albany: State University of New York Press, 1994.

Greenberg, Yudit Kornberg. "Hindu–Jewish Summits (2007–2008): A Postmodern Religious Encounter," *Interreligious Insight* 7(1) (2009): 26–39.

Gross, Aaron, and Luke Whitmore (eds.). *Dietary Regulations, Food Transactions, and Social Boundaries in Hindu and Jewish Traditions.* Special issue, *Journal of Indo-Judaic Studies* 13 (2013).

Halbfass, Wilhelm. *India and Europe: An Essay in Understanding.* Albany: State University of New York Press, 1988.

Heesterman, J.C. *The Broken World of Sacrifice: An Essay in Ancient Indian Ritual.* Chicago, IL: University of Chicago Press, 1993.

Hodgson, Marshall G.S. *Rethinking World History: Essays on Europe, Islam, and World History.* Ed. Edmund Burke, III. Cambridge: Cambridge University Press, 1993.

Holdrege, Barbara A. *Veda and Torah: Transcending the Textuality of Scripture.* Albany: State University of New York Press, 1996.

Holdrege, Barbara A. "Body Connections: Hindu Discourses of the Body and the Study of Religion," *International Journal of Hindu Studies* 2(3) (1998a): 341–386.

Holdrege, Barbara A. "Meaningless Ritual, Agonistic Sacrifice, or Ritual Taxonomy? Contending Perspectives in Vedic Studies," *Critical Review of Books in Religion* 1997 (1998b): 59–92.

Holdrege, Barbara A. "What Have Brahmins to Do with Rabbis? Embodied Communities and Paradigms of Religious Tradition," in *Judaism and Asian Religions*, ed. Harold Kasimow, special issue, *Shofar: An Interdisciplinary Journal of Jewish Studies* 17(3) (1999): 23–50.

Holdrege, Barbara A. "Interrogating Sacrifice." Paper delivered at the Annual Meeting of the American Academy of Religion, Denver, Colorado, 2001.

Holdrege, Barbara A. "The Politics of Comparison: Connecting Cultures Outside of and in Spite of the West," *International Journal of Hindu Studies* 14(2–3) (2010): 147–175.

Holdrege, Barbara A. *The Body and the Self: Hindu Contributions to Theories of Embodiment.* Forthcoming.

Holdrege, Barbara A., and Kathryn McClymond (eds.). *Beyond Hubert and Mauss: Reimagining Sacrifice in Hindu and Jewish Traditions.* Forthcoming.

Hollinger, David A. *Postethnic America: Beyond Multiculturalism.* Tenth Anniversary ed. New York: Basic Books, 2006 [1995].

Hollinger, David A. "The Concept of Post-Racial: How Its Easy Dismissal Obscures Important Questions," *Daedalus* (2011): 174–182.

Hubert, Henri, and Marcel Mauss. *Sacrifice: Its Nature and Function.* Trans. W.D. Halls. Chicago, IL: University of Chicago Press, 1964 [1898].

Johnson, Barbara C. "New Research, Discoveries and Paradigms: A Report on the Current Study of Kerala Jews," in *Indo-Judaic Studies in the Twenty-First Century: A View from the Margin*, ed. Nathan Katz, Ranabir Chakravarti, Braj M. Sinha, and Shalva Weil. New York: Palgrave Macmillan, 2007: 129–146.

Kasimow, Harold (ed.). *Judaism and Asian Religions.* Special issue, *Shofar: An Interdisciplinary Journal of Jewish Studies* 17(3) (1999).

Katz, Nathan. "From Legend to History: India and Israel in the Ancient World," in *Judaism and Asian Religions*, ed. Harold Kasimow, special issue, *Shofar: An Interdisciplinary Journal of Jewish Studies* 17(3) (1999): 7–22.

Katz, Nathan. *Who Are the Jews of India?* Berkeley, CA: University of California Press, 2000.

Katz, Nathan. "The State of the Art of Hindu–Jewish Dialogue," in *Indo-Judaic Studies in the Twenty-First Century: A View from the Margin*, ed. Nathan Katz, Ranabir Chakravarti, Braj M. Sinha, and Shalva Weil. New York: Palgrave Macmillan, 2007: 113–126.

Katz, Nathan, Ranabir Chakravarti, Braj M. Sinha, and Shalva Weil (eds.). *Indo-Judaic Studies in the Twenty-First Century: A View from the Margin.* New York: Palgrave Macmillan, 2007.

Katz, Nathan, and Ellen S. Goldberg. "The Ritual Enactments of the Cochin Jews: The Powers of Purity and Nobility," in *Ritual and Power*, ed. Barbara A. Holdrege, special issue, *Journal of Ritual Studies* 4(2) (1990): 199–238.

Katz, Nathan, and Ellen S. Goldberg. *The Last Jews of Cochin: Jewish Identity in Hindu India.* Columbia, SC: University of South Carolina Press, 1993.

Katz, Nathan, and Frank Joseph Shulman (eds.). "Bibliography about Indian Jewry," *Journal of Indo-Judaic Studies* (1999–2005) 2: 113–135 (Part I); 3: 126–132 (Part II);

5: 73–80 (Part III); 6: 79–84 (Part IV); 7–8: 100–105 (Part V).

Katz, Nathan, and Braj Mohan Sinha. "From the Editors," *Journal of Indo-Judaic Studies* 1 (1998): 5.

Lubin, Timothy. "Sacrifice by Other Means II: Brahmanical Strategies." Paper delivered at the Annual Meeting of the American Academy of Religion, Nashville, Tennessee, 2000.

Marks, Richard G. "Hindus and Hinduism in Medieval Jewish Literature," in *Indo-Judaic Studies in the Twenty-First Century: A View from the Margin*, ed. Nathan Katz, Ranabir Chakravarti, Braj M. Sinha, and Shalva Weil. New York: Palgrave Macmillan, 2007: 57–73.

McClymond, Kathryn. "In the Matter of Sacrifice." Paper delivered at the Annual Meeting of the American Academy of Religion, Nashville, Tennessee, 2000.

McClymond, Kathryn. "Death Be Not Proud: Reevaluating the Role of Killing in Sacrifice," *International Journal of Hindu Studies* 6(3) (2002): 221–242.

McClymond, Kathryn. *Beyond Sacred Violence: A Comparative Study of Sacrifice*. Baltimore, MD: The Johns Hopkins University Press, 2008.

McClymond, Kathryn. "Hinduism and Judaism," *Oxford Bibliographies Online: Hinduism*. Forthcoming.

MESAS: Department of Middle Eastern and South Asian Studies. *Emory University: Middle Eastern and South Asian Studies*, 2012. http://mesas.emory.edu/home/index.html (accessed January 4, 2013).

Neusner, Jacob. *Ancient Judaism and Modern Category-Formation: "Judaism," "Midrash," "Messianism," and Canon in the Past Quarter-Century*. Lanham, MD: University Press of America, 1986.

Newby, Gordon D. (ed.). *Encyclopedia of the Middle East and South Asia*. Forthcoming.

Pollock, Sheldon. "Deep Orientalism? Notes on Sanskrit and Power Beyond the Raj," in *Orientalism and the Postcolonial Predicament: Perspectives on South Asia*, ed. Carol A. Breckenridge and Peter van der Veer. Philadel-

phia, PA: University of Pennsylvania Press, 1993: 76–133.

Rabin, Chaim. "Loanword Evidence in Biblical Hebrew for Trade between Tamil Nad and Palestine in the First Millennium B.C.," in *Proceedings of the Second International Conference Seminar of Tamil Studies*, vol. 1, ed. R.E. Asher. Madras: International Association of Tamil Research, 1971: 432–440.

Rabin, Chaim. "Lexical Borrowings from Indian Languages as Carriers of Ideas and Technical Concepts," in *Between Jerusalem and Benares: Comparative Studies in Judaism and Hinduism*, ed. Hananya Goodman. Albany: State University of New York Press, 1994: 25–32.

Report of the Hindu–Jewish Leadership Summit, February 5–7, 2007, New Delhi, India. *The World Council of Religious Leaders*, 2007. http://www.millenniumpeacesummit.com/1st-Hindu-Jewish_Summit_Report-Final.pdf (accessed January 4, 2013).

Report of the Second Hindu–Jewish Leadership Summit, February 17–20, 2008, Jerusalem, Israel. *The World Council of Religious Leaders*, 2008. http://www.millenniumpeacesummit.com/2nd-Hindu-Jewish_Summit_Report-Final.pdf (accessed January 4, 2013).

Reynolds, Dwight F. "The Middle East and South Asia: Comparative Perspectives." Project Prospectus, University of California, Santa Barbara, 2001.

Roland, Joan. "The Baghdadi Jews of India: Perspectives on the Study and Portrayal of a Community," in *Indo-Judaic Studies in the Twenty-First Century: A View from the Margin*, ed. Nathan Katz, Ranabir Chakravarti, Braj M. Sinha, and Shalva Weil. New York: Palgrave Macmillan, 2007: 158–180.

Said, Edward W. *Orientalism*. New York: Vintage Books, 1978.

Schmidt, Frances. "Between Jews and Greeks: The Indian Model," in *Between Jerusalem and Benares: Comparative Studies in Judaism and Hinduism*, ed. Hananya Goodman. Albany: State University of New York Press, 1994: 41–53.

Schopen, Gregory. "Archaeology and Protestant Presuppositions in the Study of Indian Buddhism," *History of Religions* 31(1) (1991): 1–23.

Shulman, David, and Shalva Weil (eds.). *Karmic Passages: Israeli Scholarship on India.* New Delhi: Oxford University Press, 2008.

Smith, Brian K. *Reflections on Resemblance, Ritual, and Religion.* New York: Oxford University Press, 1989.

Spinner, Gregory. "Sacrifice by Other Means I: Rabbinic Strategies." Paper delivered at the Annual Meeting of the American Academy of Religion, Nashville, Tennessee, 2000.

Staal, Frits. *Rules without Meaning: Ritual, Mantras and the Human Sciences.* New York: Peter Lang, 1989.

Strenski, Ivan. "Between Theory and Speciality: Sacrifice in the 90s," *Religious Studies Review* 22(1) (1996): 10–20.

Swartz, Michael D. "Discourses of Sacrifice: On Rabbinic and Vedic Systems of Verbalization of Sacrifice." Paper delivered at the Annual Meeting of the American Academy of Religion, Nashville, Tennessee, 2000.

Weil, Shalva. "The Influence of Indo-Judaic Studies in Israel, or The Salience of Spirituality," *Journal of Indo-Judaic Studies* 7–8 (2004–2005): 5–11.

Weil, Shalva. "On Origins, the Arts, and Transformed Identities: Foci of Research into the Bene Israel," in *Indo-Judaic Studies in the Twenty-First Century: A View from the Margin,* ed. Nathan Katz, Ranabir Chakravarti, Braj M. Sinha, and Shalva Weil. New York: Palgrave Macmillan, 2007: 147–157.

Weinstein, Brian. "Biblical Evidence of Spice Trade between India and the Land of Israel: A Historical Analysis," *Indian Historical Review* 27(1) (2000): 12–28.

Weinstein, Brian. "Jewish Traders In the Indian Ocean – Tenth to Thirteenth Centuries: A Review of Published Documents from the Cairo Genizah," *Journal of Indo-Judaic Studies* 4 (2001): 79–94.

Weinstein, Brian. "Traders and Ideas: Indians and Jews," in *Indo-Judaic Studies in the Twenty-First Century: A View from the Margin,* ed. Nathan Katz, Ranabir Chakravarti, Braj M. Sinha, and Shalva Weil. New York: Palgrave Macmillan, 2007: 44–56.

CHAPTER 26

The Implicit Dialogue of Confucian Muslims

William Chittick and Sachiko Murata

Muslims have lived in China for well over a thousand years, tracing their lineage back to an emissary sent by Muhammad to the emperor. The first historical records of a Muslim presence date back to about 20 years after Muhammad's death, with a mission that arrived at the court in 651. Historians have found no concrete evidence of dialogue between Muslims and Confucians before the seventeenth century, when Muslims began writing about their religion in Chinese. By the end of the nineteenth century they had published several hundred books and treatises in that language, and this literature provides ample evidence that they were engaged in a constant dialogue with Confucianism, even if this seems to have taken place largely within their own books. Little evidence has appeared that the Confucian scholarly elite took notice of the Muslim writings.

The Chinese Islamic literature has sometimes been called by the hybrid word Han Kitāb (Han Qitabu 漢克塔補), the Chinese books. The authors have been called the *Huiru* 回儒, the Muslim literati, because they utilized terms and concepts that reflected the neo-Confucian synthesis brought about by scholars of the Song Dynasty. It is perhaps not without relevance that Zhu Xi (d. 1200), the most famous of the Song scholars, was a contemporary of the greatest of the Muslim synthesizers, Ibn al-'Arabī (d. 1240). The intellectual visions of both masters played major roles in shaping the Huiru worldview.

The movement to express Islamic teachings in Chinese goes back to the mid-sixteenth century, when a group of scholars decided to add the Chinese classics to the traditional Islamic canon. In his study of the history of this school of thought, Zvi Ben-Dor Benite (2005: chapter 1) explains that Hu Dengzhou 胡登洲, who died toward the end of the sixteenth century, undertook to establish a new curriculum that would impart Chinese learning in addition to the usual Arabic and Persian. Having understood that Muslims were becoming ever more ignorant of their own religion, he saw no other way for the ulama to transmit Islamic learning to monolingual Chinese. The

The Wiley Blackwell Companion to Inter-Religious Dialogue, First Edition. Edited by Catherine Cornille.
© 2013 John Wiley & Sons Ltd. Published 2020 by John Wiley & Sons Ltd.

first major literary fruit of this movement appeared in 1642 with a book by Wang Daiyu 王岱輿, who taught in Nanjing and died in Beijing. Called *The Real Commentary on the True Teaching* (*Zhengjiao zhenquan* 正教真詮), it covers the main theoretical and practical teachings of Islam in a thoroughly Confucian idiom. Benite has argued convincingly that Wang Daiyu and other Huiru saw no contradiction between their Islamic and Confucian learning. As he writes, "Chinese Muslim scholarly identity, while dialogically constructed, was one by which these scholars understood themselves as simultaneously Chinese and Muslim" (Benite 2005: 13).

The Islamic Background

Within 80 years of the publication of Wang Daiyu's book, Muslim scholars translated four Persian books on Islamic thought. As far as we know, no other Muslim texts of major theological significance were translated into Chinese before the twentieth century. The first became the most popular source for Islamic teachings in China down into modern times. The original Persian, called *The Path of the Servants from the Origin to the Return* (*Mirṣād al-'ibād min al-mabda' ila'l-ma'ād*), was written by Najm al-Dīn Rāzī (d. 1256), a Sufi teacher of Kubrawī lineage from the city of Rayy (on the outskirts of modern Tehran). At 550 pages it is longer than the other three texts put together. It was translated by Wu Zixian 伍子先, a member of an important scholarly family from Nanjing, with the title *The Fundamentals of the Return to the Real* (*Guizhen yaodao* 歸真要道), and was published in the year 1670.

Two factors were especially important in the choice to translate Rāzī's *Path of the Servants* into Chinese. First, it was recognized throughout the Persianate lands of Islam (from the Ottoman realms into Central Asia, India, and China) as one of the clearest and most comprehensive statements of Islamic teachings and practices in any language. Second, it highlights what Muslims saw as a serious lack in Confucian thought, that is, the refusal to talk explicitly about the beginning and the end, creation and eschatology. The standard terms "origin" and "return" in Rāzī's title show that the overall discussion is framed by the basic Islamic teaching that all manifest reality comes from God and goes back to him.

Rāzī's book is a masterpiece of elegant and straightforward Persian prose. By contrast, the other three translated texts express the same metaphysical vision but with a good deal of technical vocabulary. Muslim scholars probably chose these three, despite their difficulty, because of the help they could provide in formulating a philosophical vision that would rival and even surpass that of neo-Confucianism. Two of them were translated by an influential teacher named She Yunshan 舍蘊善, who flourished during the seventeenth century mainly in Kaifeng (Benite 2005: 51–54). In 1679, he published *The Classic Searching for the Real* (*Yanzhenjing* 研真經), a translation of *The Furthest Goal* (*Maqṣad-i aqṣā*) by 'Azīz Nasafī (d. ca. 1300). Nasafī, like Rāzī, belonged to the Kubrawī lineage of Sufism. The book is a short, clear, and sophisticated presentation of basic theological and cosmological teachings drawn from the two major strands of Islamic theology and metaphysics, and indeed, the two predominant strands down into early modern times. The first of these is theoretical Sufism, whose greatest teacher was

Ibn al-'Arabī, and the second philosophy, whose most influential master was Avicenna (Ibn Sīnā, d. 1037). In several Persian books, of which *The Furthest Goal* is probably the best known, Nasafī was able to simplify and popularize the teachings of both schools of thought, neither of which is known for its clarity of exposition.

She Yunshan also translated a much more difficult book, *Rays of the Flashes* (Ashi"at al-lama'āt), by 'Abd al-Raḥmān Jāmī (d. 1492), a great poet and litterateur and the most influential propagator of the teachings of Ibn al-'Arabī in the Persianate lands of Islam. He gave it the title *The Secret Inquiry into the Original Display* (*Zhaoyuan mijue* 昭元密訣). *Rays of the Flashes* is a commentary on *The Flashes*, a famous book on love by a second generation student of Ibn al-'Arabī, Fakhr al-Dīn 'Irāqī (d. 1289), who wrote it after listening to lectures by Ṣadr al-Dīn Qūnawī (d. 1274), Ibn al-'Arabī's most prolific and influential student. 'Irāqī avoided the complicated philosophical terminology of Ibn al-'Arabī and Qūnawī and expressed the ideas in the traditional imagery of love – made famous in the West by translations of the poetry of Qūnawī's friend Rūmī (d. 1273). In his commentary, Jāmī chose to explain 'Irāqī's points in the metaphysical and philosophical language typical of Ibn al-'Arabī's school of thought. The result is a dense meditation on the Divine Reality. Jāmī's approach must have rewarded careful study, for we note that the fourth book to be translated into Chinese was *Gleams* (*Lawā'iḥ*), his beautifully written short summary of Ibn al-'Arabī's metaphysics and its implications for pursuing the path to God. This appeared in the year 1724, translated by Liu Zhi 劉智, perhaps the greatest of the Huiru, about whom we will speak shortly.

If we dwell at length on these four books, it is because their content and approach throw a good deal of light on the manner in which the Huiru were able to bring about a harmonious marriage between Confucianism and Islam. By focusing on the relatively systematic explanations of Islamic theory and practice developed in the Sufi tradition, they were able to overcome the monumental obstacle faced by anyone who wants to express the teachings of an alien religion in the Chinese language. They were not so naïve as to think that conveying Islamic teachings in the language of the sophisticated intellectual tradition of China could be accomplished simply by translating and analyzing the Qur'an, even if that text is acknowledged by all Muslims as the foundation of the religion. They understood that if they were to transmit the book's message into a language other than Arabic, they would need to begin by explaining its worldview, which is no means self-evident in the book itself. Nor is it clarified by the expositions of Islamic law (the Shariah) written by jurists (*fuqahā'*) or the statements of the creed ('aqīda) written by theologians. Books on law and creed were written for practicing Muslims who wanted to be instructed in how to act correctly and believe rightly. Typical lists of the objects of belief derived from the Qur'an mention God, the angels, the scriptures, the prophets, and the day of resurrection. But what exactly do these words mean? Every thinking person – and the Qur'an frequently urges its readers to reflect on their situation in the world – needs to engage in a quest to understand what he or she believes. In the Qur'an and Islamic thought generally, the semantic fields of faith (*īmān*) and knowledge ('ilm) overlap, so Muslim scholars had little sympathy for "leaps of faith." Explication of the meaning of the objects of belief was the task undertaken by the intellectual tradition, by which we mean the three broad approaches to explaining the nature of things that can be called dialectical theology (*kalām*), theoretical Sufism (*ma'rifa*), and Hellenistic philosophy (*falsafa*), even if clear distinctions among the approaches gradually becomes more difficult to sustain over the course of Islamic history. All three were engaged in the quest to understand exactly what it is that Muslims should believe. Despite their methodological diversity – which is especially obvious before the twelfth century – these schools devoted themselves to explaining the three foundational principles of the religion: *tawḥīd* (the unity of God), prophecy, and the return to God (eschatology).

In the theoretical Sufism that became the dominant intellectual school in much of the Islamic world after the thirteenth century, the three principles were commonly discussed in terms of two basic issues: the Oneness of Being (*waḥdat al-wujūd*) and Perfect Man (*al-insān al-kāmil*). The first issue addresses tawḥīd, the unity of the Ultimate Reality. The second addresses human perfection from two points of view: the prophet as *logos*, that is, the divine archetype of human beings and the universe; and the prophet as the model to be emulated in the quest for God. These two issues provide the backdrop for Huiru thought and are given one of their most succinct and brilliant expositions in Islamic literature by Liu Zhi.

In dealing with issues of theological and philosophical explication – that is, in explaining the concepts in which Muslims are supposed to have faith – the Huiru were faced with the pre-existence of an ancient Chinese civilization represented by highly trained scholars. They had no choice but to take this tradition into account, and they did so by rethinking the Islamic worldview in terms of their own native culture. We need to keep in mind that the Huiru were not new arrivals on the Chinese scene. Unlike the Jesuits, they did not need to learn a foreign language. In contrast to Chinese Christians, they "never configured the relationship between China and Islam as oppositional. Chinese Muslims were natives of China and saw themselves as part of its landscape" (Benite 2005: 169). Nor did they share Matteo Ricci's hostility toward the grand synthesis wrought by the masters of the Song period. They were at ease with the neo-Confucian perspective of "immanent transcendence," as Tu Weiming likes to call it. Their grounding in the philosophical vision of Ibn al-'Arabī and his followers allowed them to read neo-Confucian philosophy as a nearly adequate expression of tawḥīd, the unity of the Ultimate Reality that is the first principle of Islamic thought. Moreover, the goal of Confucian learning – to become a sage – was in complete harmony with the notion of the Perfect Man. Tu Weiming (Murata et al. 2009: 592) – perhaps the only contemporary Confucian to have reflected philosophically on the Huiru perspective – sums up Liu Zhi's accomplishments in these terms:

> Inspired by both the neo-Confucian mode of thinking and Islamic philosophy, he intended to show that his intellectual and spiritual quest led him to conclude that both Confucian and Islamic wisdom point in the same direction and arrive at the same conclusion. His conviction enabled him to conduct one of the most original and systematic inquiries into the "anthropocosmic" vision of the unity between Heaven and Humanity. It seems that he intentionally rejected the strategy of justifying the truth of Islamic faith or the validity of the neo-Confucian worldview in two different languages. He opted for one consistent interpretive process to articulate his philosophy.

Liu Zhi is Chinese through and through. Far from being a missionary doing the work of a foreign church, he looked back to generations of Chinese ancestors and perceived the neo-Confucian vision as his own. As Tu Weiming (Murata et al. 2009: 608) remarks, "The Confucian legacy, like the air he breathed, was the atmosphere in which he found his personal identity." Nonetheless, Liu Zhi tells us that it took him many years to reach the point where he could articulate his synthetic vision: "Having dwelt in seclusion in a mountain forest for ten years, I suddenly came to understand that the Islamic classics have by and large the same purport as Confucius and Mencius" (ibid.: 94).

The Huiru translated books on theoretical Sufism rather than treatises on the Shariah and the creed because they knew that they could not convey the Islamic vision in an alien milieu without explaining the human situation. They translated books that address the big questions of human existence – the nature of reality itself, the structure of the cosmos, the nature of the human self, the purpose of human life. These issues are addressed in Islamic texts not by jurists, who set down the rules and regulations of everyday life, but rather by Sufis, theologians, and philosophers. Works of both philosophy and dialectical theology, however, are characterized by specific technical terminology and sophisticated methodologies that were understood only by a small scholarly elite and did not lend themselves to translation. In contrast, from early times Sufi teachers addressed not only Muslim scholars but also the common people. Unlike theologians and philosophers, who favored technical language and abstract jargon, they explained the imagery and symbolism of the Qur'an in terms of everyday human experience.

Wang Daiyu and Liu Zhi

Despite the lack of evidence for discussions among Muslims and Confucians, the Han Kitāb literature shows that many of the Huiru were engaged in a constant dialogue with Confucian thought. In what follows we look at a few examples from Wang Daiyu and Liu Zhi. If we limit ourselves to these two scholars, it is because other Huiru have not been studied in modern times.

In his two most important works Wang Daiyu follows the lead of many Confucian scholars by treating both Daoism and Buddhism as whipping boys. He is also critical of certain issues in Confucian thought, but not nearly with the same vehemence, and his terminology throughout reflects the language of neo-Confucian scholarship. A salient example of his Confucian orientation can be seen in the title of his short book, *The Great Learning of the Pure and Real* (*Qingzhen daxue* 清真大學, translated by Murata 2000: 81–112). *Great Learning* is the name of one of the four Confucian classics given pride of place in neo-Confucianism, and *Pure and Real* is a common designation for the Islamic tradition.

The first half of the Wang's *Great Learning* addresses tawḥīd in terms of what he and Liu Zhi call the "Three Ones" (*sanyi* 三一), that is, God's unity understood from three standpoints. This discussion, about which more will be said shortly, is based on the Islamic conceptualization of God in three basic ways: negatively in relation to the world, positively without regard to the world, and positively in relation to the world. Thus the divine essence (*dhāt*) is God as known only to himself, the divine names (*asmā'*) and attributes (*ṣifāt*) are God inasmuch as he may be properly described (such as living, knowing, desiring, powerful), and the divine acts (*af'āl*) are attributes of God that can only be understood in relation to the world (such as exalter and abaser, or life-giver and death-giver). In Wang Daiyu's account, the Real One (*zhenyi* 真一) is the divine essence, the Numerical One (*shuyi* 數一) is God inasmuch he has a multiplicity of names and attributes, and the Embodied One (*tiyi* 体一) is God inasmuch as he is humanly embodied in the Human Ultimate (*renji* 人極), the perfect human being who achieves, in the well-known Confucian expression, "one body with heaven, earth, and the ten thousand things."

The second half of Wang's *Great Learning* summarizes the obligations that tawḥīd imposes on human beings and explains why followers of the Three Teachings – Confucianism, Daoism, and Buddhism – fail to perceive tawḥīd adequately or live up to its demands.

Liu Zhi, who seems to have died around 1725, published the first book of what James Frankel calls the Tianfang Trilogy toward the beginning of the eighteenth century and the third some twenty years later, and he also wrote several minor but significant works. The word *tianfang* 天方, direction of heaven or heavenly square, was used to designate the Islamic tradition. The first volume of the trilogy, *Nature and Principle in Islam* (*Tianfang xingli* 天方性理), describes the worldview built on the foundation of tawḥīd and addresses issues that we can call metaphysics, theology, cosmology, and spiritual psychology. The second, *Rules and Proprieties of Islam* (*Tianfang dianli* 天方典禮), explains the rationale for Islamic praxis in a manner similar to Rāzi's *Path of God's Servants*, but in no way like the detailed manuals of jurisprudence that Muslim scholars were wont to produce in Arabic and Persian. The third, *The True Record of the Utmost Sage of Islam* (*Tianfang zhisheng shilu* 天方至聖實錄), describes the Prophet as embodying the teachings, practices, ethos, and character traits explained in the first two volumes.

Both Western and Chinese scholars have recognized Liu Zhi as the outstanding representative of the Huiru. He is the only author of the school whose major works have been studied with any care in the Western literature. The American missionary Isaac Mason published an abbreviated translation of the third volume of the trilogy as *The Arabian Prophet* (1921). We published a study and translation of the first volume as *The Sage Learning of Liu Zhi* (2009) and James Frankel devoted a thoughtful study to the second volume in *Rectifying God's Name* (2011). Frankel describes how Liu Zhi was able to present the Islamic perspective as an authentic continuation of the ancient wisdom of the sage kings and to illustrate the concordance of Islamic social, legal, and ritual teachings with those of Confucianism. Among all the Huiru books, it is this second volume that was noticed by Confucian scholars, precisely, Frankel suggests, because it focuses on social harmony rooted in the five constant virtues, the framework of Confucian social theory. This is not to imply, however, that Liu Zhi ignored the profound Islamic basis for attention to ritual and society, quite the contrary. His introductory chapters on the cosmological and psychological significance of ritual and social harmony show a rare skill in applying the abstract issues of Islamic metaphysics, as discussed in the first volume of the trilogy, to the practical considerations of life in the world.

Liu Zhi situates his Tianfang Trilogy in the Confucian context by the very title he gives to the first volume: *Nature and Principle in Islam*. "The learning about nature and principle" (*xingli xue* 性理學) is a name of the neo-Confucian perspective, clearly because of the prominence given to the two terms. Scholars have sometimes considered *xingli*, nature and principle, a compound word meaning philosophy, but to translate it this way would ignore the central importance of both concepts in Liu Zhi's book. Moreover, "philosophy" in Islamic studies is used for the specific school of thought that traces its origins back to the Greeks, and there is little trace of philosophy in this technical sense in Liu Zhi's book or in Huiru literature generally.

It is worth dwelling on the meaning of *xing* and *li* as understood by both Liu Zhi and Wang Daiyu, not least because their treatment of the terms reflects their efforts at understanding Confucian thought in a manner that would betray neither tradition. Moreover, their reading suggests that historians of Confucianism may gain some insights into neo-Confucian thought by studying the Huiru writings. This can provide one example of what Tu Weiming means when he says that *Nature and Principle in Islam* "will broaden the philosophical horizons of Confucian thinkers and compel Chinese intellectual historians to reexamine their underlying assumptions about the Three Teachings" (Murata et al. 2009: 617).

If we follow the standard interpretations of the terms xing and li offered by Sinologists and most contemporary Chinese scholars, we will surely conclude that Confucianism has few traces of religious thinking – if by "religion" we mean the theological teachings so prominent in the pre-modern West and in Islam. Indeed, since the Enlightenment, much of Western literature has portrayed Confucianism as a social philosophy that has no use for the notion of God. We can see this view prefigured in the writings of Matteo Ricci, who criticized the neo-Confucian use of the word principle to designate the Great Ultimate (*taiji* 太極), for, he said, the notion of principle does not allow for intelligence and consciousness (Frankel 2011: 173). The great historian of Chinese science Joseph Needham took a similar line. According to him, Confucianism "had no room for souls," or spirits, or anything smacking of the supernatural (Needham 1954–2004: 2: 475). The Huiru, however, offered another reading of nature and principle. Both Wang Daiyu and Liu Zhi employed nature, *xing*, to translate the Arabic word spirit (*rūḥ*) or sometimes soul (*nafs*), and they used principle, *li*, to render the words intellect (*'aql*) and soul. These three quasi-synonymous Arabic words are used throughout Islamic literature to designate the invisible, subtle reality of the human self, which is the locus of awareness, consciousness, and free will. The three terms come up constantly in any discussion of the relationship between God and man. If we translate the title of Liu Zhi's *Nature and Principle* into Arabic in a manner that would accord with his understanding of these words and the typical Arabic style of the time, it would give us something like *Kitāb al-rūḥ*, "The Book of the Spirit" (which happens to be the title of a well-known book by a fourteenth century theologian, Ibn Qayyim al-Jawziyya). Muslims who see this Arabic title would suppose that *Nature and Principle in Islam* is dealing with issues of theology and spiritual psychology, which are precisely the topics of Liu Zhi's book.

The Huiru were well aware of Confucius's reticence in talking about God or supernatural beings. Wang Daiyu remarks on it in his *Real Commentary on the True Teaching* in a chapter called "Nature and Mandate" (*xingming* 性命). Mandate is another term basic to Confucian thought and central to Huiru thinking. Wang begins the chapter by citing a saying of the Sage (*sheng* 聖), that is, Muhammad: "If you see your nature completely, then you can see the Lord." The original Arabic text reads, "He who recognizes his own soul (nafs) recognizes his Lord." Wang Daiyu explains this to mean, "To know this body is to know the Real Lord's creation and transformation. To see this nature is to see the Real Lord's mysterious mechanism" (Wang 1921: 1: chapter 11). He then remarks that Confucius rarely spoke about nature, nor did he say much about *ren*, the primary Confucian virtue, a word translated variously as humanity, humaneness, benevolence, goodness, and authentic human nature. Wang says that it was Confucius's grandson (that is, Zisi 子思) who first spoke about nature explicitly, at the very beginning of *The Doctrine of the Mean* (*Zhongyong* 中庸): "What Heaven mandates is nature; following nature is the Dao." These two sentences, he says, "are the great origin of the Learning of the Principles," that is, neo-Confucianism, "but unfortunately, they are difficult to penetrate thoroughly." To illustrate this he cites different interpretations of nature offered by Mencius, Xunzi, Hanzi, Chengzi, and others. Finally he turns to an explanation of nature and mandate that accords with Islamic teachings.

Wang Daiyu is by no means as clear and systematic as Liu Zhi, but once we compare the interpretations of nature, principle, and mandate offered by the two authors, we can see that they agree on the meanings of the words and are both drawing from Rāzī and Nasafī. Briefly, the Real Lord brings the universe into existence by issuing the mandate, which is the divine command (*amr*) mentioned in many Qur'anic verses, such as, "His only command, when He desires a thing, is to say to it 'Be!,' and it comes to be" (36: 82). The universe comes forth as a series of descending levels. Once manifestation reaches its lowest point, which is called prime matter (*hayūlā*) in Islamic philosophy and vital-energy (*qi* 氣) in Confucian thought, the creative flow reverses its direction and heads back toward the Origin. Muslim scholars call these two movements the Origin and the Return, or the Descending Arc and the Ascending Arc, and they describe the overall situation of the cosmos as "the circle of existence" (*dā'irat al-wujūd*).

Both Wang Daiyu and Liu Zhi designate the two arcs as the Former Heaven (*xiantian* 先天) and the Latter Heaven (*houtian* 後天). In Confucian thought, there is a good deal of debate about the meaning of these two terms. Typically, however, the Former Heaven is understood as the situation of the universe before manifestation and the Latter Heaven as its situation now that it has become manifest. As Liu Zhi explains with the help of a series of diagrams, the Descending Arc represents a movement from invisibility to visibility, from consciousness to unawareness, from light to darkness. When God issues the mandate, the first reality to appear is the World of Principles (*lishi* 理世), called in Arabic by names such as the World of Spirits. This world has fourteen basic levels (which Liu Zhi takes from Nasafī), representing the movement of spiritual realities from unity to multiplicity. The first level, which contains all the succeeding levels as potentialities of manifestation, is called the Nature of Continuity (*jixing* 繼性) or the Nature of the Utmost Sage (*zhishengxing* 至聖性). The first term translates the Arabic expression "the Ascribed Spirit" (*al-rūḥ al-iḍāfī*), which refers to the Qur'anic verse in which God says, "I blew into him [i.e., Adam] of My spirit" (15: 29), thus "ascribing" the human spirit to Himself. The second translates the common expression "the Muhammadan Spirit" (al-rūḥ al-muḥammadī), which is one of the many names used to refer to the Ascribed Spirit.

Liu Zhi explains that each of the fourteen descending levels of the World of Principles is more differentiated than the preceding level. "Nature" and "principle" designate the two basic sorts of spiritual realities present in this world. Following a standard neo-Confucian interpretation, he says that the two words have the same meaning, but natures designate principles that become manifest as selves, and principles designate natures that become manifest as things. Within the World of Principles itself the fourteen natures extend from the Nature of the Utmost Sage down through the natures of other sorts of sages, worthies, ordinary humans, animals, and plants, minerals, and the vast sediment. The fourteen corresponding levels of principle designate the spiritual realities lying behind the descending levels of manifestation represented in the Latter Heaven by the nine celestial spheres, the four elements, and vital-energy. In the first and fourteenth levels, nature and principle are undifferentiated. The first level of principle, called Aershi (Arabic 'arsh, meaning Throne of God), is identical with the Nature of the Utmost Sage, and the fourteenth level of principle, the vast sediment, is identical with the fourteenth level of nature, vital-energy.

None of this differentiation becomes manifest until the Latter Heaven, in the form of what Liu Zhi calls the World of Images (xiangshi 象世). This is the realm of the Ascending Arc, in which all things are traveling back toward their Origin, moving from darkness to light, unawareness to consciousness, differentiation to unity, and visibility to invisibility. In the World of Images we see that at each succeeding level – minerals, plants, animals, ordinary humans, believers, worthies, sages – interior powers like knowledge, awareness, consciousness, wisdom, compassion, and love come to be more fully actualized. The final goal of the universe is achieved when human beings, in the person of sages and worthies, return to the Origin with full awareness of the entire Circle of Existence, thereby achieving one body with heaven, earth, and the ten thousand things.

This, in brief, is the anthropocosmic vision offered by the Huiru, a vision which, in its overall contours, is congenial with both Islamic and Confucian cosmology and spiritual psychology. The purpose of describing reality in these terms is to allow people to understand where they stand in relation to God, heaven, earth, and the ten thousand things. Only on the basis of such an understanding can they set out to become sages, that is, to achieve the perfection of the human state that is the explicit goal in both theoretical Sufism and Islamic philosophy. In both Islam and Confucianism, this quest is profoundly intellectual, but it demands the transformation of the whole being. Tu Weiming (Murata et al. 2009: 596) describes what the quest for perfection involves in these terms:

> Liu was firmly convinced that his quest for Truth and Reality is an intrinsic value independent of any instrumental or strategic missionary considerations. His *Nature and Principle* is intended to show that his faith in Islam must transcend any distorted or partial representation. Rather, it is based on a worldview that offers an adequate understanding of what Truth and Reality is. Ontological insight rather than empirical investigation is the proper

method for grasping this. . . . It involves not only the brain and mind but also the heart and body. It is inexorably a transformative act. . . . It is the outcome of multifaceted intellectual reflection, rigorous spiritual exercise, persistent meditation, and profound rumination. As a form of experiential understanding, it is neither private nor subjective. Indeed, it is diametrically opposed to subjectivism and solipsism, but not at all in conflict with objectivity, disinterestedness, and impartiality.

Another salient example of the Huiru engagement with important notions of neo-Confucian thought can be found in the manner in which Wang Daiyu and Liu Zhi discuss divine unity, tawḥīd, even if they do not employ the Arabic word. As the first principle of Islamic faith, tawḥīd is given prominence in all branches of Islamic thought, though theoretical Sufism offers the most elaborate expositions of its demands on being human in the world. Both Wang Daiyu and Liu Zhi take care to differentiate the Islamic notion of unity from parallel notions found in Confucianism and Daoism. Wang Daiyu, for example frequently speaks about the three Ultimates – the Non-Ultimate (wuji 無極), the Great Ultimate (taiji 太極), and the Human Ultimate (renji 人極) – notions derived partly from Daoism and much discussed in neo-Confucianism, ever since the famous diagram of Zhou Dunyi 周敦頤 (d. 1073) (Kalton 1988: 37–42; Wing 1963: 463–64). Wang Daiyu claims that the Confucian scholars who spoke of the three ultimates failed to grasp that all three are aspects of the "Numerical One" (shuyi 數一), which is the face of the Real One (zhenyi 真一) gazing in the direction of creation and transformation.

The distinction between God's real unity and numerical unity is commonly made in Islamic texts, but Wang Daiyu's explanation seems thoroughly Chinese. He writes (1921: 1: chapter 1): "The Non-Ultimate is the beginning of the ten thousand formless things, and the Great Ultimate is the beginning of the ten thousand formed things." In other words, the Non-Ultimate is the One inasmuch as it is the beginning of the World of Principles, and the Great Ultimate is the One inasmuch as it is the origin of the World of Images. He goes on to explain (ibid.: 1: chapter 2) that these two cosmic ultimates are embraced by the Human Ultimate, which is the uncreated reality of Muhammad or the Numerical One in divinis (what Christian theologians would call the logos). The Numerical One per se, however, is simply the function (yong 用) of the Root Substance (benti 本體), which is the Real One. Concerning the Human Ultimate as the Utmost Sage, he writes (ibid.: 1: chapter 7):

> Know that the Utmost Sage is he whose substance is the Non-Ultimate and whose function is the Great Ultimate. The two wings [yin and yang] are his differentiated display and the four seasons his alteration and transformation. Heaven and earth are his covering and his carrying, and the ten thousand things are put in good order by him.

Like Wang Daiyu, Liu Zhi employs the term Human Ultimate to refer to the Perfect Man, but instead of talking about the Three Ultimates, he focuses on the Three Ones (a notion not much developed by Wang Daiyu). In the process he shows his mastery of the metaphysical exposition of tawḥīd as developed by Ibn al-ʿArabī's followers. Briefly, he explains that the Real One is the Root Substance, the Divine Essence, standing beyond comprehension by anything other than itself. The Numerical One is the function of the Root Substance, or God inasmuch as he possesses many names and attributes. The Embodied One is the Human Ultimate, the Perfect Man and fully realized sage, who has achieved one body with heaven, earth, and the ten thousand things. It is through the perfect harmony of the Three Ones that all things reach their full manifestation and realization. Thus, for example, Liu Zhi writes as follows about the Real One:

> Thus we know that it is One but also three. It is three and cannot not be three. That which is three and cannot not be three is the Real One's own act of hiding and manifesting.

> The world is where the three Ones lodge as a whole and where pervading can be manifest. Outside the world there is a world, and that is the world of the Real Principle. Inside the world there is a world, and that is the world of the Human Ultimate.

> Without the world of heaven and earth, the world of the Human Ultimate would have no assistance. Without the world of the Human Ultimate, the world of the Real Principle would have no position. Without the world of the Real Principle, the world of the Human Ultimate and the world of heaven and earth would have no way of becoming manifest by themselves. Thus the being of the world is a being that cannot not be. The being that cannot not be is the Real One's own act of hiding and manifesting.

A Note on Recent Developments

Given the prominence of dialogue among religions in modern times, it is not surprising that there have been attempts to initiate dialogue among Muslims and Confucians. One salient example is provided by Tu Weiming, from 1996 to 2008 the director of the Harvard-Yenching Institute and one of the foremost representatives of what some would call "New Confucianism." In 1993, his Harvard colleague Samuel Huntington showed him a draft of his paper, "Clash of Civilizations," and Tu passed it on to his good friend Seyyed Hossein Nasr, one of the foremost scholars of Islam in North America.

Tu's discussions with Nasr about Huntington's paper led to a series of conferences dedicated to Confucian–Islamic dialogue, most notably one held in Kuala Lumpur in 1995, at which Anwar Ibrahim was the keynote speaker, and four held in China between 2002 and 2010, sponsored by the Harvard-Yenching Institute and various Chinese universities, with much of the organizational work done by Professor Hua Tao of Nanjing University. Most of the participants in the China conferences were Chinese scholars of Islam, and all were grateful to have this relatively high-profile opportunity to discuss their work. Papers ranged over a great variety of issues, relatively few of them touching directly on the Huiru. Most of the presentations reflected the official emphasis of recent years on the social sciences, with contributions from historians, anthropologists, sociologists, and political scientists dealing with the Muslim experience of living in Chinese society. Few on the Muslim side had any more than a rudimentary familiarity with Islamic theology and philosophy, in contrast to their Huiru ancestors, but they were happy to have the opportunity to talk about social and ethical issues. The four conferences seem to have established a clear awareness of the need for Muslims and

Confucians to discuss their common issues, and all signs point to a continuation of such endeavors in the future.

Bibliography

Algar, Hamid. *The Path of God's Bondsmen from Origin to Return*. Delmar, NY: Caravan Books, 1982.

Benite, Zvi Bendor. *The Dao of Muhammad: A Cultural History of Muslims in Late Imperial China*. Cambridge, MA: Harvard University Asia Center, 2005.

Chittick, William C. and P.L. Wilson. *Fakhruddin 'Iraqi: Divine Flashes*. New York: Paulist Press, 1982.

Frankel, James. *Rectifying God's Name: Liu Zhi's Confucian Translation of Monotheism and Islamic Law*. Honolulu: University of Hawai'i Press, 2011.

Kalton, Michael. *To Become a Sage*. New York: Columbia University Press, 1988.

Mason, Isaac. *The Arabian Prophet: A Life of Mohammed from Chinese and Arabic Sources, a Chinese-Moslem Work by Liu Chia-lien*. Shanghai: Commercial Press, 1921.

Murata, Sachiko. *Chinese Gleams of Sufi Light: Wang Tai-yü's Great Learning of the Pure and Real and Liu Chih's Displaying the Concealment of the Real Realm*. Albany: State University of New York Press, 2000.

Murata, Sachiko, Chittick, William C., and Tu Weiming. *The Sage Learning of Liu Zhi: Islamic Thought in Confucian Terms*. Cambridge, MA: Harvard University Asia Center, 2009.

Needham, Joseph. *Science and Civilisation in China*. Cambridge: Cambridge University Press, 1954–2004.

Ridgeon, Lloyd. *Persian Metaphysics and Mysticism: Selected Treatises of 'Azīz Nasafī*. Richmond, Surrey: Curzon, 2002.

Wang Daiyu 王岱興. *Zhengjiao zhenquan* 正教真詮. Beijing, 1921 (and many other editions).

Wing Tsit-Chan. *A Source Book in Chinese Philosophy*. Princeton, NJ: Princeton University Press, 1963.

CHAPTER 27

A Confucian–Jewish Dialogue

Galia Patt-Shamir and Ping Zhang

The way, as *dao* or as *halakha*, begins in one's dwelling. In both Confucianism and Judaism, the way is described in terms of human relations, based on family ethics (Goldman 1995: 341). While recognition of the centrality of family is crucial for beginning a dialogue between these two traditions, differences in the understanding of family reverence emerge as the dialogue goes on, and show the uniqueness of each tradition. Unlike other inter-religious dialogues in this volume, it is important for us to note that no actual historical example of a dialogue of the kind we suggest here is to be found. Since the two traditions dwell in widely separate geographical locations, they engaged each other in no important conflicts, and encounters started no earlier than the seventh or eighth century CE. However, the encounter did not bring up engagement in true dialogue, as we show hereafter.

And yet, Confucian–Jewish dialogue is an actual practice for us, as co-authors and colleagues in the same department in Tel-Aviv University. When we met for the first time, we realized that as new faculty members, we share a (rather small) office in the Humanities building. We soon learned that while one of us is Confucian by tradition and Jewish by academic education, the other is Jewish by tradition and Confucian by academic education, and that despite the differences we share academic and practical interests. The dialogue is thus twofold, for each of us: First, a "dialogical understanding" is inherent in each of our ways of understanding. On the one hand each of us researches a tradition that is foreign to her or his own, while on the other hand we are both aware that one can understand ideas of a foreign culture only within the limits of one's own thought, and the limits are conditioned by context. Second, when we discuss ideas such as the value of learning, the accomplished personality, or the significance of the family, each of the inner dialogical understandings interacts with the other, to create yet a new, broader dialogue.

In this paper we conjure an experimental dialogue between Confucianism and Rabbinical Judaism. In the first part of the essay, we discuss one historical example of a

The Wiley Blackwell Companion to Inter-Religious Dialogue, First Edition. Edited by Catherine Cornille.
© 2013 John Wiley & Sons Ltd. Published 2020 by John Wiley & Sons Ltd.

Confucian–Jewish dialogue. In the second part of the paper we discuss the traditions' modes of theological development as "spiritual harmony" in Confucianism, as opposed to "spiritual disharmony in Judaism" (Patt-Shamir 2006)[1] and locate a common ground between the two traditions in the theme of family reverence. It is important for us to stress that by "spiritual harmony" and "spiritual disharmony" we do not imply any evaluative weight. We rather use the terms as referring back to basic inclinations for understanding world structure as well as the spur for action. While the perfection of God is by definition transcendental and thus not to be completely reached, the perfection of Way is broadened by human beings (*Analects* 15: 28). In the third part, we imagine a dialogue based on family reverence as our point of departure in understanding the uniqueness of each tradition. Our purpose is to acknowledge the differences, and to find likenesses within stark dissimilarity. We believe that only thus can a dialogue be created.

A Historical Note: A Confucian–Jewish Dialogue in Kaifeng Community

The most important example of a Confucian–Jewish encounter that brought up a significant outcome is Chinese Jews, who naturally adapted Confucian ideas to understand Judaic ones. Isolated communities developed until the nineteenth century CE around Shanghai, Harbin, and, most notably, in Kaifeng (Ember et al. 2004; Eber 2007). The shared views of Judaism and Confucianism, in particular regarding the role of the family, caused Jews in China to demonstrate flexibility in *halakhic* notions, and adapt their inherited tradition to the local ones, even if "flexibility" appears as heresy to non-Chinese Jews. In her work on the Kaifeng Jewish community, Irene Eber reveals the unexpected fact that the earliest monotheistic religion of the "West" and this ancient nontheistic tradition of the "East" share important values (Eber 1993). In particular, Jewish believers assimilated the Confucian *dao* with the Jewish *halakha*, creating a "Confucio-Jewish" faith with reference to religious scriptures from both traditions (Leslie 1972; Eber 1999).

It was usual in the Chinese-Jewish community to refer to the *Book of Mencius* (*Mengzi*) for moral ideas, to the *Book of Changes* (*Yijing*) for metaphysical issues, and to the *Records of Rites* (*Liji*) for behavioral codes. Moreover, Kaifeng Jews named their religion *tiandao*, or "the way of heaven," which was the Confucians' term for their tradition. Also, following a tradition of "matching meanings" (or "categorizing meanings" *geyi*), which was accepted in China, they applied a "creative interpretation" to identify Adam with Bangu, China's mythical first human creature – specifically as the father of the patriarch Abraham. In this spirit *Dao* served to denote the Jewish moral code and its practice, as well as the Book, the word, and the transmission. The Chinese term "heaven" (*tian*) was most commonly used for God, thereby softening the monotheistic impact on Chinese readers (Leslie 1972: 96). Other terms borrowed from Confucianism included the "five relationships" (*wulun*), to denote the basic fabric of the desired society; the "five constant virtues" (*wuchang*), to describe the fundamental moral values; and "virtue" (*de*), for understanding human moral potentiality and the ideal human personality. The name originally used for Chinese classics – *jing* – was applied in the community to Jewish scriptures as well.

Recognition of the affinity of the Jewish and Confucian forms of life is seen in written documents through an exposition of the shared history of humanity, unifying biblical allusions with Chinese religions:

> From the time of Noah and the transformation, enlightened men in western India have sought the basic principle, which created Heaven and Earth and Man;

> From the time of Abraham and the founding of the religion, men of China have spread religion, and obtained complete knowledge of Confucianism, Buddhism, and Daoism. (Shen Quan's inscription, *ibid.* 1972: 101)

In addition to the general tendency to integrate Jewish traditional beliefs with Chinese myths, more explicit attempts were made to demonstrate the similarity between Confucianism and Judaism:

> The Confucian religion and this religion agree on essential points, differing only on secondary ones . . . these principles do not go beyond the Five Relationships. Although the written characters of the scriptures of this religion are different from the script of Confucian books, yet on examining their principles, it is found that their ways of common practice are similar. (*ibid.*: 102)

The inscription cited above, in fact, presupposes an agreement between Confucianism and Judaism regarding major issues, without even having a need to explain, while the differences are agreed as "secondary" only. The inscription then, goes on to stress the Jewish moral code as a direct extension of the five relationships (ruler–minister, father–son, husband–wife, siblings, friends), in particular the love of father to son and the reverence of son to father, as well as the sovereign's benevolence to the subject and the subject's submissiveness to the sovereign. In the minds of Chinese Jews, the two traditions differ in their details alone, and share basic tenets such as rootedness in history, strict guidance for practice, admiration for know-how, valuing education and learning, family centeredness, honoring human relationships, a powerful will to survive, and a capacity to endure hardship (Goldman 1995: 329–365, 330–331).

The most important principles in Confucianism and Judaism, which accordingly were used interchangeably in the Kaifeng Jewish community, were family reverence, ritual practice and its moral significance, and reliance on oral tradition and the written word. Kaifeng Jews focused in particular on the Jewish *Yizkor* (memorial prayer) and *Yartzeit* (remembering anniversary) services for dead family members as close in spirit to Chinese ancestor worship, and they gave the services a Confucian interpretation (Leslie 1972: 101). They practiced "ancestor worship" by kneeling before the spirits of their ancestors twice a year, and making offerings to them of fruit, candy, and meat (not necessarily kosher). In particular, Heaven was coupled with reverence (*jing*), and reverence for Heaven was closely bound up with ancestral honoring (*zun*). In this way, family reverence (*xiao*) was introduced as a major religious constituent, conforming to both Jewish and Confucian ideals (Eber 1993: 244).

The Framework for Dialogue

Spiritual harmony vs. spiritual disharmony

Imagining a dialogue between Confucianism and Rabbinic Judaism, we confront in the traditions two different, and to some extent contradictory, understandings of the world. Confucians believe that the world is by nature harmonious, and harmony is the ideal of the social world. Rabbinic Judaism holds that the world is disharmonious by nature, and thus the theological method values contention. In other words not only does this disharmony motivate us, it necessarily has to be preserved. The disharmony of the universe can be seen in Biblical stories such as the creation of the world in an evolving act of separation; the expulsion of Adam and Eve from the Garden of Eden; or the necessary failure in building the Tower of Babel, which ended the dream of unifying the human world and the world of God forever (Patt-Shamir 2006: 167–240). To understand these polar frameworks, let us look briefly at some of its implications in sources from each tradition.

In Confucian *Yanzichunqiu* 7.5, Yanzi[2] says:

> Harmony is analogous to a stew. The cook uses water, fire, vinegar, minced meat sauce, salt and sour plum to cook fish and meat over firewood. The cook harmonizes these ingredients and orchestrates them by means of flavors. He accentuates the slight and attenuates the excessive. When a man of noble character consumes it, it calms his heart (Ariel, ms.).[3]

Rabbinic Judaism also uses foods as metaphors to discuss its most important classics, as Talmud Tractate Soferim says in chapter 15:

> Scriptures have been compared to water, the Mishnah to wine, and the Shas[4] to spiced-wine. The world cannot exist without water, it cannot exist without wine, and it cannot exist without spiced-wine; but a rich man enjoys all three of them. (Soncino Talmud, Soferim, Chapter 15, rule 7–8)

The Confucian text is similar to the Talmudic in its metaphors, but also in admitting and respecting the disparate elements involved. Still, the differences between the two perspectives are obvious and profound. In Confucianism, water, salt, and other ingredients generate a higher concept of the whole, namely the stew; in the Talmudic text they remain separate. This higher concept in Confucianism, which is called harmony (*he*), has a function that none of its individual ingredients can achieve, so all of them together, however different, constitute the whole and serve a single purpose. Jewish classics, namely Scripture, Mishnah, and Shas, do not produce a higher all-inclusive concept whose function is not found in any of the three, although Shas does include the other two in part or in whole.

Harmony then is a kind of "emergence" (Corning 2002) which, according to Confucianism, is *Tianrenheyi*, the interaction between Heaven and mankind as generating the one. Rabbinic Judaism describes no such emergence, but rather an unbridgeable gap between "the unified one" as God, and humankind.

Argumentative dialogue vs. inclusive dialogue

The values of spiritual harmony and spiritual disharmony influence the understanding of the relationship with the transcendental unitary entity, but also shape our patterns of communication and the possibility of dialogue.

In *Yazichunqiu*, after the passage cited above, Yan Zi further explains how the different parts of the stew should interact in the framework of harmony:

> So it is with rulers and ministers. The ruler approves a policy which contains unacceptable elements. The minister should point these out in order to make the approved policy successful. Alternatively, the ruler rejects a policy which contains acceptable elements. The minister should point these out in order to shed the unacceptable. Therefore the government is stable, is free from offences, and there is no bickering amongst the people. (Ariel ms.)

In a harmonious dialogical framework, parties who hold different opinions usually reach a clear and definite conclusion in accordance with the aspiration for social harmony. For harmonists, whatever the argument, some right answers to the questions must exist, and the dialogue leads its various participants to its resolution. While the different roles of the various parties – ruler and subject, father and son, etc. – persist, their viewpoints are bound to become one at the end of the dialogue. In this type of dialogue an essentially different viewpoint must be accommodated within the general framework at hand. Such a dialogue is "inclusive," where all parties gather under the roof of the whole and each of them, while engaging in dialogue with others, is responsible for that whole.

In a spiritual disharmonious framework, dialogue takes a form of "creative contention," that is to say argumentation is oriented toward theological difference and nuance, while differences can be held in abayance across centuries. Hence, it takes place among various parties, but not necessarily under a common roof. Participants respond to one another with reference to transcendence and the law rather than in direct relatedness among themselves. Such a dialogue is argumentative, and does not aim to reach a definite conclusion. Some practical agreements may be elaborated, but none of these is the final right answer to the question, if such an answer exists at all (see Rappel 1979: 11).

Family reverence as common ground

Therefore our main question is how we can conduct a dialogue between two traditions containing ideas so different regarding the practice of dialogue itself. How can we align the two traditions when one seeks an integrated emergence, while the other tries to remain independent? How can dialogue progress when one wants to reach a definite conclusion, while another wants primarily to list all possibilities?

For such an experimental dialogue we would like to find a platform which centers on a value that both traditions share such that the different understandings of the nature of the world and the nature of dialogue can highlight the uniqueness of each tradition rather than creating an impediment for discourse. We suggest family reverence as that platform.

By "family reverence" we refer to Confucian *xiao* and Jewish *kibbud horim*, both generally incorrectly rendered as "filial piety." Chinese *xiao* signifies a more open and undefined family feeling, which includes expressions of empathy and practices of care and honor. Roger Ames and Henry Rosemont reject the use of "filial piety" in the Confucian context (Ames and Rosemont 2006: 1). They discard the sanctimonious overtones of "piety," which are absent from *xiao*, and suggest "family reverence" instead. Our decision to extend the use of this phrase to the Jewish context rests on two foundations. First, we want to imply the existence of important common ground in the Chinese and Hebrew terms. Second, "filial piety," with its mostly Christian connotation, does not capture the idea of the Hebrew *kibbud horim*, which literally means "honoring parents" as implied in "reverence."

Moreover, the parents–children relationship involves the very first and unavoidable dialogue for most people in this world. People's behavior in this relationship largely expresses their basic notions of handling the differences between people and of connecting to each other. Lastly, family reverence is pivotal in the ethical systems of Confucianism and Rabbinic Judaism alike. In the former, family reverence is the central value which generates other values. In the latter it is the fifth of the Ten Commandments, and the very first commandment addressing inter-human relationships.

If we can conduct a successful dialogue between the two traditions on such a crucial topic, it may well mean that we can also expand the dialogue to other themes in these two traditions, and understand more about the nature and the strategies of such a dialogue.

Accordingly, in the following pages we try to find common ground between the traditions for conducting a dialogue. We wish to show how we can understand each other despite essential differences. After all, inter-religious dialogue is in part about how we can overcome the obstacles erected by our different concepts of dialogue itself.

A Dialogue Based on Family Reverence

Family reverence: natural feeling vs. commandment

Let us imagine a Confucian and a Jewish sage meeting to learn from each other. Assume that, looking for a starting point for their discussion, they choose the virtue of family reverence. The first issue they might wish to address is the source of this virtue. What makes one filial? Do we choose to be filial or is it enforced on us? Interestingly, both our discussants would agree that family reverence is not a moral choice that one makes but a necessary attitude to life. However, the roots of this necessity are quite different.

In the first chapter of *The Book of Family Reverence*, we read:

> Your physical person with its hair and skin are received from your parents. Vigilance in not allowing anything to do injury to your person is where family reverence begins; distinguishing yourself and walking the proper way (*dao*) in the world; raising your name

high for posterity and thereby bringing esteem to your father and mother – it is in these things that family reverence finds its consummation.[5]

With reference to human disposition, *xiao* is based on *innate qualities*. Every physical or mental character that one has is parental endowment. One's physical body, every hair, and every bit of skin, as well as one's tendencies and moral virtues – all are received from one's parents. For this reason nurturing our bodies is a primary expression of family reverence. In this spirit, we read in *Analects* 8: 3, in the context of his death, that Zengzi, who was known for his excellence in keeping the rites (and, mistakenly or not, as the author of the *Book of Family Reverence*), asked his students to expose his hands and legs and see that he had protected his body, hence how much he had revered his parents. So to establish our character is to glorify our parents. The point is the *continuity* which characterizes the spiritual harmonious framework; namely continuity in both spiritual and physical-biological senses. This continuity is also expressed in Chinese as "one body," (*yiti*), while body is understood in its broadest sense. Tu Wei-ming explains this body as a set of concentric circles that broaden from self through family, community, nation, and world to "beyond" (Tu 1993: 129–228). Before we were born we were integral parts of our mothers' bodies, and even earlier of our fathers' too. According to this view, our body is also characterized by *natural feeling*, which annuls the need for strife or deliberate effort for its attainment. Chapter 9 in the *Book of Family Reverence* stresses the significance of this spontaneity:

> Affectionate feeling for Parents begins at their knee, and as children take proper care of their fathers and mothers this veneration increases with the passing of each day . . .

Mencius, a great believer in inborn morality, teaches that filial piety, as a feeling, is intuitive, such that every human born is endowed with it:

> There are no young children who do not know loving their parents, and none of them when they grow up will not know respecting their elder brothers. Loving one's parents is benevolence; respecting one's elders is rightness. What is left to be done is simply the extension of these to the whole Empire. (7A: 15)

While profoundly in agreement regarding the importance of family reverence, the Jewish discussant might raise some reservations, or at least a query: how may one say that moral values are feeling-based? In monotheistic traditions the one absolute transcendental God who is omniscient is also the ultimate justification for morality; but how can family reverence be justified when there is no absolute transcendence? And why is family reverence, in particular, innate? The idea of a rebellious stubborn son (*Ben sorer u-moreh*) is well recognized in the Talmudic tradition (*Babylonian Talmud*, Sanhedrin 8.68–72); if everyone had feeling, no rebellious sons would be found. The Confucian sage, on the other hand, might ask her Rabbinic counterpart about the role of feeling in the Talmudic idea of family reverence as *kibbud horim*. Unlike the Confucian understanding that *xiao* is the natural feeling of family reverence, in Talmudic literature feeling plays little part in honoring parents. On the contrary, many stories in the Talmud show that this is accomplished by suppression of one's natural feeling, not by following it. An instance is the case of Rabbah, son of R. Huna. The latter tore up silk in the Rabbah's presence, saying: "I will go and see whether he flies into a temper or not" (*ibid.*, Kiddushin 32a).

In this story, a reaction of natural feeling on Rabbah's part should be anger, because his property has been destroyed by the parent for no good reason. Therefore his honor of parents, in this case, can be accomplished only by suppressing, or at least "overcoming" his natural feeling and definitely not as an outcome of the feeling. In other words, while feelings are certainly acknowledged in Judaism, they are neither the motivation for moral acts, nor are they responsible for morality, rather God is. Due to the framework, Talmudic discussion of honoring parents shows more tension in the parent–children relationship than early Confucian literature does. To some extent, that kind of tension justifies the imperative approach, as natural feeling can also go awry. However, if natural feeling has no necessary positive role for Jews, what, in particular, motivates family reverence?

A Rabbinic answer would probably be *the commandment*. To the Rabbinic mind, a child loves his father because it is commanded, not primarily due to his natural feeling; and the commandment is given by God. Since commandments surpass human feelings, honoring one's parents can even occur in spite of one's bad feeling about them, even if this is a result of their misdeeds. Moreover, this kind of acting against feeling does not happen through following the commandment, it exists in the commandment itself:

> Rabbi said: It is revealed and known to Him Who decreed, and the world came into existence, that a son honors his mother more than his father, because she sways him by words; therefore the Holy One, blessed be He, placed the honor of the father before that of the mother. It is revealed and known to Him Who decreed, and the world came into existence, that a son reverences his father more than his mother, because he teaches him Torah, therefore the Holy One, blessed be He, put the fear [reverence] of the mother before that of the father. (*ibid.*, Kiddushin 30b–31a)

Here we see that God formulated an essential tension within the commandment in order to rectify the naturally unbalanced human feeling in honoring and reverencing one's parents. So, contrary to the Confucian feeling-oriented family reverence, Rabbinic honoring of parents is commandment-oriented. This corresponds to the general understanding of the two traditions regarding their sources of legitimation and authority. While an early Confucian believes that *xin*, the human mind-heart, is the source of human perfection, a Rabbinic Jew believes that the source of human perfection is mainly the words of God, as commandments or Torah.

In the spiritual harmonious framework, Heaven, the Way and human beings generate an emergence of oneness. Because the Way is embodied in the human mind-heart, one should follow one's heart. In a framework of creative contention, the gap between God and human beings is unbridgeable. Human beings are limited and flawed, so the source of moral virtues can only be external – in commandments.

Immanence and transcendence, life and eternity

Just as the sources for the virtue of family reverence differ in the two traditions, so does the source for its *justification*. If *xiao* is innate, the Jewish discussant might wonder, is there any transcendence in Confucianism? Chapter 16 in the *Book of Family Reverence* suggests that:

> When at the ancestral temple the Emperor offers his respects, the ghosts and spirits acknowledge him with appreciation. When familial and fraternal deference reaches this level, the feeling resonates with the gods and spirits, shines throughout the four corners of the world, and affects everything everywhere.

It transpires that the feeling transcends the here and now, that *xiao* is rooted in a dialogical relationship with the cosmos as a single whole. "Ghosts and spirits," that is, of deceased family members, are considered part of the here and now, and through being *xiao* one becomes "divine." One's ongoing practice is profoundly relational, and therefore expands to every part of the cosmos and beyond. Through the practice of ancestral worship the relatedness is maintained with the living, but also with deceased family members, thus avoiding the separation between life and afterlife, or "here" and "beyond"; this picture presents no sense of "beyondism" whatsoever.

The "Li Yun" chapter in the *Records of Rites* describes the rites of bringing spirits, in particular ancestors' spirits, "from above" into our world (9.7), stressing that we live a common life with our deceased ancestors, in the same world, subject to the same rule (as *li*). Moreover, it explains that the sages built temples and established ancestor worship to ensure "not forgetting those to whom they owed their being" (24: 20).

Chapter 18 concludes the *Book of Family Reverence* with mourning for parents:

> When their parents are alive they are served with love (*ai*) and respect (*jing*) and when they are deceased they are served with grief and sorrow. This is the basic duty being discharged by the living, the fulfilling of the appropriate obligations (*yi*) between the living and the dead, and the consummation of service filial children owe their parents.

Family reverence transcends space and time, life and death.

Our Jewish counterpart may be quite astonished: how can transcendence and immanence be one? Aren't they inherently dichotomized, as God is from the phenomenal world? And how can life and death be treated as one continuity?

From the Confucian perspective, precisely this continuity keeps our parents in us, even when physically they are gone. No mysticism is present in this Confucian suggestion. The sense of this continuity is its obliging us, as *self-cultivators*, to be *xiao*. Being *xiao*, this continuity also gives one "a sense of immortality" while in fact it is also a sense of morality. Our own moral life in the present enables us to preserve our parents' lives in us and respect their traditions. In this way *xiao* is timeless, beyond concrete existence in time.

In the Jewish case, since *kibbud horim* is a commandment from God, it is almost transcendent by nature. In the Babylonian Talmud this transcendent nature has two basic meanings. First, honoring parents is comparable to honoring God:

It is said: Honor thy father and thy mother; and it is also said: Honor the Lord with thy substance: thus the Writ assimilates the honor due to parents to that of the Omnipresent. It is said: "Ye shall fear every man his father, and his mother"; and it is also said: "The Lord thy God thou shalt fear, and him thou shalt serve . . ." (Babylonian Talmud, Kiddushin 30b)

Secondly, if the commandment is obeyed by the children, a divine reaction follows:

There are three partners in man, the Holy One, blessed be He, the father, and the mother. When a man honors his father and his mother, the Holy One, blessed be He, says: "I ascribe [merit] to them as though I had dwelt among them and they had honoured Me." (ibid., Kiddushin 30b. See also 31a)

The transcendent nature of the commandment carries honoring parents in the Talmud beyond the limit of life; it remains valid even after the parents' death, as in Confucianism. Thus it was said, "he must honor him in life and must honor him in death" (ibid., Kiddushin 31b). Honoring parents also ensures one's life in the world to come, where death is the bridge to eternal life (ibid., Kiddushin 31a–b).

"Super–virtue" or "yielding virtue"?

In Confucianism, xiao is inborn and immanent but also the *unifying and natural source of all moral virtues*. Any concern becomes irrelevant or even ridiculous if xiao is compromised for it. In other words, to be virtuous one must first be filial. There is no sense in moral virtuosity in disregard of xiao, so one cannot be at once moral yet not filial. Since xiao is inherently in harmony with all other virtues, not only should personal considerations not interfere with family relations: under certain conditions, legal, social, political, and ethical considerations may seem subordinate. This is exemplified in the story of the Governor of She, who said to Confucius, "In our village we have an example of a straight person. When the father stole a sheep, the son gave evidence against him." Confucius's answer is quite surprising: "In our village those who are straight are quite different. Fathers cover up for their sons, and sons cover up for their fathers" (13: 18).[6] The story raised doubts regarding Confucian morality (See Liu 2007). However, the point of this story is the presupposition that being a caring family member is the root of morality, hence of the way.

The Confucian sees xiao as the basis of the family and the primary manifestation of all human-relatedness:

The gentleman devotes his efforts to the roots, for once the roots are established, the way will grow therefrom. Being good as a son and obedient as a young man is, perhaps, the root of a man's character. (1: 2, see also I: 6)

When *Analects* claims that the way grows from that idea, it implies that family reverence is being human (ren) at home. In other words, being "human" in Confucianism is first and foremost being related to others, and the first relatedness one knows is one's family. The family unit serves as the root of the Way (dao), hence is the primary foundation for all morality. Family relations and values are at the core of the general social fabric, and the journeyer of the Way takes the first steps in family relationships. Concern with kinship derives not from a vision of precedence of family members over others; rather, family is a microcosm for moral human relationships. Hence, family reverence in Confucianism can be seen as a "super virtue," namely a virtue that is crucial to the being of almost all other virtues, and that generates other virtues. Moreover, this virtue alone is deemed sufficient to bring harmony to the whole world. Anyone who upholds it is considered to uphold all other virtues and anyone who does not is considered to have failed in almost everything, no matter what he did in reality.

Hence, Chapter 14 of the *Book of Family Reverence* stresses the place of *xiao* in being an accomplished person (*junzi*) because of the ability to extend the virtue. Denouncing the father who stole the sheep is not just failure of reverence; more importantly, it is about not being *moral*. Acting according to the law and reporting and abandoning the father and his morality, while "covering" for him, facilitates taking care of him, especially of his own damaged morality. Perhaps the most fascinating aspect about the story is that children are not seen as deterministically acting out damaged familial mores – family reverence itself can heal the damages witnessed within the family, for one who is significantly attuned to *xiao*. This point can be important with regard to modern psychotherapeutic accounts of family life as primarily a place of potential (and sometimes deterministic) damage.

The idea that it is not about blind nepotistic preference is seen in Chapter 15 of the *Book of Family Reverence* on remonstrance, showing the priority of morality. In this chapter a question is whether children can be deemed filial simply by obeying. Confucius's astonished response is "What on earth are you saying? What on earth are you saying?" Then an explanation is offered, stating that in some cases remonstrance is the only response to immorality.

If a Confucian sage examined the transcendent nature of *kibbud horim*, he would probably be amazed by its similarities to Confucian *xiao*. Yet he would also be somewhat bewildered in that this transcendence did not impart to Rabbinic honoring of parents its status of a "super virtue," as with family reverence in Confucianism. Honoring parents in Rabbinic Judaism does not enjoy such a status precisely because it is a commandment, and is no more powerful than other commandments. Therefore, the Talmudic sages even believed that sometimes this commandment has to yield its priority to other commandments:

> Eleazar B. Mathia said: "If my father orders me, 'Give me a drink of water' while I have a precept to perform, I disregard my father's honor and perform the precept, since both my father and I are bound to fulfill the precepts" (Babylonian Talmud, Kiddushin 32a).

A model for politics or for economy?

As shown above, the expansive nature of *xiao* derives from the Confucian perception of family as a microcosm for human relatedness. The expansiveness of *xiao* brings it into discussions which might seem irrelevant or strange to a non-Confucian. In particular, it plays a crucial role in politics. Let us turn to the *Book of Family Reverence*, which opens with Confucius's reference to the perfect virtue of the sage kings, which made possible their harmony with all under heaven:

> "It is family reverence (*xiao*)," said the Master, "that is the root of excellence, and whence education (*jiao*) itself is born. Sit down again and I will explain it to you. . . ."

This opening statement of the *Book of Family Reverence* might be seen as astounding from a Judaic perspective. According to the passage, despite one's possible expectations, the sage kings do not excel primarily in rightness, wisdom or courage; instead, family reverence is the root of all their virtues. "But what has family reverence to do with politics?" asks the astonished discussant. The odd explanation is that by virtue of being someone's son or daughter, one is morally competent. Since morality is inherent in everyone by virtue of having parents, to be a good ruler, one needs to first and foremost honor his family. Then the explanation emerges that our physical person is received from our parents so we are obliged to cultivate ourselves: "this family reverence, then, begins in service to your parents, continues in service to your lord, and culminates in distinguishing yourself in the world."

In this spirit, Chapter 2 of the *Book of Family Reverence* presents *xiao* as a transformative tool in political life:

> When the love and reverence (of the Son of Heaven) are thus carried to the utmost in the service of his parents, the lessons of his virtue affect all the people . . .

Chapter 6 stresses that:

> From the Emperor down to the common people, the way of family reverence being inclusive and comprehensive, there should be no one concerned that they are inadequate to the task.

Implied in these passages is a harmonious attitude, in which *ethics and politics are one*; in other words, family and state are to be conducted according to one moral principle. One cannot even imagine a "good" ruler who is not faithful to his wife. "Good" has only one sense, which at all levels of society amounts to personal morality, based on *xiao*. In this way, *xiao* is associated with Confucian politics and rulership.

Rabbinic Judaism views honoring of parents differently:

> It was propounded of R. Ulla: How far does the honor of parents [extend]? – He replied: Go forth and see what a certain heathen, Dama son of Nethinah by name, did in Ashkelon. The Sages once desired merchandise from him, in which there was six-hundred-thousand [gold denarii] profit, but the key was lying under his father, and so he did not trouble him. (Babylonian Talmud, Kiddushin 31a)

The same question was repeated later in the text by R. Eliezer, quoted by Rab Judah in Samuel's name, and the answer again was the story of Dama son of Nethinah in

Ashkelon with his financial loss of "six-hundred-thousand [gold denarii]." However, this time the damage was later compensated by his selling a red heifer to the sages for the same amount (*ibid.*, Kiddushin 31a). Unlike Confucius, the use of the sum of "six-hundred-thousand [gold denarii]" is just a way to describe how far the honor can go. In the Talmudic text, this way of expressing one's honoring one's parents by counting the economic loss is quite standard.

> When R. Dimi came, he said: He [Dama son of Nethinah] was once wearing a gold embroidered silken cloak and sitting among Roman nobles, when his mother came, tore it off from him, struck him on the head, and spat in his face, yet he did not shame her. (*ibid.*, Kiddushin 31a).

> R. Tarfon had a mother for whom, whenever she wished to mount into bed, he would bend down to let her ascend; (and when she wished to descend, she stepped down upon him). He went and boasted thereof in the school. Said they to him, "You have not yet reached half the honor [due]: has she then thrown a purse before you into the sea without your shaming her?" (*ibid.*, Kiddushin 31b)

According to the *Shuowenjiezi* dictionary, the Chinese character for family reverence, *Xiao* 孝, consists of two parts. The upper part means an old person and the lower part means his child. Thus the hieroglyphic meaning of the character is "a child is physically supporting his elder" (Xue 1981: Xiao section). Literally, this was exactly what R. Tarfon did for his mother, yet for the Talmudic sages, this was not in fact sufficient to show that he upheld the honor of parents. That his mother might cause him financial damage, and that he might accept this in a well-behaved manner, is evidence of particular virtue.

Just like our assumption that a Talmudic sage would wonder what, for heaven's sake, family reverence has to do with national politics, we believe that it would be extremely hard for a Confucian sage to understand the role economics played in Talmudic honoring of parents. If family reverence is such a natural and almost holy feeling, how dare you measure it with money? Confucian sages might truly be upset on hearing the following Talmudic argument:

> "Honor" means that he must give him food and drink, cloth and cover him, lead him in and out.

> The Scholars propounded: At whose expense?

> Rab Judah said: The son's. R. Nahman b. Oshaia said: The father's. The Rabbis gave a ruling to R. Jeremiah – others state to R. Jeremiah's son – in accordance with the view that it must be at the father's expense. (Babylonian Talmud, Kiddushin 31b–32a.)

According to chapter 6 of the *Book of Family Reverence*, for common people family reverence means that "they are careful of their conduct and economical in their expenditure – in order to nourish their parents." Children are responsible not only for the cost of nourishing their parents, it is also their duty to be thrifty themselves so that the elders will have sufficient sustenance. Anyone who dared raise the Talmudic question "At whose expense?" would be considered unworthy there and then. But the Rabbinic sages not only ask the question – they answer it by placing the economic burden on the parents' shoulders: "It must be at the father's expense."

Yet this very question exposes the real difference between Confucianism's political approach, reverence, and the Rabbinic economic approach to honoring parents. Only when family members are considered economically independent is the question "At whose expense?" valid.

Guidelines for Life

Lastly we wish to refer to an essential characteristic of family reverence in both traditions, which brings us back to the role of family reverence as the common ground for dialogue; its mutual status as a *practical guide for life*. Closely akin to a ritualistic code of behavior, the *Analects* expand on the practice of *xiao* through observance of rules of conduct or rites (*li*) for parents in life and after their death (1: 11). Being filial is evinced by way of ancestral worship, in particular by observing the aforementioned three years of mourning:

> The Master said, "if, for three years, a man makes no changes to his father's ways, he can be said to be a good son." (4: 20)

In *Analects* 2: 5 a student inquires into filial practice and is answered: "Never fail to comply," that is, neither in life nor in death (see also *Doctrine of the Mean* 19). According to *xiao*, in death as in life, one reveres parents through the observance of rites. In *Analects* 17: 21, in an argument between Confucius and his disciple Zai Wo, a problem arises regarding the number of years for the mourning period. While Zai Wo believes that one year is sufficient, Confucius maintains that it has to be three years. When Zai Wo leaves the room Confucius tells his disciples that the three years' mourning period for parents is the borderline between a human (*ren*) and accomplished person (*Junzi*) who honors the family and an unfeeling petty man who fails to preserve the value. Upholding the three years' mourning ritual indicates not only one's status as a good son, but also one's full humanity. When Zai Wo wishes to shorten the three years' mourning for parents, giving sound utilitarian reasoning concerning the loss and damage it may cause, Confucius makes it clear that utilitarian reasoning is not applicable in moral practice. The practice of *xiao* reflects the Confucian form of life and requires a "form of death" too. *Xiao*, moreover it is a never-ending practice.

For Talmudic sages, *kibbud horim* furnishes a set of guidelines for humans' behavior in their daily life; this may not be treated as a superficial subject or lightheartedly, as shown in the following story:

> A widow's son asked R. Eliezer: If my father orders, "Give me a drink of water," and my mother does likewise, which takes precedence? "Leave your mother's honor and fulfill the honor due to your father," he replied: "for both you and your mother are bound to honor your father." Then he went before R. Joshua, who answered him the same. "Rabbi," said

he to him, "what if she is divorced?" – "From your eyelids it is obvious that you are a widow's son," he retorted: "Pour some water for them into a basin, and screech for them like fowls!" (Babylonian Talmud, Kiddushin 31a)

The widow's son was scolded because he was asking superficial questions without any connection to his real life. A similar question was asked later by R. Jacob b. Abbahu and was answered by Abaye, as he was beset by a real problem in his life and was ready to put the answer into practice whatever it was (*ibid.*, Kiddushin 31b).

While fundamentally different in the sense of how guidelines were set, Talmudic *kibbud horim* and Confucian *xiao* are both guidelines for daily life. Early Confucianism set those guidelines according to the guidance of sages who followed their heart-mind, just as we have seen in the argument between Confucius and Zai Wo over the duration of the mourning period. Rabbinic Judaism set these guidelines through a hermeneutic approach to the Torah and through argumentative dialogue. Even after the guidelines were set, the argument could and did continue.

Conclusion: Inter-Religious Dialogue Based on Family-Reverence

It is not our aim to suggest how the entrenched traditions of Confucianism and Judaism can change well rooted notions as an outcome of dialogue. We do believe that through the idea of the family and the value of family reverence we are able to overcome gaps that can sometimes be seen as unbridgeable. To conclude this experimental dialogue between two fundamentally different traditions, as daughters and sons of others, we regard a dialogue based on family reverence a joint contribution by Confucianism and Judaism to inter-religious dialogue.

Before proceeding, why do we see in the family a model for inter-religious dialogue? The significant gaps between participating members in different religious traditions can sometimes be a basic obstacle in religious dialogue. We hold onto fundamentally different faiths, practices, and understandings which limit our ability to understand faiths that are remote from our own. However, we all are family members, and the family is also a microcosm for differences, which presupposes diversity and dynamism. A family relates members who are old with others who can be so young that their views cannot even be expressed in words; members of different gender with different attitudes and practical preferences; members who have different backgrounds, who are related by marriage or adoption and are equally obliged to the family. Seeing the other as distinct and yet a part of the same family calls for a "negotiation of rationality" (as coined by Winch 1972: 33) and an expansion of the circle as an outcome of the different orientations. Wittgenstein's idea of "family resemblance" as resemblance in some qualities but never in all (opposed to one exclusive "essence") can illustrate the core of our model for dialogue (Wittgenstein 1953: §65–71, 31–35). We are now ready to conclude by summing up the potency of family and family reverence in inter-religious dialogue, based on the Confucian-Jewish model as presented above.

First, family reverence embodies a channel to moral life regardless of its primary justification. Either as a natural feeling (as in the Confucian case) or as commandment (as in the Jewish case), in the broad range of foundations, from innate feeling to divine commandment, family reverence is revealed as a necessary attitude in human moral life. The ability to see others as part of one's broader family can dissolve and wipe out the need for strife and unavoidable conflict, which is so necessary in inter-religious dialogue.

Second, family reverence is by definition a relatedness, rather than a divider. Either within the framework of Jewish "absolute transcendence" or of Confucian "immanent transcendence," family requires us to see the need to "transcend oneself" and search for alternative ways of reasoning and justification that are essentially different from our own. Transcending ourselves in this way, we reveal that the family gives us a power to keep living beyond the limits of our actual lives, as part of the family. In this way it "overcomes" dichotomies of immanence and transcendence, life and death.

Third, family reverence is a practice of caring. In the modern individualistic world, people tend to take care of their own development, which can sometimes interfere with others'. Whether as a "yielding-virtue" (as in Judaism) or as a "super virtue" (as in Confucianism), family reverence assumes basic care and responsibility. In the family, the responsibility for others' rights is an outcome of the incessant search for one's duty towards others, which is innate in the structure of family. Family-based dialogue offers a solid basis for duty, care, and responsibility for the other as a member in the broad human community.

Fourth, family reverence is expandable to other human realms. We tend to see the world as divided into segments of diverse political, economical, practical, and emotional interests. As a model for politics in Confucianism and for economics in Judaism, family is revealed as a microcosm that can be expanded to broader universal domains. By means of this virtue, the family as structure enlightens different perspectives that enable better understanding according to the needs of specific traditions.

Last, family reverence necessitates dialogue as ceaseless ongoing practice. A dialogue cannot be a lonely occurrence, which is enacted once and the goal can be considered as attained. The life commitment of family reverence, which both Confucianism and Judaism stress, leans on the understanding that family reverence is a practical guide for life, as tightly connected to a ritualistic code of behavior. In theory, we may talk about building our relationship with people and with the world explained through grand principles, yet in practice any relationship begins from the relation to parents. Hence, family reverence can serve as the guide to daily life, rather than some theoretical concern. As its own practice, inter-religious dialogue can enjoy its benefits.

Notes

1   Our choice of terminology follows that of Rabbi Soloveitchick, who claims: "On the contrary, out of contradictions and antinomies, there emerges a radiant, holy personality whose soul has been purified in the furnace of struggle and opposition and redeemed in the fires of the torments of spiritual disharmony to a degree unmatched by the universal *homo religiosus*." (See Soloveitchik 1991: 4.)

2   Yan Ying (ca. 500 BCE), also called Yanzi in a respectFUL way, was a politician and thinker who represented an alternative tradition of Confucianism in the state of Qi during the Spring–Autumn period in Chinese history. Traditionally, the book *Yanzichunqiu* was identified as his work.

3   The same passage also appeared in Zuo Zhuan, Duke Zhao 20th year. See also Li 2006.

4   Shas refers to the Talmud in this text.

5   All *Book of Family Reverence* references use Ames and Rosemont's translation.

6   *Analects* quotations use the Lau 1979 translation.

Bibliography

Ames, Roger T. and Henry Jr. Rosemont. *The Chinese Classic of Family Reverence: A Philosophical Translation of the Xiaojing.* Hawaii: University of Hawaii Press, 2006.

Ariel, Yoav. *Yanzichunqiu.* Manuscript.

Corning, Peter A. "The Re-Emergence of 'Emergence': A Venerable Concept in Search of a Theory," *Complexity* 7(6) (2002): 18–30.

Eber, Irene. "K'aifeng Jews Revisited: Sinification as Affirmation of Identity." *Monumenta Serica* 41 (1993): 231–247.

Eber, Irene. *The Jewish Bishop and the Chinese Bible. S I J Schereschewsky 1831–1906.* Boston: Brill, 1999.

Eber, Irene. *Chinese and Jews: Encounters between Cultures.* London: Vallentine Mitchell, 2007.

Ember, Melvin, Carol R. Ember, and Ian Skoggard (eds.). *Encyclopedia of Diasporas. Immigrant and Refugee Cultures around the World.* Vol. I: Jewish Diaspora in China by Xu Xin. New York: Springer, 2004.

Goldman, René. "Moral Leadership in Society: Some Parallels between the Confucian 'Noble Man' and the Jewish *Zaddik*." *Philosophy East and West* 45(3) (1995): 329–365.

Lau, D.C. *Confucius The Analects.* London: Penguin, 1979.

Leslie, Donald Daniel. *The Survival of the Chinese Jews – The Jewish Community of Kaifeng.* Leiden: E.J. Brill, 1972.

Li, Chen-yang. "The Confucian Ideal of Harmony," *Philosophy East and West* 56(4) (2006): 585–586.

Liu, Qingping. "Filial Piety: The Root of Morality or the Source of Corruption." *Dao: A Journal of Comparative Philosophy* 6(1) (2007).

Patt-Shamir, Galia. "Seeds for Dialogue – On Learning in Confucianism and Judaism." *Journal of Ecumenical Studies* 40(1–2) (2004): 201–215.

Patt-Shamir, Galia. "Way as Dao; Way as Halakha. Confucianism, Judaism and Way metaphors." *Dao: A Journal of Comparative Philosophy* 5(1) (2005): 137–156.

Patt-Shamir, Galia. *To Broaden the Way – A Confucian-Jewish Dialogue.* Oxford: Lexington, 2006.

Patt-Shamir, Galia. "The Value in Story-Telling: On Women's Life-Stories in Confucianism and Judaism." *Dao: A Journal of Comparative Philosophy* 9(2) (2010): 175–191.

Rappel, Dov. *The Debate over the Pilpul.* Tel Aviv: Dvir, 1979.

Slotki, Judah Jacob and Isidore Epstein. "Soferim, Chapter 15, Rule 7–8," *Hebrew-English Edition of the Babylonian Talmud.* London: Soncino, 1990.

Soloveitchik, Joseph Baer. *Halakhic Man.* Philadelphia: Jewish Publ. Soc., 1991.

Steinsaltz, Adin and Zhang Ping. *Avot: The Wisdom of Our Fathers* (Chinese). Beijing: The Press of Chinese Academy of Social Science, 1996.

Tu, Wei-ming. "Confucianism," in *Our Religions*, Arvind Sharma. New York: Harper Collins, 1993: 129–228.

Winch, Peter. "Understanding a Primitive Society," in *Ethics and Action.* London: Routledge & Kegan Paul, 1972.

Wittgenstein, Ludwig. *Philosophical Investigations*. Oxford: Blackwell, 1953.

Xu, Shen. *Shuowenjiezi*. Shanghai: Shanghai Guji Chubanshe, 1981.

Zhang, Ping. "Bridging Between the Actual and the Ideal in Early Rabbinical and Confucian Literature." Ph.D Dissertation. Tel Aviv, 2000.

Zhang, Ping. *The Jewish Way of the World – Derech Eretz Zuta* (Chinese). Beijing: Beijing University Press, 2003.

Zhang, Ping. *The Mishnah: A Study and Translation of Seder Zeraim* (Chinese). Jinan: Shandong University Press, 2011.

Zhang, Ping. "Where did the Torah come from? – a Comparative Reading of the First Chapters of *The Analects* and *Pirki Avoth*" (Chinese), in *A Dialogue between Jewish and Chinese Tradition*, ed. Chung Tsai-chun. Taipei: The Institute of Chinese Literature and Philosophy Press, 2011: 9–43.

Zhang, Ping. "Creative Tension – master–disciple relationship in Rabbinic Judaism and early Confucianism" (Chinese), in *A Dialogue between Jewish and Chinese Tradition*, ed. Chung Tsai-chun. Taipei: The Institute of Chinese Literature and Philosophy Press, 2011: 47–64.

CHAPTER 28

The Mormon–Evangelical Dialogue

Robert L. Millet

The story of how a group of Latter-day Saints began to meet and converse about religion with a group of Evangelical Protestants is rather fascinating. To some extent, it is the story of my life for the last twenty years.

The year I started the sixth grade our family moved to a small town in southern Louisiana, a tiny Cajun community made up almost completely of Roman Catholics. I remember distinctly that on the first day of class, my teacher, Mrs. Templet, asked the question: "Now is there anyone here who is not Catholic? If so, I need to know." My heart raced and my blood pressure rose. I looked about the class in a frightened and terribly shy way. I saw one boy across the room lift his hand slowly. "What are you?" Mrs. Templet asked. "I'm a Baptist," he responded, in a voice that was just above a whisper. I sat there, clearly realizing that there was not one human being in the room besides myself who had the slightest idea what a Mormon was, including the teacher. My temptation was to sit still and be quiet. But in a twinge of conscience I slowly lifted my hand into the air. "And what are you?" the teacher asked sternly. My faith failed and my strength went down the drain as I replied timidly, "I'm a Baptist too."

I was born and raised in Baton Rouge, Louisiana, and so most all of my friends were Roman Catholic or Southern Baptist. Although I was brought up in The Church of Jesus Christ of Latter-day Saints (LDS, or Mormon), I did not know many Mormons beyond those in my little congregation. We worshipped in a very small LDS branch. There was a time and a season when my family was not active in the Church, and I can remember very well attending a Vacation Bible School. As I grew up, I discovered that quite a few of my cousins were Pentecostal. So a life embedded in religious diversity is one I have known over the years. I have felt something deep down for persons of other faiths for a long time. I know what it is like to be a religious minority, and so I am a bit more sensitive to those outside the LDS faith who live in Utah, where I live.

Not long after I was appointed dean of Religious Education at Brigham Young University, one of the leaders of the LDS Church said to me, "You must find ways to reach

The Wiley Blackwell Companion to Inter-Religious Dialogue, First Edition. Edited by Catherine Cornille.
© 2013 John Wiley & Sons Ltd. Published 2020 by John Wiley & Sons Ltd.

out. You must find ways to build bridges of friendship and understanding with persons of other faiths." He said a number of other things to me but that particular charge weighed upon me for months. Some of my colleagues and I began a series of visits to other campuses. In 1991, my associate dean and I spent about four or five days at Notre Dame trying to understand better how Notre Dame as a church institution could hold fast to its religious heritage and at the same time reach forward toward academic excellence. After that, we made contact with such schools as Baylor, Wheaton College, and Catholic University.

In April, 1997, our religion faculty invited Professor Bruce Demarest, of Denver Seminary, to visit Provo and speak to us. His topic was the man Melchizedek, an enigmatic Old Testament figure, who is a matter of some interest to Latter-day Saints. Besides our own faculty, two local ministers were in attendance, one of which was Pastor Greg Johnson, who was then shepherding a small flock of Baptists in Huntsville, Utah. I happened to slip into the meeting late. During the question and answer session I referred to something that had been written by John MacArthur, Pastor/Teacher at Grace Community Church in Sun Valley, California. Greg introduced himself to me after the meeting and inquired after my interest in MacArthur's writings. I took him into my office and showed him the section of my library on Evangelical writings, including a shelf of MacArthur's books. In addition, I had read books by Evangelical writers such as John Stott, J.I. Packer, Ravi Zacharias, Philip Yancey, John Stackhouse, Randall Balmer, Billy Graham, Chuck Swindoll, Donald Bloesch, Mark Noll, George Marsden, and a whole host of others. I also had a pretty healthy section on Christian History, Roman Catholicism, and American Religious History.

Greg and I began to have lunch together about once per month to discuss our respective faiths and belief systems. We spoke of God, Christ, trinity/godhead, salvation, heaven, hell, agency and predestination, premortal existence, and other topics. We compared and contrasted, we asked questions, and we answered them. Importantly, our discussions were characterized by a mood of openness, candor, and a general lack of defensiveness. We knew what we believed, and we were committed to our own religious tradition. Neither was trying to convert the other; rather, we were making an effort to better understand one another. Our experience is one example of what can happen when men and women of good will come together in an attitude of openness, and in a sincere effort to better understand and be understood.

Since that time we have had many, many occasions, Greg and I, to eat together and to talk and listen together. One of the great unanticipated blessings of this dialogue has been the challenge of answering questions that we really had not thought about before, and articulating our perceptions in a way that would enable us to follow one another's perceptions over time. The rewards have been tremendous. In a rather informal manner, Pastor Johnson and I sought to acquire the skills and art of what our friend and colleague Richard Mouw of Fuller Theological Seminary has called "convicted civility" (Mouw 2010). It was during that time that one of my colleagues, Stephen Robinson, and Craig Blomberg, of Denver Seminary, co-authored a book titled *How Wide the Divide? A Mormon and an Evangelical in Conversation* (Blomberg and Robinson 1997).

Rich rewards have flowed from such interactions; to be able to articulate your faith to someone else who is not of your faith is a good discipline because you have to examine the adequacy of your own terminology, and you have to make sure that people not only understand you, but could not misunderstand. We discovered, for example, that Mormons and Evangelicals have a vocabulary that is very similar, but found as well that we may have different definitions and meanings for those words. Consequently, effective communication is a strenuous endeavor. To some degree, we have been forced to re-examine our own theological understandings in a way that enables us to share with each other in an informative manner.

Is This Person For Real?

Along the way, one of the challenges we faced was inevitable: the matter of trust. That is to say, Greg might ask me a question, I would give an answer, only to notice an uncomfortable look on his face, a look that bespoke his doubt as to whether I was really stating accurately what Latter-day Saints believe. It was as if he were asking – and I have been asked this a hundred times or more by others – "Are you just saying those words, or do you really mean that?" Or if I would ask him a question, I might wonder whether most Evangelicals feel the same way or whether his response was idiosyncratic to Greg Johnson. So, during the early stages, had we not been patient and persistent, we might have concluded that the other person was being disingenuous in order to keep a friendship intact.

We have, for instance, had long conversations on the themes of grace and works. At times, I was not certain that he felt I was representing mainstream Mormonism. So in order to try to convince him, I did something rather unusual. I contacted the local Brigham Young University Continuing Education office and spoke to a friend of mine that oversees lecture series beyond the Brigham Young University campus: "Frank, I need a favor." He said, "What's that?" "I need you to set up a speaking engagement in Ogden in which I deliver three lectures." I explained that I needed to do it in and around a certain time period. "Can you do that?" I inquired. He said, "Sure." So he set it up and we picked the titles and then I called Greg on the phone. I said, "Greg, I'm going to be speaking in Ogden in a few weeks. We ought to get together, have a bite to eat, and perhaps you could join me at the lectures." He agreed and we settled on the date.

There were 200–250 Latter-day Saints in attendance. I spoke on three doctrinal topics, using the Book of Mormon as my principal text, supplemented occasionally with the New Testament. The topics were the nature of fallen man, the new birth, and salvation by grace. I was stating the LDS position on these matters just as I had in my conversations with Greg, but this time there was a roomful of persons of my faith listening and taking notes. I think that was an important night for us because it helped to settle the fact that what I say is what I mean. What I say in private is what I would say in public. Consequently, one of the ways we began to grow into a meaningful friendship with each other was in the matter of trust. We came to trust that there were no ulterior motives. We believed each other. We had confidence in each other.

Debates between Mormons and Evangelicals have been common through recent decades. You can certainly draw a crowd when you have that kind of an event because people want to see the fists fly. One challenge is to value this kind of exchange and process it for what it is, without insisting on an Evangelistic conquest, a conversion, as the outcome. Too many believe that if this association does not end in a conversion then the relationship cannot have a long term purpose. But I am fully persuaded that we need to engage in one another's lives, even if the only outcome is developing a healthy friendship with a fellow human being, one from whom I can learn valuable lessons. But to engage at this relational level is much more difficult.

Pastor Johnson likes to tell the story of his encounter with a Brigham Young University religion faculty member. This particular professor became quite intrigued with the relationship Greg and I had developed, and he invited Greg to lunch just off campus. They sat down, had a little spaghetti, and the professor said: "Tell me what's going on with you and Bob Millet." Greg shared a little bit more about our friendship and some of the interactions we were having. My faculty friend said, "Well, let me get to the point, Greg. I think you are aware that Robert Millet is the dean of our religion faculty." Greg said, "Of course." "Surely you don't think he's going to convert to the Evangelical Christian way of life, do you?" Greg said, "You know, to be honest with you, I'm pretty sure he doesn't plan to do that." The professor continued: "Well, I'm assuming that as an Evangelical pastor you're not considering becoming LDS." Greg replied, "No, I'm not." In a moment of frustration, the professor blurted out, "Well what's the point?"

The Conversation Broadens

As our friendship developed over time, Greg and I began to wonder if there might be some merit in enlarging our small inter-faith circle to include other LDS and Evangelical scholars. A formal gathering of such scholars took place in the spring of 2000 at Brigham Young University in Provo, Utah. The Evangelical participants included Greg Johnson; Richard Mouw of Fuller Theological Seminary; Craig Blomberg of Denver Seminary; Craig Hazen of Biola University; David Neff of *Christianity Today*; and Carl Moser, who was at the time a doctoral student in Scotland. On the LDS side, participants included myself, Stephen Robinson, Roger Keller, David Paulsen, Daniel Judd, and Andrew Skinner, all from Brigham Young University. Names and faces have changed somewhat, but the dialogue has continued since that first gathering. Over the next nine years we came prepared (through readings of articles and books) to discuss a number of doctrinal subjects. Scholars who joined us to make presentations on specific topics included Richard Bushman (Columbia University), John Stackhouse (Regent College), and Velli-Matti-Karkkainen (Fuller Seminary). As of this writing, we have met twenty-one times.

In the early sessions, it was not uncommon to sense a bit of tension, a subtle uncertainty as to where this was going, a slight uneasiness among the participants. As the dialogue began to take shape, it was apparent that we were searching for an identity – was this to be a confrontation? An argument? A debate? Was it to produce a winner and a loser? Just how candid and earnest were we expected to be? Some of the Latter-day Saints wondered: Do the "other guys" see this encounter as a grand effort to set Mormonism straight, to make it more traditionally Christian, more acceptable to skeptical onlookers? Some of the Evangelicals wondered: Are those "other guys" for real? Is what they are saying an accurate expression of LDS belief? Can a person be a genuine Christian and yet not be a part of the larger body of Christ? A question that continues to come up is: Just how much "incorrect theology" can the grace of God compensate for? Before too long, those kinds of issues became part of the dialogue itself, and in the process, much of the tension began to dissipate.

The meetings have been more than conversations. We have visited key historical sites, eaten and socialized, sung hymns and prayed, mourned together over the passing of members of our group, and shared ideas, books, and articles throughout the year. The initial feeling of formality has given way to a sweet informality, a brother-and-sisterhood, a kindness in disagreement, a respect for opposing views, and a feeling of responsibility toward those not of our faith – a responsibility to represent their doctrines and practices accurately to folks of our own faith. No one has compromised or diluted his or her own theological convictions, but everyone has sought to demonstrate the kind of civility that ought to characterize a mature exchange of ideas among a body of believers who have discarded defensiveness. There have been those times, as well, when many of us have felt what Harvard's Krister Stendahl has described as "holy envy" – something stronger and more satisfying than tolerance, something definitely more heartwarming and even compelling than ideological indifference. No dialogue of this type is worth its salt unless the participants gradually begin to realize that there is much to be learned from the other guys.

John Stackhouse has written: "If I go no further than to think that it's okay for you to do your thing and I to do mine, then where is the incentive to seriously consider whether I should adopt your thing and abandon mine?" Further, "If one is not sufficiently sympathetic, not sufficiently vulnerable to changing one's mind, not sufficiently willing to entertain the idea that these people might just be right – then it is most unlikely that one will enter into that religion far enough to understand its essence" (Stackhouse 2002: 41, 102).

Continued Challenges

Progress has not come about easily. This is tough sledding, hard work. In my own life it has entailed a tremendous amount of reading of Christian history, Christian theology, and, more particularly, Evangelical thought. I cannot very well enter into their world and their way of thinking unless I immerse myself in their literature. This is particularly difficult when such efforts come out of your own hide, that is, when you must do it above and beyond everything else you are required to do. It takes a significant investment of time, energy, and money.

Second, while we have sought from the beginning to ensure a proper balance of academic backgrounds in history, philosophy, and theology in the dialogue, it soon became clear that perhaps more critical than intellectual acumen was a nondefensive, clear-headed, thick-skinned, persistent but pleasant personality. Kindness works really well also. Those steeped in apologetics, whether LDS or Evangelical, face a particular hurdle in this regard. We agreed early on, for example, that we would not take the time to address every anti-Mormon polemic, any more than a Christian/Muslim dialogue would spend appreciable time evaluating proofs of whether Muhammad actually entertained the angel Gabriel. Furthermore, and this is much more difficult, we agreed as a larger team to a rather high standard of loyalty – that we would not say anything privately about the other guys that we would not say in public.

Third, as close as we have become, as warm and congenial as the dialogues have proven to be, there is still an underlying premise that guides most of the evangelical participants: that Mormonism is the tradition that needs to do the changing if a greater and deeper unity is to be achieved. To be sure, the LDS participants have become well aware that we are not well understood, and that many of our theological positions need clarifying. Too often, however, the implication is that if the Mormons can only alter this or drop that, then we will be getting somewhere. A number of the LDS cohort have voiced this concern and suggested that it just might be a healthy exercise for the evangelicals to do a bit more introspection, to consider that this enterprise is in fact a *dialogue*, a mutual conversation, one where long-term progress will come only as both sides are convinced that there is much to be learned from one another, including doctrine.

A fourth challenge is one we did not anticipate. In Evangelicalism there is no organizational structure, no priestly hierarchy, no living prophet or magisterium to set forth the "final word" on doctrine or practice, although there are supporting organizations like the National Association of Evangelicals and the Evangelical Theological Society. On the other hand, Mormonism is clearly a hierarchical organization, the final word resting with the First Presidency and the Quorum of the Twelve Apostles. Thus our dialogue team might very well make phenomenal progress toward a shared understanding on doctrine, but Evangelicals around the world will not see our conclusions as in any way binding or perhaps even relevant.

This is not unlike the challenge faced by the Evangelical team involved in the ecumenical effort called "Evangelicals and Catholics Together." Despite the fact that they have issued several joint declarations such as "The Christian Mission in the Third Millennium" (1994), "The Gift of Salvation" (1997), "Your Word Is Truth" (2002), "The Communion of Saints" (2003), "The Call to Holiness" (2005), "That They May Have Life" (2006), and, most recently, "The Blessed Virgin Mary in Christian Faith and Life" (2009), the results of the interactions seem to be still questioned by individual Catholics and institutional Catholicism. On the other hand, recent LDS Official Declarations, such as "The Family, A Proclamation to the World" (1997) and "The Living Christ" (2000) were prepared and issued by the fifteen senior leaders of the Church, upon whom the responsibility rests for the determination of doctrine and policy, and these two documents enjoy near-canonical status among Mormons. Having a presiding group acknowledge, consider, and accept what an ancillary, nonecclesiastical entity proposes will be a challenge at best.

Dialogue Topics

The first dialogue, held at Brigham Young University in the spring of 2000 was, as suggested earlier, as much an effort to test the waters as to dialogue on a specific topic. But the group did agree to do some reading prior to the gathering. The Evangelicals asked that we all read or re-read John Stott's classic work, *Basic Christianity* (Eerdmans 1958) and some of my LDS colleagues recommended that we read a book I had written entitled *The Mormon Faith* (1998). We spent much of a day discussing *The Mormon Faith*, concluding that there were a number of theological topics deserving of extended conversation. When it came time to discuss *Basic Christianity*, we had a most unusual and unexpected experience. Richard Mouw asked, "Well, what concerns or questions do you have about this book?" There was a long and somewhat uncomfortable pause. Mouw followed up after about a minute: "Isn't there anything you have to say? Did we all read the book?" Everyone nodded affirmatively that they had indeed read it but no one seemed to have any questions. Finally, one of the LDS participants responded: "Stott is essentially writing of New Testament Christianity, with which we have no quarrel. He does not wander into the creedal formulations that came from Nicea, Constantinople, or Chalcedon. We agree with his assessment of Jesus Christ as presented in the New Testament. Good book." That comment was an important one, as it signaled where we would eventually lock our theological horns.

Our second gathering took place at Fuller Seminary in Pasadena. After our initial evening dinner, each participant spoke of what they had done since the last meeting, what articles or books they had published, their current research thrust, and any newsworthy issues the group might find worthwhile (a procedure that has continued to the present). In the second dialogue we chose to discuss the matter of soteriology, and much of the conversation was taken up with the relation between divine grace, faithful obedience (good works), and salvation. The Evangelicals insisted that Mormon theology did not contain a provision for grace, and that Mormons seemed to be obsessed with a kind of works righteousness. This is a matter that had come up many times before in my conversations with Evangelicals – namely that Mormons tend to be so focused on doing the right thing, doing *enough* of the right thing, and laboring tenaciously to accomplish the "work of the kingdom" that it appeared that the Saints felt that they could somehow save themselves, that in fact divine grace was not necessary.

One of the first things the Latter-day Saints in the dialogue did was to return to Mormon scriptural texts to demonstrate how often and consistent the grace of God is emphasized there. As an example, one of the Mormons, Stephen Robinson, asked the group to turn in their copies of the Book of Mormon (each participant comes prepared with a Bible and the LDS books of scripture, what is called the "triple combination") to several passages in which the text stressed the fact that we are saved only through the merits and mercy and grace of the Holy Messiah. After an extended silence, I remember hearing one of the Evangelicals say, almost in a whisper, "Sounds pretty Christian to me."

The LDS participants pointed out that what they had observed quite often among Evangelicals was what Bonhoeffer had described as "cheap grace" (Bonhoeffer 1963: 45–47), a kind of easy believism that frequently resulted in spiritually unfazed and unchanged people. I added that there were a surprising number of books by Evangelical scholars that cautioned their own people about separating justification from sanctification, that is, driving a wedge between one's conversion or salvation experience and the requisite faithfulness that ought to characterize true faith. (MacArthur 1988; Sider 2005; Willard 2006). Another LDS participant indicated that from his perspective

Evangelicals tend to have a high view of forgiveness but a low view of repentance; many sermons stress the goodness of God and the forgiveness of Jesus Christ; congregants were reminded repeatedly of the good news while receiving precious little counsel on how to repent of their sins and further of the need to demonstrate the depth of one's faith through dedicated discipleship.

In some ways, this topic – grace and works – is seldom referred to any longer among the dialogists. While both groups acknowledge that there will probably always be differences in how salvation in Christ is described between the two faith traditions, in reality we were on the same page and thus to some extent this particular issue became a theological straw man to which no one felt the need to strike a match. This dialogue was a breakthrough that we often refer to when we are in the middle of a doctrinal log jam: we ought to be just as eager to celebrate similarities as we are to define differences.

One of our dialogues took place in 2004 at the meetings of the American Academy of Religion and the Society of Biblical Literature. We had agreed as a large group to discuss the person and work of Joseph Smith. We extended an invitation to Richard Bushman, professor of History at Columbia University, to discuss with us his soon-to-be-released biography of the Mormon Prophet, *Rough Stone Rolling* (Bushman 2005). Richard quickly got everyone's attention as he turned to the Evangelical element of the group and asked simply, "Is Joseph Smith an impossibility for you?" After a long delay, he restated the question. This time someone replied: "No, not an impossibility. God can speak to us and certain individuals can have the gift of prophecy and revelation. We just do not believe God appeared or spoke to Joseph Smith."

The dialogue proceeded from there, discussing true and false prophets, whether Joseph Smith was a prophet with a large or small P (as someone put it), and whether Mormonism could be an expression of something good or Christian if Joseph Smith did not really see God (the matter of historicity). Toward the end of the meeting, one of the most prominent historians in the country, now at a major university, said: "I am not ready to accept a vision of God and Christ, an angel Moroni, or gold plates, but I am haunted by the Christianity within Mormon culture." As a follow-up, Mouw spoke at our next gathering on "The Possibility of Joseph Smith: An Evangelical Perspective," posing the question: Isn't there a way for us to examine Joseph Smith without resorting to such labels as liar or lunatic? How can Evangelicals understand Joseph Smith properly without considering the context of nineteenth-century Restorationism?

One of the most memorable of all our discussions centered around the concept of *theosis* or divinization, the doctrine espoused by Latter-day Saints and also a vital facet of Eastern Orthodoxy. For this dialogue we invited Veli-Matti Karkkainen, professor of Theology at Fuller Seminary, to lead our discussion. In preparation for the dialogue we read his book, *One With God: Salvation As Deification and Justification* (2004), as well as LDS writings on the topic. It seemed to me that in this particular exchange there was much less effort on the part of Evangelicals to "fix Mormonism" or continue another round of "tryouts for true Christianity." Instead, there was much reflection and introspection among the entire group. Mormons commented on how little work they had done on this subject beyond the bounds of Mormonism, and they found themselves fascinated with such expressions as participation in God, union with God, assimilation into God, receiving of God's energies and not his essence, and divine-human synergy. More than one of the Evangelicals asked how they could have ignored, in their encounter with Mormonism, a matter that was a part of the discourse of Athanasius, Augustine, Irenaeus, Gregory of Nazianzus, and even Martin Luther. There was much less said about "you and your faith," and far more emphasis on "we" as professing Christians, when addressing divinization and related themes.

Not long after our dialogue on deification, Richard Mouw suggested that we meet next time not in Provo, but rather in Nauvoo, Illinois. Nauvoo was of course the location of a major historical moment (1839–1846) within Mormonism, the place where the Mormons were able to establish a significant presence, where some of Joseph Smith's deepest and most controversial doctrines were delivered to the Saints, and the site from which Brigham Young and the Mormon pioneers began the long exodus to the Salt Lake Basin in February, 1846. Because a large percentage of the original dwellings, meetinghouses, places of business, and even the temple have been restored in modern Nauvoo, our dialogue was framed by the historical setting and resulted in perhaps the greatest blending of hearts of any of our dialogues. Two years later, we met in Palmyra, New York and once again focused much of our attention on historical sites, from the Sacred Grove (where Joseph Smith claimed to have received his first vision) to Fayette, where the church was formally organized on April 6, 1830. We had reaffirmed what we had come to know quite well in Nauvoo – that there is in fact something special about "sacred space." Following the Palmyra exchange, the Mormon participants insisted that Richard Mouw plan a similar experience for us in Wittenberg and Geneva! Interestingly, in the dialogue held in San Francisco in November, 2011, the decision was made to organize a major dialogue and academic conference in Germany and Switzerland on the topic "Reformation and Restoration."

After a decade of semi-annual meetings, it was decided that we should start over, delve more deeply into the topics, and prepare short written documents summarizing matters on which Mormons and Evangelicals may agree, matters on which, for the foreseeable future, we will agree to disagree, and matters that require further study and dialogue. We also agreed that our initial thrust should be at that point in Christian history where the theological friction begins, namely the years leading up to Nicea, the decisions of that and subsequent church councils regarding the divinity and humanity of Jesus; and in general the traditional Christian view of the Trinity.

Looking Ahead

We have been content heretofore with putting off the question of where these dialogues are headed, or exactly what the final product of our investigation will look like. Many of us have felt a superintending hand in the overall enterprise, and consequently trusted that whatever comes to pass is providentially intended. I would be less than honest if I suggested that the enterprise has been motivated solely by intellectual engagement, although our sessions have been immensely stimulating and enriching. I have learned that I cannot, simply cannot, take another religious tradition seriously without: (1) coming to appreciate beauty, truth, and conviction within its adherents, and recognizing in their lifestyle something commendable and even praiseworthy; (2) asking hard questions about my own tradition, including its theological consistency and relevance in a modern world; and (3) recognizing that God is moving in the hearts and lives of men and women throughout the world in ways not easily perceived.

In reflecting on his visit to Salt Lake City and the major message he offered in the Mormon Tabernacle in November 2004, Evangelical teacher and author Ravi Zacharias observed:

> The last time an Evangelical Christian was invited to speak there was 1899, when D. L. Moody spoke. . . . I accepted the invitation, . . . and I spoke on the exclusivity and sufficiency of Jesus Christ. I also asked if I could bring my own music, to which they also graciously agreed. So Michael Card joined us to share his music. He did a marvelous job, and one of the pieces he sang brought a predictable smile to all present. It was based on Peter's visit to Cornelius' home and was entitled, "I'm Not Supposed To Be Here." He couldn't have picked a better piece! I can truly say that I sensed the anointing of the Lord as I preached and still marvel that the event happened. The power of God's presence, even amid some opposition, was something to experience. As the one closing the meeting said, "I don't want this evening to end." Only time will tell the true impact. Who knows what the future will bring? Our faith is foundationally and theologically very different from the Mormon faith, but maybe the Lord is doing something far beyond what we can see. (Zacharias 2004: 2)

Few things are more needed in this tense and confused world than understanding. It really is time to stop name-calling, categorizing, and demonizing, especially among people who claim to be religious. As Joseph Smith observed in 1843, less than a year before his death:

> If I esteem mankind to be in error, shall I bear them down? No. I will lift them up, and in their own way too, if I cannot persuade them my way is better; and I will not seek to compel any man to believe as I do, only by the force of reasoning, for truth will cut its own way. Do you believe in Jesus Christ and the Gospel of salvation which he revealed? So do I. Christians should cease wrangling and contending with each other, and cultivate the principles of union and friendship in their midst; and they will do it before the millennium can be ushered in and Christ takes possession of His kingdom. (Smith 1976: 313–314).

Bibliography

Blomberg, Craig L. and Stephen E. Robinson. *How Wide the Divide? A Mormon and An Evangelical in Conversation*. Downers Grove, IL: IVP, 1997.

Bonhoeffer, Dietrich. *The Cost of Discipleship*. New York: Macmillan, 1963.

Bushman, Richard L. *Rough Stone Rolling*. New York: Alfred A. Knopf, 2005.

Karkkainen, Veli-Matti. *One With God: Salvation as Deification and Justification*. Collegeville, PA: Liturgical, 2004.

MacArthur, John F. *The Gospel According to Jesus*. Grand Rapids, MI: Zondervan, 1988.

Millet, Robert L. *The Mormon Faith: A New Look at Christianity*. Salt Lake City, UT: Shadow Mountain, 1998.

Mouw, Richard J. *Uncommon Decency: Christian Civility in an Uncivil World.* 2nd ed. Downers Grove, IL: IVP, 2010.

Mouw, Richard J. *Talking With Mormons: An Invitation to Evangelicals.* Grand Rapids, MI: Eerdmans, 2012.

Sider, Ronald J. *The Scandal of the Evangelical Conscience: Why Are Christians Living Just Like the Rest of the World?* Grand Rapids, MI: Baker, 2005.

Smith, Joseph. *Teachings of the Prophet Joseph Smith. Selected by Joseph Fielding Smith.* Salt Lake City, UT: Deseret, 1976.

Stackhouse, John G. *Humble Apologetics: Defending the Faith Today.* New York: Oxford University Press, 2002.

Stott, John. *Basic Christianity.* Grand Rapids, MI: Eerdmans, 1958.

Willard, Dallas. *The Great Omission: Reclaiming Jesus's Essential Teachings on Discipleship.* New York: Harper Collins, 2006.

Zacharias, Ravi. RZIM *Newsletter.* Volume 3, Winter 2004.

Index

Abhidharma, 189, 190, 191, 195, 197
Abhishikananda, Swami (Henri Le Saux), 37, 88, 352
Abraham, 76, 245, 250, 254–6, 398, 451
Abrahamic traditions of scriptural reasoning *see* scriptural reasoning
acculturation, Judaism in India, 421–2
action *see* social action
Activist Model of dialogue, 174–7
Adams, Nicholas, 72
Advaita tradition, 88, 199, 329, 333, 334, 335
African religions, 347
    and Christianity, 317, 322, 354
    dialogue with Islam, 311–23
Agnivesh, Swami, 292–3
aid-evangelism, 340
AIM *see* Secretariat to Aid the Implementation of Monasticism
Akbar (Abu'l-Fath Jalal-ud-Din Muhammad Akbar), 283
al-Biruni (Abu al-Rayhan Muhammad ibn Ahmad al-Biruni), 280–1, 293
Aman Panchayat, 291
Amaterasu, 264–5, 266
American Academy of Religion (AAR)
    Comparative Studies in Hinduisms and Judaisms, 421, 423, 424, 425–6, 428
American Civil Rights Movement, 212
American context for Jewish–Muslim engagement, 228–39

Anawati, Friar George, 251
ancestor worship, 452, 458, 463
androcentricity, 169–70, 172, 173–4, 385–6
Annan, Kofi, 149
anonymous Christianity, 380–1
anti-Semitism, 208–9, 210, 227, 236
Antony, Saint, 42–3
apocalypse/End Times, 216
art
    creative process, 103–5, 106, 112
    crucifixion in popular media, 214
    dialogical imperative, 99–101
    empathic relation, 111–15
    mediation, 105–11
    Mughal patronage, 283
    peacebuilding activity, 152
    presentation of difference, 101–3
Ashram movement, 89–90, 91
Asiatic Christ, 328, 329
Assisi 1986, Day of Prayer for Peace, 39, 93–4, 349–50
ATR *see* African religions
awakening, 331, 381, 382, 383, 384, 385, 390, 391
    see also nirvana/nibbana
Ayya Khema, 400, 401, 402

Ba'al Teshuva Movement (BTM), 401, 402, 406
Beck, Rabbi Leo, 210

The Wiley Blackwell Companion to Inter-Religious Dialogue, First Edition. Edited by Catherine Cornille.
© 2013 John Wiley & Sons Ltd. Published 2020 by John Wiley & Sons Ltd.